Central and East European Politics

From Communism to Democracy

Fourth Edition

EDITED BY

SHARON L. WOLCHIK
The George Washington University

JANE LEFTWICH CURRY
Santa Clara University

ROWMAN & LITTLEFIELD
Lanham • Boulder • New York • London

Executive Editor: Susan McEachern
Editorial Assistant: Katelyn Turner
Senior Marketing Manager: Kim Lyons

Credits and acknowledgments for material borrowed from other sources, and reproduced with permission, appear on the appropriate page within the text.

Published by Rowman & Littlefield
An imprint of The Rowman & Littlefield Publishing Group, Inc.
4501 Forbes Boulevard, Suite 200, Lanham, Maryland 20706
www.rowman.com

Unit A, Whitacre Mews, 26-34 Stannary Street, London SE11 4AB, United Kingdom

British Library Cataloguing in Publication Information Available

Library of Congress Cataloging-in-Publication Data

Names: Wolchik, Sharon L., editor. | Curry, Jane Leftwich, 1948– editor.
Title: Central and East European Politics: from communism to democracy /
    edited by Sharon L. Wolchik, George Washington University, Jane Leftwich Curry,
    Santa Clara University.
Description: Fourth edition. | Lanham : Rowman & Littlefield, [2018] |
    Includes bibliographical references and index.
Identifiers: LCCN 2017058150 (print) | LCCN 2017059309 (ebook) | ISBN
    9781538100899 (electronic) | ISBN 9781538100875 (cloth : alk. paper) |
    ISBN 9781538100882 (pbk. : alk. paper)
Subjects: LCSH: Europe, Eastern—Politics and government—1989– | Europe,
    Central—Politics and government—1989– | Post-communism—Europe, Eastern.
    | Post-communism—Europe, Central. | Democracy—Europe, Eastern. |
    Democracy—Europe, Central. | North Atlantic Treaty Organization—Europe,
    Eastern. | North Atlantic Treaty Organization—Europe, Central. | European
    Union—Europe, Eastern. | European Union—Europe, Central.
Classification: LCC DJK51 (ebook) | LCC DJK51.C437 2018 (print) | DDC
    947.0009/049—dc23
LC record available at https://lccn.loc.gov/2017058150

♾™ The paper used in this publication meets the minimum requirements of American National Standard for Information Sciences—Permanence of Paper for Printed Library Materials, ANSI/NISO Z39.48-1992.

Printed in the United States of America

We dedicate this edition to our families and our colleagues. We are forever grateful for our families' love and curiosity about the world. We are also grateful for the important role they play in our lives. We are grateful for our colleagues' support over the years and for all they have shared with us.

Contents

PART III: CASE STUDIES

PART IV: CONCLUSION

Illustrations

Figures

Maps

Photos

Tables

Acknowledgments

We would like to acknowledge the support of the Institute for European, Russian, and Eurasian Studies at the George Washington University, the Centre for East European Studies at the University of Warsaw, and Santa Clara University.

We thank Nancy Meyers, Bret Barrowman, Amber Footman, Isabelle Chiaradia, Michael Kilbane, Melissa Aten, Christine Cannata, Allison Beresford, Kallie Knutson, Gabriel Kelly, and Glen Kelley for their research assistance for this and previous editions of this volume. We also wish to thank Malgorzata Alicja Gudzikowska for her help in finding and getting permissions when it seemed hopeless.

We also thank Aurora Zahm for her remarkable dedication to this edition and coming to Warsaw to get it finished. Elwood Mills deserves special thanks for his seemingly unending work and patience in preparing maps and illustrations.

We thank all of our previous contributors for their patience, persistence, and diligence in preparing their contributions for the first three editions of this volume. We are especially grateful to those whom we asked to update their chapters for the fourth edition and to the new contributors to this edition.

We also want to acknowledge the intellectual debts we owe not only to Václav Beneš, to whom the first and second editions of this book were dedicated, but also to others whose mentoring and teaching have shaped our views of Central and East European affairs and comparative politics. Our colleagues and friends in Central and Eastern Europe have challenged and informed us, giving us valuable insights and untold hours of their time. For that, we owe them much. We are also grateful to the generations of students whose interactions with us helped us learn what students want and need to know about the politics of the region.

We are indebted, as always, to our families for their support in this endeavor, as in all others. This book, as our other work in this region, has been a part of their lives as well as ours, and they have shared in its creation and revision through dinner-table conversations and email and phone updates. We are gratified by their interest in Central and Eastern Europe, evident in their travel, study, and research in the region.

Finally, the idea for this book grew out of our common difficulty in finding up-to-date, accessible materials about the politics of Central and Eastern Europe after communism. But its origin actually dates to 1970, when we found ourselves beginning the study of what was then termed "Eastern Europe" with Václav Beneš at Indiana University. Our meeting at the reception for new graduate students led to a friendship that has seen us through graduate school, the births and growth of six children between us, and nearly fifty years of professional and personal triumphs and tragedies. In addition to all those we have thanked for their role in producing this book, we are grateful for each other and for our friendship.

Part I

INTRODUCTION

CHAPTER 1

Democracy, the Market, and the Return to Europe

FROM COMMUNISM TO THE EUROPEAN UNION AND NATO

Sharon L. Wolchik and Jane Leftwich Curry

In 1989, the unthinkable happened: communist rule collapsed, virtually like a house of cards, across what had been the former Soviet bloc. As Timothy Garton Ash said, "In Poland it took ten years, in Hungary ten months, East Germany ten weeks: perhaps in Czechoslovakia it will take ten days!"[1] This statement, although not entirely accurate, captures several crucial aspects of the end of communist rule: it was fast, unexpected, and unplanned.

After several decades of communism and the Cold War that most had assumed meant a Europe irreversibly divided between East and West, the countries of Central and Eastern Europe were once again free to chart their own courses. However, return to Europe and transitions from communism have not been easy for these states. Czechoslovakia, Yugoslavia, and the Soviet Union came apart, creating, from what had been eight states, twenty-nine states, nineteen of which are geographically in Europe. In the process, the collapse of Yugoslavia brought the first European war since the end of World War II. Even when their institutions were transformed to look and work like those in the established democracies of Western Europe, they often did not work in the same ways. Less than thirty years later, the democratic structures in two of what were two of Central Europe's most successful states have turned into "illiberal democracies" with free elections but political leaderships that have eliminated the independent power of the courts, the press, and other institutions that are crucial to democracy. Populist candidates and parties have also appeared elsewhere in the area.

Now, though, this shift away from democracy is happening in a Europe that has been united for more than a decade. A decade after communism collapsed and the Berlin Wall came down, the North Atlantic Treaty Organization (NATO) began to take in the states of Central and Eastern Europe. The Czech Republic, Hungary, and Poland joined NATO—once the military bulwark of the Americans and what we then called the "West Europeans" against communism. Five years later, in 2004, NATO took in the Baltic states, Bulgaria, Romania, Slovakia, and Slovenia. And, now, Croatia and Montenegro are also members. In 2004, too, the European Union (EU) took in eight of the new democracies. Romania and Bulgaria became members in 2007. Croatia became a member in 2013. Montenegro, Macedonia, and Albania remain candidate members, and Serbia has recently begun the process. After the Orange Revolution in 2004, Ukraine pushed to begin negotiations. Only Bosnia and Kosovo remain far from membership.

When communism collapsed, the new leaders and citizens in the region hoped that democracy and capitalism would take root and flourish easily and quickly. The initial realities, though, proved to be more complicated. Almost all of these states had to catch up from centuries of being the backwaters of Europe, most often as a part of someone else's empire. State economies whose failures had helped bring down communist control had to be unraveled. Political systems in which elites shared power and citizens both had a voice and took responsibility had to be devised, established, and consolidated. Finally, both the leaders and the populations had to come to grips with their communist past.

It takes time to transition

These states became part of European institutions in the decade and a half after the collapse of communism, but even the earliest and apparently most successful democratizers in Central Europe were never totally "European" in their politics or their economics. Politics and politicians in the region, over the years, have ranged back and forth from the right to the left with little in between. Populism has become more significant. Corruption is far more widespread and democracy less stable than elsewhere in Europe. The much-heralded economic reform brought private ownership and multinational corporations. At the same time, it has brought deep divisions between rich and poor, a decline in social welfare that has impacted much of the population, and, for many reasons, real disappointment in the lives they now have under capitalism.

a "broken" capitalism

Accession to the EU was the logical outcome of the fall of the Berlin Wall, but it has complicated the EU's politics and economics. The postcommunist European countries are poorer than the original members. Many of their citizens face far higher unemployment rates. As a result, their citizens are easily tempted by the possibility of working in the West, provoking fears in Britain and in many of the countries of continental Europe that these job seekers might fill the least well-paid jobs in their societies. Many citizens in this region proved to be far more skeptical of the EU than those in earlier member states. The result has been that some of these states, particularly Poland, have complicated EU debates and almost blocked key changes to EU structures and policies.

As the transition progressed, scholars debated whether these transitions would follow the models of democracy building in southern Europe (Spain, Portugal, and Greece) and in Latin America in the 1970s, or whether their precommunist history and the impact of communism made the Central and East European countries different enough from each other and from the earlier transformations that they would follow different paths.[2] This book lays out the paths—the commonalities and the differences—that have marked the transitions from communism to democracy, from centrally planned economies to the market, and from the Soviet bloc and Iron Curtain to NATO and the EU. It also looks at the causes of the backsliding by many of these countries.

The countries dealt with explicitly in this volume are those from the old European communist world that had different starts but all initially made substantial progress along the path to democracy. These include

- Poland, Hungary, the Czech Republic, Slovakia, and the Baltic states, where there was an early and decisive break with the past and a clear turn toward building democratic institutions and politics in 1989 or, in the case of the Baltic states, with the fall of the Soviet Union in 1991.
- Romania, Bulgaria, Albania, Croatia, what was then Serbia-Montenegro, Ukraine, and Macedonia, where politics took a decisive turn toward democracy more slowly or

only after critical elections or "electoral revolutions" replaced the semi-authoritarian or "illiberal democracies"[3] established after the fall of communism.

- Parts of what was Yugoslavia (Bosnia-Herzegovina and Kosovo) where outside powers sent troops and peacekeepers and ruled. Bosnia is formally independent even though its elected officials' decisions can be overruled an internationally appointed High Representative, who also has the power to remove any elected official. The independence of Kosovo has remained a highly conflictual issue: Kosovo is claimed by Serbia in its 2006 constitution as an integral but autonomous region, while Albanians in Kosovo have declared their independence.

This volume does not deal with East Germany, the former German Democratic Republic, which went through many of the same processes in its shift to democracy but in the context of reunification with West Germany rather than as a separate state.

The Rocky Roots of Central and Eastern Europe

History has not been kind to the peoples in the east of Europe. The landscape of the region is a mosaic of different nationalities that have their own languages, religions, and cultures. For most of their histories, the peoples of this region did not have their own states. They were underlings first of each other and then of the empires of Europe: the Ottoman Empire in the south, the Russian Empire to the east, and the Austro-Hungarian and Prussian empires to the west. In those empires, they were not the leaders. Instead, most served the empires' needs for food, cheap labor, or bureaucrats. Most often, they struggled to develop or preserve their national identities against attempts to assimilate or control them. Thus, when they became independent states, most after World War I, virtually all but what became Czechoslovakia were economically behind and politically troubled.[4]

The division into empires created a second layer of difference in this area. The lines drawn between the empires were more than geopolitical divisions. They resulted in clear differences in the trajectories of these states toward democracy and industrialization. Nearly a century after the empires collapsed, the differences between these states in the way their democracies work or do not work fall along the same lines as the empires' divisions of the nineteenth century. When new states were formed and old states re-created after World War I, the empires' boundaries reappeared in the differences in the economies and infrastructure of the new states. Each empire had made its capital the focus. The train lines went back and forth to Berlin, Vienna, and Moscow, not between Warsaw and Krakow or Prague and Bratislava.

The areas of southeastern Europe that became Serbia, Montenegro, Macedonia, Bulgaria, Bosnia, Albania, and parts of Romania and Croatia were loosely ruled by the Ottoman Empire beginning in the thirteenth century. The Ottomans did little to develop this area. Corruption glued the empire together. It also brought it down after local nationalism began to increase and the European empires, led by Austria-Hungary, moved in to take the pieces they could of most of these areas. Before World War I, Serbia, Bulgaria, Albania, and Romania were formally independent but internally torn apart. The battles that emerged over their borders and who belonged where have continued since. Their economies were based largely on subsistence agriculture.

Map 1.1.   Central and Eastern Europe Today

The Russian Empire in Europe encapsulated the Baltic states (Latvia, Lithuania, and Estonia) the eastern part of Poland and part of Ukraine. Unlike the Ottoman rulers, Russia's goal was to Russify and hold tight to these lands and their populations. In spite of Russia's stranglehold, though, these nations retained their memories of national glory and religions that were, at best, not Russian and, most often, anti-Russian. Many of

Map 1.2. Empires in Central and Eastern Europe, 1800

lots of resistance not'l pride

their intellectuals escaped to Western Europe and the United States, creating strong ties with the West that defied Russia's attempts to seal the borders, keep out new democratic ideas, and make them "Russian." The Poles were the most determined. They fought against Russian control with uprisings and underground organizations that began in the 1700s when Russia, Austria, and Prussia partitioned Poland. Under Russian rule, Poland, Ukraine, and the Baltics remained largely agricultural economies with only a few pockets of industry and mining.

Until World War I, the German Empire extended into what is now western Poland. The Germans in western Poland and in the Czech Lands of Bohemia and Moravia had a long history of dominance and were also a large part of the population in much of this area. They dominated the economies of both western Poland and the border regions of what came to be Czechoslovakia. These areas were industrialized, and their agriculture was the most modernized in Central and Eastern Europe.

The Austro-Hungarian Empire encompassed the Czech Lands, Slovakia, Hungary, Croatia, Slovenia, part of Poland, and what is now western Ukraine, as well as Bosnia after 1878. If foreign control can be good, Austrian control was. In the areas ruled from Vienna (the Czech Lands, parts of Poland and Ukraine, and Slovenia), industrial development and local governance were allowed and encouraged. Citizens from these states participated in regional government and the Diet in Vienna. Schooling took place in German and also in the local languages. The Czechs flourished under Austrian rule; Bohemia and Moravia came to account for the majority of the industry in the empire. Citizens in the Hungarian part of the empire (Slovakia and Croatia) had fewer opportunities to develop national movements. In Slovakia, there was little education available beyond the elementary level in Slovak and, particularly after the 1870s, Slovaks came under heavy pressure to assimilate and adopt Hungarian as their language. Non-Hungarians had few political rights or opportunities to participate in politics even at the regional level. Opportunities for education and participation in local governance were somewhat greater in Croatia under Hungarian rule. However, given the domination of political life in Hungary by the landed aristocracy, there were few incentives for the development of industry. Apart from Budapest, much of the region remained dependent on agriculture.

WWI spurred new boundaries

World War I marked the birth of a new constellation of states in the east of Europe. It was triggered by the assassination of Austrian archduke Ferdinand in Sarajevo by a Serbian who wanted Bosnia to be part of Serbia, not the Austro-Hungarian Empire. After the war, US President Woodrow Wilson's call for national self-determination for the peoples of Europe was reflected in the carving up of the old empires into nation-states. The boundary lines of the states established at this time were far from perfect. The results created serious problems within and between states in the interwar period and are evident in political conflicts between ethnic groups even today.

The Russian Revolution in 1917 and the attempts to spread the revolution beyond Russia created new ideological pressures and divisions that further complicated the political fortunes of these fragile new states. Ukraine had a brief period of independence that ended when it was conquered by Bolshevik armies in 1921. In Hungary, communist supporters led by Béla Kun established a short-lived experiment with communism, the Hungarian Soviet Republic. Ousted after only a few months, this experiment discredited the idea of communism in Hungary and contributed to Hungarian antagonism toward the Soviet Union. The communists also tried but failed to spread their revolution to Slovakia and Poland.

At the end of the war, the Treaty of Versailles drew the borders of the new Europe. However, although national self-determination was the call, ethnic groups were intermingled when the borders were drawn. The desire of the Allies to punish Germany, Austria, and Hungary; the establishment of communism in Russia; and the constellation of military forces on the ground instead determined the borders of the new Europe. To punish Germany and Austria, the lands of the German and Austro-Hungarian empires were cut apart. Hungary was most affected. As the result of the Treaty of Trianon of 1920, Hungary lost two-thirds of its territory and roughly 60 percent of its population to its neighbors.[5] Since many of the areas Hungary lost were populated largely or in part by ethnic Hungarians, citizens and leaders in the shrunken Hungary saw this loss as unjust. The popular response to Trianon, "No, no never," was played out in the efforts of Hungarian leaders to reverse the treaty and regain Hungary's "historical lands," an effort that dominated Hungarian politics and poisoned its relations with its neighbors during the interwar period. Bulgaria also was punished; it lost land to Greece, Romania, and Yugoslavia. With the breakup of Austria-Hungary, Germans lost their dominant positions in what became Czechoslovakia and the newly re-created Polish state.

The boundaries of the new states of Czechoslovakia and Yugoslavia brought together ethnic groups that were very different in their religions, cultures, economies, and levels of development. These differences were most divisive in Yugoslavia. There, the languages and religions, as well as the empires under which the different ethnic groups had developed, varied greatly. The political opportunities and experiences of the main groups in these countries also differed widely in the new states. Instead of being on equal footing, one group dominated the others in each state.

The Polish territories straddled German areas in the West and areas with mixed Lithuanian, Ukrainian, and Polish populations in the East. Like Poland, Romania emerged as a multiethnic state patched together from pieces of very different European empires. As in Czechoslovakia and Yugoslavia, the new leaders of these states had to create unified states from peoples who came with very different histories and resources. Very often, states were created from national groups whose historical memories included conflict with or resentment of each other.

The interwar period began with high hopes of building democracy in the new states. However, with the exception of Czechoslovakia, these new democracies disintegrated rapidly into autocracies. Only Czechoslovakia, Hungary, and Poland had more than fleeting moments of democracy. In Hungary and Poland, these ended with authoritarian regimes under military rulers. In Bulgaria, Romania, and Yugoslavia, royal dictatorships quickly replaced parliamentary rule. In Albania, which had maintained its independence at the Paris peace conference despite the plans of many of its neighbors and the larger powers to partition it, parliamentary rule was disrupted by a coup and, in 1928, the proclamation of a monarchy by Ahmet Zogu.

Ruled by combinations of bureaucratic and military elites, supplemented in some cases by representatives of the rising industrial class, these governments paid little attention to the needs of citizens, who, after a brief period, had few avenues for effective political participation. As authoritarian governments usurped the powers of parliaments, most of the numerous small political parties that had begun to be active were outlawed. Citizens were channeled into movements or parties loyal to the government.[6] Communist parties were established in 1921 in all of these states. They too were soon outlawed in most cases. Extremist parties and movements, particularly those on the far right, such as the Iron Guard in Romania and the Arrow Cross in Hungary, flourished and were a real threat to political stability. In Bulgaria, the radical Internal Macedonian Revolutionary Organization ruled parts of the country briefly.

With the exception of Czechoslovakia, which was one of the most developed nations in the world during the interwar period because of the concentration of 70–90 percent of Austria-Hungary's industry in Bohemia and Moravia, these countries remained largely (Poland and Hungary) or overwhelmingly (the others) agrarian. The new leaders of all these states aggressively tried to industrialize. They achieved some success in the 1920s. Growth rates at this time were higher in Poland and Romania than in France or Germany. However, their economies continued to be heavily dependent on agriculture. In the less than twenty years between the wars, none of the largely agrarian states were strong enough to develop their infrastructures, build up their industry, or compete on the world market. Indeed, economic conflict over land distribution and ownership amplified ethnic conflict. The trauma of the Great Depression derailed early efforts to develop and increased the susceptibility of these economies to foreign penetration and economic and political domination. The degree of development these states did achieve also proved problematic from a political perspective. The bureaucracies and leaders of these new states proved incapable, in most cases, of meeting the increased demands for services and infrastructure that urbanization created. They also were generally unsuccessful in incorporating the growing working class into the national political community.

In the end, it was the actions of outside powers and the advent of World War II that brought about the end of the interwar system in Central and Eastern Europe. The inability of the interwar leaders to resolve old issues, such as ethnic conflict, or deal with the new demands resulting from the development that did occur, however, played a role by increasing their vulnerability and making them easy prey for outside manipulation.

World War II was the watershed event for the fledgling democracies in Central and Eastern Europe. None of the new states had the time or resources to build real defenses against a German onslaught. The first steps to war began when the Germans took the Sudetenland from Czechoslovakia with the approval, in the now infamous Munich Agreement, of Italy, France, and Britain in September 1938. After that, the move toward war continued with the Molotov-Ribbentrop Pact for the division of Poland between the Soviets and the Germans, and their simultaneous invasions of Poland in 1939. The German invasion triggered French and English declarations of war against Germany, starting World War II. Bulgaria, Hungary, and Romania fought alongside the Germans as part of the Axis powers. Albania was essentially occupied by the Italians and then the Germans. Only at the end of the war did Romania manage to leave the Axis camp. Slovakia and Croatia emerged as "puppet states" of the Axis powers, although Croatia also was eventually occupied. Poland, the Czech Republic, the rest of former Yugoslavia, the Baltic states, and western Ukraine were occupied by Germany. In 1941 (the 149th anniversary of Napoleon's attack on Russia), the German-Soviet pact collapsed, and German troops swept across Poland into the Soviet Union.

World War II would prove devastating for Poland, Ukraine, Yugoslavia, and the Baltic states, all of which suffered great loss of life as well as physical destruction. In the

Map 1.3.   Central and Eastern Europe, 1914

others, although the physical damage was less, the destruction of their political and social leadership was dramatic. The sizable Jewish and Roma minorities, as well as many of the intellectuals and others who were perceived as threats or who fought against the Germans, were decimated by the Holocaust. The complicity of some domestic leaders in the deportation of the Jews to the death camps and the collaboration of some with the Nazis further diminished their moral claims to leadership once the war was over.

The Allied leaders of Britain, the Soviet Union, and the United States began to plan for Germany's defeat and the resurrection of Europe in 1943. At Yalta, the second of three conferences between British, US, and Soviet leaders, Britain and the United States essentially agreed to let the Soviet Union have a dominant role from Berlin east. By the end of the war, the slaughter of millions of Jews and Roma, various boundary changes, the shift of Poland's borders to the west, the expulsion of Germans from Poland and Czechoslovakia, and population exchanges in border areas made most of these states more homogeneous ethnically than they had been before the war. The Western Allies pushed provisions for free, competitive elections as soon as the war ended. With the partial exception of the 1946 elections in Czechoslovakia and the 1945 elections in Hungary, however, these did not happen. After the war, western Ukraine and the Baltic states were incorporated into the USSR. The other Central and East European states found themselves in the Soviet sphere of influence.

The Imposition of Communist Rule

In many of these states, communist rule came with the Soviet armies. Soviet Ukraine was retaken from the German armies in 1943 as the Soviets moved west, and the western part of Ukraine, which had been part of Poland in the interwar period, was incorporated into the Soviet Union as Poland's borders were pushed west. The Soviet army then conquered the Baltic states and much of Central and Eastern Europe as it fought the Germans and marched to meet the Allied forces in Berlin. As they pushed the German forces out, the Soviets installed a "baggage train government"[7] led by communist leaders who had spent the war years in the Soviet Union and returned with the Red Army in Poland. In Czechoslovakia, a coalition government of communist and noncommunist leaders was allowed to rule the reunited country until 1948. Hungary and Bulgaria, as Axis powers, were simply occupied by the Soviet Union, although other political forces were allowed to play some role in Hungary until 1947. Soviet troops also brought handpicked Romanian communists with them when they marched into Romania, which had switched from the Axis to the Allies in 1944.

In Yugoslavia and Albania, the Soviets played a very limited role in establishing communism. Although the Soviet army helped liberate Belgrade, Josip Broz Tito and the Partisans liberated most of Yugoslavia through guerilla warfare against the German occupiers. Most of the aid they received came from the Western Allies. The Partisans thus came to power largely through their own efforts. In the process, they also often fought nationalist Croatian ustaše forces and Serbian četniks who, in turn, fought each other and the Axis occupiers. The Soviet role in establishing communism was also negligible in Albania, where resistance fighters with Yugoslav and Western support ousted the occupiers and established a provisional communist government in 1944.

In Czechoslovakia and Hungary, a period of modified pluralism followed the end of the war. Soviet forces withdrew from Czechoslovakia after the war but remained in Hungary. Although, initially, the Communist Party had a number of advantages in both countries, other political forces were able to play a role in political life for several years. In Hungary, the Communist Party was far less popular than its main political rival, the Smallholders Party. In the election of 1945, the Smallholders received 57 percent of the vote; the Hungarian Communist Party and the Social Democrats each received 17 percent. Over the next two years, the Communist Party's membership increased greatly, and party leaders succeeded in gradually restricting the freedom of action of other political parties and discrediting their leaders. The ultimate step in this process was the manipulated election held in 1947 in which the Communist Party emerged as the strongest political force. In Czechoslovakia, where the Communist Party won the largest number of votes in the generally free elections of 1946, decreasing support for the party and changes in the international environment led the communists to orchestrate a government crisis in February 1948. After the democratic ministers in the coalition government resigned, a government dominated solely by the Communist Party took power.

When communist governments took over after the war, they installed their men and women at the local level and in the key ministries so that they controlled the economy, military, and police. Parties on the far right were tarred as collaborators and outlawed soon after the end of the war. The timing varied, but in all cases, noncommunist parties were either eliminated or allowed to exist under Communist Party control to mobilize sectors of the population unlikely to become members of the party. The socialist parties from before the war were forced to merge with the communist parties. Communists who had fought against the Germans in their countries were purged in favor of those who had come from the Soviet Union with the Red Army. This process generated purge trials and attacks on communist and noncommunist intellectuals and workers for their connections with the West, the prewar regime, or criticism of the new socialist state.

At the same time, communist rulers had to start rebuilding from the destruction of the war. For the Polish communists, this process meant rebuilding most of the major cities and industries. In other countries, this task was less monumental. However, in all, there were population shifts and the need to create functioning economies. This process included the collectivization of all agricultural land into farms owned by the state or cooperatives farmed by large groups of farmers. This was a bitter pill for those who, less than a generation before in many cases, had received their own plots. It also meant drawing young people from the farms to the cities to build and run new industries. In the 1950s, propaganda portrayed these developments as the great glory of these new socialist states. The dramatic growth in industry also resulted in a great deal of upward social mobility, as a generation went from being peasant children to being educated workers who went on to leadership positions. The old elites were pushed aside in the process.

Communist Rule and Its Realities

Communist rule was intended to put everything under the supervision and direction of the Communist Party and to ensure that the various states in the Soviet bloc were themselves supervised and directed by the Soviet Union. No aspect of life or politics was to be excluded. Everything was owned and controlled by the governments, which in turn were led by the Communist Party. Ostensibly, this arrangement was to speed up the transformation Karl Marx predicted, in which industrialization first brought capitalist exploitation of the working class and then increasing equality and power for the working class. However, since these were not the states or the economic conditions where Marx had said this transition would occur, Vladimir Lenin's turning of Marx on his head was used to justify establishing communist rule in places where the Industrial Revolution was delayed. The promise was that the state, rather than capitalists, would develop and own industry and transform the working class into the ruling class.

In reality, the institutions and policies that were associated with communist rule in Central and Eastern Europe failed both economically and politically. As developments throughout the communist period in the region illustrate, in most cases, the Soviet model was not welcomed or implemented by the population, but imposed from above. It also came into conflict with underlying conditions and values in many of these societies.

The irony of communist rule in the east of Europe is that it never worked as it claimed and was never monolithic. As early as 1947, the Soviet bloc had its first breakaway. In the period immediately after he came to power, Tito in fact implemented the Soviet model more quickly (to be detailed below) than Stalin wanted, given his hopes that communist parties would come to power peacefully in Italy and France and his emphasis on "national roads to socialism." Tito refused to accept Soviet interference in Yugoslav affairs and also offended Stalin with his plans for a "Balkan Union" under Yugoslav leadership. Disagreement over the speed with which Yugoslavia was moving to establish a communist system and its own control of the secret police led to an open break between the two leaders. Soviet advisors withdrew, and Tito became the icon of evil in communist rhetoric.

The break meant that the fragile multiethnic state of Yugoslavia was on its own, without access to Soviet bloc supplies or markets and, because it remained communist, without immediate aid from the West either. To explain away the split, Tito charged that Soviet-style communism was ideologically incorrect and proposed real decentralization of decision-making in the party and government. In 1952, the party changed its name to the League of Communists of Yugoslavia, a step that symbolized its intention to lead by example rather than force. Over the next two decades, power devolved to the republics and away from the center. The Yugoslav leadership also instituted a system of "workers' self-management" that involved workers in decision-making in factories, even though management retained a good deal of power. Tito also became one of the founders of the nonaligned movement and positioned Yugoslavia between the Western and Eastern blocs.

Ironically, its neighbor, Albania, would isolate itself from the West and the Soviet Union and its East European allies. In response to de-Stalinization in the Soviet Union and Khrushchev's peacemaking with Yugoslavia in the mid-1950s, Albania turned to China. That alliance grew stronger in the late 1960s when Albanian leader Enver Hoxha followed the Chinese in declaring an Albanian Cultural Revolution. In the late 1970s, when China normalized its relations with the United States, Albania isolated itself from the outside world, making it a law that it would take no foreign aid.

Although Yugoslavia remained a one-party system in which no organized political dissent was allowed, Tito's innovations allowed a degree of openness in debate within the country and contact with the West that no other communist government in the region permitted. Many of the institutional innovations the Yugoslavs tried were directed at giving different ethnic groups a stake in maintaining a unified state. The system, in the end, gave each republic a veto over decision-making at the federal level. This system worked for a decade after Tito's death. But it failed to overcome the divisions that played out in a series of brutal wars between the former republics in the 1990s.

After communist governments were established in the rest of the region, they implemented far-reaching institutional and policy changes. This process, which began in earnest after the Stalin-Tito rift and the February 1948 coup in Czechoslovakia, involved copying the Soviet experience in all areas. The early emphasis on the need to find national roads to socialism gave way to efforts to create a uniform system of political and economic organization throughout the region by 1948. The Soviet model that Central and East European leaders emulated was the model that existed in the Soviet Union at the time, which was the Stalinist pattern of political and economic organization, economic development, and social and value change. In 1989 and 1991 when communist rule collapsed, this model left the countries in the region with an elaborate set of institutions and huge bureaucracies involved in coordinating and directing the economy as well as the state apparatus. The fused nature of political and economic power both contributed to the end of communism and complicated the transition away from it.[8]

The Communist Party was charged throughout this period with having the "leading role" in the system. Its goal as a party was not to win elections. Those victories were guaranteed because there was, in normal circumstances, only one candidate per seat, and, whether or not he or she was a party member, the Communist Party selected that candidate. Its goal was to serve as the "vanguard of the proletariat" and to lead the state in the name of that proletariat. Membership in the party was selective rather than elective. To be one of the 10–20 percent of the population in the party required that people apply, serve a long candidacy, and be approved by the party as members.

The Communist Party was organized hierarchically from the primary party organizations found in every workplace up to the Politburo or Presidium led by the first secretary. Its basic rule was "democratic centralism." This organizational principle required all decisions made at the top to be supported and carried out by all party members without question. In reality, though, party membership had very little to do with any commitment to the ideology. It was, most often, simply a ticket to upward mobility. Decisions were not made by the membership and its elected bodies but by a huge party bureaucracy (*apparat*) that managed not only internal party issues such as organization, ideology, and propaganda but also directed and supervised the work of each state institution. It did this through a system of parallel hierarchies, whereby party leaders supervised and directed the workings of each state institution at every level of government.

At the very top of the Communist Party, the Politburo—or Presidium, as it was sometimes called—members allocated to themselves the key party and state offices. From their perch, they served as the "interlocking directorate," coordinating the various branches of the party and state. Information came up to them from the various party organizations and bureaucracies, and their directives were translated downward. From the top down, the Communist Party structures were the skeleton of the state. The party selected or approved the managerial or politically significant personnel working at all levels of the state bureaucracy and economy (*nomenklatura*), channeled information between the top and bottom, took ultimate responsibility for all major policy, coordinated the work of different sectors of the state, and provided ideological guidance.

Although the Communist Party controlled and directed all political life, everyone was expected to participate in the system. In contrast to the interwar period, when a wide variety of charitable, professional, political, and interest organizations flourished in most of the region, the associational life of these countries was brought almost entirely under the control of the Communist Party. An elaborate system of mass organizations, ranging from trade unions to children's organizations, served as "transition belts" to carry the party's directives to the population and mobilize ordinary people to carry out the party's bidding.

Elections were also regularly held for national, regional, and local government bodies. The candidates for these positions (party and nonparty members), as in the Soviet case, were selected and assigned by the Communist Party, one for each open seat, even if they were not party members. Elections were to demonstrate support rather than to select. Opposition was shown by not voting or by crossing out the candidate. As the 99 percent turnout rates demonstrated, opposition, however meek, was virtually impossible in this system.

The Soviet model also included a system of economic institutions and policies as well as a strategy of economic transformation that subordinated economic life to the party's direction and control. These economies were centrally planned economies with a large, party-directed planning apparatus. Decisions about what would be produced, how much, where, and for whom, as well as what workers of different ranks were to be paid and what each product would cost, were made by the state Planning Commission. All parts of the economy from agriculture and industry to social welfare and the arts were owned and run by the state. The Planning Commission's decisions were based on general policy goals set by the Communist Party leadership rather than the market. Often, these policy goals were established for political reasons and were not based on economic rationality.

The establishment of state ownership of most, if not all, economic assets began almost as soon as the communists took power. Communist leaders expanded the process of nationalizing industry that started in most of these countries immediately after the end of the war. In line with Soviet practice, they adopted rapid industrialization as a goal. They also emphasized heavy industry, particularly metallurgy and mining, to the detriment of light industry, agriculture, and the service sector. Collectivization of agriculture was another component of the model. In many cases, peasants who had only recently received land confiscated from expelled Germans or collaborators resisted fiercely. Communist elites also reoriented foreign trade away from traditional patterns with the rest of Europe to the Soviet Union and other communist countries.

The impact of this model on economic performance varied at first by the initial level of development of each economy. Stalinist economic policies worked best, at first, in the least developed countries in the region. There they produced rapid growth rates and urbanization as well as high rates of social mobility. The inefficiencies of centralized economies and Stalinist strategies of development eventually plagued and doomed all the economies of the region. However, in the economies that began with a higher standard of living and industrialization, these failings became evident more quickly. Shortages of basic goods and the lack of adequate services resulted in poor worker morale and low rates of productivity. There was little incentive to innovate. As a result of these failings, these economies could not compete on the world market. These dismal economic conditions were facts of life everywhere in the region. What the population got from state control of the economy was cradle-to-grave welfare, very low-cost housing, guaranteed employment, little pressure to work hard, and prices that virtually never changed even as products disappeared from the shelves. To cope with the shortages and disappearances of goods, elaborate personal systems of barter and an entire second economy based on illicit trade emerged and became a prime part of the "marketplace" wherever it was possible.

so much control

Communism, though, involved far more than state ownership and Communist Party elite control of the state and the economy. The system demanded public conformity and loyalty. Direction and control of the media and public discussions blocked criticism of the system, its leaders, and their decisions. It also discouraged support for alternative institutions and beliefs. All the media were organized as the mouthpieces of the party, which ensured that views other than those the party sanctioned did not get reported. Lest the population see how others lived, travel and communications in and out of the country were controlled and restricted.

The Soviet model also involved social change and efforts to change the population's value systems. Elimination of most private property served to undermine the economic base of the old elites and minimize the resources they could use to resist the new system. In the process, it also helped to turn the social hierarchy virtually upside down. Restrictions on the ability of the children of the upper and middle classes to obtain higher education

Photo 1.1. This wood-processing plant was abandoned in eastern Poland (Ruciana Nida) as a result of the economic transition, leaving hundreds out of work in the area. (Hanna Siudalska)

and admissions procedures that gave children of workers and peasants preference also promoted changes in the status of members of different social groups. Wage structures that rewarded manual labor in priority branches of the economy such as heavy industry, mining, and construction more than work in the "nonproductive" sectors of the economy, such as education, medicine, retail trade and public catering, and administration, served the same purpose. Even when these policies faded away in the 1970s and 1980s in some of these countries, the old national elite was disadvantaged in comparison to the men and women who had risen from peasants to working class in the 1950s and then moved up through the Communist Party. They had the power in the state and party to buy themselves into the new economy in ways many who had fought the system or had come out of the intelligentsia did not.

Political leaders also used education, art and culture, and leisure activities to try to change popular values. The humanities, social sciences, and even many of the hard sciences that did not contribute to national defense suffered from an infusion of ideology into their content. Certain disciplines, such as sociology, were branded bourgeois sciences and banned outright in the 1950s in Poland, Hungary, and Yugoslavia and far longer elsewhere. Anti-religion campaigns were used to try to wean the population away from religion and toward a belief in Marxism–Leninism as a worldview everywhere but Poland. The goal was the creation of "new socialist men" (and women) who put "the collective" above individual interests and who worked tirelessly for the promotion of socialism. In the arts and culture in communism's early years, the doctrine of "socialist realism" required that all artistic expression be directed toward political ends.

Communism was also a system in which the leaders had little trust in those they worked with or in the population as a whole. The Soviet model was not chosen by the population, but was imposed from above. In most cases, the communist leaders who imposed it were in turn also chosen by outside actors (the Soviet leadership). The changes the model required were far-reaching and affected all areas of life. As a result, these regimes relied heavily on coercion. The secret police were an important tool to control dissent and punish opponents and were also used to provide information to the party leadership on what the population did and thought. The military hierarchy was paralleled by a political force in the military to make sure soldiers and officers were politically trained. In the end, it was a society that was watched and directed from all sides.

This pattern was expanded into relations among communist parties and rulers. The central Soviet party in Moscow controlled what the party units, and through them, governments, did in the Baltics, Ukraine, and elsewhere in the Soviet Union. Although formally independent, the other states in what came to be the Soviet bloc were not truly independent. Their party leaders had to be approved by the Soviet leadership, to consult with them and follow their lead on all aspects of domestic and foreign policy, and to work with their neighbors only under Soviet supervision. The result was that changes in the Soviet Union or elsewhere in the bloc impacted all its members.

Formally, all of the members of the Soviet bloc (which did not include Yugoslavia and, after 1961, Albania) were members of the Warsaw Pact and the Council for Mutual Economic Assistance (Comecon or CMEA). The Warsaw Pact, a response to the formation of NATO, organized all the military units of the Soviet Union and the Central and East European states under the command of the Soviet military leadership. It had elaborate plans as to who would do what for both offensive and defensive battles in Europe.

Perhaps more importantly, it allowed for a monitoring of the preparedness and attitude of the various nations' troops and also forced bloc states to coordinate their military hardware.

Comecon, the Council for Mutual Economic Assistance, was the economic trade organization that coordinated the economies of these states. It too was led by the Soviet Union. Through Comecon, Soviet interests were played out in the distribution of economic specialties to individual Central and East European countries other than Yugoslavia and Albania (and, after 1961, Romania), the direction of trade within the bloc and with the West and Third World, and the management of all currency exchange, since the currencies of Soviet bloc states could not be exchanged outside the "ruble zone" as currency values were set as much for political reasons as for economic ones. In the process, tasks were divided up, so no country could be economically independent.

Map 1.4. Axis and Allies, December 1941

In the early communist period, Soviet control played a critical role in determining the course of events in the region. After the death of Stalin in March 1953 Soviet, control shifted from direction to guidance and from prescription to proscription. The leaders of Central and East European countries were urged to come to some sort of accommodation with their populations. The Soviet leadership served more as a watchdog, lest orthodoxy be challenged too vigorously, rather than the director of events. However, although the Soviet model could be reformed and adapted, there were limits. The Communist Party had to retain its "leading role." There could be no criticism of the Soviet Union or a turn from the Warsaw Pact to the West. Twice, popular demands on the street and disillusionment within the party went beyond these limits. Both times, in Hungary in 1956 and Czechoslovakia in 1968, Soviet or Warsaw Pact troops invaded, put down the revolt, and installed "safe" leaders.[9] When the recognition of Solidarity as the only independent trade union in the communist world in Poland in 1980 led to challenges to the party's leading role, Poland's communist leaders under General Wojciech Jaruzelski imposed martial law in December 1981 to prevent a Soviet-led invasion.

On a day-to-day basis, though, the whole system worked to prevent things from spinning so far out of control. Individual leaders worked their way up through the ranks. They knew the Soviet leaders well enough to easily estimate what would be tolerated and what would not. What they did not know they were told in meetings with the Soviet leaders. Soviet troops were stationed in every country (except Romania, Yugoslavia, and Albania—all of which were far enough away to be able to have separate foreign policies). Long-established economic ties and dependence on cheap Soviet oil and natural gas further tied the bloc together. The Iron Curtain that divided Berlin snaked between East and West economically, politically, and militarily.

Yet, even with these controls and this grand divide, the Soviet model was modified over time in each country. The "Polish Road to Socialism," after Stalin's death and the Polish upheavals in 1956, brought in a nationalist leadership that was able to trade tolerance from its population for private agriculture, small-scale private industry, and legal rights for the Catholic Church, to which 98 percent of Poles belonged. As part of its mission in Comecon in the 1970s, Poland actively sought trade with the West. In the late 1980s, Poland's communist leaders turned to Solidarity to share power and the responsibility for improving Poland's disastrous economic performance, only to lose the first partially free election in communist Europe in 1989.

In the 1960s, Romania took its own road. Its communist leaders imposed a form of communism that was both nationalist and highly repressive. Consumer needs were denied in order to support Romania's international position. Romania withdrew from Comecon because it was pressed to become a purely agricultural state and from direct participation in the Warsaw Pact's invasion of Czechoslovakia. It deviated from Soviet foreign policy by maintaining relations with Israel and China when the Soviet Union broke them. And, the West courted it because of its foreign policy independence. All of this was both tolerated and used by the bloc. It provided them with a channel to two critical international actors, the West and China. However, Romania also served as the demonstration case of how repressive communist rule could become.

Hungarians also took advantage of the opening that the death of Stalin and disunity among the Soviet leadership created to challenge the communist system in the mid-1950s. In what has now been recognized as the Revolution of 1956, Hungarians fought Soviet troops in the streets of Budapest. When Hungarian leaders declared the country's neutrality and announced plans to adopt a multiparty system, the Soviets invaded again. After a period of harsh repression, Hungarian leader János Kádár presided over a process of gradual reform. Adopting the slogan "He who is not against us is with us," Kádár shifted to a more conciliatory posture toward the population that has been described as "goulash communism." In the late 1960s, the Hungarian leadership allowed progressively more elements of the market in an attempt to stimulate the economy. Private enterprises proliferated, and state-owned firms' earnings were determined more by what they produced than by what the plan ordered. To further improve the economy and regain the support of its alienated population, the "Kádár Compromise" also came to include the gradual withdrawal of the Communist Party from many areas of life and a corresponding increase in room for debate and independent activity. Hungary also followed Poland in shifting the balance of its trade with the bloc and the West. In the process, Hungary's economy moved further than any other toward the market.

In the late 1960s, Czechoslovakia also experienced a period of reform. A delayed response to de-Stalinization and the failing of the economy, this process of renewal and reform at the elite level gained a mass following in early 1968. When Alexander Dubček and his colleagues proved unable or unwilling to rein in calls for even greater freedom, the Warsaw Pact once again intervened to "protect" socialism from its enemies. The so-called Brezhnev Doctrine enunciated at this time justified the invasion as the right of the Soviet Union and other socialist states to ensure that socialism was not threatened in any socialist country and reaffirmed the Soviet Union's role as the arbiter of the limits of reform.

As part of the Soviet Union, the Baltic states and Ukraine experienced shifts in policy and the degree of openness that occurred elsewhere in the USSR as leaders changed after Stalin's death. However, although de-Stalinization allowed somewhat more room for the republics to chart their own courses, the Soviet system remained highly centralized. Moscow often interfered in republic affairs to quell excessive nationalism or particularism on the part of the republic's Communist Party leaders as well as their populations. National movements continued to develop in the 1970s and 1980s, however. These movements were particularly strong in the Baltic states, where the memory of independent statehood in the interwar period was still very much alive.

The Collapse of Communism

Much as Communist Party leaders and their minions tried to claim that communism was creating a better world, it did not. The plan failed to encourage or allow for the research and development needed for the economies to be effective or even to replace outdated and failing machinery. After the 1950s, workers no longer worked out of fear. They worked for a better life. However, in what was most often an economy of shortages with salaries paid whether or not workers and their factories produced, there was little incentive for productivity. And, so, as the machinery failed and workers did less and less, productivity dropped. With this, there was a vicious circle. Lacking the new equipment that Western firms had, communist economies sank further, and productivity decreased as did what was available on the market, so workers had even less reason to work. As less and less was available and the wait for apartments remained decades long, the population grew more alienated. At the same time, the continuing shortages meant that those with power claimed as much as they could for themselves. Corruption and connections were decisive in what people got and how they lived.

When Mikhail Gorbachev came to power in the Soviet Union, he tried to deal with the crumbling of the communist system. Soviet reforms moved from merely trying to "accelerate" production by making people work harder to revealing the faults in the system through glasnost and making an effort to restructure the economy through perestroika to widespread changes in how the state and the party worked and the expansion of opportunities for people to organize independently and make their views known. The other countries in the bloc were pressed to follow the direction of the Soviet Union. For hardliners in Czechoslovakia, East Germany, Bulgaria, and Romania, the reforms were far from welcome. For the Poles and the Hungarians, they were a justification to go even further in reforms they were already making. For all of the countries in Central and Eastern Europe, as well as the Soviet Union itself, the reforms were destabilizing. Not only did the once stable limits of reform suddenly seem flexible, but, as the Soviet leadership focused on solving its own serious problems, it in effect cut Central and East European communist leaders loose to please their populations while propping up their own economies and paying market prices for once cheap Soviet energy resources.

In the end, the softening of Soviet rule and the mounting pressures by young people and others who wanted more, systems that were increasingly unable to deal with their failings, and the disillusionment of the party faithful started the fall of the Soviet bloc dominoes, and it could not be stopped. Where there was an established opposition, the changes were smoother than where no opposition had been able to form or survive. But the system fell apart everywhere outside the Soviet Union in 1989, and in 1991, the Soviet Union itself broke up.

Changes in the Soviet Union under Gorbachev and the Soviet leadership's decision to allow Central and East European countries to go their own ways (the so-called Sinatra Doctrine) clearly were important factors in bringing about the end of communism in the region. Similarly, Boris Yeltsin's decision to recognize the independence of the Baltic states in August 1991, after the abortive hard-line coup, and the dissolution of the Soviet Union in December of that year opened the way for the Baltic states and Ukraine to become independent states again. Developments in countries such as Poland and Hungary, which were at the forefront of the process of change, and the fall of the Berlin Wall also influenced developments elsewhere. But while outside factors facilitated the process and, in some cases, acted as the catalyst for the changes, the collapse of these systems also reflected the deep economic and political crises that communist systems had created in all of these states.

The end of communism in the region differed in the speed of the process, the extent of citizen involvement, and the level of violence involved. If we combine these dimensions, four main patterns emerge. The first occurred in Poland and Hungary, where the end of communist rule most closely resembled the pacted transitions in Latin America and southern Europe. In both, reformist leaders in the Communist Party negotiated the end of communism with representatives of the opposition in roundtable discussions. In Poland, the regime and Solidarity leaders agreed to hold semi-free elections in June 1989. Although the agreement guaranteed the party's candidates certain seats, Solidarity won an overwhelming victory and formed the first government not dominated by the communists since the end of World War II.

In Hungary, where the opposition was much smaller, its leaders used issues connected with the Revolution of 1956 to open roundtable negotiations with reformers in the Communist Party. In what was, in some ways, the most remarkable case, the Hungarian communists negotiated themselves out of power without any significant pressure from mass public action other than the peaceful crowds that came to the streets for the reburial of the leaders killed after the 1956 revolt, which gave the process of change a public face. In 1990, presidential and parliamentary elections formalized the change of regime agreed upon in 1989. In both the Polish and Hungarian cases, the end of communism reflected a longer-term process of opposition organization and change within the party as well as in the broader society.

In East Germany, Czechoslovakia, and Romania, the collapse of communism came about suddenly, as the result of massive citizen protests. The process began in East Germany, where peaceful demonstrations led by activists in several cities gained momentum and became explicitly political once the Hungarians opened their borders and allowed large numbers of East Germans trying to reach West Germany through Hungary to do so. In November 1989, the fall of the Berlin Wall, the most potent symbol of the division of Germany into two halves, had repercussions around the world and encouraged citizens in other communist states to press for change in their own countries.

Photo 1.2.   Deputy Prime Minister Mieczysław Rakowski (in photo) meets with the crew of the Gdańsk shipyard, where he criticized the activities of Solidarity. The emergence and tolerance of Solidarity for fifteen months in 1980 and 1981 and the martial law regime that followed were the final protest and repression before 1989, when the authorities gave in. Rakowski went on to become the last communist prime minister and, after the 1989 defeat of communist candidates, the last head of the Polish United Workers' Party. (Stefan Kraszewski/PAP)

In Czechoslovakia, the beating of peaceful protestors in Prague, who had gathered on November 17 to commemorate a student killed by the Nazis in 1939, led to mass demonstrations in Prague and Bratislava that quickly spread to other towns and cities. Aware that the Soviet leadership would not come to their aid, Czech and Slovak leaders yielded power in negotiations with the opposition twenty-one days after the beginning of the demonstrations. The election of Václav Havel as president by a parliament still dominated by the Communist Party in December capped the victory of what came to be called the Velvet Revolution for its peaceful nature.

Mass demonstrations also brought down the extremely repressive, personalized dictatorship of Nicolae Ceauşescu in Romania. Protests in Transylvania spread to the capital and other cities. In contrast to the cases above in which Communist Party leaders yielded power peacefully, Ceauşescu's secret police force, the Securitate, fired on the peaceful demonstrators. When this action failed to stop the protests, Ceauşescu's opponents within the Communist Party engineered a coup. Nicolae Ceauşescu and his wife, Elena, who was also very deeply involved in the regime's politics, were tried in what can only be described as a show trial and executed on Christmas Day.

In Bulgaria and Albania, the transitions occurred in two stages. In the first, less repressive Communist Party leaders took over from the old guard. These leaders were, in turn, replaced by the opposition in later elections. In Bulgaria, the reformed Communist Party won in multiparty parliamentary elections in 1990, although the opposition gained a significant number of seats in parliament. The opposition won the 1991 elections only to lose to the reformed communists, now the Bulgarian Socialist Party, in 1994. It was only in the mid-1990s that a coalition of the democratic opposition returned to power. In Albania, the Communist Party won the 1990 multiparty elections. The newly formed opposition was able to form a noncommunist government only after the 1992 elections.

The transition from communist rule in Yugoslavia differed in many important ways from the end of communist rule elsewhere in the region. In Yugoslavia, the end of communism coincided with the breakup of the country. It also occurred in a series of wars that resulted in a large number of deaths as well as large waves of refugees as the result of "ethnic cleansing," widespread physical destruction, and economic devastation. With the exception of Slovenia, which succeeded in defending its independence in a three-week war in 1991, the transition to postcommunist rule in the states formed from Yugoslavia followed a very different path, one complicated by the impact of the wars and the need to come to terms with their aftermath.

In the Baltic states, the transformation was torturously close and yet impossible until the whole Soviet Union collapsed. The Lithuanians in 1990 and the Latvians in 1991 tried to declare independence, only to have the Soviets move in. It was only during the crisis in Russia that developed after the attempted coup in the summer of 1991 that movements for independence were able to succeed in Latvia, Lithuania, and Estonia. In all three, groups that had originally supported cultural autonomy gained adherents within the respective communist parties, which also supported self-determination and later independence.

In Ukraine, activists centered in the western part of the country gained supporters in the late 1980s and early 1990s. After Yeltsin recognized the independence of the Baltic states in August 1991, Ukraine's leaders declared Ukrainian independence. As in a number of postcommunist states, the first free elections in Ukraine resulted in the election of a former Communist Party functionary. Political life in Ukraine moved in a markedly democratic direction only after the Orange Revolution defeated President Leonid Kuchma's handpicked candidate and brought Viktor Yushchenko to power in 2004.

The Transition from Communism

Despite the many ways in which they differed from each other and the different ways communism developed in each of their countries, the leaders of Central and Eastern Europe had to resolve a number of similar crises after the end of communist rule. The most visible of these were summarized by the election slogans of most political parties in the first free elections in these countries: "Democracy, the market, and a return to Europe." In the first area, the new elites had to create or re-create democratic political institutions, values, and practices. The process involved dealing with the economic and political power of the Communist Party and revising the legal system and constitutional structures to make them compatible with democracy, the establishment of a multiparty system, the re-pluralization of associational life, and the recruitment and training of new leaders. They also had to counteract the influence of communism on the political values and attitudes of the population and foster new values supportive of democracy.

The economic aspect of the transition was equally daunting. In addition to privatizing state assets and fostering development of new private enterprises, the new leaders in the *economy* region also had to devise redistribution policies to restore property confiscated by the state to its rightful owners or heirs. They needed to redirect trade patterns, particularly after the disbanding of the Comecon and the end of the Soviet Union, and begin to deal with the environmental devastation that communist patterns of development created. They also had to deal with the requirements of international financial institutions and the economic and social consequences of the dramatic drop in production that accompanied the shift to the market.

These policies had their counterparts in the arena of foreign policy. In addition *foreign* to asserting their independence on the world stage and negotiating the withdrawal of *policy* Soviet troops when necessary, the new elites undertook a series of actions to reclaim what they perceived to be their rightful place in Europe. Many of these focused on efforts to join European and Euro-Atlantic institutions, with particular emphasis on the EU and NATO. As of this writing, most of the postcommunist states of Central and Eastern Europe have achieved these goals. In most of the remaining countries, political elites continue to push for inclusion.

The transition from communist rule has also had social and psychological dimensions. *social* In the first area, there has been a major change in the social structures of these countries. New (or old, previously prohibited) groups, such as entrepreneurs, and numerous occupations associated with the rapid development of the previously neglected service and financial sectors have emerged. The status of different social groups has also changed. With the shift to the market, restitution of property, and the end of most state subsidies, visible income differentials, which were previously small, increased. Social inequality, poverty, and unemployment also increased substantially. While some people were able to take advantage of the new opportunities available in politics, the economy, and society, many others were not. For the latter group, the end of communist rule entailed largely new hardships, particularly in the early postcommunist period when production and the standard of living fell dramatically in most countries. The division of society into winners (those who were young, well educated, and urban) and losers (older, less skilled workers, those living in rural areas, and single parents, as well as many women) in turn had important political repercussions.

The end of tight political control and the opening of borders, coupled with the uncertainty and disruptions created by the transition itself, exacerbated old social pathologies and problems, such as alcoholism, juvenile delinquency, prostitution, violence in the home, drug use, and street crime, and allowed new problems to emerge. Organized crime, trafficking in persons, smuggling, and the sex trade are among the most visible of these. Certain social issues, such as tensions between various ethnic groups, the widespread discrimination against and marginalization of the Roma, and the xenophobia and anti-Semitism that often poison political discussions, all had existed in the communist era but were taboo. Now they are recognized as problems and discussed openly,[10] although they all too often continue to serve as sources of violence and repression. Support for extreme nationalist parties and the development of skinhead movements, particularly in economically depressed regions, are further reflections of these trends.

The experience of living in a time in which most aspects of life, from political choices to the organization of daycare, were in flux also had predictable psychological consequences in the region. Although these effects were most widespread among those for whom the transition brought largely new hardships, they also affected those who could be seen as winners. As one Czech student put it soon after communism fell in that country, "Under communism, it was a question of whether I was allowed to do things; now it is a question of whether I will prove capable of doing them." Greater uncertainty as well as far greater choices, coupled with new pressure to perform well at work, increased competition, and the specter of unemployment, all contributed to the stress individuals and families experienced, even among those groups fortunate enough to be able to take advantage of new opportunities.

The Role of International Organizations and Outside Actors

In contrast to the interwar period in which outside actors either largely ignored the region (the United States, Great Britain, France) or had designs on it (Italy, Germany, and at times the USSR), the international climate has been far more favorable to the success of efforts to create stable democracies and market economies and engineer a return to Europe in the postcommunist period. All of these countries have received substantial economic and democracy-building assistance from the United States, the EU, and many individual European countries. The postcommunist states have also been the recipients of economic assistance and loans as well as a great deal of advice from international financial institutions such as the International Monetary Fund and World Bank. The latter, as well as the EU, have exerted significant influence not only on the policies adopted by successive governments in the region, but also, in many cases, on the institutional design of these societies and polities.[11] In the case of the successors to former Yugoslavia, the international community intervened with negotiators, military force, and peacekeepers to resolve or prevent conflict. It also, in the form of the International Criminal Tribunal for former Yugoslavia at The Hague, set standards of cooperation that delayed or sidetracked the beginning of negotiations for EU accession and NATO membership for several of these countries.

Membership in European organizations did facilitate far greater contact with the rest of Europe and introduced new influences, both positive and negative, that go far beyond even the dense web of official contacts that link these states to older members and each other. Now that some of these states are part of the EU and others are working to join, their leaders also face new challenges as EU members. These include establishing themselves so that their interests are considered in debate and decision-making, and balancing the demands of their membership in both European and transatlantic organizations. Their success in establishing themselves as key members of the European community was demonstrated in 2014 by the election of Poland's president, Donald Tusk, as president of the European Council. Two years later, the "Three Seas Initiative" brought the states between the Adriatic, Baltic, and Black Seas together to strengthen the voice of the Central and East European states in this area (including Austria) in the EU and also to increase the ties and cooperation between the states in this area in terms of transport, energy sources, and economic development.

At the same time that joining European and Euro-Atlantic institutions has brought many benefits to the countries involved, the asymmetrical nature of the relationship between these countries and these institutions, as well as powerful Western countries, has also led, predictably, to resentment and skepticism on the part of certain segments of the population in all of these countries, who ask whether they have traded rule by Moscow for rule by Brussels, the seat of the EU and NATO headquarters.[12] The impact of this backlash on politics in the region should not be underestimated, as is clear from the success of Viktor Orban and his Fidesz Party in Hungary not only in the 2010 and 2014 elections but also in moving Hungary from a liberal democracy to an "illiberal democracy," as he has termed it, where the courts and media are closely controlled and nationalist and populist rhetoric and policy are the focus. Small and large protests happen but they have been relatively powerless. The Law and Justice Party in Poland took much the same path after its victory in the presidential and parliamentary elections in 2015. It moved rapidly to impose anti-EU populist ideology and Catholic religious principles as well as to diminish the independence of the courts and to transform the public media and the educational system. At the same time, it appealed to those who thought they "lost" in the transition with economic policies of increased social welfare. The center-right and left parties have essentially collapsed after having been leaders in Polish politics for decades. As Law and Justice pushed its platform, though, it triggered massive public protests. The most dramatic of these came, first, when the Law and Justice party tried to make any abortion illegal in January 2017 and, second, when it passed laws putting the entire court system under the party's control. In both cases, there were massive protest marches that resulted in the draconian laws being put aside. However, the shift to the right has not stopped, and threats to democracy continue to increase in Poland.

Elsewhere, a quarter of a century after democracy was established all over Central and Eastern Europe, smaller radical anti-system and populist parties have emerged and people have taken to the streets to make demands for and against them. In part, this was a product of the disappointment of many with what they got from their new systems. It was also encouraged by the surge of largely Muslim refugees from Syria and elsewhere in 2015. Pressure by the EU for states to take in refugees triggered reactions both by governments in Poland and Hungary as well as in the Czech Republic and from citizens elsewhere against taking these refugees and then against the EU for making decisions for its member countries.

The leaders of these postcommunist states have tried different policies in dealing with issues they have faced since the end of communist rule. They have had varying degrees of success in meeting their common challenges and those specific to their societies. The chapters that follow examine these developments. The first section provides an overview of the main political, economic, foreign policy, and social issues postcommunist leaders have faced. The second part of the book focuses on these issues as they have been dealt with in individual countries. Chapters in this section also discuss questions of particular importance in the countries examined. As the pages to follow illustrate, the success of leaders in Central and Eastern Europe in dealing with these challenges has varied, as has the response of the international community to these states. In the process, many of these countries have gone forward and backward on their roads to democracy. What has seemed to be success has often been followed by failure. Just as underlying realities in the region led to diversity in the way communist institutions, policies, and ideology played themselves out in particular countries, so too the transition from communism, though it has involved the same tasks for all, has reflected the diverse social, economic, and ethnic composition of these countries as well as their individual histories and political traditions.

Notes

1. Timothy Garton Ash, *The Magic Lantern: The Revolution of '89 Witnessed in Warsaw, Budapest, Berlin, and Prague* (New York: Random House, 1990), 78.

2. See debate between Terry Lynn Karl, Philippe C. Schmitter, and Valerie Bunce in the following articles: Philippe C. Schmitter with Terry Lynn Karl, "The Conceptual Travels of Transitologists and Consolidologists: How Far to the East Should They Attempt to Go?" *Slavic Review* 53 (Spring 1994): 173–85; Valerie Bunce, "Should Transitologists Be Grounded?" *Slavic Review* 54 (Spring 1995): 111–27; Terry Lynn Karl and Philippe C. Schmitter, "From an Iron Curtain to a Paper Curtain: Grounding Transitologists or Students of Postcommunism?" *Slavic Review* 54 (Winter 1995): 965–78; and Valerie Bunce, "Paper Curtains and Paper Tigers," *Slavic Review* 54 (Winter 1995): 979–87.

3. Fareed Zakaria, *The Future of Freedom: Illiberal Democracy at Home and Abroad* (New York: W. W. Norton, 2003).

4. Barbara Jelavich, *History of the Balkans, Vol. 2, 20th Century* (Cambridge: Cambridge University Press, 1983), 128–31.

5. Lonnie R. Johnson, *Central Europe: Enemies, Neighbors, Friends* (Oxford: Oxford University Press, 1996).

6. Andrew Janos, "The One-Party State and Social Mobilization: East Europe between the Wars," in *Authoritarian Politics in Modern Society*, ed. Samuel P. Huntington and Clement Henry Moore (New York: Basic Books, 1970), 204–36.

7. Zbigniew Brzezinski, *The Soviet Bloc, Unity and Conflict* (Cambridge, MA: Harvard University Press, 1960).

8. See Bartlomiej Kaminski, *The Collapse of State Socialism: The Case of Poland* (Princeton, NJ: Princeton University Press, 1991); and Valerie Bunce, *Subversive Institutions: The Design and Destruction of Socialism and the State* (Cambridge: Cambridge University Press, 1999).

9. Brzezinski, *The Soviet Bloc*.

10. See Zoltan D. Barany and Ivan Volgyes, eds., *Legacies of Communism in Eastern Europe* (Baltimore, MD: Johns Hopkins University Press, 1995); and James R. Millar and Sharon L. Wolchik, eds., *The Social Legacy of Communism* (Cambridge: Cambridge University Press, 1994).

11. See Wade Jacoby, *The Enlargement of the European Union and NATO: Ordering from the Menu in Central Europe* (Cambridge: Cambridge University Press, 2004); and Jan Zielonka and Alex Pravda, eds., *Democratic Consolidation in Eastern Europe* (New York: Oxford University Press, 2001) for discussion of the influence of the EU in the region.

12. Ronald H. Linden and Lisa Pohlman, "Now You See It, Now You Don't: Anti-EU Politics in Central and Southeast Europe," *European Integration* 25 (December 2003): 311–34.

Part II

POLICIES AND ISSUES

CHAPTER 2

The Political Transition

Valerie Bunce

The collapse of the communist regimes and communist states from 1989 to 1992 produced a number of remarkable changes in the political and economic landscape of Europe's eastern half. In particular, during the brief span of three years, authoritarian regimes gave way to political orders that were, albeit to quite varying degrees, more competitive and more respectful of civil liberties. In addition, twenty-two new states arose from the rubble of the Soviet Union, Czechoslovakia, and Yugoslavia, while one communist state, the German Democratic Republic, merged with its neighbor, the German Federal Republic, to reconstitute a single Germany. As a result, a region once composed of nine states featured by the end of the Cold War twenty-nine—if we include all of the successor states of the former Soviet Union, together with Central and Eastern Europe and the Balkans. At the same time, open market economies, again to varying degrees, replaced state-owned, centrally planned, and highly protectionist economies. Finally, the post–World War II separation of Europe into two halves ended, not just because of the economic and political liberalization of the east, but also because of the eventual eastward expansion of three international institutions: the Council of Europe, the North Atlantic Treaty Organization (NATO), and the European Union (EU). In short, 1989–1992 constituted a revolution in Central and Eastern Europe—in state boundaries, in the organization and practice of politics and economics at home and abroad, and, finally, in elite and mass identities and political preferences.

This chapter assesses the political side of this revolution. In particular, I compare patterns of regime transition in Central and Eastern Europe since the dramatic events of 1989, draw some generalizations about what has transpired and why, and place these changes in the larger context of the global spread of democratic governance. My discussion is divided into two parts. In the first section, I focus on the short-term political consequences of the collapse of communism, or the forms of governance that came into being during the early years of the transition from 1989 to mid-1996. Of interest here are such questions as the following: Did the end of Communist Party hegemony lead, as many expected, to the immediate rise of democratic politics, or do we in fact see a more complicated political story? To what extent were the early political dynamics of postcommunist Europe typical or distinctive when compared with the collapse of dictatorships and regime change in other parts of the world? Finally, what factors seem to provide the most compelling account of the first stage of the political transition in postcommunist Europe?

In the second part of this chapter, I shift my focus to developments beginning in the latter part of 1996 that continued through mid-2017. Here, the discussion addresses three notable trends. The first is the remarkable ability of the new states in the region to endure (and several more to form), and the second is the expansion of democratic polities since the mid-1990s. This expansion represents two convergent developments: the fact that most of the first democracies in the region stayed the political course, coupled with the failure of the remaining and more authoritarian regimes in the area to maintain their political momentum. In this sense, there have in fact been several waves of democratization in postcommunist Europe, with the first occurring immediately after the fall of state socialism and the second occurring roughly a decade later. The final trend is less reassuring about the future of democracy in the region. Several countries long thought to be the most durable democracies in Central and Eastern Europe—that is, Poland and especially Hungary—are experiencing major challenges to democratic politics from right-wing populist politicians and parties.

Postcommunist Political Diversity

By 1996, one could identify three types of political regimes in postcommunist Central and Eastern Europe.[1] The first, which included Poland, the Czech Republic, Hungary, Slovenia, Lithuania, and, less perfectly, Estonia and Latvia (because of some political discrimination against their Russian minorities), was a democratic order, characterized by political arrangements that combine free, fair, and competitive elections that are regularly held; representative institutions that convert public preferences as expressed through elections into public policy; rule of law, or rules of the political game that are accepted by both elites and publics and applied consistently across time, space, and circumstances; and extensive civil liberties and political rights guaranteed by law. Because of all these features, democracy in general, and in these cases in particular, can be understood as a way of organizing politics that rests on accountable government.[2] What is striking about Poland, the Czech Republic, and the other countries listed above at this time, therefore, was that they managed to move quickly to full-scale democracy.

The second type of regime in the region at this time was authoritarian. In authoritarian states, political arrangements lack the characteristics noted above, thereby producing governments that have neither the incentives nor the capacity to be accountable to their citizens. Authoritarian regimes, in particular, lack the institutionalized competition, individual rights, and procedural consistency that translate individual preferences into public policy through elections and representative government. This combination of traits describes the politics during the period under discussion in two of the successor states of Yugoslavia (Croatia and Serbia-Montenegro). Here, it is interesting to note that, despite the efforts of their dictators, Franjo Tuđman in Croatia and Slobodan Milošević in Serbia-Montenegro, some political pluralism was in evidence—most notably in the capitals of Zagreb and Belgrade, where oppositions had a presence and where publics, even in the face of fraudulent elections, still managed to deny their dictators decisive electoral support.

Photo 2.1.   Remembering Václav Havel, Prague, Czech Republic. (Davidlohr Bueso)

Finally, the remaining countries in the region, Albania, Bosnia (but only after the Dayton Peace Accords of 1995 had demilitarized the country and provided a skeletal form of government), Bulgaria, Macedonia, Romania, Slovakia, and Ukraine—a group of countries roughly equal in number to the full-scale democracies at this time—fell between the extremes of dictatorship and democracy. They were what can be termed "hybrid regimes," that is, political arrangements that feature some of the formal characteristics of democracy, such as representative institutions and political competition, but fall short of the liberal standard as a result of unfair elections, extensive corruption, irregular recognition of civil liberties, significant biases in the media, opposition parties that are poorly organized in comparison with parties in power led by authoritarians, and weak ties between political representatives and the citizenry. Also common in this category are several other characteristics that undermine the development of accountable government—in particular, rapid turnover in governments (a characteristic that Poland also shared), an inability of citizens to counteract the power of the state through associational ties with each other (or what has been termed "civil society"), and a sharp divide between urban and rural politics, with the latter more consistently supportive of authoritarian rule.[3]

In short, in the first stage of the transition from state socialism, we find three characteristics. The first is political diversity. Put simply, the deregulation of the political, economic, and social monopoly of the Communist Party that occurred throughout Central and Eastern Europe from 1989 to 1991 was not followed necessarily by the rise of democratic politics. In this sense, the Central and Eastern Europe of this period presented an important lesson. There can be a substantial lag, and even no relationship, between two developments that are often assumed to be tightly intertwined: the decline of authoritarian rule and the rise of democratic politics. Second, regime change in this region was largely peaceful but sometimes violent. The Baltic states' attempts to separate themselves from the Soviet Union invited a short-term violent response on the part of the Soviet leadership. The merger in Yugoslavia between two issues—the future of the regime and the future of the state—produced very different political trajectories among the republics that made up the state and a war from 1991 to 1995 that left 140,000 people dead (according to the International Center for Transitional Justice) and undermined democratization in those successor states that served as the major site of this conflict, Croatia and Bosnia, while in the process shaping developments in their neighbors, particularly Macedonia and Serbia-Montenegro. The fall of Nicolae Ceauşescu in Romania in 1989 was also violent. These contrasts aside, however, it is striking that where regime transition was accompanied by violence, the result was either a hybrid regime or a dictatorship. Thus, democracy and a peaceful adjudication of conflicts—with the latter often serving as one definition of democratic governance—were closely associated with one another in the Central and East European transitions.

Finally, there were significant differences across the region in the resources, cohesion, and political goals of both the communists and the opposition. For example, while the communists were quick to embrace the liberal political and economic agenda of the opposition in the Baltic countries, Poland, and particularly Hungary and Slovenia, they were more resistant in the remaining cases. Serbian political dynamics under Milošević are the most extreme example of this resistance. At the same time, oppositions varied greatly. Whereas in the Baltic countries, Poland, the Czech Republic, Hungary, and Slovenia, the opposition was large, sophisticated, relatively cohesive, and committed to liberal politics, in the remaining countries, the opposition tended to suffer from a number of problems. For example, Bulgaria saw divisions over the best way to build capitalism and democracy and become an effective political force, and in both Serbia and Slovakia, elite struggles over political power and manipulation of national tensions in order to maintain authoritarian control and stave off demands for democracy demobilized and often marginalized the liberals.[4] Elements of this pattern can also be seen, more recently, in Macedonia.

Comparative Perspectives: The Puzzles of Diversity

Was the diversity of postcommunist political dynamics and political pathways in the first half of the transformation surprising or predictable? The answer is that for many analysts, the political patterns of postcommunism, as summarized above, were in fact unexpected. This was the case whether we refer to specialists on comparative democratization or specialists on postcommunist Europe.

At the time that communism collapsed, there had already been a clear trend, in evidence since the mid-1970s, suggesting that the decline of authoritarian rule led invariably to the rapid and peaceful rise of democratic politics. This was precisely what had happened, for example, in one state after another in both Latin America and southern Europe (though the Portuguese case was an exception). In addition, the dichotomous thinking of the Cold War, which had framed political dynamics and therefore political assumptions in the international order for forty-five years, made it easy to presume that

Photo 2.2. General and former president Wojciech Jaruzelski and former president Lech Wałĕsa at a debate on Poland's past. (*Rzeczpospolita*)

there were only two political choices in the world: democracy or dictatorship. Thus, if the hegemony of the Communist Party was challenged and dictatorship rested on this hegemony, and, just as importantly, if the Soviet Union failed to back up communist rule in its client states and at home and, indeed, failed in the more profound sense of being able to continue functioning as a regime, a state, a regional hegemon, and a superpower, then in the wake of its collapse, it was widely thought, democratic revolutions would follow both within the Soviet Union and throughout the Soviet bloc. As we have seen replayed in reactions to the Arab "spring" from 2010 to 2011 and in US debates about Iraq from 2002 to the present, moreover, many assumed not just that the political world offered only two regime options but also that if dictators and dictatorships were subtracted from the equation, publics would necessarily rise up to embrace the democratic cause—and be able to translate these preferences in relatively quick order into well-functioning democratic institutions and procedures. Democracy, in short, was natural and easy, and these characteristics would be revealed once the distorting effects of dictatorship were removed.[5]

From these perspectives, therefore, the assumption was that the end of dictatorship constituted the beginning of democracy—and full-scale democracy at that. Such an optimistic reading of the future was unusually tempting in the wake of 1989, given the rapid and region-wide character of the collapse of Communist Party control and the dependence of these regimes and their specific economic and political features on that control. This position, however, was as flawed in the postcommunist world as it would be a decade later in Iraq and Afghanistan and several decades later in Egypt.[6] Oppositions can be fractious, dictatorships invariably have supporters, constructing democratic institutions in weak states can be difficult, and publics can care as much about their personal circumstances as about governmental forms. Moreover, the fall of dictatorships can be partial, not complete.

Scholars specializing in the postcommunist region had different expectations—though these were also inaccurate in some respects.[7] For some scholars, the emphasis had long been on the striking similarities among the communist states—similarities that spoke not just to common ideological texts but also to the foundational role of the Soviet Union as the "inventor" and then the "exporter" of state socialism. In all of these cases, communist regimes were governed by a single Communist Party that enjoyed a monopoly on power, money, and social status and was committed to rapid socioeconomic development through control of the allocation of both labor and capital. It is puzzling, therefore, that the structural and ideological similarities across this region—similarities far greater than those found, for example, among dictatorships in Latin America or southern Europe during the 1960s and 1970s—could have translated so quickly into such differences, not just in political regimes, as already noted, but also in economic regimes. Thus, capitalism replaced socialism very quickly in Poland, Hungary, the Czech Republic, the Baltic states, and Slovenia, whereas socialist economics, especially with respect to state control over the economy, remained in place to varying degrees in the other countries in the region. Commonalities, therefore, in the most basic building blocks of politics and economics—for example, state control over politics and the economy—gave way very quickly to diversity.

For other specialists, there was widespread recognition that these countries entered the transition with variable mixtures of assets and liabilities, such that postcommunism would not produce, especially in the early stages, identical political dynamics—the similarities in the institutional "skeletons" of these systems notwithstanding. In this sense, diversity was expected. Not expected, however, was the range of regimes that appeared, with the most improbable group comprising those countries that made a quick and thoroughgoing transition to democratic politics. As some observers were quick to note, of the many countries in Central and Eastern Europe that had experimented with democratic politics during the interwar era, only one—Czechoslovakia—had managed to survive until World War II with democratic institutions and procedures intact. Even in that case, however, the inclusiveness of the polity and the extent of political and certainly economic equality among the nations that shared that state at the time were both in some question.[8] In short, little of the political past could be recycled to support democratic change. As a result, democracy was assumed to be, at best, an uphill struggle—in direct contrast, for example, to the Latin American transitions to democracy that occurred in the 1970s and 1980, where the norm was redemocratization, not building democracy from scratch.[9]

Many analysts also recognized the considerable costs of the state socialist brand of authoritarian rule due to its unusually penetrative and despotic character. These were dictatorships that, while less and less brutal over time in most cases, were nonetheless extraordinarily ambitious. By owning and planning the economy, monopolizing political power, sealing borders, and atomizing publics, these dictatorships seemed committed to the destruction of some of the most elementary building blocks of democratic life—for example, interpersonal trust, respect for the law, confidence in political institutions such as political parties, and participation in associations independent of the state, such as labor unions, clubs, professional associations, and the like. The autonomy of individuals and groups, so important for countering the power of the state in a democratic order, therefore, had been severely limited by the communist experience. Economic decline during the last years of state socialism, moreover, would also seem to have constrained the rise of democracy, especially since the political regime transition in question would be tied to an unusually costly economic transition. Indeed, it is not just that Central and Eastern Europe featured—and still features—a much lower level of economic development than Western Europe, which many have read as undermining democratic governance, but also that citizens in Central and Eastern Europe experienced a far greater decline in living standards in the first half of the 1990s than one saw during the Great Depression, when nearly half of Europe's democracies, we must remember, had collapsed.[10]

When we compare the perspectives of specialists in the postcommunist region and those of specialists on recent democratization in other regions, therefore, we find a clear contrast. Whereas the former tended to underpredict democracy, assuming, in effect, that many more regimes would fall into either the hybrid or authoritarian camp, specialists on comparative democratization had the opposite problem: they overpredict democratic rule. In both cases, the political diversity of the region—at least by the mid-1990s—was puzzling. How then can we explain why some countries in Central and Eastern Europe moved decisively in a democratic direction, while others moved less decisively and thereby combined elements of democracy and dictatorship, and still others remained authoritarian but in forms different from the communist model?

Explaining Early Political Pathways

A number of plausible factors would seem to be helpful in accounting for the differences among postcommunist regimes during the early stages of the transition. One could suggest, for example, that a key consideration would be the age of the state. As a number of studies have suggested, in the West, states were built long before the possibility of democratic politics either entered or could enter the political agenda. State building is a nasty process, wherein political leaders, wanting to secure their access to people and economic resources and to deny that access to their competitors, use their militaries, local allies, and rudimentary bureaucracies to solidify their political and economic control over a spatially defined group. Rather than negotiate each time they need money and troops, they prefer to create more permanent arrangements—or what subsequently became known as states. The essence of state building, therefore, to borrow from Charles Tilly, is that wars make states, and states make wars.[11]

The demand for democracy in the West, therefore, took place after state building. Once people have lived together for some time in a common state and operate within an increasingly integrated and interactive political and economic context, they can learn to define themselves as members of a common political community, or nation. In the process, they can also embrace a common political project that redefines the relationship between citizens and the state by arguing that states cannot just be coercive or just provide citizens with security. Instead, they are expected to do more—by recognizing citizens as equal, by guaranteeing political rights, and by creating accountable government.

The necessary sequencing of these developments—or spatial consolidation of political authority followed by growing pressures for accountable and legitimate governance—would seem to suggest that the key difference in Central and East European political trajectories after communism is whether the state is new—and thereby committed to the draconian politics and economics of state building—or better established and, because of prior integration of the economy and settlement of borders and membership in the nation, more responsive to political demands for equality and rights. Indeed, precisely this contrast led Dankwart Rustow to argue more than forty years ago that democracy can only enter into the realm of political choice when issues involving membership in the nation and the boundaries of the state have been fully resolved.[12]

The problem here, however, is that the variations in postcommunist political trajectories are not predicted by the age of the state. Just as some of the long-standing states in Central and Eastern Europe, such as Bulgaria and Romania, were hybrid regimes in the first half of the 1990s, some of the newest states in that period—Slovenia, the Czech Republic, and the Baltic states—were in the group of early and robust democracies. Even more interestingly, in the cases of Slovenia and the Czech Republic, the states were in fact completely new formations—in contrast to Estonia, Latvia, and Lithuania, which had been independent states during the interwar years as a result of the Russian Revolution and the breakup of the Russian empire.

Might the differences be explained by ethnic and religious diversity? Again, it is logical to assume that democracy is harder to construct when many nations share the same state, when national differences coincide with differences in economic resources and political power, when previous governing arrangements play diverse groups off one another, and when national minorities spill over into neighboring states, thereby generating tensions about the legitimacy of existing boundaries. However, this factor does not distinguish well among the Central and East European countries either. Both Poland and Albania, for example, have national homogeneity despite their very different political pathways immediately after communism, and the robust democracies of Estonia and Latvia have unusually high levels of diversity, defined here as the size of the second largest ethnic community.

This leaves us with two remaining hypotheses. One is that variation in democratization reflects differences in the mode of transition. Put succinctly, transitions engineered by bargaining between opposition and incumbent elites are more likely to produce democratic government than transitions that occur in reaction to mass protests—a contrast that has been used to explain differences in democratizing dynamics in Latin America and southern Europe. The problem here is that most of the transitions in Central and Eastern Europe involved mass—indeed massive—mobilization, and all of the most successful transitions, except in Hungary, took place in response to mass protests. The other hypothesis targets differences in the nature of politics during communism. Here, the argument is that the more liberalized regimes during communism would have laid more of the groundwork for democracy after communism—for example, because their communists were reform-minded and because opposition forces had more opportunities to expand their support and develop sophisticated political strategies for winning power.

However, the strong democracies within our group are in fact divided between those that experienced more hard-line communist rule—Czechoslovakia and the Baltic countries—and more reformist regimes—Slovenia, Poland, and Hungary.[13]

Explaining Diversity

How, then, can we explain the early patterns of postcommunist politics? We can begin to answer this question by recognizing the importance of the age of the state and the difficulties introduced by what was for many states in this region a simultaneous transition to a new regime and a new state. For states that were already defined at the time of the transition from communism, the key factor that shaped subsequent political pathways seems to have been the outcome of the first competitive election. In particular, where the opposition won handily (Poland and Hungary), we see quick and sustained democratization. By contrast, where power was more equally divided between the communists and the opposition (as in Romania and Bulgaria), the result was a hybrid regime.

But is this argument in fact a tautology, in that when communists win, dictatorships follow; when the opposition wins, democracy follows; and, finally, when they are neck and neck, a synthesis of the two options materializes? Despite the logic of this observation, there are in fact several reasons to be more confident that the argument about initial electoral outcomes is illuminating. One is that this line of explanation also captures variations in economic reform, with rapid reforms following a clear victory of the opposition, resistance to such reforms when the communists win, and a pattern of "fit-and-start" reforms when electoral outcomes are more evenly divided. Another is that there is no particular reason to assume that, if the opposition wins, it will necessarily embrace democratic politics—though in every one of the established states it did. Oppositions, after all, can want many things. Third, it is notable that this argument flies in the face of the generalization in the literature on Latin America and southern Europe that "balanced transitions"—or those in which the opposition and the authoritarians are evenly balanced in their power and form political pacts with each other as a result—lead to the most successful transitions to democracy. With this type of equality, it has been argued, both sides feel secure enough to proceed with regime change. Thus, what seems tautological in Central and Eastern Europe is in fact counterintuitive in other regional contexts.[14]

This leads us to a final point, which helps us deal with the problem of what "causes the cause." Initial electoral outcomes in the contest between authoritarians and opposition forces correlate in turn with patterns of protest during the communist era. To put the matter succinctly, one can conclude that, at least in Central and Eastern Europe, rapid progress toward democracy seems to have depended on a dynamic wherein the development of a strong opposition during communism translated, with the end of the party's monopoly, into an unusually strong political showing in the first elections, which augured well for the future and quality of democratic governance. In this sense, the proximate cause, or variations in electoral outcomes, alerts us to a more distant cause, or variations in opposition development during communism.

We can now turn to the new states in the region—or the Baltic countries, the Czech Republic, Croatia, Macedonia, Serbia-Montenegro, Slovakia, Slovenia, and Ukraine.

(Because of the war and its subsequent development as an international protectorate, Bosnia is left out of the comparison.) Here, a key issue seems to be whether the nationalist project connected with a liberal or illiberal political project—or whether defending the nation was understood to require, or at least be consistent with, democracy or dictatorship. For those countries (then republics) that had nationalist demonstrations or movements during communism (Croatia in the early 1970s, Serbia-Montenegro in the early 1980s, and Slovakia in the late 1960s), the resulting dynamics divided the opposition into democrats and nationalists while weakening public support for the communists and pushing them to bear down on nationalism and to resist any political and economic reforms that might expand opportunities for nationalism to reinvigorate itself. As a result, when communism collapsed, either communists became nationalists in order to maintain dictatorial power (as in Serbia-Montenegro and Slovakia), or the nationalists, facing discredited communists, rejected liberal politics in order to take power (as in Croatia). In either case, democracy was poorly served, whether the communists, the nationalists, or some combination of the two emerged triumphant. By contrast, where nationalist mobilization materialized only when communism began to unravel (as in the Baltic countries, Macedonia, and Slovenia), the nationalist ideology was defined in a liberal way such that nationalist and liberal forces came together to form a powerful opposition, and communists, not as politically isolated or as compromised as in the first set of cases, had little choice, in terms of either personal preferences or self-interest, but to defect to the liberal cause. Ukraine is also an example of late mobilization. However, because of the east-west divide in Ukraine with respect to identity, history, and economic interests, there were more obstacles to democratic change in that country than the others.

In short, we find two pathways. In the older states, regime change was a product of the balance of power between the communists and the opposition forces and, to push the causal process further back in time, the development of a capable opposition during the communist era, whereas in the new states, the key factor seems to have been varying combinations of nationalism, liberalism, and communism, with the particular combination strongly affected by when nationalist mobilization took place and the effects of this timing on the preferences and popularity of both the communists and the nationalists. Put more simply, one can suggest that patterns of political protest during communism, albeit playing out in different ways in republics versus states and introducing different political options, seemed to play a critical role, once the communists lost their political monopoly, in either ushering in democratic politics or compromising the democratic political agenda.

Durability of New States and New Democracies

If many observers were surprised by political outcomes in Central and Eastern Europe in the first phase of the transition, they were even more surprised, given these early developments after the fall of communism, by what transpired in the second phase. From 1996 to 2016 we find three political trends, with the first two both indicating and contributing to greater stability in the region and the third one having the opposite effect. First, while the new states that formed in the region from 1991 to 1992 have remained, much to the surprise of many analysts, they have been joined in recent years by several other new states. Thus, in the late spring of 2006, Serbia-Montenegro divided into two separate states, Kosovo (once a part of Serbia-Montenegro) became an independent state in 2008–2009, and the Russian Federation expanded in size at the expense of its neighbor, Ukraine, as a result of its annexation of Crimea (a peninsula in southeastern Ukraine) in the spring of 2014.[15] While the international community recognizes the new states of Montenegro and Kosovo (though the Russian government and a few others have objected to the latter) and, thus, Serbia's new name and boundaries, it views the sudden boundary changes of Russia and Ukraine as illegitimate. Several aspects of the Crimean case make it very different from the other two. One is that the key international actor involved in the reformulation of boundaries gained territory as a result of its engagement. Russia, in short, was a far more "interested" observer with respect to Crimea than were the United States or the EU in the cases of Montenegro and Kosovo. Second, in contrast to Kosovo, the citizens of Crimea did not need to be protected from attacks launched by their own government. Finally, the hastily held referendum that purportedly legitimated Crimea's secession from Ukraine was not a referendum on independence (as had been the case for Kosovo and Montenegro) but rather a choice about whether to remain in Ukraine or join the Russian Federation. That referendum, moreover, took place with Russian troops already in control of the peninsula and in the absence of any international monitors.

The relative stability of borders in this region since 1992 speaks to several factors. One is that opportunities for redefining boundaries tend to be fleeting, occurring primarily during the unusual circumstances of a conjoined shift in domestic and international regimes, as had happened from 1989 to 1992 when communism collapsed, the Soviet Union was dismembered, and the Cold War ended. Another is that state dissolution during the earlier tumultuous period succeeded to some degree in providing a closer alignment of national and state borders and, with that, an expansion in the legitimacy of both the regime and the state. Finally, powerful actors in the international community tend to resist border changes because they see an opening up of the question of borders as highly destabilizing for both domestic and international politics. To question existing borders is to invite minority communities throughout the region—and certainly their leaders—to demand states of their own. Such demands are tempting in many cases, because they empower minority leaders, while allowing them to ignore other, more pressing issues that might challenge their political influence—for example, rising corruption, poor economic performance, and a decline in the quality of democratic life.

Recent developments in both Montenegro and Kosovo, however, remind us that the borders in southeastern Europe remained in some flux for many years after the collapse of communist regimes and states. Indeed, in sharp contrast to their words and deeds in other parts of the world, including the Caucasus and Russia, major players in international politics, such as the United States and the EU, grew increasingly unwilling and unable to support the borders of Serbia-Montenegro as established during the wars that accompanied the dissolution of the Yugoslav state from 1991 to 1995. Thus, beginning in 1997, the Montenegrin political leadership began to question the value of its federal relationship with Serbia. In 2003, the EU, eager to keep borders intact, brokered a deal whereby Montenegro agreed to stay within the larger, but quite decentralized, state until 2006, when a referendum would be held on the question of Montenegrin independence.

In the spring of 2006, this referendum did take place, and a majority (though not an overwhelming one) of Montenegrins expressed their desire to establish their own state. Quickly following the referendum, Serbia and Montenegro went their separate ways.

The situation in Kosovo has been different. Following the US-led NATO bombing campaign in 1999 to protect Albanian inhabitants in Kosovo from the increasingly repressive actions of the Milošević regime, the United States, with EU support, defined Kosovo as an international protectorate. When it became increasingly clear that Kosovo could not be reintegrated with Serbia, because of the institutional precedents set by its postwar status, the strong support of the majority within Kosovo for independence, and continuing tensions between the Serbian and Albanian communities coinhabiting the province, the United States took the lead, with EU support, in providing verbal, economic, and technical support for a gradual transition in Kosovo to sovereign statehood.[16] This culminated in a February 2008 declaration of independence. For Serbian publics and politicians, the departure of Kosovo has been a good deal more controversial than the exit of Montenegro. Moreover, widespread poverty, the dearth of state institutions that could be recycled from the past, and continuing tensions between the Serbian and Albanian communities living in Kosovo have also rendered the state-building project there a more difficult and prolonged venture than in Montenegro. Thus, while the establishment of the Montenegrin state took place relatively smoothly and quickly, the same has not been the case for Kosovo.[17]

The second trend in the region since the mid-1990s is the growing homogenization of the regimes in Central and Eastern Europe, given the expansion of democratic orders (albeit of varying quality). This development reflected two trends: on the one hand, nearly all of the first democracies stuck and indeed deepened, an outcome one cannot necessarily have expected, especially in view of the constraints on democratization, noted earlier, as a result of the authoritarian past and the stresses of economic reform; on the other hand, the hybrid democracies of the first stage have, in virtually every case, shifted to the democratic camp in the second stage, while the regimes that were initially dictatorships all moved in a liberal direction, thereby joining the hybrid category and sometimes moving in an even more liberal direction (see table 2.1). It is safe to conclude, therefore, that the Baltic states, the Czech Republic, Slovakia, Slovenia, Bulgaria, Romania, and Croatia, all EU members, are very likely to continue as democratic regimes in the future. At the same time, Albania, Bosnia, Macedonia, Serbia, and Montenegro have all made significant progress since 2000 in building more democratic polities.

There are, however, three important exceptions to this "happy" pattern of democratic progress throughout the region. One is Ukraine, which had made some strides in building democracy in the aftermath of the Orange Revolution in 2004 but experienced continuing problems with corruption and, following the election of Viktor Yanukovych as president in 2010, a decline in democratic performance. Following widespread popular protests in Ukraine against Yanukovych's unexpected turn away from the EU in the late fall of 2013, the government collapsed and Yanukovych fled to Russia (which had been a close ally), Russia annexed Crimea, and Russia launched a covert campaign to destabilize eastern Ukraine. In May 2014, a new president, Petro Poroshenko, was elected, and in October of the same year, a new parliament was elected. Despite their commitment to economic and political reforms, however, the new government has made limited progress,

Table 2.1. **Freedom House Rankings for Central and East Eu**
2006-2017

Country	2006	2008	2010	2011	2012	2013	2014			
Albania	3	3	3	3	3	3	3			
Bosnia-Herzegovina	3.5	3.5	3.5	3.5	3	3.5	3			
Bulgaria	1.5	1.5	2	2	2	2	2	2	2	2
Croatia	2	2	1.5	1.5	1.5	2	1.5	1.5	1.5	1.5
Czech Republic	1	1	1	1	1	1	1	1	1	1
Estonia	1	1	1	1	1	1	1	1	1	1
Hungary	1	1	1	1.5	1.5	1	1.5	2	2	2.5
Latvia	1	1.5	2	2	2	1.5	2	2	2	1.5
Lithuania	1	1	1	1	1	1	1	1	1	1
Montenegro		3	2.5	2.5	2.5	2.5	2.5	3	3	3
Poland	1	1	1	1	1	1	1	1	1	1.5
Romania	2	2	2	2	2	2	2	2	2	2
Serbia	2.5	2.5	2	2	2	2.5	2	2	2	2.5
Slovakia	1	1	1	1	1	1	1	1	1	1
Slovenia	1	1	1	1	1	1	1	1	1	1
Ukraine	2.5	2.5	3	3.5	3.5	2.5	2.5	3	3	3

Source: Freedom House's "Freedom in the World" (http://www.freedomhouse.org/report-types/freedom-world).

Note: The cumulative average of political rights and civil liberties scores is based on a scale of 1 to 7, with 1 considered free and 7 considered unfree.

especially with respect to reducing corruption. The ability of the government to carry through on reforms, of course, has been severely compromised by the continuing crisis in eastern Ukraine.

The remaining exceptions are Hungary and Poland—two countries that, from the early 1990s onward, were widely viewed as the front-runners in the race to democracy and capitalism in Central and Eastern Europe. In both cases, democracy has eroded following the sweeping victories of right-wing nationalist parties in parliamentary elections—the Civic Alliance, or FIDESZ, in the case of Hungary in 2010, and the Law and Justice Party in the case of Poland in 2015. The leaders of both parties have used their parliamentary majorities to wage a war on democracy by, for example, undercutting civil liberties and political rights, purging the judiciary and the bureaucracy, exerting more state control over the media and civil society groups, and using extremist rhetoric and policies—for example, in response to the refugee crisis—to carry out their culturally conservative and nationalist agendas. Prime Minister Victor Orban's attack on Hungarian democracy, however, poses the greater threat, in part because he is far more corrupt than his Polish counterpart, in part because he has been more aggressive in changing the Constitution and taking on issues of personal and academic freedom, and in part because his assault on democracy has been going on longer, that is, seven years.[18]

The recent developments in Poland and especially Hungary and backsliding under Yanukovych in Ukraine notwithstanding, it is fair to conclude that a democratic Central and Eastern Europe has finally come into being. In this sense, the pessimists have been oven wrong, whereas the optimists seem to have been validated—with one important qualification. As the division of this chapter suggests, democratization in Central and Eastern Europe has come in two stages. The first wave, as already outlined, featured an immediate and sharp break with the communist past, or a process wherein massive demonstrations, a large and unified opposition embracing liberal politics, and communists who were marginalized (as in the Czech Republic), ideologically sympathetic to the goals of the opposition (as in Hungary and Slovenia) or sufficiently self-interested in the face of a powerful opposition to recognize the logic of defecting from dictatorship (as in the Baltic countries), combined to end the old order and lay the groundwork for competitive elections, which the forces in support of democratic politics then won handily. Although this scenario describes what happened with most of the "early democratizers" in the region, some variations on these dynamics should be noted. Thus, in both Poland and Hungary—the two countries that, in effect, jump-started the collapse of communism in 1989—the critical political turning point was in fact a roundtable between the communists and the opposition forces (with the roundtable following significant protests in Poland in the fall of 1988 and the roundtable in Hungary strongly influenced by the surprising political outcome of the Polish precedent). In both cases, the roundtable set the stage for subsequent elections, which were semi-competitive in Poland and fully competitive in Hungary. In both cases, noncommunist governments were formed and predictably fueled the democratic momentum.

The second wave, or developments that took place in Albania, Bulgaria, Croatia, Macedonia, Montenegro, Romania, Serbia, Slovakia, and Ukraine from 1996 to 2014, has entailed one overarching similarity. Founding elections in all of these cases had compromised the transition to democracy—either through the victory of the ex-communists, who were divided in their commitments to democratic politics, or through the victory of nationalist oppositions, who were often more illiberal than their ex-communist counterparts. However, subsequent elections changed the political balance in ways that, in contrast to the earlier period of transition, better served a democratic outcome. In this sense, a key issue in all of these countries was the growth of political competition during the transition—a pattern that we also find in the first democracies and that, because it produced turnover in governing parties and coalitions, contributed to the deepening of democratic politics.

The dynamics of the second round of democratic transitions in Central and Eastern Europe, however, varied in detail. In Bulgaria, Romania, and Slovakia, the key issue was the eventual rise of a more effective liberal opposition that was able to win power and, for the first time, form a durable and effective government. We find a different dynamic in Albania, Croatia, Macedonia, and Montenegro. Here, the key issue was the growing incentives for the ex-communists, reacting to an opposition that was either liberal or illiberal but in both instances highly competitive, to embrace the liberal cause as a means of weakening the incumbents, differentiating themselves, and thereby accumulating political power.

The final dynamic was in Serbia, where we see a replay, in effect, of the first transitions to democracy in the region, albeit a decade later—a process that also took place, three years later and informed by the Serbian precedent, in Georgia in 2003 and in Ukraine in 2004. In Serbia, mass protests in the fall of 2000 in reaction to an attempt by the increasingly corrupt and politically repressive ex-communists to steal the election,

Photo 2.3.   Berlaymont building with "Welcome Bulgaria Romania to the EU." (European Commission)

enabled the opposition—a coalition as broad as that seen, for example, in Czechoslovakia in 1989—to win power over the long-governing ex-communists. This sharp break with the past, however, was not so sharp, as the subsequent instability of Serbian politics indicated—consider, for example, the continuous squabbling between the Serbian president and the prime minister, the inability of elections to reach the constitutionally required level of turnout, the assassination of Prime Minister Zoran Đinđić in the spring of 2003, and the continued popular support for the antidemocratic Radical Party by a substantial minority of Serbian citizens. The outcome of the presidential elections held in June 2004 and thereafter; the acceptance of Montenegro's declaration of independence in 2006; the use of the International Court of Justice to challenge Kosovo's declaration of independence in 2008 significant progress in both economic reforms and economic performance; the impressive Serbian record since 2000 with respect to civil liberties, political rights, and free and fair elections; and, finally, the commitment of once antidemocratic parties to the democratic project, however, suggest that Serbia is indeed on the road to democracy.

These details aside, all of these "second-wave" democracies are interesting in that the shift from either dictatorship to democracy or from hybrid to full-scale democracy took place in response to elections that brought to power governments with the incentive and the capacity to change the country's political course.[19] But this leaves two obvious questions. Why did the "laggards" in stage one all move in a more democratic direction in stage two? And how can we explain, more generally, the recent convergence in regime types in Central and Eastern Europe?

Explaining the Second Wave: Domestic Factors

In contrast to the explanations offered with respect to the first stage of the transition, the explanations of the second stage are much less parsimonious. Indeed, the importance of both domestic and international factors, both of which pushed in a similar liberalizing direction, is striking. On the domestic side, we can point to two influences. One is suggested by the fact that if we look at postcommunist Eurasia as a whole (or add to our Central and East European group the remaining twelve Soviet successor states), we find a high correlation between contemporary political arrangements and the duration of Communist Party rule. All of the states of interest in this volume are democratic, and they all became communist after World War II. By contrast, the record of democracy in those Soviet successor states where communism had been in place since World War I is far more mixed, featuring, for example, clear-cut dictatorships, such as in Belarus and Uzbekistan, low-quality democracies, such as in Ukraine, and formerly relatively democratic orders that have moved decisively in a dictatorial direction, such as in Armenia and Russia. The durability, albeit continued fragility, of democracy in Moldova—the only Soviet successor state, aside from the Baltic countries and the western part of Ukraine, to have been added to the Soviet Union after World War II—makes this comparison even more instructive. Just as strikingly, given the Armenian, Russian, and Belarusian cases, there have been no cases of democratic breakdown in Central and Eastern Europe since the end of Communist Party hegemony (though the period of Vladimír Mečiar's rule in Slovakia after the breakup of the Czechoslovak federation certainly compromised Slovak democratic performance in the short term, and the same can be said about Poland since 2015 and Hungary since 2010).

Why is the length of Communist Party rule so important? Two plausible factors come to the fore. First, a longer experience with communism means deeper penetration by communist ideology, institutions, and practices—penetration secured in part by the number of generations that lived under communist rule. This could make a transition to democracy more difficult, because of the absence of democracy-supporting institutions and values and because of the constraints on the development of a viable political opposition. The second reason is also historical in nature but asks us to think in broader terms about what this correlation means. The countries of concern in this volume all have a long history of close connections with Western economies, cultures, and political ideas—a history abruptly ended by the rise of communism during and immediately after World War II. The geographical proximity to the West, therefore, may have been important in laying the groundwork, once opportunities for political change presented themselves, for subsequent democratic development. The ability of these countries to withstand the challenge of communism, of course, was aided by the brevity of the communist experience—especially, for example, the unusually brief duration of Stalinization, when the most antidemocratic aspects of state socialism were imposed.[20]

The second domestic factor focuses particularly on those countries where illiberal nationalists came to power after the deregulation of the Communist Party's monopoly, that is, Slovakia, Croatia, and Serbia. In all three cases, the liberal opposition, having been divided and demobilized by the struggle over the national question, finally managed to regroup and remobilize and thereby win elections. The literature on both nationalism and democratic transitions is in fact silent about when and why once successful illiberal nationalists lose power and politicians with a more liberal agenda take their place, focusing far more on the question of why some transitions to democracy feature a central political role for illiberal nationalists. In response to the first and largely unexplored question, we can identify two striking commonalities in our three cases: the opposition was able to focus on the threats and costs of one leader in particular (Mečiar, Tuđman, or Milošević), and international actors, including the EU, the United States, and transnational networks of nongovernmental organizations, played an important role in providing support to the opposition—for example, training them in the art of resistance, providing electoral monitors, and helping them organize campaigns to increase voter registration and electoral turnout. International influences, in short, were critical—a dimension that I will now address more systematically.

International Influences

As noted above, geography played a role in the second wave of democratization. However, its impact was also expressed in international dynamics. If the events of 1989, or the region-wide collapse of Communist Party hegemony, indicated the power of diffusion when neighboring states have similar domestic structures, similar historical experiences, and similar external constraints (such as Soviet control), then diffusion, we might suggest, can still operate after these momentous events. Here, it is important to remember that there was in fact a great deal of interaction among the states of concern in this volume during the communist era. For example, oppositions in Poland, Hungary, and Czechoslovakia were in contact with each other during communism; the rise of the Solidarity movement in Poland in 1980 influenced opposition development in the Baltic states and in Bulgaria before the dramatic developments at the end of the decade; and protests in Central and Eastern Europe during the communist era invariably called for adoption of some features of the Yugoslav alternative model of communism. While this pattern did not guarantee by any means that these countries would all follow identical pathways once the hold of the communists weakened, it did mean that developments in one country had the potential to influence developments elsewhere in the region—for example, demonstrating that democracy was possible in the first stage of the transition and, later, helping weaker opposition forces in, say, Bulgaria, Romania, and Slovakia to acquire the strategies needed to move their less democratic countries in a more liberal direction. Indeed, changes in Slovak politics in the second half of the 1990s influenced subsequent political changes in Croatia and Serbia—and Georgia and Ukraine, for that matter. In this way, over time the region converged in both its political and economic forms—as it had in the past, only in an illiberal way and then with the additional nudge of a hegemon, the Soviet Union, committed for reasons of security and ideology to dictatorship.

The importance of geography, or the spatial side of politics, also alerts us to several other international factors. One is the global wave of democratization. By the turn of the twentieth century, a majority of the world's population lived in democratic orders—an unprecedented situation and one that contributed to developments in Central and Eastern Europe by rendering democracy perhaps the "only game in town." That the countries under discussion are in Europe, of course, also mattered, especially given the role of the Helsinki Process, beginning in the 1970s, in solidifying a European norm of democracy and human rights and, indeed, in providing the opposition in Central and Eastern Europe during the communist era with greater resources to question their regimes' legitimacy and performance.

This leads to a final international variable: the EU. As numerous scholars have argued, the EU has had two effects in Central and Eastern Europe.[21] It has provided a clear standard for democratic politics (and capitalist economics) by which both publics and elites in this region can measure regime performance, and it has provided powerful incentives for those countries to meet (and continue to meet) EU standards—for example, by offering advice on the construction of liberal orders and by holding out the promise of markets, financial support, and the legitimacy that comes from being coded as European and, therefore, part of a prosperous, stable, secure, and, to use the language of many Central and East Europeans, "normal" community. Many scholars and Central and East European citizens, of course, debate whether the EU has been such a powerful force for democracy. Does the EU, for example, make democracy both possible and doable, or has it merely courted those countries that were already on the road to democratic government? Does the EU secure sovereignty for the postcommunist countries or undermine their newly won sovereignty by reducing domestic policy control? Do the economic benefits of joining the EU outweigh, especially in the short term, the costs of preparing for membership—which include not just meeting a huge number of expensive conditions but also facing the constraints imposed by EU markets, the protectionism of older members, and the EU's commitment in recent years to austerity measures in the face of the global economic crisis? Has the EU encouraged competition or merely strengthened those already in power, thereby contributing to inequalities in power and money? Finally, does EU membership produce equality among countries through the creation of a single Europe, or has the eastward expansion of the EU effectively created a hierarchy, sundering the rich western members from their poor eastern cousins and dividing the east, in turn, into countries designated as either current or possible future members and those countries that, because of geography, have no hope of joining and may, as a result, be isolated and thereby locked into authoritarian rule?

While insightful in certain respects, these concerns must be placed alongside two incontrovertible facts. First, all of the countries that have recently joined the EU (though contemporary Hungary and Poland are exceptions, and the EU is currently considering ways to make them pay for their declining democratic performance) or applied for candidate status evince clear improvements over time in democratic assets. Second, there is a clear correlation between prospects for joining the EU and the breadth of the domestic political spectrum. Put simply, we have witnessed in Central and Eastern Europe a sharp decline in most countries (though, again, Hungary and Poland are recent exceptions) of extremist political voices and the convergence of political parties around support for the EU (though public support of the EU, it must be recognized, varies over time within countries as well as among them). For example, after returning to power in 2003, the Croatian Democratic Union, a party that had formerly ruled over Croatia as a dictatorship, went further than its more "moderate" predecessor in embracing EU membership as its primary policy goal. Similarly, Tomislav Nikolić, the president of Serbia from 2012 to May 2017, has done the same, despite a long record of opposition to the EU and support for illiberal Serbian nationalism. We can, of course, debate whether political moderation, as in most of the second-wave democracies, is a consequence of the EU's influence or a function of purely domestic developments. However, the fact remains that political leaders in Central and Eastern Europe, either early in the transition or later, have come to believe that joining the EU is critical for their own political futures and for concerns about identity, money, stability, and security that are critical to voters.

However we construe this dynamic, improvements in democratic performance in such areas as rule of law, state provision of civil liberties and political rights, and moderation in the political values and attitudes of citizens and politicians alike are associated with EU membership. In the rush to embrace the EU, other ways of meeting goals, such as international security and economic growth, as offered by the extreme right and especially the extreme left, have lost political support, either during the accession process or in the years immediately following membership. With respect to the latter dynamic and the second round of democratization in Central and Eastern Europe, extremist parties have either gone into decline or chosen to adapt. Thus, just as political competition increased in all of the countries in Central and Eastern Europe that had lagged in democratization, the structure of competition itself changed through the decline in political polarization. The EU may very well have played a key role in that process.

What is critical to recognize, however, is that these generalizations about the impact of the EU on narrowing the ideological spectrum apply less well in 2017 than they did five and certainly ten years ago. Like Western Europe, some countries in Central and Eastern Europe—most obviously, Poland and Hungary—have experienced a resurgence of right-wing nationalism. The popularity of the EU has also declined.

Conclusion and Some Speculation

In this chapter, I have argued that the transition to democracy in Central and Eastern Europe has proceeded in two stages. In the first stage, from 1989 to the first half of 1996 (with the Romanian presidential elections constituting the turning point), there were variable regime outcomes, with half of the region moving quickly to democracy and the other half either stuck in dictatorship or perched precariously between the two regime extremes. In this period, the key issue was the development of oppositions during communism and the extent to which they embraced liberal politics and were able to win in the first competitive elections. In the second period, 1996–2014, the "laggards" in democratization all moved in a liberal direction. In this case, the causes were multiple, including diffusion effects within the region, the role of the EU, the declining capacity of authoritarian leaders to maintain power through exploitation of cultural differences, and limited constraints on democratization because of what was, from a broader regional standard, a shorter history of Communist Party rule. As a result, the pronounced political diversity of Central and Eastern Europe in the immediate aftermath of the collapse of communism and communist states declined. Just as state boundaries tended to endure, so too democratization spread. Indeed, even the exceptional cases of Montenegro and Kosovo and their secession from Serbia could be construed as an investment in a more authentic democratic politics for all three parts of the original Serbian-Montenegrin federation.

The patterns of democratization in Central and Eastern Europe, together with their underlying causes, present us with several important questions that are relevant to this region and, more generally, to the study of recent transitions to democratic rule. What do we mean by regime outcomes? Does it make sense to argue that some countries in Central and Eastern Europe succeeded or failed to become democratic orders after communism, or does it make more sense to argue that the countries in this region were differentially situated to build democratic orders, with the result that democratization took longer in some cases than in others? The analysis presented above suggests that the latter interpretation is more compelling. This implies that there are differences in the assets and obstacles to democratization and that these differences affect how long a transition can take, even after the evident decline of authoritarian rule.

The time horizons we use to evaluate democratization, therefore, are critical in two ways. First, we can draw premature conclusions about political pathways after authoritarianism if we rush to judgment. Second, we may need different explanations for these pathways, depending on when we choose to step back and evaluate political patterns. In this sense, there seems to be no single road to democratic politics, especially if we allow ourselves to recognize faster versus slower transitions.

But does this mean that, given time, democracy is inevitable? Given the nearly region-wide victory of democracy in Central and Eastern Europe by 2016, or twenty-six years into the transition, we might be tempted to draw such a conclusion. However, there are ample reasons to be skeptical. One is that there are still significant differences in the quality of democratic governance in Central and Eastern Europe. For example, Macedonia has faced repeated instability rooted in the intersection between ethnic diversity and interparty competition, political support for conservative nationalist parties and conservative politicians with inconsistent commitments to democracy has increased in recent years in Bulgaria and especially Poland and Hungary, and the shift to the democratic column in Croatia and especially Serbia is of relatively recent vintage. In addition, other waves of democratization in the past, while admittedly not as global in their reach as the current wave, have been followed by democratic breakdowns. Here, the contemporary examples of Poland and especially Hungary serve as cautionary tales of being too quick to generalize about democratic change. This is especially the case since, in the third wave in particular, we have seen few examples of the collapse of democracy but more examples of a subtler deterioration in democratic performance. Moreover, the current global wave reveals a disturbing pattern: the rise of more and more hybrid regimes, which could tip in either political direction and, at the same time, could endure as halfway houses built on political compromises that promote stability at the cost of corruption and checkered economic performance. Still another consideration is that democratization in Central and Eastern Europe, as I have repeatedly emphasized throughout this chapter, is strongly advantaged by the long connection of this area to Western Europe and, more recently, by the influence of international institutions such as the EU. That recognized, however, it is also the case that populism in Western Europe has influenced politics in Central and Eastern Europe (and vice versa), and that the EU is poorly set up to deal effectively with challenges to democracy in its member states. To put the matter succinctly, the EU's political and economic leverage is much greater with states that are seeking membership than with states that are already members.

Finally, Central and Eastern Europe is distinctive in another way that has also invested in democratic political outcomes. This is a region that does not force dominant international powers, such as the United States, NATO, or the EU, to choose between security concerns and democracy promotion—a choice that was evident throughout the Cold War and that undermined, as a result, democratic politics. Even after the Cold War, this choice is being made again with regard to US policy toward Russia, Central Asia, the Caucasus, and Pakistan.

Democratization in Central and Eastern Europe, therefore, as in southern Europe beginning in 1974, while proceeding in stages, has nonetheless been strongly aided in ways that are largely unavailable to many other countries that have participated in the third wave. Unlucky throughout its history, especially in comparison with Western Europe, Central and Eastern Europe at this time—in comparison with other regions undergoing regime change—has become, in these respects, lucky. Domestic and international factors are largely working together to support democratic rule, whereas both sets of factors in the past had usually pushed these countries in the opposite direction.

These advantages, however, must be judged alongside some constraints on democratization that are likely to become even more apparent in the future. One issue is the declining capacity of the EU to provide incentives for new members, candidate members, and countries with association agreements to deepen the dynamics of both democratization and economic reform. The problem here is that the EU is very divided from within; it is perceived by many publics, whether inside or outside the EU, as too bureaucratic and too removed from its various citizenries to represent their interests and speak for them; it is facing deep economic problems; and it is in the midst of addressing the departure of the United Kingdom from the EU as a result of the verdict of the British voters in June 2016. As a result, the EU is unlikely in the near future, precisely because of all these problems, to expand to include such new but precarious democracies as Albania, Bosnia, Macedonia, Montenegro, Serbia, or Ukraine. The EU, in short, is less willing and able to invest in the newest democracies than it was in the case of the first and most robust democracies in the region. In this sense, the north-south divide in Central and Eastern Europe is likely to continue.

In addition, there is the continuing problem in many of these countries of significant corruption and expanding socioeconomic inequality—with the latter often correlated with cultural cleavages. These developments can contribute to political polarization, especially in hard economic times—as we have seen, for example, in Hungary and Poland. Moreover, most of the regimes in the region feature weak political parties—as institutions that structure the political preferences of mass publics, serve as the primary linkages between citizens and their governments, and shape, especially through elections and parliaments, the course of public policy. The "party" problem, in combination with a severe economic crisis, helps explain political polarization and deterioration in the quality of democracy in Hungary. Yet another issue for even the well-established democracies in the region is the very high level of political cynicism (whether citizens focus on the performance of democratic institutions or on specific politicians), coupled, not surprisingly, with often low voter turnouts. Throughout the region, therefore, we find both continuing weakness in democratic institutions and public disappointment with the democratic experiment. Democracy, therefore, while region-wide, is flawed, and these deficiencies, while unlikely to be fatal to democracy, will necessarily define the boundaries and the consequences of political competition for many years to come.

Study Questions

1. Is it accurate to say that the end of communism led to an immediate and region-wide transition to democracy in Central and Eastern Europe?
2. What are the key differences between democracy and authoritarianism?
3. What are hybrid regimes?
4. How typical have the experiences with region transition in Central and Eastern Europe been in comparison with such transitions in other parts of the world?
5. What have been the key differences in the political evolution of regimes in Central and Eastern Europe since the fall of communism, and what key factors account for these differences?
6. How important was the EU for the spread of democracy in Central and Eastern Europe?
7. What do the recent politics of Poland and Hungary tell us about the durability of democracy?

Suggested Readings

Michael Bernhard and Jan Kubik, eds. *Twenty Years after Communism: The Politics of Memory and Commemoration*. Oxford: Oxford University Press, 2014.

Bunce, Valerie. "Global Patterns and Post-Communist Dynamics." *Orbis* 50 (Autumn 2006): 601–20.

Bunce, Valerie, Michael McFaul, and Kathryn Stoner-Weiss, eds. *Democracy and Authoritarianism in the Postcommunist World*. New York: Cambridge University Press, 2009.

Bunce, Valerie J., and Sharon L. Wolchik. *Defeating Authoritarian Leaders in Postcommunist Countries*. New York: Cambridge University Press, 2011.

Gagnon, Charles P. *Myth of Ethnic War: Serbia and Croatia in the 1990s*. Ithaca, NY: Cornell University Press, 2004.

Mungiu-Pippidi, Alina, and Ivan Krastev, eds. *Nationalism after Communism: Lessons Learned*. Budapest: Central European University, 2004.

Stroschein, Sherrill. *Ethnic Struggle, Coexistence and Democratization in Eastern Europe*. New York: Cambridge University Press, 2014.

Vachudova, Milada Anna. *Europe Undivided: Democracy, Leverage, and Integration after Communism*. Oxford: Oxford University Press, 2005.

Zielonka, Jan, ed. *Democratic Consolidation in Eastern Europe*. Oxford: Oxford University Press, 2001.

Websites

Radio Free Europe/Radio Liberty: http://www.rferl.org

Freedom House, "2014 Nations in Transit Data": http://www.freedomhouse.org/report-types/nations-transit#.VzAizM5Z9ac

World Bank, "Worldwide Governance Indicators": http://www.info.worldbank.org/governance/wgi/index.aspx#home

Notes

1. The tripartite political division of the region in the immediate aftermath of communist regimes has been analyzed by several scholars. See, e.g., Valerie Bunce, "The Political Economy of Postsocialism," *Slavic Review* 58 (Winter 1999): 756–93; M. Steven Fish, "The Determinants of Economic Reform in the Postcommunist World," *East European Politics and Societies* 12 (Winter 1998): 31–78; and Michael McFaul, "The Fourth Wave of Democracy and Dictatorship: Noncooperative Transitions in the Postcommunist World," *World Politics* 54 (January 2002): 214–44.

2. There are many competing definitions of democracy. Perhaps the most helpful summary of these debates can be found in Robert Dahl, *On Democracy* (New Haven, CT: Yale University Press, 1998).

3. Since the early 1990s, hybrid regimes have become the most common outcome of the global wave of democratic change that began in the mid-1970s. See Larry Diamond, "Thinking about Hybrid Regimes," *Journal of Democracy* 13 (April 2002): 3–24; Steven Levitsky and Lucan A. Way, "The Rise of Competitive Authoritarianism," *Journal of Democracy* 13 (April 2002): 51–65. See also Marina Ottaway, *Democracy Challenged: The Rise of Semi-Authoritarianism* (Washington, DC: Carnegie Endowment Press, 2003).

4. On the issues of demobilization of the liberals in these two countries, see V. P. Gagnon, *The Myth of Ethnic War: Serbia and Croatia in the 1990s* (Ithaca, NY: Cornell University Press, 2004); and Kevin Deegan-Krause, "Uniting the Enemy: Politics and the Convergence of Nationalisms in Slovakia," *East European Politics and Societies* 18 (Fall 2004): 651–96.

5. See, e.g., Samuel P. Huntington, *The Third Wave: Democratization in the Late Twentieth Century* (Norman: University of Oklahoma Press, 1991); Guillermo A. O'Donnell, Philippe C. Schmitter, and Laurence Whitehead, eds., *Transitions from Authoritarian Rule,* vols. 1–4 (Baltimore, MD: Johns Hopkins University Press, 1986); and Giuseppe Di Palma, *To Craft Democracy* (Berkeley: University of California Press, 1991).

6. On the unexpected problems encountered after the fall of Saddam Hussein, see Larry Diamond, "What Went Wrong in Iraq?" *Foreign Affairs* 83 (Summer/Fall 2004): 34–56; and Peter Galbraith, "Iraq: Bush's Islamic Republic," *New York Review of Books* 52 (August 11, 2005): 6–9.

7. A useful summary of these arguments can be found in Grzegorz Ekiert and Stephen Hanson, eds., *Capitalism and Democracy in Central and Eastern Europe: Assessing the Legacy of Communist Rule* (Cambridge: Cambridge University Press, 2003).

8. Carol Leff, *National Conflict in Czechoslovakia: The Making and Remaking of a State, 1918–1987* (Princeton, NJ: Princeton University Press, 1988).

9. See, especially, O'Donnell, Schmitter, and Whitehead, *Transitions*; and M. Steven Fish, *Democracy from Scratch: Opposition and Regime in the New Russian Revolution* (Princeton, NJ: Princeton University Press, 1995).

10. See Nancy Bermeo, *Ordinary People in Extraordinary Times: The Citizenry and the Breakdown of Democracy* (Princeton, NJ: Princeton University Press, 2003).

11. Charles Tilly, *Coercion, Capital and European States, AD 990–1992* (London: Basil Blackwell, 1992).

12. Dankwart Rustow, "Transitions to Democracy: Toward a Dynamic Model," *Comparative Politics* 2 (April 1970): 18–36.

13. See Terry Lynn Karl, "Dilemmas of Democratization in Latin America," *Comparative Politics* 23 (Spring 1990): 28–49; and Valerie Bunce, "Rethinking Recent Democratization: Lessons from the Postcommunist Experience," *World Politics* 55, no. 2 (January 2003): 167–92.

14. Bunce, "The Political Economy," 756–93; McFaul, "The Fourth Wave," 214–44; and Valerie J. Bunce and Sharon L. Wolchik, "Favorable Conditions and Electoral Revolutions," *Journal of Democracy* 17, no. 4 (October 2006): 5–22.

15. Valerie Bunce and Aida Hozic, "Diffusion-Proofing and the Russian Invasion of Ukraine," *Demokratizatsiya* 24 (September 2016): 345–456.

16. International Commission on the Balkans, *The Balkans in Europe's Future* (Sofia: Secretariat Center for Liberal Strategies, 2005).

17. Elton Skendaj, *Creating Kosovo: International Oversight and the Making of Ethical Institutions* (Ithaca, NY: Cornell University Press, Washington, DC: Woodrow Wilson Center, 2014).

18. David Ost, "Grappling with the Hungarian and Polish New Right in Power," *Newsnet* 56 (August 2016): 1–4.

19. For a comparison of these two waves, see Valerie Bunce and Sharon Wolchik, "A Regional Tradition: The Diffusion of Democratic Change under Communism and Postcommunism," in *Democracy and Authoritarianism in the Postcommunist World*, ed. Valerie Bunce, Michael McFaul, and Kathryn Stoner-Weiss (New York: Cambridge University Press, 2009).

20. The importance of geographical proximity to the West has appeared in a number of studies that have attempted to explain variations among postcommunist political and economic trajectories. See, e.g., Jeffrey S. Kopstein and David A. Reilly, "Geographical Diffusion and the Transformation of the Postcommunist World," *World Politics* 53 (October 2000): 1–37.

21. See, e.g., Milada Anna Vachudova, *Europe Undivided: Democracy, Leverage, and Integration after Communism* (Oxford: Oxford University Press, 2005); Wade Jacoby, *The Enlargement of the European Union and NATO: Ordering from the Menu in Central Europe* (Cambridge: Cambridge University Press, 2004); and Ronald H. Linden, ed., *Norms and Nannies: The Impact of International Organizations on the Central and East European States* (Lanham, MD: Rowman & Littlefield, 2002).

CHAPTER 3

Re-Creating the Market

Sharon Fisher → economist, IHS Markit → a business consulting firm

Transforming the economies of Central and Eastern Europe was probably the most complicated aspect of the transition from communism. At the start of the reform process, there was no single model for how the changes should be carried out. The postcommunist transition was unique. Unlike with the transitions in Latin America and elsewhere in the world, there was no real market economy on which to build, so the old state economy had to be dismantled as a market economy was developed. Thus, reforms happened in a rather haphazard way, and most knowledge of the transition process was formed after the fact.

Defining the "success" of a country's transition can be difficult, as some former communist states gained international recognition for certain reforms (such as privatization) but were laggards in other areas (such as banking reform). Some countries that initially appeared to be on a rapid path toward a market economy eventually slowed down, while the opposite occurred in other cases. In most countries, foreign observers perceived the success of reforms much differently than the domestic population did, and reformist politicians often suffered in elections. Regardless, it is generally agreed that the most successful economic transitions in the region were those of the eight countries that joined the European Union (EU) in May 2004. Still, even among those countries, there have been great variations, and the global economic crisis of 2008–2009 as well as the subsequent Eurozone debt drama had a surprisingly negative impact on several of the new member states.

In retrospect, initial conditions and the strength of the commitment of successive governments to reforms appear to have been the two most important factors in determining the economic success of Central and East European countries.[1] In regard to the initial conditions, the Central and East European countries began the transition from communism from somewhat disparate starting points. Some, such as Hungary and Poland, had a head start: they had begun reforms during the final years of the communist era. Others, such as the Czech Republic, benefited from a strong manufacturing tradition. The more advanced countries in the region were generally those with close proximity to Western markets, whether because of historical traditions or the ease of trade and investment ties with the EU. Geographic proximity made it easier to attract foreign direct investment (FDI) and turn from trade with the former Soviet Union to Western Europe. For example, despite being substantially behind the Central European countries at the end of the communist era, the three Baltic states benefited in the transition period from cooperation with their Nordic neighbors. The countries that experienced the bulk of their industrialization during the communist era often had a more difficult economic transition, especially when they were far from Western markets.

The other key factor determining the success or failure of the initial economic reforms was the policy approach of the new postcommunist governments. While the political developments in each individual country had a substantial impact on the way market-oriented reforms were carried out, the economic situation also had a major effect on politics, as fickle populations frequently shifted their support from government to opposition depending on which side was promising prospects of greater well-being. It is important to keep in mind that frequent changes in government, often brought on by popular dissatisfaction with how the economic reforms worked, contributed to a lack of continuity in the reform process throughout the region.

The way communism ended in the various countries of Central and Eastern Europe also had a significant impact on the approach governments took to economic reforms. According to the European Bank for Reconstruction and Development, the presence of a noncommunist government in the initial transition period is strongly correlated with the character of reforms in subsequent years.[2] Communists or former communists initially remained in control in Bulgaria, Romania, Ukraine, and Albania but were ousted in Poland, Hungary, Czechoslovakia, and the three Baltic states. As a result, reforms were considerably faster in the latter countries in the early 1990s. Once the pace was set, successive governments generally continued with the reform process, even when the reformed communists came to power. By the middle to late 1990s, prospects for EU accession also helped push them along on the reform path.

The Demise of Central Planning

Formally, communist economic policy was based on a protection of workers' interests through a "dictatorship of the proletariat." In practice, however, the Communist Party leadership controlled all social and economic organizations and made all major decisions about the economy. All appointments, including the managers of enterprises, had to be approved by the party, whether by the Central Committee or local organs. Those who formed the party *nomenklatura* (defined as a list of people from which high-level government appointments were selected) were provided with special rights and privileges to motivate them.

A key element of communist economic policy was "collective ownership," or nationalization of the means of production. Private ownership of land and the means of production were abolished without compensation, while lower classes benefited from social promotion. Agriculture was collectivized with the installation of communist rule. Only in Yugoslavia and Poland was private farming allowed. Central planning was another important aspect of communist economic policy, with a focus on quantity rather than on quality or profit. Prices in this system were regulated, and fixed prices at both the wholesale and retail levels meant that open inflation was never a problem. With regard to labor, the communist system offered full employment. Those who did not work were considered "parasites." A balanced budget, on the surface at least, was another element of the communist economic program.

Foreign trade was regulated by the Council for Mutual Economic Assistance (CMEA) trading bloc, established by the Soviet Union, Bulgaria, Czechoslovakia, Hungary, Poland, and Romania in 1949. The CMEA was formed in response to the US Marshall Plan's offer of economic aid to some of these countries (which the Soviet Union insisted they refuse). Within the CMEA (also known as Comecon), a system of international specialization was laid out so that different goods were produced in different parts of the region to meet Soviet needs (and also those of the bloc as a whole), particularly in the military sector. This policy ensured that no state could stand alone economically. It did not work like a common market; instead trade was negotiated and conducted bilaterally, with oversight by the Soviet Union.

The communist economic system was, even at its best, a tragedy of errors. Central planning meant that bankruptcy was not a possibility. State subsidies were used to keep unprofitable firms afloat. Maintaining a balanced budget thus would have been a challenge if there had been open accounting. Even though most countries' budget deficits were quite small, they created substantial imbalances. The only way to cover deficits was through foreign borrowing or printing more money.

Economic plans focused on production rather than personal consumption. There was similarly little investment in health care, transportation, housing, and services. Moreover, there was a complete disregard for the environmental effects of production. The pricing system encouraged an intentional lowering of quality by producers and contributed to shortages. After all, decisions were made at the Central Planning Commission based on political goals. Citizens relied on their personal connections to obtain goods and services, and the gray economy grew steadily. This meant that corruption was rampant, a trend that has continued well into the second decade of the twenty-first century. Although socialism was supposed to create individuals committed to the common good, most people were focused primarily on providing for their families.

Because domestic prices were regulated nationally, there was no link between domestic and foreign prices. As a result, currencies were not convertible. There were official and unofficial exchange rates. An overvalued domestic currency provided little reason to export goods outside the region as long as countries did not have debts they needed to repay to foreign creditors. By the end of the communist era, some 60 to 75 percent of trade was conducted with other CMEA members, and many of the goods produced were not competitive in the West.

Before long, the communist economic system began to show signs of strain. As these economies faltered, some countries implemented limited economic reforms. Hungary launched its so-called goulash communism in 1968. In Poland, after several failed attempts, market reforms were begun a final time in 1982. In Yugoslavia, the communist system was considerably more liberal and the economy less plan-oriented and more "self-managing" than in other countries in the region. In the late 1980s, the Yugoslav regime introduced extensive market-oriented reforms. However, most other regimes were reluctant to make any significant policy changes. Even after Mikhail Gorbachev launched partial reforms in the USSR during the late 1980s, countries such as Czechoslovakia, East Germany, Bulgaria, Romania, and Albania maintained a hard-line stance until the fall of communism in 1989.

In those countries that did introduce reforms, there was a clear pattern. The reach of the plan (the number of things it regulated) was cut. Power was delegated from branch ministries to enterprise managers to help decentralize decision-making. Economic incentives were promoted. Pricing was made more flexible and market-oriented. Inflation was made a fact of life. The establishment of small private enterprises was permitted. Foreign trade was partially liberalized. Since substantial distortions remained, other, new problems emerged. For example, as unemployment was legalized, jobless benefits were introduced, so a higher share of state revenues had to be devoted to social welfare.

By the late 1980s, the communist system was in precarious shape. Most countries experienced severe economic crises with falling output, profound shortages of consumer goods, accelerating inflation rates, widening current-account deficits, and rising foreign debt. Failing to deliver the expected growth, economic reforms instead called into question the legitimacy of the entire communist system with its claim of superiority over capitalism. Countries such as Poland and Hungary were forced to borrow heavily from abroad to spur investment and consumption in an effort to raise growth rates and appease the population. As the liabilities to foreign lenders increased, debt service also rose, and international credits began to dry up by the end of the decade. Many countries in the region were forced to reschedule their foreign debts.

During the last years of the communist era, the only relative "success stories" were Hungary and Czechoslovakia. Czechoslovakia managed to steer clear of major imbalances, despite the hard-line approach of its communist system. Meanwhile, Hungary had transformed itself into a socialist market economy while maintaining some degree of economic balance, although foreign debt did rise substantially. Both countries avoided the debilitating shortages that plagued other economies in the region.[3]

Macroeconomic Stabilization

As they transformed toward capitalism, most Central and East European countries inherited strong macroeconomic and external disequilibria from the communist system, including budget imbalances based on overarching social welfare systems and high levels of foreign debt. Even countries like Czechoslovakia, which had relatively stable and positive initial macroeconomic conditions at the outset, had to deal with the inflationary impact of price liberalization and the effects of the collapse of trade with the USSR. Across the region, advisors from organizations such as the International Monetary Fund (IMF) gave technical assistance to devise macroeconomic stabilization programs based largely on methods that were applied in developing countries. Even as governments implemented these programs, it was unclear how effective they would be. After all, postcommunist transitions were unprecedented in the scope of the changes required.

Macroeconomic stabilization programs included price liberalization, restrictive monetary and fiscal policies, and foreign trade liberalization, accompanied by a sharp devaluation of the domestic currency, making it weaker against international currencies such as the US dollar. These measures were aimed at stabilizing the economy and allowing for the introduction of structural changes, including enterprise privatization and reforms of the banking sector and social welfare system.

The main debates on the transition focused not on what needed to be done but rather on how to sequence and pace the reforms. Some argued that demonopolization of industry was required before prices were set free to prevent firms from simply hiking prices. In the stabilization package, there was also considerable debate over the extent of the currency devaluation and how much interest rates should be shifted. Devaluation helped to improve external trade balances, allowing for international stabilization. Nonetheless, it also raised the price of imports of consumer and industrial goods, thereby contributing to higher inflation. The small- or medium-size open economies in Central and Eastern Europe were particularly vulnerable to these cross-pressures.

In terms of speed, reformers were divided into proponents of "shock therapy" versus "gradualism." The gradualists argued for relatively lax monetary and fiscal policies and a slower transfer of assets from the state to the private sector, with the aim of protecting the population from the social consequences of reforms. With time, it became clear that none of the countries that consistently advocated a gradual approach were successful reformers.

PRICE LIBERALIZATION

Among the countries that launched reforms before 1989, only Hungary broadly liberalized prices under the communist regime. Elsewhere in Central Europe, the "big-bang" approach to price liberalization was used after the fall of communism. Poland took the lead in January 1990, and Czechoslovakia followed a year later. When "big bangs" happened, market forces set prices for consumer durables and nonfood items, so shortages disappeared as the population's ability to purchase goods diminished. But politicians and consumers were often reluctant to give up fixed prices on essentials such as food (particularly bread and meat) and gasoline because such a step would impoverish a population that expected economic gains under the new capitalist system. In the end, many governments dropped price controls only because of their inability to continue providing subsidies. In most Central and East European countries, rents, public transport, and utilities remained under state control throughout the 1990s and even into the first decade of the twenty-first century. Prices were often set below the real costs because price hikes were seen as politically risky. In Slovakia, for example, consumer prices for natural gas did not reach world market levels until 2004; regulated rents in the Czech Republic remained well below market prices through 2006.

Price liberalization caused inflation to surge throughout the Central and East European region in the initial transition years. Most countries experienced triple- or quadruple-digit price growth after the fall of communism. Those increases were largely a result of filling out the imbalances from the previous regime, particularly where countries printed money to cover budgetary expenditures. The former Czechoslovakia, where the state maintained a balanced budget under communism, had the smallest increase in inflation following the launch of price liberalization, and inflation never reached triple digits. In contrast, countries such as Ukraine and rump Yugoslavia, where macroeconomic stabilization programs initially failed, suffered from hyperinflation.

Several key lessons regarding price liberalization can be drawn from the postcommunist transitions in Central and Eastern Europe. First, the initial liberalization had to be as comprehensive as possible. Any additional deregulation of prices proved to be extremely complicated, spurring passionate public debates and broad opposition. Second, greater distortions of initial price levels required more comprehensive deregulations, even as the distortions made price hikes more difficult for the public to stomach due to the large increase over communist-era levels. Third, populations willingly accepted price deregulation when it was accompanied by a change in the system. In fact, nowhere in the region did price liberalizations stir widespread protest.[4] Finally, high levels of inflation are incompatible with economic growth. In contrast, countries that did not experience hyperinflation were able to moderate the declines in gross domestic product (GDP) during the early transition years.

RESTRICTING MONETARY POLICY

The liberalization of prices in Central and Eastern Europe usually involved higher increases in inflation than were initially expected. This inflation resulted in demands for a loosening of control over monetary policy. Many countries in the region, in fact, maintained low interest rates in the initial transition years. This discouraged savings and contributed to a low level of trust in local currencies. Although this negatively affected average citizens, it benefited politically connected individuals because they could obtain loans at low real interest rates.

Eventually, monetary authorities shifted from expanding the money supply to restricting it, with the aim of keeping inflation down. Their policies involved, instead, a slow growth in the money supply, even a negative growth in real terms. These policies were also accompanied by large increases in interest rates to make them higher than the rate of inflation. In Ukraine, for example, real interest rates were set at a high of 200 percent in spring 1996.[5] This policy of high interest rates discouraged domestic borrowing and encouraged saving and investment. Perhaps more important was the impact high interest rates had in reducing risky lending practices. In each country's transition, "success" required that monetary authorities eventually find a balance between the two extremes of high versus low interest rates to support economic growth.

BALANCING FISCAL BUDGETS

Because the main source of financing for budget deficits comes from the printing of money, fiscal policy is closely linked to monetary policy as an important element in stabilizing economies undergoing transformation. The persistence of fiscal imbalances poses serious risks for the sustainability of long-term economic growth because it triggers higher inflation rates. Thus, a first step in the macroeconomic stabilization programs in Central and Eastern Europe was a dramatic reduction of fiscal deficits, so that revenues and expenses in the state budget became more balanced. By reducing state expenditures and increasing revenues, the new elites sought to ensure that the fiscal reforms would provide the necessary funds to sustain a radical stabilization program. Balanced budgets were especially crucial in those countries that were very indebted because the financing of fiscal deficits contributed to rising inflation and made it difficult to satisfy creditors. A balanced budget became a main criterion for receiving IMF financing and other credits from international financial markets. Governments in the region struggled to balance the demands of their constituents with the austere fiscal targets required by international financial institutions.

Initially, fiscal deficits were driven largely by the high expenditures associated with the oversized public sector and the collapse of revenues due to production declines in the transition process. On the expenditure side, the first step transitional governments took was to eliminate consumer price subsidies, especially for basic food products. The second step involved cutting subsidies for state enterprises. This step proved much more difficult to implement because it contributed to higher levels of unemployment. As firms sought profitability, they typically laid off workers. Pressures for more state expenditures emerged through public demands for higher social spending in the form of social welfare programs and pensions. Most countries in the region maintained enterprise subsidies throughout the 1990s in at least a few key but inefficient sectors, most notably agriculture, mining, and energy. Eventually, direct subsidies were frequently replaced by indirect subsidies, with state companies getting cheap credits from state-owned banks.

On the revenue side, an entirely new taxation system was necessary. Under the new system, personal income and consumption taxes accounted for a larger share of total tax revenues, thereby taking the burden off enterprises and helping them maintain competitiveness. The first step was to replace the communist-era "turnover tax" with the value-added tax (VAT), a consumption tax levied at each stage of production based on the value added to the product at that stage; the final consumer ultimately bears the tax burden. In contrast, the turnover tax was utilized under the previous system on a discretionary basis. Goods considered socially necessary were subsidized by negative tax rates. In the new system, VAT rates were typically around 20 percent, often with lower rates for necessities such as food and medicines.

The second important element in reforming the revenue side of the budget was the establishment of personal income taxes. Under communism, personal income taxes were insignificant. In the transition period, three alternative models were used: a social democratic approach with high progressive income taxes that went up to more than 50 percent of gross income for the wealthiest citizens (Hungary and Ukraine); a standard model with a progressive system taxing individuals between 12 and 40 percent of their income; and the Baltic model (Estonia, Latvia) with a flat personal income tax—the same percentage for everyone.

The third step involved the establishment of a corporate tax system that was legislated rather than being subject to negotiations between managers and their government supervisors, as it had been during the communist era. Most countries initially chose to impose a flat profit tax of 30 to 35 percent.[6]

Another major concern of the transition countries was the need for an efficient and effective collection system. After all, since "taxes" were not really a part of a state economy, there was no real infrastructure for tax collection and enforcement. Under communism, taxes were automatically transferred to the budget through the state-owned banking system. In the new regimes, there was a need for institutions, people, and funds to manage the new tax system. Most of the Central and East European countries were relatively successful in establishing a strong, relatively unitary revenue service. The countries of the Commonwealth of Independent States (CIS) had more problems. In most cases, the introduction of the VAT proved successful in boosting revenue collection. With regard to personal income tax, the Baltic approach proved by far the most successful in terms of revenue collection because it was simple and easy to enforce. The progressive tax systems found elsewhere merely encouraged underreporting and avoidance.

CURRENCY CONVERTIBILITY AND EXCHANGE RATE REGIMES

Currency convertibility and the unification of exchange rates were important prerequisites for foreign trade liberalization. As already mentioned, communist regimes had no link between domestic and foreign prices, making currencies inconvertible for international payments. Most former communist countries immediately adopted a fully convertible current account, allowing for trade in goods and services. In contrast, convertibility was introduced only gradually on capital accounts, which govern the transfer of financial assets. The Baltic states emerged in the forefront of the reforms aimed at bringing capital-account convertibility.[7]

In regulating the currency, policy makers began the transition with an initial devaluation that accompanied the introduction of a stabilization program. While two or more different exchange rates had existed in communist systems, including the official and black market rates, this could not happen in economies that were joining the world economy. So a single, official exchange rate had to be established. The devaluation was introduced to improve trade imbalances by making imports more expensive and exports cheaper. After the initial devaluation, governments adopted one of four types of exchange rate regime: floating rates (in which the currency floats freely without intervention from the central bank), pegged rates (where the currency's value is fixed against that of another currency or basket of currencies to provide a nominal anchor), crawling pegs (a pegged exchange rate regime where the reference value is shifted at preestablished times), and currency boards (in which foreign exchange reserves are used to back the currency).

FOREIGN TRADE LIBERALIZATION

Under communism, trade in the Central and East European region was handled through the CMEA. That system was disbanded in January 1991. At that time, the USSR began demanding payment for raw materials in Western currencies and at world market prices. Thus, the USSR signaled that it was no longer willing to subsidize the rest of the region by exporting hard goods and importing soft goods in exchange for political loyalty. Similarly, the Central and East European countries were no longer willing to accept political domination in exchange for Soviet subsidies. While many analysts initially thought that the CMEA's demise would significantly increase trade within the region by removing many of the impediments associated with the old structures, the opposite occurred. The collapse of demand in the Soviet Union caused sharp declines in interregional trade. For the Central and East European countries, the postcommunist transition required a major redirection of trade. These transitional economies needed to find export products that would be competitive on world markets in order to service their debts.

Trade liberalization was carried out through a shift to tariffs, accompanied by reductions in tariff rates. This was reflected in the abolition of the many administrative restrictions on the import and export of industrial products from the old system. That shift had the advantage of making trade regulation more transparent and compatible with the General Agreement on Tariffs and Trade and later the World Trade Organization. Trade liberalization began in manufacturing and gradually shifted to sensitive areas such as services and agricultural trade. The Central European countries and Estonia initially had the most success in the first phase of liberalization, introducing tariffs and reducing tariff rates in 1990 through 1991.

Trade liberalization was important for several reasons. Opening the domestic markets to imported products from the West helped satisfy consumption-starved citizens. Moreover, trade liberalization pushed countries forward in their structural adjustment; given the small size of the domestic markets, competition in most countries could only happen from imports. External economic relationships also contributed to stabilizing the economy by forcing domestic inflation into line with international rates.

In addition to foreign trade liberalization, currency convertibility, and exchange rate policy, there were two other important aspects of external economic relations: developing new market-friendly institutions to promote economic integration within the region and gaining access to preferential trading arrangements in the international economy such as the EU. The Central European Free Trade Agreement was established in 1992 by Hungary, Poland, and Czechoslovakia with the aim of testing regional cooperation prior to EU integration. It was soon enlarged to include other countries from the region. In the USSR, all former republics except for the three Baltic states joined the CIS in 1991. Most Central European and Baltic countries had signed association agreements with the EU by the mid-1990s. These agreements served to boost exports and consolidate the opening of markets. General Agreement on Tariffs and Trade/World Trade Organization membership also helped to guarantee the maintenance of free trade. In May 2004, eight Central and East European countries took the final step in international economic integration and became full EU members. They were joined in January 2007 by Bulgaria and Romania and in July 2013 by Croatia.

Structural Reforms

The achievement of macroeconomic stabilization paved the way for the launch of structural reforms, creating an investment climate conducive to the entry of new businesses, including small and medium enterprises. In centrally planned economies, all means of production, transportation, and financial intermediation had been owned by the state. As a result, firms had few incentives to produce high-quality goods. Long-term investment was limited. Moreover, in planned economies, no consideration was given to profitability. Firms were often grossly overstaffed, with employees working at half capacity because of shortages of inputs for production. The initial path toward transition involved removing barriers to private business. This required the establishment of an institutional framework conducive to the development of a market economy. Governments had to develop commercial, labor, and tax codes that provided the base for the creation of new businesses, while also paving the way for privatization and labor market reforms. Of all the institutions that had to be developed, the establishment of a two-tiered banking system was the most critical.

Fiscal reform played a double role in the transformation process of the former socialist countries. In addition to being a key element in the stabilization efforts, it was also part of the structural adjustment program. Under communism, companies had provided social protection to their employees. The state took over that role in the new regime. This required a transformation of the entire social welfare system through a process referred to as "rightsizing" government.

PRIVATIZATION

Privatization was a crucial aspect of the restructuring process because, most significantly, it improved the efficiency of resource allocation and contributed to stronger budget constraints on enterprises. Private firms divested themselves of unprofitable sectors and laid off excess employees. Privatization also had positive spillover effects throughout the economy. It helped spur the development of entrepreneurial spirit. Moreover, receipts from privatized enterprises improved the state's fiscal position as it struggled with reforms. Finally, although the privatization process itself was often plagued by corruption, the sale of state-owned firms eventually contributed to a reduction in the power of government policy makers by establishing new, private owners.

The privatization process across Central and Eastern Europe began through the sale of small-scale enterprises, typically through auctions, direct sales, or giveaways, or through restitution schemes that returned properties to their precommunist owners. Restitution was also used with respect to land and housing. While Hungary and Poland had allowed for small private businesses in the 1980s, in hard-line regimes such as Czechoslovakia, 99 percent of the economy remained in state hands up until the fall of communism. Despite these very different starting points, small-scale privatization was accomplished with relative ease and was close to completion within one to two years in most countries.

The sale of state-owned companies became more complicated when countries began selling off medium- and large-scale enterprises. Privatization agencies were created to choose which firms should be sold and to establish the rules and regulations for the sales. The main methods used were manager-employee buyouts (MEBOs), voucher schemes, direct sales, initial public offerings (IPOs), and public tenders. The strategies varied between countries. Countries typically chose one main method and combined it with a mix of other approaches.

Privatization through MEBOs involved selling the enterprise to the current management and employees at discounted prices or sometimes simply transferring ownership without a cash payment. That is why the approach is often referred to as an "insider" model. While MEBOs are relatively quick, simple, and popular with the workers, they are also inefficient. Use of the MEBO method slowed the restructuring of the enterprise's management and operations; required continued state support, given the dearth of funds the employees and managers had for investment; failed to bring in the required market expertise; and left the state with little or no monetary compensation for the sale of the enterprise. Slovenia is the only country from the Central and East European region that had real success in using the MEBO approach, probably because its economy was already well integrated with Western Europe when the transition started.

The voucher or coupon method involved the transfer of shares in state-owned companies to citizens. In this method, citizens are given coupons for nominal sums (or sometimes for free). They trade these coupons for shares in firms or investment funds. The main advantages of the coupon method have been its speed, relative ease of administration, and equitability. In Central and East European countries, coupon privatization was presented as a way of garnering public support to continue market reforms by turning citizens into shareholders. Nonetheless, like the MEBOs, coupon programs failed to bring in the funds needed for enterprise restructuring. Another downside was that the diffusion of ownership translated into weak corporate governance, which, narrowly defined, refers to the relationship between a company and its shareholders. Both the coupon and MEBO methods allowed for the transfer of property in capital-starved economies, but state budgets did not benefit from the temporary boost in revenues that privatization can bring. The coupon method was first launched in Czechoslovakia in 1992 and later copied in other countries before eventually falling out of favor.

Many Western market analysts see issuing stock on securities markets at a predetermined price in an IPO as the most transparent way of selling off state corporations. That method can also reap large revenues for the government. However, IPOs were seldom used in the Central and East European region because of the lack of developed financial markets in the transitioning countries.

Direct sales and public tenders were among the most common forms of privatization in Central and Eastern Europe. These were usually managed by the state privatization agency. In theory, direct sales go to the highest bidder. However, in practice, corruption can be rampant in direct sales due to the lack of transparency. Unlike direct sales, public tenders are based not on the level of privatization proceeds but rather on the premise of achieving the highest long-term economic growth potential. Thus, sales are negotiated with buyers who must present a business plan that takes into account such factors as employment, investment, and performance guarantees. These schemes require that the enterprises for sale be attractive enough to find investors willing to make a long-term commitment. The tender method is more difficult in the short term because negotiations can take a long time and revenues from the sales are generally not as high as in the case of direct sales. Another downside is that the rules for the tender are set at the discretion of state officials. Nonetheless, the short-term disadvantages are typically more than offset by the long-term benefits. The public tender method has been seen as the most successful privatization method in the Central and East European region.

PRIVATIZATION STRATEGIES IN THE VISEGRAD COUNTRIES

The four countries of the Visegrad Group—so named for the Hungarian town of Visegrad, where the meeting that formed the group was held—are the Czech Republic, Hungary, Poland, and Slovakia. These countries approached privatization in radically different ways in the early 1990s. Hungary first focused on creating an institutional and legal framework for the new capitalist system and addressed the problem of limited domestic capital by beginning early with sales to foreign investors. That proved a wise approach since the new foreign owners replaced the socialist-era managers and removed what could have become a powerful force with the potential to obstruct market-oriented reforms. In privatizing, the Hungarians stuck to traditional methods such as public tenders and IPOs, largely avoiding experimentation with alternative forms such as voucher schemes, restitution, and employee buyouts. Most of Hungary's lucrative state properties had been sold off by 1997, allowing deep restructuring to take place earlier than in the other three Visegrad countries.

Czech and Slovak privatization began when the two nations were still part of the same country. The Czech-devised voucher scheme was launched in an effort to transfer property to private hands as quickly as possible. The program compensated for the lack of domestic capital by offering shares to the population for a symbolic price. This move was aimed at broadening public support for reforms. There was an element of nationalism in the Czech scheme. The desire to keep firms in domestic hands was greatest for strategic companies such as banks, telecoms, utilities, and other "family jewels." A major flaw of the coupon program was that, unlike the Hungarians, the Czechs failed to first create an adequate legal and institutional framework. Insufficient regulation allowed for high levels of abuse, including insider trading and asset stripping. Moreover, because most shares were put in investment funds—many of which were controlled by banks that remained in state hands—corporate governance was absent, unemployment remained unnaturally low, and the banking system ended up in shambles. Only after an economic crisis in 1997 did the Czech Republic shift its approach and focus on public tenders. Key firms in the banking and energy sectors were sold to foreign investors.

After Slovakia gained independence in 1993, the second wave of voucher privatization was canceled. Privatization initially ground to a halt until political elites had devised ways of benefiting from the sale of state assets. From 1994 to 1998, privatization focused mainly on MEBOs and direct sales, usually to political allies of then Prime Minister Vladimír Mečiar at rock-bottom prices. That approach appealed to nationalists as the ruling parties stressed their aim of shunning foreign investment and instead creating a domestic entrepreneurial class. As a result, many politically connected but incompetent owners led their empires to ruin, causing great damage to the economy. After the change of government in 1998, Slovakia shifted to an approach similar to that in the Czech Republic with international tenders for key firms in the banking, telecom, and energy sectors. In both cases, the financial sectors were in such poor shape by the late 1990s that there were few protests when the banks were finally sold to foreign investors.

In its approach to privatization, Poland used a mix of different methods, depending on the orientation of the government in power at the time. In the early transition years, privatization was slower in Poland than in Hungary and the Czech Republic. But it accelerated in the latter part of the 1990s after the financial and legal framework had been established. While initially not as open to foreign investors as the Hungarians, the Poles were more welcoming than the Czechs and Slovaks.

Despite the different paths taken in the early 1990s, the approaches of all four countries converged by the end of the decade as they prepared for the competitive pressures of EU accession. As demonstrated by the Slovak and Czech cases, it was possible to prevent key firms from coming under foreign control for some years. However, the results were often not positive, as domestic owners frequently appeared more concerned with their personal interests than with those of their firms and employees. In contrast, foreign investors generally led the economic recoveries throughout the region, providing improved management techniques and know-how, boosting production and exports, and preparing the economies for the shock of full EU membership.

"RIGHTSIZING" GOVERNMENT

Rightsizing government is a matter of adapting the public sector to the needs of a capitalist economy. While the stabilization programs dealt with such issues as cutting enterprise and price subsidies and introducing a new taxation system, the structural reform programs required that the government take over certain social welfare functions previously performed by state enterprises, including the provision of health care, housing, and kindergartens.

This process involved several dilemmas. First of all, there was no "optimal" size for government in established Western economies. Indeed, data from the Organization for Economic Co-operation and Development indicate that 2015 general government spending accounted for about 29 percent of GDP in Ireland versus 57 percent of GDP in Finland. Second, the public sector experienced severe shocks during the transition. As declines in GDP and fiscal pressures reduced funding for social welfare programs, issues of poverty and inequality became more urgent. Rightsizing does not necessarily mean cutting the size of the public sector, however. While the state's declining role is crucial with regard to enterprise development, it must expand in other areas, such as regulatory activities (including antitrust, securities, and bankruptcy mechanisms) as well as unemployment insurance and other labor market policies.

Under communism, central government tax revenues averaged about 50 percent of GDP and reached as high as 61 percent in Czechoslovakia in 1989. That was far higher than warranted by the level of economic development.[8] During the transition, states faced the challenge of taking on more social welfare functions while at the same time reducing budget deficits. In practice, that was especially complicated since people were accustomed to relying on the welfare state. In the early transition years, governments set up generous unemployment schemes with long payment periods covering a large share of former salaries. Benefits also applied to new entrants to the labor market. As unemployment rates rose, however, the generosity of the schemes declined. Although public sectors decreased in size substantially in the early years of the transition, they remained large: budget revenues accounted for 42 to 47 percent of GDP in Central Europe by 1995.[9]

Countries adopted a variety of approaches to fiscal reform. Radical reformers such as Czechoslovakia, Estonia, and Latvia started early with balanced budget targets. The record shows this was a wise decision, given that delayed attempts at balancing were unsuccessful in Poland, Hungary, and Lithuania. In the latter cases, the habit of generous social spending was difficult to break for political reasons. Despite a favorable starting point in the Czech Republic and Slovakia, fiscal deficits surged in those countries during the latter part of the 1990s, partly due to the high cost of bailing out the banking sector and also because of the soft-budget constraints related to off-budget funds. The official state budget deficit reached about 1 to 2 percent of GDP in the Czech Republic during 1997 and 1998; however, the hidden deficit was almost three times that size.[10]

Fiscal reforms became especially important as privatization wrapped up. In the early years of the transition period, some governments used privatization revenues to finance more spending, helping to compensate for the gap between domestic savings and private investment needs. As the countries approached the end of the transition, however, the international financial community discouraged such practices and called on countries to use privatization revenues to pay off government debts.

LABOR MARKET REFORMS

Under central planning, unemployment did not exist. Governments introduced identity cards. Each citizen was required to have a place of employment or prove that he or she was legitimately out of the labor force. Factories were built in areas with high levels of joblessness. Collective farms and large enterprises helped to absorb residual unemployment. The maintenance of full employment meant that many workers received wages in excess of their contribution to their firms' revenues. Thus, the full-employment policy functioned as a disguised form of unemployment compensation.

A key aspect of the postcommunist transition was to transfer employment from the public to the private sector. In a market economy, companies locate plants where they can maximize profits, not reduce unemployment. Access to transport, electric power, and raw materials is a crucial factor and often more important than labor costs. Delivery times and transport costs are also key, so manufacturers often prefer to have plants closer to clients and markets. Thus, growth has been concentrated near big cities or Western borders. Large plants in out-of-the-way locations are frequently loss makers.

All of the countries in the region witnessed a rise in unemployment during the early years of the transition. In certain respects, the emergence of unemployment can be seen as a healthy development, a sign of the rationalization of production and employment. Enterprises had incentives to shed redundant workers as they faced firmer budget constraints, particularly in industries with declining competitiveness. Meanwhile, farms shed labor as agricultural subsidies fell. Still, the increase in unemployment was much greater in some countries than in others. In Central and Eastern Europe, layoffs were much more common during the 1990s than in the CIS, where less restructuring took place.

During the 1990s, governments fought the layoffs without much success. They did make it more difficult for companies to cut their workforces, however, by imposing high severance pay requirements along the West European model. Financial pressures forced enterprises to utilize other mechanisms to reduce labor costs, such as early retirement schemes and wage arrears, with the latter especially prevalent in the CIS countries. In an effort to deal with rising unemployment rates, some governments introduced active labor market policies such as public works projects, job retraining programs, and employment subsidies, especially for unskilled groups such as Roma. Active labor market policies were often mixed with passive policies such as changes in taxation laws and regulations governing the hiring and firing of employees.

While active labor market programs are not always effective in the long run, cutting high payroll taxes and approving legislation that makes it easier for companies to hire and fire workers have had a more substantial impact on job growth. Also important are changes in the jobless benefits system aimed at encouraging the unemployed to find work, as benefits are sometimes set too high in relation to the minimum wage. Deregulation of rents can help encourage labor mobility, as can improvements in the banking sector that allow for the growth of mortgage lending.

Some countries have tried to use FDI as a way to bring down unemployment rates. Nonetheless, much of the FDI in the region was initially related to privatization. Foreign investors who buy existing firms do not always provide more jobs. Governments often require that investors agree to keep employment at a certain level; however, eventually, the workforce has to be cut to raise productivity. Greenfield investment—which entails the construction of a new plant—is much more beneficial in terms of job creation, but attracting investors is tough, given the stiff competition among countries. Although some investors were attracted by the region's low wages, there was little to stop those firms from moving further eastward once salaries edged closer to West European levels, especially if wage growth was not matched by increased productivity.

Hungary is the one Central and East European country that achieved substantial success in using FDI as a job-creation policy. After reaching double digits between 1992 and 1995, Hungarian unemployment rates fell to around 6 percent from 2000 to 2004. That reduction occurred thanks partly to government incentives for foreign investors, especially those who invested in regions with high levels of unemployment, such as eastern Hungary. By 2000, Hungary was experiencing labor shortages in certain areas,

Photo 3.1. Children playing outside a run-down apartment building in Bulgaria. (*Kapital Weekly*, Bulgaria)

as the country's population had been declining since 1980. Although labor availability improved temporarily during the 2008–2009 global economic crisis and its aftermath, talent shortages reemerged as a pressing challenge in 2016–2017, with Hungary's unemployment rate falling back to just over 4 percent during the latter year.

For most countries, the development of small and medium enterprises remains the only real answer to cutting unemployment. Many countries in the region were slow to develop legal frameworks conducive to substantial growth of small business. Moreover, the slow development of the lending market also delayed progress, as banks were hesitant to lend to small enterprises because there was little recourse if they did not pay their debts, as long as courts did not function properly. In contrast, mortgages were a safer bet for banks since property could be used as collateral.

Since the postcommunist transition began, unemployment rates in Central Europe and the Baltic states have rarely reached as high as 20 percent, although divergent demographics have contributed to wide variations in jobless rates among countries (see table 3.1). Variations among regions within a given country were also substantial since poorly functioning housing markets limited labor mobility. The younger populations in Poland and Slovakia meant that unemployment rates were considerably higher than in Hungary during most of the postcommunist transition, particularly among youth. However, high emigration rates helped trigger a steep reduction of unemployment in Poland by the mid-2010s, bringing the jobless rate down to one of the lowest in the region by 2016.

Table 3.1.   Unemployment Rates for Central and East European States, 1998–2016 (Percentage)

Country	1998	2004	2008	2012	2016
Kosovo	n/a	39.7	47.5	30.9	27.5
Bosnia-Herzegovina	n/a	21.5	23.4	28.0	25.4
Macedonia	34.5	37.2	33.8	31.0	23.7
Montenegro	18.5	27.7	16.8	19.7	17.7
Serbia	12.2	18.5	13.6	23.9	15.3
Croatia	17.2	13.8	8.6	15.8	13.3
Albania	16.7	14.7	12.8	13.0	10.3
Slovakia	12.7	18.4	9.6	14.0	9.6
Latvia	14.0	11.7	7.7	15.0	9.6
Ukraine	5.6	8.6	6.4	7.6	9.3
Slovenia	7.4	6.3	4.4	8.9	8.0
Lithuania	13.2	10.9	5.8	13.4	7.9
Bulgaria	12.2	12.1	5.6	12.3	7.6
Estonia	9.2	10.1	5.5	10.0	6.8
Poland	10.2	19.1	7.1	10.1	6.2
Romania	6.3	8.0	5.6	6.8	5.9
Hungary	8.7	6.1	7.8	11.0	5.1
Czech Republic	6.5	8.3	4.4	7.0	4.0

n/a = not available
Source: Eurostat, IHS Markit.
Note: Countries are listed by 2016 rank.

In general, Balkan countries have experienced much higher jobless rates than those in Central Europe, often reaching or exceeding 30 percent. That was partly a result of the wars of the 1990s and low levels of FDI. Kosovo, which declared independence from Serbia in February 2008, has faced some of the highest unemployment rates of the region, surpassing 50 percent of the labor force in 2001 and 2002 before falling to about 28 percent by 2016. While unemployment levels in the Balkans have been unbearably steep, jobless rates are thought to be considerably lower in reality because of the strong informal economy in those countries. Still, long-term unemployment remains a serious challenge for policy makers in the Balkan region, and jobless rates remained in the double digits throughout the region in 2017.

Macroeconomic Trends

TRANSITION RECESSIONS AND RECOVERIES

Certain elements of the communist economic system had strongly negative implications for the transition process, even for those countries that had already begun reforms. The causes of recession in the transitions can be divided into macro- and microelements. Macroelements include the effects of high inflation; the impact of the stabilization program, with contradictory fiscal and monetary policies spurring reductions in aggregate demand; and the collapse of intraregional trade, which had negative effects on both export demand (reducing aggregate demand) and import supply (reducing aggregate supply). Microelements of the transitional recessions included problems in coordinating production when the collapse of central planning left enterprises unprepared to find new buyers for their outputs and suppliers for their inputs. The communist regime had left managers with poor marketing skills.

The countries that recovered most quickly from the recession generally had favorable initial conditions. It is no accident that the Central European economies were the first to begin recovering, followed by the Baltic states. Other factors helped limit the term of the transition recession, including a rapid reduction in inflation; the implementation of institutional and policy changes at the micro level to allow for the introduction of competitive market forces; rapid growth in the private sector without excessive restrictions; a geographic redirection of trade away from traditional markets and toward the EU; and sectoral restructuring, allowing for rapid growth in the service sector.

The countries that faced special difficulties with stabilization were those struggling the most with the legacies of the old system. Many of the countries in Central and Eastern Europe were new, established in the early 1990s after the collapse of the USSR, Yugoslavia, and Czechoslovakia. They struggled simultaneously with state- and nation-building concerns and defining and defending their borders. As a result, economic reform was often not their top priority. Many had no previous experience with macroeconomic management. Problems also arose from having been part of dysfunctional currency areas, such as the ruble (former USSR) and dinar (former Yugoslavia) zones. In Ukraine, as in other former Soviet countries, the initial use of the ruble was a major impediment to macroeconomic stabilization and a significant cause of inflation, as each country in the ruble zone had an incentive to pursue expansionary macroeconomic policies because some of the resulting inflation would be exported to other countries in the region.

All Central and East European economies experienced large declines in GDP (15–70 percent) between 1989 and 1993. After the onset of the initial postcommunist recession, Poland was the first to begin to recover (1992), followed by the rest of Central Europe in 1993 through 1994. Poland, in 1996, was the first to reach its 1989 level of GDP, with Slovenia and Slovakia not far behind. In contrast, Ukraine experienced one of the most serious transition recessions in the entire Central and East European region. Its economy did not begin to experience GDP growth until 2000.

It is difficult to compare pre- and post-transition GDP given the different ways of using statistics and the deliberate falsification or omission of unfavorable data under the old regime. GDP statistics exaggerated the true decline in economic welfare that occurred during the transition. In the communist system, output levels were often over-reported for the sake of plan fulfillment. On the other hand, once the transition began, enterprises faced incentives to underreport in order to avoid taxes and divert output to the gray economy. Another factor was the so-called forced substitution practice: the lack of substitutes gave buyers little choice but to purchase goods available under the old system that were not really desired. After the transition began, better substitutes were often imported, reducing GDP but, at the same time, increasing consumer welfare.

As with GDP data, official measures of inflation exaggerated the declines in economic welfare associated with postcommunist inflation. Price liberalization only made explicit the hidden inflationary pressures that had existed in the previous system. The higher prices that resulted from liberalization reduced households' real income on paper, but they also allowed households to purchase whatever they could afford without having to wait in line or endure forced substitution. This trade-off—higher prices and lower real incomes in exchange for less waiting and forced substitution—benefited some people and rendered others worse off. It did not, however, connote automatic impoverishment. Moreover, the higher prices that occurred after liberalization were a partial reflection of the higher product quality that resulted from price liberalization and the creation of a buyer's market.

SECOND-STAGE STABILIZATION

In the transition process, it is important to distinguish between first- and second-stage macroeconomic stabilization programs. The first stage occurred from 1990 to 1993 during the early part of the postcommunist transition. Some countries that started out well later showed signs of imbalance and had to implement second-stage programs. This happened in Hungary in 1995 with the Bokros Plan, as well as in the Czech Republic (1997–1999), Slovakia (1998–2000), and Poland (2001).

The justification for second-stage stabilization programs differed depending on the country, and a variety of solutions were implemented. For example, in the case of Slovakia, the country was on the verge of an acute economic crisis by the time of the September 1998 parliamentary elections because of poorly designed structural and macroeconomic policies, particularly during the years 1994 to 1998. The government's expansive fiscal policy was among the main causes of the crisis. It involved public financing of large infra-structure projects and state guarantees for bank loans. Another reason for the crisis related to inadequate bank regulation, contributing to serious problems with nonperforming loans. A third cause was the privatization strategy, which favored domestic over foreign buyers and thus generated high current-account deficits financed by foreign borrowing instead of inflows of FDI. The impact of those policies was exacerbated by the central bank's attempts to maintain a fixed exchange rate regime. This meant that monetary policy had to be tightened, sending interest rates upward and contributing to increased insolvency among Slovak enterprises. A solution to the credit crunch necessitated intervention in macroeconomic management and in the banking and enterprise sectors. That included austerity measures aimed at stabilizing public finances and reducing the current-account deficit, restructuring and privatizing the state-owned banks, and easing and accelerating bankruptcy proceedings.[11] With stabilization largely achieved by 2002, the country was then able to move on to more advanced reforms.

THE GLOBAL CRISIS OF 2008–2009

Thanks to the impact of second-stage stabilization programs, compounded with the positive effects of EU integration, the average GDP in Central Europe and the Balkans surged by some 6 to 7 percent annually between 2004 and 2007. Strong GDP growth was accompanied by a sharp drop in unemployment rates in most of the new EU member states and candidate countries. By 2007, rising labor shortages were seen as one of the main problems facing the more advanced countries of the region.

When the global crisis struck in the United States and Western Europe, Central and Eastern Europe initially seemed relatively immune. However, the first signs of recession in Central Europe emerged in the final months of 2008, as falling demand in Western Europe contributed to sharp declines in industrial output and exports. By early 2009 unemployment rates were rising, and many analysts warned of imminent catastrophe across the region. Indeed, the crisis highlighted certain imbalances, particularly regarding high current-account deficits and external debt (see "External Economic Trends" below), which became harder to finance as credit tightened. In addition, the region faced sharply declining inflows of FDI, as global companies scaled back their investments. Another key source of foreign-currency earnings—remittances from citizens working abroad—also became scarcer. Even the new EU member states were not immune to the impact, as the crisis hit Hungary and the three Baltic states especially hard. The IMF and EU stepped in to help remedy the situation, allowing the afflicted countries to avoid default. Nonetheless, most Central and East European countries experienced sharp declines in GDP during 2009, in many cases the largest drops since the early 1990s. Poland, Albania, and Kosovo were the only countries in the region to avoid recession in 2009. Whereas Poland's large domestic market and flexible exchange rate helped to shield the country from troubles elsewhere, Kosovo and Albania avoided recession due to their relative economic isolation.

THE EUROZONE DEBT CRISIS

Just as a recovery from the global crisis was underway in the region, a new set of economic challenges emerged, as a sovereign debt crisis that began in Greece spread through several other Eurozone member states. Slovenia was the only country in Central and Eastern Europe to experience the Eurozone debt crisis directly, as deteriorating bank assets due to a rapidly rising level of nonperforming loans led to calls for an EU bailout in 2013. Still, the government was reluctant to turn toward the Eurozone for help and instead drew up plans to recapitalize the sector and transfer nonperforming assets to a bad bank, much like in Slovakia and the Czech Republic during the second-stage stabilization process of the late 1990s. In December 2013, three Slovenian banks were bailed out, and a fourth requested recapitalization in April 2014.

Indirect and secondary effects of the Eurozone crisis were felt across Central and Eastern Europe. Countries with strong economic links to Italy and Greece saw reduced revenues from exports, workers' remittances, and investment. By 2012 and 2013, the crisis had widened and deepened, pulling much of Europe into a double-dip recession. In Central and Eastern Europe, a deteriorating export performance was matched by weak consumer confidence and investment. The situation was further exacerbated by the need to cut budget deficits and public debt following the upward surge in 2009. Otherwise healthy economies such as the Czech Republic were punished by the government's enthusiasm for fiscal austerity, pulling the country into a long-running recession. Other countries in the region managed to find a balance between austerity and growth, but even these economies saw a sharp slowdown. By 2013, GDP in most Central and East European countries remained below the levels seen prior to the 2008–2009 crisis. The only exceptions were Kosovo, Albania, Poland, Slovakia, Macedonia, and Montenegro. By 2016, the economies of Croatia, Latvia, and Slovenia still remained below precrisis levels.

External Economic Trends

BALANCE OF PAYMENTS

Current-account balances in Central and Eastern Europe have fluctuated considerably during the transition period (see table 3.2). By the mid-1990s, most countries in the region had balances within respectable limits, with deficits of about 5 percent of GDP or less, while some countries even recorded surpluses. However, deficits shot back up between 1996 and 1998, as access to external financing grew. In many countries, current-account gaps narrowed in subsequent years, particularly where second-stage adjustments took place. Nevertheless, current-account deficits for the region expanded again between 2004 and 2008, as EU enlargement eased access to credit. There were some notable exceptions, though. Excluding the CIS countries, the Czech Republic had the lowest current-account deficit in Central and Eastern Europe in 2008 (at less than 2 percent of GDP), followed by Slovenia, Slovakia, and Poland (all at about 5 to 6.5 percent of GDP). It is no coincidence that those four countries had the easiest time weathering the global downturn of 2008–2009.

The level of the current-account deficit is often closely linked with the gap between exports and imports of goods, particularly in the less developed countries of the region. While foreign trade balances in the Central European countries have generally remained at reasonable levels (and have sometimes been in surplus), Balkan countries such as

Table 3.2. Current-Account Balances for Central and East European States as a Share of GDP, 1995–2016

Country	1995	2004	2008	2010	2016
Slovenia	−0.4	−2.8	−5.3	−0.2	6.8
Hungary	−3.4	−8.5	−7.0	0.3	4.9
Bulgaria	−0.1	−6.4	−21.9	−1.8	4.3
Croatia	−15.7	−20.6	−8.7	−1.4	2.7
Estonia	−4.1	−12.2	−8.9	1.7	2.6
Latvia	0.4	−11.7	−12.7	2.1	1.5
Czech Republic	−2.3	−4.2	−1.7	−3.3	1.0
Poland	0.6	−5.5	−6.7	−5.4	−0.2
Slovakia	2.0	−8.8	−6.3	−4.7	−0.7
Ukraine	−3.1	10.7	−7.1	−2.2	−0.7
Lithuania	−13.6	−7.7	−13.8	−0.5	−1.0
Romania	−4.7	−8.3	−12.2	−5.2	−1.9
Macedonia	−6.7	−8.2	−12.6	−2.1	−3.1
Serbia	n/a	−13.2	−21.2	−6.4	−4.0
Bosnia-Herzegovina	−9.3	−15.5	−13.5	−5.8	−4.4
Kosovo	n/a	−7.3	−11.9	−11.7	−9.2
Albania	−0.5	−5.0	−15.7	−11.3	−9.6
Montenegro	n/a	n/a	−49.4	−22.7	−19.0

n/a = not available
Source: IHS Markit.
Note: Countries are listed by 2016 rank.

Kosovo, Bosnia-Herzegovina, and Albania have been plagued with very low export-to-import ratios. As a result, those countries must rely on high surpluses on the "current transfers" account (which includes foreign grants and workers' remittances from abroad) to keep overall current-account deficits in line. Even so, current-account deficits in the Balkans have tended to be much higher than those in Central Europe, often reaching well into the double digits. Throughout the broader region, the balance of trade in services, which includes transport, travel, and other services, has generally been in surplus. That is especially true in countries with thriving tourism sectors such as Croatia and Montenegro. One factor that has introduced an element of uncertainty into the level of the current-account gap has been the rising income deficits, as foreign investors send their earnings home. Large income deficits have been especially apparent in Central European countries that have attracted significant levels of FDI.

Generally, a current-account deficit of more than 5 percent of GDP is seen as unsustainable. A negative current-account balance must be compensated for by a positive financial account. This can stem from inflows of foreign direct and portfolio investment as well as long- and short-term foreign loans. If supported by inflows of FDI rather than by foreign borrowing, high current-account deficits were not seen as overly worrying. Indeed, Estonia's current-account gap reached about 9 to 15 percent of GDP between 2002 and 2007, a time when economic growth was strong, inflation was low, and budget balances were in surplus. Nonetheless, large external deficits raise a country's vulnerability amid a global downturn, and Estonia was one of the first countries to be hit during the crisis of 2008–2009.

FOREIGN DIRECT INVESTMENT

Privatization deals involving foreign investors were initially unpopular in some Central and East European countries, as people feared that their governments were "selling out." That was particularly true when firms in certain strategic sectors were sold. Nonetheless, experience has shown that all of the Central and East European countries have needed to attract foreign capital in order to provide the investment resources and expertise necessary to fuel growth. FDI brings modern technologies, know-how, new forms of management, and an altogether different corporate culture. Thus, foreign investment is recognized as a way of speeding up the restructuring of companies and helping to improve their overall competitiveness. It also accelerates a country's access to global markets. Foreign-owned companies have often had much stronger export sales than domestic ones, particularly during the early transition years.

Much of the FDI in the Central and East European region was initially concentrated in a few manufacturing branches, such as automobiles and automotive components, electronics, food processing (particularly soft drinks, beer, dairy products, and sweets), tobacco, and construction materials. Investments in retail trade were also significant. From the mid-1990s, states began selling their shares in the strategic utilities, telecom, and banking sectors, with foreign investors often gaining significant stakes. FDI in the banking sector has been especially important, bringing in more competition, a greater variety of products, and higher levels of expertise.

Although there are many advantages to investing in the Central and East European region, transition economies are, in certain respects, risky for foreign investors. Labor regulations and taxes are frequently complex and subject to rapid change, depending on the whims of policy makers. Relatively high levels of corruption and insider trading exist, and many countries in the region have experienced serious problems with corporate governance, as company managers have often felt little responsibility to shareholders. Company registration has also been difficult, with barriers to small business and smaller-scale investors. Privatization negotiations have frequently been long and difficult, with significant political interference. Meanwhile, bankruptcy procedures have been complicated by an inadequate justice system. Finally, exchange rate volatility has added substantial risk.

During the 1990s, most of the FDI in the region went to Poland, Hungary, and the Czech Republic, all of which proved to be good locations for investment due to the rapid liberalization of foreign trade, proximity to Western markets (resulting in low transportation costs), relatively large domestic markets, high levels of technical education, much lower labor costs than in their West European neighbors, and relatively good infrastructures. Moreover, the fact that the three countries were seen as front-runners in the EU accession process made investment especially attractive.

As it became clear that additional countries would be included in the first wave of the EU enlargement process, FDI also rose rapidly elsewhere. Many of the countries that scored high cumulative levels of FDI per capita did so by virtue of their small size, while the opposite was true for Poland. With Croatia and Montenegro the most notable exceptions, FDI inflows were typically greatest in the countries that made the fastest progress in EU integration. Investors in the new EU member states have the advantage of

Photo 3.2. Warsaw's city center. (Malgorzata Alicja Gudikowska)

operating in the same legal and regulatory environment as their main markets. Moreover, EU membership is generally seen as a guarantee of a certain degree of political stability as well as the existence of enforceable contracts, should problems occur. More risky countries require higher returns to make the investment worthwhile. While Serbia has achieved considerable success in attracting FDI since the fall of Slobodan Milošević in 2000, most investments have been linked to privatization.

Moving Forward

Some ten to twelve years after the transition began, the more advanced countries in the Central and East European region had completed the vast majority of the postcommunist economic reforms. That was particularly true in the case of the eight states that joined the EU in May 2004. As the postcommunist transition neared completion, the leading economies shifted their focus instead to issues also facing their counterparts in Western Europe and elsewhere in the world, including taxation, pension, and health-care reform. At the same time, the Central and East European countries have to deal with the emergence of poverty, growing disparities in income, and demographic challenges. Other key concerns for the eleven Central and East European countries that joined the EU between 2004 and 2013 are preparation for joining the Eurozone and the convergence of incomes with the wealthier West European economies. By the start of 2018, only five new member states (Slovenia, Slovakia, Estonia, Latvia, and Lithuania) had adopted the euro, and the Eurozone debt crisis and general uncertainty have diminished political will in most countries that currently remain outside the common currency area.

TAXATION REFORM

Accession to the EU spurred a third round of taxation reforms in many of the Central and East European countries, with the aim of raising competitiveness, simplifying the taxation system, and ensuring a reduction in budget deficits. Fiscal policies are carefully scrutinized once countries join the EU, as the Maastricht criteria for Eurozone entry requires that budget deficits remain below 3 percent of GDP. The need to meet the Maastricht criteria was a key impetus for fiscal reforms in Slovakia between 2002 and 2006, for example. Nonetheless, the Maastricht budget requirements are also important in providing a basis for healthy medium- and long-term economic growth. If budget deficits are not brought under control, macroeconomic balance could be threatened, particularly once privatization revenues run out.

There are several justifications for introducing more competitive taxation policies. First of all, initial transfers from the EU budget were considerably lower with the 2004 enlargement round than in the case of countries such as Portugal and Greece. Thus, the new member states had to rely on other factors to spur development with the aim of catching up with richer EU countries (see table 3.3). Strong investment inflows are seen as a prerequisite for the more rapid GDP growth needed to help countries reach the income levels in Western Europe. Once in the EU, however, member states are limited in the kinds of incentives they can offer to foreign investors. Many of the perks provided by Hungary in the 1990s are no longer permitted. Moreover, the new EU member states have struggled to attract investments that are not based on low wages alone, given that salaries are rising as the countries become increasingly integrated with the West. Thus, fiscal reform provided a relatively simple way for these countries to bring in more

Table 3.3.   GDP per Capita, 2004–2016

Country	2004	2008	2014	2015	2016
Czech Republic	78	84	86	87	88
Slovenia	86	90	82	83	83
Slovakia	57	71	77	77	77
Lithuania	49	63	75	75	75
Estonia	54	69	76	75	75
Poland	50	55	67	68	68
Hungary	61	62	68	68	67
Latvia	46	59	64	64	65
Croatia	55	63	59	59	60
Romania	34	49	55	56	58
Bulgaria	34	43	46	47	49
Montenegro	29	41	41	42	45
Macedonia	27	32	36	36	37
Serbia	30	36	37	36	37
Bosnia-Herzegovina	22	29	31	31	32
Albania	20	25	30	29	29

Source: Eurostat, February 2018.
Note: Countries are listed by 2016 rank. Calculated in purchasing power standard (PPS) terms; EU-28 = 100.
   PPS calculates GDP by taking into account differences in prices across countries.

investment. By 2017, five of the new member states had surpassed the level of GDP per capita in Greece, although that achievement was met partly thanks to the poor economic results in the latter country. Three new member states (the Czech Republic, Slovenia, and Slovakia) had met or surpassed the level of GDP per capita in Portugal.

In the older EU countries, the so-called European social model, characterized by strong labor unions and the need for consensus in social dialogue, makes reforms difficult. In contrast, the new member states have found it easier to implement sweeping changes. Slovakia was the regional leader in introducing a taxation system that was both simple and attractive to investors, and the reforms met with very little formal protest. Whereas Estonia introduced a flat income tax in the early years of its transition, spurring several other countries to follow suit, Slovakia became the first to adopt that approach at a more advanced stage of transition. Slovakia's flat tax took effect in January 2004, just months before the country's EU entry. Slovakia's taxation changes applied not only to individuals, but also to corporations, all at a flat rate of 19 percent. Moreover, the country's VAT rate was unified at 19 percent, while the government canceled the inheritance, dividends, real estate transfers, and gift taxes. Although considerable doubts emerged before those changes took effect, the impact on tax collection was surprisingly positive. That was particularly true with regard to the corporate income tax, as the new system helped to reduce tax evasion.

Slovakia's tax changes triggered reform efforts elsewhere in Europe as well. In 2004, Poland's corporate income tax rate was reduced to the same level as in Slovakia, while the rate in Hungary was brought down to just 16 percent. The Czech Republic began to gradually lower its corporate income tax rate starting in 2004, reaching 19 percent by 2010. Initial reactions from countries such as Germany and France to tax reforms in the new member states were not positive, and Slovakia and other so-called neoliberal states were accused of "tax dumping." Some older member states called for the harmonization of taxation rates within the EU to prevent firms from moving eastward to benefit from more advantageous conditions. However, the prospect of harmonization proved challenging, and countries like Austria and Germany were forced to substantially reduce corporate tax rates to maintain competitiveness with their eastern neighbors. The tax changes in Central Europe and the Baltic states also inspired EU hopefuls in the Balkans and elsewhere. Serbia imposed a flat corporate tax rate of just 10 percent in August 2004, which at the time was the lowest rate in Europe. Montenegro went one notch lower in January 2006, with a 9 percent rate. A number of countries in the region adopted a flat tax on personal income as well.

After the surge in budget spending in 2009, Central and East European countries have been under pressure to reduce deficits, leading many to backtrack on earlier reforms and raise taxes. Several countries in the region—including Slovakia, the Czech Republic, and Montenegro—have been forced to abandon the flat tax on personal income, as governments introduced a series of austerity measures including higher tax rates for wealthier residents. Some countries raised the corporate tax and VAT rates as well.

SOCIAL POLICY REFORM

Social policy is one of the most difficult aspects of the reform process, as such changes are extremely unpopular politically. The Visegrad countries inherited very comprehensive social safety nets from the communist period, featuring such perks as free health care, free education through graduate school, extensive paid maternity leave for women, and full pensions, even if no contributions had been made. Many of those policies were maintained during the 1990s. Thus, the Central European countries were considered premature welfare states, with social security benefit levels found in countries with much higher per capita GDPs. By contrast, the CIS countries generally had underdeveloped welfare states during the transition period, given their difficult budgetary constraints.

In carrying out reforms, a key concern was to better target the benefits provided to reach the people who needed them the most. Much of the traditional safety net was regressive, with the bulk of the subsidies going to those who were already relatively well-off. For example, across-the-board subsidies for household electricity and natural gas were especially beneficial for people with large homes, while those with smaller dwellings received less. Thus, one way of addressing that imbalance was to raise household electricity prices to market levels, while providing subsidies for lower-income people.

Another key question relates to which agencies and levels of government should be charged with administering benefits. Two conflicting principles exist in that regard. First, if policies are made by national governments, statewide standards are established. Thus, a country avoids the situation in which regions compete for business by lowering taxation rates and providing fewer benefits. At the same time, however, putting policy making in the hands of regional or local governments may help promote experimentation and provide more accountability. There is no single standard in the EU; France embodies

Photo 3.3. Upscale stores with imported and domestic luxury goods, like this one in a mall in Warsaw, are now common in much of Central and Eastern Europe. (Monika Szewczyk)

the first option and Germany the latter approach. Several of the new EU member states, including Poland and Slovakia, have implemented administrative reforms aimed at achieving decentralization.

The pension system has been a key concern of policy makers in the realm of social welfare reform, particularly in countries such as Hungary, where the aging population would have resulted in a fiscal meltdown if reforms were not implemented. Pension reforms generally include raising the retirement age, taxing working pensioners, shifting the formulas by which pensions are indexed, and moving toward a system based on employee contributions. International organizations such as the World Bank urged Central and East European countries to privatize their pension systems, in line with the models developed by Chile and other Latin American countries. Thus, countries were encouraged to shift from a pay-as-you-go system, where today's workers pay the benefits for current retirees, to one with personal accounts. The new approach is often referred to as a "three-pillar system," with the first pillar consisting of a downsized pay-as-you-go scheme and the second pillar comprising personal accounts. The third pillar is optional and refers to voluntary private savings accounts. The new approach to pensions was intended to encourage savings while at the same time improving the long-term health of state finances.[12]

Hungary and Poland were the first countries in the Central and East European region to pursue pension reform along the Chilean model, transforming their pension systems in 1998 and 1999, respectively. Latvia (2001), Bulgaria, Croatia, and Estonia (all 2002), Macedonia (2003), Lithuania (2004), Slovakia (2005), Romania (2008), and the Czech Republic (2013) followed, with variations from country to country. The costs of switching from one system to another were quite large. Nonetheless, privatization revenues provided a good source of funding, helping to make the reforms socially acceptable by avoiding large hikes in taxation rates. Participation in the new pension system was generally mandatory for new workers but optional for older citizens.

Initially, the personal accounts were more popular than expected among older workers, signaling distrust in the old system and expectations of higher yields from private funds.[13] Nonetheless, the economic uncertainty in Europe that began in 2008 contributed to a changing attitude toward private pension accounts. As was the case with the flat tax, pension reforms frequently fell victim to the fiscal difficulties around the region following the 2008–2009 crisis. In an effort to reduce budget deficits and public debt, several countries introduced a reduction in the level of funds going into personal accounts. The most dramatic backtracking occurred in Hungary, where the pension system was effectively renationalized in 2011. Amid rising fiscal pressures, Poland moved in early 2014 to take control of government bonds that were previously held by private pension funds, transferring them to the state-run system. Moreover, Poles were discouraged from remaining in the private system. Poland's 2015–2019 cabinet took another step backward by reducing the retirement age in October 2017, undoing the reforms of its predecessor. Despite the rising skepticism elsewhere, the Czech Republic introduced its own three-tier system in 2013, making participation in the second-tier voluntary. Nevertheless, the center-right government that launched the Czech pension reforms failed to gain a political consensus, and the cabinet that took over in early 2014 dismantled the new system.

ADOPTING THE EURO

The eleven Central and East European countries that acceded to the EU between 2004 and 2013 are all expected eventually to join the Economic and Monetary Union (EMU), meaning that they will use the euro as their national currency. In order to do so, they must first meet the criteria on inflation, interest rates, fiscal deficits, national debt, and exchange rate stability laid out in the EU's 1992 Maastricht Treaty. Inflation must fall below the "reference value," with the rate of consumer price inflation not exceeding the average in the three best-performing EU member states (excluding those countries with negative inflation) by more than 1.5 percentage points. Likewise, average nominal long-term interest rates must be no higher than 2 percentage points above the three best-performing member states. The general government budget deficit must be less than 3 percent of GDP, while public debt must be below 60 percent of GDP. Prior to entering the Eurozone, each country must join the Exchange Rate Mechanism–II (ERM-II), which serves as an EMU waiting room. On entry to the ERM-II, a country pegs its currency to the euro, keeping the exchange rate within 15 percent of its central rate. A country must remain in the ERM-II for two years without a currency devaluation before it may adopt the euro.

The EU does not judge these criteria equally. A revaluation of the currency against the euro is more tolerable than a devaluation. One somewhat flexible criterion concerns public debt, as countries with debt over the 60 percent limit have been accepted into the Eurozone in the past, so long as the overall share was declining. Although Eurostat data indicate that Hungary and Croatia were the only new member states to exceed the public debt threshold in 2011–2012, Slovenia joined them in surpassing the 60 percent mark in 2013–2016. In the case of Slovenia, the surge in public debt in 2013 was directly related to the bank bailouts.

Three of the new Central and Eastern Europe member states (Estonia, Slovenia, and Lithuania) entered the ERM-II in June 2004. All three countries initially hoped to adopt the euro in 2007, which was the earliest possible date for the new member states. Nonetheless, only Slovenia was given approval by the European Commission to join the EMU in 2007, as both Estonia and Lithuania were delayed by inflation rates above the Maastricht limit. Having joined the ERM-II almost one year after its Baltic neighbors (in May 2005), Latvia initially expected to join the Eurozone in 2008. However, as in Estonia and Lithuania, stubbornly high inflation delayed EMU membership for Latvia. Inflation was a particular challenge in the Baltic states because their currency pegs did not allow for exchange rate fluctuations, meaning that real appreciation had to occur through inflation.

At the time of EU accession, the four Visegrad countries all had problems that would prevent them from adopting the euro in the near term. Public finances were seen as the biggest obstacle for Poland, Hungary, the Czech Republic, and Slovakia. Rising to the challenge, Slovakia launched major fiscal reforms between 2003 and 2005 and joined the ERM-II in November 2005. Although the change in government following the June 2006 parliamentary elections presented some risks with regard to both fiscal policy and inflation, Slovakia's euro adoption occurred on schedule in January 2009.

Slovakia's Eurozone entry happened just in time, as the global crisis would have set the country off course in 2009, particularly on the fiscal front. As budget deficits surged in 2009 (see table 3.4), most of the new EU member states outside the Eurozone were expected to experience further delays in EMU entry. Already in 2008, several of the

Table 3.4. General Government Budget Deficit as a Share of GDP, 2009–2016

Country	2009	2013	2014	2015	2016
Romania	−9.5	−2.1	−1.4	−0.8	−3.0
Poland	−7.3	−4.1	−3.5	−2.6	−2.5
Slovakia	−7.8	−2.7	−2.7	−2.7	−2.2
Hungary	−4.6	−2.6	−2.1	−2.0	−1.9
Slovenia	−5.9	−15.1	−5.4	−2.9	−1.9
EU-28	−6.6	−3.3	−3.0	−2.4	−1.7
Croatia	−6.0	−5.3	−5.4	−3.3	−0.9
Estonia	−2.2	−0.2	0.7	0.1	−0.3
Latvia	−9.1	−1.0	−1.6	−1.2	0.0
Bulgaria	−4.1	−0.4	−5.5	−1.6	0.0
Lithuania	−9.1	−2.6	−0.7	−0.2	0.3
Czech Republic	−5.5	−1.2	−1.9	−0.6	0.7

Source: Eurostat, October 2017.
Note: Countries are listed by 2016 rank.

new member states had deficits that were above the 3-percent-of-GDP Maastricht limit. Estonia was the only new member state to see its deficit fall within the Maastricht limit in 2009, and the country adopted the euro in January 2011. Latvia made great strides in reducing its budget gap after the 2008–2009 crisis and won approval to join the common currency zone in January 2014. Lithuania adopted the euro in 2015.

Even after the larger Central European countries meet the Maastricht criteria, Eurozone accession may be pushed back further for political reasons. It makes sense for small countries such as the Baltic states to accede to the Eurozone as soon as possible. Advantages include reduced exchange rate risks, lower interest rates, and the elimination of transaction costs associated with maintaining a national currency. Those factors help attract investment and contribute to real economic convergence. Nonetheless, some politicians and economic analysts in the larger Central European countries have been more hesitant, preferring to maintain a national currency as long as possible in order to have more control over domestic economic policy. Although the currency instability that was associated with the 2008–2009 global crisis made some skeptics in the larger countries more amenable to rapid EMU entry, sentiment shifted away again during the subsequent Eurozone debt drama.

DEALING WITH POVERTY AND DEMOGRAPHIC CHALLENGES

Countries in the Central and East European region began the transition with among the lowest levels of income inequality in the world; however, that situation has been changing. Eurostat data indicated that by 2015 Bulgaria, Lithuania, and Romania had the highest risk-of-poverty or social exclusion rates in the entire EU. Still, other new EU member states, such as the Czech Republic and Slovenia, ranked among the best performers. While high inflation impoverishes society as a whole, stabilization programs can harm certain groups, particularly those living on fixed incomes or reliant on the state for transfers. The incidence of poverty also appears to be associated with high jobless rates, particularly when combined with states' increasing frugality in providing unemployment benefits. The loss of a stable income is the main cause of poverty throughout the region.[14] In terms of demographic groups, poverty is generally found more frequently among citizens with low levels of education and skills, those living in rural areas, those with large families, and women, children, and the elderly.

Although poverty and inequality have emerged as a real problem in some CIS countries, they are generally less severe in Central and Eastern Europe than in other transitional societies. That may be partly due to the high levels of literacy in the postcommunist world, the close proximity to Western Europe, and better-targeted social benefits. Some citizens supplement their incomes with household garden plots and occasional employment; others work in the informal economy. Many urban families depend on relatives in the countryside for certain agricultural goods. Populations in countries such as Albania have survived mainly thanks to foreign assistance and workers' remittances, as citizens move to Greece and Italy in search of work, sending their earnings back home to their families. Despite rising poverty levels in the 1990s, purchases of consumer durables also increased significantly in many countries, partly due to the declining prices of such goods relative to salaries.

Poverty levels may stop growing or even decline once a country's economy strengthens; however, certain groups will likely continue to suffer. The situation is particularly severe among Roma, whose share of the total population varies from less than 1 percent in Poland to nearly 10 percent in Slovakia. In absolute terms, Romania has by far the biggest Romani population, at an estimated 1.8 million. Throughout the region, Roma generally have lower levels of education than the rest of the population. For example, an estimated 1 million Romanian Roma are illiterate. They frequently face racial discrimination in hiring, resulting in much higher jobless rates than among the rest of the population. Moreover, the housing of Roma is often poor and sometimes lacks electricity and running water.[15] Although efforts have been made by various governments and international institutions to alleviate poverty among Roma, the obstacles are great and progress has been slow.

Another unwelcome consequence of the transition has been a significant brain drain from Central and East European countries to Western countries, especially among young, educated people who speak foreign languages. This trend has intensified since EU accession, which allows for the free movement of labor to richer West European countries. Countries hit especially hard by external migration include the three Baltic states, Romania, Bulgaria, and Poland, contributing to serious demographic challenges for policy makers over the medium to long term. Migration is likely to continue until economic opportunities and wages converge with those in more developed countries.

When Is the Transition Complete?

Despite the challenges still faced throughout the Central and East European region, many countries have managed to emerge from the shadow of communism. In economic terms, the transition is deemed complete when soft-budget constraints are eliminated and formerly state-owned companies begin performing like competitive enterprises. Thus, the end of the transition is defined as the point at which the wide differential in the productivity of labor and capital among new versus old firms that existed at the start of the transition has eroded. It marks a time when there are no more distinctions between old, restructured, and new companies.[16] Policy makers are no longer focused on issues specific to the postcommunist transition and instead face problems shared by more advanced, Western economies.

Whereas most of the new EU member states have reached the end of the postcommunist transition period, at least in economic terms, significant challenges remain in many of the Balkan and CIS countries. Fortunately, the states that are further behind have the advantage of being able to study the various reform models implemented by their counterparts in Central Europe and the Baltics to determine the appropriateness of specific policies in their own countries. That may help the Balkans and CIS to move forward more rapidly, once they adopt a consistent pro-reform course.

Study Questions

1. Which countries in Central and Eastern Europe have had the most successful economic transitions? Have there been any surprises?
2. Which countries in the region remain the most dependent on the Russian market?
3. Privatization took many forms in Central and Eastern Europe. Which methods were the most successful in ensuring stable growth and employment?
4. Why did the global economic crisis hit Central and East European countries so hard? Which countries remain most vulnerable to future crises?
5. Why have some countries in Central and Eastern Europe been eager to adopt the euro as quickly as possible, while others have been hesitant?

Suggested Readings

Aåslund, Anders. *Building Capitalism: The Transformation of the Former Soviet Bloc*. Cambridge: Cambridge University Press, 2002.

Connolly, Richard. "The Determinants of the Economic Crisis in Post-Socialist Europe." *Europe-Asia Studies* 64, no. 1 (2012): 35–67.

Ekiert, Grzegorz, and Stephen E. Hanson, eds. *Capitalism and Democracy in Central and Eastern Europe*. Cambridge: Cambridge University Press, 2006.

European Bank for Reconstruction and Development (EBRD). *Transition Report 2000: Employment, Skills and Transition*. London: EBRD, 2000.

Frydman, Roman, Kenneth Murphy, and Andrzej Rapaczynski. *Capitalism with a Comrade's Face*. Budapest: CEU Press, 1998.

Funck, Bernard, and Lodovico Pizzati, eds. *Labor, Employment, and Social Policies in the EU Enlargement Process: Changing Perspectives and Policy Options*. Washington, DC: World Bank, 2002.

Keereman, Filip, and Istvan Szekely, eds. *Five Years of an Enlarged EU: A Positive Sum Game*. Berlin: Springer, 2010.

Lavigne, Marie. *The Economics of Transition: From Socialist Economy to Market Economy*. 2nd ed. New York: Palgrave Macmillan, 1999.

World Bank. *Transition: The First Ten Years*. Washington, DC: World Bank, 2002.

Websites

Eurostat: http://epp.eurostat.ec.europa.eu (EU statistics)
V4 Revue: http://visegradrevue.eu (analysis from Central Europe)
EUbusiness, "Eastern and Central Europe": http://www.eubusiness.com/regions/east-europe (economic news from Central Europe)

Notes

1. See World Bank, *Transition: The First Ten Years* (Washington, DC: World Bank, 2002), chap. 2.

2. European Bank for Reconstruction and Development (EBRD), *Transition Report 2000: Employment, Skills and Transition* (London: EBRD, 2000), 18–19.

3. For more on the communist economic system and its collapse, see Anders Aåslund, *Building Capitalism: The Transformation of the Former Soviet Bloc* (Cambridge: Cambridge University Press, 2002), chaps. 1 and 2.

4. The first three lessons are noted by Anders Aåslund. See Aåslund, *Building Capitalism*, 167–68.

5. Aåslund, *Building Capitalism*, 238.

6. See Aåslund, *Building Capitalism*, 227–32.

7. Aåslund, *Building Capitalism*, 171.

8. Aåslund, *Building Capitalism*, 222.

9. See EBRD, *Transition Report 2000*, 55, 69.

10. World Bank, *Transition*, 53.

11. Slovakia's second-stage stabilization policies and their causes are discussed in Katarína Mathernová and Juraj Renčko, "'Reformology': The Case of Slovakia," *Orbis* (Fall 2006): 629–40.

12. World Bank, *Transition*, 81–83; and Aåslund, *Building Capitalism*, 344–5.

13. World Bank, *EU-8 Quarterly Economic Report* (April 2005).

14. EBRD, *Transition Report 2000*, 106.

15. Arno Tanner, "The Roma of Eastern Europe: Still Searching for Inclusion," Migration Policy Institute, May 1, 2005, http://www.migrationpolicy.org/article/roma-eastern-europe-still-searching-inclusion.

16. World Bank, *Transition*, xix.

CHAPTER 4

Civil Society and Political Parties

GROWTH AND CHANGE IN THE ORGANIZATIONS LINKING PEOPLE AND POWER

Kevin Deegan-Krause

Communism fell and democracy rose because of complex geopolitical interactions and powerful structural forces, but amid the turmoil small groups of thoughtful, committed citizens were the ones who actually brought about big changes. Fledgling civil society organizations and political parties promoted democratic values and built new institutions that helped prevent a return to dictatorship. If we want to understand how Central and Eastern Europe has changed and what we might expect for its future, we need to look not only at the big questions of constitutions, markets, and national identity but also to the concrete and local experience of civil society and political parties. This chapter will set down basic definitions for civil society and political parties, consider the difference between the two, and then discuss how they developed in the region with particular attention to laws, values, organizations, and their impact on society.

What We Mean by Civil Society and Political Parties

Civil society and political parties are different, but they are similar enough to share a chapter because they inhabit an "in-between" space. "Civil society" in particular is often defined by what it is *not*. It is not "the family," "the state," or "the market" but rather a sphere of activity located between these in which "institutions, organizations and individuals . . . associate voluntarily to advance common interests."[1] More recent and specific definitions try to recast this negative space into a positive set of values. Roberto Foa and Gregorz Ekiert define civil society as

> the realm of organized social life that is open, voluntary, self-generating, at least partially self-supporting, autonomous from the state, and bound by a legal order or set of shared rules [and which] involves citizens acting collectively in a public sphere to express their interests, passions, preferences, and ideas, to exchange information, to achieve collective goals, to make demands on the state, to improve the structure and functioning of the state, and to hold state officials accountable.[2]

"Civil society organization" is the generic term for any institutional unit of civil society, and this term includes all those interest groups, service groups, clubs, think-tanks, foundations, churches, and any other institutions that fit the definition's requirements by being voluntary, independent, and oriented to public, collective goals.

Parties are *not quite* the same as civil society organizations. They are sometimes easier to spot because they often use "party" in their name, but not all parties use that label and not everything with that label is a party. One of the most widely used definitions sets up two criteria: a party is an "institution that (a) seeks influence in a state, often by attempting to occupy positions in government, and (b) usually consists of more than a single interest in the society and so to some degree attempts to "aggregate interests."[3] The lines between civil society organizations and parties are sometimes blurry, but the general rule is that parties seek "influence from within the government" while civil society organizations work from outside and that parties take a more "comprehensive view of the public interest and political agenda" while civil society organizations focus more narrowly on a few specific agenda items.[4] Political parties together form broader collectives called "political party systems" that describe how parties relate to one another: their alliances and feuds, the issues they fight about, and their relative positions on the political spectrum.

Understanding Civil Society in Central and Eastern Europe

HOW CIVIL SOCIETY DEVELOPED IN A CHAOTIC REGION

Civil society in Central and Eastern Europe faced widespread destructive pressure under communism, but when that pressure lifted, civil society organizations rapidly emerged to play an important role in the postcommunist period. The development of civil society has not been smooth, however. The mid-1990s were a time of particularly difficult adaptation, and civil society organizations in the south of the region faced the most severe challenges.

The seizure of power by communist parties in the late 1940s did profound damage to civil society in Central and Eastern Europe, but its problems began much earlier. Professional associations, discussion circles, charitable societies, and other groups began to flourish in the late 1800s industrialized cities such as Prague and Budapest, but they were much slower to develop in the countryside and in countries to the south and east. Further growth was made more difficult both by the economic crises of the 1920s and 1930s, which starved civil society of resources, and by the emergence of authoritarian leaders who saw civil society as a threat to their rule and tried to suppress its activity. When communist parties took over after World War II, they also attacked independent civil society but from a different direction. Communists were willing to allow clubs and associations—and even to help build them—but only on the condition that they became completely dependent on the state. Communist parties in the region actively used what remained of civil society as "transmission belts" for mobilizing support (or at least the appearance of support) for government efforts, and they made major efforts to create a "dense network of large associations" while at the same time ensuring that these were "tightly controlled by the party-state."[5]

At the same time, another kind of civil society began to emerge beneath the surface. Dissidents who rejected the overwhelming power of the communist regimes began to work together to organize their opposition even though they faced the constant risk of political persecution and legal prosecution. Most of these organizations remained fragmented and hidden from view except in rare instances when (as in Poland) they could find protection from other institutions such as trade unions or the Catholic Church or when (as in Czechoslovakia) leaders of dissident organizations openly accepted imprisonment as the price of speaking out. Yet, whenever pressure from above eased—as it did in Hungary in 1956, in Czechoslovakia in 1968, in Poland in the late 1970s, and across the region in the late 1980s—organizations such as these showed a strong capacity to organize, and they quickly mobilized marches and other acts of public opposition along with newspapers, informal schools, and help for the families of those who were fired or jailed.

As communism weakened and the Soviet Union withdrew support, an independent civil society again began to emerge from several directions: the increased strength of independent dissident groups, the increased independence of formerly state-run groups, and the creation of many wholly new civil society organizations. In the northern and western countries of the region, these organizational networks played critical roles in pushing some governments into negotiations and pushing others out of office. In the south of the region, significant activity by civil society organizations also helped to end the communist monopoly in Yugoslavia, but much of that effort became bound up in ethnic conflicts about the groups would control the state.

As a vibrant and voluntary alternative to the tired and oppressive state apparatus of communism, civil society played a key role in the democratic transitions but popular enthusiasm eventually waned. As many of the most skillful activists turned their attention to parliament and the government, and as many of the smaller, less-connected organizations saw their resources dry up, many skeptics believed that civil society simply could not overcome the destructive historical legacies of suppression by interwar dictators followed by subservience under communist rule. History was not destiny, however, and instead of shriveling up, civil society organizations adapted to the new circumstances with new goals and new forms of organization. Civil society survived and in some places it even thrived.

MEASURING CIVIL SOCIETY ACROSS TIME AND SPACE

How can we assess the state of civil society? The region of Central and Eastern Europe is diverse and rapidly changing, and there are simply not many tools for making good comparisons. Of the available measures, one of the best is the Varieties of Democracy (V-Dem) project that asks scholars to estimate the strength of civil society for every year, past and present. Figure 4.1 summarizes the views of experts about whether civil society enjoyed "autonomy from the state" and whether citizens could "freely and actively pursue

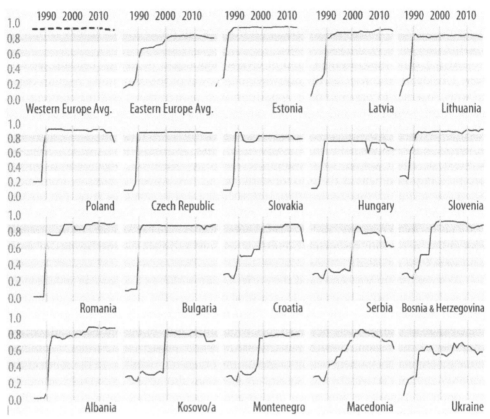

Figure 4.1.   Overall Strength of Civil Society over Time (Core Civil Society Score)
Source: V-Dem 2017.

their political and civic goals, however conceived." In every country in the region, the autonomy of civil society rose sharply from extremely low levels in the late 1980s to higher levels in the early 1990s and then remained fairly strong.[6]

A closer look at individual countries, however, shows some significant variation. The data show two fairly distinct regional patterns and a few variations. In the northern and western countries of the region (especially in the eight countries that entered the European Union [EU] in 2004), the graphs show that civil society followed an almost identical pattern, strengthening rapidly from exceptionally low civil society under communism and then remaining relatively strong in subsequent decades. In the south and east, the graphs show much more variation, with some repeating the pattern above—especially in Romania and Bulgaria—and others experiencing more gradual climbs and lower peaks. While most countries in the region remained close to the levels they reached in the late 1990s, Hungary, Serbia, and Macedonia have shown noticeable declines. Even with the drop, however, they have stayed well above their mid-1980s levels (unlike countries to the east such as Russia whose civil society experienced the same initial rise but by 2016 had fallen back to the levels of the late communist era).

DIMENSIONS OF CIVIL SOCIETY GROWTH AND CHANGE

These broad, all-purpose measurements are useful for making big comparisons, but they do not tell the whole story because civil society can succeed or fail in many different ways. Helmut Anheier and Lisa Carlson argue that civil society has multiple dimensions. Their "Civil Society Diamond" breaks down the analysis of civil society into four different categories:

- *Space:* "What is the legal and political space within the larger regulatory environment in which civil society operates; and what laws and policies enable or inhibit its development?"
- *Values:* "What values underlie civil society; what values, norms and attitudes does it represent and propagate; how inclusive and exclusive are they; and what areas of consensus and dissent emerge?"
- *Structure:* "How large is civil society in terms of institutions, organizations, networks, and individuals; what are its component parts; and what resources does it command?"
- *Impact:* "What is the contribution of civil society to specific social, economic and political problems?"[7]

Space: What Institutions Shape Civil Society?

All organizations work within broader frameworks of rules and resources that they cannot completely control. The "in-between" nature of civil society makes it especially dependent on decisions that are made somewhere else, whether by families, by firms or, especially, by governments. But the relationship with government is complicated. Civil society needs government to act but not too much. On the one hand, civil society organizations cannot function without some degree of public order or formal legal status that allows them to protect their organizational identity, oversee membership, and manage accountability and finances. Many civil society organizations, furthermore, depend on government for financial support, either directly through subsidy or indirectly through tax codes that promote voluntary donations. On the other hand, civil society needs governments to refrain from getting involved because governments that become too intrusive in their regulation (either accidentally or intentionally) can undermine the positive efforts of civil society organizations, scare off membership, and threaten their essential independence.[8] The communist era is perhaps the best example of a government that intrudes too much—to the point of undermining and even criminalizing anything it did not like—while the chaos of some countries in the early postcommunist era demonstrates the way that civil society needs government to enforce the rule of law.

Some countries in Central and Eastern Europe in the postcommunist era have found it more difficult than others to maintain this complicated equilibrium. Since the mid-1990s, the United States Agency for International Development (USAID) has issued annual reports on civil society's "legal environment" with special attention to questions about how well governments register, tax, regulate, and respect the independence of civil society organizations. The results follow familiar regional patterns: the legal environments in most countries in the north and west of this region have consistently received high marks as "supportive" while most countries in the south and east of the region received the lower assessment of "evolving" because of problems such as administrative harassment, fines, and deliberate refusal to register new organizations. Positive change did occur in most countries as they began to enact more streamlined rules on tax exemptions, donations, and accounting procedures, but improvement remained slow.[9] A few declines, by contrast, were severe, most notably in Hungary, whose once widely praised nonprofit legal environment descended into "an atmosphere of intimidation" with the rise of Viktor Orbán's "illiberal democracy" model. Now the atmosphere is characterized by "accusatory statements by the government" and "ongoing administrative harassment" including police raids on organizations distributing civil-society-related grants from the Norwegian government.[10]

Values: What Are Civil Society's Motivations?

Even a supportive legal structure will not produce a strong civil society if a society's underlying values do not contribute to individuals volunteering the time, money, and effort that civic efforts require. Under these circumstances, even a high degree of public support may not produce positive results if the values nurtured by civil society organizations are too sharply at odds with one another or with the fundamental values of democracy.

The first question for a successful civil society is whether anyone cares. Other spheres of action—governments, firms, and families—have carrots and sticks that allow them to exert leverage and get what they want, but civil society organizations have no sticks to force cooperation and even carrots are in short supply because of the famous "free-rider" problem that allows some people stand by and take advantage of the social benefits produced by civic engagement of others.

In the early years of postcommunism, the incentives won out and large parts of the populations of many countries demonstrated the core values that sustain civil society. At first, only a courageous few risked severe punishment to organize into groups and take small-scale actions. They typed multiple copies of forbidden texts, organized small discussions and events, and even mounted legal defenses of others facing prison as the Committee to Protect the Workers (KOR) did after the 1970 strikes in Poland and the civil-rights advocacy group Charter 77 did in Czechoslovakia. As organized groups got stronger and sensed lack of resolution from the communist governments in the 1980s, ever-larger numbers turned out for collective protests and introduced an independent spirit into once-subservient communist-era associations. Many of the leaders of these efforts came from the earlier opposition groups: Lech Wałęsa, the shipyard worker who became head of the Solidarity organization and movement in Poland, had been in the workers' group created by the intellectual group formed in 1976, Committee to Protect the Workers, KOR, and Václav Havel, the playwright who helped lead mass demonstrations in Prague in November 1989, had spent years in prison for his activity as spokesperson for the Czech dissident group, Charter 77.

Many of the leaders of dissident groups and civil society organizations went on to prominent government positions—Wałęsa and Havel became the presidents of their respective countries—but, at the grassroots level, the victory was less obvious. As early public enthusiasm for demonstrations waned, the corrosive effects of communism on the values of civil society members became increasingly apparent. According to Marc Morjé

Howard, communism's tendency to force people into supportive organizations and then label those activities as "voluntary" produced a low level of generalized trust in society as a whole and encouraged the narrow relationships of trust based on the close-knit "private and informal networks" that people built for self-protection. The end of communism did not immediately break these habits, and the economic slumps and political crises of postcommunism led to a deep dissatisfaction that encouraged many people to "withdraw even further from public activities."[11]

More recent evidence, however, indicates that instead of withdrawing completely, people in the region shifted their civil society participation to other, less-obvious activities. Fao and Ekiert have found that, although the level of many civil society behaviors in Central and Eastern Europe falls considerably below those of Western Europe, the gap is narrowing.[12] Small-scale studies and local opinion polls show that the idea of "volunteering" is losing some of the stigma of the communist era and that some segments of the population have begun to adopt West European patterns of charitable giving and philanthropy.[13]

The values of civic engagement, however, can do more harm than good if citizens are engaged in the pursuit of destructive goals. Simone Chambers and Jeffrey Kopstein mince no words when they confront the problem of "bad civil society," by which they mean groups that embody the civil society ideals of voluntary mutual engagement among individuals but in the service of "hate and bigotry."[14] Ugliness, of course, is in the eye of the beholder, and fears about the violence of football fan clubs such as the Czech Ultra Sparta, the intolerance of conservative religious organizations such as the Polish nonprofit Radio Mariya, or the nationalism of patriotic organizations such as Croatian Disabled Homeland War Veterans Association, exist alongside fears about the danger to the social order posed by what many see as morally permissive Gay Pride Parades or the "anti-patriotic cosmopolitanism" of organizations funded by Hungarian billionaire George Soros. In reality, though, the potential sources of "bad civil society" in Central and Eastern Europe represent only a tiny share of the sector as a whole. Far from the extremes, most civil society organizations in East and West alike act to help the needy, solve practical problems, and engage together on hobbies and areas of mutual interest.

Structure: What Are Civil Society's Capacities?

Even when legal civil society merely provides open space for people with similar goals or interest to interact, it requires organizations with formal names, bylaws, members, and resources. How these are structured can have a huge impact on whether people can use civil society to reach their goals. Along with its review of legal frameworks, USAID has also evaluated civil society based on the measures membership, management, fundraising, training, and partnerships with other sectors along with the transparency and accountability of civil society organizations.[15] These show rapid growth in the capacity of civil society in the early 1990s followed by a long period of overall stability. During this stable period, however, big changes were happening under the surface. A three-decade analysis of Poland, conducted by Ekiert, Kubik, and Wenzel, found that the submissive associations of the communist era faced major challenges caused both by the loss of state resources and the acquisition of a new and unfamiliar independence. Many formerly communist-led unions, associations, and organizations either simply collapsed or limped along with inherited memberships and little sense of direction. At the same time, new professional associations, unions, and clubs emerged as fresh-thinking alternatives to communist-era groups and other groups emerged to meet needs that had not existed under communism such as campaign watchdog organizations, chambers of commerce, and homeless shelters. In the process, civil society's "center of gravity shifted from the large, membership-based, formal organizations, such as trade unions and professional associations (mostly inherited from the old regime), to a highly diverse sector of small, professionalized NGOs that rely on voluntary involvement and public as well as private funding."[16] In Poland's case, there are "tens of thousands" of "small organizations run by professional staffs that rely on public funding, fundraising, and volunteers" and "focus on a wide range of local and national issues and initiatives."[17] Poland is not unique. Countries across the region exhibit similar patterns with the most effective associations of the old regime being "complemented by the dynamic growth of new organizations," together creating "a diverse, competitive, and balanced associational sphere."[18]

Along with this organizational transition came new patterns of economic impact and funding. Although civil society plays a significant role in serving people's needs and stabilizing the political system, it remains a relatively small part of the economy. A 2013 study by Johns Hopkins University found that the nonprofit sector in the Czech Republic, for example, accounted for just under 2 percent of all jobs and economic activity, though the direct impact was slightly larger when adjusted to include volunteers, and the indirect, nonmonetary effects were even more significant.[19] Because civil society organizations did their work with relatively few financial resources, wealthy outside institutions could, by devoting only a tiny fraction of their own resources, have an outsized impact on the organization and direction of civil society. During the 1990s and early 2000s, the EU and the United States, together with private philanthropists such as George Soros, funded hundreds of consultants and contributed hundreds of millions of dollars to strengthen civil society organizations in the hopes of helping to consolidate democracy. Although these efforts appear to have played a big role in creating the basic infrastructure for civil society, there were limits. Critics argue this funding failed to achieve many of its goals because recipients were concentrated in a relatively thin layer of elite nonprofits with international connections rather than among local-level organizations with fewer connections.[20] This dependence on outside resources also led to problems for civil society in the north and west of the region that had been the first to get aid either in donations or advisors. By the time the other countries in the region were felt to be ready to get aid, special-funding programs for soon-to-be EU member states had begun to dry up. Other outside donors then focused their efforts on the more vulnerable democracies of the south and east.

Impact: How Does Civil Society Shape Its Surroundings?

The impact of civil society, then, depends on the combination of the rules that govern it, the values that shape it, and the organizational capacity of its organizations. A recent report by the World Economic Forum offered a long list of tasks that civil society organizations perform in any society: "watchdog" over public institutions; "advocate" for awareness of social issues; "service provider" to meet societal needs; "expert" to provide well-crafted solutions; "capacity builder" and "incubator" to make future efforts possible; as well as "representative," "champion," and "definer of standards" to identify voices that otherwise go unheard and bring them into existing systems of governance.[21] To what extent does civil society in Central and Eastern Europe actually fulfill this role?

During the late stages of communism, dissidents excelled in the role of champion of the people against the regime. In the absence of rival parties or opposition newspapers, the small and vulnerable civil society organizations were representatives of the society and its concerns by talking and writing as openly as they could about societal problems including everything from corruption to industrial pollution as well the quality and availability of vegetables. As democratically elected governments emerged in the early stages of postcommunism, civil society added watchdog functions. Over time, much of the watchdog role shifted to political parties that sought to keep one another in check, but civil society organizations continued to advocate on issues that did not have any strong political representation of their own. During this same period, civil society organizations also began to respond directly to public needs and became increasingly involved in providing services, even if they often lacked the funding to really solve the problems they were addressing.

The surveys by USAID measure the impact of civil society using two main factors: advocacy, the ability of organizations to "communicate their messages through the media to the broader public, articulate their demands to government officials, and monitor government actions to ensure accountability," and service provision, "the range of goods and services that [civil society organizations] provide and how responsive these are to community needs and priorities."[22] Civil society organizations across the region rank higher for their advocacy than for their service provision. This is understandable because civil society groups generally have fewer resources than governments, and it is usually more expensive to provide services than to advocate. Furthermore, even with foreign support, civil society organizations usually cannot afford to provide wide-reaching services without assistance from the domestic government. The barriers to advocacy, by contrast, are more uneven and depend heavily on how governments treat civil society. In the most extreme cases, governments emphasize the threat posed by civil society. Hungarian Prime Minister Viktor Orbán, for example, claimed that policy advocates from civil society organizations "are being paid by foreigners" who use this access to government "to apply influence on Hungarian political life."[23] Orbán subsequently escalated tensions with a law whose administrative procedures threatened to force the closure of Central European University, a social science-oriented institution based in Budapest and funded by Hungarian refugee and human rights advocate George Soros.

In response, many of these civil society organizations have tried to get around these barriers by turning to more public forms of protest. Hungarian civil society has responded not only with significant demonstrations but also with numerous smaller efforts that that range from serious investigation of corruption by government officials to successful gofundme.com campaigns for creating parodies of government anti-immigrant billboards ("Come to Hungary, *we've* got jobs in London").

In a similar vein, Poland's 2016 Black Monday Women's March to oppose a government antiabortion law progressed quickly from online protest ideas—calls for women to boycott work and to gather in public wearing black—to mass demonstrations of women and men in more than sixty Polish cities, which closed down many businesses and government offices and ultimately helped push the government into withdrawing the legislation. Less than a year later, the government's attempt to subordinate the independence of the courts (chapter 9) led to yet another series of mass demonstrations in front of the government and the Supreme Court and in cities around the country (including a group claiming to represent the earlier women's organization, along with opposition political parties and angry citizens). In this latter case, demonstrations did not deter Polish parliament but did strengthen the case for Poland's president's to veto the initial bills even though they had been initiated by his own party.

Although the concerted efforts of a strong civil society have been unable to check the efforts of a government that has both the desire and the parliamentary votes necessary for undermining democratic accountability. But, the absence of victory does not mean total defeat and, even if civil society is not the "make-or-break" factor in preventing the return to dictatorship, it is still important because it reinforces support for the everyday work of democratic institutions, builds connections among citizens that may later help with mobilization, and helps secure the well-being of those who are hit hardest by political and economic decline.

Indeed the true impact of civil society—the full expression of its values and its capacity—is often only apparent when these organizations find themselves under pressure. Attempts by the governments of Slovakia, Croatia, and Serbia to impose authoritarian rule in the mid-1990s led to strong and effective response by civil society organizations, revealing strengths that had been honed under four decades of resistance to communism combined with new tactics learned from around the world. Working independently of political parties (though accepting European and American financial and technical assistance), these organizations produced "rock the vote" tours, sought to boost turnout with a campaign built around the slogan "It's not all the same to me," and prepared civil disobedience that could detect and respond to evidence that the government had manipulated election results. While these efforts probably could not have defeated the government without an equally effective campaign of cooperation by parties in the political opposition, they certainly helped increase the new government's majority and gave it political breathing room in its first years of operation. These efforts also provide one of the earliest examples of Central Eastern civil society as an international influence in its own right since leaders from Slovakia helped advise their counterparts in Croatia in the following year, and representatives of both groups went on to advise civil society organizations in Serbia in 2000 and in Georgia and Ukraine in the early 2000s.

Understanding Political Parties in Central and Eastern Europe

Civil society raised the curtain on democracy in Central and Eastern Europe, but political parties stole the show.[24] Civil society organizations moved to the margins and transformed into a solid, stable sector of service providers and advocates. Political parties jumped to

Photo 4.1. Black Monday Women's Strikes in 2016 against the legislation which would criminalize all abortions. (Adam Lach, NAPO)

the center of the political stage, transformed to keep up with changing circumstances and then transformed again and again to keep up with opponents who were changing too. In the process, Central and Eastern Europe produced complicated party systems with many parties and rapid shifts in names and membership as well as programs. Many of those parties built themselves in traditional ways, around economic and cultural issues and ties to specific voting groups, but others burst in with new ideas and new ways of organizing.

HOW POLITICAL PARTIES DEVELOPED IN A CHAOTIC REGION

Central and Eastern Europe lacked party competition between 1948 and 1989, but it certainly never lacked political parties. In every country of the region, a single, dominant Communist Party controlled every political institution and, though there were periodic elections, voters usually faced the choice of voting for the sole Communist Party–approved candidate on the ballot or risking party disapproval (or worse) by failing to vote or making the ballot invalid with an "X" across the ballot or writing in "No." When they had a "choice," the other parties on the ballots were subordinate to the Communist Party that were sham opposition, loyal to the Communist Party but presenting themselves as representing specific groups, like the peasants in the case of the Polish Peasant Party, for whom the Communist Party had no appeal.

The communist monopoly on power ended by the early 1990s. Communist parties did not. In most countries of the region, the successors of the various communist parties proved resilient and, while most were pushed out of office in the first years after 1989, some actually managed to stay in governing coalitions and others returned to power in coalitions at the next election through a combination of internal reform, strong organization, and voters' desire for economic protection. Some broke apart and others changed their names to "Socialist" or "Reform" or "Labour"; but, since they began with a huge membership base and still retained some member loyalty, most were successful in translating the membership and inherited resources—funds, offices, and bureaucratic connections—into strong results in the early competitive elections.

Competing against the communists in these elections were parties representing all of the various forces that had previously opposed communist rule—those who favored freer markets or sought more civil liberties—as well as those with strong religious belief or national identity, and those with strong ecological concerns or other specific interests such as larger pensions or higher farm supports (or even more specific interests such as the Czech Republic's "Independent Erotic Initiative" and "Friends of Beer"). In some countries, these extremely disparate forces managed to band together into one or more large anti-communist movements. In others, they found that cooperation more difficult. Although all of the anti-communist movements ultimately splintered into many parts, some of the fragments went on to become strong parties in their own right. Many of these new parties took as their models the kinds of parties found in Western Europe: liberal parties supporting free markets, Christian democratic parties supporting moral values, ethnic parties supporting their own particular cultural groups, and social democratic parties (other than the communist successors) supporting moderate redistribution of wealth and income. Many other parties remained difficult to pin down in those familiar terms but possessed well-known leaders who could attract votes. During the 1990s, some of these leader-driven parties (often allied with nationalist groups) sought to stifle competition and return to one-party rule. Croatia's Franjo Tuđman, Serbia's Slobodan Milošević, Slovakia's Vladimír Mečiar, and Ukraine's Leonid Kuchma all used their executive powers to defeat or eliminate (and in some cases, apparently, kill) political opponents who threatened to hold them accountable. They all, to varying degrees, manipulated electoral rules and procedures to try to stay in power. Through a combination of illness, political miscalculation, and popular counterpressure, however, none of the four succeeded in bending the political system fully to his will (unlike parallel cases in Russia and Belarus).

By the mid-2000s, every country in the region had developed a reasonably robust political party system in which entities recognizable as political parties actively competed fairly over jobs and taxes and minority rights and other predictable, if mundane, issues. The emergence of regularized party competition did not necessarily produce stable party systems, however, and the 2000s and 2010s brought significant disruptions by new political parties that capitalized on public dissatisfaction with politics and the apparent corruption of the newly entrenched postcommunist leaders. Often led by celebrities from nonpolitical backgrounds (ranging from an ex-king to the manager of a supermarket chain, and including colorful figures such as television investigative journalists and game-show hosts), these parties promised cleaner government based on new ways of thinking ("neither left nor right but forward") but they usually found it difficult to deliver on these promises and faced their own outsider challenges in the elections that followed. Parties such as Positive Slovenia (the manager), Lithuania's Party of National Resurrection (the game-show host), the Czech Republic's Public Affairs (the journalist), and the National Movement of Simeon the II (the king) rose quickly and then disappeared without a trace one or two election cycles later, leaving space for another new party in its wake.

MEASURING POLITICAL PARTIES ACROSS TIME AND SPACE

The challenges of assessing parties are different than those of civil society. Gathering statistics on individual parties is fairly easy because governments keep specific lists of what count as a party and when parties compete they compete almost exclusively using the common currencies of votes and seats. But there's no easy way to judge the overall health of a party system. The number of parties and the speed of change provide two good starting points because there are dangers on *both* sides: too many parties can be as dangerous as too few, and too little change can be as destructive as too much.

Fragmentation: How Many Parties?

There is no way, in the abstract, to decide on the right number of parties in a political party system. Without at least two parties, it is hard to imagine meaningful competition, but every addition to the party system makes it more unlikely that a majority will agree on who will run the government and what policies it will pursue. Figure 4.2 shows the sizes of political party systems in Central and Eastern Europe using a mathematical formula designed to deal with the problem of how to count parties with vastly different sizes, especially tiny parties.[25] A measure of less than 2.0 on this scale suggests that one party is significantly larger than all the rest combined, while a measure of more than 6.0 indicates a number of parties so large that cooperation becomes difficult. Figure 4.2 shows that the average in Central and Eastern Europe has declined from the high-end of the normal range in the early 1990s to a middle position that is now in line with political party systems in Western Europe.

Unlike the graphs for civil society strength, the graphs of fragmentation do not show any clear geographic patterns. Slightly larger party systems were more common in the north, particularly the Baltic countries of Estonia, Latvia, and Lithuania, which tended to hover between five and six systems with below-average levels of fragmentation were more common in the south and east of the region (with the sole exception of Bosnia and Herzegovina where the constitution separates voting along ethnic lines and multiple parties can compete successfully for support within each of the three major ethnic groups). Only a few countries fell below the threshold indicating one-party dominance and it was rare for any single party to command a majority of the seats in parliament. Some of these single-party-dominant periods were short-lived, such as Bulgaria and Lithuania during the mid-1990s, and Slovakia in the early 2010s, but a few other countries have seen more consistent one-party dominance, especially Montenegro, where the Party of Democratic Socialism has dominated over other parties since 1992 and nearly

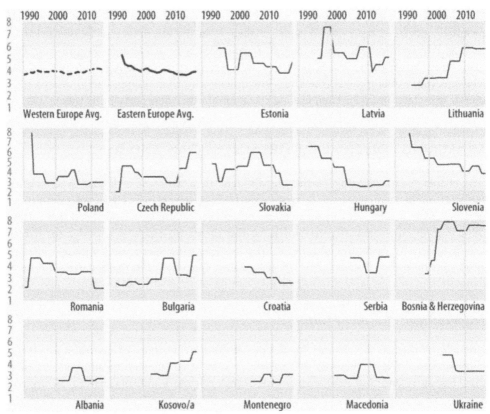

Figure 4.2.   Effective Number of Parliamentary Parties in Central and Eastern Europe over Time

Source: Casal Bértoa, Ferdinand, "Database on WHO GOVERNS in Europe and Beyond," 2017, (http://whogoverns.eu).

always controlled a parliamentary majority, and Hungary, where the party Fidesz gained a two-thirds majority in parliament in 2010 against a fragmented opposition and then repeated that performance in 2014.

Volatility: How Much Change?

The first decade of democracy in any country is often a time of extreme party system change in political party systems as voters and politicians try various options before deciding to settle down. Central and Eastern Europe experienced similar changes but never actually came to rest. Calculating party volatility is measured here by the changes in every party's vote share from one election to the next. Like fragmentation, volatility has "danger zones" at both the high and low ends: constant change means that voters and politicians cannot make intelligent guesses about what will happen next and, therefore, cannot make long-term plans. Infrequent change gives parties little incentive to listen to voters.

Volatility in Central and Eastern Europe started high and has remained high. Even the relatively conservative measurements used in figure 4.3 show that about one-third of all voters changed their minds from one election to the next, resulting in a volatility of about 30 percent during the first postcommunist decade. This was three times as high as in Western Europe during the same period. Volatility dropped to around 20 percent in the second postcommunist decade with one-fifth of all voters changing their minds. Then, instead of declining further toward what had been West European levels, it began to rise again in the mid-2000s and remained high in the 2010s and West European levels also rose in this later period.

As with fragmentation, the location and timing of volatility reflect broad regional differences. To the extent that there is any geographical pattern, it is the opposite of what occurred in civil society. The most extreme volatility levels emerged in the northern and western states rather than those in the south and east (though, even in those countries,

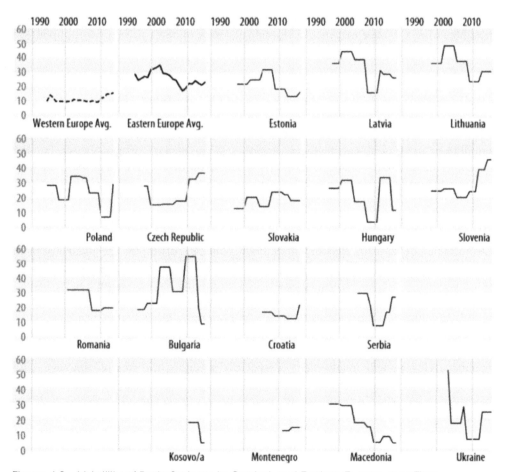

Figure 4.3. Volatility of Party Systems in Central and Eastern Europe over Time
Source: Casal Bértoa, Ferdinand, "Database on WHO GOVERNS in Europe and Beyond" (http:// whogoverns.eu).

the level of change has been well above West European levels). Part of the explanation lies in the fragility of political parties themselves. Furthermore, economic problems and corruption scandals do not just weaken parties' support among voters, they kill parties outright or cause them to splinter into many pieces, and new parties pop up out of nowhere to fill the open spaces. Because this kind of volatility depends on the choices of parties and their leaders, and most did not come into politics with the same party loyalties as their counterparts in Western Europe, the region's volatility is quite unpredictable. In some countries, such as Slovakia, the changes have occurred frequently but at a relatively moderate level. In other countries, such as Hungary, the Czech Republic, Bulgaria, and Slovenia, periods of stability ended with massive changes to the party system. Sometimes, the self-inflicted wounds were sudden: a leaked recording of a Hungarian prime minister's profanity-filled admission that "we lied morning, noon and night," revelations in Poland of top politicians conversations in expensive restaurants about their planned luxury vacations and contemptuous comments on voters, and a police anti-corruption raid on the office of the Czech prime minister. In other countries, the changes reflected the hope for a better alternative as was the case with the return of Bulgaria's former king as a possible savior, and the emergence in Slovenia of a wave of new parties run by nonpolitical outsiders.

DIMENSIONS OF POLITICAL PARTY GROWTH AND CHANGE

As with civil society, these broad measurements only scratch the surface. A deeper understanding of parties can use the same categories as the analysis of civil society, but the questions are different—how are parties regulated? How do they compete? How are they organized? And how do they govern?

Space: What Institutions Shape Political Parties?

Democracies depend on elections and, since political parties are the main actors in the electoral process, they are subject to a significant amount of regulation. As in other regions of the world, the countries of Central and Eastern Europe have distinct regulations about how parties apply for formal registration (often requiring a petition with a minimum number of signatures) and preventing parties from using the same or similar names or acronyms as established parties and how they interact with their members with a requirement that party leaders submit, periodically, to election by party members. Government involvement is especially strong in the area of campaigns and finance. Almost every country in the region requires full disclosure of donations and places limits on what individuals and organizations can donate and prevents or limits what foreign organizations can give as well as how much parties can spend. In return, nearly all countries provide free media time for campaign advertisements and most provide a public subsidy (in some countries as much as $10 for each vote a party receives over a certain threshold).[26] Lawmakers justify these rules and subsidies as part of an effort to reduce the dependence of parties on hidden private interests; but, the enforcement of disclosure requirements in many countries often depends on what party is in power and the generous subsidies to victorious parties are seen by many as an attempt to create a cartel to exclude potential rivals.[27]

Of all laws related to parties, by far the most important is the choice of an electoral system, particularly in terms of the rules that determine how votes are translated into seats in parliament. Except for presidential elections, where there can only be one winner, the winner-take-all system of voting for individual candidates is extremely rare in Central and Eastern Europe (and even in the region's presidential voting systems the winner is not simply the one with more votes than anybody else; if no presidential candidate wins an outright majority of 50 percent plus one vote, then the top two candidates must face each other in a second round of voting held several weeks later). Instead of winner-take-all, countries in Central and Eastern Europe preferred the proportional representation model of continental Western Europe where voters cast ballots for political parties and the share of seats in parliament roughly matches each party's share of the vote. (Only the parliaments of Lithuania and Hungary have consistently used winner-take-all systems to elect individual candidates from single-member districts, and even in these systems they use the proportional representation system to elect a significant share of the parliament). If proportional representation often fails to produce *exactly* proportional results, it is because most systems also try to reduce fragmentation by imposing a "vote threshold" that prevents a party from getting *any* seats at all unless its overall vote share exceeds a certain threshold of about 5 percent. When many of these smaller parties are excluded, it can help to magnify the performance of larger parties. In Poland in 2015, for example, the threshold excluded five significant parties with a total of nearly 16 percent of the overall vote. A result in an above-the-threshold party such as Law and Justice could benefit from having its 37.8 percent share of the vote translated into 51.1 percent of all seats in parliament.

Because electoral laws and electoral systems define the gateway into political power, they can be tempting targets for political manipulation. During the first decade of postcommunism, leaders in Slovakia, Croatia, and Serbia made significant changes in electoral laws—switching seats from proportional to winner-take-all, raising the size of the threshold, changing the ability of parties to band together in coalitions—often at the last moment, in order to knock opposition parties off balance, and these were often successful, though, in the long run, they tended to strengthen political oppositions and unify their efforts. In subsequent decades, such attempts have been less blatant, but parties in power continue to adjust the legal space of party competition for their own benefit, especially in countries to the east and south such as Ukraine, Albania, Montenegro, and Macedonia, which scored lower on measurements of integrity of the electoral process especially because of problems with government use of state media, voters excluded from election rolls, and opaque party finance. Hungary faced particular scrutiny for manipulated district boundaries in its winner-take-all section (a phenomenon known in the United States as "gerrymandering") and for its restrictive electoral regulations.[28]

Values: What Do Political Parties Fight About?

The only value that political parties in a democracy can be expected to agree on is the value of democracy itself (and even that is not a certainty). Fighting about values is

Photo 4.2. Law and Justice Party majority voting for their legal reforms. (Adam Lach, NAPO)

what parties do and the party system is the main realm in which rival visions of a better world can come into clearer focus. Those visions take different forms depending on the preferences of the party. For clarity, political scientists group them into three main categories of appeals: charisma, clientelism, and program.

While "charisma" is notoriously resistant to a precise definition, it is found when individual leaders demonstrate they (and they alone) have solutions to their voters' deepest fears. Since charismatic parties depend on a personal connection with the leader, they often disregard ideology and the specifics of how to solve the problem and emphasize the leader's ability to get things done. Many of these parties (though not all) even bear the leader's name: "Palikot's Movement" and "Kukiz '15" in Poland, "We Are Family-Boris Kollar" in Slovakia, the "People's Party of Dan Diaconescu" in Romania, and many others.

Clientelism involves direct transfers of resources between parties and supporters, ranging from cash for votes to jobs for supporters to subsidies for particularly supportive clans, industries, or neighborhoods. Research by Herbert Kitschelt finds that parties in the south and east of the region use the most clientelism but that even the less clientelist Baltic and Višegrad countries used such tactics more than the Western Europe average (though not much more than Greece, Italy, Portugal, and Spain).[29] Parties in the north and west tend to rely most on hidden "wholesale" clientelism at the national level in which firms receive lucrative government contracts in exchange for hidden cash payments that parties use to pay for expensive election campaigns. Parties in the south and east also engage more frequently in "retail" clientelism at the local level, such as the use of local community services to encourage turnout among favorable voting groups reported in Bulgaria and Romania and even the individual cash-for-votes transactions identified in analyses of Ukrainian elections.

While charisma and clientelism are important for specific parties, the most important differences between Central and Eastern European parties—and the strongest sources of competition—occur on the programmatic level. Some early observers expected that precommunist and communist legacies would sentence the region to unproductive struggle over personalities and payments, but parties across the region quickly adopted specific policy positions and began to compete along internationally recognizable issue dimensions. Several common patterns began to emerge quite soon in almost every country in the region:

- *Economics.* Emerging parties immediately clashed over whether markets or the government would exert the dominant influence over economic activity. The battles took many forms: whether to lower taxes to attract investment or raise taxes to provide more public services in education and health care; whether to focus on the well-being of pensioners or the opportunities for students; whether to keep industries safely in state hands or raise revenue by privatizing them to the highest bidder; and whether those bids must come from domestic buyers or from wealthier foreign investors with less commitment to the country's well-being. Social democratic and socialist parties across the region (including some Communist-party successors) were the most frequent promoters of government intervention in the economy, facing off against pro-market parties that used labels such as "civic," "free," or "liberal" (in the classical, "small-government" sense of the word).
- *Culture.* Clashes over cultural values varied from country to country to a greater degree than economic questions, but the cultural issues tended to revolve around respect for norms of religion and moral authority such as abortion, homosexuality, and restoration of church property previously confiscated by communists. These values, championed by parties with labels such as "Christian" or "people's" were initially stronger in countries with Roman Catholic traditions such as Poland and Slovenia, but similar emphasis has subsequently emerged also in parties in the northern Baltics and Romania and other countries across the region. In some countries, parties emerged on

the opposite end of this dimension with calls for a free choice of lifestyle and morals, and in the absence of strong interest in ecological questions, it is on these questions of cultural freedom that the region's "green" parties often focused their efforts.

• *Ethnicity.* Most countries in Central and Eastern Europe have a sizeable ethnic minority with a distinct language and culture, and minority groups in those countries almost invariably led to competition between political parties of a minority group that sought more rights and resources and parties of the majority group.[30] The ethnic dimension sometimes also encouraged conflicts among parties of the ethnic majority about whether to demand majority dominance or to adopt a more conciliatory stance. Nearly every country in the region produced at least one sizeable party that went beyond praise of the majority ethnic group to call for stronger steps against potential internal threats such as the dangers posed by minority groups—often secession or criminality—and potential external threats such as a flood of migrants, a loss of national identity due to globalization or EU rules, or mistreatment of people from the same ethnic group living in neighboring countries. Although such extreme right ("nationalist" constitutes yet another meaning of "right" in the region) parties have appeared across the region—from "Attack" in Bulgaria to "All for Latvia!"—their direct role in politics has been relatively minor, though larger parties with only slightly more moderate positions have led governments in Poland, Slovakia, Hungary, Croatia, and Serbia.

In some ways, party competition along these three dimensions has come to resemble the West European model, and recent research finds that over time voters in Central and Eastern Europe have come to agree with party positions almost as much in the east as in the west.[31] In other ways, however, the dimensions are different. Whereas in Western democracies, the preference for higher taxes and spending usually aligns with a more open approach to moral judgments, this connection was almost wholly absent in Central and Eastern Europe countries such as Slovakia. It has actually been reversed in others such as Hungary, Poland, Romania, and Bulgaria where those who wanted more government involvement in the economy often sought a much stronger government hand on questions of morals and national identity. This, in turn, blurred common political labels so that a party that supports welfare spending but rejects gay marriage might call itself either "left" (as in Slovakia) or "right" (as in Poland and Hungary).[32]

Although economic, cultural, and ethnic issues played the most important role, parties also fought about issues that did not have obvious parallels in Western Europe:

• *Democracy.* Nearly all parties in the region claimed to support "democracy" but many still sometimes disagree about what the term *means* and some see democracy as entirely consistent with significant power in the firm hand of a charismatic leader who can put for restrictions on rival branches of government or opposition parties or public protest in order to preserve a higher goal such as public order, national unity, or moral cultural values. Such conflicts have led to near collapses of democracy in Slovakia, Croatia, and Serbia in the 1990s and Ukraine in the 2000s and continue in some form to the present especially in Montenegro, Macedonia, Hungary, and Poland where governments have taken steps to weaken or subordinate potential sources of accountability such as courts, oversight agencies, and the mass media. The conflicts in Hungary and Poland are particularly worrisome because these countries, once exemplars of democracy in the region, have begun to see a political sorting of the population between those who are willing to tolerate a firmer political hand and those who are not. As long as advocates of the strong hand hold a parliamentary majority capable of constitutional change, the democratic system remains at risk.

• *Corruption.* The use of state resources for private gain has become a major issue in Central and Eastern European politics, but corruption does not follow the ordinary rules of issue competition. Parties in power cannot easily defend the corruption that may have happened on their watch (and it is often quite significant), so they try instead to talk about their experience or redirect public attention to other issues where they can make stronger claims. On the other side stand antiestablishment parties—often newly created with assertive, clever marketing and celebrity leaders from outside the political realm— which identify corruption as the single most important issue and argue that there is no difference between any of the existing parties, all of which should be replaced.

Closely related to the debates over democracy and corruption is the growing importance of populism. The subject is difficult to discuss because "populism" has developed many overlapping and contradictory meanings over recent decades and often becomes a slur used to describe the unexpected success of an opponent (we are "popul*ar*" but they are "popul*ist*"). If populism still has any meaning, it involves the sweeping rejection of elites on behalf of virtuous ordinary people.[33] Many (though not all) of the radical right parties discussed above have strong populist elements, but populists do not always have strong anti-immigrant or anti-minority tendencies. The most recent crop of populists in Central and Eastern Europe call for a thorough housecleaning but do not offer many details on policy positions, something that is readily apparent even in the new parties' names: "For Latvia from the Heart," "The Party of National Resurrection" (Lithuania), "Dawn" (Czech Republic), "Ordinary People" (Slovakia), "Positive Slovenia," "Bridge" (Croatia), "Save Romania Union," and "Will" (Bulgaria).[34] Without a solid programmatic structure, these parties have rarely survived for long, and the closer they have gotten to power the more fragile they proved to be, since once in office they have often proven to be just as corrupt as the parties they railed against.

Structure: How Do Parties Organize and Build Relationships with Voters?

Relationships between parties and voters depend not only on issues but also on how parties organize themselves to draw in potential supporters. As with civil society, the organizational structures in Central and Eastern European parties are somewhat weaker than those of Western Europe, but the lower average levels of membership and member activity conceal a wide variation. Parties in Central and Eastern Europe follow every possible organizational style from the deep, extensive organization of former communist parties (carried over from when they were in power) to the intangible webs of social media and celebrity marketing that characterize some newer party efforts. These organizational methods are not all created equal. The lightweight celebrity and social media method offers a recipe for short-term electoral success but this usually only works once and, according to a long-term study by Margit Tavits, a party's long-term survival and sustained influence still is greatest if they have more traditional organizations with paid employees, office spaces, and frequent membership activities.[35] Some new parties have begun to understand the advantages of organization "on-the-ground," but then have found that they cannot build such structures without diverting their already strained human and financial resources away from the difficult work of becoming an effective party in parliament or government. Many of these pay the price in the next election and find themselves replaced by even newer parties that then face the same dilemma.[36]

Even the parties that have succeeded in establishing deeper societal roots have not necessarily followed expected patterns. Traditional ideas of "class" voting—laborers voting for left-wing parties, for example—have remained weak since the fall of communism despite increasing social inequalities, but parties have found other ties that can connect them to social groups. Ethnic voting patterns in particular are so strong that nearly all members of minority populations vote for ethnically defined parties such as the "Democratic Union for Integration" supported by ethnic Albanians in Macedonia, the "Movement for Rights and Freedoms" supported by ethnic Turks in Bulgaria, and various parties supported by ethnic Hungarians in Romania and Slovakia and by ethnic Russians in the Baltics. Religious patterns also shape party support (especially in Roman Catholic countries) because frequent churchgoers give strong support to parties with clear positions on cultural morality. They sometimes refer to themselves as Christian Democrats. Major differences in party choice have also emerged between younger city dwellers with high education and potential for advancement who support parties such as Slovakia's "Freedom and Solidarity" or Slovenia's "Party of the Modern Center" and older voters living in the countryside with few opportunities to get ahead who support parties such as Poland's "Law and Justice" and the Croatian Democratic Union.

Impact: How Do Political Parties Turn Values and Votes into Policy?

The main way that parties shape their surroundings is by winning elections and using their power to determine government policy. The question of where to focus their electoral efforts is made easier by the fact that almost all the constitutions of the region create centralized, parliamentary systems of government. This means that political power in the region rests mainly in national-level legislatures and in prime ministers and cabinets that are chosen by the parliament and serve only as long as they can maintain parliamentary support.[37] Furthermore, since proportional representation means that few parties win majorities in parliament, prime ministers are usually forced to depend on coalitions of several parties that have agreed to work together. The impact of parties thus depends on their ability to work with other parties and at the same time maintain their own internal unity.

Coalitions are difficult work, and finding one or more appropriate partners for the long run is difficult. Most of the region's coalitions parties share values on at least one of the major dimensions, whether economic, cultural, or national. No combination is easy but some governments found common cause or pliant partners that received support for specific issues: in Hungary, for example, the nominally left-leaning Hungarian Socialist Party could agree on morality issues (and some economic ones) with the culturally liberal Free Democrats, while in Poland the pro-market Civic Platform was willing to take care of some of the rural interests of the Polish Peasants' Party. But the lure of power has even brought bitter enemies into the same government, such as the decision of the Slovak

National Party to join with the "Bridge" party of ethnic Hungarians in the 2016 coalition of Slovakia's Prime Minister Robert Fico. These combinations face constant challenges, however, and the increasing importance of other dimensions where the partners do not agree can break a government, as can scandals, and other factors such as the illness or death of a leader. On average, governments in the region have served out only about half of their possible terms before a crisis in cooperation among parties has led to a new prime minister, a new coalition, or new elections that shuffle the parliament and cause the whole process of coalition building to start over again.[38]

Civil Society and Political Parties Looking Forward

Communism in Central and Eastern Europe lasted for four decades. Postcommunism is now approaching the same age. Whether it lives longer than its predecessor will depend in no small part on the functioning of civil society and political parties. At the moment, those two intertwined sectors look reasonably healthy in most of the region. Civil society organizations and parties have not fully replicated their counterparts in Western Europe, either in form, density, or strength, but in most cases, they bear a fair resemblance to the institutions of successful democracies elsewhere in the world.

But that does not mean that there is no reason for concern. Some of the dangers are immediately familiar, most notably the Hungarian example of what happens when one organization—in this case a political party—becomes both strong and ambitious enough to drive its rivals—both parties and civil society organizations—into submission. Strong civil society and robust party systems cannot alone prevent the return of chaos or autocracy (especially when promoted by powerful foreign interests such as Russia), but they are the best hope.

Other challenges stem not from the region's history and geography but from elsewhere in the rapidly changing world. Civil societies and parties re-emerged in Central and Eastern Europe just as the world was rushing to an entirely new model of communication and organization that was both more flexible and more fragile. In older democracies, these innovations faced inertia from well-entrenched organizations, but in Central and Eastern Europe the fall of communism meant that alternatives were much weaker. The resulting loose organization of civil society and rapid turnover of political parties may not pose an immediate threat, but the region must figure out how to ensure stability and plan for the future despite with organizations that do not expect to survive the next election or the next funding cycle. Though this next revolution lacks the drama of 1989, the decisions of parties and organizations of Central and Eastern Europe still deserve our close attention.

Study Questions

1. What functions do civil society and political parties have in common? How are they different?
2. How have civil society organizations changed from their role under communist rule to their role in the political change of the 1990s to their role in today's democracy?

3. How do civil society organizations differ geographically across Central and Eastern Europe? Which countries stand out as different from their neighbors and what is different about them?
4. How do electoral laws and electoral systems shape what political parties are like in Central and Eastern Europe?
5. What kinds of value conflicts shape the competition among political parties in Central and Eastern Europe? How do these differ from (or resemble) the competition in your own country?

Suggested Readings

Anheier, Helmut K., and Lisa Carlson. *The Civil Society Diamond: A Primer*. CIVICUS: World Alliance for Citizen Participation, 2001. Available online: http://www.civicus.org/view/media/CDMethodologyPrimer2.pdf.

Berglund, Sten, Joakim Ekman, Kevin Deegan-Krause, and Terje Knutsen. *The Handbook of Political Change in Eastern Europe*. 3rd ed. Cheltenham, UK: Edward Elgar, 2013.

Ekiert, Grzegorz, Jan Kubik, and Michal Wenzel. "Civil Society and Three Dimensions of Inequality in Post-1989 Poland." *Comparative Politics* 49 (April 2017): 331–50.

Foa, Roberto Stefan, and Grzegorz Ekiert. "The Weakness of Postcommunist Civil Society Reassessed." *European Journal of Political Research* 56 (2017): 419–39.

Howard, Marc Morjé. *The Weakness of Civil Society in Post-Communist Europe*. Cambridge: Cambridge University Press, 2003.

Mudde, Cas, and Cristobal Rovira Kaltwasser. *Populism: A Very Short Introduction*. Oxford: Oxford University Press, 2017.

Post, Robert C., and Nancy L. Rosenblum, eds. *Civil Society and Government*. Princeton, NJ: Princeton University Press, 2001.

United States Agency for International Development (USAID). *The 2015 CSO Sustainability Index for Central and Eastern Europe and Eurasia*. 2015. Available online: https://www.usaid.gov/sites/default/files/documents/1861/Europe_Eurasia_CSOSIReport_2015_Update8-29-16.pdf.

Ware, Alan. *Political Parties and Party Systems*. Oxford: Oxford University Press, 1996.

Websites

Varieties of Democracy (V-Dem) Project, https://www.v-dem.net
Party Systems and Governments Observatory, https://whogoverns.eu
Political Data Yearbook Interactive, http://www.politicaldatayearbook.com

Notes

1. Helmut K. Anheier and Lisa Carlson, *The Civil Society Diamond: A Primer* (CIVICUS: World Alliance for Citizen Participation, 2001), 3. Available online: http://www.civicus.org/view/media/CDMethodologyPrimer2.pdf.

2. Roberto Stefan Foa and Grzegorz Ekiert, "The Weakness of Post-Communist Civil Society Reassessed," *European Journal of Political Research* 56 (2017): 421.

3. Alan Ware, *Political Parties and Party Systems* (Oxford: Oxford University Press, 1996), 5.

4. Nancy L. Rosenblum, "Primus Inter Pares: Political Parties and Civil Society," *Chicago Kent Law Review* 75, no. 2 (2000): 493–529, available at http://scholarship.kentlaw.iit.edu/cklawreview/vol75/iss2/9.

5. Grzegorz Ekiert, Jan Kubik, and Michal Wenzel, "Civil Society and Three Dimensions of Inequality in Post-1989 Poland," *Comparative Politics* 49 (April 2017): 335.

6. See Michael Coppedge, et al., "V-Dem [Country-Year/Country-Date] Dataset v7.1," Varieties of Democracy (V-Dem) Project, 2017. Measurements conducted by the international nongovernmental organization Civicus and the United States Agency for International Development (USAID) tell similar stories.

7. Anheir and Carlson, *The Civil Society Diamond*, 6.

8. See Robert C. Post and Nancy L. Rosemblum, eds., *Civil Society and Government* (Princeton, NJ: Princeton University Press, 2001), 8–12.

9. United States Agency for International Development (USAID), *The 2015 CSO Sustainability Index for Central and Eastern Europe and Eurasia*, 2015. Available online: https://www.usaid.gov/sites/default/files/documents/1861/Europe_Eurasia_CSOSIReport_2015_Update8-29-16.pdf.

10. János Kornai, "Hungary's U-Turn," *Capitalism and Society* 10, no. 1 (2015): 6. Available online: http://www.kornai-janos.hu/Kornai_Hungary's%20U-Turn.pdf.

11. Marc Morjé Howard, *The Weakness of Civil Society in Post-Communist Europe* (Cambridge: Cambridge University Press, 2003), 10.

12. Ekiert, Kubik, and Wenzel, "Inequality in Post-1989 Poland," 339.

13. Ekiert, Kubik, and Wenzel, "Inequality in Post-1989 Poland," 339.

14. Simone Chambers and Jeffrey Kopstein, "Bad Civil Society," *Political Theory* 29, no. 6 (2001): 844.

15. USAID, *The 2015 CSO Sustainability Index*.

16. Ekiert, Kubik, and Wenzel, "Inequality in Post-1989 Poland," 334.

17. Ekiert, Kubik, and Wenzel, "Inequality in Post-1989 Poland," 333.

18. Ekiert, Kubik, and Wenzel, "Inequality in Post-1989 Poland," 335.

19. Lester M. Salamon, S. Wojciech Sokolowski, Megan A. Haddock, and Helen S. Tice, *The State of Global Civil Society and Volunteering* (Baltimore, MD: Johns Hopkins University Center for Civil Society Studies, 2013), 2–3.

20. Christine Mahoney and Michael J. Beckstrand, "Following the Money: European Union Funding of Civil Society Organizations," *Journal of Common Market Studies* 49, no. 6 (2011): 1339.

21. World Economic Forum, *The Future Role of Civil Society*, 2013, 9. Available online: http://www3.weforum.org/docs/WEF_FutureRoleCivilSociety_Report_2013.pdf.

22. USAID, *The 2015 CSO Sustainability Index*.

23. Viktor Orbán, Prime Minister Viktor Orbán's Speech at the 25th Bálványos Summer Free University and Student Camp. Website of the Hungarian Government, 2015. Available online: http://www.kormany.hu/en/the-prime-minister/the-prime-minister-s-speeches/prime-minister-viktor-orban-s-speech-at-the-25th-balvanyos-summer-free-university-and-student-camp.

24. Much of the work in this section derive from a chapter written with Zsolt Enyedi on "Voters and Parties in Eastern Europe" that is forthcoming in Adam Fagan and Petr Kopecký, eds., *The Routledge Handbook of East European Politics* (UK: Routledge, 2017).

25. Fragmentation is tied to the number of parties but it is not just of a matter of counting the number of parties on the ballot. The formula for fragmentation weighs both the number and size of parties so that a few big parties will register low fragmentation while many small parties will register high fragmentation and a mix will register a level in between.

26. Marijn Van Klingeren, Margarita Orozco, Joost van Spanje, and Claes de Vreese, "Party Financing and Referendum Campaigns in EU States, European Parliament Directorate-General for

Internal Policies." Available online: http://www.europarl.europa.eu/RegData/etudes/STUD/2015/519217/IPOL_STU(2015)519217_EN.pdf.

27. Fernando Casal Bértoa and Ingrid van Biezen, eds., *The Regulation of Post-Communist Party Politics* (UK: Routledge, forthcoming 2018).

28. Pippa Norris and Max Grömping, "Populist Threats to Electoral Integrity: The Year in Elections 2016–2017." Electoral Integrity Project, 31–35. Available online: https://www.electoralintegrityproject.com/data/.

29. Herbert Kitschelt, Clientelism and Party Competition. Lecture delivered at Central European University, March 8, 2017. Available online: https://sites.duke.edu/democracylinkage/files/2014/12/2.5.Kitschelt.pdf.

30. Some countries such as Poland, Croatia, Romania, Slovenia, and Serbia formally reserve a small number of seats for representatives of small ethnic minorities that otherwise might not be able to pass the parliamentary threshold, though these often sided with the parliamentary majority in the hope of gaining tangible benefits for the group.

31. Robert Rohrschneider and Stephen Whitefield, *The Strain of Representation* (Cambridge: Cambridge University Press, 2012).

32. Jan Rovny and Erica Edwards, "Struggle over Dimensionality: Party Competition in Western and Eastern Europe," *East European Politics & Societies* 26, no. 1 (2012): 56–74.

33. Cas Mudde and Cristobal Rovira Kaltwasser, *Populism: A Very Short Introduction* (Oxford: Oxford University Press, 2017).

34. A similar phenomenon has subsequently had a profound effect on political competition in Italy (Five Star Movement), Spain (We Can and Citizens), Greece (The River), and France as well as in Asia, Latin America, and the United States.

35. Margit Tavits, *Post-Communist Democracies and Party Organization* (New York: Cambridge University Press, 2013).

36. Tim Haughton and Kevin Deegan-Krause, "Hurricane Season: Systems of Instability in Central and East European Party Politics," *Eastern European Politics and Societies* 29, no. 1 (2005): 61–80.

37. Although many countries in the region have popularly elected presidents, most of those presidents have relatively weak positions in the overall political system.

38. Courtney Ryals Conrad and Sona N. Golder, "Measuring Government Duration and Stability in Central Eastern European Democracies," *European Journal of Political Research* 49 (2010): 119–50.

CHAPTER 5

Ethnicity, Nationalism, and the Challenges of Democratic Consolidation

Zsuzsa Csergő

As Central and East European societies emerged from communism in the early 1990s, people throughout the region expressed their preference for democracy, free markets, and the European Union (EU). Many in the West expected the EU to supersede the political ideology of nationalism, which has traditionally pursued the establishment of territorially sovereign, culturally homogeneous nation-states. In earlier centuries, efforts to achieve such congruence between the political and national units in Europe involved aggressive efforts to change state boundaries, eject or assimilate nonconforming groups to "purify" the nation, or encourage minority populations to repatriate to other countries.[1] By the end of the 1980s, such methods of nation-state creation were no longer acceptable in the western part of the continent. Leading scholars of democratic development in other regions, too, argued for a new paradigm to address the need for democracies to accommodate ethno-cultural diversity.[2] In Central and Eastern Europe, European integration seemed to offer the best prospect for moving beyond the era of the traditional nation-state.

A lesson that much of the scholarly literature about nationalism drew from West European development in this period was that, if democratization and marketization could progress unhindered, politics grounded in ethnic and national identity would lose its relevance, and more advanced—rational, individualist, and inclusive—notions of citizenship would take its place. These were the thoughts voiced from within the Iron Curtain during the communist decades by dissident Czech, Hungarian, Polish, and other intellectuals who articulated alternative visions of a free society and spoke poignantly about universal human values and inalienable individual rights and freedoms. Against the backdrop of such expectations, the story of Central and Eastern Europe after the collapse of the communist regimes is filled with reasons for disappointment. After decades of democratization and Europeanization in the 1990s and 2000s, signs of autocratization appeared in a growing number of countries in the region in the 2010s. This chapter provides an account of how ethnicity and nationalism played a role in these trajectories as defining features of institutional development before and after democratization and EU membership.

Even after the initial euphoria over the end of communism, the voices expressing themselves most forcefully spoke about "nationhood" and, in the overwhelming majority of cases, exalted the supposed inalienable rights of groups rather than of individuals. Ethnically conceived national groups all over the postcommunist countries of Central and Eastern Europe viewed democratization as the opportunity finally to achieve or consolidate sovereignty over territories they claimed as their "national homelands." National aspirations contributed to the collapse of all three multinational federations (the Soviet Union, Yugoslavia, and Czechoslovakia). Of the seventeen countries commonly considered to belong to this region, twelve were established or reestablished after 1989 along national lines. Only five countries continued within their existing borders. Conflicts over nation-building became significant features of the difficult process of regime change in most of these states.

Nationalism not only remained relevant after the collapse of communism but also emerged as the most powerful ideology that most important and popular political elites and parties advanced and that publics in these countries found appealing. At the same time, the desire to "return to Europe" and join Western institutions was also a very significant motivation throughout the region. In some cases, aspirations to strengthen national cultures while joining an integrated Europe seemed fully compatible. For instance, people throughout the West cheered the fall of the Berlin Wall, which led to the subsequent reunification of the German state. Although wary of the disintegration of the Soviet state, Westerners also celebrated the reestablishment of the three Baltic states as examples of forward-looking, Western-oriented nationalism. When mass nationalist violence broke out in former Yugoslavia, however, influential public voices in the West began asking whether Central and East Europeans were returning to their violent past rather than transitioning into a peaceful and prosperous future in a common European home. Some argued that ancient hatreds made the rebirth of nationalism inevitable in such places as the Balkans.[3] Others argued that the process of democratization engendered manipulative elites' interest in employing nationalism.[4] Such arguments are often associated with a debate between "primordialism" and "constructivism" in nationalism scholarship. The first label describes explanations based on the assumption that enduring elements of ethnic kinship serve as "primordial" sources of nationalism. The second label describes arguments that emphasize the significance of institutions, particularly the modern state, and the role of political actors in "constructing" nationhood.[5] An increasing number of scholars today question the usefulness of these labels and aim to develop more nuanced explanations for the salience of ethnicity and nationalism in contemporary societies.[6]

Developments in other parts of the world since 1989 have demonstrated that neither the popular appeal of nationalism nor the problems that this ideology poses for democratic governance are specific to the postcommunist region. Wherever political elites design nationalist strategies, the process reveals sources of tension rooted in the "Janus-faced" character of nationalism: as with other political ideologies, nationalism is forward-looking in the sense that it articulates a vision of the future; at the same time, nationalist strategies almost always call for turning to the past for self-definition.[7] When nationalists claim self-government rights for "the nation" on a "national" territory or "homeland," they usually offer a certain interpretation of history to justify these claims. Whether such a historiography relies on historical evidence is less important than the degree to which it can foster a sense of shared history and purpose. To express this idea, "national myth" is the term most often used to describe national stories. Some national myths have been

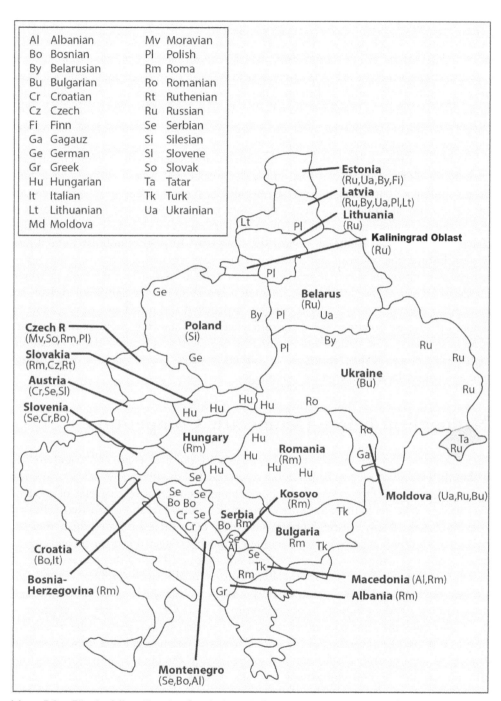

Al	Albanian
Bo	Bosnian
By	Belarusian
Bu	Bulgarian
Cr	Croatian
Cz	Czech
Fi	Finn
Ga	Gagauz
Ge	German
Gr	Greek
Hu	Hungarian
It	Italian
Lt	Lithuanian
Md	Moldova
Mv	Moravian
Pl	Polish
Rm	Roma
Ro	Romanian
Rt	Ruthenian
Ru	Russian
Se	Serbian
Si	Silesian
Sl	Slovene
So	Slovak
Ta	Tatar
Tk	Turk
Ua	Ukrainian

Estonia (Ru,Ua,By,Fi)
Latvia (Ru,By,Ua,Pl,Lt)
Lithuania (Ru)
Kaliningrad Oblast (Ru)
Belarus (Ru)
Czech R (Mv,So,Rm,Pl)
Slovakia (Rm,Cz,Rt)
Austria (Cr,Se,Sl)
Slovenia (Se,Cr,Bo)
Poland (Si)
Ukraine (Bu)
Hungary (Rm)
Romania (Rm)
Moldova (Ua,Ru,Bu)
Kosovo (Rm)
Serbia
Bulgaria
Croatia (Bo,It)
Bosnia-Herzegovina (Rm)
Macedonia (Al,Rm)
Albania (Rm)
Montenegro (Se,Bo,Al)

Map 5.1. Ethnic Minorities in Central and Eastern Europe, 2014. The map includes minorities over 0.2 percent of the population in the latest official census for each state.

more successful than others in accommodating ethnic diversity. The so-called civic type of nationalism, which builds community on shared political traditions, is potentially more inclusive than "ethnic nationalism," which requires members of the nation to share a common ethnicity. Nonetheless, even countries commonly considered textbook cases of "civic nationalism," such as Britain, France, and the United States, reveal significant similarities to "ethnic nationalism," as schools, churches, the media, the military, and various other state and private or public institutions perpetuate unified national stories and literatures and mental maps of national homelands.[8]

In many instances, the national myth contains stories about ethnic competition over territory, invoking memories of past ethnic dominance and subordination, which continue to influence current state- and nation-building processes. Yet not all ethnic groups engage in national competition. A key difference between ethnic and national groups is that, although ethnic groups aim to reproduce particular cultures, only national groups claim self-government rights on a particular territory.[9] In postcommunist Central and Eastern Europe, the majority and minority groups that articulated competing notions of self-government rights were national groups that defined "nation" on the basis of ethnic markers—most commonly language, in some cases religion. Yet significant differences emerged in the way national aspirations were articulated and posed against one another. Before offering explanations for these differences, the following pages provide a brief account of state- and nation-building in the period that preceded democratization, highlighting processes that created the conditions in which postcommunist democratization and nationalism subsequently took shape.

Nationalism before Democratic Competition

The pursuit of modern nation-states by nationalist political elites and counter-elites within the Hapsburg Empire began in the second part of the nineteenth century, and the dynamics of these efforts revealed the fundamentally competitive character of modern nationalism. Whether in the framework of the multinational Hapsburg state (reconstituted after 1867 as the dualist Austro-Hungarian Empire) or its successor states, the nationalist policies that a dominant ethnic group adopted invariably triggered resentment and engendered conflicting nationalist aspirations from other groups. During this process, national literatures emerged in vernacular languages, and national historiographies were written and became justifications for nationalist demands. Czechs and Hungarians defined their national myths and aspirations in opposition to Austria's Germans. After the creation of the dualist state, the same pattern remained characteristic in both parts of the monarchy. In the Austrian part, Czechs and Slovenes challenged German cultural dominance and articulated unsuccessful calls for national sovereignty. In the Hungarian part, the nationalist movements of non-Hungarians (Slovaks, Croats, and Romanians) encountered rejection by Hungarian elites.[10] Besides challenging one another, nationalist political elites also competed for international support and legitimization for their conflicting notions of national power. The complex matrix of these domestic and international interests led Austria-Hungary into World War I and, at the end of the war, resulted in the dissolution of the monarchy into its successor states.

When the victorious powers agreed to establish the successor states at the end of World War I, they relied on the Wilsonian principle of national self-determination. The demographic patterns of the region, however, made the delineation of clear "national" borders impossible. The states created to bring justice to previously subordinate national groups of the monarchy also became multinational, with new "titular" nations attempting to establish political and cultural hegemony over national minorities. Although relations of dominance and subordination were reversed after the dissolution of the Austro-Hungarian state, the same pattern of nation-building continued, with multiple groups sharing the same state but holding conflicting notions about legitimate territorial sovereignty. Incompatible narratives about the "justice" of the post–World War I settlements became part of conflicting national historiographies that have remained significant sources of tension over territorial sovereignty in the region.

Sovereignty is a fundamental principle of political organization and also one of the most contested because it takes different forms, and these forms are at times incompatible with one another. As J. Samuel Barkin and Bruce Cronin observe, "There has been a historical tension between state sovereignty, which stresses the link between sovereign authority and a defined territory, and national sovereignty, which emphasizes a link between sovereign authority and a defined population."[11] This tension had become particularly apparent in Central and Eastern Europe by the mid-nineteenth century and remained salient throughout the region's history. Yugoslavia, created to provide southern Slav peoples with a common state, in reality comprised a diversity of national groups that maintained strong prejudices and reproaches against one another. A famous expression of Slovene prejudices, for instance, is the 1927 statement by Catholic party leader Anton Korošec: "In Yugoslavia it is thus: the Serbs rule, the Croats debate, and the Slovenes work."[12] Even in Czechoslovakia, where the leadership established the strongest democratic institutions in the region, large national minority populations remained discontented with their status and continued to challenge the legitimacy of the new state.

With the political principle of national self-determination internationally legitimized, competing nationalist aspirations crystallized in the interwar period and formed the basis for strategies that later escalated into some of the atrocities committed during World War II. The Hungarian government focused its efforts on regaining lost territories and population. Wary of this Hungarian policy of irredentism, neighboring governments that had gained significant territories from historic Hungary designed aggressive economic and cultural policies to achieve more effective control over those territories and their inhabitants. Greater Romania, for example, based its institutional policies primarily on reordering the ethnic hierarchy in Transylvania in favor of Romanian dominance.[13] Hungarian organizations forcefully challenged these policies. Similarly, in Czechoslovakia, many Germans and Hungarians joined political parties that challenged the legitimacy of the state. These groups felt vindicated when Adolf Hitler dismembered Czechoslovakia in 1938, occupied the Czech Lands, and helped to redraw contested political borders throughout the region. The supposed right of the sizable German-speaking population of interwar Czechoslovakia, the Sudeten Germans, to belong to a common German nation-state served as a pretext for Hitler's destruction of the Czechoslovak state. After Germany's show of military might, the governments of Hungary, Romania, and Slovakia (a state that Hitler helped create) each became Hitler's allies at various times of the war, trusting that their participation on the victor's side would help them establish, reclaim, or maintain sovereignty over mutually claimed "national" territories and peoples. As a result of Hitler's policies, the Hungarian government was able to reannex two regions with majority Hungarian populations (the southern region of Czechoslovakia in November 1938 and northern Transylvania between 1940 and 1944). These sudden reversals of fortune were as traumatic to the Slovak and Romanian inhabitants of these territories as they had been for Hungarians after World War I. After the defeat of the Axis powers at the end of World War II, the post–World War I borders were reestablished, and the conditions for nationalist policies changed significantly.

The evolution of Polish state- and nation-building provides another example of traumatic shifts in territorial and ethno-cultural boundaries in the context of great power politics. By the end of the eighteenth century, the territories that had once been part of the medieval Polish kingdom were split among the Russian, German, and Austrian empires. When an independent Polish state was created at the end of World War I, that state incorporated an ethnically diverse population with complex histories of competition that provided significant sources of conflict during the interwar period. This multiethnic society was devastated during World War II. After the division of Poland by the Soviet Union and Germany in 1941, the violence perpetuated on that territory (primarily through state-designed strategies of ethnic cleansing but also through violence committed by social actors) annihilated one-third of the population—including almost the entire population of Polish Jews and large numbers of Poles, Ukrainians, and other ethnicities.[14] The peace agreements at the end of World War II re-created a Polish state but within territorial boundaries that were moved significantly to the west. The boundary shift was coupled with ethnic cleansing ("unmixing") of a different kind: millions of ethnic Germans from the western part of the new Polish state were forced out of their homes and moved to postwar Germany, and large numbers of Poles and Ukrainians were forced to resettle in the west.[15] As a result of these traumatic territorial and demographic changes, the Polish state turned from a long history of ethnic diversity to significant ethnic homogeneity.

Nationalist competition contributed also to the collapse of Yugoslavia in 1941, when Hitler and Benito Mussolini divided the state among Germany, Italy, Hungary, and Bulgaria and established, in the center of the former federation, a Croatian state ruled by the fascist Ustaša. In the bloody civil wars that engulfed Yugoslavia in subsequent years, the Ustaša government led a violent campaign against Jews, Roma, Serbs, and other groups; Yugoslav Partisans fought to defend villagers against terror; and the extreme nationalists among Serbian Četniks engaged in revenge attacks against ethnic Croatians, Muslims, and Partisans. By the end of the war, over one million people were killed, including Serbs, Croats, Bosnian-Herzegovinian Muslims, Danube Swabians (a German-speaking ethnic group), Jews, Slovenes, and Roma.

Against the backdrop of such violence, many communist leaders in the region, among whom ethnic minorities were represented in disproportionately high numbers, viewed internationalism as an appealing alternative to nationalism. Although communism provided leaders with unprecedented power to conduct "social engineering," none of these regimes succeeded in creating homogeneity in societies where multiple groups had earlier competed for national rights. There emerged no sizable "non-national" Yugoslav population in Yugoslavia, or Czechoslovak population in Czechoslovakia, capable of holding

Photo 5.1. Roma refugee camp in Zvecan, north of Kosovo, November 1999. Although the exact figure is unknown, millions of Roma live in often substandard conditions throughout Central and Eastern Europe and often have disproportionately high unemployment rates. (Lubomir Kotek/OSCE)

these federations together when the communist regimes began collapsing in 1989. The Soviet state was similarly unable to engender nonnational identities and loyalties.

Despite an initial emphasis on internationalism, in practice, nationalism remained a key organizing principle during the communist period.[16] In Yugoslavia, communist leader Josip Broz Tito made the eradication of national antagonisms his primary goal in 1945 and suppressed all overt manifestations of ethnic sentiment. Nonetheless, by the end of the 1960s, Slovenian, Croatian, Serbian, and other national identities were reasserting themselves in literature and the arts, and by the mid-1970s these groups had achieved self-government in the constituent republics of the Yugoslav federation. In the other part of the region that fell under Moscow's dominance, each of the "brotherly states" of Central and Eastern Europe pursued its own brand of nationalism in domestic politics.[17] The postwar Czechoslovak government, for instance, declared ethnic Germans and Hungarians collectively guilty of having contributed to Hitler's destruction of Czechoslovakia and gained Soviet approval for the expulsion of these ethnic groups from the country. Based on the so-called Beneš Decrees (named for the state's president, Eduard Beneš), Czechoslovakia expelled the overwhelming majority of ethnic Germans to Germany and a large percentage of the Hungarian population, including much of the Hungarian educated class, to Hungary.[18] Those who remained in the state were denied citizenship rights until 1948. Despite such a drastic policy to achieve an ethnic balance favoring the state's two titular groups, the Czechs and the Slovaks, a significant number of Hungarians remained in the Slovak part of Czechoslovakia. Throughout the communist decades, they were subject to economic, cultural, and educational policies that severely restricted their ability to reproduce their culture and improve their socioeconomic status. The relationship between the Czechs and the Slovaks was also tense from the beginning of cohabitation. Initial notions of a unified Czechoslovak identity were soon replaced by efforts to loosen Prague's control over the Slovak part of the land in a federative structure that better represented national interests.

Compared to Czechoslovakia, the postwar Romanian communist government adopted more minority-friendly policies. Because the ethnic Hungarian party was instrumental in the communist takeover in Romania, Hungarian minority leaders gained Moscow's support in achieving full citizenship rights, participation in the government, and the right to maintain cultural and educational institutions. The same Soviet government that in Czechoslovakia gave its full support to President Beneš's policies to expel the German and Hungarian minorities, in Romania facilitated the establishment of regional autonomy for Hungarians in Transylvania in 1952. Although this autonomous region was short-lived, the first communist-dominated Romanian government was much better disposed toward minorities overall than was the Beneš government in Czechoslovakia.[19] As the influence of ethnic Hungarian leaders in the Communist Party weakened, however, the government launched a nationalizing strategy that severely weakened the political status and social structure of the Hungarian community in Transylvania. Beginning in the mid-1960s, the government of Nicolae Ceaușescu launched a ruthless strategy to consolidate a centralized unitary national state. Ethnic Germans were offered incentives to immigrate to West Germany, and Hungarians were subjected to administrative, economic, and educational policies aimed at their assimilation. Against such a backdrop, ethnic Hungarians unsurprisingly played a significant role in the collapse of the Ceaușescu regime in December 1989.[20]

Of the unitary communist states in the region, Poland and Hungary were the only two that did not have sizable national minority groups. The small ethnic communities that existed in these states presented no systematic challenge to majority cultural dominance. Within the framework of the Moscow-led communist camp, the Hungarian government also indicated little interest in influencing the conditions of ethnic Hungarians living in the neighboring states. Under such circumstances, the significance of the national principle appeared less prominent in either case than it did in the region's multinational states. Yet the absence of internal national minorities did not make nationalist motivations irrelevant in these countries. In Poland, national aspirations contributed to the emergence of Solidarity, the most powerful anti-communist movement in the region in the 1980s. In Hungary, interest in the national principle strengthened by the end of the 1980s, especially with regard to Hungarian minorities living in the neighboring states.

Democratization and Nationalist Competition

With the collapse of communism came the promise of change, and for majorities and minorities alike, change brought a chance to redefine old ideas of citizenship and self-government. At the beginning of the process, most societies in the region experienced a unifying spirit of euphoria over the collapse of repressive regimes.[21] Democratization offered unprecedented opportunities for these societies to articulate differences through competitive elections, political parties, and parliamentary debates. The EU offered a model of political integration and a way of transcending the nationalist competitions of the past. Yet the most influential political actors throughout the region articulated their intentions to achieve both stronger national sovereignty and European integration.

The international institutions that most of the newly elected governments aspired to join—the North Atlantic Treaty Organization (NATO), the Council of Europe, the Organization for Security and Co-operation in Europe (OSCE), and the EU—insisted on peaceful negotiations about sovereignty issues. As various majority and minority groups in the region asserted claims to "national" self-government, Western international institutions reasserted the principle of individual rights, but they also began adopting an impressive number of documents calling for the protection of the rights of minority cultures. These documents signaled increased international awareness that many states incorporate multiple nation-building processes and that tensions arising from these situations must find lasting solutions acceptable to all parties involved.[22]

Despite the relative consistency of international expectations and the shared objective of Central and East Europeans to return to a "common European home," the conditions under which this goal could be harmonized with nationalist aspirations varied. Consequently, there were significant variations in the way nationalism manifested itself throughout the region. The differences revealed themselves in the goals that leaders and groups articulated and the strategies they designed to achieve those goals. An overwhelming nationalist goal in the region was to establish national entities by creating new states (e.g., in former Yugoslavia and Czechoslovakia) or to reestablish precommunist state borders (in the Baltic region). Another form of nationalism pursued national dominance in existing states, despite minority opposition to this strategy (Romania and Bulgaria).

A third form aimed at strengthening a common sense of nationhood beyond state borders (Hungary). The pages that follow offer explanations for these differences in nationalist strategy, emphasizing the influence of preexisting state structure (federal or unitary), national composition (whether national strategies involved internal or external national minorities), and the choices of national elites (to what extent majority and minority elites were willing to negotiate their claims within the emerging democratic institutions, employing the prospects of NATO and European integration in the process).

FROM MULTINATIONAL FEDERATIONS TO NATIONAL STATES

The nationalist movements that pursued state formation emerged in the three multinational federations: Czechoslovakia, the Soviet Union, and Yugoslavia. Although each of the three dissolving federal states was ethnically diverse, only a limited number of groups defined themselves in national terms and claimed rights to national self-government. In each case, the titular groups of substate administrative units were most likely to claim such rights. These were the Serbs, Slovenians, Macedonians, Montenegrins, and Croatians in former Yugoslavia; the Czechs and Slovaks in former Czechoslovakia; and the Estonians, Latvians, and Lithuanians in the former Soviet Union. In each case, those engaged in state formation had to answer the following questions: What would be the physical boundaries of the successor states? What would "the nation" mean within those boundaries? Who belonged to the new political community and under what terms? And what should happen to those who did not belong? In all cases, the political elites who led the movements for national independence played a very important role in shaping the debates about these questions. In the great majority of cases, nationalist claims were negotiated peacefully, within the channels of democratic political competition. In other cases, however, democratic forms of parliamentary debate and party competition were unable to contain national conflicts, and these conflicts escalated into devastating wars.

DEMOCRATIZATION DERAILED: NATIONALISM IN THE BALKANS

In former Yugoslavia, the substate borders of the republics did not coincide with people's mental maps of "historic homelands." Consequently, national self-determination became a vehemently contested idea in the Balkans, as multiple national groups living in a mixed demographic pattern claimed the same territory as "their own," and each group turned to a different national myth and conflicting interpretation of past relations of dominance and subordination, sacrifice and victimization.

Serbs and Croats composed the majority of the state's population as well as the overwhelming majority in the three largest republics—Serbia (and its autonomous provinces, Kosovo and Vojvodina), Croatia, and Bosnia-Herzegovina. Approximately 24 percent of Serbs lived outside the Republic of Serbia and 22 percent of Croats lived outside Croatia. Tensions between these two groups influenced interethnic relations throughout Yugoslavia. Montenegrins generally identified with Serbs, and Muslims lived intermixed with Serbs and Croats. Only Slovenia and Macedonia, with their very small Serbian and

Croatian populations, were not drawn into Serbian-Croatian competition.[23] In such a context, successive unilateral declarations of independence by nationalist elites contributed to a cycle of conflict that marked the entire decade of the 1990s and caused devastation and horror not seen in Europe since World War II.

The unilateral declaration of independence triggered military intervention even in Slovenia, where no other groups had articulated competing national claims for the same territory. The fight for independent Slovenia, however, was relatively uneventful compared to the brutal wars that followed in other parts of the disintegrating state. The Yugoslav army, by late 1991, had evolved into primarily a Serbian army. In the absence of Serbian claims for Slovenia as a "national homeland," European mediation quickly convinced the Yugoslav army to withdraw and hand over sovereignty to the Slovenian state in October 1991.

In other Yugoslav republics, where majority and minority political elites advanced competing and mutually incompatible claims for the same "national homeland," these claims mobilized large-scale ethnic support that led to violent conflict. The Serb Democratic Party in the Krajina region of Croatia, for instance, immediately challenged the emerging Croatian movement for an independent state by demanding administrative and cultural autonomy for the Serb-majority region. Unable to achieve this goal immediately, the leaders of the four Serb-controlled areas declared the formation of the Serb Autonomous Region of Krajina in January 1991 and added in March the same year that this region would "dissociate" from an independent Croatia and remain within Yugoslavia.

This sequence of unilateral declarations of national sovereignty exacerbated an already existing distrust and hostility among these groups and helped trigger a devastating war in Croatia. The government of Croatia on one side and the Yugoslav state presidency, as well as local Serbian authorities, on the other employed armed forces to resolve the crisis. The war ended in 1995 with the help of US and European mediation, after brutal destruction in Croatian cities and villages, great suffering among the civilian population, and "ethnic cleansing" on both sides that resulted in the displacement of more than a half-million refugees. Today, the Serbian minority represents only slightly more than 4 percent of Croatia's population.

Competition over national sovereignty became particularly vicious in Bosnia-Herzegovina, a republic in which three groups began their armed fight for an acceptable state design in April 1992. The Party of Democratic Action, representing the majority Muslim population, advocated an independent and unitary Bosnia-Herzegovina, with no internal territorial division along national lines. The Serb Democratic Party first rejected separation from Yugoslavia and fought for a separate state in the Serb-populated areas— in the hope of future reunification with other Serbian-inhabited territories of (former) Yugoslavia. The Croatian Democratic Union allied itself with the Muslim party against the Bosnian Serbs but also staged its own secessionist attempt in Herzegovina from 1993 to 1994—a conflict resolved only through strong international pressure, which led to the formation of a Muslim-Croat federation. The war over the fate of Bosnia-Herzegovina lasted from 1992 to 1995 and involved the engagement of the Serbian and Croatian militaries as well as NATO forces. Although all three groups committed atrocities, Serbian troops were responsible for more crimes than their counterparts, and the Muslim population suffered most grievously.[24]

Photo 5.2. Croatian refugees fleeing from Bosnian forces in June 1993 near Travnik, when the Herzegovinian Croats turned on the Bosnians, creating an internal disaster. The Serbs reportedly sat in the hills laughing. (Jim Bartlett)

The Dayton Peace Accords, reached through international mediation in 1995, created a loose confederation that holds the Muslim-Croat federation and the Serb republic in the common state of Bosnia and Herzegovina, dividing the Muslim-Croat federation into separate national cantons and allowing the Bosnian Croats to maintain a close link with the Croatian state. Although the Serb Democratic Party no longer dominates politics in the Republika Srpska of Bosnia-Herzegovina, the main political parties representing the Serb population have continued to articulate desires for an independent state.

The other territory over which some of the most violent nationalist conflicts emerged outside Bosnia-Herzegovina was Kosovo, a region that features prominently in the Serbian national myth. Before 1990, Kosovo was part of the Serbian republic of Yugoslavia but had a majority ethnic Albanian population. In 1990, Kosovo lost its autonomy under the emerging rule of Slobodan Milošević. As a result, the Albanians in this province were systematically excluded from institutions of political and economic power, and their means of cultural reproduction (such as education in the Albanian language) were virtually eliminated from state-sponsored institutions. When the opportunity for democratization presented itself, Albanian members of the Kosovo Assembly articulated the Kosovar Albanians' right to national self-determination as early as 1990. In September 1991, they organized a referendum in which an overwhelming majority of Kosovars (99.8 percent) voted for independence. After significant efforts to achieve independence through peaceful civil disobedience and the gradual construction of a "parallel state" (e.g., parallel institutions of education and health care), the National Movement for the Liberation of Kosovo (KLA) became impatient with this strategy and began a series of violent attacks against Serbs (police officers and civilians) in Kosovo. Serbian authorities responded with a massive offensive in July 1998, forcing the KLA to withdraw into the hills. The Serbs then began a ruthless and systematic process of ethnic cleansing, which resulted in approximately seven hundred thousand ethnic Albanian civilians from Kosovo being expelled from their villages and forced to flee to Albania or Macedonia. Despite international intervention, including two months of massive NATO bombings against military and industrial targets also in Serbia, the Serbian government refused to agree to an independent Kosovo. When Serb forces finally agreed in a June 1999 peace agreement to withdraw from Kosovo, the agreement guaranteed the continued territorial integrity of Yugoslavia (Serbia-Montenegro), including the province of Kosovo, which has been under UN administration since 1999. However, following the collapse of negotiations over the final status of Kosovo between local and international actors and the publication of a UN report calling for the independence of the former Serbian province[25] (albeit under international supervision), the Kosovo Assembly adopted a unilateral proclamation of independence on February 17, 2008. Swiftly recognized by the United States and some (though not all) EU member states, Kosovo's independence remains challenged by Serbia. Tensions over the border have decreased after an EU-brokered deal in April 2013 recognized Serb majority areas of Kosovo as autonomous at the municipal level; yet, Kosovo suffers from weak state capacity and remains under considerable international supervision.[26]

INDEPENDENCE AND EU INTEGRATION: THE BALTIC STATES

The Baltic states of Estonia, Latvia, and Lithuania were reestablished without significant border disputes within the territorial boundaries that these states had before their forcible annexation to the Soviet Union in 1940. Although Russians had dominated the institutions of power at both the federal and republic levels and ethnic Russians had settled in these republics in significant numbers, there were no significant disputes over national territorial borders between Russian nationalist politicians and the leaders of independence movements in the Baltics.

An important factor in the absence of territorial disputes was that, although Russians were the ethnic group closely associated with Soviet federal power structures, the ethnic Russian population in the Baltic republics overwhelmingly comprised relatively recent settlers whom the native population viewed as colonizers. As the formerly dominant ethnic group in the Soviet Union, the Russians remaining in the Baltic states stood to lose the most at independence. Yet ethnic Russians articulated no systematic challenge to nationalist aspirations in the Baltics. The new states, with their prospects for European integration, offered better socioeconomic conditions than neighboring Russia. Rather than demanding self-government, let alone secession and unification with Russia, ethnic Russian political organizations contested the exclusionary aspects of citizenship and language laws and lobbied European institutions to pressure these governments to adopt more minority-friendly policies. At least at the beginning of the 1990s, speaking the

Russian language did not signify ethnic or national identity in these states in the same way that language was the primary marker of Latvian, Estonian, or Lithuanian identity. The Russian-speaking population included people of different ethnicities who had switched to Russian as the language of advancement to higher status. Consequently, no commonly shared national myth existed among Russian speakers in the Baltic states that could have become the grounds for national sovereignty claims.[27] The only sizable historical minority in the Baltic region was the Polish minority in Lithuania. Although of roughly the same size as the state's Russian minority (at the time, each made up roughly 10 percent of the population), the Polish minority articulated a stronger challenge to majority nation-building than Russians in any of the three states—including Estonia and Latvia, where Russians made up a much higher proportion of the population.

The policies of the Russian government in Moscow constituted another significant factor accounting for differences between nation-building processes in the Yugoslav and Baltic regions. With over one hundred thousand Red Army troops stationed in the Baltic republics when the Soviet Union collapsed, many had feared violent Russian opposition to independence. Nevertheless, the Russian government agreed to withdraw these troops relatively quickly. In contrast to the Serbian leadership's involvement in mobilizing Serbian minorities in the secessionist republics and providing them with military resources, the Russian government aimed instead to eliminate discriminatory citizenship and language legislation in these countries through indirect pressure on their governments and complaints brought to European institutions.

In pursuit of national states, Baltic governments adopted policies to establish national dominance over the institutions of the new state. After 1990, there was a strong sense among these populations that democratization should bring national justice. Even though they were formally titular ethnicities in their republics during Soviet occupation, the share and status of indigenous ethnic groups had decreased dramatically due to large-scale deportation campaigns against the native population, the emigration of great numbers of Balts to the West, and the massive influx of Russians (see table 5.1).

As a result of these changes, Russian became the predominant language in the public domain, especially in the urban centers. The relationship between Russian and the titular national languages during the Soviet era remained that of one-sided bilingualism despite language legislation adopted in the final years of Soviet political reform that aimed at "emancipating" the Baltic languages. Non-Russians had to be fluent in Russian in order to function fully and advance socioeconomically, but Russian speakers were not learning the languages of the republics in which they resided.[28]

Decades of aggressive linguistic Russification, however, seemed only to reinforce the Balts' national aspirations, and the notion that Russian presence represented "illegal occupation" became a significant building block in strategies of state reconstruction. After achieving independence in 1991, each of the three governments adopted citizenship and language policies that established the dominance of the titular language in the state. The policies of nationalist state-building were most aggressive in Latvia, where the ratio of the native population compared to the Russian-speaking population was the highest, and most moderate in Lithuania, where the ratio of the Russian minority was the lowest. In Lithuania, all residents who had lived in the republic before independence obtained citizenship simply by applying. In Estonia and Latvia, only citizens of the interwar

Table 5.1. Ethnic Composition of the Baltic States

Nationality	Percentage of Population
Ethnic Composition of Estonia (2008 Census)	
Estonian	68.7
Russian	25.6
Ukrainian	2.1
Belarusian	1.2
Finn	0.8
Other	1.6
Ethnic Composition of Latvia (2009 Census)	
Latvian	59.3
Russian	27.8
Belarusian	3.6
Ukrainian	2.5
Polish	2.4
Lithuanian	1.3
Other	3.1
Ethnic Composition of Lithuania (2009 Census)	
Lithuanian	84.0
Polish	6.1
Russian	4.9
Other or unspecified	3.9

Source: CIA, The World Factbook 2013, https://www.cia.gov/library/publications/the-world-factbook.

Estonian and Latvian states before Soviet annexation in 1940 and their descendants had an automatic right to citizenship. Citizenship laws required other residents to pass a language-proficiency test in order to become citizens of the reestablished states, even though during the Soviet era hardly any Russian school taught Latvian. As a result, roughly a third of the population of Estonia and Latvia was excluded from citizenship.[29] Citizenship laws also disadvantaged ethnic Russians in the distribution of resources. The 1991 Latvian privatization law, for instance, excluded noncitizens. In Estonia, property restitution similarly discriminated against Russians.[30]

In general, the story of state- and nation-building in the Baltic region is about harmonizing national sovereignty with European integration. "Returning to Europe" and obtaining protection from future Russian reannexation by joining the EU were inextricable parts of the pursuit of national sovereignty in this region.[31] Employing the powerful leverage that these motivations provided, European institutions—especially the OSCE's High Commissioner on National Minorities, the Council of Europe, and the EU—applied strong pressure on the Baltic governments to adopt more inclusive citizenship laws and more pluralistic educational and language policies that complied with "European norms."[32] After 1998, the governments of Estonia and Latvia began adopting amendments to their citizenship laws that made the naturalization of "nonhistoric" minorities easier. International pressure has been less successful in influencing them to liberalize their language policies. Language legislation in both states also continues to reflect a nationalist state-building strategy, although in most cases restrictive language legislation was only moderately implemented.[33] Tensions over language use continue. In Latvia, a new bilingual curriculum introduced in 2002 and 2003 required that minority-language schools teach certain subjects exclusively in Latvian. In Estonia, a 2007 education reform introduced similar requirements. In both states, policies that mandate the exclusive use of the majority language in subjects considered significant for the reproduction of national cultures, such as history and music, have reinforced fears among Russian speakers that majorities intend to erase Russian culture from these states.[34] Still, state-minority relations remained peaceful, and Russophone minority actors continued to pursue claims for minority integration through electoral politics, relying particularly on strength in local government in major cities.[35]

In successor states of the Soviet Union, the parallel processes of democratization and EU integration described in this section unfolded only in the Baltic states. A brief account of developments in Ukraine helps to highlight how internal divisions over EU membership and national identity can contribute to a major state crisis in a post-Soviet European successor state where political elites failed to establish credible democratic institutions. Although the appeal of democratization is strong in Ukrainian society, the idea of EU membership remains deeply divisive. Given Ukraine's geographic position between the EU and Russia, the ambivalence about European integration has implications beyond the "Euroskepticism" found in current EU member states. A significant segment of Ukraine's political elite and public favors the pursuit of EU membership, but a sizable portion of the state's Russian speakers, especially in the eastern region close to the Russian border, is more interested in maintaining close ties with Russia. The Russian government, meanwhile, strongly opposes the idea of Ukraine's incorporation into Western political and security institutions. The combination of these conditions reinforced skepticism also among EU leaders about the prospects for Ukraine's inclusion in the European integration project. Given the large size of the Ukrainian territory and population in comparison with the Baltic states and the magnitude of Ukraine's socioeconomic problems, the prospects for Ukraine's EU integration remain weak, especially after the 2008 financial crisis. Although Ukraine became part of the EU's "Eastern Partnership" initiative,[36] this framework provides European institutions with no leverage to influence policies affecting interethnic relations in a partner state or to shape bilateral relations between Ukraine and Russia.

Ukraine includes a large Russian-speaking population with ambivalent attitudes toward the Ukrainian national identity pursued through policies designed in the state center. Under such conditions, a significant crisis of trust in the government can lead to a major state crisis in which even the political borders of the state become contested.[37] The evolution of the 2013–2014 Ukrainian state crisis manifests this logic. Ukraine's political elites failed to establish credible democratic institutions for the state created after 1991. President Viktor Yanukovych's decision to violently repress antigovernment demonstrations, which began in Kiev in November 2013 in response to the government's refusal to sign an association agreement with the EU, led to a major state crisis. The escalation of this crisis—involving the aggressive intrusion of the Russian state through a military annexation of the Crimean Peninsula, followed by secessionist mobilization in Eastern Ukraine, all in the name of protecting Ukraine's Russian-speaking population— highlights not only the failure of democratization in Ukraine but also the continued salience of ethnicity in the politics of sovereignty and legitimacy in the region.

Russian support for secessionism in Ukraine heightened concerns about state sovereignty and regional security in the Baltic states, where the integration of large Russophone minorities remained a major challenge of democratic consolidation. Concerns about the future of the EU—which gained significance in this region after the 2008 "Euro crisis" and became magnified by the Syrian refugee crisis and Brexit in 2015–2016—reinforced fears among national majority populations that the Putin government would successfully mobilize Russophone "kin" majorities against the states in which they live.[38]

THE "VELVET DIVORCE" AND ITS AFTERMATH: THE CZECH AND SLOVAK STATES

In contrast with the violent conflicts over national sovereignty in former Yugoslavia and the powerful support for independence in the Baltic republics, the independent Czech Republic and Slovakia were created after the peaceful dissolution of Czechoslovakia in 1992. Some accounts of the separation emphasized cultural differences between Czechs and Slovaks and assigned a significant weight to Slovak aspirations for a national state.[39] Yet separation was not primarily the outcome of ethnic division between Slovaks and Czechs. Rather than the result of large-scale popular mobilization for independence, as in the Baltic states, the creation of independent Czech and Slovak states was an outcome negotiated among the political leaders of the two parts of the federation with only limited public support.[40] At the same time, each of these states was established democratically, by elected governing bodies, and in the absence of significant popular opposition.[41]

As with the separation of the Baltic states, a key reason for the absence of violent conflict over the dissolution of Czechoslovakia was that no disputes emerged between Czechs and Slovaks over state borders, as the two groups did not initiate mutually exclusive "national homeland" claims to the same territory. Before the first establishment of Czechoslovakia in 1918, Slovaks had lived within the Hungarian kingdom for ten centuries, and the old territorial border remained a substate boundary in Czechoslovakia. After decades of coexistence with the prospect of mobility within a common state—first in interwar Czechoslovakia and then in communist Czechoslovakia—no sizable Czech national minority developed in Slovak territory or Slovak historic minority in the Czech Lands that would articulate a substate national challenge to either of the new states. Another important reason why the Czech and Slovak divorce lacked significant controversy was that the Hungarian minority in the Slovak part of the state, a historic minority with competing homeland claims in the southern region of Slovakia, did not challenge the Slovaks' right to independence.

For reasons described earlier in this chapter, at the time of independence, the Czech Republic was one of the least ethnically diverse states in the region (see table 5.2). Czech political leaders therefore faced few challenges to pursuing a single, dominant culture in the new state. Of all the ethnicities in the state, the Roma continue to constitute the largest and most distinct cultural group, with a share of the population estimated at between 2 and 3 percent. Official policies and popular attitudes toward this minority after the creation of the new state indicated that the national majority had little desire to accommodate Roma culture. Citizenship laws limited the rights of Roma to become

Table 5.2. Ethnic Composition of the Czech Republic (2011 Census)

Nationality	Percentage of Population
Czech	64.3
Moravian	5.0
Slovak	1.4
Other or unspecified	29.3

Source: The Czech Statistical Office (Český statistický úřad). Czech Demographic Handbook 2013. Available at: http://www.czso.cz/csu/2013edicniplan.nsf/engt/8E001797ED/$File/4032130116.pdf.

Table 5.3. Ethnic Composition of Slovakia (2011 Census)

Nationality	Percentage of Population
Slovak	80.7
Hungarian	8.5
Roma	2.0
Czech	0.6
Ruthenian	0.6
Ukrainian	0.1
Other or unspecified	0.5

Source: Statistical Office of the Slovak Republic. 2011 Population and Housing Census. Available at: http://portal.statistics.sk/files/table-10.pdf.

naturalized in the new state. On the level of local government, anti-Roma efforts included attempts to segregate swimming pools, construct walls separating Roma and Czech inhabitants, and provide subsidies for Roma willing to emigrate. The relatively small size and fragmentation of the Roma population, however, prevented these incidents from becoming a matter of broader debate about Czech national exclusivism.[42]

National aspirations found a more complex social context in newly independent Slovakia.[43] Before 1993, the primary question of Slovak national sovereignty had been whether an independent Slovak state was necessary to fulfill national aspirations. After the creation of Slovakia, the key question became how a Slovak "nation-state" could materialize on a territory that incorporated a relatively large, geographically concentrated, and politically well-organized historic Hungarian community (see table 5.3). During the first period of independence, from 1992 to 1998, the Slovak political parties in power, under the leadership of Prime Minister Vladimír Mečiar, opted for traditional nationalist policies.[44] In an attempt to suppress minority claims for substate institutional autonomy, these policies were aimed at establishing Slovak majority control over all institutions of government and cultural reproduction. Restrictive language legislation adopted in 1995 was designed to strengthen the status of the Slovak literary standard against dialects and to exclude minority languages from the spheres considered most important for the reproduction of national cultures: local government, territory markings, the media, and the educational system. Hungarian minority parties forcefully challenged these policies and pressed for a pluralist Slovak state. Employing the methods of party competition and parliamentary debate, Hungarian minority political elites asked that Slovakia's historic Hungarian minority be recognized as a state-constituting entity. To guarantee the reproduction of Hungarian minority culture in Slovakia, they demanded substate forms of autonomy, at various times emphasizing either the cultural, educational, or territorial aspects of self-government. Despite internal debates among Hungarian parties about the best institutional forms, they agreed on the importance of language rights and claimed the right to use the Hungarian language in the southern region of Slovakia in all public spheres and the educational system.

Majority–minority debates over these questions marked the first decade of democratization in Slovakia. The Mečiar government's policies of increasing centralized control over society also created sharp divisions within the Slovak majority. Based on their agreement about the necessity of moving Slovakia away from a recentralizing authoritarian regime, the Slovak and Hungarian parties in opposition eventually formed a strategic electoral alliance that defeated the Mečiar government in the 1998 parliamentary elections. This Slovak-Hungarian electoral alliance was able to form a governing coalition that changed the course of Slovak nationalist policies in the following years. Even though debates about minority self-government and language equality continued and often reflected vehement disagreements, the prospect of European integration provided a significant incentive to both majority and minority moderate parties to negotiate peacefully. They managed to design policies that, while preserving the predominance of the majority language throughout the country, gradually included the minority language in ways that satisfied the main aspirations of minority parties articulated from the beginning of the 1990s. The return of national exclusivist parties to the government after 2006 raised questions about the future of minority accommodation in the country. The controversy over the June 2009 amendments to the Slovak language law restricting minority language use in official business reveals the limits of international pressure in the post-EU accession period, when the conditionality of prospective EU membership can no longer constrain majority policy makers. Still, the prospect of a more minority-friendly approach to nation-building in the future remains open. The coalition government formed after the 2010 parliamentary elections included a new Hungarian-Slovak party called "Bridge," which placed particular emphasis on interethnic reconciliation. This party became part of coalition governments also after the 2012 and 2016 parliamentary elections. Although these changes in government had no significant impact on minority policy in Slovakia, electoral and party politics remains the primary form of majority–minority contestation also in Slovakia.

Consolidating National States: Nation-State or Pluralism?

The unitary states of Bulgaria, Hungary, Poland, and Romania continued their existence within unchanged state borders after the communist collapse. The absence of state collapse and new state creation, however, did not make nationalist ideology irrelevant in these countries. Wherever majority national elites chose to define the postcommunist state as the unitary "nation-state" of the majority national group, and the government engaged in aggressive policies to create majority dominance over sizable ethnic and national minority groups, nationalism became a deeply divisive political strategy.

Photo 5.3. With the expansion of the European Union, West European tourists have come in large numbers to places like this Hungarian village in Transylvania. Many buy "ethnic gifts" at new shops like this one. (Dana Stryk)

FROM NATIONALIST COMMUNISM TO DEMOCRATIC NATIONALISM: ROMANIA

As in other multiethnic societies in the region, the legacies of past relations of dominance and subordination between ethnic groups continued to influence majority and minority perspectives in Romania about what "national sovereignty" should mean. With the end of World War II, the contested borders of the state were redrawn again, largely along the same lines created after World War I, and Romania fell under the influence of the Soviet Union.[45] Despite the ruthlessness of anti-Hungarian policies enacted during the dictatorship of Nicolae Ceaușescu, members of the Hungarian minority maintained a strong sense of national identity. Only days after the bloody December 1989 revolution that toppled perhaps the most repressive communist dictatorship in the region, ethnic Hungarians formed a political party that commanded the overwhelming majority of the votes of their population of 1.6 million in every subsequent election, and they became a significant force in the Romanian parliament (see table 5.4).

Rather than discarding the nationalist policies of the Ceaușescu period, however, the government of Ion Iliescu, after 1990, designed a new constitution that defined the state as a "nation-state" based on the unity of an ethnically determined Romanian nation. The regime based its power on alliances with ultranationalist Romanian parties of the left and right and instituted minority policies that in some ways were more restrictive than their counterparts during the Ceaușescu dictatorship. The new constitution

Table 5.4.   Ethnic Composition of Romania (2011 est.)

Nationality	Percentage of Population
Romanian	83.4
Hungarian	6.1
Roma	3.1
Ukrainian	0.3
German	0.2
Other	0.7
Unspecified	6.1

Source: CIA, *The World Factbook 2017*. Available at: https://www.cia.gov/library/publications/the-world-factbook/docs/profileguide.html.

affirmed Romanian as the only official language in Romania. Laws adopted on public administration and public education also severely restricted the use of minority languages and became sources of intense controversy between the Romanian government and the Hungarian minority party. Like its counterpart in Slovakia, the Hungarian minority party demanded the right to Hungarian-language cultural and educational institutions and to use that language in local and regional government. The Hungarians pressed for these demands through bargaining and negotiations with majority parties willing to compromise on national issues. Although all Romanian parties rejected Hungarian claims to substate autonomy, moderate Romanian parties were willing to form an electoral alliance with the Hungarian party, and—much in keeping with events in Slovakia—this strategic alliance defeated the Iliescu government in 1996, formed a coalition government, and began to change Romanian nation-building policies. Even though the Iliescu government returned to power in the 2000 elections, the prospect of membership in NATO and the EU had become significant enough for the regime to expand the rights of language use in the spheres most important for minority cultural reproduction.[46] Although Romania was considered a "laggard" in democratic consolidation and EU accession (admitted together with Bulgaria in 2007, while eight other Central and East European states had become EU members in 2004), postaccession Romanian governments remained more supportive of minority-friendly policies (including language policies) than their Slovak counterparts. Hungarians in Romania have voted overwhelmingly for the same moderate umbrella minority party since 1990, which has been part of Romanian coalition governments since 1977, playing a key role in the relative stability of the Romanian political system. The question remains open, however, about the ability of this minority party to sustain its mobilizational capacity among an increasingly discontented minority electorate.[47] The challenges of minority inclusion remain significant also in Romania. The demand for substate territorial autonomy in a Hungarian-majority region is highly divisive, and the marginalization of Roma minorities remains a significant unresolved issue.

Nation Building across State Borders

Besides cohabitating with a national majority in the same state, most ethnic and national minorities in this region also have neighboring "kin-states"—that is, states in which their ethnic kin compose a titular majority.[48] A growing interest emerged among the governments in such kin-states to adopt legislation that would grant preferential treatment to ethnic kin living in other states. The constitutions of several states, such as Albania, Croatia, Hungary, and Macedonia, contain commitments to care for the well-being of kin living abroad. Several governments, such as in Bulgaria, Hungary, Poland, Romania, Russia, Serbia, Slovenia, and Slovakia, adopted legislation to provide benefits to ethnic kin living abroad. Although these constitutional clauses and benefit laws differ in their specific content, ranging from cultural and economic benefits to dual-citizenship rights, their common characteristic is that they support the preservation of national identity and aim to contribute to the fostering of relationships between a kin-state and those outside its borders who define themselves in some sense as conationals.[49]

HUNGARY AND VIRTUAL NATIONALISM

The Hungarian state's nation-building strategy after 1990 is the clearest example of the trans-sovereign type of nationalism in the region. This type of nationalism does not pursue a traditional nation-state through territorial changes or the repatriation of ethnic kin within its borders. Instead, it aims to maintain a sense of common cultural "nationhood" across existing state borders.[50] Close to 3 million ethnic Hungarians live in Hungary's neighboring states. In an integrated Europe, they compose one of the largest historical minority groups. After the collapse of communist regimes, Hungarian political elites were aware that revisionism was an unacceptable proposition if they wanted to join an integrated Europe. Instead of pressing for border changes, they created a network of institutions that link Hungarians living in the neighboring countries to Hungary while encouraging them to remain "in their homeland" and, in effect, withstand assimilation where they reside. To complement these cross-border institutions, the Hungarian government expressed support both for EU membership for Hungary and its neighbors and for Hungarian minority demands for local and institutional autonomy in their home states. According to the logic of these policies, if Hungary and all of its neighbors became EU members, and the EU provided a supranational, decentralized structure for strong regional institutions, then Hungarians could live as though no political borders separated them.

Although the "virtualization of borders" appeared attractive to many Hungarians, the idea found little appeal among the majority political parties in neighboring countries. Seven states neighboring Hungary include ethnic Hungarian populations, and five of these states were newly established after the collapse of communist federations. As discussed earlier in this chapter, the majority national elites in both newly created and consolidating national states were highly reluctant to weaken their sovereignty and accommodate multiple nation-building processes in their territories. Thus, Hungarian efforts unilaterally to "virtualize" borders in the region triggered tensions between Hungary and its neighbors.

The adoption in June 2001 of the Law Concerning Hungarians Living in Neighboring Countries (commonly known as the Hungarian Status Law)—which defined all ethnic Hungarians in the region as part of the same cultural nation and on this basis offered a number of educational, cultural, and even economic benefits to those living in neighboring states—triggered significant attention from policy makers in the region, European institution officials, and scholars of nationalism.[51] The competitive dynamics of nation-building in the region and its potentially large-scale regional impact made the Hungarian strategy particularly controversial. The governments of Romania and Slovakia, the two states with the largest Hungarian populations, expressed concern that the legislation weakened their exclusive sovereignty over ethnic Hungarian citizens and discriminated against majority nationals in neighboring countries. Although these neighboring governments themselves had adopted similar policies toward their own ethnic kin abroad, controversy over the Hungarian Status Law brought Hungary's relations with these neighbors to a dangerously low point. The fact that all of these governments were keenly interested in EU membership eventually helped them compromise. Hungary signed a bilateral agreement with Romania and altered the language of the law in response to European pressure in 2003. Yet the controversy over the Hungarian Status Law foreshadowed the challenges of reconciling European integration with the continuing power of divergent and competing national aspirations. The divisiveness of cross-border nationalism became particularly visible after 2010, when the newly elected Hungarian government began adopting legislation that made it easier for ethnic Hungarians living in neighboring countries to become Hungarian citizens and gain nonresident voting rights. These acts triggered strong resentment in Slovakia and also deepened political divisions in Hungary. The strong showing of the vehemently xenophobic Movement for a Better Hungary (Jobbik) in the 2009 European Parliament elections, together with this party's increasing success among the Hungarian electorate—in obtaining parliamentary seats in the 2010 elections and gaining 20 percent of the votes in the 2014 parliamentary elections—reveals the salience of exclusivist nationalism despite the earlier successes of democratic consolidation. The new Hungarian constitution adopted in 2011 is also criticized for provisions that can indirectly sanction discrimination against Hungary's large Roma minority. The Fidesz government relied increasingly on nationalist populism to legitimize a shift to autocratization in Hungary. Prime Minister Viktor Orbán featured himself as a trailblazer of "illiberal democracy," understood as a government based on ethnically conceived nationalism. After 2015, the government successfully instrumentalized the Syrian refugee crisis to brand itself as the defender of the nation and of European Christianity. In the same spirit, a set of laws was adopted in 2017 to undermine those nongovernmental organizations and institutions that represent and encourage critical attitudes about ethnic exclusivism and populist nationalism (e.g., the Central European University of Budapest and human rights nongovernmental organizations).[52]

Nationalism and the Fragility of Democracy

Although European organizations uphold the principles of liberal democracy, respect for ethnic diversity, human rights, and dignity, democratization in the Central and East European societies that became EU member states did not lead to a broad acceptance of liberal-individualist understandings of citizenship. Nor did nationalism result in horror perpetuated in the name of ethnic kin throughout the region. Given the dramatic collapse of states and regimes during the 1990s, the relatively low occurrence of violent conflict associated with these changes was remarkable. The promise of European integration altered the conditions under which nationalist interests could be articulated.

The specific goals that nationalist leaders and groups articulated in the 1990s and 2000s, as well as the means by which they pursued those goals, varied across the region. Most of the former titular groups of multinational federations sought national independence. Where substate boundaries within the disintegrating multinational federation had coincided with the territories that titular groups defined as their historic homelands and secession encountered no significant challenge from other groups, nationalist state-building unfolded without significant violence. In these cases, the prospects for integration into Western institutions helped reinforce initial interests in democratization. Examples of such nonviolent (or relatively nonviolent) state formation include the reestablishment of the Baltic states of Estonia, Latvia, and Lithuania; the secession of Slovenia and Macedonia; and the creation of independent Czech and Slovak states.

Where the state-building aspirations of a group encountered forceful challenge by another group claiming the same territory as a historic homeland within a dissolving federal state and the dominant political elites opted for unilateralism over sustained negotiation across ethnic lines, nationalist mobilization led to devastating wars. This was the situation in the former Yugoslav republics of Croatia, Bosnia-Herzegovina, and the Serbian autonomous province of Kosovo. Competing national elites in these cases opted for national sovereignty or its violent denial even at the most horrific costs, and future prospects for European integration did not figure significantly in their calculations—despite the fact that, before the communist collapse, Yugoslavia had been better connected to international institutions than Soviet bloc countries. European integration gained primacy in nationalist strategy only in Slovenia, where belonging to Europe constituted a strong element of national identity, and with no significant national minority, the issue of national sovereignty was most easily resolved.

Lithuania provides an important lesson about the significance of the choices that majority and minority political elites make in nationalist competition. In the same period that Croatian and Serbian majority and minority elites were fighting a devastating war in the southeastern part of the continent, the leaders of the Lithuanian national majority and the Polish minority opted for a consensual resolution of the tension over mutually claimed homelands. Eager to satisfy European expectations, they engaged in a bilateral and peaceful negotiation over the issues of autonomy and minority rights.

Governments in Bulgaria, Romania, and all of the multiethnic successor states of dissolving federations had to determine whether the democratic state could pursue the traditional nationalist aim of the political-cultural congruence of the nation or accommodate minority cultures in a more pluralist state. Excepting Croatia, Serbia, and Bosnia-Herzegovina, in all of these states, majority and minority political parties remained committed to democratic means of negotiating their competing notions of sovereignty.

Complicating matters even further, many governments in the region juggle the dual roles of home state (in relation to their titular nation and national minorities living on their territory) and kin-state (in relation to ethnic kin populations living outside their territory). Such cases have prompted officials in European institutions to begin designing a common set of norms to assure minority protection and permit kin-states to build relations with external minorities while continuing to uphold the principle of state sovereignty.[53]

Harmonizing the principles of state sovereignty and individualism with the practice of multiple nation-building within and across state borders will remain a continuing challenge. In this sense, postcommunist member states are no different from their West European counterparts, where the strengthening of nationalist sentiment is also revealed in electoral politics. Concerns about the impact of nationalism on democratic consolidation are no longer confined to the "new democracies" of Central and Eastern Europe. Rather, this region provides invaluable lessons about the sources of conflict as well as about the strategies of peaceful democratic contestation.

Study Questions

1. State borders have changed many times in Central and Eastern Europe following the awakening of national movements in the second half of the nineteenth century. What were the most significant border changes, and in what ways have they exacerbated the competitive logic of nationalism and the problem of noncongruence between state and national boundaries?
2. Explain the "Janus-faced" character of nationalism and the way it has influenced postcommunist democratic development in Central and East European countries. In what ways can we say that nation-building policies in this region have been both forward-looking and at the same time turned to the past?
3. Bearing in mind the significance of preexisting institutions, national composition, and the choices made by political elites, what seems to set apart the violent ethnic politics of the former Yugoslavia from the largely peaceful evolution of majority–minority conflicts in the rest of Central and Eastern Europe?
4. Most ethnic minorities in Central and Eastern Europe have kin-states in the region, and most governments have enacted legislation to extend various kinds of benefits to ethnic kin living abroad. Discuss the reasons why kin-state nationalism is controversial in this region and how it affects the evolution of democratic government and European integration.
5. The enlargement of the EU to include democratized postcommunist states is commonly viewed as a source of success in democratic consolidation and interethnic peacemaking in significant parts of Central and Eastern Europe. At the same time, the reassertion of Russian regional power under Vladimir Putin's government is viewed as a factor that weakens the prospects for democratic consolidation and can even endanger state stability in the successor states of the Soviet Union. What is the role of these processes of regional influence in explaining the successes and failures of nation-building and minority inclusion throughout the postcommunist region?

Suggested Readings

Brubaker, Rogers. *Nationalism Reframed: Nationhood and the National Question in the New Europe.* Cambridge: Cambridge University Press, 1996.
Bunce, Valerie. "Peaceful versus Violent State Dismemberment." *Politics and Society* 27, no. 2 (1999): 217–37.

Csergo, Zsuzsa. *Talk of the Nation: Language and Conflict in Romania and Slovakia.* Ithaca, NY: Cornell University Press, 2007.

Csergo, Zsuzsa, and James M. Goldgeier. "Nationalist Strategies and European Integration." *Perspectives on Politics* 2, no. 1 (2004): 21–37.

Gagnon, V. P., Jr. *The Myth of Ethnic War: Serbia and Croatia in the 1990s.* Ithaca, NY: Cornell University Press, 2004.

Gellner, Ernest. *Nations and Nationalism.* Ithaca, NY: Cornell University Press, 1983.

Hale, Henry. "Explaining Ethnicity." *Comparative Political Studies* 37, no. 4 (May 2004): 458–85.

Hroch, Miroslav. "From National Movement to the Fully-Formed Nation: The Nation-Building Process in Europe." *New Left Review* 198 (1993): 3–20.

Kallas, Kristina, "Claiming the Diaspora: Russia's Compatriot Policy and Its Reception by Estonian-Russian Population," *Journal on Ethnopolitics and Minority Issues in Europe* 15, no. 3 (2016): 1–25.

Kelley, Judith. *Ethnic Politics in Europe: The Power of Norms and Incentives.* Princeton, NJ: Princeton University Press, 2004.

King, Charles. *Extreme Politics: Nationalism, Violence, and the End of Eastern Europe.* Oxford: Oxford University Press, 2010.

Kymlicka, Will, and Magda Opalski. *Can Liberal Pluralism Be Exported? Western Political Theory and Ethnic Relations in Eastern Europe.* Oxford: Oxford University Press, 2001.

Laitin, David. *Identity in Formation: The Russian-Speaking Populations in the Near Abroad.* Ithaca, NY: Cornell University Press, 1998.

Livezeanu, Irina. *Cultural Politics in Greater Romania: Regionalism, Nation Building, and Ethnic Struggle, 1918–1930.* Ithaca, NY: Cornell University Press, 1995.

Roeder, Philip. "The Triumph of Nation-States: Lessons from the Collapse of the Soviet Union, Yugoslavia, and Czechoslovakia." In *After the Collapse of Communism,* edited by Michael McFaul and Kathryn Stoner-Weiss, 21–57. Cambridge: Cambridge University Press, 2004.

Schulze, Jennie L. *Strategic Frames: Europe, Russia, and Minority Inclusion in Estonia and Latvia.* Pitt Series in Russian and Eastern European Studies. Pittsburgh, PA: University of Pittsburgh Press, 2017.

Snyder, Jack. *From Voting to Violence: Democratization and Nationalist Conflict.* New York: W. W. Norton, 2000.

Snyder, Timothy. *Bloodlands: Europe between Hitler and Stalin.* New York: Basic Books, 2010.

Subotic, Jelena. *Hijacked Justice: Dealing with the Past in the Balkans.* Ithaca, NY: Cornell University Press, 2009.

Tesser, Lynn. *Ethnic Cleansing and the European Union: An Interdisciplinary Approach to Security, Memory and Ethnography.* Basingstoke, UK: Palgrave Macmillan, 2013.

Tismaneanu, Vladimir. *Fantasies of Salvation: Democracy, Nationalism, and Myth in Post-Communist Europe.* Princeton, NJ: Princeton University Press, 1998.

Waterbury, Myra. *Between State and Nation: Diaspora Politics and Kin-State Nationalism in Hungary.* Basingstoke, UK: Palgrave Macmillan, 2010.

Wimmer, Andreas. *Ethnic Boundary Making: Institutions, Power, Networks.* New York: Oxford University Press, 2013.

Notes

1. Ernst Gellner, *Nations and Nationalism* (Ithaca, NY: Cornell University Press, 1983), 1; and Andreas Wimmer, *Waves of War: Nationalism, State Formation, and Ethnic Exclusion in the Modern World* (Cambridge: Cambridge University Press, 2012).

2. Alfred Stepan, Juan J. Linz, and Yogendra Yadav, *Crafting State-Nations: India and Other Multinational Democracies* (Baltimore, MD: Johns Hopkins University Press, 2010).

3. Robert Kaplan, *Balkan Ghosts: A Journey through History* (New York: Vintage Books, 1993); and Mischa Glenny, *The Balkans 1804–1999* (New York: Viking, 2000).

4. Jack Snyder, *From Voting to Violence: Democratization and Nationalist Conflict* (New York: W. W. Norton, 2000); and Roger Petersen, *Western Intervention in the Balkans: The Strategic Use of Emotion in Conflict* (Cambridge: Cambridge University Press, 2011).

5. Anthony D. Smith, *Nationalism and Modernism: A Critical Survey of Recent Theories of Nations and Nationalism* (London: Routledge, 1998); Rogers Brubaker, *Nationalism Reframed: Nationhood and the National Question in the New Europe* (Cambridge: Cambridge University Press, 1996); and Kanchan Chandra, ed., *Constructivist Theories of Ethnic Politics* (New York: Oxford University Press, 2012).

6. Henry Hale, "Explaining Ethnicity," *Comparative Political Studies* 37, no. 4 (May 2004): 458–85; and Andreas Wimmer, *Ethnic Boundary Making: Institutions, Power, Networks* (Cambridge: Cambridge University Press, 2013).

7. Tom Nairn, "The Modern Janus," in *The Break-Up of Britain: Crisis and Neo-nationalism*, ed. Tom Nairn (London: New Left Books, 1977).

8. Taras Kuzio, "The Myth of the Civic State: A Critical Survey of Hans Kohn's Framework for Understanding Nationalism," *Ethnic and Racial Studies* 25, no. 1 (2002): 20–39.

9. For a political self-determination theory of territory, see Margaret Moore, *A Political Theory of Territory* (New York: Oxford University Press, 2015).

10. For a historical account, see Hugh L. Agnew, *The Czechs and the Lands of the Bohemian Crown* (Stanford, CA: Hoover Institution Press, 2004). About nationalism and competition, see Anthony W. Marx, *Faith in Nation: Exclusionary Origins of Nationalism* (Oxford: Oxford University Press, 2003). About resentment as an important motivation for nationalism, see Liah Greenfeld, *Nationalism: Five Roads to Modernity* (Cambridge: Cambridge University Press, 1992).

11. J. Samuel Barkin and Bruce Cronin, "The State and the Nation: Changing Norms and the Rules of Sovereignty in International Relations," *International Organizations* 48 (Winter 1994): 107–30. See also Stephen Krasner, ed., *Problematic Sovereignty: Contested Rules and Political Possibilities* (New York: Columbia University Press, 2001), 1–23.

12. Quoted in Arnold Suppan, "Yugoslavism versus Serbian, Croatian, and Slovene Nationalism," in *Yugoslavia and Its Historians: Understanding the Balkan Wars of the 1990s*, ed. Norman M. Naimark and Holly Case (Stanford, CA: Stanford University Press, 2003), 126.

13. Irina Livezeanu, *Cultural Politics in Greater Romania: Regionalism, Nation Building, and Ethnic Struggle, 1918–1930* (Ithaca, NY: Cornell University Press, 1995).

14. See Timothy Snyder, *Bloodlands: Europe between Hitler and Stalin* (New York: Basic Books, 2010).

15. For accounts of the significance of these processes of ethnic "unmixing" for the postcommunist political and social development of the region, see Rogers Brubaker, *Nationalism Reframed: Nationhood and the National Question in the New Europe* (Cambridge: Cambridge University Press, 1996); and Lynn Tesser, *Ethnic Cleansing and the European Union: An Interdisciplinary Approach to Security, Memory and Ethnography* (Basingstoke, UK: Palgrave Macmillan, 2013).

16. See Valerie Bunce, *Subversive Institutions: The Design and the Destruction of Socialism and the State* (Cambridge: Cambridge University Press, 1999).

17. About national ideology in Romania, see Katherine Verdery, *National Ideology under Socialism: Identity and Cultural Politics in Ceaușescu's Romania* (Berkeley and Los Angeles: University of California Press, 1991). For the national question in Czechoslovakia, see Sharon Wolchik, *Czechoslovakia in Transition: Politics, Economics, and Society* (London: Pinter, 1991).

18. Vojtech Mastny, "The Beneš Thesis: A Design for the Liquidation of National Minorities, Introduction," in *The Hungarians: A Divided Nation*, ed. Stephen Borsody (New Haven, CT: Yale Center for International and Area Studies, 1988), 231–43.

19. Bennett Kovrig, "Peacemaking after World War II," in *The Hungarians: A Divided Nation*, ed. Stephen Borsody (New Haven, CT: Yale Center for International and Area Studies, 1988), 69–88.

20. Peter Siani-Davies, The *Romanian Revolution of December 1989* (Ithaca, NY: Cornell University Press, 2007).

21. Vladimir Tismaneanu, *Fantasies of Salvation: Democracy, Nationalism, and Myth in Post-Communist Europe* (Princeton, NJ: Princeton University Press, 1998).

22. These documents include the Commission on Security and Cooperation in Europe's (CSCE's) Copenhagen Document (1990), also known as the European Constitution on Human Rights, which included a chapter on the protection of national minorities; the Council of Europe's (CE's) European Charter on Regional and Minority Languages (1992); the United Nations Declaration on the Rights of Persons Belonging to National and Ethnic, Religious and Linguistic Minorities (1992); the CE's Framework Convention for the Protection of National Minorities (1995), which is commonly considered a major achievement as the first legally binding international tool for minority protection; and the Organization for Security and Co-operation in Europe's (OSCE's) Oslo Recommendations regarding the Linguistic Rights of National Minorities (1998).

23. Aleksa Djilas, "Fear Thy Neighbor: The Breakup of Yugoslavia," in *Nationalism and Nationalities in the New Europe*, ed. Charles Kupchan et al. (Ithaca, NY: Cornell University Press, 1995), 88.

24. Djilas, "Fear Thy Neighbor," 102.

25. United Nations, *The Comprehensive Proposal for Kosovo Status Settlement* (New York: United Nations Office of the Special Envoy for Kosovo, March 26, 2007).

26. For different scholarly perspectives on the international consequences of Kosovo's unilateral declaration of independence, see the special issue titled "Self-Determination after Kosovo," published in *Europe-Asia Studies* 65, no. 5 (July 2013).

27. Zsuzsa Csergo and James M. Goldgeier, "Kin-State Activism in Hungary, Romania, and Russia: The Politics of Ethnic Demography," in *Divided Nations and European Integration*, ed. Tristan James Mabry, John McGarry, Margaret Moore, and Brendan O'Leary (Philadelphia: University of Pennsylvania Press2013), 89–126.

28. For Soviet language policy, see Rasma Karklins, *Ethnopolitics and Transition to Democracy* (Washington, DC: Woodrow Wilson Center Press and Johns Hopkins University Press, 1994), 151–52.

29. Graham Smith et al., *Nation-Building in the Post-Soviet Borderlands: The Politics of National Identities* (Cambridge: Cambridge University Press, 1998), 94.

30. Julie Bernier, "Nationalism in Transition: Nationalizing Impulses and International Counterweights in Latvia and Estonia," in *Minority Nationalism and the Changing International Order*, ed. Michael Keating and John McGarry (Oxford: Oxford University Press, 2001), 346.

31. Rawi Abdelal, *National Purpose in the World Economy* (Ithaca, NY: Cornell University Press, 2001); David J. Smith, "Minority Rights, Multiculturalism and EU Enlargement: The Case of Estonia," *Journal on Ethnopolitics and Minority Issues in Europe* 14, no. 4 (2015): 79–113; and Zsuzsa Csergő and Ada Regelmann, eds., *Europeanization and Minority Political Action in Central and Eastern Europe*, special issue published in *Problems of Post-Communism*, 64, no. 5 (2017).

32. Judith Kelley, *Ethnic Politics in Europe: The Power of Norms and Incentives* (Princeton, NJ: Princeton University Press, 2004). For a more skeptical view of the power of this leverage, see Bernd Rechel, ed., *Minority Rights in Central and Eastern Europe* (London: Routledge, 2009).

33. Rasma Karklins, "Ethnic Integration and School Policies in Latvia," *Nationalities Papers* 26, no. 2 (1998): 284.

34. Ojarrs Kalnins, "Latvia: The Language of Coexistence," *Transitions Online,* September 1, 2004, http://www.to.cz/TOL/home; Gerli Nimmerfeldt, "Integration of Second Generation Russians in Estonia: Country Report on TIES Survey in Estonia," *Studies of Transition States and Societies* 1, no. 1 (2009): 25–35; and Tatjana Bulajeva and Gabrielle Hogan-Brun, "Language and Education Orientations in Lithuania: A Cross-Baltic Perspective Post-EU Accession," in *Multilingualism in Post-Soviet Countries,* ed. Aneta Pavlenko (Toronto: Multilingual Matters, 2008), 122–48.

35. Licia Cianetti, "Representing Minorities in the City: Education Policies and Minority Incorporation in the Capital Cities of Estonia and Latvia," *Nationalities Papers* 42, no. 6 (2014): 981–1001.

36. The Eastern Partnership was established in 2008 as a venue for improving the EU's relations with neighboring states.

37. Maria Popova and Oxana Shevel, "What Doesn't Kill Ukraine," *Foreign Policy,* March 12, 2014.

38. Jenne L. Schulze, *Strategic Frames. Europe, Russia, and Minority Inclusion in Estonia and Latvia* (Pittsburgh, PA: University of Pittsburgh Press, 2017).

39. See Gordon Wightman, "Czechoslovakia," in *New Political Parties of Eastern Europe and the Soviet Union,* ed. Bogdan Szajkowski (Detroit, MI: Longman, 1991), 67; and Jiri Musil, "Czech and Slovak Society," in *The End of Czechoslovakia,* ed. Jiri Musil (Budapest: Central European University Press, 1995), 92.

40. Sharon Wolchik, "The Politics of Transition and the Break-Up of Czechoslovakia," in *The End of Czechoslovakia,* ed. Jiri Musil (Budapest: Central European University Press, 1995), 240–1; and Abby Innes, "Breakup of Czechoslovakia: The Impact of Party Development on the Separation of the State," *East European Politics and Societies* 11, no. 3 (Fall 1997): 393.

41. About negotiated transitions, see Juan J. Linz and Alfred Stepan, *Problems of Democratic Transition and Consolidation: Southern Europe, South America, and Post-Communist Europe* (Baltimore, MD: Johns Hopkins University Press, 1996), 316.

42. Zsuzsa Csergo and Kevin Deegan-Krause, "Liberalism and Cultural Claims in Central and Eastern Europe," *Nations and Nationalism* 17, no. 1 (January 2011): 85–107.

43. Kevin Deegan-Krause, *Elected Affinities: Democracy and Party Competition in Slovakia and the Czech Republic* (Stanford, CA: Stanford University Press, 2006).

44. The primary force behind national exclusivist policies was the Slovak National Party, which exerted pressure on the main governing party, Movement for a Democratic Slovakia. See Tim Haughton, "Vladimír Mečiar and His Role in the 1994–1998 Slovak Coalition Government," *Europe-Asia Studies* 54, no. 8 (2002): 1319–38.

45. For the history of the interwar period, see Joseph Rothschild, *East Central Europe between the Two World Wars* (Seattle: University of Washington Press, 1974).

46. Zsuzsa Csergo, *Talk of the Nation: Language and Conflict in Romania and Slovakia* (Ithaca, NY: Cornell University Press, 2007).

47. Tamás Kiss and István Székely, "Shifting Linkages in Ethnic Mobilization: The Case of RMDSZ and the Hungarians in Transylvania." *Nationalities Papers* 44, no. 4 (2016): 591–610.

48. Brubaker, Nationalism Reframed.

49. Szabolcs Pogonyi, *Extra-Territorial Ethnic Politics, Discourses and Identities in Hungary* (Basingstoke, UK: Palgrave Macmillan, 2017).

50. Zsuzsa Csergo and James M. Goldgeier, "Nationalist Strategies and European Integration," *Perspectives on Politics* 2 (March 2004): 26.

51. Zoltán Kántor et al., eds., *The Hungarian Status Law: Nation Building and/or Minority Protection* (Sapporo, Japan: Slavic Research Center, 2004); and Myra Waterbury, *Between State and Nation: Diaspora Politics and Kin-State Nationalism in Hungary* (Basingstoke, UK: Palgrave Macmillan, 2010).

52. András L. Pap, *Democratic Decline in Hungary: Law and Society in an Illiberal Democracy* (Abingdon, UK: Taylor & Francis, 2017).

53. See *Report on the Preferential Treatment of National Minorities by Their Kin-State* (adopted by the Venice Committee at its forty-eighth plenary meeting, Venice, October 19–20, 2001), http://assembly.coe.int/ASP/Doc/XrefViewHTML.asp?FileID=10094&Language=EN   (accessed August 25, 2014).

CHAPTER 6

Transitional Justice and Memory

Vello Pettai and Eva-Clarita Pettai

In the study of politics, Eastern Europe represents a region that allows us to study stirring phenomena like the dynamics of popular protest, the rebirth of democracy, and the development of new national identities. It does so, however, in response to the preceding period of severe political and social repression that, in the case of Central and Eastern Europe, lasted some five decades, while in Ukraine, it lasted more than seven decades. Although this oppression went through several phases and had clear variations from country to country, it encompassed not only restrictions on free speech, association, and travel but also more horrific human rights violations such as widespread surveillance, indiscriminate arrest, mass deportation, and summary killing. Moreover, much of what had happened was kept secret, known only through individual recollections and family stories. While liberation between 1989 and 1991 was an exhilarating event for all of these peoples, it also came with hard questions about how to deal with this past: Who should be held to account? How should victims be acknowledged? How should the country as a whole remember this era? As each society struggled with these issues, it also became apparent that the periods of Nazi and communist rule in the region had not been a mere interregnum or hiatus; for many, it was seen as a national ordeal that would mark the identity and politics of these peoples for decades to come.

The process of reckoning with past regime abuse and people's suffering is generally called "transitional justice." Postcommunism is only one of three broad contexts in which this increasingly global phenomenon has occurred, the others being after military regimes (such as in Argentina or South Korea) and after civil wars (such as in Sierra Leone or Sri Lanka).[1] What is special about the crimes and abuses of communist rule is that they were more pervasive and subtler than those in other regimes. Therefore, while Central and East Europeans could draw on certain transitional justice lessons from other countries, they also had to deal with specific communist-era legacies, such as dismantling extensive secret police networks or returning thousands of buildings and other forms of property that had been nationalized by the communist authorities. Beyond this, because communist rule had followed World War II and the brutalities of Nazi occupation, many of these countries actually had to right the wrongs of two periods of repression almost simultaneously. Third, while transitional justice in Central and Eastern Europe was strongly focused on "righting the wrongs" of the preceding regimes, it also had a forward-looking commitment to rebuilding democratic values, rule of law, and societal trust that would help to undergird the region's return to the Western world.

Yet, all of these similarities notwithstanding, the countries of Central and Eastern Europe have also varied considerably in terms of not only the timing and scope of transitional justice measures adopted by the new governments, but also the levels of political controversy that have accompanied these policies. Some countries like the Czech Republic were early and aggressive implementers of transitional justice, while others, such as Bulgaria, have been late and halting. Some countries, like Poland, have seen recurring waves of political debate over the need for such policies, while others, like Estonia, seem almost to have "closed the books" on these matters. In any case, none of the Central and East European states has been able to avoid dealing with the past, as Poland's first postcommunist prime minister put it, by "drawing a thick line" and simply moving forward.

Moreover, as more and more time has elapsed since the collapse of communism, the question of how to deal with the past has gradually shifted from being an immediate issue of what to do with the remnants of the old system to a process of forming a common national memory of those troubled times. The oppressors of the former regime and their victims are no longer alive or they are not as prominent in these societies as they once were. New dimensions of political and social life, such as European Union (EU) membership, socioeconomic development, or a resurgent Russia, have also often overtaken transitional justice. Debate about the Nazi and communist eras has frequently shifted toward how this past should be remembered and commemorated, depicted and framed, taught and communicated. This phenomenon has been called the politics of memory. Unlike transitional justice, which focuses on specific individuals or groups, the politics of memory looks at how politicians seek to influence society as a whole by propagating a certain "correct" version of history and thereby craft particular historical identities for the longer term. Yet, here too, there are many national differences, in terms of not only how historiography has evolved, but also how politicians have tried to instrumentalize commemorative events, institute certain national memorial days, and sometimes even adopt formal laws on how the past should be named and remembered in the public sphere.

Different Dimensions of Postcommunist Transitional Justice

We begin by taking a closer look at transitional justice and laying out two important frameworks for analyzing this phenomenon. The first takes a time perspective and examines not only how quickly or slowly new democratic governments in Central and Eastern Europe adopted certain transitional justice measures but also how far back in time the regime abuses were that these measures sought to rectify. The second framework involves understanding the range of specific measures countries could adopt concerning transitional justice. Here, the issues concern the degree to which countries deal with both perpetrators and victims of past regime abuse, as well as the legal level at which these measures are implemented.

When new democratic governments come to power, often their first priority is to deal with the immediate aftermath of the prior regime.[2] This is not easy, however, since the necessary criminal procedures or laws for prosecuting offenses like human rights violations will not have existed under the legal codes left over from the communist era. In this respect, new democracies always face a dilemma. Either they can implement quick, but perhaps also arbitrary, justice (by banning, say, all former communist party members from politics regardless of what they did as members) and, thereby, undermine the principles of rule of law which democracy itself stands for. They can take time to pass new legal frameworks, but in so doing may lose momentum in the process as a whole (as certain suspects flee into exile or disappear into obscurity). Much will depend on the strength of the new democratic governments themselves. Where democratic leaders are in a strong position politically, they can adopt a number of transitional justice policies quickly. Where former rulers were able to negotiate their departure from power and remain active in political life, progress on transitional justice may be slower. Several electoral cycles may be needed before political forces committed to dealing with the past can regain power and begin to adopt relevant measures. In these cases, we often speak of "late," "delayed," "second-wave," or "post-transitional" justice.

In Central and Eastern Europe, the Velvet Revolution in Czechoslovakia allowed new leaders to push for speedy adoption of laws that not only cleansed the civil service of former communists but also offered rehabilitation and compensation to political prisoners under the former regime. Although Czechoslovakia later broke up through the Velvet Divorce, the Czech Republic continued implementation of these steadfast policies (while Slovakia did not). Albania was also a case of quick action on transitional justice under the Democratic Party elected in 1992. The new government moved swiftly to replace former communist officials with its own loyalists. It also passed legislation seeking to bar ex-communists from standing for future elected office. However, because many of these measures began to be used for very partisan purposes, the Democratic Party soon became unpopular. The ex-communist Socialist party was returned to office in 1997, and transitional justice essentially stopped.

In Lithuania, Hungary, and Poland, another combination ensued, as ex-communists were able to return to power within just a few years of the transition, and thereby stall transitional justice measures relatively quickly. At the same time, right-wing forces were able to reestablish control later on and thereafter undertake what was mentioned above as delayed transitional justice. Conservative parties in Lithuania, for example, regained control of government in 1996, and then began a series of truth and justice initiatives lasting for many years. In Poland, the rise to power of the Law and Justice Party in 2005 also opened up a new wave of transitional justice, including a more aggressive policy preventing former secret police employees from working in the public sector.[3] Bulgaria, Romania, and Ukraine, meanwhile, represented cases where ex-communist parties remained relatively strong throughout the 1990s (even when in the opposition), and, as a result, transitional justice remained weak all around.

Another dimension of time important for studying transitional justice relates to the fact that communist rule in Central and Eastern Europe lasted for more than four decades and in Ukraine upward of seven. The consequence of this was that in some countries it was easier for politicians to address regime abuses that were farther back in time than to confront those where perpetrators may have still been active in society. Establishing a historical truth commission to look into the 1956 uprising in Hungary, the 1941 Stalinist deportations in Latvia, or the 1932–1933 Holodomor famine in Ukraine—even if it named specific persons involved—was politically a less audacious act of transitional justice than trying to put late communist officials on trial or establish expensive reparations programs for former dissidents. Morally speaking, both types of justice were important, especially in terms of understanding the whole communist era. However, when we want to understand why some countries addressed certain regime abuses and not others, we can see that some issues were costlier to tackle politically than others.

Indeed, the two time dimensions mentioned here were often intertwined. When new democratic governments did not have the political muscle to directly confront former communist leaders, they could focus on dealing with historical instances of repression. Likewise, when left-wing governments were in power and they had little interest in dwelling too much on the immediate past, they could still demonstrate a degree of *bona fides* regarding transitional justice by sponsoring measures that addressed decades-old injustices without fear of undermining their own political legitimacy. Sometimes governments could come to power many years after democracy had been established and then seek to take on tough transitional justice issues like putting an ex-communist leader on trial, such as Poland did against Wojciech Jaruzelski and Czesłav Kiszczak.

Photo 6.1. General Wojciech Jaruzelski, president of Poland in 1989 and 1990 and former head of the Polish military, was tried for attacks on demonstrators in Gdańsk during the 1970 demonstrations. The trial ran for nearly a decade and then was dropped in 2013 due to his age and illness. (Adam Chelstokski/FORUM)

But when this combination of time dimensions (late, but aggressive transitional justice) took place, the relevance of the act was often diminished, since the leaders were likely to be very old and the charges more difficult to sustain.

A second overarching framework on the basis of which transitional justice processes in Central and Eastern Europe can be compared involves scrutinizing the breadth of different measures that are undertaken. When governments abuse their power or repress their citizens, justice should, in theory, encompass both punishing the perpetrators and acknowledging the victims. In reality, however, it may be the case that the latter is easier than the former. Offering compensation or rehabilitation to a deportee is often simpler to carry out than proving the legal culpability of the secret police official who ordered the deportation. This means that one aspect of studying transitional justice concerns looking at how much countries are able to deal with one or the other side of this same coin.[4]

Furthermore, even when a country addresses both perpetrators and victims, it may do so at three different levels of policy. On the one hand, classical transitional justice begins with enacting *criminal-judicial* legislation that would allow for the prosecution and trial of former regime officials responsible for human rights violations. Likewise, however, it is important to recognize that criminal-judicial legislation can pertain also to victims, in the sense of reversing erstwhile convictions imposed during show trials or politically motivated prosecutions. This is known as rehabilitation. A step lower in terms of policy involves *administrative-political* measures that can deprive perpetrators of certain political rights or privileges, while restoring or according such benefits to victims. Again, these tracks need not take place at the same time, but they both involve mid-level policy measures that will often be enacted by law but can also be implemented through administrative decisions. Lastly, certain truth measures can be seen as having purely *symbolic-representative* value in terms of shaming perpetrators or acknowledging the suffering of victims. As such, they would appear to have the least consequence. However, for individual perpetrators or victims these can still be important, as when a perpetrator's professional career may be damaged by having been exposed as a one-time secret informant, or when a victim's feeling of dignity is restored when he or she is able to gain access to surveillance files compiled by the security services, or participate in official ceremonies commemorating past repressions.

In the sections that follow, we will bring examples of all of these policy variants of transitional justice. However, we will also try and show where different time dimensions manifested themselves. That is, we will see how some of these types of action were taken early on following the collapse of communism and others were sometimes pursued years later. Likewise, we will observe that certain policy measures were more prevalent toward more historical injustices, while others pertained mainly to more recent communist repression.

CRIMINAL-JUDICIAL JUSTICE: PROSECUTION AND REHABILITATIONS

Few Romanians alive during the collapse of communism will ever forget what they felt when they heard in December 1989 that their country's ruler Nicolae Ceaușescu and his wife Elena had been tried and summarily executed barely three days after they fled from power. This was an example of immediate criminal justice vis-à-vis a former repressive leader akin to what one might imagine happens stereotypically when a society tired of being subjugated by a ruthless dictator rises up for revenge. Needless to say, the trial conducted over the Ceauşescus was not a formal court procedure. After he and his wife were caught, they were "tried" by their military captors and put before a firing squad. This illustrates one of the first challenges that many postcommunist countries faced when they tried to criminally prosecute former leaders: What law should or could be applied toward communist-era repression so that it would not be considered retroactive or *post hoc* justice? How could evidence be gathered for such culpability, how should such trials or procedures take place, and what should constitute proper punishment if an accused were found guilty?

New leaders in three countries in the region, the former East Germany, Poland, and Bulgaria, actively sought to put prominent communist officials on trial; however, their strategies in this regard slightly differed. Both Germany and Poland sought to build cases against Erich Honecker and Wojciech Jaruzelski, respectively, that centered on their role in ordering the direct killing of civilians. In Honecker's case, it involved his responsibility for issuing a policy to shoot people trying to cross the border to West Germany surreptitiously. For Jaruzelski, it concerned a command to open fire on workers striking in 1970 at the Gdansk shipyards. Ultimately, however, both of these trials failed, not only because of the defendants' delaying tactics and their advanced age by the mid-1990s, but also precisely because it was difficult to prove culpability so high up in the chain of command. The case against the longtime head of Bulgaria's Communist Party, Todor Zhivkov, was for a more banal offence of misappropriating state funds. In his case (along with a number of other defendants in the trial), the prosecution was more successful, and multiyear prison terms were handed down because these were provable offenses. The only successful prosecutions for actual political repression were of mid- and lower-level officials such as border guards or security personnel, who were tried and found guilty of manslaughter in specific incidents. Officials in Germany carried out more than five hundred such prosecutions, while in the Czech Republic, the number was around fifty.[5]

In Hungary, a different difficulty emerged when, during the early 1990s, authorities attempted to carry out a form of more retrospective justice by seeking criminal charges against those who had been involved in killing during the 1956 revolution or forty years earlier. Repeatedly, the Hungarian parliament passed legislation enabling the relevant prosecutions to begin; each time, however, the Hungarian Constitutional Court issued rulings declaring such amendments illegal as they overrode the statute of limitations that existed for manslaughter under Hungarian law.[6] Eventually, the court acknowledged that the statute of limitations would not apply if repressions during the 1956 uprising constituted a war crime or a crime against humanity, since these notions derived from international law. This opened up a new legal avenue for prosecutors, and a number of trials were launched, including against Béla Biszku, a top-ranking communist official from 1956 who had publicly asserted that the reprisals had been justified.

The proposition that communist-era repression constituted in many cases a full-scale crime against humanity without any statute of limitations became a prevalent legal approach in the Baltic states as well. For these countries, the motivation was even more acute, since repression during the 1940s had included multiple waves of mass deportation, most prominently in 1941 and 1949. During those years, more than 180,000 people had been herded into cattle cars and forced to resettle in remote areas of Siberia or sent into the Gulag. Countless individuals died along the way, while even more perished later amidst the harsh labor and living conditions. Many of the responsible agents of the Soviet secret police at the time, the NKVD, continued to be alive in the 1990s. The parliaments in Estonia, Latvia, and Lithuania therefore reworked their criminal codes in order to lay out statutes against not only war crimes and crimes against humanity but also genocide. They used these provisions to begin several hundred investigations (particularly in Lithuania), which resulted in nearly sixty convictions. However, as in many other countries, many of the accused died during trial proceedings, or they were given suspended sentences because of their advanced age.

Judicial authorities were also heavily involved in the process of rehabilitating victims of communist-era repression. Laws clearing individuals of conviction for politically motivated crimes were passed across the region as soon as democracy was reestablished. One example was Czechoslovakia, where barely six months after the Velvet Revolution, parliament adopted a rehabilitation law that invalidated a wide range of convictions that had been carried out against dissidents and other opponents of the regime based on specific, political offenses listed in criminal law. It sufficed to simply rescind these statutes and annul all convictions issued on their basis in order to carry out rehabilitation. At the same time, other cases were more ambiguous, such as when people had participated in some anti-regime demonstration, but were convicted for simply "hooliganism." These cases often needed to be reexamined before rehabilitation could be granted. Lastly, many countries (such as the Baltic states) adopted laws that went farther back in time in order to deal with the victims of Stalinist repression during the 1940s and 1950s. In these instances, prior convictions were also readily overturned, since extrajudicial tribunals had often handed them down. Nevertheless, there were also rehabilitated individuals who had actually committed crimes. In Lithuania, officials were forced to rescind rehabilitation for several dozen individuals, after it came out that although these people had been tried for anti-Soviet activity in the late 1940s, they had also been linked to the repression and killing of Jews during the Nazi occupation. Serbia and Croatia, meanwhile, rehabilitated a number of controversial figures from World War II following their conviction by postwar communist tribunals despite much controversy among legal and academic experts.

POLITICAL-ADMINISTRATIVE TRUTH AND JUSTICE: LUSTRATION AND COMPENSATION

Transitional justice in Central and Eastern Europe has most often been associated with lustration, or the process of investigating, exposing, removing, and possibly sanctioning individuals for different degrees of communist-era collaboration that did not involve a formal criminal offense. In reality, this phenomenon involved three separate policy dimensions. First, what level of prior participation in the regime would be seen as warranting lustration? Second, what kind of more precise administrative sanction would be imposed for that involvement? And third, how would the screening of existing state employees as well as the vetting of future employees be organized?[7]

Regarding the first dimension, most countries concentrated their attention on those who had most directly been responsible for repression: full-time agents and employees of the former security services. Therefore, some form of screening and vetting legislation targeting these people was adopted at some point in almost every country of the region. Closely related to this category, however, were the thousands upon thousands of informants and collaborators of the secret police, whom most countries also sought to subject to lustration in some way. Yet, here the verification process was not so easy, since it was never clear whether operative files from the secret services (also often seized after the democratic transition) could really be trusted to determine someone's degree of involvement given that agents of the police may have tried to embellish their successes within the system. This kind of ambiguity often gave pause for thought in some countries such as Estonia, where informants of the Soviet KGB were never actively pursued even though lustration legislation allowed for this. Meanwhile, other countries such as Albania cast their net in a different direction and included as subject to lustration all those who had been members of the Politburo and Central Committee of the former communist party as well as communist-era parliamentary deputies and presidents of the Supreme Court.[8] In other words, a number of *ex officio* positions from the past regime could be included within the circle of lustration, irrespective of what these people had actually done in office.

On the second question of determining appropriate sanctions, most countries would begin with a ban on employment in the civil service (especially for former secret police agents). In some countries, however, the notion of civil service was extended beyond simple administrative positions to include not only the courts, but also high-level management positions in state-owned companies (the Czech Republic) or even university management positions (Poland). This implied a maximum effort to keep former regime individuals out of the democratic state. Moreover, Lithuania would also seek to bar these people from working in many areas of the private sector, such as banking, detective services, or the legal profession. Although this 1999 version of the country's lustration law would eventually be overturned by the European Court of Human Rights, it did lead, in the very beginning, to many private firms firing individuals alleged to have been involved with the Soviet KGB.[9]

A strong level of formalized noncriminal sanctioning of former regime officials was adopted in Latvia, which after 1996 screened all candidate lists for parliamentary and local elections and authorized the central electoral commission to make public the names of all those who had been listed somehow in leftover KGB files. Moreover, if a court had formally proven a person's collaboration with the Soviet security forces, he could be removed from the electoral list. In other words, the country effectively denied former agents their right to stand for public office, which the European Court of Human Rights did uphold in the initial term, but eventually declared a violation of European human rights law in 2008.

To deal with this entire process of personnel review (the third important policy dimension), countries in the region established a variety of administrative offices and procedures. The Czech Republic had perhaps the most rigorous system, requiring individuals seeking to retain or obtain employment in the public sector to request a formal lustration certificate from a special section of the Ministry of Interior tasked with reviewing available files from the former secret police, the StB. In this respect, the burden of proof was put on each individual to directly vindicate himself before being allowed into the system. Poland and Hungary enacted milder procedures, both in terms of limiting the scope of government posts under review to high-ranked elected officials (and not all civil servants) as well as by making the screening process less onerous. For example, under Poland's 1997 legislation, individuals were required to sign a declaration disclosing any prior collaboration with the old regime. Thus, in theory, one could admit collaboration and, in so doing, be exonerated and free to seek high elected office. If one lied on one's declaration, a special court could review the evidence and reveal the person's name in public. However, these proceedings were generally conducted behind closed doors, so this quickly became a battle cry among conservatives like the Kaczyński brothers for a more rigorous lustration procedure. Lastly, Estonia took one of the most liberal approaches, specifying that current and future state employees merely sign an "oath of conscience" that they had not engaged in communist-era repression. Moreover, these documents would remain simply on file unless another individual or prosecutor specifically contested them. In this respect, the Estonian system presumed that individuals were telling the truth before they were scrutinized (and not the other way around). Moreover, this system came to an end relatively quickly (December 2000), instead of being extended in duration as in the Czech Republic.

Needless to say, all of these different approaches endured various levels of criticism for being either too lax or too severe.[10] Moreover, when particularly respected politicians were brought down by these provisions (such as Juris Bojārs in Latvia, a one-time prominent member of the Latvian independence movement, but also ex-major in the KGB), it became obvious that cleaning out the skeletons in the closet would be tricky. Yet, beyond these formal procedures and their attempts to adhere to some degree of rule of law, the phenomenon of "informal lustration" also flared in each postcommunist country, as politicians traded accusations of possible collaboration by their opponents and the news media both amplified these debates and provided fodder of its own through investigative reporting and public speculation. This was the crossfire to which two prime ministers in Poland (Jan Olszewski and Jozef Oleksy) would be subjected during the first half of the 1990s before Poland even had a lustration law. In Bulgaria and Romania, this frenzy accelerated in the 2000s partly as a response to insufficient lustration policies being passed in the first place.[11]

This continuous politicization and instrumentalization of lustration controversies also indicates why (in contrast to many other transitional justice measures) these policies have, most often, been subject to a ratcheting up or a tightening many years after democracy has been consolidated. In other words, a time dimension is clearly evident in this domain, such that many analysts have spoken of "late lustration" when examining, for example, how both Romania and Poland tried to stiffen their policies in 2006.[12] These kinds of shifts have also made explaining lustration a complicated affair. While structural issues such as type of democratic transition may have mattered in the initial term, there have also been many wildcards in play when one considers how sensationalist media revelations can have unforeseen consequences for public opinion or political posturing. These waves of controversy have also been criticized for undermining one of the very objectives of transitional justice: to rebuild trust in society and the new democratic system.

Turning to the victim side of political-administrative transitional justice, it is perhaps no surprise that countries that decided to legally rehabilitate victims of repression also often worked out additional, administrative forms of reparation, including granting those individuals monetary compensation and/or other social privileges. Ideally, this type of transitional justice involved adopting formal legislation that would accord certain individuals special legal status as "repressed persons" and make them eligible for particular benefits. Lithuania adopted such a law in 1997 specifying no less than three dozen types of repression or persecution individuals may have suffered during either the Soviet or Nazi German occupations from 1939 to 1991, and making all of them entitled to special standing.

In terms of monetary compensation, former political prisoners in the Czech Republic, for example, received a base payment of roughly $83 per month of incarceration under the communist regime, while in Bulgaria those who had been held in labor camps or imprisoned could receive up to $1060 per month of detention, as would former prisoners in Romania.[13] Meanwhile, in some countries like Poland, interesting dividing lines emerged on temporal grounds. The country's original 1991 compensation law limited benefits to those who had suffered from 1944 to 1956, thereby making the measure largely a retrospective one. Many members of the Polish Senate objected to this restriction, saying that this would belittle suffering that had happened after the end of Stalinist terror. At the same time, a number of more recent victims of repression (especially those who had been imprisoned during the martial law period after 1980) believed that compensation for them would cast in a somewhat disparaging light the pro-democracy struggle that these people had waged simply out of their convictions. Moreover, many politicians born out of the Solidarity movement were uneasy about making themselves personally eligible for such benefits. The expansion of compensation policy in Poland therefore remained a thorny issue for years to come.

In the Baltic states, the focus was overwhelmingly on measures to compensate suffering for the victims of the 1940s' deportations. All three countries tailored their pension systems and even some privatization schemes to count time spent in Siberia as part of a victim's years of gainful employment. Lithuania also paid such victims direct compensation, although this raised certain ambiguities, since it was the Soviet authorities who had deported these people; therefore, some found it questionable that the new Lithuanian state should take on this burden instead of, say, Russia as the USSR's successor state.[14]

A further administrative type of reparative justice for victims involved the restitution of any property taken away by the communist authorities. Sometimes this concerned political prisoners or deportees, who had had their homes or other property seized by the communist state. For these victims, the process of restitution was relatively easy. However, a much broader form of this policy involved the restitution of property that had been nationalized by the communists usually during the beginning of their regime. Here the question was should all of these former owners and their descendants get back their property, and if so, in what manner? Moreover, property had to be differentiated into at least five forms: agricultural land, dwellings and buildings, nonphysical property such as stocks, property that had been demolished or destroyed during war, and church or religious community property. Concerning agricultural land, restitution processes generally proceeded smoothly, since in most Central and East European countries (with the exception of Poland), agriculture had been collectivized, and this meant that all arable land was in state hands. In most instances, it was not difficult to review whatever land records existed prior to nationalization and to develop procedures for the return of this land, even if in the short term it went to smallholders and would prove counterproductive from the perspective of developing a new and strong agricultural sector.[15]

More controversial was the policy of returning houses and apartment buildings to former owners, especially if those dwellings now had new tenants and these people would suddenly become renters not to the state but to private owners.[16] Not only would this process require years of bureaucratic effort (verifying former ownership claims and negotiating among often multiple claimants and their descendants) but also, in social terms, so-called "forced renters" would often be pressured to leave these homes so that restituted owners could undertake renovations or develop their properties for more profitable gain. In theory, this kind of housing transformation was supposed to help revive real estate as such and make it more productive (especially in downtown urban areas). However, in reality, it came at the cost of considerable social disruption. In many cases, municipal authorities lacked alternative housing for such forced renters. Controversy would also flare over whether émigrés would be allowed to get back property abandoned decades earlier; in Estonia and Latvia they would, in the Czech Republic and Lithuania not. Politically, the issue would remain charged for many years.

This was one reason why some governments such as Lithuania, Hungary, and Poland opted for more restrictive rules, such as offering claimants only compensation, especially if the prior dwelling, commercial enterprise, or land had since been substantially changed or privatized. In legal terms, this was justified as still constituting justice, since property rights were construed as meaning a right to a certain value or good, and not an absolute right to a particular object. Restitution could therefore also take the form of privatization vouchers or other certificates, which could be used for the purchase of alternative property. Lastly, property restitution policy often shifted over time, as different governments would attempt to either speed up or slow down these processes depending on their political persuasion. At the same time, the courts often stepped in to maintain some kind of consistency in the process. Hence, Lithuania's courts would stymie conservatives' attempts to expand restitution efforts in the late 1990s, while Estonian courts would often side with former owners even after lawmakers in that country sought to curtail some of the restitution provisions.

A final area of contention concerned religious property. In many countries, officials had to negotiate extensively with the Catholic Church concerning the return of not only churches, but also agricultural lands and other property. Likewise, the restitution of Jewish property that had been seized or abandoned as part of the Holocaust but that had never been returned or compensated by the subsequent communist authorities was very difficult. Many Central and East European countries were reluctant to take on these claims, arguing that, in most instances, the individual claimants were no longer citizens or residents of these countries and were therefore ineligible under existing law. Furthermore, many governments demurred on recognizing Jewish community property, especially if it pertained to social welfare establishments like hospitals or schools. Lastly, acknowledging Jewish claims in cities like Warsaw, Vilnius, or Riga promised to open up large swaths of property to either restitution or expensive compensation. A number of international associations such as the World Jewish Restitution Organization put pressure on governments to resolve these issues. In 2011, Lithuania passed a special law on "good will compensation," allocating over $50 million over a ten-year period to a special restorative fund. Efforts to pass similar legislation in Latvia and Poland have failed.

SYMBOLIC-REPRESENTATION JUSTICE: TRUTH-SEEKING AND RECOGNITION

A final cluster of transitional justice measures represents those actions that are seemingly of mere symbolic value in that they do not impose tangible punishment on perpetrators nor offer reparations to victims. However, they do play a substantive role in determining society's overall understanding of its past or they contribute to individual truth revelation, healing, and/or reconciliation. Again, we can divide these measures in terms of their focus on perpetrators and victims, though often measures in this field will cover both groups.

Almost all countries of Central and Eastern Europe have periodically adopted parliamentary or other solemn declarations condemning their prior communist regime.[17] For example, in 1991, the Czechoslovak Federal Assembly issued a statement on the 1948–1989 period of "non-freedom" through which it characterized its former government as having systematically violated human rights and its own laws. This stance was reaffirmed in 1993 after the Velvet Divorce, when Czech legislators adopted a new "Act on the Illegality of the Communist Regime and Resistance to It." In that document, the parliament specifically listed ways in which the regime had suppressed people's free will, violated human rights, restricted property rights, and committed other crimes and abuses. Moreover, the Act asserted that "[t]hose who implemented the Communist regime as officials, organizers, and agitators in the political and ideological sphere, are fully responsible for the[se] crimes." Later, a group of opposition MPs contested the Act in the Czech Constitutional Court, claiming that the Act established an illegal principle of collective guilt vis-à-vis former communists. Interestingly, the Court rejected that appeal, saying, "The constitutional foundation of a democratic State does not deny the Parliament the right to express its will as well as its moral and political viewpoint by means which it considers suitable and reasonable within the confines of general legal principles."[18]

Some years later, the Slovak parliament passed a similar resolution decrying the "immorality and illegality of the communist system," while Bulgaria denounced its erstwhile Communist Party for (among other things) "purposefully and deliberately ruining the values of European civilization . . . the moral and economic decline of the State . . . [and] employing permanent terror against people who disagree with the system of ruling."[19] At the same time, a statement denouncing the role of the Slovenian Communist Party in sustaining the erstwhile Yugoslav regime failed to pass the Slovenian parliament in late 1997.[20]

In the Baltic states, such declarations have been even more poignant, as they have generally blamed a specific country, the Soviet Union, for their communist suffering. In this respect, the Balts have largely externalized their condemnation of communist rule onto the USSR—and by implication to the Russian Federation as the successor state to that one-time occupier. As the Latvian parliament declared in 1996,

[t]hroughout the occupation, the Soviet Union conducted a targeted genocide against the Latvian people, in breach of the Convention on the Prevention and Punishment of the Crime of Genocide of 9 December 1948. The occupation regime killed innocent people, carried out several mass deportations and other repressive policies, cruelly punished those, who with or without arms fought for the restoration of Latvian independence, and unlawfully expropriated Latvian citizens without compensation and suppressed freedom of expression.[21]

In many instances (such as the Czech Republic instance mentioned above), political declarations have also sought to laud resistance fighters and dissidents against the regime or have otherwise drawn attention to the victims alongside condemning the perpetrators. Sometimes these declarations have also been the start of the rehabilitation procedures described earlier.

Still another approach to identifying perpetrators and victims in the national psyche is through truth commissions and other bodies, where the past is researched, discussed, and clarified. Although no country in postcommunist Europe established the kind of public truth commission pioneered famously in postapartheid South Africa, many countries began the process by convening special parliamentary commissions to study individual periods of repression, such as Poland during the 1981 military crackdown, Hungary in 1956, and Czechoslovakia in 1968.[22] A special Bundestag Enquête Kommission conducted more systematic examinations of regime abuses in Germany, and a comparable multiyear inquiry was conducted by the Slovenian parliament in the early 1990s.

Even more broadly, a number of countries appointed commissions made up of historians, cultural figures, and other prominent individuals to examine the crimes and legacies of these regimes in societal terms. Often known as "historical commissions," such bodies were established in Estonia, Latvia, Lithuania, and, later, Romania.[23] In Estonia, the "State Commission for the Examination of Repressive Policies Carried Out During the Occupations" was launched in March 1992, barely six months after the reestablishment of independence.[24] It was also one of the longest standing bodies, operating until 2005. While its focus was mostly historical (looking into the "crimes of genocide" committed by the Nazi German and Soviet regimes), one of its lasting legacies was to publish extensive lists of victims of the Soviet deportations during the 1940s. A second group of historical commissions was created in the Baltic states during the late 1990s, when external pressure from international Jewish organizations and the United States succeeded in getting the countries to establish new truth bodies (mostly composed of historians) that would investigate both the Holocaust and Soviet repression in these states. Although each of the Baltic commissions was distinctive in terms of its composition and its operating style, they were all tasked with helping to identify both perpetrators and victims during the half-century of foreign rule in these countries.[25]

By contrast, the Presidential Commission for the Analysis of the Communist Dictatorship in Romania was established much later (in 2006) and was a more political body aimed at discrediting the former Ceaușescu regime in the face of repeated returns to power by ex-communist parties during the 1990s and early 2000s. The commission's final report constituted an extensive investigation into the inner workings of both the erstwhile secret police, the Securitate, and the communist party, arriving at the conclusion that in many respects the regime had committed "genocide." Nevertheless, the public impact of the commission and its report was limited, with few of its recommendations ever implemented.[26] Far more successful was the 2003–2004 International Commission on the Holocaust in Romania, led by Elie Wiesel. Its final report contributed to much more public awareness, including the creation of a Holocaust commemoration day.

In many respects, the most direct pathway to truth revelation came through the opening of former regime archives, both in relation to former wrongdoers and their victims. The most innocuous version of this approach was to allow individuals to see whatever information the former secret services had collected personally to them. This was often of importance to those who had been repressed, arrested, or deported. While the names of former security agents or other related individuals would usually be blacked out, it would still be possible for citizens to discover what the regime had once thought about them or undertaken against them. The pioneer in this kind of openness was Germany, where the *Stasi-Unterlagenbehörde* organized free access to almost all of the former GDR's secret files for anyone interested in viewing them.

At the same time, any kind of transparency in terms of former secret archives often brought stark public conflicts when insufficient systems had been put in place for lustration. A case in point was Slovenia, where lawmakers failed to pass lustration legislation in 1997 and just a few years later a Slovene diplomat, Dušan Lajovic, made public on the internet a database of more than one million files from the Slovene branch of the Yugoslav secret police, the UDBA. Yet, because the files were simply a listing of all individuals who had ever come under the agency's purview (including common criminals), it was impossible to tell whether any single person named in the files had actually had a more specific or suspect relationship to the UDBA. Needless to say, names of prominent members from almost all of Slovenia's political parties turned up in the database, and this prompted an archetypal round of finger-pointing among the politicians. However, what is relevant here is the phenomenon of mass release of archival documents. For, a similar episode occurred in Poland, when, in February 2005, journalist Bronisław Wildstein released online a list of 240,000 people allegedly linked to the former secret services. In order to get a better handle on these potential leaks, the Lithuanian Genocide and Resistance Research Center decided to publish, on its own, historical files from the Lithuanian KGB dating back to the 1940s and 1950s. Latvia likewise decided to make its available KGB documents public in May 2018, but only after a commission of academics and experts had reviewed all of the materials.

A related question to all of this was, of course, who was taking care of the files and what kinds of government agencies have been developed more broadly to examine the communist past? Scholars have begun to comparatively analyze these organizations, finding that many of them are extremely broad in their functions and tasks.[27] Not only are many involved with facilitating access to files or organizing commemorative activities, but they may also be called upon to verify lustration processes, certify rehabilitation claims, or provide prosecutors with archival evidence for criminal trials against communist-era officials. The Institute of National Remembrance in Poland, known under its Polish abbreviation IPN, is a vivid example, as it has departments not only for historical research and national education, but also for vetting government officials and for "the prosecution of crimes against the Polish nation." It has more than a dozen regional offices and delegations, totaling more than a thousand employees. Likewise in Lithuania, the Genocide and Resistance Research Center is involved in all aspects of transitional justice and memory work. Meanwhile, almost all the countries of the region have prominent museums portraying the history of the communist period, be it the House of Terror in Budapest, the Occupation Museum in Riga, or the Sighet Museum in Romania.

It is, therefore, no surprise that these commemorative efforts have increased particularly during the 2000s, since the process of dealing with the communist past has begun to shift from direct transitional justice policies and measures to a much wider and often more diffuse process of national memory construction. To be sure, memory debates have been present in the region since the early 1990s, while controversies over certain politicians' communist pasts will surely arise again in the future. However, the broad proportion of these phenomena has slowly begun to invert.

Social Memory, Master Narratives, and "Memory Wars": New and Old Battlegrounds

"Memory" is a term whose use has grown exponentially in the social sciences over the last two decades. It can be deceptive, however, in the sense that it no longer tends to mean only what people remember in their mind, but also what entire nations see as their history or their self-perceptions of who they are in historical terms. It is, therefore, often very difficult to pin down what is studied under "memory" and, by extension, the "politics of memory." For our purposes, we will examine this phenomenon as it relates to transitional justice. In many respects, the two are comparable: the kinds of truth and justice measures that a nation seeks will depend on how people view the past repression of a regime. So, in a sense, memory molds transitional justice. If the regime was seen as being soft (as is often said of Hungary), less transitional justice will be needed. At the same time, transitional justice measures can also begin to craft national memory when lustration laws, for instance, begin to reveal just how many people were involved with the old system, or when historical commissions are tasked to form an official assessment of a certain event. Even courts are part of national memory construction when they issue verdicts in relation to former regime perpetrators and thereby hand down a kind of judicially certified version of repression history.

In this section, we will therefore study how transitional justice and memory are often intertwined. We will look at how memory issues were present already at the beginning of the democratic transitions, but also at how they have grown in importance, as the communist era has itself become more distant history. Measures that are, formally speaking, part of transitional justice increasingly have an effect on crafting historical understandings as well, in particular for younger generations who have had less or no personal experience under the communist regime. As the thirtieth anniversary of the collapse of communism approaches, there is debate not only about what communism once was, but also about how it collapsed and who played what role in that process. Indeed, even the first elements of transitional justice undertaken in the 1990s are slowly becoming subject to memory contestation.

When we go back to the heady days of 1989, we see that memory was already very much at the forefront of the democratic revolutions, accentuating the wide array of other grievances against the regimes with respect to failed economic performance,

Photo 6.2. The Three Crosses Monument, also known as the Solidarity Monument, was put up in December 1980 after the Solidarity Trade Union had been legalized. It commemorates the shipyard workers killed during the 1970 shipyard workers' strikes when the government attacked the striking shipyard workers as they marched outside the shipyard. This monument is now at the entrance to the Solidarity Center in Gdansk. (Aurora Zahm)

environmental devastation, or social alienation. Long neglected or silenced experiences of the early communist period, including occupation, mass arrests, extrajudicial executions, deportations, and show trials, poured into the open and stoked a large part of the rejection of the communist regimes once liberalization occurred in the mid-1980s. In Poland, stories about the mass shooting of officers by the Soviets in Katyń had been part of family narratives and later dissident political activities ever since the 1970s. In the Baltic states, details slowly emerged about the scope and significance of having lost independent statehood in 1940 and then being subjected to Stalinist deportations. For Czechoslovakia, the fateful dates of 1938, 1948, and 1968 became rallying cries of the Velvet Revolution and served as an important empowerment for those calling for change.

Yet, historical memory also emerged as a divisive element in these turbulent times of regime change. The most ominous case was the former Yugoslavia where the ideas and symbolism of the Serbian *Chetnik* and Croatian *Ustasha* extreme-right organizations experienced a revival and provided nationalists with "weapons of destruction" to fuel already simmering interethnic tensions in the region.[28] Likewise, reemergent memories of interethnic violence and of forced resettlement after border shifts between, for example, Poland and its neighbors Lithuania and Ukraine had potentially destructive power.

The question of how to remember the history of a twentieth century that had been in an ideological straightjacket for decades was thus crucial and highly political in the postcommunist processes of democratization and state-building. Through public commemoration, the rewriting of textbooks, the renaming of spaces and streets, the creation of new museums, and numerous other acts, these countries sought to reclaim power over their recent history. The outcome of this process was generally a past reframed into one of national victimization and oppression. On the one hand, this narrative served an important political purpose of providing a sense of unity in times of economic hardship and political instability. It helped to get over some of the social atomization that the communist regime had promoted and developed a sense of purpose as the countries faced a new era of rebuilding. At the same time, it often swung the pendulum of national memory very starkly in a nationalist direction, to the chagrin of not only certain minority groups in these same countries but also more broadly in Europe and internationally. A recent example could be witnessed in Ukraine, where decommunization legislation in 2015 led to the dismantling of Soviet-era monuments, street renaming, and a rather aggressive rewriting of World War II history.

One of the most blatant memory tools at the disposal of states is to adopt laws criminalizing the denial, condoning, or gross trivialization of certain historical events. While such laws have long existed in many European countries in relation to the Holocaust, a number of Central and East European nations have complemented this domain with so-called "memory laws" (*lois mémorielle*) concerning Stalinism and communism. Hence, Poland incorporated within its 1998 law creating the IPN, a provision allowing for up to three years of imprisonment for "anyone who publicly and contrary to the facts denies" communist and Nazi crimes (Art. 55). The Czech Republic issued a similar law in 2001, as have Slovenia, Latvia, and Lithuania. In addition, some countries (Lithuania, Poland, Hungary, and Romania) have sought to ban the public display of communist symbols such as the hammer and sickle (alongside the swastika).

Another element worth noting in relation to memory processes (and in partial contrast to transitional justice) is that they have not always been top-down or imposed by government. Nonstate actors have also been instrumental in fostering public memorialization of the entire communist era as criminal. In the Baltic states, and especially in Lithuania, former deportees and repressed people constituted a strong voice in the national conservative political camp, seeking to advance a staunch anti-communist narrative of national suffering and heroism through education and other public activities. Moreover, one such nonofficial activity involved organizing international public tribunals that would feature legal experts from different countries who would reexamine the crimes committed by the regimes and evaluate communist ideology from a legal perspective. The first such tribunal took place in Vilnius in 2000, organized by civil society organizations and supported by several public figures, resulting in a "judgment" that would condemn communism as a criminal doctrine responsible for, among other things, genocide and crimes against humanity. A similar citizen tribunal was held in 2006 in Cluj, Romania. Although these bodies lacked any formal legal standing, they sought to use the terminology of international criminal and humanitarian law in order to influence national narratives of the communist regime and of national victimization.[29]

Yet, delving into the past has meant not only revealing communist regime crimes, but also shedding new light on the mass killing of Jews and other minorities during the war in this region that Timothy Snyder would later term the "bloodlands" of Europe. Already in the early 1990s, the emerging master narratives of national victimhood and the overarching tendency in public commemoration and historical writing to externalize responsibility for any past wrongdoing clashed with tales of local collaboration with Nazi perpetrators, of locally initiated anti-Jewish pogroms, and of killing squads involved in the mass shooting of civilians, especially Jews. In some cases, the realization of long-neglected historical truths about local complicity in the extermination of Jewish life in the region gave birth to painful, yet ultimately healthy, public debate and national introspection. Thus, the debates and new research following the 2001 publication of Jan Gross's book about the killing of Jews in Jedwabne by their Polish neighbors constituted a genuine shift in Polish perceptions of the German occupation period. However, certain historical revelations as well as outside accusations against individual states voiced by international actors, such as the Simon Wiesenthal Centre, also provoked resistance among local populations, and the ensuing public debates and political rhetoric revealed that many anti-Semitic myths and stereotypes still existed in societal discourses. Moreover, the preoccupation of Western historians and state officials with the history and memory of the Holocaust and its local collaborators was perceived by many East European politicians and intellectuals as, at best, ignorant, and, at worst, negligent of the suffering that had been inflicted on the region by Stalin. Scholars of European and transnational memory have thus come to talk of "memory wars" (Etkind) and of "battleground Europe" (Leggewie), at the center of which they see the history and memory of the Holocaust and the Gulag pitted against each other in an unfortunate competition of collective victimhood that held little value for advancing knowledge and awareness about the history of World War II and its aftermath of state violence.[30]

With the enlargement of the EU and the direct incorporation of Central and Eastern Europe into European politics, memory was transposed further onto the pan-European level. After 2004, many of the national historical research institutes that had been involved in transitional justice along with a number of related history museums teamed up into a novel set of memory agents, who would begin appearing at EU-sponsored conferences and hearings, lobbying for European parliamentarians to acknowledge the criminal character of the communist regimes.[31] In particular, Baltic, but also Hungarian, Czech, and Polish, members of the European Parliament were at the forefront of lobbying their colleagues to pass legislation or adopt resolutions that would condemn communism and call for Europe-wide commemoration. Eventually, the parliament adopted a pair of resolutions in which the crimes of Stalinism were condemned and remembrance pledged. The latter included the creation of a "European Day of Remembrance for Victims of Stalinism and Nazism" on August 23, the day of the signing of the so-called Molotov-Ribbentrop Pact in 1939 that divided up Eastern Europe between the two dictators.[32] The EU has also financed a number of NGO projects and networks related to commemoration such as the "Platform of European Memory and Conscience."

A second memory-related phenomenon that seemed to kick in around the 2000s was a more anthropological notion of communist nostalgia. The concept gained currency in political science as scholars sought to explain how ex-communist parties in many countries were returning to power in open elections. Later, it became an explanation for the rise of populist parties, with the conclusion being that voters were nostalgically looking for a return to social equality and order. Among other social scientists (and, in particular, social anthropologists), the study of nostalgia was embedded in the notion of postsocialism and examined memories of past everyday life. Especially among older age cohorts as well as in countries that had experienced more liberal forms of communist rule, such as in the former Yugoslavia and Hungary, a sense of "not everything was bad" seemed to exist. Yet, as numerous studies of communist nostalgia have pointed out, it is, in fact, rarely the case that people yearn for the return of the old communist system as such; rather, it has been an expression of their dissatisfaction with existing socioeconomic conditions and their perceived lack of equality in society. In this sense, nostalgia is but a label referring to what Velikonja has called "retrospective utopia"—a notion of a better life that is as much a projection into the past as it is into the future.[33]

Finally, with time elapsing since the end of communism and the triumph of the democratic revolutions, the memories of that particular period have themselves become an object of contestation. In some countries, the contrasting narratives of that period continue to have a strong hold on the political landscape, as partisan leaders on the right try to frame the negotiated transitions of the late 1980s, for example in Hungary and Poland, as a betrayal of the nation by the liberal elites of that time. Thus, the 2005 lustration campaign by the Polish Law and Justice Party was less about actually changing or expanding an already existing law than it was about framing the liberal political elite of the country as corrupted by former communists. In Romania, memories of the 1989 overthrow of Ceaușescu and the subsequent takeover by a second tier of communist elites remain contested and reappear in the political discourse especially during elections. Hence, the way in which 1989/1991 is being publicly remembered tells us a lot about not only party-political cleavages, but also deeper cultural and structural undercurrents that define social and political life in this part of the world.[34] Politics in most of the countries that experienced peaceful revolutions in 1989 and 1991 is extremely polarized, or "fractured," as political elites seem to be split along seemingly irreconcilable narratives of the not so distant past. Indeed, much of the populist rhetoric of the so-called illiberal leaders in the region (such as Poland's Jarosław Kaczyński, Hungary's Viktor Orbán, or Slovakia's Robert Fico) builds on a narrative of the "incomplete revolution of 1989" and on allegations of national treason committed by the liberal, cosmopolitan elites of the early 1990s.

Conclusion

Studying politics in Eastern Europe involves examining and renaming multiple, successive layers of political development and change. The post-1945 period of communist rule is, of course, an essential starting point, but so are the subsequent regime transition, the institutionalization of democratic politics, the challenges of EU accession, and now, in some cases, the dangers of democratic backsliding. Transitional justice and memory politics fit into this landscape as accompanying processes aimed at establishing an understanding of what happened during communist rule as well as what to do about that afterward. The two phenomena begin with an overarching aspiration to bring some kind of "truth" and "justice" to this repressive past. This is why these two terms are frequently used as synonyms for everything that had to do with coming to terms with the past. However, it is clear that these two goals are, at best, very ambiguous, if not to say subjective. No matter how hard societies may try to work out different degrees of accountability and/or develop adequate forms of reparation, there will always be uncertainty about whether the full truth has been established or justice really achieved. This explains why transitional justice can also be a protracted and recurring political issue. There will probably never be a moment where all people agree that these two processes have been completed and that the books can indeed be closed. Rather, these issues remain hanging in the air, open for attachment to additional political or economic grievances, as we saw with the discussion of communist nostalgia or when making sense of the rise of Viktor Orbán in Hungary or the Kaczyńskis in Poland. Truth and justice are therefore inherently slippery phenomena, since they are largely in the eye of the beholder. As political analysts, we can, at best, try and sort out the different dimensions of this wide-ranging process. But full explanations are difficult to come by, given precisely the way truth and justice were intertwined and interact with so many other political strategies and societal issues.

Still, given that some countries have clearly engaged in greater degrees of transitional justice and memory politics than others, scholars have offered different accounts as to why this might be so.[35] Some point to differing communist-era historical legacies with regard to regime legitimacy as explanatory variables. Thus, in some cases, like Hungary or ex-Yugoslavia, the regimes introduced economic reforms that allowed for certain freedoms already long before the 1980s. In other cases, such as Poland or even Soviet-Lithuania, local communist elites managed to pursue successful "national communist" strategies, thereby making it feel like the communist period had perhaps not been so divisive or fracturing as to warrant extensive transitional justice.

A second explanatory level looks at how more conciliatory modes of regime transition itself led to differing degrees of interest in "pursuing justice" during subsequent years. The more negotiated the precise transition, the less radical the transitional justice process would be—not only because of a certain degree of societal reconciliation, but also because elites from the previous regime would continue to be part of the political process and could tamp down impulses for transitional justice. So, the Czech Republic, which had a very abrupt break with the former regime, also had the most decisive array of transitional justice policies, while Poland and Hungary (with their roundtable talks during the transition) opted for milder measures vis-à-vis the past. Third, patterns of doing transitional justice have also been influenced by states' constitutional arrangements (such as the role of popularly elected presidents or the power of constitutional courts) as well as driven by the politics of the moment (electoral conflicts, institutional power games, or other political policy decisions). In other words, irrespective of prior influences, the communist past has sometimes been simply a political football for different political actors, and this too has caused the process of transitional justice and memory to ebb and flow over the last three decades. This is the framework that best explains later waves of transitional justice such as when countries decide to toughen their lustration laws or expand victim benefits. It also increasingly accounts for when memory politics comes to the fore in political discourses and mobilization strategies.

All of this goes to show that transitional justice needs to be studied not only across countries, but also over time. Not only have countries differed in comparison to each other, they have also gone up and down in terms of their preoccupation with these issues over the years. This makes finding a single approach to the phenomenon almost impossible. Everything depends on the type of comparison that is chosen. Moreover, as this chapter has sought to demonstrate, "transitional justice" as such is in reality a composite of at least three levels of policy adopted in response to either perpetrators or victims, enacted either right after a democratic transition or many years later, and aimed at redressing repressive acts committed toward the end of the former regime or going back many decades beforehand. All of these dimensions are important to map out before more specific analysis can begin.

Likewise, scholars have reflected on whether transitional justice has any kind of downstream effect on other democratic processes.[36] That is to say, apart from the moral ambitions of transitional justice (to achieve "truth" and/or "justice"), we can also ask whether transitional justice helps to improve elite political culture, respect for rule of law, trust in political institutions or democratic values in society. Research in this area has been inconclusive, since transitional justice is unlikely to be the sole explanatory variable for these phenomena. For example, low or high levels of trust in political institutions may be caused by other factors such as policy performance or levels of corruption. Nevertheless, this perspective on transitional justice is an important one, since it asks the broader question of what transitional justice is good for.

Finally, we have seen that transitional justice is increasingly blended with and perhaps even superseded by memory politics, since political contests are more and more about how society will remember and perceive the communist era and less about how to deal with recent crimes. Perspectives have begun to shift from how to deal with the past to how that past was dealt with. This does not imply that this debate will become wholly historical or only among historians, any more than this has happened with, say, questions of slavery and the Civil War in the United States or the Holocaust and World War II in Germany. Politics remain a crucial element in these debates, since it will influence how each nation crafts its historical identity. If communism is remembered primarily as victimhood (as many conservative parties would like), this will influence not only certain domestic political orientations but also relations with the rest of Europe in terms of a desire to continue recasting broader European historical identity. If other, more varied narratives emerge, this may relativize the place that communist and transitional justice will hold in Central and East European politics.

Study Questions

1. What forms and dimensions of transitional justice can we find in Central and Eastern Europe?
2. What controversies and problems have emerged after transitional justice measures have been implemented?
3. How do you think communism should be remembered in the national memories and/ or histories of the countries of Central and Eastern Europe?
4. What relevance do these stances have for today's political development in the region?

Suggested Readings

Assmann, Aleida, and Linda Shortt, eds. *Memory and Political Change*. London: Palgrave Macmillan, 2012.

Blacker, Uilleam, Alexander Etkind, and Julie Fedor, eds. *Memory and Theory in Eastern Europe*. London: Palgrave Macmillan, 2013.

Koposov, Nikolay. *Memory Laws, Memory Wars: The Politics of the Past in Europe and Russia*. Cambridge: Cambridge University Press, 2017.

Lebow, Richard Ned, Wulf Kansteiner, and Claudio Fogu, eds. *The Politics of Memory in Postwar Europe*. London: Duke University Press, 2006.

Müller, Jan-Werner, ed. *Memory and Power in Post-War Europe: Studies in the Presence of the Past*. Cambridge: Cambridge University Press, 2003.

Nalepa, Monika. *Skeletons in the Closet. Transitional Justice in Post-Communist Eastern Europe*. Cambridge: Cambridge University Press, 2010.

Nedelsky, Nadya. "Divergent Responses to a Common Past: Transitional Justice in the Czech Republic and Slovakia." *Theory and Society* 33, no. 1 (2004): 65–115.

Pakier, Malgorzata, and Bo Strath, eds. *A European Memory? Contested Histories and Politics of Remembrance*. New York: Berghahn Books, 2010.

Pettai, Vello, and Eva-Clarita Pettai. "Dealing with the Past: Post-Communist Transitional Justice." In *Routledge Handbook of East European Politics*, edited by Adam Fagan and Petr Kopecky. London: Routledge, 2017.

Teitel, Ruti G. "Transitional Justice Genealogy." *Harvard Human Rights Journal* 16 (2003): 69–94.

Notes

1. Because of our focus on *postcommunist* transitional justice, we will not cover in this chapter transitional justice processes related to the ethnic (or civil) war in many parts of former Yugoslavia. While it is true that a number of the truth and justice measures that have been undertaken vis-à-vis

these conflicts (such as legal trials against war criminals or the memorialization of victims) are similar to the measures we outline here, in many instances they have also been linked to international criminal law (the International Criminal Tribunal for the former Yugoslavia, ICTY) or they have become internationalized political issues (serving as conditionality elements for European Union accession). The type of postcommunist transitional justice that we examine here (i.e., in relation to former communist leaders and the former communist regime) has been very limited in countries such as Croatia, Serbia, Macedonia, or Bosnia-Herzegovina.

2. Ruti G. Teitel, *Transitional Justice* (New York: Oxford University Press, 2000).

3. In Slovenia, too, resurgent center-right parties tried to pass different transitional justice measures in the late 1990s, but each time they failed to get a requisite majority in parliament.

4. Claus Offe, "Coming to Terms with Past Injustices," *European Journal of Sociology* 33, no. 1 (1992): 195–201; Neil J. Kritz, "The Dilemmas of Transitional Justice," in *Transitional Justice: How Emerging Democracies Reckon with Former Regimes. General Considerations*, ed. Neil J. Kritz (Washington, DC: US Institute of Peace Press, 1995), 1: xix–xxx; and Noel Calhoun, *Dilemmas of Justice in Eastern Europe's Democratic Transitions* (New York: Palgrave Macmillan, 2004).

5. Jon Elster, *Closing the Books: Transitional Justice in Historical Perspective*; and Muriel Blaive, "The Czechs and Their Communism, Past and Present. In Inquiries into Past and Present," in *IWM Junior Visiting Fellows' Conferences, Vol. 17*, ed. D. Gard et al. (Vienna: IWM, 2005).

6. Frigyes Kahler, "Communist Terror in 1956 and the Rule of Law," *Hungarian Review* 4, no. 1 (2013): 49–62.

7. See also Roman David, "From Prague to Baghdad: Lustration Systems and Their Political Effects," *Government and Opposition* 41, no. 3 (2006): 347–72. For an explanatory model of lustration based on institutional rules and strategic interaction, see Monika Nalepa, "The Institutional Context of Transitional Justice," in *Routledge Handbook of Comparative Political Institutions*, ed. Jennifer Gandhi and Ruben Ruiz-Rufino (Oxon: Routledge, 2015), 389–403.

8. Mark S. Ellis, "Purging the Past: The Current State of Lustration Laws in the Former Communist Bloc," *Law and Contemporary Problems* 59, no. 4 (1997): 181–96; and Robert C. Austin and Jonathan Ellison, "Albania," in *Transitional Justice in Eastern Europe and the Former Soviet Union: Reckoning with the Communist Past*, ed. Lavinia Stan (London: Routledge, 2009), 176–199.

9. Eva-Clarita Pettai and Vello Pettai, *Transitional and Retrospective Justice in the Baltic States* (Cambridge: Cambridge University Press, 2015).

10. For accounts regarding the Polish case, see Matt Killingsworth, "Lustration after Totalitarianism: Poland's Attempt to Reconcile with Its Communist Past," *Communist and Post-Communist Studies* 43, no. 3 (2010): 275–84.

11. Cynthia Horne, "'Silent Lustration': Public Disclosures as Informal Lustration Mechanisms in Bulgaria and Romania," *Problems of Post-Communism* 62, no. 3 (2015): 131–44.

12. Cynthia M. Horne, "Late Lustration Programmes in Romania and Poland: Supporting or Undermining Democratic Transitions?" *Democratization* 16, no. 2 (2009): 344–76; and Kieran Williams et al., "Explaining Lustration in Central Europe: A 'Post-Communist Politics' Approach," *Democratization* 12, no. 1 (2005): 22–43.

13. Roman David and Susanne Y. P. Choi, "Victims on Transitional Justice: Lessons from the Reparation of Human Rights Abuses in the Czech Republic," *Human Rights Quarterly* 27, no. 2 (2005): 392–435; and Lavinia Stan, *Transitional Justice in Post-Communist Romania* (Cambridge: Cambridge University Press, 2013).

14. The issue of reparations for Soviet-era damages remains a highly contentious issue in Baltic-Russian relations. Both Latvia and Lithuania have put together detailed compensation claims to the Russian Federation, something that Moscow has dismissed outright.

15. Csilla Kiss, "Hungary," in *Encyclopedia of Transitional Justice*, ed. Lavinia Stan and Nadya Nedelsky (Cambridge: Cambridge University Press, 2013), 2: 230–6.

16. Mark Blacksell and Karl Martin Born, "Private Property Restitution: The Geographical Consequences of Official Government Policies in Central and Eastern Europe," *Geographical Journal* 168, no. 2 (2002): 178–90; Lynn M. Fisher and Austin J. Jaffe, "Restitution in Transition Countries," *Journal of Housing and the Built Environment* 15, no. 3 (2000): 233–48; and Csongor Kuti, *Post-Communist Restitution and the Rule of Law* (Budapest: Central European University Press, 2009).

17. In this subsection, we will concentrate on declarations that specifically condemn a country's former communist party or ruling elite as opposed to communism as an ideology or social system. Given the distinction we are seeking to make between transitional justice and memory, we see the denunciation of former rulers as part of the former, while the censure of communism is seen as the latter.

18. Full text in Neil J. Kritz, *Transitional Justice: How Emerging Democracies Reckon with Former Regimes. Laws, Rulings, and Reports* (Washington, DC: US Institute of Peace Press, 1995), 3: 428–31.

19. Nadya Nedelsky, "Czechoslovakia, and the Czech and Slovak Republics," in *Transitional Justice in Eastern Europe and the Former Soviet Union: Reckoning with the Communist Past*, ed. Lavinia Stan (London: Routledge, 2009), 37–75. National Assembly of Bulgaria, "Law on Declaring the Criminal Nature of the Communist Regime in Bulgaria," May 5, 2000.

20. Tamara Kotar, "Slovenia," in *Transitional Justice in Eastern Europe and the Former Soviet Union: Reckoning with the Communist Past*, ed. Lavinia Stan (London: Routledge, 2009), 200–21.

21. Latvijas Republikas Saeima, "Deklarācija 'Par Latvijas Okupāciju,'" August 22, 1996.

22. Timothy Garton Ash, "Trials, Purges and History Lessons: Treating a Difficult Past in Post-Communist Europe," in *Memory and Power in Post-War Europe: Studies in the Presence of the Past*, ed. Jan-Werner Müller (Cambridge: Cambridge University Press, 2002), 265–82.

23. Lavinia Stan, "Truth Commissions in Post-Communism: The Overlooked Solution?" *Open Political Science Journal* 2 (2009): 1–13.

24. Vello Pettai, "State Commission for the Examination of Repressive Policies Carried out during the Occupations," in *Encyclopedia of Transitional Justice*, ed. Lavinia Stan and Nadya Nadelsky (Cambridge: Cambridge University Press, 2013), 161–167.

25. Eva-Clarita Pettai, "Negotiating History for Reconciliation: A Comparative Evaluation of the Baltic Presidential Commissions," *Europe-Asia Studies* 67, no. 7 (2015): 1079–101.

26. Monica Ciobanu, "Criminalising the Past and Reconstructing Collective Memory: The Romanian Truth Commission," *Europe-Asia Studies* 61, no. 2 (2009): 313–36; and Alina Hogea, "Coming to Terms with the Communist Past in Romania: An Analysis of the Political and Media Discourse Concerning the Tismăneanu Report," *Studies of Transition States and Societies* 2, no. 2 (2010): 16–30.

27. Georges Mink, "Institutions of National Memory in Post-Communist Europe: From Transitional Justice to Political Uses of Biographies (1989–2010)," in *History, Memory and Politics in Central and Eastern Europe: Memory Games*, ed. Georges Mink and Laure Neumayer (Basingstoke, NY: Palgrave Macmillan, 2013), 155–70.

28. Ilana R. Bet-El, "Unimagined Communities: The Power of Memory and the Conflict in Former Yugoslavia in Memory and Power," in *Post-War Europe: Studies in the Presence of the Past*, ed. Jan-Werner Müller (Cambridge: Cambridge University Press, 2002), 206–22.

29. *Anti-Communist Congress and Proceedings of the International Public Tribunal in Vilnius "Evaluation of the Crimes of Communism" 2000* (Vilnius: Ramona, 2002); and Lavinia Stan, *Transitional Justice in Post-Communist Romania* (Cambridge: Cambridge University Press, 2013).

30. Alexander Etkind et al., *Remembering Katyn* (Cambridge: Polity Press, 2013). Claus Leggewie, "Battlefield Europe: Transnational Memory and European Identity," *Eurozine* (April 28, 2009), http://www.eurozine.com/battlefield-europe; and Aleida Assmann, "Transnational Memories," *European Review* 22, no. 4 (2014): 546–56.

31. Georges Mink, "Institutions of National Memory in Post-Communist Europe: From Transitional Justice to Political Uses of Biographies (1989–2010)," in *History, Memory and Politics in Central and Eastern Europe: Memory Games*, ed. Georges Mink and Laure Neumayer (Basingstoke: Palgrave Macmillan, 2013), 155–70; and Laure Neumayer, "Integrating the Central European Past into a Common Narrative: The Mobilizations around the 'Crimes of Communism' in the European Parliament," *Journal of Contemporary European Studies* 23, no. 3 (2015): 344–63.

32. While all of the Central and East European members of the EU have adopted this day onto their national calendars, only Sweden has taken the date on board among West European countries.

33. Mitja Velikonja, "Lost in Transition: Nostalgia for Socialism in Post-Socialist Countries," *East European Politics & Societies* 23, no. 4 (2009): 535–51. See also Joakim Ekman and Jonas Linde, "Communist Nostalgia and the Consolidation of Democracy in Central and Eastern Europe," *Journal of Communist Studies and Transition Politics* 21, no. 3 (2005): 354–74; and Maria Nikolaeva Todorova and Zsuzsa Gille, *Post-Communist Nostalgia* (New York: Berghahn Books, 2010).

34. Michael Bernhard and Jan Kubik, eds., *Twenty Years after Communism: The Politics of Memory and Commemoration* (New York: Oxford University Press, 2014).

35. For a good overview of explanatory models for transitional justice, see Lavinia Stan, "Conclusion: Explaining Country Differences" in *Transitional Justice in Eastern Europe and the Former Soviet Union: Reckoning with the Communist Past*, ed. Lavinia Stan (New York: Routledge, 2009), 247–70.

36. Cynthia M. Horne, "Assessing the Impact of Lustration on Trust in Public Institutions and National Government in Central and Eastern Europe," *Comparative Political Studies* 45, no. 4 (2012): 412–46; see also the chapters by Lynch and Marchesi and by David in *Post-Communist Transitional Justice: Lessons from Twenty-Five Years of Experience*, ed. Lavinia Stan and Nadya Nedelsky.

CHAPTER 7

The EU and Its New Members

FORGING A NEW RELATIONSHIP

Ronald H. Linden

After the extraordinary changes of 1989, virtually all of the newly democratizing states of Central and Eastern Europe made overtures to join the three major organizations of what was generally referred to as "Europe": the Council of Europe, the North Atlantic Treaty Organization (NATO), and the European Union (EU) (see table 7.1). They wanted to do so for a number of reasons. Some were practical: to allow the people of the region to partake of the prosperity and security that the EU and NATO, respectively, had afforded the West European states since the end of World War II. Some were psychological and symbolic: to heal the division of Europe and return to where they would have been had the Cold War not cut them off, and to be included among the world's democracies. This chapter offers some background on the region's international environment before 1989 and then examines the process undertaken by the Central and East European states to join the EU. A discussion of the challenges the new members and the EU itself face now and going forward follows. The chapter ends with some questions raised for political science and for discussion. As the chapter by Joshua Spero in this volume deals with NATO accession, this chapter does not discuss those issues.[1]

Eastern and Western Europe before 1989

After World War II, the two parts of Europe moved in different directions, economically and politically. After being prevented by Joseph Stalin from participating in the US-funded Marshall Plan to rebuild Europe, Central and Eastern Europe was absorbed into the Soviet-dominated economic and political system and its organizations. All of the Central and East European states (except Yugoslavia) became members of the Council for Mutual Economic Assistance, founded in 1949, and the Warsaw Pact, the Soviet-dominated military alliance, established in 1955. Most importantly, they were bound by bilateral economic, political, and military ties to the Soviet Union. Trade was sharply curtailed with the West and reoriented toward the Soviet Union (see table 7.2). Five-year plans approved by the respective communist parties ruled the region's economies, and private economic activity was reduced to insignificance or eliminated altogether.

Table 7.1. Membership in European Organizations

Country	Date of Joining or Status with Organization		
	Council of Europe	European Union	NATO
Albania	7/13/1995	Candidate	4/1/2009
Bosnia-Herzegovina	4/24/2002	Potential candidate	MAP[d]
Bulgaria	7/5/1992	1/1/2007	3/29/2004
Croatia	11/6/1996	7/1/2013	4/1/2009
Czech Republic	6/30/1993	5/1/2004	3/16/1999
Hungary	11/6/1990	5/1/2004	3/16/1999
Kosovo	n/a	Potential candidate	KFOR[e]
Macedonia	11/9/1995	Candidate	MAP[d]
Montenegro	5/11/2007	Candidate	7/5/2017
Poland	11/26/1991	5/1/2004	3/16/1999
Romania	10/7/1993	1/1/2007	3/29/2004
Serbia	6/3/2006[a]	Candidate	Partnership for peace
Slovakia	6/30/1993	5/1/2004[b]	3/29/2004
Slovenia	5/14/1993	5/1/2004[b]	3/29/2004
Ukraine	11/9/1995	Association agreement[c]	NATO–Ukraine Commission

Sources: Council of Europe (http://hub.coe.int); European Union (http://europa.eu); European Council, "EU Relations with Ukraine," http://www.consilium.europa.eu/en/policies/eastern-partnership/ukraine/; NATO (http://www.nato.int).
[a] Continued membership of state of Serbia and Montenegro, dating from April 3, 2003.
[b] Eurozone member.
[c] A "new generation" agreement providing for political association and economic integration, including a free trade area but not membership, was signed in 2014 and came into effect in 2017.
[d] Membership Action Plan; consultation process with NATO aimed at membership but which does not guarantee membership.
[e] Kosovo Force; NATO-led security force in place since 1999.

Table 7.2. Reorientation of Trade: Share of Central and Eastern Europe's Trade with Western Europe by Year

Country	Imports				Exports			
	1928	1989	1995	2002	1928	1989	1995	2002
Bulgaria	61.6	13.7	38.4	51.3	64.5	7.8	38.6	55.6
CZ/SL	54.8	15.4	45.4	62.0	43.9	16.5	45.7	64.2
Hungary	32.4	30.9	61.5	57.5	25.0	24.2	62.8	73.5
Poland	54.5	27.7	64.7	67.5	55.9	30.5	70.1	67.3
Romania	50.2	7.8	50.9	63.9	53.9	17.5	54.5	68.0

Sources: For 1928 and 1989, Susan M. Collins and Dani Rodrik, *Eastern Europe and the Soviet Union in the World Economy* (Washington, DC: Institute for International Economics, 1991), 39, 40. For 1995 and 2002, European Bank for Reconstruction and Development, *Transition Report 2003* (London: EBRD, 2003), 86. Data for 1928 and 1989 reflect trade with European countries that became or were members of the European Community; data for 1995 and 2002 reflect trade with members of the European Union. For 1995 and 2002, the average for the Czech Republic and Slovakia was used.

As a result, while Western Europe regained economic vitality, established convertible currencies, and began to participate actively in global trade and investment, Central and Eastern Europe did not. The states of the region did recover from the war and did make progress in providing basic goods and services for most of their populations, especially in comparison to the low level of economic development that had characterized most of the region (except for the Czech Lands) before the war. But the region was cut off from the stimulant of international trade competition, was not open to Western investment, and was in fact obliged to render economic support to the USSR, providing an estimated $20 billion worth of technology, machinery, skills, and manufactured goods in the first fifteen years after the war.[2]

The region remained a marginal global economic actor for the entire period of the Cold War. All of the Central and East European states together provided only 4.5 percent of the world's exports—equal to about one-third of the amount West Germany alone provided. The typical Central and East European state received from the USSR nearly 40 percent of its imports and sent to the USSR more than one-third of its exports.[3] None of the region's currencies were convertible, even in transactions among themselves. On the other hand, the region was shielded from sharp jumps in the price of internationally traded commodities like oil because these were provided to the region at the Council for Mutual Economic Assistance "friendship price" (a periodically adjusted fraction of the global price). Thus, the region's socialist economies avoided sharp recession and had little price inflation, but by the late 1970s and 1980s, they also began to show little or no growth.[4] The states of the region also received a substantial trade subsidy from the Soviet Union because they were able to purchase energy and other resources at lower than world prices in exchange for "soft" goods (i.e., those not salable in the West).[5] When Mikhail Gorbachev became the leader of the Soviet Union in 1985, he moved to change this "international division of labor" to adjust to economic realities. The revolutions of 1989 intervened, and the Central and East European states found themselves thrown onto the harsh playing field of the global economy without the experience or economic mechanisms to compete.

The Courtship of the EU: Toward the "Big Bang"

What is today an organization of twenty-eight countries with more than 500 million people began in the aftermath of World War II as a limited attempt to link key parts of the economies of former enemies France and Germany. In 1951, the European Coal and Steel Community was founded by those two countries, plus Italy, Belgium, the Netherlands, and Luxembourg. In the landmark Treaty of Rome of 1957, the European Economic Community was created to complement the European Coal and Steel Community and a new European Atomic Agency. These three were combined in 1965 into the European Community (EC). The members created a parliament and modified other parts of the organization, but over the next two decades, the organization grew slowly in terms of both number of members (adding the United Kingdom, Ireland, and Denmark in 1973, Greece in 1981, and Spain and Portugal in 1986) and areas of policy responsibility. By the time the Berlin Wall fell in 1989, the EC still had only twelve members, but it had committed itself (through the Single European Act of 1986) to creating the mechanisms for a single European economy. The Treaty on European Union, referred to as the Maastricht Treaty after the Dutch town in which it was signed in 1992, renamed the organization the EU and began to move the members toward more unified economic functioning as well as stronger common political institutions. Austria, Finland, and Sweden joined in 1995, bringing the number of members to fifteen. In 2002, the common European currency, the euro, was introduced in eleven of the member states.

After the overthrow of communism, the Central and East European states moved to try to join the EU as soon as possible. Hungary and Poland formally applied in 1994; Romania, Slovakia, and Bulgaria in 1995; and the Czech Republic and Slovenia in 1996. By that time, all had held at least one set of open elections deemed proper by international observers; had created conditions for the exercise of citizens' rights of expression, assembly, and participation; and were seeing the birth—in some cases, explosion—of political parties and interest groups. The states of the region also rejected the idea of recreating the Soviet-era economic or political alliances in any new form in favor of joining the most successful and attractive international organization in history, the EU. That organization had never had to consider such a potentially large simultaneous expansion before. Moreover, in previous enlargements, the candidates for membership were not only functioning democracies but had also established capitalist and Western-oriented economic systems. In Central and Eastern Europe, by contrast, the countries seeking membership were only just starting the process of creating such systems, were much more numerous, and, most importantly, were significantly poorer than even the poorest EU member. Among potential candidates, for example, the gross domestic product (GDP) per capita of Poland (the largest) was just over two-thirds that of Greece, the poorest EU member, and only 40 percent of the average of all EU members (see table 7.3).

It is not surprising, then, that the EU moved somewhat slowly to establish and implement standard procedures for bringing the Central and East European states into the organization. Along with financial assistance to help these states reform their economies (see below), the EU signed a series of association agreements, called the Europe Agreements, to govern trade with the Central and East European states. At the 1992 European Council at Lisbon, the organization for the first time pledged to help the Central and East European states not just to reform their economies but ultimately to become members of the organization. At the Copenhagen Council in 1993, the EU set forth the basic criteria that the new members would have to meet to be admitted. These criteria included stability of institutions guaranteeing democracy, the rule of law, human rights, and respect for and protection of minorities; the existence of a functioning market economy as well as the capacity to cope with competitive pressure and market forces within the union; and the ability to take on the obligations of membership, including adherence to the aims of political, economic, and monetary union.[6]

To fulfill these criteria, applicants were obliged to accept and pass into legislation the codes, practices, and laws in place in the EU, referred to as the *acquis communautaire*. Starting in 1998, all of the applicant countries were evaluated annually to assess their progress toward establishing democratic practices, including the rule of law, the exercise of political rights by the population, and the protection of minority rights. Economic assessments judged the countries' movement toward establishing a market economy, including privatization, fiscal and monetary control, and openness to foreign investment. Each applicant's ability to undertake the "obligations of membership" was assessed by measuring the adoption of measures laid out in the *acquis*, covering, for example, agriculture, transportation, environmental policy, and justice and home affairs (e.g., the countries' legal systems, including courts, police, rights of accused, and use of the death penalty).[7] In all, there were thirty-one chapters of standards by which these countries were judged, and only when all chapters had been "closed," or judged satisfactory by the European Commission, were invitations for membership issued. That happened for

**Table 7.3. Gross Domestic Product per Capita of New and Old
EU Members GDP in PPS per Inhabitant, 2001 (EU-15 = 100)**

Luxembourg	190
Ireland	118
Netherlands	115
Denmark	115
Austria	111
Belgium	109
Finland	104
Italy	103
France	103
Germany	103
Sweden	102
United Kingdom	101
Spain	84
Cyprus	74
Slovenia	70
Portugal	69
Greece	65
Czech Republic	59
Hungary	53
Slovakia	48
Poland	41
Estonia	40
Lithuania	39
Latvia	33
Bulgaria	25
Romania	24
Turkey	23

Source: Eurostat, *Towards an Enlarged European Union* (Brussels: European
Commission, n.d.).
Note: In this chart, gross domestic product per capita is calculated on the basis
of purchasing power standard (PPS), which takes into account differences in
prices across countries.

eight Central and East European states in 2002, leading to their simultaneous admission (the "Big Bang") in May 2004.[8] For Romania and Bulgaria, however, there were thirty-five chapters, and these two countries were subject to "enhanced monitoring" by the Commission. They were permitted to join as of January 1, 2007, but under an unprecedented "Cooperation and Verification Mechanism" that obliges them to report on their progress in judicial reform, the fight against corruption, and, in Bulgaria's case, the fight against organized crime.[9] In 2005, Croatia began formal negotiations and in July 2013 became the twenty-eighth member of the EU.

The Costs of Joining

For most Central and East European states, making the transition to democratic practices with regard to individual freedoms, elections, political institutions, and parties was challenging. Although the countries' populations desired such institutions and practices after four decades of Communist Party rule, not all of the states moved equally quickly. In some cases, communist-era practices—and people—remained powerful, as, for example, in Slovakia and Romania. It took electoral defeats in these cases to improve the EU's opinion and these countries' chances for joining the organization.

For Central and East European governments, adapting their countries' political and legal processes to European norms involved making adjustments in a variety of policy arenas. Elimination of the death penalty and laws against homosexuality, for example, was required. Improvements in the legal system, including the formation of independent judges and constitutional courts, were needed in most cases. One of the most common areas of pressure lay in the EU's criticism of the countries' treatment of their Roma minorities. Numbering over 4 million and scattered throughout the region,[10] Roma minorities suffered both legal and economic discrimination, exclusion from employment and political power, and, in some cases, actual physical harassment.[11] Even leading candidates for membership such as the Czech Republic were subject to criticism by the EU for restrictive citizenship laws and hostile actions toward Roma.[12]

The EU's involvement in minority issues in the region produced some skepticism even as it provided an opportunity for domestic minority groups and nongovernmental organizations to utilize EU influence on their behalf to secure better treatment from their governments. For example, the EU insisted that the candidate states implement full recognition and guarantees of minority rights that in some cases did not apply in member states.[13]

Photo 7.1.   EU Enlargement Day in May 2004. The flags of Cyprus, the Czech Republic, Estonia, Hungary, Latvia, Lithuania, Malta, Poland, the Slovak Republic, and Slovenia are raised at an EU building, marking their accession to the union. (European Committee, 2007)

Setting up appropriate Western-style parliamentary and electoral institutions and getting them running in forms that the EU would approve were relatively simple tasks compared to the process of wrenching the economies into line with EU expectations. These states were not as economically developed, had not traded in a competitive world market, and did not have the resources to make the economic transition without substantial pain. The Central and East European economies were more agricultural, less productive, used more energy and human resources to produce the same number of goods as the West, and, for the most part, produced goods that were not competitive on the world market. To make matters worse, the goods these states could potentially sell globally were precisely those that the EU specialized in—farm products, steel, textiles—and the EU was at first not eager to open its markets. Within a few years, however, tariff and quota restrictions on Central and East European exports to Western Europe were removed and trade shifted sharply from East to West (see table 7.2). Still, given the uncompetitive nature of these economies, it took several years before any could achieve significant positive trade balances.

Production in most of the Central and East European states declined dramatically and it took until the end of the decade for most of Central and Eastern Europe to reach the economic levels of 1989 and even longer for Romania and Bulgaria.[14] Unemployment, which had not officially existed under socialism, soared, reaching more than 12 percent of the workforce on average throughout the region. Part of the adjustment to EU economic policies involved improving the environment for competition, eliminating government support of industries, ending price controls, and allowing bankruptcies. The EU also exerted pressure to allow foreign investment on a nondiscriminatory basis, meaning that experienced, successful West European companies would be free to buy up valuable assets in these states, now available at bargain basement prices. After 1989, the region attracted more than $170 billion in foreign direct investment (through the year 2004), with the bulk going to the three Central European states, Poland, Hungary, and the Czech Republic. While proceeding slowly on formal admission, the EU did move to provide the region with substantial economic aid through its PHARE program.[15] Other programs were added, like the Special Accession Programme for Agriculture and Rural Development and the Instrument for Structural Policies for Pre-Accession programs. Together, more than €20 billion ($23,399,800,000) was allocated to new members in what was termed "pre-accession aid," though some continued even after they became members.

Perhaps the major challenge to the accession process involved agriculture. Since its formation, the EU has supported farmers by controlling imports, supporting prices, and providing direct payments through the Common Agricultural Policy.[16] Common Agricultural Policy payments constitute the single largest item in the EU budget. With 7 million new farmers (and 40 percent more agricultural land) added by Central and East European accession to the 6 million already in the EU, the organization realized that it could not afford to extend to the new members the generous agricultural subsidies it had been providing to farmers in the EU-15 states. Moreover, in global trade negotiations, the EU has pledged to reduce the level of its subsidies. Hence, as part of these states' accession, direct payments to Central and Eastern Europe's farmers were at first a fraction of those paid to farmers in Western Europe and were increased gradually.[17]

The Politics of Membership

When the EU was founded, the driving idea was to link continental Europe's major economic powers, France and Germany, so inextricably as to make future wars between them impossible. As other functions became part of common responsibility, such as control of nuclear energy, control of agricultural production, and external trade ties, the organization not only grew in complexity but also added members. Great Britain's membership had been vetoed by France in 1963 and was delayed for ten years, but adding democratic Portugal, Spain, and Greece in the 1980s and the relatively rich, capitalist Austria, Sweden, and Finland in 1995 was not controversial. However, adding eight or ten economically weak states that had operated as one-party dictatorships and state-run economies for four decades was not popular. Public opinion surveys among the members of the EU consistently showed a lack of enthusiasm for enlargement in most EU member states. Despite public ambivalence, movement toward membership proceeded, reinforcing the idea among some that the organization operates with a "democratic deficit"—that is, that decisions are made by distant elites who are not responsible to anyone and reflect bureaucratic imperatives in Brussels more than the desires of their constituents.[18]

In Central and Eastern Europe, though, accession to the EU was generally very popular. Public opinion polls in the 1990s showed that majorities of the populations in the region strongly supported joining the EU. In general, Central and East European populations trusted the EU and saw joining as the right thing to do for their country.[19] Support was not equally high throughout the region, however, as the costs of adjustment and the uneven distribution of such costs among the population became evident. In a 2002 survey, for example, only one-third of Estonians and Latvians thought that membership would be "a good thing," while more than two-thirds of Hungarians and Bulgarians thought so.[20] In most cases, as countries moved closer to joining the EU, public support for doing so fell off somewhat before rebounding.[21] Referenda on joining were held in each of the Central and East European countries due to join in 2004 and produced positive—though in some cases, close—votes.[22] In the Croatian referendum in 2012, two-thirds of those voting supported accession, but the turnout (43 percent of eligible voters) was the lowest of any new member state.[23] By 2011, among the new member states, public views of the benefits of EU membership were similar to those held in countries with longer membership, but there was somewhat more uncertainty as to whether EU membership was a "good thing" than in the older member states.[24]

Apart from accommodating legal, political, and economic systems to the demands of the *acquis*, for several of the new members, some issues provided a possible challenge to the depth of their commitment to join. Many worried that their inexperienced and weaker economies, especially in the agricultural sector, would not be able to compete with rich, subsidized EU enterprises. There was concern that West Europeans would buy up their countries' low-priced assets and land, leaving local people unemployed and without property. For their part, some politicians in the EU feared that economic dislocation and the attraction of the more prosperous West would produce a vast labor migration once borders were erased and full EU citizenship, including the right to live anywhere, was extended eastward. In the end, several countries were granted transition periods during which they could retain control over agricultural land purchase. But the "free movement of persons" was also limited for the new members, with restrictions remaining in place for not less than two and possibly up to seven years.[25]

Border issues continue to be complicated for some new members. All the new members were obliged to move toward adopting the provisions of the Schengen Treaty (1985) operating among most EU states. This treaty allows for free movement of citizens within the EU but mandates strict enforcement and guarding of the EU's external borders. With that border now pushed eastward, Poles and Hungarians living in Ukraine, for example, found visiting their ethnic kin in new EU member states more difficult and expensive than it had been before. The need for visas suggested a second-class status and depressed the substantial cross-border economic activity that had grown up. Gradually, the EU approved visa-free travel for citizens of the Western Balkans and noncandidate countries like Moldova, Georgia, and Ukraine.[26] But a major challenge to coherent border policies occurred when hundreds of thousands of refugees began to travel through the region as they fled wars and upheaval in the Middle East and North Africa (see below).

Most of the new members also face serious issues in terms of compliance with environmental regulations. This chapter of the *acquis* includes extensive regulations affecting power generation (especially nuclear power), water, air cleanliness, and the burning of fossil fuels. Accommodating EU standards has been enormously expensive for these states and, in some cases, has obliged them to close down some power plants altogether. To ensure their entry, for example, Lithuania and Bulgaria agreed to close their nuclear reactors, which had the effect of increasing their dependence on Russian sources of energy.

Croatia, the EU's newest member, faced the most comprehensive and exacting scrutiny by the Commission due in part to criticisms of the poor performance of Romania and Bulgaria, which joined in 2007. As with those states, the issue of action against corruption slowed negotiations, which lasted six years. Evidence of the EU's persuasive power was the fact that Croatia arrested and tried its own former prime minister, Ivo Sanader, on corruption charges in 2010. But legacy issues from the state's time as part of Yugoslavia remained. Most difficult politically was Croatia's obligation—as part of its adherence to the Copenhagen criteria—to arrest and extradite those alleged to have committed war crimes during the wars with Serbia or in Bosnia. As the Croatian government acted on these demands and former military leaders were arrested and extradited, progress toward membership resumed.[27] (See chapter 16 on the successors to Yugoslavia.)

For all of the Central and East European states, the period after 1989 and before 2004 represented a wrenching shift in both real and symbolic terms. These states had been part of the Soviet Union's external empire for the four decades after World War II, and over the years, Moscow had used political and economic ties and Soviet-dominated regional organizations to maintain control. When challenges emerged, as happened in Hungary in 1956 and in Czechoslovakia in 1968, the USSR had been willing to use force to keep the countries subordinate. Only in 1989 did the USSR, under Mikhail Gorbachev, refrain from intervening to prevent far-reaching democratic change and the return of full sovereignty to the states of this region. The irony is that having finally achieved full control over their own affairs, the leaders of the newly democratic Central and East European states, with their populations' agreement, moved relatively quickly to surrender key parts of that sovereignty to a different power center, the European

Union. All were willing to remake virtually all of their institutions and practices to conform to standards set by Brussels. Finally, fifteen years after the revolutions that toppled dictatorships in Central and Eastern Europe, and only after the EU was satisfied that national laws and institutions accorded with its norms, the eastern and western parts of Europe were formally reunited.

The EU and the Region: Achievements and Challenges

CHANGING THE INSTITUTION AND THE SETTING

The enlargement of the EU to the east obliged the organization to adapt its governing structure. Voting mechanisms in the European Council and the number of representatives in the European Parliament were adjusted, though the organization failed to reduce the size of the European Commission. (All twenty-eight members still nominate one commissioner.[28]) Though the EU grew dramatically in size and power since the end of the Cold War, eastern expansion turned out to be one indicator of the high watermark in the growth of both dimensions. In 2005, a proposed European Constitution was defeated in referenda in Holland and France. A new, less ambitious Reform Treaty (referred to as the Lisbon Treaty) was drafted and finally ratified in 2009. The new treaty reflects Europe's emergence as an international actor, providing for the new political posts of President of the European Council and High Representative for Foreign Affairs and Security Policy. It also reflects a desire to improve decision-making and reduce the democratic deficit by strengthening the ability of the European Parliament to affect decisions.[29]

In terms of changes in the states, the gains from EU enlargement were multiple and substantial: durable security was established in a region known for conflict, the Central and East European countries were bound together and to Western Europe economically and politically, and the painstaking creation of democratic institutions and societies was initiated and supported.

For the first time in modern history, the possibility of military conflict in the heart of Europe is virtually nonexistent. Most of the Central and East European states have joined those in Western Europe as full members of both the EU and NATO. Others in the Balkans, including virtually all parts of what was once Yugoslavia, aspire to join these organizations. Across the membership area, international warfare of the type seen in the last century seems as unlikely as war between France and Germany. The significance of the organization's success on this dimension was thrown into sharp relief by the occurrence of military action just outside the EU domain in Georgia in 2008 and in Ukraine in 2014. Economically, the region's trade and investment are overwhelmingly tied to fellow members (see below), and by 2015, the single-currency Eurozone had grown to nineteen members and included five CEE states (Slovakia, Slovenia, Estonia, Latvia, and Lithuania).

In addition, the EU's aim of promoting democratic institutions and practices in the region has been broadly successful. By 2005, the first "graduating class" of EU joiners from the region were declared to be "no longer in transit" by Freedom House, using an annual assessment of democratic processes.[30] Table 7.4 shows the effect of EU involvement. By

2008, the Democracy Scores (1 being the best and 7 the worst) had improved in eight of eleven CEE members of the EU compared to the 1991–2000 period. The average Democracy Score for "New EU members" that year was 2.33 while the average for the Balkans was 4.03 and for the former Soviet states, 5.84.

CHALLENGES

Preserving Democracy

Building democracy is an arduous process—especially in a region with precious little democratic history—and gains are fragile. Even with as powerful an actor as the EU as a motivator and guide, movement forward is not guaranteed—especially once the chief prize, membership, is achieved. The slow, often unwieldy processes of democracy test the public's patience, and those seeking greater power are willing to exploit grievances and threats (real and imagined) to weaken democratic institutions. Thus, some democratic "backsliding" has occurred in Central and East Europe (note the decline in table 7.4 in the average score from 2.28 in 2005 to 2.57 by 2013). As figure 7.1 illustrates, that decline has continued—dramatically in some cases.

As these indicators show, EU membership has not prevented the erosion of democracy in several CEE states. Hungary and Poland represent the greatest challenge to the EU's much-lauded "soft power" and the very values it professes to represent.

In Hungary in 2010, the conservative Alliance of Young Democrats (FiDeSz), in coalition with the Christian Democratic People's Party, won a two-thirds majority in parliament. Since then, the Government of Prime Minister Viktor Orbán has adopted many measures, including a new constitution, that strengthen the hand of the ruling party, weaken electoral opposition, and erode the independence of the media, judiciary, and central bank. These and other measures have drawn criticism from the Council of Europe, the European Commission, and the European Parliament, which in May 2017 declared that such developments "have led to a serious deterioration in the rule of law, democracy and fundamental rights which is testing the EU's ability to defend its founding values."[31]

The EU faces a similar challenge to its ability to protect democracy in Poland, where the government of the PiS (Law and Justice) party, in power since 2015, has adopted similar measures (see chapter 9 on Poland). Lacking enough votes in the Sejm (parliament) to change the constitution, the government in the fall of 2017 adopted legislation to ensure PiS control of the country's judiciary, including the Constitutional Tribunal and Supreme Court. After repeated warnings, the European Commission took the unprecedented action of invoking Article 7 of the Lisbon Treaty and declared there to be "a clear risk of a serious breach of the rule of law in Poland." While urging the Polish government to undo these measures, it invited the European Council to accept the Commission's judgement and take action, which could involve sanctions costing Poland its EU voting rights.[32]

The underlying foundation of democratic attitudes can also erode, as the demands of economic and party competition and the forces of global change test public commitment to the still new systems. Surveys have shown a growing dissatisfaction with the way democracy operates in the region and a stubborn lack of trust in political parties and democratic institutions, such as presidents and parliaments.[33] In 2009, a PEW survey showed

Table 7.4. Democracy Scores for Central and Eastern Europe, the Balkans, and States of the Former Soviet Union

	1999–2000	2001	2002	2003	2004	2005	2006	2007	2008	2009	2013
New EU Members											
Bulgaria	3.58	3.42	3.33	3.38	3.25	3.18	2.93	2.89	2.86	3.04	3.18
Croatia	4.46	3.54	3.54	3.79	3.83	3.75	3.71	3.75	3.64	3.71	3.61
Czech Republic	2.08	2.25	2.46	2.33	2.33	2.29	2.25	2.25	2.14	2.18	2.14
Estonia	2.25	2.13	2.00	2.00	1.92	1.96	1.96	1.96	1.93	1.93	1.96
Hungary	1.88	2.13	2.13	1.96	1.96	1.96	2.00	2.14	2.14	2.29	2.89
Latvia	2.29	2.21	2.25	2.25	2.17	2.14	2.07	2.07	2.07	2.18	2.07
Lithuania	2.29	2.21	2.21	2.13	2.13	2.21	2.21	2.29	2.25	2.29	2.32
Poland	1.58	1.58	1.63	1.75	1.75	2.00	2.14	2.36	2.39	2.25	2.18
Romania	3.54	3.67	3.71	3.63	3.58	3.39	3.39	3.29	3.36	3.36	3.50
Slovakia	2.71	2.50	2.17	2.08	2.08	2.00	1.96	2.14	2.29	2.46	2.57
Slovenia	1.88	1.88	1.83	1.79	1.75	1.68	1.75	1.82	1.86	1.93	1.89
Average	2.41	2.40	2.37	2.33	2.29	2.28	2.27	2.32	2.33	2.39	2.57
Median	2.27	2.21	2.19	2.10	2.10	2.07	2.11	2.20	2.20	2.27	2.32
The Balkans											
Albania	4.75	4.42	4.25	4.17	4.13	4.04	3.79	3.82	3.82	3.82	4.25
Bosnia	5.42	5.17	4.83	4.54	4.29	4.18	4.07	4.04	4.11	4.18	4.39
Macedonia	3.83	4.04	4.46	4.29	4.00	3.89	3.82	3.82	3.86	3.86	3.93
Yugoslavia	5.67	5.04	4.00	3.88	n/a	n/a	n/a	n/a	n/a	n/a	n/a
Serbia	n/a	n/a	n/a	n/a	3.83	3.75	3.71	3.68	3.79	3.79	3.64
Montenegro	n/a	n/a	n/a	n/a	3.83	3.79	3.89	3.93	3.79	3.79	3.82
Kosovo	n/a	n/a	n/a	n/a	5.50	5.32	5.36	5.36	5.21	5.11	5.25
Average	4.83	4.44	4.22	4.13	4.20	4.10	4.05	4.05	4.03	4.04	4.21
Median	4.75	4.42	4.25	4.17	4.00	3.89	3.82	3.82	3.82	3.82	4.09

Non-Baltic Former Soviet States

Armenia	4.79	4.83	4.83	4.92	5.00	5.18	5.14	5.21	5.21	5.39	5.36
Azerbaijan	5.58	5.63	5.54	5.46	5.63	5.86	5.93	6.00	6.00	6.25	6.64
Belarus	6.25	6.38	6.38	6.46	6.54	6.64	6.71	6.68	6.71	6.57	6.72
Georgia	4.17	4.33	4.58	4.83	4.83	4.96	4.86	4.68	4.79	4.93	4.75
Kazakhstan	5.50	5.71	5.96	6.17	6.25	6.29	6.39	6.39	6.39	6.32	6.57
Kyrgyzstan	5.08	5.29	5.46	5.67	5.67	5.64	5.68	5.68	5.93	6.04	5.96
Moldova	4.25	4.29	4.50	4.71	4.88	5.07	4.96	4.96	5.00	5.07	4.82
Russia	4.58	4.88	5.00	4.96	5.25	5.61	5.75	5.86	5.96	6.11	6.21
Tajikistan	5.75	5.58	5.63	5.63	5.71	5.79	5.93	5.96	6.07	6.14	6.25
Turkmenistan	6.75	6.83	6.83	6.83	6.88	6.93	6.96	6.96	6.93	6.93	6.93
Ukraine	4.63	4.71	4.92	4.71	4.88	4.50	4.21	4.25	4.25	4.39	4.86
Uzbekistan	6.38	6.42	6.46	6.46	6.46	6.43	6.82	6.82	6.86	6.89	6.93
Average	5.31	5.41	5.51	5.57	5.66	5.74	5.78	5.79	5.84	5.92	6.00
Median	5.29	5.44	5.50	5.54	5.65	5.72	5.84	5.91	5.98	6.13	6.23

Source: Freedom House, https://freedomhouse.org/sites/default/files/NIT2013_Tables_FINAL.pdf.
Note: The Democracy Score ranges from 1, the highest level, to 7, the lowest level and is an average of ratings for Electoral Process (EP); Civil Society (CS); Independent Media (IM); National Democratic Governance (NGO\1); Local Democratic Governance (LGO\1); Judicial Framework and Independence (JFI); and Corruption (CO).

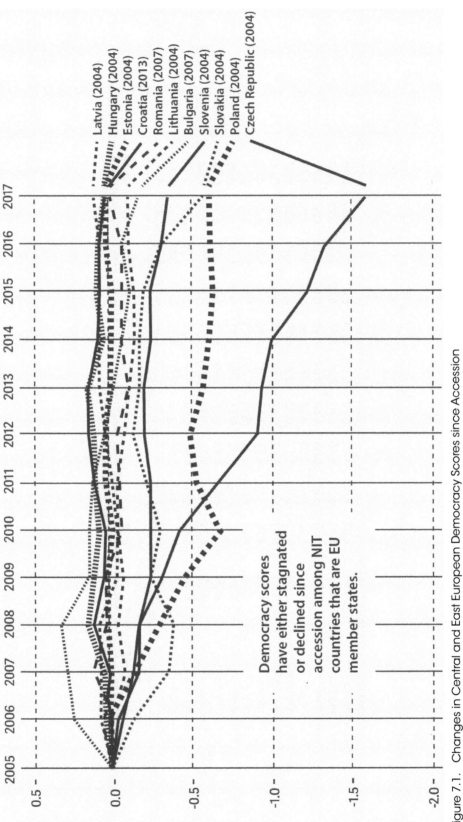

Figure 7.1.   Changes in Central and East European Democracy Scores since Accession
Source: Freedom House, Nations in Transit 2017.

Table 7.5. Support for Democracy

Most countries lack majority support for democracy as best form of government

Percentage who say . . .

	Democracy is preferable to any other kind of government	*In some circumstances, a nondemocratic government can be preferable*	*For someone like me, it doesn't matter what kind of government we have*
Greece	77	15	6
Lithuania	64	15	17
Georgia	55	19	21
Croatia	54	19	23
Armenia	53	13	32
Romania	52	28	17
Czech Republic	49	27	22
Hungary	48	26	21
Poland	47	26	18
Bosnia	46	22	26
Estonia	46	29	20
Bulgaria	39	34	23
Belarus	38	35	17
Ukraine	36	31	23
Latvia	34	30	26
Russia	31	41	20
Moldova	26	44	19
Serbia	25	28	43

Source: "Democracy, Nationalism and Pluralism," *Religious Belief and National Belonging in Central and Eastern Europe,* Pew Research Center, May 10, 2017. Survey conducted June 2015–July 2016 in eighteen countries. "Don't know/refused" responses not shown. Available at: http://www.pewforum.org/2017/05/10/democracy-nationalism-and-pluralism/; see Appendix A "Methodology" for details.

that support for the multiparty system had steeply declined in Bulgaria, Lithuania, and Hungary, while staying flat, or nearly flat, in Poland, the Czech Republic, and Slovakia.[34] A survey in 2017 (see table 7.5) showed a disturbingly weak support for democracy, with only Romania, Croatia, and Lithuania among the CEE EU members showing majority preference for democracy compared to other systems. Equally troubling, the survey shows a strong minority embracing a political indifference that makes them vulnerable to populist, all-purpose solutions proposed by nationalist parties and actors hostile to democracy.[35] But such parties have also been successful in Western Europe, and especially compared to developments in the non-EU Balkans or post-Soviet states (see table 7.4), democratic stability has been established in the region, with the EU's help and in less than a generation.

Managing Migration

With the collapse of the Arab Spring movement for democracy and especially the worsening of the civil war in Syria, Europe has seen a migration inflow of unprecedented proportions. At the end of 2014, just over fifty thousand people had fled war, poverty, and hopelessness in the Middle East and North Africa to seek asylum in Europe. By the end of

2015, that number exceeded 1.3 million. Most were trying to reach the richer countries of Europe, especially Germany, but to do so, they had to traverse CEE states, notably Serbia and EU member Hungary. By the end of 2015, more than 177,000 refugees were camped in Hungary, the highest number *per capita* in Europe. Despite their commitments to the EU, several Central and East European members rejected the idea of taking in refugees and challenged the EU's right to make such policy.

Anti-immigrant and anti-Muslim fears were exploited by populist parties in each of these countries, but the problem was exacerbated by the EU's inability to construct an effective and equitable solution. With thousands dying in the Mediterranean and the burden of rescue and settlement falling disproportionately on Greece, Italy, and Hungary, EU interior ministers, in an unusual majority vote, adopted a plan in 2015 to distribute by quota some 120,000 arriving refugees (plus 40,000 previously agreed to). Despite these meager numbers compared to the overall numbers and the fact that less than 10 percent would be settled in Eastern Europe, four CEE states (Hungary, Slovakia, the Czech Republic, and Romania) voted against the plan. Hungary built barriers on its borders (in violation of Schengen Treaty principles) and later, along with Slovakia, sued the EU in the European Court of Justice, unsuccessfully, to try to block the plan. With the quota plan producing weak results (just over eighteen thousand resettlements by spring 2017), the EU itself took legal action against the Czech Republic, Hungary, and Poland because of their failure to comply with the deal.[36] Unable to coordinate among themselves, the EU signed an agreement with Turkey in 2016 that obliged that country to halt the outward flow of refugees in return for more a more favorable approach by the EU toward Turkey's accession plans and the provision of visa-free travel (something virtually all of the Balkan candidate members had been granted).

The CEE states are not the only EU members to resist the distribution of migrants, but this very public resistance by new democracies and new members represents a clear rejection of both the values and idea of the supranational organization. At the same time, it provides a powerful focus for those domestic forces willing to demonize both "the other" and external actors like the EU for political gain.[37]

Economic Struggles

When the Central and East European states joined the EU in 2004 and 2007, they were obliged to commit to eventually joining the Eurozone. In this subset of EU members, a single currency operates and states' fiscal (budget) autonomy is limited. Five CEE states have joined so far (Slovenia, Slovakia, Estonia, Latvia, and Lithuania) but the two largest East European economies, Poland and Romania, have not.

Nevertheless, all of the Central and East European joiners have become tightly entwined with the economic dynamics of their European partners. EU countries are the principal source of foreign direct investment, and by 2012, EU partners took nearly two-thirds of all exports from Central and Eastern Europe. Such exports are crucial to the economies of the region, accounting, for example, for 40 percent of the GDP in the Czech Republic and 30 percent in Hungary, the Slovak Republic, and Slovenia from 2007 to 2009.[38]

In 2008, an international economic crisis hit, begun by a deep recession in the United States and then Europe. With both investment funds and the market for exports sharply reduced, poorer EU states that had counted on cheap credit began instead to borrow, at first to cover domestic needs and then—at much less attractive rates—to cover earlier borrowing. With unsustainable debt building in Greece, Ireland, Spain, and Portugal, the EU was obliged to act. It did so at the behest of richer "paymaster countries," Germany, the Netherlands, and Finland, and imposed severe austerity programs in return for aid.

At the same time, new centrally controlled institutions of the EU were created, like the European Stability Mechanism in 2012, with access to €500 billion ($584,685,000,000) in lending capacity and a "European Fiscal Compact" that includes automatic "correction mechanisms."[39] The European Central Bank began providing long-term, low-interest loans to banks. The combined effect of these actions did work to make the annual budget situation in Italy, Portugal, and Spain somewhat more manageable, and modest growth returned to the Eurozone in 2014 and has continued. The price paid (unwillingly by some members) has been stronger central EU policies and institutions, especially those affecting Eurozone countries, and a sharpening of divisions between Europe's "haves" and "have nots."

The 2008 global economic crisis and the slowdowns in the Eurozone rippled across Central and Eastern Europe as well. Deep recessions occurred in Hungary, Croatia, Bulgaria, Slovenia, and the Slovak Republic, as well as in the Baltic states. Only Poland was able to maintain growth. In many new member countries, economic crisis led to political change. Governments in Croatia, the Czech Republic, and Eurozone members Slovenia and Slovakia succumbed to early collapse. Hostility to costly bailouts was also evident. When successive bailouts for Greece were being considered in 2015, Slovak Prime Minister Robert Fico said, "Let no one ask Slovaks who earn €550 to €600 [a month] and get pensions of €250 to €300 to put money together and send out a €1 billion."[40]

The Central and East European states rebounded quickly and, in fact, have shown growth that outpaces Western Europe. But public opinion in the east, like that across most of Europe, has shown fading faith in the EU.[41] In the region, distrust of the EU is strongest in the Czech Republic, Slovenia, Hungary, and Slovakia but is not dramatically different (except for the CR) than that seen, on average, across Europe.[42] Economic dissatisfaction, corruption, and opposition to EU directives, especially on migration and democratic practice, has strengthened the electoral showing of nationalist parties across the region. In Hungary, policies at odds with EU preferences twice led to suspensions of EU development funds. At one point, Prime Minister Orbán compared the EU's action to Soviet-style interference.[43] The return to growth in both parts of Europe may ease electoral pressure, but the fundamental issues of how to make the single market work and how to make the EU as a whole work for the benefit of all will continue to challenge Europe, east and west.

Dealing with Russia

Another dimension of the EU's international role became decidedly more complicated because of the admission of eleven Central and East European states, three of which were once part of the Soviet Union and virtually all of which have diverging histories with, and views of, Russia. Russia is a key economic partner of the EU—its fourth largest trading partner. More importantly, it is the leading supplier of Europe's oil and gas imports, which account for four-fifths and three-fifths of European energy use, respectively. EU countries get most of their oil and gas from outside the region, and in both cases, Russia is the dominant supplier.[44] Dependence on Russian energy is not evenly distributed, with the proportion being much higher among the Central and East European states. Hungary, the Czech Republic, and Slovakia, for example, get nearly all their natural gas from Russia. That fact, plus historical paths that have included both liberation from the Nazis and occupation by the communists, produces a range of attitudes toward Putin's Russia. The Baltic states, Poland and Romania, for example, prefer that the EU take a tough stand on sanctions imposed on Moscow after its seizure of the Crimean Peninsula from Ukraine in 2014 and its support of rebels in the eastern part of that country. These states tend to see a more imminent threat to their hard-won sovereignty, while others, notably the Czech Republic and especially Hungary, are more willing under their current governments to seek greater cooperation and fewer penalties in relations with Russia.

Foreign policy has always been the weakest policy area of EU coordination. Adding so many states with a range of attitudes toward Russia plus high levels of energy dependence produces a complex map of possible responses to Russia. And this was before new uncertainties emerged about the level of US commitment toward the region after the election of Donald Trump.[45]

The EU and the Region: Going Forward

While the issues of democracy, economic health, refugees, and dealing with Russia find the CEE states center stage in the development of the EU, the future form and actions of the organization itself will have a significant impact on the peoples and countries of the region even as their own politics will be a factor in shaping the new EU. In this respect, three major dynamics will test the relationship between the "new" Central and East European members and the now sixty-year-old organization.

BREXIT

For the first time in its history, the EU has seen a member, Great Britain, opt to leave the community. And not just any member, but its third largest in terms of population and economy and its most militarily capable member. The EU will be reduced economically and face uncertain trade and investment ties with the United Kingdom. A new, as yet undetermined, status for EU citizens in the United Kingdom will have to be negotiated. The EU's global power, assertion of international role, and governing values will almost certainly be diminished.

For the CEE states, the ramifications are many. Great Britain had been one of the strongest proponents of enlargement to the East as well as the EU member most firm in its critical attitude toward Russia. Thus, countries like Poland and the Baltic states will lose a critical ally in those policy debates within the EU. At the same time, the United Kingdom's "special relationship" with the United States gave strongly pro-US countries in the region, like Poland, an organic connection to Washington within the EU that will now be gone.

More concretely, more than one million people have left East Europe to live and work in the United Kingdom since accession, increasing the connection between East and West and sending valuable remittances back home. After the UK vote, overall immigration to the United Kingdom slowed with the inflow of Poles, Lithuanians, and others from CEE slowing dramatically.[46] Brexit negotiations may or may not provide protection for EU citizens inside the United Kingdom, but for now, the attraction of moving west—once automatic—is called into question.

ENLARGEMENT AND INFLUENCE

For the EU, the questions of enlargement and influence are related. In postcommunist Central and East Europe, Brussels saw itself as helping to extend the benefits of democracy and economic vibrancy to a region cut off for decades by the Cold War. This enlargement was generally welcomed by the leaderships and populations of the CEE states. "Completing" the process by adding states that emerged from the breakup of Yugoslavia has proven more challenging.

In 2003, the EU committed itself to continuing enlargement to include all of the states in what is referred to as "the Western Balkans."[47] Slovenia joined the organization in the first wave of enlargement in 2004, and Croatia did so in 2013. Macedonia, Montenegro, Albania, and Serbia are termed "candidate members" (like Turkey), and Bosnia-Herzegovina and Kosovo are labeled "potential candidates."

As with the earlier accessions, for some Balkan states, there are special obstacles to membership. In Bosnia-Herzegovina, constitutional reform that would strengthen the country's ability to act as a unified entity is stalled despite vigorous EU involvement. (See chapter 16 on the post-Yugoslav states.) Macedonian progress toward membership is blocked by Greek objections to the country's name.[48] Kosovo, which declared independence from Serbia in 2008, is not recognized by five EU members or, crucially, by candidate member Serbia. However, in 2013, EU High Representative Catherine Ashton succeeded in brokering a power-sharing agreement that affects the northern part of the new country where most members of the Serb minority live.[49] Slow movement toward normalization of relations, though rocky, has continued and was a product of the desire of both sides to enhance their prospects for EU membership and an important positive result of the EU's Western Balkans policy.[50]

The struggles noted above—especially over policy on refugees and the slide away from democratic progress—have reinforced a deep "enlargement fatigue" among the leadership and people of the EU. Among all the EU publics, nearly half are opposed to further enlargement; among those living in the new CEE members, though, a majority favor enlargement.[51] With the EU divided on so many crucial issues, it seems unlikely that any of the Balkans states will find enough support for membership very soon.

Other states on the periphery of Europe, for example, Moldova, Armenia, Azerbaijan, Belarus, and Ukraine, have not been offered a "membership perspective." Instead, the EU hopes to exercise influence—and movement toward democracy and an open economy—by offering association agreements through its "Eastern Partnership" program begun in

2008.[52] The record has been mixed, but nowhere more problematical than with the largest non-EU "neighbor," Ukraine.

UKRAINE

Ukraine has a bifurcated history and ethnic composition (see chapter 17 on Ukraine) and only a brief record as a self-governing country. From its independence following the collapse of the USSR in 1991, the EU and especially some members like Poland have been eager to push it toward democratization, a more open, better-run economy, and a stronger relationship with the EU.

During the contested presidential elections at the end of 2004 (the Orange Revolution), the EU did not accept the election of Viktor Yanukovych and pushed strongly for new, fair elections. These made Viktor Yushchenko president. Ukraine was granted the status of "functioning market economy" and was considered a "priority partner country." EU-Ukrainian relations have been governed by a Partnership and Cooperation Agreement dating from 1998, and the EU has been the country's largest trading partner and the largest donor of technical assistance. Long negotiations eventually produced an association agreement, even though Viktor Yanukovych did succeed in becoming president in 2010. This agreement, the first of its kind for Partnership countries, was to provide for a stronger form of "political association" with the EU, including domestic reforms, and deeper economic ties, including the establishment of a free trade area.

Those very ties, however, alarmed Russia, which saw this as further Western incursion into a region in which it claims "privileged interests."[53] During 2013, a combination of political pressure and economic incentives (such as a lower price for natural gas) persuaded President Yanukovych to suspend plans to sign the association agreement. As a result of this action and accumulated frustrations with corrupt and ineffective government, huge demonstrations erupted in central Kyiv (labeled the "Euromaidan") that culminated in Yanukovych's fleeing the country to Russia in February 2014.

When a new interim government was formed, Russia continued to warn it against signing the agreement with the EU. At the same time, Moscow took advantage of upheaval in the country and secessionist sentiment in the Crimean Peninsula to forcibly wrest that territory from Ukraine. The EU, along with the United States, condemned the political machinations that accompanied this action, such as a referendum in which 96 percent of voters approved joining Russia, and applied targeted sanctions against Russian and pro-Russian Ukrainian elites. International condemnation notwithstanding, Crimea was annexed to Russia on March 21, 2014. The same day, the Ukrainian government signed the political provisions of the association agreement. The EU began immediately to implement free trade measures between the EU and Ukraine as part of a package of economic and political support measures designed to bolster Ukraine's economy and sovereignty.[54]

New presidential elections were held in May, even while a full-scale rebellion erupted in the eastern part of the country, led by forces opposed to the Kyiv government and supported by Russia. In June 2014, new president Petro Peroshenko signed the association agreement with the EU, including its provisions for a Deep and Comprehensive Free

Trade Agreement, which took effect in 2016. The EU is now Ukraine's largest trading partner and the full association agreement came into effect in 2017.[55]

The EU and the United States have applied an ever-widening package of sanctions against actors and sectors in the Russian economy because of their "illegal annexation of territory and deliberate destabilization of a neighboring sovereign country."[56] In mid-2016, these became linked to the implementation of the Minsk Agreements signed by Russia, Ukraine, Germany, and France in 2015 to put an end to the conflict. (See chapter 17 on Ukraine.) But the EU's leverage with Russia, as its largest export partner and leading investor, is blunted by its own dependence on Russian energy and by divisions within the EU over how best to deal with Moscow. For example, plans to greatly expand the supply of Russian gas directly to Germany (circumventing Ukraine and the CEE states) through a second Nord Stream pipeline have drawn severe criticism from several members and European Council president Donald Tusk.[57] Some, like Hungary, have gone ahead to sign their own deals with GAZPROM, Russia's dominant gas supplier.[58]

The broader question for the EU—and its eastern members—is whether it will continue to have influence beyond its borders, in places where membership is not "on offer" or where major external powers, like Russia, oppose that influence. Georgia and Moldova, for example, have also signed association agreements, including Deep and Comprehensive Free Trade Agreements. The EU is the largest trading partner for both and their citizens, like those of Ukraine, enjoy visa-free travel in the EU. Joining the EU is still the goal for most of the states of the Western Balkans.[59] Still, going forward, the EU will be smaller and still divided on a range of issues. But "hard" power was never its strength and division on the continent is not new. The question now is whether the EU's vaunted "soft" power—the appeal of its governing values and system—will still be as powerful.[60] The "new" democracies of Central and East Europe—now less new and, in some cases, less democratic—will have an important say in answering that question.

Implications for Political Science

A central problem in the study of world politics has always been the question of why states act in certain ways. Do they do so out of considerations of pure power (the realist point of view), because of the nature of their governments (the liberal point of view), because of changes in their identity (the constructivist point of view), or because of the role of international institutions (the liberal institutionalist point of view)?[61] If a state's behavior seems to conform to the dictates of other more powerful states, is this because it has no choice, because it truly associates itself with the behavioral norms of its neighbors, or because it sees gains in acting that way?

The case of the Central and East European states accepting and implementing the norms of the EU provides a real-world experiment for such theories, though, like all such experiments, only an approximate one.[62] In the real world, states cannot be put in laboratories with some variables held constant and others allowed to vary. But for the years since the revolutions, the states of Central and Eastern Europe and their paths represent an observable group of outcomes that can be studied comparatively. These states, with different cultures and histories and different experiences of conflict, all became democratic and were freed from the dominant power that had ruled their region. They all had strong economic and political incentives to join the EU. Their leaders and populations all claimed to want to adhere to democratic norms, and in most cases, they moved to do so, at least until after EU membership was achieved.

Yet, as this chapter and others in this volume have shown, both before and after the "Big Bang," the states of this region diverged, both from each other and from most of the countries that emerged directly from the USSR—for example, Ukraine. Grzymala-Busse, among others, suggests that now, a decade after Europe was formally reunited, divergences among Central and East European states are greater than those separating "east" from "west" Europe. Pointing to the rise of populism across the continent, she says, "If anything, the real divide runs between mainstream European political elites and large swaths of voters disappointed in what they perceive as the failure of their representatives to respond to their concerns."[63]

Exploring these differences and their contemporary implications leads us to numerous questions, both in the realm of international relations as well as comparative political studies. First, why were the newly liberated Central and East European states so willing to dance to the EU's tune? What combination of incentives or threats were applied and with what effect?[64] Second, what will happen now that membership (the major incentive) has been achieved?[65] Third, what external influence can the EU exert—especially in its new reduced form—beyond its borders? On the international stage, has the once dominant "soft power" influence of the EU been defeated by the hostility of local regimes to democracy and the "hard power" capabilities of traditional states like Russia?[66]

A fourth, a broadly ominous question is whether democracy, once achieved, can be reversed. The histories of Weimar Germany and post–Cold War Russia suggest that it can. But in both of those cases, there were few effective instruments of international engagement to support democracy. In the case of the EU and the states of Central and East Europe, there have been and continue to be instruments available to the "normative hegemon" (the EU).[67] And overall, the region has seen a persistence of democratic and economic reforms, even in the face of significant challenges. But in some cases, most notably Hungary and Poland, democratic practices have been seriously weakened, and the EU has been unable to reverse that trend. If that is the case, from the perspective of the EU and other major democracies, like the United States, the policy question is what, if anything, can be done to halt the slide? From the scholarly vantage point, we want to know why democracy succeeds, persists, and becomes robust in some countries but fails in others. What combination of domestic and international factors make the difference?[68]— a bigger question than this chapter or this book, to be sure, but one which the recent experience of East Central Europe and its intensive interaction with the EU can help answer.

Study Questions

1. What seems to explain the different paths to democracy and an open economy seen in Central and Eastern Europe? Is it determined by the past, or culture, or by contemporary political dynamics?

2. How do you explain the willingness of the Central and East European states to comply with comprehensive demands of the EU for membership so soon after regaining independence of action after the collapse of the Soviet alliance system?

3. Is there a link between economic success and democratization? Is democracy more successful in those Central and East European countries that are doing better economically, like Poland?

4. What are the factors that will explain the outcome in the tug-of-war over democracy between the EU as an organization and some of the states of Central and Eastern Europe? Will the EU and its members become less democratic or more so?

5. What strengths and weaknesses does the EU bring to the struggle for influence with Russia over Central and East Europe and the Balkans?

Suggested Readings

Bechev, Dimitar. *Rival Power: Russia in Southeast Europe*. New Haven, CT: Yale University Press, 2017.

Berend, Ivan T. *From the Soviet Bloc to the European Union: The Economic and Social Transformation of Central and Eastern Europe since 1973*. New York: Cambridge University Press, 2009.

Grabbe, Heather. *The EU's Transformative Power: Europeanization through Conditionality in Central and Eastern Europe*. New York: Palgrave Macmillan, 2006.

Haughton, Tim, ed. *Party Politics in Central and Eastern Europe: Does EU Membership Matter?* New York: Routledge, 2011.

Jacoby, Wade. *The Enlargement of the European Union and NATO: Ordering from the Menu in Central Europe*. Cambridge: Cambridge University Press, 2004.

Lewis, Paul, and Radoslaw Markowski, eds. *Europeanising Party Politics: Comparative Perspectives on Central and Eastern Europe*. Manchester: Manchester University Press, 2011.

Linden, Ronald H., ed. *Norms and Nannies: The Impact of International Organizations on the Central and East European States*. Lanham, MD: Rowman & Littlefield, 2002.

Pop-Eleches, Grigore, and Joshua Tucker. *Communism's Shadow: Historical Legacies and Contemporary Political Attitudes*. Princeton, NJ: Princeton University Press, 2017.

Schimmelfennig, Frank, and Ulrich Sedelmeier. *The Europeanization of Central and Eastern Europe*. Ithaca, NY: Cornell University Press, 2005.

Vachudova, Milada. *Europe Undivided: Democracy, Leverage, and Integration after Communism*. Oxford: Oxford University Press, 2005.

Websites

European Bank for Reconstruction and Development: http://www.ebrd.com/pages/homepage.shtml

European Union: http://europa.eu/index_en.htm

European Union, "Enlargement": http://europa.eu/pol/enlarg/index_en.htm

Freedom House: https://freedomhouse.org/; *Nations in Transit*: https://freedomhouse.org/report-types/nations-transit

M. E. Sharpe, *Problems of Postcommunism*: http://www.mesharpe.com/mall/results1.asp?ACR=PPC *Transitions Online*: http://www.tol.org

Visegrad Group: http://www.visegradgroup.eu/

Notes

I would like to thank Shane Killian, Kristen Flanagan, and Isabel Ranner for their research on this chapter.

1. For a discussion of the enlargement of the Council of Europe, see Peter Leuprecht, "Innovations in the European System of Human Rights Protection: Is Enlargement Compatible with Reinforcement?" *Transnational Law and Contemporary Problems* 8 (1998): 313–36.

2. Paul Marer, "Has Eastern Europe Become a Liability to the Soviet Union? (III) The Economic Aspect," in *The International Politics of Eastern Europe*, ed. Charles Gati (New York: Praeger, 1976), 65.

3. James L. Ellis, "Eastern Europe: Changing Trade Patterns and Perspectives," in *East European Economies: Slow Growth in the 1980s*, US Congress, Joint Economic Committee, 99th Cong., 2nd sess., March 28, 1986, 17, 24. Figures are for 1980.

4. Thad P. Alton, "East European GNP's Domestic Final Uses of Gross Product, Rates of Growth, and International Comparisons," in *Pressures for Reform in the East European Economies*, US Congress, Joint Economic Committee, 101st Cong., 1st sess., October 20, 1989, 81.

5. Michael Marrese and Jan Vanous, *Soviet Subsidization of Trade with Eastern Europe* (Berkeley, CA: Institute of International Studies, 1983).

6. These criteria can be seen on the European Union Law website, http://eur-lex.europa.eu/summary/glossary/accession_criteria_copenhague.html.

7. These annual reports can be searched on the website of the European Commission at: https://ec.europa.eu/neighbourhood-enlargement/countries/package_en.

8. In case a Central or East European state failed to fulfill its commitments in certain areas (internal market, justice, and home affairs) after accession, "safeguard clauses" were included in the Accession Treaty, allowing for "appropriate measures" to be taken by the European Commission to ensure full compliance. The full text of the Accession Treaty can be seen on the website of the European Parliament at: http://www.europarl.europa.eu/enlargement_new/treaty/default_en.htm.

9. For background on this process and the reports, see "Mechanism for Cooperation and Verification for Bulgaria and Romania," European Commission, http://ec.europa.eu/cvm/progress_reports_en.htm.

10. Estimates and censuses vary widely on the number of Roma. The best comparative assessment can be found in Zoltan Barany, *The East European Gypsies* (New York: Cambridge University Press, 2001), 157–64.

11. Dena Ringold, *Roma and the Transition in Central and Eastern Europe: Trends and Challenges* (Washington, DC: World Bank, 2000).

12. See Lynn M. Tesser, "The Geopolitics of Tolerance: Minority Rights under EU Expansion in East-Central Europe," *East European Politics and Societies* 17, no. 3 (Summer 2003): 483–532.

13. Michael Johns, "Do as I Say, Not as I Do: The European Union, Eastern Europe and Minority Rights," *East European Politics and Societies* 17, no. 4 (Fall 2003): 682–99.

14. Economic data can be found in the annual *Transition Reports* published by the European Bank for Reconstruction and Development in London, http://www.ebrd.com/news/publications/transition-report/transition-report-201617.html.

15. The term "PHARE" was derived from the French title for the assistance program originally designed for Hungary and Poland and later expanded to all the Central and East European countries.

16. For background on the CAP, see "The Common Agricultural Policy (CAP) and Agriculture in Europe—Frequently Asked Questions," European Union, http://europa.eu/rapid/press-release_MEMO-13-631_en.htm.

17. "Enlargement and Agriculture: An Integration Strategy for the EU's New Member States," European Union, http://europa.eu/rapid/pressReleasesAction.do?reference=IP/02/176&format=HTML&aged=1&language=EN&guiLanguage=en.

18. See Peter Mair, "Popular Democracy and EU Enlargement," *East European Politics and Societies* 17, no. 1 (Winter 2003): 58–63.

19. Public opinion polls on enlargement can be found at "Public Opinion and the Enlargement," European Commission, http://ec.europa.eu/commfrontoffice/publicopinion/topics/enlargement_en.htm.

20. European Commission, *Candidate Countries Eurobarometer 2002* (Brussels: European Commission, 2002), http://ec.europa.eu/commfrontoffice/publicopinion/archives/cceb/2002/cceb_2002_highlights_en.pdf.

21. European Commission, *Eurobarometer 2003.2: Public Opinion in the Candidate Countries* (Brussels: European Commission, 2003), http://ec.europa.eu/commfrontoffice/publicopinion/archives/cceb/2003/2003.2_full_report_final.pdf.

22. Referenda results for states joining in 2004 can be seen in Györgi Szondi, "The Eastern European Referendum Campaigns on the Accession to the European Union—A Critical Analysis," *Journal of Public Affairs* 7 (2007): 55–69, 59.

23. Andrea Čović, "Referendum Briefing No 18 Croatia's EU Accession Referendum, 22 January 2012," European Parties Elections and Referendums Network, http://www.sussex.ac.uk/sei/documents/epern-ref-no18.pdf.

24. Eurobarometers can be retrieved from http://ec.europa.eu/commfrontoffice/publicopinion/index.cfm.

25. "Report on Results of the Negotiations on the Accession of Cyprus, Malta, Hungary, Poland, the Slovak Republic, Latvia, Estonia, Lithuania, the Czech Republic and Slovenia to the European Union," European Commission, https://ec.europa.eu/neighbourhood-enlargement/sites/near/files/archives/pdf/enlargement_process/future_prospects/negotiations/eu10_bulgaria_romania/negotiations_report_to_ep_en.pdf.

26. Yan Matusevich, "Terms and Conditions Apply: Georgia and Ukraine's Visa-Free Victory," *Open Democracy Russia*, June 2, 2017.

27. For background and a timeline of Croatia's accession, see "Croatia," European Commission, Enlargement, http://ec.europa.eu/enlargement/countries/detailed-country-information/croatia.

28. The website of the European Commission is http://ec.europa.eu/index_en.htm. Nomination to the Commission does not automatically ensure approval. In 2010, the Bulgarian nominee to be commissioner of humanitarian aid was obliged to withdraw because of criticism in the European Parliament. Stephen Castle, "Bulgarian Drops Candidacy for European Commission," *New York Times*, January 19, 2010.

29. For a summary and explanation of the Lisbon Treaty, see http://europa.eu/rapid/press-release_MEMO-09-531_en.htm?locale=en. For discussion of the background and changes, see "The 'Treaty of Lisbon,'" *EurActiv.com*, http://www.euractiv.com/future-eu/treaty-lisbon/article-163412.

30. Freedom House, "Outlook for New Democratic Spring," *Nations in Transit 2005*. Available at: https://freedomhouse.org/report/nations-transit-2005/essay-outlook-new-democratic-spring.

31. Jan Strupczewski, "European Parliament Chastises Hungary on Rights, Eyes Sanctions Process," *Reuters*, May 17, 2017; "EU Criticism Mounts of Hungary's Crackdown on Foreign Universities," *Euronews*, June 4, 2017; "EU Threatens Hungary with Legal Action over Constitution," *EurActiv.com*, April 15, 2013; and Alexandra Sarlo and Maia Otarashvili, "Can the EU Rescue Democracy in Hungary?" *Eurasia Review*, August 1, 2013.

32. European Commission, "Rule of Law: European Commission Acts to Defend Judicial Independence in Poland," Brussels, December 20, 2017; and Alice Cuddy, "What Is 'Article 7'

and Why Was It Triggered against Poland?," *Euronews*, December 20, 2017. The Commission also brought a case against Poland in the European Court of Justice for a similar measure affecting the country's lower courts.

33. Richard Rose, *Understanding Post-Communist Transformation* (London: Routledge, 2009).

34. *The Pulse of Europe 2009: 20 Years after the Fall of the Berlin Wall,* Pew Global Attitudes Project, 2009.

35. Holly Case, "Shape-Shifting Illiberalism in East-Central Europe," *Current History* (March 2017): 112–15; and Michael Minkenberg, *The Radical Right in Eastern Europe: Democracy under Siege?* (New York: Palgrave Macmillan, 2017).

36. "EU to Sue Poland, Hungary and Czechs for Refusing Refugee Quotas," BBC News, December 7, 2017; and Aria Bendix, "EU Takes Legal Action against Czech Republic, Hungary, and Poland," *The Atlantic,* June 14, 2017.

37. "The East European Response to the 2015 Migration Crisis," Special Issue, *Slavic Review* 76, no. 2 (Summer 2017).

38. Jan Cienski, "Exports Buoy Fragile Recovery in Central and Eastern Europe," *Financial Times,* August 26, 2013, 4; and Mark Allen, "The Impact of the Global Economic Crisis on Central and Eastern Europe," IMF, http://www.imf.org/external/region/bal/rr/2011/022511.pdf.

39. Andrew Walker, "What Is the European Stability Mechanism?" BBC News, July 7, 2015. For the text of the "Fiscal Compact," see http://europa.eu/rapid/press-release_DOC-12-2_en.htm.

40. Lucia Virostkova, "Slovakia Takes Hard Look at Greek Talks," *EUobserver,* June 12, 2015.

41. European Commission, *Standard Eurobarometer* 85 (Spring 2016), 13. Available at: http://ec.europa.eu/commfrontoffice/publicopinion/index.cfm/Survey/getSurveyDetail/yearFrom/1974/yearTo/2016/surveyKy/2130.

42. European Commission, *Standard Eurobarometer* 85 (Spring 2016), 13. Available at: http://ec.europa.eu/commfrontoffice/publicopinion/index.cfm/Survey/getSurveyDetail/yearFrom/1974/yearTo/2016/surveyKy/2130, Annex.

43. Simon Taylor, "Orbán Accuses EU of Colonialism," *EuropeanVoice.com,* March 16, 2012.

44. Eurostat, "EU Imports of Energy Products—Recent Developments," May 10, 2017.

45. Linda Kinstler, "What Trump Means for Central and Eastern Europe," *The Atlantic,* November 28, 2016.

46. Christopher Hope, "Net Migration from Eastern Europe to Britain Slows to a Trickle after Brexit Vote," *The Telegraph,* May 25, 2017.

47. See the "Presidency Conclusions" of the Thessaloniki European Council, Council of the European Union, June 19 and 20, 2003, http://www.consilium.europa.eu/uedocs/cms_data/docs/pressdata/en/ec/76279.pdf.

48. For background on this dispute, see Sinisa Jakov Marusic, "Macedonia-Greece Name Dispute: What's in a Name?" *Balkan Insight,* June 30, 2011, http://www.balkaninsight.com/en/article/background-what-s-in-a-name.

49. Dan Bilefsky, "Serbia and Kosovo Reach Agreement on Power-Sharing," *New York Times,* April 19, 2013.

50. Stefan Lehne, "Serbia-Kosovo Deal Should Boost the EU's Western Balkans Policy," *Carnegie Europe,* April 23, 2012. For a review of the relationship since then, see United Nations, Security Council, "Rising Tensions Shrink Space for Dialogue between Serbia, Kosovo, Secretary-General's Special Representative Tells Security Council," February 27, 2017.

51. European Commission, *Standard Eurobarometer,* Table of Results, 83 (Spring 2015), 172. http://ec.europa.eu/commfrontoffice/publicopinion/archives/eb/eb83/eb83_anx_en.pdf.

52. See "Eastern Partnership Roadmap 2012–13: The Multilateral Dimension," European Commission, SWD (2012) 108 final, May 15, 2012; and "Joint Declaration of the Prague Eastern Partnership Summit, Prague, May 7, 2009" 8435/09 (Presse 78) Brussels, May 7, 2009.

53. Andrew Kramer, "Russia Claims Its Sphere of Influence in the World," *New York Times*, August 31, 2008.

54. For a text of the agreement, see "EU-Ukraine Association Agreement," European External Action Service, https://eeas.europa.eu/node/10420_en. See also European Council, "EU Relations with Ukraine," http://www.consilium.europa.eu/en/policies/eastern-partnership/ukraine/.

55. European Council, "EU-Ukraine Summit, 12–13/07/2017," http://www.consilium.europa.eu/en/meetings/international-summit/2017/07/12-13/. European External Action Service, "EU-Ukraine Association Agreement enters fully into force," 01/09/2017; http://eueuropaeeas.fpfis.slb.ec.europa.eu:8084/headquarters/headquarters-homepage/31591/eu-ukraine-association-agreement-enters-fully-force_en.

56. "Statement by President Barroso and President Van Rompuy in the Name of the European Union on the Agreed Additional Restrictive Measures against Russia European Commission—STATEMENT/14/244 29/07/2014," European Union, http://europa.eu/rapid/press-release_STATEMENT-14-244_en.htm. Sanctions have been repeatedly "prolonged" in time and occasionally "extended" to include more individuals and companies in Russia. See European Council, "Timeline—EU Restrictive Measures in Response to the Crisis in Ukraine." http://www.consilium.europa.eu/en/policies/sanctions/ukraine-crisis/history-ukraine-crisis/.

57. Georgi Gotev, "Commission Passes the Nord Stream 2 Buck to Member States," *Euractiv*, June 9, 2017. Rochelle Toplensky, "Tusk Adds Voice to Calls for Greater EU Control over Nord Stream," *Financial Times*, June 5, 2017.

58. Gabriella Lovas and Zoltan Simon, "Hungary Commits to Russia Gas Route as Poland Looks to U.S.," *Bloomberg*, July 7, 2017.

59. Ryan Heath, "The Race for EU Membership," *Politico*, December 15, 2016.

60. Karen E. Smith, "Is the European Union's Soft Power in Decline?" *Current History*, (March 2014): 104–9.

61. See James E. Dougherty and Robert L. Pfaltzgraff Jr., *Contending Theories of International Relations* (New York: Addison Wesley Longman, 2001), for a review of international relations theories.

62. Among those who see the postcommunist region as providing a "natural experiment," see Judith Kelley, "International Actors on the Domestic Scene: Membership Conditionality and Socialization by International Institutions," *International Organization* 58 (Summer 2004): 425–57.

63. Anna Grzymala-Busse, "An East-West Split in the EU?" *Current History* (March 2016): 89–94 (quote is p. 92).

64. See, e.g., the discussion in Milada Vachudova, *Europe Undivided: Democracy, Leverage, and Integration after Communism* (Oxford: Oxford University Press, 2005).

65. See the discussion in Tim Haughton, "When Does the EU Make a Difference? Conditionality and the Accession Process in Central and Eastern Europe," *Political Studies Review* 5 (2007): 233–46.

66. Karen E. Smith, "The European Union in an Illiberal World," *Current History* (March 2017), 83–87. On the difference in types of power, see Joseph S. Nye Jr., "Hard Power, Soft Power and the 'War on Terrorism,'" in *American Power in the Twenty-First Century*, ed. David Held and Mathias Koenig-Archibugi (Cambridge, UK: Polity Press, 2004), 114–33.

67. Thomas Diez, "Normative Power as Hegemony," *Cooperation & Conflict* 48, no. 2 (June 2013): 194–210.

68. Ulrich Sedelmeier, "Anchoring Democracy from Above? The European Union and Democratic Backsliding in Hungary and Romania after Accession," *Journal of Common Market Studies* 52, no. 1 (2014): 105–21.

CHAPTER 8

Security Issues

NATO AND BEYOND

Joshua Spero

After the fall of the Berlin Wall, the Warsaw Pact's dissolution marked the institutional end of the Cold War and Europe's division into two competing blocs, one dominated by the Soviet Union and the other by the United States. In the process, the North Atlantic Treaty Organization (NATO) ceased to be focused on protecting the West from a potential communist attack. Instead, getting NATO membership became a key incentive for former communist states to transition toward democracy and European integration. In the early years of the twenty-first century, the old NATO allies and their new partner nations moved to doing cooperative crisis management across the continent and thrust the Alliance into working beyond Europe.

Today, NATO stands at another crossroads with its members determining the next steps toward greater political-military integration between old and new members, as serious transatlantic disagreements with the United States grow and aggression from Russia against NATO's periphery increases. Consequently, this nearly seventy-year old post–Cold War Alliance continues to integrate its militaries into a unique multilateral command structure, already transitioning beyond the post-9/11 era, but confronting dangers to its survival, yet again, because of rising interallied tensions during relative peacetime.

How European democratization and integration will continue depends on developments between Russia and NATO, particularly the independent nations between East and West, including some that were formerly part of the USSR; non-NATO nations between North and South, some formally neutral and now European Union (EU) members; and those remaining in NATO, but institutionally exiting form the EU (United Kingdom). Given the 2014 Russia-Ukraine war that reinvigorated NATO's focus on its 1949 treaty's Article V collective defense commitment, the potential for greater regional conflicts on NATO's periphery and political differences between allied and non-NATO partner nations will challenge NATO's expansive twenty-first-century crisis management and cooperative security roles. However, the bottom line for NATO always is its collective action focus, where alliance cohesion stems from its members' collective contributions politically, economically, and militarily, especially the twenty-first-century contributions from non-NATO nations, some of which are not in Europe itself.[1] Thus, to avoid regional wars that threaten Europe's relative continental peace, NATO's long-term cohesion, military partnerships, and operational resiliency are needed to provide the peaceful linchpin that bridges Europe's ongoing political divides.

Even with the Russia-Ukraine war, NATO's post–Cold War focus has shifted from protecting Europe's Cold War division toward bringing all of Europe together, managing conflicts within Europe, and grappling with international terrorist networks, especially after September 11, 2001. It was to achieve these challenging goals that NATO aided and then took in the states of Central and East Europe, as they transformed their military forces and NATO leaders deemed these states, "democratic." During this period of rapid change, NATO forces were deployed outside NATO member-state territories as peacekeepers, peace enforcers, and then as fighters in Bosnia, Kosovo, Macedonia, Afghanistan, Iraq, and Libya.

The Warsaw Pact and Its Legacy

The inclusion of former Warsaw Pact members in NATO did not mean simply shifting players on a chessboard. The Warsaw Pact was formally established in 1955 as a response to the establishment of NATO to enforce existing Central and Eastern European subordination to Moscow as satellite nations and to match the NATO "threat." From weapons production to a politicized military leadership, the pact linked the militaries of the Soviet Union and its satellites together under Soviet control. Yugoslavia remained the only state in this region to avoid Warsaw Pact membership. After the invasion of Czechoslovakia in 1968, Albania withdrew from the Warsaw Pact, and Romania, which did not participate in the invasion, pursued its own independent foreign policies while still remaining a pact member.

Although high-level officers from Central and Eastern Europe remained part of the Warsaw Pact's hierarchy, Soviet officers and commanders controlled planning and military action. One way the Soviets controlled the Warsaw Pact was by enforcing a policy of equipment interoperability. To do this, they insisted that all Warsaw Pact forces share the same equipment and fit Soviet anti-NATO specifications. From airplanes to guns, interdependence was further enforced by not allowing any single country to produce all weapons and by giving states specific tasks under the direction of the Warsaw Pact and the Council for Mutual Economic Assistance. This intertwining of military control structures, therefore, prevented members from acting independently.

For the Soviet Union and Warsaw Pact, political control over all aspects of the military remained as important as military prowess and professionalism. The only military maneuvers the pact actually conducted were in 1968 to counter the liberalization in Czechoslovakia known as the Prague Spring. Later, although the Warsaw Pact did not intervene, the threat of maneuvers pressured Poland during the 1980–1981 unrest to impose martial law. For the conscripts and professional military, political and military training went hand in hand. Required military service for men out of school or during their college careers focused on indoctrination, though such indoctrination rarely succeeded. Even military oaths referred to defending the bloc and the Soviet Union rather than individual homelands.

The USSR also ensured the military reliability of the Warsaw Pact via the joint command and Warsaw Pact maneuvers. Pact forces upheld the mission of protecting

Map 8.1. Warsaw Pact and NATO States, 1989

the Soviet bloc. In the event of NATO action, each military was assigned a specific task. Ostensibly designated for offensive planning against the West, the pact lasted almost forty years until 1991. After the pact's collapse in 1991, crack troops from Soviet forces remained stationed along the Iron Curtain border between the East and West.[2]

After 1989, however, the pact itself immediately became a vestigial organization as newly democratizing Central and East European leaderships turned westward for economic and political guidance. The Soviet army's intervention in Latvia and Lithuania, then still part of the Soviet Union, in early 1991 to stop popular demands for independence made the Warsaw Pact's existence, even as a historical marker, unacceptable to Central and East European leaders. Soon after the intervention, the foreign ministers of Poland, Czechoslovakia, and Hungary demanded dissolution of pact military structures. In June 1991, the pact's foreign and defense ministers met to end its military functions. Nine months later, the USSR dissolved.[3]

Central and East European leaders whose countries had once been Warsaw Pact members now contended with dismantling the pact's Soviet-dominated political-military structures. For these countries to become members or partners of NATO, the once "ideological enemies" had to become trusted allies. A complete restructuring and reconstruction required several steps. First, each country needed to develop different, individual military chains of command separate from Russia's military. Second, each Central and East European country had to make a complete shift to Western weapons and equipment. Third, the logic for large militaries dependent on draftees needed to be rethought. The withdrawal of Soviet troops from the German Democratic Republic (East Germany), Poland, Czechoslovakia, and Hungary and their return to the USSR, a country whose economy at this point could not meet its population's demands, also had to be negotiated.

To join NATO, Central and East European states began restructuring their militaries and redefining civil-military relations, doing away with old pact weaponry, and investing in new equipment to fit NATO specifications. Professional high-ranking military officers from pact forces needed to become partners—at least "partners for peace"—with their old enemies. For these states, even with support and aid from the West, the cost of retooling militaries and committing to NATO membership was extremely high, given the costs of transition from communism and transition of the senior officers, many of whom were educated in Soviet military academies. But this first opportunity to become "official" parts of the West seemed worth the price, especially given some prominent political democratization debates across Central and Eastern Europe in the early 1990s over how quickly to change communist security structures and integrate westward rather than try to remain neutral.

When NATO was established in 1949, its members (Belgium, Canada, Denmark, France, Great Britain, Iceland, Italy, Luxembourg, Netherlands, Norway, Portugal, and the United States) agreed that the Soviet Union and its Eastern bloc posed the main threat to Western security. NATO members committed to defend each other if any non-NATO nation attacked a NATO member. This guarantee was focused mainly against a Soviet bloc invasion of the West. The security umbrella NATO provided in the early 1950s extended to vital sea-lanes from Greenland to Iceland and Britain. When NATO did expand, it strengthened its defense in 1952 during the Korean War by having Greece and Turkey become members to contain the Soviet Union on NATO's southeastern border. In 1955, the Federal Republic of Germany joined, putting NATO on the Iron Curtain's border dividing Germany and Europe as a whole, and in 1982, Spain was integrated into NATO. The membership of these two countries increased NATO's strategic depth and promoted democratization in those countries. In 1978, NATO reaffirmed its members' equal commitments by agreeing that 3 percent of each member's budget would be devoted to NATO.

The process of inclusion and developing NATO strategy avoided the strict Warsaw Pact hierarchical approach. Although a US general always headed NATO, the United States, which was the largest NATO donor, had limited influence in the organization because the many European-based US forces were separate from NATO. Joint maneuvers were "joint" rather than dominated by one leader over other countries. No attempt to meld these armies and the foreign policies of NATO states was allowed in the absence of an active threat. There was also no political training for forces involved in NATO missions.

Although many Cold War crises erupted in Europe and tensions between Greece and Turkey flared regularly, no attacks against NATO members occurred from outside NATO. Its troops did remain on high alert during the Berlin and Cuban crises, but they were never fully activated. Nonetheless, the presence of Soviet troops in Berlin, close to NATO's eastern borders, during the 1961 Berlin crisis and the Soviet-led Warsaw Pact invasion of Czechoslovakia in 1968 necessitated continual NATO vigilance against potential Soviet threats. Even after Western policy began to shift toward détente with the USSR, the United States and Western Europe continued to modernize their nuclear arsenals to defend Europe, if necessary. Ultimately, NATO held together even as the revolutions of 1989 changed European security rapidly.[4]

NATO's Redefinition

The collapse of communism first in Central and Eastern Europe and then the USSR exacerbated NATO's internal disagreements over the nature and purpose of the alliance given the lack of any clear "Soviet" threat. NATO's focus shifted rapidly during the initial postcommunist period from potential Soviet threats to NATO's enlargement, bringing the former Central and Eastern European "enemy states" into NATO. However, the eruption of violence in Yugoslavia—the first post–World War II large-scale violence within Europe—quickly complicated the postcommunist transition and dual enlargement processes, just as NATO began redefining critical threats. Yugoslavia's disintegration in 1991, during a decade of armed conflicts as that country broke apart, proved difficult for NATO because members, such as Germany, France, and the United Kingdom, maintained different commitments toward and concerns about the emerging independent post-Yugoslav nations. Subsequent NATO intervention at several key junctures in the post-Yugoslav wars challenged NATO's unity.

NATO's effort to deal with the new European reality began right after the Warsaw Pact collapsed, with the November 1991 New Strategic Concept. This strategic approach focused on a new European security policy with former pact countries before any of them fully transformed. NATO's transformation continued at the 1994 Brussels Summit, where the groundwork for NATO's post–Cold War role was set out by establishing combined joint task forces to support Europe's security and defense identity. Such an initiative was intended to strengthen European states' ability to work more effectively together and take more initiative. This allied shift, though, led to ongoing debate over NATO's role that lasted through the 1999 Washington Summit celebrating NATO's fiftieth anniversary and integrating its three newest members—the Czech Republic, Hungary, and Poland.

NATO Expansion: Integrating the East

At the same time that NATO searched for a new mission and better balance between Europe and America, Central and Eastern European leaders pressed to join NATO to affirm their Westernization and guard against Russian instability. NATO opted for a policy of inclusion to fulfill its long-term goal of a Europe "whole and free" but hesitated to enlarge immediately. In reality though, the process had begun, before the Warsaw Pact collapsed, at a NATO summit in London in July 1990, when NATO invited the Soviet Union and Warsaw Pact members "to establish regular diplomatic liaison with NATO."[5] Once the pact disbanded, NATO launched the North Atlantic Cooperation Council to

Photo 8.1.   NATO flag-raising ceremony marks the accession of the Czech Republic, Hungary, and Poland to the alliance. They were the first postcommunist countries to join NATO. In March 2003, Bulgaria, Estonia, Latvia, Lithuania, Romania, Slovakia, and Slovenia also joined, followed by Croatia and Albania in 2009. (NATO photos, 1999)

include former communist countries, without moving toward formal enlargement.[6] After the USSR disintegrated, NATO included some former Soviet republics in the North Atlantic Cooperation Council.

The North Atlantic Cooperation Council promoted dialogue on common security concerns with Central and Eastern Europe and post-Soviet states. The dialogue bridged the former East-West divide and started practical cooperation. It also helped Central and East European politicians understand how defense rooted in democracy-based politics, and national security encompassing civil emergency planning signified more than just military priorities. The 1994 Brussels Summit moved NATO leaders closer to enlargement by establishing the Partnership for Peace (PfP), which included those countries deemed "able and willing to contribute to European security."[7] PfP eventually involved all Central and Eastern European and post-Soviet states (except post-Yugoslav states at war during the 1990s) that desired to join and fulfilled the criteria for democratic and military reform. At the same time, membership was extended to Finland, Sweden, Austria, and Switzerland, established democracies that had maintained neutrality during the Cold War. Although the more democratic countries of Central and Eastern Europe saw PfP's establishment as more of "a policy for postponement," PfP addressed some of their key security concerns and established norms for partners wanting to contribute to common European security.[8] The Central and Eastern European states that initially participated in PfP became the core group of new states in the expanded European security process. Participation in extended political and military coordination for search and rescue,

Photo 8.2. NATO summit in 1994, where the Partnership for Peace program was established. Currently, thirty-five countries are members of the program. (NATO photos, 1999)

humanitarian assistance, and peacekeeping operations not only set the stage for NATO membership for some PfP partner nations but also established crucial ties for NATO operations beyond member territories.

The PfP process provided the foundation for membership invitations issued to Poland, Hungary, and the Czech Republic at the July 1997 Madrid Summit since NATO deemed these country transitions successful at "produc[ing] political, economic, social and military security." During this summit, NATO also restructured PfP to allow members' actual involvement in NATO military operations. When NATO extended membership invitations, it underscored that "no European democratic country . . . would be excluded from consideration" in future enlargements.[9]

These initial invitees joined NATO on its fiftieth anniversary, on March 12, 1999. As they joined, NATO launched its Membership Action Plan (MAP) to prepare nine more states for possible membership invitations (Albania, Bulgaria, Estonia, Latvia, Lithuania, Romania, Slovakia, Slovenia, and Macedonia). MAP initiation depended not just on military readiness but also on continuing democratization and market expansion. In order to become acceptable members of NATO, MAP nations were required to become

Map 8.2.   European Members of NATO, 2014

"producers" of security through equitable treatment of ethnic minorities, good neighbor relations with surrounding countries, and democratic oversight of the military.[10]

By the 2002 Prague Summit, many countries involved in the MAP process were deemed to have successfully fulfilled the action plan. As a result, NATO issued invitations to a large number of MAP countries, overcoming Russian opposition to having NATO integrate former Soviet republics. After Lithuania, Latvia, and Estonia were invited to join, NATO's eastern borders with Russia were extended. NATO also expanded into southeastern Europe with the addition of Bulgaria, Romania, and Slovenia; Slovakia was also included in this round of expansion. When these seven new members, comprising both former Soviet and former Yugoslav states, joined NATO in 2004, they demonstrated the impact of NATO on democratization and military cooperation. At successive NATO summits in Bucharest (2008) and on NATO's sixtieth anniversary in Strasbourg/Kehl (2009), Albania and Croatia joined the alliance, and Montenegro joined Macedonia as a MAP country, with the latter integrating into the Alliance in 2017 after the Warsaw Summit. After the 2003 Rose Revolution in Georgia and the 2004 Orange Revolution in Ukraine, both of those countries expressed their desire to become MAP countries as NATO membership shifted to southeastern Europe and Eurasia. Given the sensitivity of inviting countries bordering Russia and former Soviet republics outside the Baltic nations, particularly in the aftermath of the Russo-Georgian War in summer 2008, NATO hesitated to issue MAP invitations to Georgia and Ukraine. Yet, NATO attempted to maintain its long-term commitment to keep an "open door" policy for PfP and Euro-Atlantic partners to join NATO, including Russia.[11]

The Costs of Membership

Membership in NATO originally provided the fastest road for Central and Eastern European countries to join the West and shed their communist past. For former communist and postcommunist leaders, membership signified that their countries had freed themselves from Soviet dominance and reinforced their mantle of Western democracy. Poland's president, Aleksander Kwaśniewski, personified the ability of former communist leaders and states to transform into democracy-based NATO contributors. Despite being a former communist, on becoming president of Poland, Kwaśniewski actively led Poland's efforts to attain NATO membership. When Poland was accepted into NATO, he championed this step as proof that Poland had become a successful postcommunist democracy. NATO membership became most popular in Poland, among the original entrants, because of the country's long-held fear of Russian threats and its mantle as the first postcommunist country to elect a noncommunist leadership in June 1989. Membership was less significant for Hungarians and Czechs because of their greater sense of geographical security and their much smaller armies. But NATO's membership and security guarantee under Article V collective defense served as proof of change, hope for protection, and promise of investment and foreign aid.

All of these benefits came with real costs. Although former pact members often invested far more in the military during the communist period, NATO membership remained expensive. Transitioning from their old force structures, purchasing Western equipment, and making force commitments, as well as contributing financially, cut deeply into the budgets of these former pact states as they tried to become members of the EU. NATO membership did become a requirement for transitioning "into the West." Although it was a guarantee of security and not officially linked to EU membership, it emerged as a prerequisite for joining the EU. As a result, economic conditions in new NATO countries initially worsened. Indeed, soon after the first entrants joined NATO, their economies declined precipitously, although only in part as a result of the costs of membership. Given these costs, the need to stay within the fiscal budget deficit limits imposed by the EU on these same new NATO members only posed more economic challenges.

The issue of "guns versus butter," then, signified real trade-offs: funding social programs in areas such as unemployment, education, and health care, making necessary infrastructure investments in roads and train lines to fulfill EU demands, or funding modernization to meet NATO demands. These choices occurred in a context in which the economies, even in their worst periods, were in far better shape than during communism, at least until the 2007–2008 global economic crisis. The monies paid for development of the military could double, as they did in the early years in Poland, Hungary, and the Czech Republic, and the percentage of the budget going to the military remained relatively stable. Now, given the potential political backlash against the economic failure to "fund" the expected lifestyle improvements for large portions of the population, state expenditures on defense became politically difficult to justify. Yet, some of these northeast, Central, East, and southeast European NATO members increased their military expenditures domestically and their budgetary contributions to NATO as a result of Russia's annexation of Crimea from, and years-long battles along, Eastern Ukraine since 2014. Ironically, these newer frontline allies, particularly Poland, Estonia, and Romania, already contribute more to NATO militarily than many older NATO members. Along with key long-time, crucial members with sea-lanes, Norway and Britain, these new and old NATO members increased their GDP defense percentages—and, more importantly, hosted new NATO nations doing exercises and began building new military command and joint force structures on NATO's land/sea frontier areas with Russia.[12]

These recent NATO operational and strategic developments, especially on newer allied territories and along sea areas, attempt to balance with significant operational requirements in Afghanistan, Iraq, and Libya such substantial force and controversially financial contributions, some for over a decade. On the one hand, the prospect of having forces in Afghanistan and Iraq seemed to bring with it the promise of involvement in postwar reconstruction and alignment with the prestigious United States. On the other hand, it meant that new NATO members, also in most cases either new EU members or EU aspirants, got labeled as "Trojan horses" for US policy interests within NATO and within the EU. Contributing militarily to NATO—or to US-led operations in Afghanistan and/or Iraq—arguably strengthened new members' and aspirants' integration into Europe institutionally in the first decade of NATO enlargement. European integration and the Eurozone crisis also pressured already fragile aspirant and new member economies as the global recession's impact endangered national budgets. These political and economic challenges reduced NATO's effort in Libya, where air operations remained limited as the Europeans, with France and Britain in the lead, depended on US military logistics and resupplies to reinforce those on land. Therefore, throughout the early postrecession years, wary publics in aspirant and new member countries often voiced skepticism of further NATO and EU enlargement.[13]

NATO's New Roles: Deploying outside Europe and Reconsidering Collective Defense

In the early and mid-1990s, even as NATO debated its role and integrated new members into the alliance, NATO forces deployed with old and new members in ways never before attempted. In 1996, as part of the 1995 Dayton Peace Accords that ended the Bosnian War, NATO and PfP nations contributed to the Implementation Force set up to enforce the fragile peace agreement. When the Implementation Force's mission officially ended in December 1996, they continued to serve as members of the successful Stabilization Force, reinforcing Bosnia's rebuilding effort with the Organization for Security and Co-operation in Europe. This on-the-ground involvement, which was replayed in the Kosovo Force deployments to maintain the peace after NATO's bombing, also ended the Serb-Kosovar Albanian conflict and ethnic cleansing of Albanians that occurred in 1998 and 1999. Indeed, the seventy-eight-day NATO bombing campaign over Serbia and Kosovo drew NATO offensively into war, saving hundreds of thousands of Kosovar Albanians but reaching a new juncture in the defensive alliance's history, as nearly one thousand Serbs were killed.[14]

Photo 8.3.   Polish and American soldiers during NATO training in Eastern Poland. (PAP Agency)

NATO's involvement in former Yugoslavia's wars severely tested the alliance's cohesion. Since the Kosovo bombing campaign failed to gain a UN mandate, real difficulties erupted in 1999 when NATO needed consensus on military intervention in Serbia and Kosovo. Although the postbombing Kosovo Force operation did receive a UN mandate, justification for new military actions using old provisions complicated NATO's post–Cold War missions because different allies had different ties and commitments to Serbia. More complications emerged from the interests of some new NATO members and PfP partners who opposed military action in Kosovo, in contrast to their positions concerning the Bosnian settlement. For the United States, NATO's involvement in Bosnia and then Kosovo occurred primarily because the United States wanted to enforce peace and counter large-scale Serb aggression militarily without entering into a politically untenable commitment of US ground forces. For most European NATO members, the worst post–World War II European violence raised the need to stem huge refugee inflows across Europe from former Yugoslavia, which created serious socioeconomic burdens.[15]

NATO's political decision to make the Balkans part of NATO's "area of responsibility" led, in addition to actions in Bosnia and Kosovo, to NATO force deployments in Macedonia, where they successfully prevented conflict. These deployments occurred before any of the Balkan states, including the newly independent post-Yugoslav nations, became NATO members. The hope was that the 2004 accession of Slovenia, Romania, and Bulgaria would increase Balkan stability by demonstrating to the other states in the region that NATO membership remained possible. These newly admitted states soon started advocating and formulating policy inside NATO to include the rest of the Balkans (Croatia, Albania, and Macedonia, as well as Bosnia-Herzegovina, Serbia, and Montenegro). In the aftermath of September 11, 2001, prior integration of PfP members into NATO and advanced NATO ties to PfP partners also meant that the United States could use Balkan as well as Central Asian military bases to support operations in Afghanistan. Consequently, new NATO member Poland, particularly, and other PfP nations, with NATO allies, contributed ground force contingents to Afghanistan and later Iraq, while comparable multinational units also continued to be stationed in Kosovo and Bosnia.[16]

Since 9/11, NATO has struggled to reshape its defense capabilities to deal with the new risks of global terrorism. Due to these new globalized terrorist threats, NATO has included states in the Caucasus and Central Asia as participants, though they are not NATO members or potential members. It also has prompted more cooperation among NATO members against globalized terrorist networks, increasing the amount of shared intelligence and shared preparation for expanded nuclear, chemical, biological, or radiological threats. The risks, for NATO members, of undertaking collective defense increased dramatically after 9/11. Immediately after the attacks, NATO members invoked the Article V clause for the first time, ironically to support and protect the United States. Although the United States only supported the implementation of the NATO collective defense enactment weeks later, NATO ambassadors unanimously voted on September 12, 2001, to invoke Article V. Once the United States finally sought NATO support in the aftermath of 9/11, NATO planes and ships began to protect the continental United States. Then, in 2002, when the United States needed reinforcement in Afghanistan, some NATO members and PfP partners joined US forces there. In 2003, the United States requested that NATO take the lead on one of the Afghanistan operations. In the

NATO-led International Security Assistance Force in Afghanistan, Poland and the Czech Republic, among other NATO allies, led PfP member troops from Romania, Bulgaria, Ukraine, and Slovakia in combat. After the 2003 US–British-led invasion of Iraq, these NATO and PfP partner nations also contributed forces, as they did for counterinsurgency missions to rebuild Afghanistan. Poland commanded one of the three multinational sectors in Iraq alongside the United States and Britain.[17]

In the long run, the 9/11 attacks triggered significant splits within NATO, reflecting differing threat perceptions and approaches to coalition building in NATO-led operations. Even though NATO membership involves a commitment to a broader set of responsibilities and wider geographical areas of engagement, most recently clarified in the New Strategic Concept in 2010, disputes arose among old and new NATO members over the Iraq War. Of the original NATO states, only Great Britain, Spain, Italy, and the Netherlands provided military forces. The newer NATO states, particularly Poland and Romania, committed themselves in the early part of the war and sent either forces or specialized noncombat support units, despite strong popular opposition.[18] Not only did strains exist among NATO members over the war in Iraq from 2003 to 2011, but most NATO states remain unwilling to increase their defense budgets despite the widening gap in military capabilities and investment between the United States, its longtime allies, and new members. NATO's International Security Assistance Force mission in Afghanistan, which moved the alliance's focus away from European territorial defense, also lacked consensus as members differed on the importance of missions performed outside Europe.[19] Intraallied consensus faces continued challenges as most NATO nation forces transitioned from Afghanistan in 2014 and transferred security to Afghanistan, a decision taken at NATO's May 2012 Chicago Summit and reinforced at NATO's September 2014 Wales Summit. Yet, allies committed to remain in Afghanistan for training, advising, and assistance missions for the nation's security forces and civilian and military institutions. Given the reality of continued instability in Afghanistan, NATO and Afghanistan agreed to initiate NATO's Resolute Support Mission in January 2015 and advanced at NATO's Warsaw Summit in July 2016—and this doesn't involve alliance combat forces in the wake of the Russia-Ukraine war since 2014.[20]

Such intraalliance tensions over force deployments beyond Europe also led to tensions within the alliance and with Russia over NATO's more recent strategic focus on the Black Sea, the Caucasus, and Central Asia, as well as over future NATO membership for Ukraine and Georgia. In an attempt to dilute and weaken NATO, Russia has tried to influence NATO debates about membership for Ukraine and Georgia. To a certain extent, Russian leaders see their Central and East European counterparts as working to bring countries that border Russia, and that Russia regards as within its sphere of interest, westward into NATO. However, Russian leaders also believe that many NATO allies remain hesitant to vote on new members, as many states do not want to irritate Russia, whose cooperation NATO needs for missions outside Europe and on whom many of the states in Western Europe largely depend for their energy needs.[21] Consequently, between 2008 and 2009, it was mainly the United States and the Central and East European states that supported potential NATO membership paths for Ukraine and Georgia. Although NATO allies voiced significant concern over Russian military tensions with Ukraine—particularly concerning the transit of Russian energy supplies to Europe via Ukraine, the Russo-Georgian War, and Russia's territorial annexation of Crimea—NATO found itself facing larger security dilemmas outside Europe where NATO either needed Russia's cooperation or NATO nations refused to confront Russia militarily. Thus, disagreements among members concerning how best to deal with the threat of periodic cutoffs of Russian oil and natural gas supplies for Western Europe via Central and East European pipelines and NATO military deployment commitments abroad, let alone within Europe, continually hampered NATO consensus on further enlargement.[22]

Paradoxically, Russian endeavors to counter NATO actions relied even more effectively on debating within the NATO-Russia Council, at least before the Russia-Ukraine crisis. Though alliance decisions occur at the North Atlantic Council, the highest NATO body, which excludes non-NATO PfP partners such as Russia, Russian concerns raised in the NATO-Russia Council affect the decisions arrived at by NATO members.[23] Before the Russo-Georgian War worsened NATO-Russia ties, Russia threatened NATO on future NATO MAP invitations for Ukraine and Georgia. Russian speeches at the NATO headquarters and consistently after the NATO April 2008 summit threatened military intervention in Ukraine and Georgia if MAP invitations emerged. These threats caused major reactions in European capitals. Such Russian threats also set the stage for more antagonistic politico-military maneuvering to disrupt NATO consensus, particularly in the aftermath of the Russo-Georgian War in August 2008.[24]

The geopolitical impact of the Russo-Georgian War on NATO-Russia relations became clearer both in NATO's suspension of NATO-Russia Council sessions for several months and in NATO taking some decisions that favored Russian military strategy. NATO's sixtieth-anniversary summit in April 2009 demonstrated how the Russian military incursions in Georgia had slowed inroads toward alliance made by recent members and aspirant partners. The alliance distanced itself from enlargement with Ukraine and Georgia and retreated on missile defense in Poland and the Czech Republic. Divisiveness among allies grew over Russian military threats on NATO's eastern periphery, especially the postwar breakaway Georgian regions in Abkhazia and South Ossetia. The reduced commitment to enlargement and slowed MAP progress for Ukraine and Georgia evident in NATO declarations underscored allied divergence.[25] Indeed, the US missile defense system initiative in Poland and the Czech Republic before the April 2009 NATO summit initially gained alliance support. However, by the summit's end, NATO developments veered away from a US–Central European–NATO effort and, in fact, began to focus on a US-NATO-Russian one.[26] The April 2009 summit's declaration appeared to affirm Russian military objectives.[27] Russian arguments against missile defense influenced such important Western European leaders as Germany to diverge from its Central and East European and US counterparts.[28] Dissension in NATO also emerged as NATO nations downplayed Iranian threats to Europe, while Russia rejected proposed US antiballistic missile defenses based on Russian territory. By the fall of 2009, the deal to trade US missile defense systems in Poland and the Czech Republic for suspension of sales of Russian S-300 surface-to-air missile systems to Iran emerged in US-Russian negotiations.[29]

By NATO's May 2012 Chicago Summit, NATO enlargement remained on the back burner, while NATO theater ballistic missile defense appeared to take priority. Such missile defense concentrated on Turkey and threats from the Syrian civil war rather than from Iran. At the same time, NATO allies and partners began to cooperate on some missile defense via the NATO-Russia Missile Data Fusion Center and joint Planning Operations Center. But the Russia-Ukraine crisis, particularly after Russia's annexation of Crimea in March 2014, ruptured NATO-Russia ties, suspending the NATO-Russia Council, again. Even given the slowdown in enlargement, missile defense, and official NATO-Russia ties, the Alliance's impact throughout northeastern, Central, Eastern, and southeastern Europe grew politically and operationally as the Russian-Ukrainian war escalated in 2014 and Russian military pressure spurred divisiveness within NATO.[30]

Although significant alliance tensions with Russia rose resulting in new efforts to reverse declining NATO nation resource contributions to the alliance's trilateral approach of collective defense, crisis management, and cooperative security, NATO nations came to terms with Russia's renewed threats on NATO nation borders. To confront the rapidly increasing threats, among others, of regional civil wars, massive refugee flows, and expanding international terrorist networks from North Africa and the Middle East, NATO slowly revitalized one of its original, core missions to counter large-scale military threats continentally in Europe during the past several years. The uprisings across North Africa and the Arab nations between 2011 and 2013 resulted in NATO's air mobilization from spring through the summer of 2011 in Libya. Remarkably, the UN Security Council gave unanimous approval to have NATO regionally help Libyans seek refuge within Libya as the country disintegrated. In Operation Unified Protector, NATO protected civilians from mass slaughter primarily with sortie and air-strike missions, a regional role that the Arab League supported. Yet, even as the initial UN mandate for NATO action in Libya received Russian support, primarily because NATO's leading nations pledged not to use the alliance offensively, Russia's approval evaporated when NATO determined to strike Libyan military forces as a means of protecting Libyan civilians. Hence, continued tensions within NATO and with Russia over Libya compounded intra-alliance tensions preceding the Russia-Ukraine crisis, while concerns persist about future out-of-area missions. Even more tellingly, although the United States pushed France and Britain to take the lead in Operation Unified Protector, without US logistical and operational military reinforcement for the sortie and strike missions, NATO's Libyan operation might have collapsed. Clearly, some of the lessons emerging from Unified Protector pointed toward long-lasting failures in full alliance interoperability and long-term European NATO member defense cuts. After the UN-mandated and NATO-led operation in Libya, such negative NATO military trends give pause to other out-of-NATO area operations, particularly as NATO returns to its collective defense mission in new ways not considered since the end of the Cold War. Time will tell since large-scale upheaval hampers Libya and, regionally, Morocco, Algeria, Tunisia, Egypt, Mali, Niger, Sudan, and Somalia, in combination with upheavals projected from Syria, Jordan, Israel, Yemen, Iraq, Iran, Afghanistan, and Pakistan, as security dilemmas across North Africa, the Middle East, and Southwest Asia portend more threats to NATO's members and partners in Europe and Eurasia. Particularly destabilizing to these nations and regions are al-Qaeda's terrorist network offshoots and emergence of the Islamic State—with ironic potential that, as NATO begins building up its collective defense capabilities against a possible Russian military threat along the Alliance's periphery, NATO nations and Russia may find common ground in trying to counter such international terrorist networks intent on greater attacks against Russian, European, and North American targets.[31]

NATO Today and Tomorrow

The fate of the next phase for NATO's transformation and its impact on its newest members of the past two decades certainly remains challenging, especially in ways not often understood for burden-sharing on the Alliance's three key pillars: collective defense, crisis management, and cooperative security. Resilience, agility, innovation, and adaptation are key to the pragmatic allied determination to continue transforming NATO by putting a "persistent federated approach" into practice. To counter arguments over obsolescence and faltering collective defense commitments,[32] Allied Command Transformation, one of NATO's new twenty-first-century military leaderships—the only integrated military command structure outside of Europe in Norfolk, Virginia—reinforces NATO's three pillars and federated approach:

> With a persistent connection between the Alliance decision-making structures and national structures, danger signs could be spotted earlier, and the necessary assets available in members' inventories to monitor and if necessary to react to developments could be employed with much greater agility and effectiveness.[33]

Pivotally, NATO's Warsaw Summit in July 2016, building on the transformative initiatives promulgated at its Wales Summit from September 2014 for implementation, began revitalizing the Alliance operationally, strategically, and politically. By reinvigorating its collective defense capabilities and focusing for the first time on new member nation territories, NATO leaders began concentrating on better political coordination regarding differing national strategic threat perceptions and interests. NATO nations forged new discussions and debates about the definition of its Article V defenses, potentially opening the way for nonmilitary responses to threats against allies, particularly when new challenges constantly put the Alliance on guard from outside and within: not only increasing its collective defense requirements against Russian aggression countering expansive international terrorist networks and growing cyberattacks, and girding for larger refugee migrations, but also finding greater Allied Partner cooperative crisis management to try handling authoritarian trends in key front-line allies, Turkey and Poland. Given NATO's new strategic depth with new Allied territories to defend against these conventional and unconventional twenty-first-century threats, some from aggressive nation-states, others by hostile nonstate actors, Allies and Partners moved to bridge their differences politically, confronting challenges to Alliance integrity. NATO's cohesion only remains as strong as its transatlantic linkages to Canada and the United States, especially as Great Britain exits the EU and Russia divides Allies, most dangerously splitting Germany from the United States. Thus, Allies quickly began implementing far-reaching operational changes since 2015 in NATO's command and force structure eastward, led by the United States and Britain to reinforce the Alliance's three pillars along NATO's vastly larger periphery.[34]

Importantly, several years ago, many European leaders also realized that their Eurozone economic dilemmas need not preclude them and their societies from contributing more militarily and more concertedly to the regional and international security NATO provides Europe. Even as European allies and partners remain dependent on the

US military for out-of-Europe NATO military operations, some burden-sharing problems have declined as Europeans recognized within NATO the necessity for reinvigorating the Alliance's security across Europe. Subsequently, to avoid hollowing out NATO and reduce intra-alliance dysfunction, NATO's territorial defense rather than significant out-of-NATO-area expeditionary capabilities have become the priorities. As a result, there is already a redirection of resources, personnel, and strategy to NATO's periphery, demonstrating interallied cooperation and cohesion to manage crises better and start preparing more effectively against invasion.[35]

All Europeans face the reality that, unless they keep contributing more militarily, not only raising defense budget increases to 2 percent of GDP, when that is possible, but also expanding critical interallied information sharing, training, exercising, and operations planning, NATO needs to accelerate on the US allied initiatives launched at the NATO 2014 Wales and 2016 Warsaw Summits. Indeed, the long-running debate over NATO versus EU resources continues to challenge the security vulnerabilities that Europeans believe are most significant.[36] After all, the growing conflicts in North and Central Africa, the Middle East, and Southwest Asia endanger NATO allies and partners, particularly with globalized terrorist networks, constant on-the-ground attacks and cyberattacks throughout Europe and North America, and mass migrations of people from non-European war zones.

Yet, even taking these out-of-Europe concerns into account, NATO's revitalization stems, once again, from its age-old adage regarding traditional fears of Eastern threats and maintaining its allied cohesion: Russia's growing military redeployments on and along the non-NATO Eastern Ukrainian border area, along the three Baltic NATO nation borders, the Kaliningrad Russian region that splits Poland from the Baltic nations, and the Black Sea bastion spanning allies Turkey, Bulgaria, and Romania—and PfP Partners, Ukraine, and Moldova. As NATO redefines Europe eastward, the northeast, Central, East, and southeast European nations no longer delineate the border of West and East or North and South, but act as bridges to the East from the heart of Europe. They need NATO's backing as long as threats exist from an increasingly authoritarian Russia and some of its unreformed PfP partners along NATO's eastern periphery, even those located on Afghanistan's borders.[37]

As the heads of state agreed at NATO's 2016 Warsaw Summit, building form their commitment at the 2014 Wales Summit, the potential turning point in NATO's post-9/11 transition to its new stage of adaptation, perhaps the key to the Alliance's survival, emerged from this short statement in its lengthy Communiqué:

> NATO has responded to this changed security environment by enhancing its deterrence and defense posture, including by a forward presence in the eastern part of the Alliance, and by suspending all practical civilian and military cooperation between NATO and Russia, while remaining open to political dialogue with Russia.[38]

The outcome of this strategic and operations-planning statement entailed significant increases in the US, British, Canadian, and German battalion-sized battle groups deployed consistently and voluntarily for rotational training and exercising on NATO eastern periphery territories (Estonia, Lativa, Lithuania, and Poland). First, reassurance on these forces and equipment buttressed NATO's new Readiness Action Plan on defense and crisis response for hybrid warfare and covert paramilitary operations, both crucial missions coordinated with the EU. Tacitly, these new defense projections targeted potential Russian aggression and globalized terrorist network attacks. Second, NATO's Response Force involved two key facets for phased implementation: immediate reinforcement of "Assurance Measures" and long-term force posture for "Adaptation Measures."[39]

These "measures" involved a series of steady force increases focused on rapid implementation and deployment: NATO's Very High Readiness Joint Task Force, exercising since 2015 and comprising France, Germany, Italy, Poland, Spain, Turkey, and the United Kingdom; SMART Defense/Connected Forces Initiatives between NATO and national forces for eight future Force Integration Units/Headquarters; a Combined Joint Expeditionary Force delineating a division-size land element with air, maritime, and special forces components; Multinational Corps Headquarters in northeastern Europe, reinforced for multinational division headquarters in Poland, and the establishment, from a Romanian effort, of a multinational framework brigade to advance integrated training of Allied units in a Multinational Division Headquarters/Southeastern Europe/Black Sea region; Joint Surveillance and Reconnaissance Initiative; increased Allied Ground Surveillance; expanded Airborne Early Warning and Control Force; and Enhanced Cyber Defense Policy. According to NATO, such "Assurance Measures" remain "flexible and scalable in response to the evolving security situation, and will be kept under annual review by the North Atlantic Council," to include reinforcement efforts to help Turkey, given its frontline status to the Middle East and North Africa.[40]

Consequently, membership in NATO, as well as in the EU, for all its costs, remains necessary to becoming part of a democratized Europe in the twenty-first-century and as a force for promoting democratic values, to the greatest extent possible. Although some NATO and EU member states are weak in consolidating or maintaining durable democracies, they appear unlikely to revert to communism or deep-seated authoritarianism. Instead, they need the pull the Alliance provides for its leaders, as NATO peacefully pushes Europe's security and stability eastward.

Ultimately, 2014 became pivotal to NATO's reemergence as the security institution of Europe. NATO's revival may well solidify because of Poland's key frontline border with Ukraine and its keen ties with Ukraine's post–Cold War leaders. Furthermore, Germany's unique leadership linkages with Russia since the Cold War's collapse buttress the Poland-Germany partnership with Europe and the United States. For great powers and international institutions trying to bring an end to the Russia-Ukraine war, this Poland–Germany bridge-building maintains West-East consultation and economic linkages to Ukraine and Russia. Having emerged with postcommunist Poland in 1989 under the Solidarity trade union and underground dissident movement to play the key Central and East European role[41] in unifying Germany for twenty-first-century Europe's integration, the Poland–Germany heartland bridge will significantly influence, more than separately, the next EU and NATO moves for Ukraine, Russia, and beyond.[42]

Since the NATO Alliance constantly faces new threats, the Allies soon need to decide on a New Strategic Concept process so that NATO continually adapts and transforms institutionally.[43] The real challenge becomes managing or successfully overcoming the geostrategic maneuvering between and among Russia, the new members of the alliance, and older member states, in the face of the smaller role of the United States in Europe—and, likely, internationally.[44] From NATO's creation, the USSR and now Russia have long wanted to dilute NATO politically and militarily, if not cause its collapse.[45] Yet, NATO's survival depends on how well it manages intra-alliance political differences over its operations and strategic planning in Europe and beyond—strengthening alliance resources and capabilities. Ironically, while a NATO out-of-area failure in Southwest Asia/Afghanistan might imperil alliance unity and possibly the alliance's future, interallied differences over the transatlantic linkages could destabilize the Alliance itself. This fraying of the decades-old political enlargement and military integration process for so many new Eastern members—and their Eurasian partners—more than likely might harm European and US national security strategies if leaders don't strengthen and heal the transatlantic link.

Study Questions

1. Is NATO the effective security institution for Europe in the twenty-first century?
2. How significantly has NATO's mission changed since the end of the post–Cold War era?
3. Should NATO have deployed forces from its contributing member and partner nations beyond the borders of its member states, starting in the mid-1990s for the first time?
4. What might be the most useful institutional relationship NATO could have with the EU?
5. How might NATO consider its options if the United States decides to have its NATO allies take much more responsibility in the years ahead, or even withdraw significantly from NATO's integrated military command structure?

Suggested Readings

Alexander, Yonah, and Richard Prosen. *NATO: From Regional to Global Security Provider.* Lanham, MD: Lexington Books, 2015.

Asmus, Ronald. *Opening NATO's Door: How the Alliance Remade Itself for a New Era.* New York: Columbia University Press, 2002.

Collins, Brian J. *NATO: A Guide to the Issues.* Westport, CT: Praeger Security International, 2011.

Duignan, Peter. *NATO: Its Past, Present, and Future.* Stanford, CA: Hoover Institution Press, 2000.

Goldgeier, James. *Not Whether but When: The U.S. Decision to Enlarge NATO.* Washington, DC: Brookings Institution, 1999.

Hodge, Carl C. *NATO for a New Century: Atlanticism and European Security.* Westport, CT: Praeger, 2002.

Hoffmann, Stephanie C. *European Security in NATO's Shadow.* Cambridge: Cambridge University Press, 2012.

Johnston, Seth. *How NATO Adapts: Strategy and Organization in the Atlantic Alliance since 1950.* Baltimore, MD: Johns Hopkins University Press, 2016.

Kaplan, Lawrence S. *NATO Divided, NATO United: The Evolution of an Alliance.* New York: Praeger, 2004.

Kay, Sean. *NATO and the Future of European Security.* Lanham, MD: Rowman & Littlefield, 2003.

Mayer, Sebastian, ed. *NATO's Post-Cold War Politics: The Provision of Security.* London: Palgrave Macmillan, 2014.

Michta, Andrew A. *The Limits of Alliance: The United States, NATO and the EU in North and Central Europe.* Lanham, MD: Rowman & Littlefield, 2006.

Moore, Rebecca C. *NATO's New Mission: Projecting Stability in a Post–Cold War World.* New York: Praeger, 2007.

Papacosma, Victor S., Sean Kay, and Mark R. Rubin, eds. *NATO after Fifty Years.* Wilmington, DE: Scholarly Resources, 2001.

Hyde-Price, Adrian, and Mark Webber, eds. *Theorizing NATO: New Perspectives on the Atlantic Alliance.* London: Routledge, 2016.

Ivanov, Ivan Dinev. *Transforming NATO: New Allies, Missions, and Capabilities.* Lanham, MD: Lexington Books, 2013.

Simon, Jeffrey, ed. *NATO Enlargement: Opinions and Options.* Washington, DC: National Defense University Press, 1996.

Sloan, Stanley R. *NATO, the European Union and the Atlantic Community.* 2nd ed. Lanham, MD: Rowman & Littlefield, 2005.

Sloan, Stanley R. *Permanent Alliance?: NATO and the Transatlantic Bargain from Truman to Obama.* New York: Bloomsbury Academic, 2010.

Sloan, Stanley R. *Defense of the West: NATO, the European Union and the Transatlantic Bargain.* Manchester, UK: Manchester University Press, 2016.

Spero, Joshua B. *Bridging the European Divide: Middle Power Politics and Regional Security Dilemmas.* Lanham, MD: Rowman & Littlefield, 2004.

Yost, David. *NATO Transformed: The Alliance's New Roles in International Security.* Washington, DC: United States Institute of Peace, 1999.

Yost, David. *NATO's Balancing Act.* Washington, DC: United States Institute of Peace, 2014.

Websites

NATO on Twitter: https://twitter.com/NATO
NATO on YouTube: https://www.youtube.com/NATO
North Atlantic Treaty Organization (NATO): http://www.nato.int

Notes

The previous version of this chapter in the second edition of this volume was coauthored by Jeffrey Simon and Joshua Spero, based on Simon's chapter from the first edition.

1. Joshua B. Spero, "Considering NATO's Long-Term Revitalization," *E-International Relations,* July 30, 2014, http://www.e-ir.info/2014/07/30/considering-natos-long-term-revitalization/ (accessed August 14, 2014).

2. Zbigniew Brzezinski, *The Grand Failure: The Birth and Death of Communism in the Twentieth Century* (New York: Collier, 1989).

3. Andrew Michta, *East Central Europe after the Warsaw Pact: Security Dilemmas in the 1990s* (New York: Greenwood, 1992).

4. Jeffrey Simon, ed., *European Security Policy after the Revolutions of 1989* (Washington, DC: National Defense University Press, 1991).

5. Heads of State and Government, "London Declaration on a Transformed North Atlantic Alliance," meeting of the North Atlantic Council in London, July 6, 1990, paragraph 7.

6. Heads of State and Government, "Rome Declaration of Peace and Cooperation," meeting of the North Atlantic Council in Rome, Press Release S-1(91)86, November 8, 1991, paragraph 11.

7. "Declaration of the Heads of State and Government Participating in the Meeting of the North Atlantic Council in Brussels," Press Communiqué M-1(94)3, January 11, 1994, paragraph 13.

8. These occurred in the form of individual partnership programs (IPPs), which involved broad cooperation in the planning and review process, peace support operations, moves to ensure transparency, and the development of democratic oversight of the military.

9. Heads of State and Government, "Madrid Declaration on Euro-Atlantic Security and Cooperation," meeting of the North Atlantic Council in Madrid, July 8, 1997, paragraph 8.

10. North Atlantic Treaty Organization (NATO), "Study on NATO Enlargement," in *NATO Handbook*, October 8, 2002, http://www.nato.int/docu/handbook/2001/hb030101.htm (accessed January 11, 2010); and "Membership Action Plan (MAP)," *Topics*, April 2, 2009, http://www.nato.int/issues/map/index.html (accessed January 11, 2010).

11. Sean Kay, *Global Security in the Twenty-First Century: The Quest for Power and the Search for Peace*, 2nd ed. (Lanham, MD: Roman & Littlefield, 2011); and Andrew A. Michta, "NATO Enlargement Post-1989: Successful Adaptation or Decline?" *Contemporary European History* 18, no. 3 (2009): 363–76.

12. Kedar Pavgi, "NATO Members' Defense Spending, in Two Charts," *Defense One*, June 22, 2016, http://www.defenseone.com/politics/2015/06/nato-members-defense-spending-two-charts/116008/?oref=d-river (accessed May 25, 2017); and Sigurd Neubauer, "Norway, an Exemplar of NATO Burden-Sharing: What the Alliance Can Learn from Oslo," *Foreign Affairs*, January 2, 2017, https://www.foreignaffairs.com/articles/norway/2017-01-02/norway-exemplar-nato-burden-sharing (accessed May 24, 2017); and David Shlapak and Michael W. Johnson, "Outnumbered, Outranged, and Outgunned: How Russia Defeats NATO," *War on the Rocks*, April 21, 2016, https://warontherocks.com/2016/ 04/outnumbered-outranged-and-outgunned-how-russia-defeats-nato/ (accessed May 25, 2017).

13. Joshua B. Spero, "Great Power Security Dilemmas for Pivotal Middle Power Bridging," *Contemporary Security Policy* 30, no. 1 (April 2009): 147–71; Sean Kay, "Indecision on Syria and Europe May Undermine America's Asia Pivot," Commentary and Analysis, *War on the Rocks*, July 8, 2013, http://warontherocks.com/2013/07/indecision-on-syria-and-europe-may-undermine-americas-asia-pivot (accessed August 20, 2013); and Andrew A. Michta, "After the Summit: NATO Must Invest Real Money to Stay in Business," *The American Interest*, July 10, 2016, http://www.the-american-interest.com/2016/07/10/nato-must-invest-real-money-to-stay-in-business/ (accessed May 25, 2017).

14. Ivo H. Daalder and Michael E. O'Hanlon, *Winning Ugly: NATO's War to Save Kosovo* (Washington, DC: Brookings Institution, 2000).

15. Steven L. Burg and Paul S. Shoup, *The War in Bosnia-Herzegovina: Ethnic Conflict and International Intervention* (Armonk, NY: M. E. Sharpe, 1999); and Sabrina P. Ramet, *Thinking about Yugoslavia: Scholarly Debates about the Yugoslav Breakup and the Wars in Bosnia and Kosovo* (Cambridge: Cambridge University Press, 2005).

16. Joshua Spero, "Paths to Peace for NATO's Partnerships in Eurasia," in *Limiting Institutions: The Challenge of Eurasian Security Governance*, ed. James Sperling, Sean Kay, and S. Victor Papacosma (Manchester, UK: Manchester University Press, 2003), 166–84.

17. *East Europe's New Role in the Middle East*, Special Report, Woodrow Wilson International Center for Scholars, January 2004.

18. Joshua B. Spero, "Beyond Old and New Europe," *Current History* 103, no. 671 (March 2004): 135–38.

19. Zbigniew Brzezinski, "An Agenda for NATO," *Foreign Affairs* 88, no. 5 (September–October 2009): 2–20; and Karl-Heinz Kamp, "Toward a New Strategy for NATO," *Survival* 51, no. 4 (August–September 2009): 21–27.

20. NATO, "Chicago Summit Declaration on Afghanistan: Issued by the Heads of State and Government of Afghanistan and Nations Contributing to the NATO-led International Security Assistance Force (ISAF), NATO, May 21, 2012, http://www.nato.int/cps/en/SID-1BBDB541-FD5ACE96/natolive/official_texts_87595.htm (accessed August 20, 2013); NATO, "Wales Summit Declaration: Issued by the Heads of State and Government Participating in the Meeting of the North Atlantic Council in Wales," Press Release (2014) 120, September 5, 2014, http://www.nato.int/cps/ic/natohq/ official_texts_112964.htm (accessed may 25, 2017); and NATO, "Warsaw Summit Declaration on Afghanistan: Issued by the Heads of State and Government of Afghanistan and Allies and their Resolute Support Operational Partners," Official Texts (Chronological), Press Release (2016) 121, July 9, 2016, http://www.nato.int/cps/en/natohq/official_texts_133171. htm?selectedLocale=en (accessed May 24, 2017).

21. Adrian Karatnycky and Alexander J. Motyl, "The Key to Kiev," *Foreign Affairs* 88, no. 3 (May–June 2009): 106–20; and Charles King, "The Five-Day War," *Foreign Affairs* 87, no. 6 (November–December 2008): 2–11.

22. Svante E. Cornell et al., *Regional Security in the South Caucasus: The Role of NATO* (Washington, DC: Johns Hopkins University, 2004); Paul Gallis, *NATO and Energy Security* (Washington, DC: Congressional Research Service, 2006); and Joshua Spero, "NATO's Precarious Future," *International Affairs Forum* (UK: Taylor & Francis), December 2013, http://www. tandfonline.com/doi/abs/10.1080/ 23258020.2013.864886?journalCode riaf20-.U9kS2lYk_1r (accessed May 25, 2017).

23. "Chairman's Statement in Meeting of the NATO-Russia Council in Defence Minister's Session in Brussels," NATO-Russia Council, June 13, 2008, http://www.nato-russia-council.info/ htm/EN/documents13jun08.shtml (accessed August 22, 2009).

24. Oksana Antonenko, "A War with No Winners," *Survival* 50, no. 5 (October–November 2008): 23–36.

25. NATO Final Communiqué, "Meeting of the North Atlantic Council at the Level of Foreign Ministers Held at NATO Headquarters, Brussels," NATO, December 3, 2008, http://www.nato. int/docu/pr/2008/po8-153e.html (accessed August 19, 2009).

26. "NATO Chief Expects Joint Missile Defense with Russia by 2020," *RIA Novosti*, December 17, 2009, http://en.rian.ru/world/20091217/157273894.html (accessed December 28, 2009).

27. NATO, "Strasbourg/Kehl NATO Summit Declaration: Issued by the Heads of State and Government Participating in the Meeting of the North Atlantic Council in Strasbourg/Kehl," section 54, April 4, 2009, http://www.nato.int/cps/en/natolive/ news_52837.htm (accessed August 22, 2009).

28. Eugene Rumer and Angela Stent, "Russia and the West," *Survival* 51, no. 2 (April–May 2009): 91–104.

29. "U.S., Russia Trade European Missile Defense System for S-300 SAMs," *RBC Daily*, September 24, 2009, available at *RIA Novosti*, http://en.rian.ru/papers/20090924/ 156242202. html (accessed December 28, 2009); and Oliver Thränert, "NATO, Missile Defence and Extended Deterrence," *Survival* 51, no. 6 (December 2009–January 2010): 63–76.

30. NATO, "2012 Chicago Summit Declaration: Issued by the Heads of State and Government Participating in the Meeting of the North Atlantic Council in Chicago, NATO, May 20, 2012, http:// www.nato.int/cps/en/SID-1BBDB541-FD5ACE96/natolive/ official_texts_87593.htm (accessed August 20, 2013).

31. Rebecca C. Moore, *NATO's New Mission: Projecting Stability in a Post–Cold War World* (New York: Praeger, 2007); V. P. Malik and Jorg Schultz, eds., *Emerging NATO: Challenges for Asia*

and Europe (New Delhi: Lancer, 2008); James W. Peterson, *NATO and Terrorism: Organizational Expansion and Mission Transformation* (New York: Continuum, 2011); Stephanie C. Hoffmann, *European Security in NATO's Shadow* (Cambridge: Cambridge University Press, 2012); and Kimberley Martin, *Reducing Tensions between Russia and NATO*. Council on Foreign Relations, Special Report #79, March 2017.

32. Michael D. Shear, Mark Landler, and James Kanter, "Europe: In NATO Speech, Trump Is Vague about Mutual Defense Pledge," *New York Times*, May 25, 2017, https://www.nytimes.com/2017/05/25/world/europe/donald-trump-eu-nato.html (accessed May 26, 2017); and Anne Applebaum, "For the U.S.-European Alliance, Everything has Changed," *Washington Post*, May 28, 2017, https://www.washingtonpost.com/opinions/global-opinions/for-the-us-european-alliance-everything-has-changed/2017/05/28/5b42e5dc-43b9-11e7-a196-a1bb629f64cb_story.html?utm_term=.eafd993f201a (accessed May 30, 2017).

33. "A Federated Way Ahead for NATO in an Age of Complexity: Food for Thought Paper," The International Institute for Strategic Studies, February 2017, prepared with the support and cooperation of NATO Allied Command Transformation (http://www.act.nato.int/).

34. NATO, "Warsaw Summit Communiqué: Issued by the Heads of State and Government Participating in the Meeting of the North Atlantic Council in Warsaw 8–9 July 2016," Official Texts (Chronological), Press Release (2016) 100, July 9, 2016, http://www.nato.int/cps/en/natohq/official_texts_133169.htm (accessed May 25, 2017); Hans Binnendijk, Daniel S. Hamilton, and Charles L. Barry, "Alliance Revitalized: NATO for a New Era," *The Washington NATO Project*, Center for Transatlantic Relations School of Advanced International Studies Johns Hopkins University, April 2016, https://transatlanticrelations.org/wp-content/uploads/2016/08/NATO-Alliance-Revitalized-Report_Key_CORRECTED-VERSION_EURO.pdf (accessed May 26, 2017); François Heisbourg, "The Future of the U.S. Alliance System: Will It Survive the Trump Presidency?" *Foreign Affairs*, December 5, 2016, https://www.foreignaffairs.com/articles/2016-12-05/future-us-alliance-system (accessed May 30, 2017); Elizabeth Braw, "Next Steps for NATO: The Necessity of Greater Military Interoperability," *Foreign Affairs*, November 27, 2016, https://www.foreignaffairs.com/ articles/2016-11-27/next-steps-nato (accessed May 30, 2017); and Josef Joffe, "The Folly of Abandoning Europe: The Case against U.S. Retreat," *Foreign Affairs*, December 12, 2016, https://www.foreignaffairs.com/articles/europe/2016-12-12/folly-abandoning-europe (accessed May 30, 2017).

35. NATO, "Framework for Future Alliance Operations," Supreme Allied Commander Transformation and Supreme Allied Commander Europe, August 2015, http://www.act.nato.int/publications-ffao (accessed May 31, 2017); Judy Dempsey, "The Merkel Way, The Macron Way," Judy Dempsey's Strategic Europe/Carnegie Europe, May 31, 2017, http://carnegieeurope.eu/strategiceurope /?fa=70105 (accessed May 31, 2017); and Jeremy Shapiro, "This Is How NATO Ends: With the Quiet Shuttering of an Irrelevant Brussels Office Building in September 2020," *Foreign Policy*, February 15, 2017, http://foreignpolicy.com/author/jeremy-shapiro/ (accessed May 24, 2017).

36. Joshua B. Spero, "European Union Security Challenges," *International Affairs Forum*, July 2011, http://ia-forum.org/Content/ViewInternalDocument.cfm?ContentID=7863 (accessed August 20, 2013); and Judy Dempsey, "Judy Asks: Will Trump Make Europe Stronger?" Judy Dempsey's Strategic Europe/Carnegie Europe, May 31, 2017, http://carnegieeurope.eu/strategiceurope/?fa=70123 (accessed May 31, 2017).

37. NATO, "Backgrounder: Interoperability for Joint Operations," NATO Public Diplomacy Division, July 2006, http://www.nato.int/nato_static/assets/pdf/pdf_publications/20120116_interoperability-en.pdf (accessed May 30, 2017); Sean Kay, "NATO Revived? Not So Fast," *War on the Rocks*, March 6, 2014, http://warontherocks.com/2014/03/nato-revived-not-so-fast (accessed April 12, 2014).

38. NATO, "Warsaw Summit Communiqué," paragraph 11.

39. NATO, "Warsaw Summit Communiqué," paragraphs 36 and 37; and NATO, "Strategic Foresight Analysis: 2015 Interim Update to the SFA 2013 Report," Headquarters Supreme Allied Commander Transformation, http://www.act.nato.int/strategic-foresight-analysis-2015-report (accessed May 31, 2017).

40. NATO, "Warsaw Summit Communiqué," paragraph 36; and Jonathan Eyal, "The Real Problems with NATO: What Trump Gets Right, and Wrong," *Foreign Affairs*, March 2, 2017, https://www.foreignaffairs.com/articles/europe/2017-03-02/real-problems-nato (accessed May 24, 2017).

41. Spero, "Great Power Security Dilemmas," 160–61.

42. Joshua B. Spero, "An East-West Bridge for Ukraine," *Duck of Minerva*, April 4, 2014, http://www.whiteoliphaunt.com/duckofminerva/2014/04/an-east-west-bridge-for-ukraine.html (accessed April 12, 2014).

43. Andrew A. Michta, "A Common Threat Assessment for NATO?" Judy Dempsey's Europe/Carnegie Europe, February 16, 2017, http://carnegieeurope.eu/ strategiceurope/68017 (accessed May 25, 2017); and Stanley R. Sloan, "Don't Expect a New NATO Strategic Concept Any Time Soon," *Atlantic Council*, February 24, 2017, http://www.atlanticcouncil.org/blogs/new-atlanticist/don-t-expect-a-new-nato-strategic-concept-any-time-soon?tmpl=component&print=1 (accessed May 24, 2017).

44. Sean Kay, "Is NATO an Alliance for the 21st Century?" in *NATO's Current and Future Challenges*, ed. S. Victor Papacosma, Occasional Papers 6 (Kent, OH: Kent State University, 2008); Sean Kay, "The Russia Crisis Proves the Case for the Asia Pivot," *War on the Rocks*, March 27, 2014, http://warontherocks.com/2014/03/the-russia-crisis-proves-the-case-for-the-asia-pivot/ (accessed April 12, 2014); Julie Smith and Jim Townsend, "It's Mattis and Pence to the Rescue of the Transatlantic Alliance," *Foreign Policy*, February 13, 2017, http://foreignpolicy.com/2017/02/13/its-mattis-and-pence-to-the-rescue-of-the-transatlantic-alliance/ (accessed May 25, 2017); and Judy Dempsey, "NATO and the EU Had Better Prepare for a Tempestuous Relationship with the U.S. Administration," Carnegie Europe, May 26, 2017, http://carnegieeurope.eu/strategiceurope/?fa=70090 (accessed May 30, 2017).

45. Andrew A. Michta, "Central Europe and NATO: Still Married, but in Need of Counseling," *Center for European Policy Analysis*, Report No. 29, December 2009; Colin Dueck, "Trump, Europe, and the Quest to Save NATO," *War on the Rocks*, February 3, 2017, https://warontherocks.com/2017/02/trump-europe-and-the-quest-to-save-nato/, (accessed May 24, 2017); and Tomáš Valášek, "A New Transatlantic Security Bargain," Carnegie Europe, May 23, 2017, http://carnegieeurope.eu/2017/05/23/new-transatlantic-security-bargain-pub-70050 (accessed May 30, 2017).

Part III

CASE STUDIES

Map 9.0. Poland

CHAPTER 9

Poland

THE POLITICS OF "GOD'S PLAYGROUND"

Jane Leftwich Curry

Poland was the first and one of the most successful transitions from communism to Western-style democracy in 1989 when the Central and East European transitions began. After a difficult beginning, its economy not only transformed very quickly into a Western-style capitalist economy, but, even during the European economic crisis beginning in 2008, it had one of the highest growth rates in the European Union (EU). It was also the leading Central and East European state in the EU and a strong advocate for aid to and inclusion of countries to its east. Poland's politics changed with the 2015 presidential and parliamentary elections when Law and Justice, a populist right-wing party, won enough seats to control the presidency and both houses of the parliament.

Once in power, it moved to take control of the courts, media, and educational system, imposing nationalist and populist policies as well as policies on issues such as barring abortion long demanded by the Catholic Church. At the same time, it increased (or promised to) social welfare benefits for its core supporters, most of whom felt they had lost out in the economic transformation and not been heard by the Civic Platform government. As a result, Poland is now on Hungary's path toward "illiberal democracy" where the opposition is increasingly powerless to do anything more than demonstrate against government policies in the streets.

The story of how Poland became both the leader in the democratization process in Central and Eastern Europe and one of the first states to have its democratic institutions weakened by populism began long before 2015. Poland's history set the stage both for the relative liberalism of Poland's communism and its move toward "illiberal democracy" in which the institutions of democracy function but the power of any opposition in the system is limited at best. It went from being the largest country in Europe, sitting as it did in the "heart of Europe,"[1] to, by 1795, not existing. It was split between the Russian, German, and Austrian empires. Only in the smaller Austrian section of Poland could Polish be used anywhere in public outside of the churches. So, Catholicism became not only the religion of most Poles but also a central element of Polish national identity, the importance of which was heightened by Poles' battles to reclaim what they saw as their country and the presence of other nationalities within what became Poland after the World War I settlements.

Those boundaries drawn in the Versailles Peace Treaty at the end of World War I made Poland a multiethnic state: fully one-third of the population was not ethnically

Polish. This new state was burdened by having to establish national structures, deal with a diverse population of peoples with long histories of conflict, and build an economy and infrastructure out of the pieces of the three empires. Democracy and capitalism enjoyed brief success in the initial years of independence only to be virtually washed away by the Great Depression. From their history, Poles learned to maintain their culture and national identity, defined as it was by "being Catholic" and opposing outside oppression. At the same time, the divisions between the empires remained embedded not only in where the trains ran but also in the differences that still exist today in the regional economies and political leanings of the three regions.

Poland was devastated during World War II. In September 1939, the Molotov-Ribbentrop Pact divided it between the Germans and the Soviets. Then, in 1941, the Germans turned on the Soviets, took over all of Poland, and used it as a base from which to attack the Soviet Union and annihilate Jews from Poland and other countries, as well as a large number of ethnic Poles. Large numbers of Poles fought in a national underground (the Home Army) against the Russians and Germans, while a far smaller group, identifying with communism (the People's Army), fought the Germans and the nationalist underground. Ultimately, one-third of Poland's population perished (including almost all of its Jewish population); its capital, Warsaw, was razed to the ground; and much of its industrial base and many other cities were destroyed.

Polish Communism

Soviet troops brought a communist regime in as a "baggage-train government" when they marched across Poland and pushed the Germans out in 1945. That new leadership was an uneasy alliance between Polish communist officials who had spent the war in the Soviet Union and communists who had fought in the small pro-communist underground. These new rulers had to rebuild most of the country and, at the same time, impose unwelcome communist rule.

In the process, many of the factories and much of the infrastructure that had survived were taken back to the Soviet Union to rebuild its own infrastructure. To add to the complications of rebuilding, in postwar agreements, the boundaries of Poland were moved far to the west into what had been Germany and most of Poland's eastern territories were annexed by the Soviet Union. With this shift came a massive population transfer: most Germans in what became western Poland were forced out or went willingly to Germany. There were battles between Poles and Ukrainians. Many Poles who lived in what had been eastern Poland were moved or were forced west to settle the areas the Germans had vacated.

The Communist Party, PUWP, took control of the government and established state ownership of much of Poland's economy. With this came Stalinist terror; but, it was more restrained than elsewhere in Central Europe because the top leaders knew the Communist Party had been seen as "Russian" and unwelcome in Poland while the Catholic Church was very closely identified with "being Polish." So, the Catholic Church was allowed to function openly and have religious and secular organizations throughout the communist period. At the same time, there were many who gained from the ongoing reconstruction and industrialization when large numbers of new industries were built and young peasants moved to cities to work in factories. In the process, a whole new working class was established and educated.

With the deaths of Joseph Stalin in 1953 and Poland's Stalinist leader, Bolesław Bierut, in March 1956, fear and control decreased. In the summer of 1956, Polish workers demonstrated in the Western city of Poznań, demanding "bread and freedom" and calling out, "The press lies." Polish troops fired on the demonstrators, killing almost a hundred. Open intellectual protests spread throughout Poland in the fall. Many Polish United Workers' Party (PUWP) members demanded reforms in the party itself. The party leadership tried to end this "Polish October" by bringing back Władysław Gomułka, the party leader jailed in the Stalinist period for his independence. When he was returned to power, he started "a Polish road to socialism," allowing private farming, small private enterprises, more freedoms for the Catholic Church, and greater freedom for public discussion. From then on, Poland remained on its own "freer" road.

These events were the first in a series of revolts against communism's failings, including student and intellectual demonstrations in 1968 and workers' strikes and demonstrations that were triggered by price increases and economic failures in 1970, 1976, and 1980. After each of the workers' demonstrations, the communist authorities made concessions to maintain their hold and buy support and then failed to meet their promises. With each uprising, though, the opposition grew and became more organized until, after the 1976 workers' demonstrations, the Workers' Defense Committee (KOR) formed to aid arrested workers and their families. It produced underground publications to let people know about their rights and about human rights violations in Poland and to encourage independent thinking. By the late 1970s and early 1980s, this opposition had flowered into a massive underground press empire, a number of human rights organizations, and a whole alternate cultural milieu, including a "Flying University" offering courses and instructors not permitted in the communist educational system.[2] It was from this opposition, in combination with the shipyard workers who had demonstrated and lost in 1970, that Solidarity would emerge a decade later.[3] After 1989, when the communists inadvertently negotiated themselves out of power, these two organizations, KOR and Solidarity, produced many of the elites of democratic Poland.

When Edward Gierek took over as head of the Party after the December 1970 Gdańsk shipyard strikes, he promised Poles their lives would improve. To jump-start the economy and provide for a higher living standard, Poland borrowed from the West to build new factories with Western equipment and began importing Western consumer goods. The loans were supposed to pay for themselves with earnings from the export of products to the West. However, the plan did not work: much of the money was wasted, Polish goods did not sell, and Poland had to borrow more and more just to pay the interest on its debts. By the beginning of the 1980s, the shelves of Polish stores were bare and Poland was in the midst of a debt crisis with $8.1 billion—far more than its ready cash and assets would cover—of its over $20 billion debt to the West due in 1980.

The government was so desperate in 1980 to placate Western creditors without touching off demonstrations that it imposed price increases on food staples (as required by Western creditors), region by region, with instructions to local leaders to negotiate pay increases if there were strikes or demonstrations. By August, rolling price increases on food had been imposed across the country, last of all, in the seacoast towns where the 1970 riots had brought down the Gomułka regime.

In response to the price increases, workers in the Gdańsk shipyards went on strike and simply refused to negotiate pay increases. Under the leadership of dissident worker, Lech Wałęsa, workers occupied the shipyards in Gdańsk and other Baltic towns, demanding not just the economic and social welfare benefits communism had promised but also the right to have an independent trade union, the right to strike, and more media freedom so that they would know what was really going on. Intellectuals joined them. Workers from other places in Poland sent messages of support and some joined in support strikes. In August, the Polish government conceded to the workers' demands by negotiating and signing the Gdańsk Agreement. Solidarity was the first independent trade union in the communist world and became a national movement for economic and political change in Poland.

Poles had been further emboldened to stand up to their leaders by the election of Karol Wojtyla, the former archbishop of Kraków, as pope in 1978 and his triumphant return to Poland in June 1979. He returned as a conquering hero. His trip was organized and run by Church volunteers rather than the government, even as he was feted by communist leaders and the population alike. This gave Poles a sense that they did not need the government to organize.

The rise of Solidarity was dramatic. By the end of its first year, more than one-third of the population had joined the movement. A farmers' Solidarity and a students' union also had formed and forced the government to recognize them. Workplaces organized. Many party members joined Solidarity and sought to bring its openness into the PUWP. Independent press and discussions appeared everywhere. Solidarity elections and a national congress were held. Solidarity, at its height in 1981, had over 10 million members, easily the majority of Poland's workforce.

Popular demands on the government increased. Poland's economy simply could not work well enough to feed its population, much less provide the gains the Gdańsk Agreements promised. As the economic situation worsened, strikes and demonstrations became the order of the day. Food supplies were in such short supply that they were rationed, and individuals had to use their connections to get the meat and other necessities they could not get with their rations.

The strikes and hardships of "real socialism" in Poland created friendship groups that helped people survive and informal professional groups that helped counter the controls in the communist system. These groups, as well as the high level of social resistance, also allowed alternative elites to establish themselves; provided the personal ties between groups that would help in the transition; and gave people organizing experience that facilitated what would be Poland's negotiated transition.

The government could only make more and more political concessions, even as the Soviet Union and other Soviet bloc states pressed for a crackdown. For Polish leaders and their allies, the potential for chaos and threat of contagion were all too real. Party leader and head of the Polish military, Wojciech Jaruzelski, and those around him were convinced, by the end of 1981, that the Soviet Union would invade if popular actions and government concessions went any further.

On December 13, 1981, Jaruzelski declared martial law and the freedoms Solidarity had enjoyed for fifteen months ended with a Polish military "takeover." Solidarity and other independent groups were declared illegal and shut down. Thousands of Solidarity and intellectual activists, as well as some top PUWP leaders accused of corruption and mismanagement during the Gierek era, were interned. Polish soldiers and police were on the streets when people woke up. Military officers supervised factories, schools, media, and government offices for months. Media freedom and free discussion ended. Individual parishes and Catholic organizations provided havens for discussion and distributed donations of food and clothing that were provided both by other Poles and, ultimately, by Western governments and organizations. Most Poles were too shocked to act. The United States and some other Western countries imposed sanctions on Poland. Martial law continued formally for a year and a half but the last internees were released only after three years.

Until the mid-1980s, the economic situation remained severely troubled. The sanctions imposed by the United States and some other Western countries remained in place. Some activists were interned and Solidarity and the other independent organizations were illegal; but, an active underground movement functioned and dissident publications and activities proliferated. At the same time, the difficulties of daily life amid constant shortages meant that most individuals focused on feeding and supplying their families rather than engaging in open political protest.

The weaknesses of the old communist system that made it more open than other communist systems also complicated the transition. Poland was, by 1989, over $40 billion in debt to the West[4] and still enmeshed in the Soviet bloc economic system. This meant that its options for economic reform were limited by the other Soviet bloc states and the need to satisfy its Western creditors. Its opposition, which had been the strongest in the communist world well before Solidarity's heyday in 1980–1981, had ideological divisions. From the 1970s on, most Poles had real knowledge of and very high expectations for democracy and capitalism because they had been guest workers in the West, had ties to family members there, and had an elite that tried to buy them off with its openness to the West. The image of democracy and capitalism they took away from this was of prosperity, not inequality. In Poland, they learned to work around or oppose the system. They did not learn, however, how to function as citizens in a normal democratic system. In the end, the communist-era reforms left them with high hopes for democracy, little practice working within a democracy, and an economy of foreign debt, inflation, and failed factories.

Transition from Communism

By the late 1980s, Poland's economy had failed to rebound and provide what Poles thought they had been promised. The communists' efforts to win support or even draw in some workers and intellectuals had largely failed. Much of Poland's population was alienated from both Solidarity and the communist government. Random strikes with no specific goals worried both Solidarity leaders and the communists. To deal with this alienation, communist leaders reached out to the opposition as they tried to get the economy moving by decreasing controls on prices and forcing factories to be self-supporting. When none of these maneuvers worked, the government, with the support of the Catholic Church, sought Solidarity leaders' agreement to begin discussions on systemic change. Church leaders helped bring the two sides together and facilitated Roundtable talks between them.

No one thought communism would end. For the rulers, the Roundtables were a way to hold on to power by getting Solidarity to share responsibility for Poland's problems and move toward a new, more open system of government over the next four years. For

Solidarity's self-appointed representatives, their most important goal was to force the relegalization of Solidarity as a trade union (something the government conceded on the first day of the public Roundtables). The population hoped that the Roundtable agreements would protect the economic guarantees of a social welfare state and that the freedoms of the Solidarity era would be returned. The Catholic Church wanted the Roundtables to stabilize Poland and ensure its interests and position.

After five months of private discussions and nine weeks of public discussions, the two sides agreed to defer decisions on economic reforms and move ahead with political reforms and partially free parliamentary elections designed to reassure the Soviet Union by ensuring that the PUWP and its former allies held a majority of seats in the main house (Sejm) and that Solidarity and other nonparty people were just "junior partners." So, 65 percent of the seats in the Sejm were designated for candidates who had been in one of these communist-era parties and 35 percent of the seats were designated for candidates who had not belonged to a party in the communist era. In the process, they created a system that broke taboos but did not initially violate the Soviet Union's old limits.

The Polish political system was redesigned to have a second legislative chamber (the Senate) and a president elected by the two houses together. Finally, forty seats in the Sejm were reserved, in this first election, for the so-called National List of the regime's notables and reformers. The new Senate, as a trade-off, was elected without any constraints. A majoritarian election system, in which those who did not get a majority had to run in a second election, was used for both "party" and nonparty seats in the Sejm and new Senate as well as for the National List.

The results of the elections on June 4, 1989, defied all expectations. Candidates Solidarity identified as theirs (signaled by posters showing the candidate with Lech Wałęsa) won every nonparty seat in the Sejm and all but one in the Senate. Only a few of the Communist Party candidates, however, got the requisite majority to win in the first round. Most of the "Party" seats had to be decided in the second round. All but the two men whose names were at the bottom of the National List lost in the first round. Few who lost in the first round ran again in the second.[5] The presidency (elected by the Sejm and Senate) went, as had been tacitly promised, to Jaruzelski, the man who had both called for the hated martial law and championed the Roundtable talks. His victory was the result of a political compromise Solidarity leaders engineered to placate Communist Party and military hard-liners in Poland and hard-line leaders elsewhere in the Soviet bloc.

The 65 percent majority established for the Communist Party and its old allies did not hold. The smaller parties, long Trojan horses to draw peasants and small entrepreneurs into the system, broke with the PUWP and joined Solidarity. That reversed the percentages for the "establishment" and the "opposition" in the Sejm: people elected as PUWP members, as a result, held 35 percent of the seats, and 65 percent of the seats were held by Solidarity and its new allies from the old system.

The Soviet leaders accepted the results. But no one knew what would happen next. Solidarity deputies' platform had been against communism but had no actual plans for what would change and how. Communist-era deputies had expected to share power with nonparty members. They had no plan for what to do when they were in opposition.

A new, noncommunist government was formed in September 1989. Tadeusz Mazowiecki (longtime Catholic editor, dissident, and advisor to Solidarity leader Lech Wałęsa) was named prime minister on Wałęsa's recommendation. He formed a unity

Photo 9.1. Solidarity poster that covered the streets of Poland the morning of the June 1989 elections, based on a Gary Cooper poster for the film, *High Noon*.

government of dissident intellectuals, experts in economics, specialists from the parties formerly aligned with the Communist Party (PUWP), and three communist ministers to manage the most important ministries for Soviet interests: the Ministry of Interior (police and spy services), the Ministry of Defense, and the Ministry of Foreign Trade. Western-educated economist Leszek Balcerowicz was named minister of finance and deputy prime minister to manage economic reform.

What had been the Solidarity monolith against the communists dissolved into many factions. Faced with minority party membership after forty years of party rule, PUWP deputies wanted as little to do with the rejected system as possible. By January 1990, PUWP had dissolved itself and passed its resources on to the new Social Democratic Party of the Polish Republic (SLDRP).

Solidarity and communist deputies all worked to cut-and-paste the communist constitution to fit the election results and the Roundtable Accords. They excised from the constitution provisions like the "leading role of the party" and the promise of fealty to the Soviet Union. All national symbols dropped their communist elements. Then, under pressure from the United States and Western Europe, the Sejm passed bills instituting "shock therapy" economic reform (the Balcerowicz Plan) for rapid privatization, foreign aid, and investment. This program—coupled with the inflation that began after the last communist government freed most food prices so they skyrocketed with the reforms (while salaries remained stable)—triggered a drop in the purchasing power of the zloty by 40 percent at the end of the plan's first month (January 1990) and brought a rapid end to popular euphoria over communism's end and Poland's "return to Europe."

Political Institutions

Until 2007, governance was based on the "Small Constitution" of 1992 that merely codified the additions and deletions made in 1990 to take "communism" out of the communist-era constitution and define the basic powers of the major institutions. It did not, however, provide a framework to establish, coordinate, and balance what institutions could and could not do. So, until the final constitution was completed, legislators legislated powers for themselves and whatever president or prime minister was in office simply claimed the right to act and, in the process, set a precedent. As a result, the final constitution was a product of proposals from various political parties and also, particularly in the case of the powers of the presidency, of what the five presidents since 1990 had done and not done that had worked or angered people.

Wojciech Jaruzelski, as a remnant of the defeated regime, did only what he was asked to do by the Solidarity government and parliament. His successor, Lech Wałęsa, the former leader of Solidarity, took control by ignoring the restrictions on presidential powers. Two years into his rule, he faced a very divided parliament. There were deadlocks with the government, public opposition to and disgust with his style of leadership, and even claims, among former supporters, that he had been a secret agent.

Aleksander Kwaśniewski, who was elected president in 1995 and again in 2000, took a very different position from his predecessors. Given the public attacks on his party (SLD) and on him for being from the legacy party to the old PUWP, Communist Party, he focused on disproving stereotypes about communists. He was a "by-the-book" president, taking no more power than was constitutionally mandated. In his first term, he had an SLD and Peasant Party parliamentary majority, so legislation was passed and conflicts avoided. After the 1997 parliamentary election, he worked with the right-wing parliamentary coalition by avoiding direct conflict and presenting himself as a professional. He was able to get parliament's support for the constitution, which he had played a key role in developing. In his presidency, he focused on international diplomacy, negotiating Poland's entrance into the North Atlantic Treaty Organization (NATO). In the process, he returned prestige and the faith of the public to the presidency.

As a result of these experiences, the 1997 constitution reined in the powers of the presidency and increased the powers of the prime minister and cabinet. It also attempted

Photo 9.2. The leaders of all sides of the Polish Roundtable—Tadeusz Mazowiecki (prime minister from 1989 to 1991), Lech Wałęsa (president of Poland from 1991 to 1995), and Aleksander Kwaśdniewski (president from 1995 to 2005)—after signing the accords in 1989. (Forum)

to ensure that presidential and parliamentary elections would, only infrequently, be in the same year by having the president elected for five years and the parliament for four.

The president got the right to step in and name a prime minister only if the Sejm was too divided to agree. The prime minister and his cabinet can be removed only by a vote of no confidence by the parliament. The prime minister is responsible for selecting his cabinet and presenting his choices to the Sejm for approval.

The powers of legislation are concentrated in the Sejm. The Senate, on the other hand, is primarily a body to review and revise Sejm legislation and serve as a moderator in conflicts. In this system, the powers of the presidency were counterbalanced by those of the parliamentary bodies and the prime minister. The government also has the explicit responsibility to lead the policy-making process in domestic and foreign affairs, carry out the laws passed by the parliament, put forth regulations when authorized by the Sejm, and manage the state budget. Finally, the president and prime minister must cosign all laws.

A Constitutional Court was established to determine whether laws and international agreements are constitutional and also adjudicate disputes over whether the actions of individual institutions are constitutional. The fifteen justices are to be chosen by the Sejm for staggered nine-year terms so that no one political group can name all the justices. Lower-level courts' judges were to be selected and nominated by bodies of legal experts who could judge their competence and, then, be appointed by the Sejm. All this assumed, however, that the three branches of government were not controlled by the same party and that the politicians in power respected the constitutional provisions.

In 2001, SLD returned as the dominant party in parliament, balanced against a fragmented right wing. By default, Poland moved back to a semi-presidential state, with Kwaśniewski appointing economist Marek Belka as prime minister and taking leadership in areas like foreign policy that were the constitutional purview of the presidency.

In 2005, Lech Kaczyński of the Law and Justice Party was elected president. The parliamentary elections that followed resulted in his party being the largest in the Sejm. Because it did not have a majority, though, it formed a government with two small radical right-wing parties (Samoobrona, or Self-Defense, and the League of Polish Families). Kaczyński named his identical twin brother, Jarosław, prime minister. The two brothers, as president and prime minister, expanded their powers by claiming that anyone who disagreed with them had been a communist or agent and should be purged. They also put into effect a review process of the old secret police files that made them public and allowed for the removal of individuals from public office based on the contents of their files. This made opposition to their government risky.

In 2007, Jaroslaw Kaczyński's coalition government fell apart, triggering early parliamentary elections. They were held on October 24, a month after the government dissolved and showed popular disaffection with the right-wing coalition's attacks about who did what in the past. A movement spearheaded by young people to get out the vote brought the more policy-focused center left Civic Platform to power.

The party's centrist leader, Donald Tusk, became prime minister. He worked to modernize the bureaucracy, so the government would be more responsive. He and his coalition reversed what the Law and Justice coalition had done in foreign affairs by moving back to closer relations with Germany. Tusk's positive and professional style of leadership, as well as Poland's economic health during the recession, made him a popular leader. He then faced constant attacks and vetoes of legislation by Lech Kaczyński who, essentially, pushed against these shifts by using his presidential veto powers and publicly attacking his enemies as "communists."

When Lech Kaczyński began his campaign for a second term as president in 2010, public opinion polls showed that he was not popular enough to win. He escalated the rhetoric in his battle for power with Tusk. In foreign policy, he battled with the prime minister, Donald Tusk, over who could speak for Poland. So, after Prime Minister Tusk represented Poland in the official Russian-Polish commemoration of the Katyn Massacre, the slaughter of Polish officers by Soviet soldiers at the start of World War II, Kaczyński, as president, organized his own delegation of political leaders and families of the men slaughtered to the site in Russia. The plane carrying them crashed in Smolensk, Russia, killing all aboard and beginning a political battle between Polish and Russian authorities led by his twin brother, as head of the Law and Justice Party, over whether the accident was the result of pilot error, bad landing conditions, or a Russian attack. Jarosław Kaczyński also began a battle with Civic Platform over how to memorialize his brother that continues today with a demonstration in front of the presidential palace on the monthly anniversary of the crash.

In the special election in 2010 to replace his deceased brother as president, Jarosław Kaczyński, the Law and Justice candidate, lost to Civic Platform's candidate, Bronislaw Komorowski. This again put both the parliament and the presidency in the hands of one party. Civic Platform remained popular and cohesive under Komorowski and Tusk. Poland continued to do well economically although there were tax increases and demonstrations over the low incomes of professionals in health care and education.

Photo 9.3. The late president Lech Kaczyński congratulating his twin brother, Jarosław Kaczyński, on his swearing in as prime minister in 2006. He left office in November 2007. (*Rzeczpospolita*)

The tide turned in 2015. Law and Justice won an early election triggered by Tusk's resignation as prime minister to become the first East European to be president of the European Council. Its victory over Civic Platform was triggered by revelations from a series of secret tapes of high officials from Civic Platform and the former communist SLD party talking about their foreign vacations and impatience with "Poles" and a growing disaffection among Poles outside the major cities. The votes for the moderate left Civic Platform also were splintered by the fragmentation of the old left and the appearance of candidates, including an unknown rock musician who came in third in the first round of the presidential race in 2015 with a youthful protest vote. As a result, Komorowski lost the presidency in the second round to a relatively unknown candidate of Law and Justice, Andrzej Duda.

In the parliamentary election that followed, where barely half of the eligible voters voted, Law and Justice ran as a moderate center-right party that was going to "listen" to the voters. It won the most votes (37.58 percent) and got a bare majority of the seats in the Sejm as well as the Senate because the left was so fragmented that parties and coalitions other than Civic Platform did not get the requisite 5 percent of the votes for a party to get seats nor did the coalitions get the requisite 7 percent. Its win was both a result of the divisions in the left and also a general exhaustion among Poles who lived in poorer regions of Poland and felt they had not benefitted from the strength of the Polish economy. Young people joined as they also felt shut out from getting their own apartments or good jobs.

In office, Law and Justice has proved to be far from centrist. Jarosław Kaczyński is the dominant figure in the party even though he has no formal role other than being a deputy to the Sejm. In rapid succession, once it was in power, the party moved to put the Constitutional Court under its control by refusing to recognize the justices appointed earlier by Civic Platform and, when those justices did not step down, refusing to recognize and publish the court's decisions as is required for them to be legally binding. Then, it passed legislation that effectively took control of state radio and television and put it under a new body Law and Justice developed and appointed in 2016. A year later, it moved to take control of the courts at all levels by putting them, along with the Prosecutor's Office, under the control of the minister of justice. These changes triggered a summer of demonstrations and then were partially blocked by a veto from the president against his own party's laws. In addition, it has changed the Polish school system and increased "patriotic" education in literature and history while decreasing science and foreign languages. Its "educational reform" also made it easier for teachers to be fired for deviating from the line. It has also taken steps to hamper the private media and NGOs by putting up barriers to their receipt of foreign support. In keeping with its support among the most traditional Catholics, it attempted to make all abortions illegal in 2016 until it was forced to back down, at least temporarily, in response to the massive Black Monday strike of women. Economically, it has served its base and the interests of the Catholic Church by providing 500 zlotys (more than $100) monthly for every child more than one in a family. It has promised to build a million new, cheap apartments for young people who feel frozen out of owning their own apartments. And, it also reduced the retirement age to sixty-five for men and sixty for women. In foreign policy, it has increasingly taken an anti-EU stance.

Parties and Elections

After 1989, Poland not only had to develop a new political system but it also had to develop political parties. The Citizen's Committees that formed in 1989 essentially had no platform other than being against the Communist Party, PUWP, and its traditional allies, the Polish Peasant Party and the Democratic Party, which represented the small-scale peasant farmers and private entrepreneurs that had been allowed to function in Poland after 1956. Once the Communist Party was defeated in 1989, rather than establishing clear and stable policy options, parties and elections were focused on individual battles between political leaders. The clearest divide, among voters and parties, was initially between those who saw the communist system in a positive light and those who identified with the Catholic Church. This divide was often more significant than specific economic interests in determining how people voted in the first two decades.[6] As a result, Poland has had one of the lowest levels of electoral participation, seldom more than a few points over 50 percent.

The initial elections themselves were marked by increased ideological fragmentation, parties came and went. Only the former communists had the resources for and tradition of party organization and offices. Newer parties ran, most often, out of leaders' homes or church buildings. This led to instability and to a real personalization of politics that made it difficult for voters to develop a real connection to what were often ephemeral parties and candidates that had no clear policy commitments.

In the long run, these fluid and irresolvable noneconomic divisions meant that the battles in Polish politics have been more over divisive issues of the past and religion than over how best to deal with the economy and what the state should do for people. As a result, without alternative policies for soluble problems, political rhetoric has often focused on charges and countercharges.

The first elections after 1989 were local government elections, held before the duties and new powers of the various levels of local government had been established or there were clear policy alternatives. It was a series of battles among the individual candidates. At the same time, a campaign by Lech Wałęsa and his followers started to force Jaruzelski's resignation and pass a law for direct popular election of the president. Jaruzelski conceded to this pressure and resigned. The law was changed, so the first presidential election was held in 1990.

Shifting loyalties and voting for someone new who seemed to promise dramatic improvement in living conditions and, on the right, condemned all opponents then became the pattern in Poland. Two other long-term features of party affiliation in Poland also began at this point. One was the regional difference in party support between the prosperous west, with its big cities that supported pro-reform candidates and the impoverished east, and other areas where factories had gone bankrupt and small-scale agriculture failed. They supported the "right" with its promises of social welfare and condemnation of the "communists." While almost all politicians recognized the authority of the Catholic Church, it was the right that committed to Catholic social policies. The left, on the other hand, even if it was connected with the former Communist Party, avoided ties with the past.

Initially, a plethora of tiny parties emerged, making coalitions difficult if not impossible after the initial free elections. In the early parliamentary elections of 1991, one hundred parties ran candidates, and twenty-nine parties were elected in the Sejm's proportional representation elections. The Senate was also fragmented after its elections. In addition to two warring Solidarity-based parties and the Solidarity trade union, there were various small right-wing parties that condemned both the former communists and Solidarity deputies for the losses "caused by" the Balcerowicz Plan, in a campaign marked by nationalist and religious rhetoric. Only the former communists, the Social Democratic Party of the Polish Republic (in what was eventually the SLD), remained unified.

So divided was this parliament that, within two years, it was unable to make policy and turned in on itself. In the process, the largest of the many parties in the Sejm pushed through two laws that impacted party politics. First, to cut down on the fragmentation of the Sejm, political parties were required to win 5 percent of the national vote and coalitions 7 percent to hold seats in the Sejm. This has meant that many small parties ran for election but do not get enough votes to qualify and, as a result, the percentages of seats larger parties get are sometimes far more than their percentage in the vote. Second, the Sejm legalized a system allowing parties represented in parliament to receive national government funding for their campaigns if they won at least 3 percent in the election. The amount of this funding was proportional to the number of seats a party won in the Sejm or Senate.

In 1993, this electoral law resulted in the SLD, with only 20.41 percent of the votes, and its former allies, the renamed Polish Peasant Party, with 15.4 percent of the vote, winning 60.5 percent of Sejm seats. The nine right-wing parties that ran could not form a coalition, and none reached the 5 percent of the vote required to hold seats in parliament, so they got no seats even though, together, they polled 34.45 percent of the vote.

After the era of Communist Party rule, the very word "party" and the notion of being a party member had negative connotations, so, until the 2015 elections, most of the groups that ran for elections eschewed the word "party" and did not build structures or enroll members. Candidates, even from the most established parties, have had to invest their own money in campaigns. Only if they win seats in parliament are they at least partially reimbursed by the state. The expenses of being in parliament are paid through their party directly from the parliament's budget.

This funding did not result in political parties with permanent structures. Initially, only the former communists (SLD) had the infrastructures typical of European parties. That was because they and their subsidiary parties in the communist era, the Peasant Party and the Democratic Party for small entrepreneurs started ahead because they inherited their parties' communist-era buildings, equipment, and membership lists, as well as old members who had long organized for the party. These cadres of old party workers were willing to work for the SLD and the Peasant Party, even though they voiced a pro-capitalist ideology. They did this because the other parties attacked or shunned anyone who had been in communist-era parties. But, by 2015, the postcommunist SLD had sold off the former buildings of the PUWP and its former loyalists were no longer active. It was then not even able to get enough votes to have a seat in the parliament.

The other political groups in Poland initially did not have the resources or desire to invest in increasingly expensive permanent infrastructures and offices. In the early years of Poland's democracy, some, mostly right-wing, parties received support and facilities from the Catholic Church in exchange for advocating strongly for its interests. But, in the years between elections, even the more successful parties remained essentially "couch parties," focused on individual leaders and existing only during political campaigns and in their formations in the Sejm and Senate. Until the reformation of Law and Justice after Kaczyński's defeat in 2010, most center and right-wing parties had no formal membership and owned no property. Leaders and parliamentary deputies only held together because they got funding, beyond their salaries, from their party in parliament. Even the dominant party between 2007 and 2015, Civic Platform, did not build a strong party organization. It basically functioned as a Western catchall party focused on its strong and popular leadership.

Parties' ideologies were unstable and confusing at best. The Democratic Left Alliance (SLD), cast off its Marxist ideology already in 1989 and voted for the Balcerowicz Plan. It then shifted to advocating for "trickle-down economics," claiming that the poor would gain from excess profits in a capitalist economy. Its leader, Aleksander Kwaśniewski, in the presidential races in 1995 and again in 2000, ran as a modern, pro-capitalist, European leader who was above the political fray. The SLD, once it won the 2001 parliamentary election, became known for corruption at its lower levels and, as a result, lost its popular support. Kwaśniewski's attempt to save the left by linking those from the old Solidarity who stood for workers' rights and social democracy—who had never gotten an electoral foothold—and the SLD together in a group called Left and Democrats in the 2007 elections failed. Little remains of the left except for small groups of young politicians who advocate for what are marginal issues in Poland.

The initial political center of Mazowiecki (Freedom Union) could not disassociate itself from the losses people had suffered due to the Balcerowicz Plan that it had voted in as one of its first pieces of substantial legislation in 1989. As a result, its candidates were defeated in the 1990 presidential election and the 1991 parliamentary elections and then returned to government in 1995 as an element of the Civic Platform. This center party has stood against Polish nationalism and for establishing a liberal market economy, democratization, and a return to Europe. Although some of its leaders were lay Catholic opposition leaders during the communist era, this center has not supported giving the Catholic Church a dominant voice in legislation.

In 2001, Civic Platform won 12.7 percent of the votes, coming in second to the Democratic Left Alliance with its 41.0 percent. In 2007 and 2011, the Civic Platform won the parliamentary as well as the presidential election in 2010. It has maintained a pro-European and pro-free market position and supports a strong Polish presence in the EU. Equally important to its strength for a decade was its reputation for rational and reasoned political action rather than a politics marked by strong rhetoric of charges, and countercharges, seen as a negative characteristic of the right. But, in 2015, it was unable to hold on to power.

The one long-term party to hold seats in every parliament since the first free elections in 1989 has been the Polish Peasant Party. It is an outgrowth of the communist-era peasant party. And, it has been in coalitions with both sides. Initially, it focused on the interests of the agricultural sector; more recently, it has positioned itself as a moderate party supporting both economic development and a preservation of social supports. In the 2005 election, it did lose some of its peasant supporters to the radical Self-Defense Party; in 2007, however, it regained voter support as a party not involved in the ideological fights and also as the one major party that did not support the war in Iraq. It barely got enough votes to hold seats in the Sejm in 2015 when peasants were drawn by the economic promises of the Law and Justice Party.

The right wing has focused on the bitterness of Poles, particularly those in the east and small towns and peasant areas, over what they lost in the rapid shift to capitalism. Like earlier right-wing parties, they advocate for social welfare and protecting workers even as they rail against communist-era repression, the profits "communists" and the others have made by using their positions to buy up valuable properties during the transition as well as communists' supposed connections to Russia and the old secret police. Most right-wing parties, including the Law and Justice and, earlier, the Solidarity Action Coalition and the League of Polish Families, also, implicitly or explicitly, have supported Catholic religious values and Church authority. In identifying themselves as Polish nationalists, most have opposed Poland's deep involvement with both the West and the governments of the former Soviet states. As such, they did not fully support joining the EU.

The most powerful and long-standing of these parties, Law and Justice, built its platform around attacks on the corruption of government officials and "the elite"; promises to end inequality and to punish communists and their agents by, at the least, excluding them from power; and, finally, Polish nationalism and support for Catholic Church

Photo 9.4.   Blocked by the police, opposition protestors protest the monthly memorial of Lech Kaczynski's death. (Malgorzata Alicja Gudzikowska)

positions. Since Law and Justice emerged out of the Solidarity coalition in 2001 with Lech Kaczyński, then minister of justice, as its leader, it has been in and out of power. The party has had seats in the Sejm and Senate from 2001 on. In 2005, the right had enough seats to form a coalition with the more centrist Civic Platform and have its leader, Lech Kaczyński, elected in the presidential race.

Jarosław Kaczyński, after losing the election to replace his twin brother and the former president, Lech Kaczyński after his death in 2010, worked to build a loyal cadre of party members into "local circles," often in coordination with the right-wing Catholic organization base that had formed around the so-called Radio Marjla family and its leader, Father Tadeusz Rydzyk. This made it possible for Law and Justice to get the most votes in the 2015 election and, since the left had fragmented into so many tiny parties that none met the 5 percent barrier to get seats, to hold a majority of the seats in parliament. Those "local circles" have held the party members together and allowed Kaczyński to place relative unknowns, dependent on him for their positions, as candidates in various electoral districts in the 2015 campaign. Then, these "local circles" helped ensure the party's victory. The "local circles" also reward their members with opportunities like being bussed to Warsaw to see Donald Trump speak in July 2017 and events like the monthly mass and memorial for Lech Kaczyński, which Jarosław Kaczyński leads. These events trigger opposition demonstrations which, in turn, strengthen Law and Justice to members sense that they need to stay together because the opposition is presented as a threat when it demonstrates and the police put up barricades.

Civil Society

Unlike the rest of the postcommunist world, Poland had well-established and independent civil society groupings in the communist period. The Catholic Church, already in the mid-fifties, not only held religious services but also had intellectual organizations and its own press. Informal intellectual opposition groupings as well as increasingly restive official professional associations existed as well. The various intellectual opposition groups that emerged in the mid-seventies had clear leaders known to the public, produced elaborate and regular sets of publications, ran an alternative educational system, and provided legal and financial support for individuals working in the opposition or workers punished for their participation in demonstrations. Professional associations also acted more independently than their equivalents elsewhere in the Soviet bloc as they pressed for privileges and power for their members. In addition, the shortages in the economy and complications in getting things done in the system resulted in Poles being part of elaborate friendship networks that often involved personal ties between those in the regime and those in the opposition.

These institutions, after being significant forces in ending communism, rapidly lost out in the transition. The informal networks were no longer necessary. Professional groups could not work as they had earlier because there was now competition for jobs between professionals and the state did not control workplaces. And, while established opposition groups and Solidarity retained their symbolism, they lost popular support when they had to be for something (particularly the painful economic reforms) rather than simply against communism. Their authority was also tarnished by allegations and revelations that some members had connections with the communist-era secret police.

The Catholic Church also saw its power shift. At its zenith in the eighties, it was able to function in ways that were not possible for religious institutions elsewhere. It also benefitted from having a Polish Pope who played an active role in Polish politics. Local priests were critical as a base and then mediator during the Gdansk shipyard strikes and the formation of Solidarity. In the martial-law years, individual churches served as havens for the opposition and also distribution centers for donated food and clothing for the needy during martial law. Church leaders would then serve as the intermediary and guarantor for the Roundtable talks and the elections that followed.

Local churches and the national hierarchy have since inserted themselves directly into politics, pressing public officials with demands to enact policies the Church wanted and supporting individual candidates and parties. The Catholic Church and the parties it supports have been able to legislate policies that have not been supported by large segments of the population like requiring religious education in all schools and imposing strict limits on abortion.

These gains have also created problems for the church. Although Poland remains one of the most Catholic countries in Europe (88 percent of its citizens identify as Catholic, although only 58 percent claim to be practicing[7]), the number of births out of wedlock and the number of abortions continue to increase. While many politicians were and are wary of going against the church's wishes, increasing numbers of Poles see the church as having too much influence in politics and ignore many of its directives.[8] Liberal Catholic intellectual organizations have largely folded because they are no longer needed, given the freedoms of the media and public discussion that now exist. And, the church hierarchy no longer controls religious messages. The right-wing, privately owned Radio Maryja, with its xenophobia, racism, and anti-Semitism, has become so powerful and popular that the church hierarchy cannot moderate it or stop it.[9]

As the economic transition reduced the free time and resources of most people, new civil society institutions have failed to become players in politics. Initially, Western foundations created or funded civil society organizations in Poland. Most of these lasted only as long as the funding from the outside did. Other organizations appeared. Some were charities for needy groups, but most focused on providing special benefits and privileges for their members or substituting for poor state services. They have not been significant political actors or avenues for popular participation in politics.

The Economy and Social Problems

The economy was the Achilles' heel of Poland's leaders in the communist period and during the transition. It benefited from the aid it received early on from the United States and Western Europe and, when it was preparing to enter the EU, from the EU. Poland's economy had the highest growth rate of any EU country during the European recession that began in 2008. But, many Poles, especially the elderly, those who live outside of the big urban agglomerations, and the less educated, saw and see themselves as losers, even when Poland's economy is strong.

When communism ended in 1989, Poland was an economic disaster. The reformers inherited a failed economy built on the Soviet model of state ownership with small private as well as collective farms. It was further distorted by communists' attempts to jump-start the economy in the 1970s by borrowing heavily from the West to build new factories, raise salaries, and import Western goods to satisfy the population. This made it the third most indebted country in the world by 1990.[10] It also had allowed Poles to go abroad to work and to start their own small firms. That meant reformers faced a population with higher expectations than elsewhere, a crushing debt to both the West and East as well an economic system that was already partly privatized. Its population had higher expectations and its economic reformers had less flexibility because Poland was so in debt to the West and East.

This meant that decisions about how to transform the economy were dependent on the approval of Western creditors because Poland needed debt reduction as well as Western aid to survive and change. As a result, economic reform began with "shock therapy," in the form of the Balcerowicz Plan. This ended all price controls and simultaneously froze salaries. In the process, prices rose dramatically and then fell, the Polish zloty because convertible to Western currencies, trade barriers and government subsidies for state enterprises ended, and interest rates increased for borrowing.

The initial results were disastrous for most individuals. By the end of January 1990, individual purchasing power was reduced to nearly half of what it had been at the end of 1989. Registered unemployment went from 0.3 percent in December 1989 to 6.5 percent a year later, jumping to 11.4 percent in December 1991 and 16.4 percent in 1993.[11] Declines in all the major economic indicators for the next two years were equally dramatic. Gross Domestic Product (GDP) dropped over 18 percent. In the first month of 1990 alone, industrial production dropped 30 percent, and the purchasing power of wages and salaries went down more than one-third. Peasant incomes fell by about half. Polish agricultural goods lost out on the domestic market to better-packaged and heavily subsidized Western goods that were often cheaper than their now unsubsidized Polish equivalents. Old state cooperatives and private enterprises that had survived the communist era collapsed because they could not compete with mass-produced Western goods or pay soaring costs for rent, materials, and salaries. At the same time, a small group of wealthy "owners and consultants" emerged. By 1993, the economy had begun an upswing that lasted through the mid-1990s, when it slowed perceptibly and economic growth hovered around 5 percent per year in the mid-1990s.

Even as the economy grew, however, there were problems. Growth happened only in specific areas where new technology brought productivity increases and job losses. The export sector lagged behind, leaving Poland with a serious deficit. Inflation remained high. For a large percentage of Poles, the new buildings and foreign investments in the major cities were coupled with bankruptcies of the factories and other institutions that had kept the smaller cities and rural regions alive. These triggered significant regional unemployment outside the major cities in what was known as "second Poland" and a slide into poverty for a majority of the population, even as a small but ever-increasing number of people grew wealthy from the changes. These socioeconomic divisions lasted for decades, creating the embittered population that turned to right-wing populist parties and elected Law and Justice, PiS, twice.

The solution for the government was to push privatization. New small firms, largely based on imports and street trade, blossomed. They often began by working around the existing rules, selling on the street, and paying little or no tax. Many state stores were simply privatized by their employees. As a result, the share of employment and the national income in the private sector grew from less than one-third to more than half of the Polish economy by 1993, even though larger and weaker state firms continued on, virtually untouched by privatization.

The next step proved extremely complex and contentious. Solidarity leaders advocated moving toward employee ownership and maintaining cooperative enterprises. Leszek Balcerowicz, as deputy prime minister and minister of finance in the first postcommunist government, and his supporters wanted simply to privatize state industries as quickly and completely as possible by establishing a stock market and letting weak industries go bankrupt. Only after eleven draft laws were rejected did this Margaret Thatcher–style privatization become law.

In the end, Poland's privatization was piecemeal, done largely through foreign investment and mass privatization. Those firms that were viable were consolidated into national investment funds. In this process, only 512 of the 8,453 state firms were included. As a result, initially, only about 2 percent of the total workforce was involved. Much of the money earmarked to prepare firms for privatization went to managers rather than to upgrading and reorganizing the firms. Every adult Pole got a share certificate for 180 zlotys (about $40) to invest in these funds. For most Poles, this minimal "mass privatization" was far from enticing. Rather than enlivening the market, the process caused the worth of the firms and the certificates to fall to less than half their original value.[12]

Most foreign direct investment involved government and private firms buying up state firms and Western businesses moving in to renovate or replace them or open new businesses. The bulk of new investments were in construction and the opening of huge foreign-based supermarkets and discount stores. In the end, the Polish economy, 75 percent of which was in private hands by 2000, became a "subsidiary economy" of foreign firms. At the turn of the century, after these initial investments, foreign investment decreased dramatically: between 2000 and 2002, direct foreign investment dropped from $9.341 billion to $4.131 billion.[13]

There were serious political complications in both mass privatization and foreign direct investment. For most Poles, privatization seemed to hurt rather than help. Newly privatized firms were often sold or transformed to make money for their managers. Wages and work conditions in many foreign firms, particularly in the large supermarkets, were often below Polish standards. Almost 75 percent of banking services has been controlled by Western capital and large parts of other key institutions, such as the media, some postal services, and telephone services, are owned or partly owned by outside interests. Many Poles felt Poland was being sold off, at bargain prices, to the West. The public's disgust at not getting the benefits it had expected from capitalism has been magnified by accusations and revelations of corruption involved in selling off, with huge tax and price breaks, Polish industries and resources to Western firms and Russian interests.

The growth in Poland's GDP during the 2008 European recession was largely the result of the impact of the funding the EU gave to prepare Poland's economy and infrastructure for accession; the comparatively small amount of its GDP invested in exports most of which were agricultural products; the slowness of its banking sector to modernize and lower its standards for loans or make large loans in foreign currency; and the fact that Poland had not joined the Eurozone. This meant that the Polish economy was not affected by the economic problems of many West European states when the recession hit. It also meant Poland had its own funding for investment projects. Its agricultural sector, after having opposed joining the EU, found itself actually benefiting from Poland's membership. Not only did the EU provide substantial agricultural aid as Poland was joining, but Poland's small, traditional farms found a valuable niche as producers of organic foods.

For all of Poland's macroeconomic successes, those gains did not help large sectors of the population. The percentage of Poles who were unemployed grew, and the worth of most workers' earnings dropped because of increases in inflation. To keep the state sector solvent, many (mostly larger) state plants that could not easily be sold to private investors were closed down or sold off at low prices. Because so much of Poland's industry had been concentrated in single-industry towns and regions, outside the major cities, these changes created areas of mass unemployment in what came to be known as "second Poland." It resulted in disaffection with the Civic Platform (PO) in Poland's small towns and less industrialized areas.

By the 2015 election, the economy, again, became a political issue. The national debt has remained lower than in many other European states, but it still has been more than 50 percent of its GDP since 2009. Efforts to reduce that debt by cutting state costs and benefits hurt the most vulnerable parts of the population. The pressure of unemployment on the economy has grown as the loss of jobs elsewhere in Europe forced Poles who had left to work or study abroad to return, increasing the level of unemployment in Poland. It was made worse, politically, because those who returned had seen how the people in the West they worked for lived and, unlike their predecessors who had worked abroad for short periods during the communist period, the money they earned abroad and brought back did not go far. Then, with the conflict in Ukraine in 2014, the already large flow of

Ukrainians coming into Poland to take poorly paid jobs as guest workers exploded as large numbers of refugees from the war and economic collapse took refuge in Poland. They soaked up some of the jobs students and unqualified workers would normally have taken.

While, comparatively, life was better than it was after communism fell or even in the early 2000s, the disparities between the under and unemployed and the urban middle and upper classes angered those who felt they were losers and so supported Law and Justice because of its commitment to increase social welfare supports for large segments of the population. To date, the payments to families for children and increases in welfare payments have resulted in more individual spending; but, there are real risks for the economy in the long run.

Social Conditions

There have been real gains for many in the population since 2005 when 17 percent of the population lived below the government-established social minimum (enough income to cover not only food and housing but also clothes, limited cultural events, and education) and 26 percent of children lived in poverty.[14] By 2013, unemployment hovered around 10.3 percent, down from 19.1 percent in 2004, with approximately 27.3 percent registered unemployment among youth, down from 39 percent in 2004. Much of this was long-term unemployment. The decreases in poverty and unemployment occurred, in large part, because the elderly population decreased. The cohort of young people entering the labor market also was much smaller than it had been previously because, as of 2010, nearly 2 million were working abroad and many others were attending universities. Those gains, though, are not all permanent. By 2013, many young people going into the labor market, after working abroad or finishing their educations, found there were no jobs for them. Although, under Law and Justice, the age for mandatory retirement has been decreased.

The impact of these inequities and demographic changes was, from the beginning, aggravated by the economic reforms' negative effect on the very aspects of social welfare that were "givens" in the communist era—free education and health care and guaranteed pensions. That, coupled with EU pressures for a low budget deficit, made either reforming or supporting social services and having a welfare system difficult at best.

These trends have also been aggravated by the heightened demand on and costs to the state for health care and education as well as unemployment assistance and pensions. The economic reforms increased the cost of basic necessities dramatically, even as privatization and the commitment to an exchangeable currency and meeting EU requirements decreased the money the state could spend on such services. So, doctors and teachers have experienced a steady decline in their salaries and financial support for hospitals, schools, and other social welfare institutions has dried up. Initially, this was buffered because the wealthier segment of the population could use new private hospitals, clinics, and schools. Many professionals also shifted to the new private sector in education and health care where salaries were higher, worked multiple jobs, or left the country.

All this increased Poles' sense of the inequality in their society. The results of these social demands and the inability of the state to meet them have resulted in a number of problems. Unemployment and family support funds have been, most often, so limited that no one can live above the biological minimum level on only unemployment benefits or the family subsidies regions give out. So, most of the unemployed have drifted away into the gray economy of illegal trade and crime. Particularly in the rural areas and small towns, poverty became a steady state. And, the divisions between the well-off and those who are less well-off seem much more dramatic.

State support of the poor has been limited at best. After 1989, Jacek Kuron, a long-time member of the opposition and the first noncommunist minister of social welfare, fought for decent unemployment benefits and even set up his own soup kitchens as a model for private action to deal with problems for which there was no government money. Only after the 1997 election was there an attempt to create coherent public programs to reorganize the health-care and pension systems and their funding. But by 2005, neither the right-wing Solidarity Electoral Action government nor its social democratic successor had been able to implement effective reforms in these areas. Hospitals closed down for months at a time because of lack of funds. The Constitutional Court declared a health-care reform law unconstitutional in 2002, leaving the health-care system to function with no legal structure for more than a year until a new law was passed in 2004. The crisis in the public sector has decreased slightly with the passage of some health-care and education legislation, but it is far from over. Salaries for public-sector employees remain a major political issue and resulted in some medical personnel going on hunger strikes in 2017.

Transitional Justice

Transitional justice in Poland, after a delayed beginning, officially focused on three processes: trying leaders accused of ordering attacks on major demonstrations, lustrating politicians listed as agents in secret police files, and setting up programs for recognizing and getting information out on long-ignored moments in Polish history. Ironically, public opinion surveys show that these processes have not been of great interest to the population; they have, however, been significant in political battles.

Because Poland's negotiated revolution included communists in the Roundtables and in the first postcommunist government, many of the leading dissidents initially were reluctant to punish the men and women of the former regime, its secret police, and its network of agents. This led to their "drawing a thick line" between the past and present. The files stayed in the police offices and secret police officials continued to work, often supervised by the men they had monitored. The first and partial lustration law was passed only in 1996.

Before 2007, individual politicians were "lustrated" (barred from public office for having served as agents of the secret police) only if they lied in the declaration required of each candidate and some state officials by claiming not to have been such an agent. These declarations were posted in election district polling stations but did not deter voters from supporting strong candidates even if they admitted to having been agents. If they were challenged and a top government official was found to have lied on his forms, he was given the choice of either simply resigning from his positions or going through a trial in a special, closed court.

In the void this delay in opening the files caused, politicians on the right made accusations and claimed to have proof that their political opponents had been agents in what was "wild lustration." This forced politicians on the left to move to establish a legal process for dealing with the past, complicated as it was by the secret police files having remained in the hands of the police so they were vulnerable to being destroyed or tampered with.

In 2006, the Law and Justice Party pushed through legislation expanding the requirement for lustration to the legal, media, and education professions, as well as to other state offices, and opening up the police files of those who had been spied on not just to the victims but to journalists and scholars as well. That legislation was largely rejected by the courts because it violated European human rights standards. Then, in 2007, the Institute of National Memory was opened after a more developed and broader law was passed.

With the opening of files and lustration, charges of political enemies having been an agent of the secret police or the Soviet Union, as well as references to the past, remain regular parts of political discourse. To the extent that they had credibility, these attacks not only muddied political battles but also the public image of the church and the opposition movement, both prime targets for secret police pressure. And although most of the victims and perpetrators are now dead or elderly and there is little political support for the politics of attacks, the secret police and their agents remain a popular topic in Polish film, and "who did what" is of interest to younger generations as well.

Pressure from the right also resulted in trials of Wojciech Jaruzelski and others around him. These trials have been for the killing of workers in 1970 (although Jaruzelski did not sign the order and was not in the area when the attacks happened) and for the imposition of martial law. The trial for the 1970 killings dragged on for years. In 2007, based on documents in the files taken over by the Institute of National Memory, a trial of Jaruzelski and his close associates over the declaration of martial law in 1980 began as well. Both trials drew little public interest and ended because the defendants were too old and ill even to attend the trials. Ultimately, they had no effect on public opinion: a significant part of the population saw martial law as "the lesser evil."

The Institute of National Memory has also taken an active role in historical discussions of the atrocities of World War II and events in the communist period by publishing books, sponsoring meetings, and even producing games designed to remind people of what happened and Polish heroism and teach youth about the problems of life in communist systems.

At the same time, new museums and monuments have been opened on issues ignored in the communist era: the Warsaw Uprising at the end of the war, the history of Jews in Poland, and repression under the communists. The content of these museums and the "telling" of much of modern Polish history has become an increasingly contentious issue under Law and Justice with legal actions against people who refer to "Polish death camps" or blame Poles for killings during the War. In recent years, there have also been battles over who really was the leader of Solidarity—Lech Walesa or Lech Kaczyński. Even the Warsaw Uprising celebrations, which had been prohibited under the communists, were targets when there was an attempt to have Lech Kaczyński and the others in the plane crash honored with those who were heroes of the Warsaw Uprising.

By November, 2017, this increasingly heated nationalist and anti-immigrant rhetoric helped trigger massive nationalist demonstrations against Jews and Muslims on a newly established "Independence Day."

Foreign Policy

Poland's foreign policy since 1989 has tried to bridge three worlds: the United States, Western Europe, and the former Soviet bloc. Given the strength of the Polish lobby and the size of the Polish economy and unpaid debt, US interests were early and powerful players, as were West European interests. After the collapse of the Soviet Union, Poland advocated for the Baltic states and Ukraine, particularly in the EU. It also has worked to aid any democratization in Belarus.

For all the initial government's interest in returning to Europe, it was impossible for Poland to turn away from what was the Soviet Union totally. The Soviet responses were key to how the Poles designed the limits of their transition. The Soviet Union and former Soviet states that border Poland (Ukraine, Belarus, and Russia) had been established legal and black markets for Polish goods. Russia was also the major source of energy resources for Poland. So, Poland's eastern neighbors could not simply be ignored. So, the leaders of Poland turned to the West even as they dealt and remained tied to the East.

Former Soviet peoples' desire to go to the West or have their systems follow Poland's model proved to be a blessing. Initially, Poles worried that there would be a mass exodus out of these poorer states, flooding Poland with refugees. Instead, they got a plethora of skilled laborers from Ukraine and other former Soviet states ready to work at low wages in Poland to cover their expenses in their home countries. Conversely, foreign policy leaders came to value the idea of Poland as a bridge between the East and West. In playing this out, Poland has been far more engaged than other countries in Central and Eastern Europe in working with countries to the east and advocating for their democratization. Aleksander Kwaśniewski, as a former communist and president of Poland, was asked by the then Ukrainian president, Leonid Kuchma, to lead top-level negotiations. He formed a group of negotiators—including the then president of Lithuania and Javier Solana, as head of the EU Foreign Affairs section, along with a Russian representative—which helped negotiate an end to the Orange Revolution with the leaders on both sides of the dispute. And then, once Russian engagement in Ukraine began in 2014, Polish politicians were the leaders in NATO and the EU pushing for strong stands against the repression and Russian actions.

This balancing act was complicated as it was coupled with incentives, largely for those on the left, to get legitimacy by being welcomed by US leaders, NATO, and the EU. For all of Poland's former politicians, especially the former communists, it was critical for them to stress their Western ties and the fact that reforms were required for Poland to rejoin Europe as a part of the transatlantic alliance. It fell to the right wing to emphasize Polish nationalism and the risks and costs of alignment with both the EU and Russia. Those on the right have been inclined to picture Poland as being sold off to Western (and former Soviet) interests. Hence, the Euroskeptic candidates in European Parliament elections were, most often, from right-wing parties in Poland.

It was further complicated by the need to respond to the demands of membership in the EU and NATO or to US demands. Although Poland was the central geographic corridor for NATO and the EU's expansion eastward, it initially lagged in making the necessary reforms. It also did not always side with the Europeans in economic and political matters. In fact, Poland was long called by some "America's Trojan horse." When faced with a choice between American and European producers, it leaned toward US products. At the same time, for Poles, the United States' refusal to lift its visa requirement, as it has for the other Central European countries, has been a serious issue, especially now that Poles have money and there is no longer any real incentive for them to work, illegally as they did in the past, in the West.

NATO membership was an important symbol of Poland's turn to the West. It was, for Poles, a guarantee that they were safe from their eastern neighbors, even though there was no commitment, until Russia's intervention in Ukraine, to protect Poland in the event of an attack. The costs of joining and retooling its military were partially cushioned by Western aid it had received earlier to smooth its movement into NATO. After Britain, Poland was one of the first European states to join the "coalition of the willing in Iraq," with a sizable contingent of troops that governments on both the right and left maintained, and one of the last to withdraw. In response to Russian actions in Ukraine, NATO agreed to station rapid response forces in Poland.

In the summer of 2016, Poland's relationship with NATO and the United States grew more complicated. On the one hand, it hosted the NATO Summit in 2016. At that Summit, though, Poland was criticized for the weakening of its democratic institutions by Barak Obama and, more indirectly, by other leaders. On the other hand, the meeting involved a commitment to having a NATO defense force in Poland.

Poland's membership in the EU was guaranteed by its geographic position. Even if it lagged in its preparations, it could not be ignored and could not have its membership delayed. Many in Poland and the West feared the results of Poland's inclusion in the EU, even as they cheered this visible end to the division of Europe. Many thought Poles would leave en masse to work in Western Europe. To calm fear of what came to be known as "the Polish plumber," provisions were enacted allowing countries not to give Central and East Europeans work permits for long-term stays for the first seven years after they were allowed in the EU. But until the 2008 recession, the emigration of Poles to Great Britain and Ireland proved a boon for those economies. Then, in 2016, they were targets of the Brexit vote.

In its east, Poland now has one of the most heavily guarded borders in the world (built with West European money) to keep emigrants from getting into "Europe" through Poland. And yet, Poland's neighbors from Ukraine and Belarus can enter with only a visa—given out for free at embassies and consulates. So, Poles have been able to maintain their temporary-worker labor force and provide a haven in times of political repression in Belarus and Ukraine. This new border had unexpected side effects: it cut off or reduced the "grey market" trade that had been "big business" for eastern Poland, where factories were so poorly developed and produced such low-quality goods that they could only trade with the even poorer countries to the east.

EU subsidies and special provisions eased the major concerns about the domestic impact of entry into the EU and also the fear that Germans would retake their prewar property in western Poland. The EU responded to the latter concern by ruling that, for the first seven years after Poland joined the EU in 2004, foreigners could not purchase Polish land.

Poles' limited enthusiasm for joining the EU was clear in the initial vote for EU membership in May 2003, when 77 percent of those who went to the polls voted yes for membership—less than in any other Central and East European state except the Czech Republic and Slovakia—after an active government campaign in favor of joining. In the elections for the European Parliament in June 2004 (less than two months after May 1, 2004, when Poland officially joined the EU), only 20.4 percent voted, and of those, 55 percent supported candidates from parties that were, at best, skeptical of the EU. In the 2009 EU elections, participation had risen slightly to 24.5 percent, and the Euroskeptic vote had decreased, with 44 percent of the Polish vote (and half the seats) going to Civic Platform candidates. In the 2014 election, Polish votes were essentially split between Euroskeptics and supporters of the EU with pro-EU parties getting a total of 51.95 percent of the votes for parties large enough to place (Civic Platform, 32.15 percent and the SLD and Polish Peasant Party, 19.8 percent) and the Euroskeptic parties that got seats getting 38.5 percent (with Law and Justice getting 31.7 percent of the total vote and a small Congress of New Rights, 6.8 percent).

As a result, Polish policy toward the EU has been split. The social democratic government treated membership in NATO and the EU as its great achievement. The Law and Justice government that began in 2005 was Euroskeptic, painting itself as the defender of Polish interests and the traditional Catholic faith in the EU. When a majority of Poland's deputies were on the Euroskeptic right, Poland did not always go along with standard EU procedures. Poland was a leader in the demand that the EU constitution define Europe as a Christian society. Polish deputies have also worked to increase its power in the EU, going so far in 2007 as to nearly block an agreement on vote counting provisions for the new EU constitution. A last-minute compromise delaying the new voting system ultimately placated the Poles.

The victory of the Civic Platform in 2007 resulted in a dramatic turn toward closer ties with Western Europe and the United States, despite the objections of President Kaczyński. Prime Minister Donald Tusk rapidly developed close ties with Angela Merkel of Germany and other West European leaders. His work with these leaders facilitated his election to head the Council of Europe, giving him even greater influence in European policy toward Russia.

As it has moved westward in its foreign policy, Poland has also maintained strong ties with Russia and the former Soviet states. In the process, Polish governments have tried to ensure continued access to Russian energy resources and markets. The Polish economy has also benefited from the cheap laborers that have come west to Poland to work. As the European recession began and politics grew more troubled elsewhere, Poland, led by Donald Tusk, became a model for politics in the region and a leader in Europe itself.

Polish foreign policy, explicitly and implicitly, advocated for democratization in the countries to its east. When Russia under Vladimir Putin became more authoritarian and popular upheavals took place in Georgia and Ukraine in 2003 and 2004, Poland's ability to maintain itself as a bridge between East and West declined. Russian-Polish relations, along with Polish-Belarusian relations, have grown colder, with Russia circumventing Poland in building an oil pipeline from Russia to Germany. But the conflict never went so far as to threaten Polish supplies of Russian energy.

In 2013, beginning with the Euromaidan, Poles were engaged. When Russia entered Crimea, Polish foreign minister Radoslaw Sikorski took the lead in pressing NATO, the G7, and the EU to take a strong stance against Russian aggression. In Poland, Poles watched the events closely and collected clothes and money to help the Ukrainians. And Poland moved to provide financial support for Ukraine until International Monetary Fund and other monetary aid could be agreed on and delivered to Ukraine.

The Law and Justice government has been critical of leading European states, including its neighbor Germany. It also is attempting to weaken the power of the larger EU states and Russia by beginning an organization of the states between the Baltic, Adriatic, and Black Seas (twelve Central and East European states, two Baltic states—Lithuania and Estonia, and Austria). Its goal is to both strengthen these smaller states by giving them a united voice and decrease their dependence on Russia and Germany for infrastructure, energy, and trade. At its first major meeting in Warsaw in July 2017, Donald Trump spoke and encouraged these states to increase their trade with the United States in this area.

Conclusion

The grand irony of the Polish transition has been that Poland was the furthest from Soviet-style communism (with the exception of Yugoslavia) before the transition began, had the best-developed civil society, and was the first state to begin the transition. Of the former communist states that are new entrants to the EU, Poland is the largest country with the biggest economy. Yet its initial transition, while clearly oriented toward democracy and capitalism, was one of the most troubled, with the public quite willing to vote out regime after regime; serious economic problems, even when it had the fastest-growing economy in the region; and real popular disaffection with both the economy and politics. In the end, the weakness of Poland's communist regime and the success of the former communists in returning to power as pro-democracy politicians not only opened the door for a negotiated transition but also made it difficult for the new capitalist and democratic system to satisfy its constituents.

Poland entered the EU haunted by old problems. For many individuals, the pains of the economic transition and the gap between their expectations and reality delegitimized the new system. Its failure to provide employment for youth decreased young people's excitement about building a "new Poland." The original reformers and the communists who turned democrats lost credibility, leaving Poland's political system with few successful parties that participated in the change or are supported because of their work on economic reform and Poland's new position as a part of NATO and the EU. At the same time, Poland's delay in dealing with the past and the secret police files on agents, who came to symbolize the evils of communism, made the past a political football to shut down opposition and explain away economic failures.

But with the recession in Europe, Poland's problems with reform worked to its advantage. Poland had been less successful, after the transition, in getting foreign investment, opening up lending, and borrowing to modernize its economy. That meant it had not taken the steps that backfired for other countries. Politically, the back-and-forth of Polish politics destroyed both the ideological left and right. It reduced people's expectations of politics and politicians. And it left Poland with only a center of less ideological parties and a population with few expectations of their government.

After the presidential and parliamentary elections of 2015, Poland turned sharply to a populist, right-wing ideology that was supported by the people in the small towns and agricultural areas who felt they had "lost out" as a result of the transition and Westernization of Poland when Law and Justice candidates won both elections. This has led to the new leadership seeking to play a stronger and more independent role and being more critical of "the West." It has also led to a condemnation by the European Parliament in April 2017, of Poland's violations of European democratic norms with its moves, among others, to control the court system. The parliament then directed the European Commission to take action to sanction Poland in what has been a sharp turnaround in Poland's position in the EU.

Study Questions

1. Why was Poland's communism less repressive and more inclined to liberalization of the economy and some aspects of society than that of other states? How did this impact the nature of the transition?

2. What were the key elements in Poland's history that made its communist rule different from other Central and East European states? What were the differences?

3. Why was Poland's transition a fully negotiated one, and how did this impact the nature of the initial government and the making of its critical decisions? What have been its long-term effects?

4. How was the Poland's economic transition begun? What was the political effect?

5. What are the structures of the government and the powers of the different branches of the government in postcommunist Poland? How was this system developed?

6. What has been the impact on Poland's political system of the election of Law and Justice in 2015? How has it changed the political system? What have its economic policies been? Who do they benefit?

7. What were the key political parties in Poland?

8. Why was civil society strong in communist Poland and weak in postcommunist Poland?

9. What have Poland's relations with the West and with the East been?

Suggested Readings

Curry, Jane L., and Luba Fajfer. *Poland's Permanent Revolution.* Washington, DC: American University Press, 1995.

Davies, Norman. *The Heart of Europe: The Past in Poland's Present.* Oxford: Oxford University Press, 2001.

Garton Ash, Timothy. *The Polish Revolution: Solidarity.* New Haven, CT: Yale University Press, 2002.

Kowalik, Tadeusz. *From Solidarity to Sellout.* Translated by Eliza Lewandowska. New York: Monthly Review Press, 2012.

Websites

Center for Public Opinion Research: http://www.cbos.pl/EN/home_en/cbos_en.php
Gazeta.pl: http://www.gazeta.pl (general news website with limited English translation)
Government Central Statistical Office: http://stat.gov.pl/en/
Polish Ministry of Foreign Affairs: http://www.msz.gov.pl/en/ministry_of_foreign_affairs
Warsaw Voice: http://www.warsawvoice.pl (weekly English-language publication)

Notes

God's Playground is a two-volume history of Poland by Norman Davies (New York: Columbia University Press, 1982). In the title of this definitive history of Poland, Davies makes the point that Poland has been the country most conquered and fought over in Europe and has undergone successive experiments and disasters.

1. Norman Davies, *The Heart of Europe: The Past in Poland's Present* (Oxford: Oxford University Press, 2001).

2. Padraic Kenney, *Carnival of Revolution* (Princeton, NJ: Princeton University Press, 2002).

3. Jane Curry and Luba Fajfer, *Poland's Permanent Revolution* (Washington, DC: American University Press, 1995).

4. David S. Mason, "Poland," in *Developments in East European Politics*, ed. Stephen White, Judy Blatt, and Paul G. Lewis (Durham, NC: Duke University Press, 1993), 45.

5. Those two probably won only because, for the National List, voters could use a single *x* to mark out all the candidates on the two-column National List ballot. The names at the bottom of the two columns often fell below the *x* and so were not counted as being crossed out.

6. Miroslawa Grabowska, *Podzial postkomunistyczny: Spoleczne podstawy polityki w Polsce po 1989 roku* (Warsaw: Wydawnictwo naukowe Scholar, 2004).

7. CBOS, "Religinosc: 2013" (yearly report).

8. Beata Roguska and Bogna Wciorka, "Religijnosc i stosunek do kosciola," in *Nowa rzeczywistosc*, ed. Krzysztof Zagorski and Michal Strzeszewski (Warsaw: Dialog, 2000).

9. Agnieszka Cybulska et al., "Demokracja w praktyce," in *Nowa rzeczywistosc*, ed. Krzystof Zagorski and Michal Strzeszewski (Warsaw: Dialog, 2000), 80–84.

10. http://www.nytimes.com/1991/03/16/business/poland-is-granted-large-cut-in-debt.html

11. World Economy Research Institute, *Transforming the Polish Economy* (Warsaw: World Economic Research Institute, 1993), 6.

12. Barbara Blaszczyk and Richard Woodward, *Privatization and Company Restructuring in Poland*. Report No. 18 (Warsaw: CASE, 1999).

13. *Rocznik statystyczny 2004* (Warsaw: GUS, 2005), 597.

14. Daniele Checchi, Vito Peragine, and Laura Serlenga, "Fair and Unfair Income Inequalities in Europe," DP No. 5025, IZA, June 2010, http://ftp.iza.org/dp5025.pdf.

Map 10.0. The Czech and Slovak Republics

CHAPTER 10

The Czech and Slovak Republics

TWO PATHS TO THE SAME DESTINATION

Sharon L. Wolchik

In November 1989, mass demonstrations in Prague, Bratislava, and other cities caused the hard-line communist system in Czechoslovakia to fall. Preceded by nearly twenty years of stagnation, the Velvet Revolution, as these events came to be called, ushered in a broad process of change designed to reinstitute democracy, re-create a market economy, and reclaim the nation's rightful place on the European stage. It soon became evident, however, that the impact of the transition in the Czech Lands and Slovakia, as well as the perspectives and ambitions of political leaders in the two areas, differed significantly.

After the peaceful breakup of the common state and the creation of two independent states in January 1993, the transition process diverged considerably. Progress in the Czech Republic was recognized by that country's admission to the North Atlantic Treaty Organization (NATO) in the first round of NATO expansion in March 1999. In Slovakia, by way of contrast, the antidemocratic actions of the government of Vladimír Mečiar and lack of progress in privatization cast doubt on Slovakia's fitness to join the Western club of nations and resulted in the country's exclusion from the first round of NATO expansion. The victory of the opposition in Slovakia in the 1998 parliamentary elections put the country back on track, a fact recognized in Slovakia's inclusion in the second round of NATO expansion in 2004 and its accession, along with the Czech Republic, Poland, Hungary, Latvia, Lithuania, Estonia, and Slovenia, to the European Union (EU) in the same year.

Leaders in both countries continue to face numerous challenges in consolidating democratic governance. Thus, political attitudes and values still reflect an amalgam of precommunist, communist, and postcommunist influences at the mass and elite levels, civil society remains weak, and the political party systems are still fluid. In both, coalition governments have proved fragile and corruption, particularly at the elite level, is an ongoing political issue. There are also significant problems in both countries in terms of incorporating minorities and dealing with the inequalities of opportunity and outcome created by the shift to the market. However, both remain among the most successful cases of transition in the region.

Precommunist History

Many of the differences between the Czech and Slovak republics date to the precommunist era. Prior to the creation of an independent Czechoslovak state in 1918, both regions were part of the Austro-Hungarian Empire. In contrast to several other ethnic groups in the region, neither Slovaks nor Czechs, after the Battle of White Mountain in 1620, had a native nobility. However, the Czech Lands were ruled by Austria, whereas Slovakia formed part of the Hungarian kingdom for nearly a thousand years. As a result, the Czechs had greater opportunities to develop a mass-based national movement and participate in politics in Bohemia and Vienna. The Czech Lands also became the center of the empire's industry.

In Slovakia, however, efforts to Magyarize, or Hungarianize, the population prevented the formation of a broad-based national movement. These efforts, which were particularly strong after 1878, also kept Slovaks from receiving secondary or higher education in their own language. In contrast to the Czech Lands, which were among the most developed parts of the empire, Slovakia remained predominantly agrarian. Tax codes designed to preserve the political power of the landowning aristocracy in Hungary stifled industrial development, although numerous mining and other centers, largely inhabited by Germans, did develop.

A final difference between the two regions was evident in the sphere of religion. Both peoples were predominantly Roman Catholic, but the population in the Czech Lands was far more secular than that in Slovakia, where levels of religious observance were much higher. There were also important differences in the relationship between Catholicism and national identity, as well as in the role of Protestantism in the two areas. Although the Czech national movement that developed in the nineteenth century included Catholic figures and symbols, such as Saint Wenceslas, Protestant figures, such as Jan Hus, the fifteenth-century precursor of Martin Luther who called on the church to reform and was burned as a heretic in 1415, were equally if not more important, and Catholicism played a relatively small role in the development of Czech national identity. A small Protestant minority in Slovakia also played an important role in efforts to create a national revival. However, Catholic figures and, in the interwar period, Catholic priests and the church were much more closely linked to the emerging sense of Slovak identity. Slovaks were also much more likely to attend church and turn to church ceremonies to mark major life passages such as birth, marriage, and death.[1]

These differences came to the fore very soon after the formation of the Czechoslovak Republic in 1918. The result of efforts by leaders in exile such as Tomáš Masaryk and Milan Štefánik, as well as the need to fill the void created by the fall of the Austro-Hungarian Empire at the end of World War I, the new state, which came to include Ruthenia in 1919, brought together regions at very different levels of development, populated by peoples with very different experiences.

The impact of these differences was evident throughout the interwar period. The government in Prague was committed to industrializing Slovakia and closing the gap in development levels between the two parts of the country. However, very little progress was made in this respect before the Great Depression plunged Czechoslovakia, as much of the rest of the world, into economic decline. Levels of unemployment skyrocketed, and emigration increased.[2]

Other policies of the government also fed Slovak dissatisfaction. Faced with the need to staff bureaucratic positions vacated by Hungarians, the government turned to the generally better-educated Czechs. Czech administrators, as well as Czech businessmen and specialists who came to Slovakia as part of the development effort, frequently provoked resentment. The expansion of opportunities for education in the Slovak language during the interwar period led to a significant increase in the numbers of Slovaks with secondary and higher education, but there were relatively few Slovaks with these qualifications at the beginning of the period.[3] The unitary nature of the state, which was a centralized government based in Prague, also provoked dissatisfaction among many Slovaks, who came to feel that they had merely traded rule from Budapest for rule from Prague.

As a result of these factors, support for nationalist groups grew in Slovakia. Founded by Father Andrej Hlinka, the Slovak People's Party (after 1925, Hlinka's Slovak People's Party; after 1938, Hlinka's Slovak People's Party–Party of Slovak National Unity) gained an increasing share of the vote in Slovakia. As Adolf Hitler gained power in Germany, many leaders and members of the party adopted the trappings of Nazism and looked to Hitler to support their goal of an independent Slovak state.

The German minority in the Czech Lands also became increasingly dissatisfied with the state. Konrad Heinlein's Sudeten German Party received the overwhelming share of the vote of the Germans in the Sudetenland, and the dissatisfaction of this group provided the pretext for Hitler's demand at the September 1938 Munich Conference that Czechoslovakia cede the Sudetenland to the Third Reich. Faced with the unwillingness of his British, French, and Russian allies to come to Czechoslovakia's aid, President Eduard Beneš acceded to Hitler's demands. Beneš also agreed to autonomy for Slovakia in October 1938. These steps only temporarily spared his country, however, as the Germans invaded on March 15, 1939, and established the Protectorate of Bohemia and Moravia under German control. Slovak leaders, threatened with invasion as well if they did not comply with Hitler's demands that they declare independence, declared Slovakia an independent state on March 14, 1939. This independence was largely illusory, and the Slovak state adopted many of the policies of the Nazis, including sending most of the country's Jews to the death camps.

Czechoslovakia was the only state in the region to retain democratic government until it was ended by outside forces. The interwar democratic system, which is often idealized, was certainly more successful than those in neighboring states in dealing with many of the pressing issues of the day. Progressive labor and occupational safety legislation and an extensive social welfare system succeeded in incorporating the growing working class and deflecting dissent. Elite political culture, heavily influenced by President Masaryk, also played an important role in supporting democracy, although the country, in fact, had a dual political culture as evident in the large size of the legal Communist Party.[4] The dominant role of the *pětka*, the five-party coalition that ruled the country for much of this period and often set policy in discussions among party leaders outside parliament, resulted in a form of democracy dominated by disciplined political parties and their leaders. The interwar leadership was less successful in dealing with ethnic issues than with social problems, a weakness that eventually contributed to the end of the interwar state.

Inhabitants of the Czech Lands and Slovakia had different experiences during World War II. Both areas experienced lower levels of human and property loss than states such as Poland and Yugoslavia, which had large, active resistance groups and were the scenes of heavy fighting. Occupied by the Germans, the Czech Lands were considered a source of manufactured goods and labor for the Nazi war effort. Beneš formed an exile government in Britain, but aside from sporadic acts against German rule, there was little armed resistance, particularly after the Germans retaliated for the assassination of the Protector by burning the village of Lidice to the ground. Although they had little real autonomy, many Slovaks saw the Slovak state led by Jozef Tiso as the realization of Slovak aspirations for independence. As Hitler's ally, Slovakia was also spared heavy destruction. In August 1944, Slovak anti-Nazi opposition leaders staged what has come to be known as the Slovak National Uprising against the Germans in central Slovakia. This action came to be seen after the war as a symbol of Slovak resistance and a counter to the policies of the Slovak state.

Most Jews in both the Czech Lands and Slovakia perished in the Holocaust. Roughly ninety thousand Jews lived in the Czech Lands before the outbreak of World War II. In 1942 alone, fifty-five thousand of them were sent to Theresienstadt; many of these were later deported to Auschwitz and other death camps. An estimated eighty thousand Czech Jews, or 90 percent of the community, perished in the course of the war. In Slovakia, only fifteen thousand of the estimated ninety thousand Jews survived.[5]

With the exception of the area of western Bohemia around Plzeň, which was liberated by US troops, Czechoslovakia was liberated by the Red Army. Afterward, the country was reestablished according to its interwar boundaries with the exception of Subcarpathian Ruthenia, which became part of the newly expanded Ukrainian Soviet Socialist Republic. From 1945 until February 1948, the country experienced a modified form of pluralism. The Communist Party enjoyed certain advantages, including control of the ministries of information, the interior, and agriculture, but other political parties existed and were free to participate in political life. In the 1946 elections, which were generally considered free and fair, although the political spectrum was truncated because several parties were banned for collaborating with the Nazis, the Communist Party emerged as the most popular party with 38.6 percent of the vote. Declining support on the eve of the scheduled 1948 elections, coupled with changes in Joseph Stalin's plans for the region in light of the beginning of the Cold War, led the party to instigate a government crisis in February 1948 over control of the police. The democratic members of the government resigned, and after President Beneš accepted their resignations, a government clearly dominated by the Communist Party took power.

The Communist Experience

After the February coup, the Czechoslovak communist leadership began implementing the Soviet model in earnest. The few political parties allowed to continue to exist were subordinated to the Communist Party, which became the only effective political party. The new government also stepped up the nationalization of industry, which had begun under the previous government, and aggressively collectivized agriculture. A central planning board was established to set binding five-year plans based on reorienting the country's economy to focus on heavy industry to the neglect of light industry, the consumer and service sectors, and agriculture. Efforts were also made to industrialize Slovakia, which was much less developed economically than the Czech Lands at the outset of the communist period.

As in other states in the region, the leadership also implemented measures designed to change the social structure by improving the status of previously disadvantaged groups, such as workers and farmers, and remove the privileges of the previous elites. The associational life of the country was simplified. Most voluntary organizations were outlawed and replaced by large, unitary mass organizations under the control of the party. The independent media were disbanded, and a system of strict control of information and censorship was established. The party also asserted its control in the areas of education, culture, and leisure. Political criteria became important for admission to higher education, and the content of education was politicized. The elites also made efforts to use culture and leisure to propagate values and behaviors consistent with Marxism-Leninism. As part of the latter effort, the regime undertook a brutal campaign against religion that resulted in the takeover and desecration of numerous churches, and the party's control of those priests allowed to continue to function.

Since the changes involved in implementing the Soviet model affected almost every area of life and were not chosen by the population but rather imposed from the top down, it is not surprising that the leadership came to rely increasingly on coercion. The purge trials in Czechoslovakia were among the harshest in the region, and numerous high party officials, including the secretary-general of the party, Rudolf Slánský, as well as Vladimír Clementis and several other Slovak party leaders, were executed after highly publicized show trials.[6]

Czechoslovakia remained a model Soviet satellite throughout the 1950s and early 1960s. An uprising in Plzeň after Stalin's death in 1953 was quickly put down. The regime survived de-Stalinization, which led to the Revolution of 1956 in Hungary, and popular protests and strikes in Poland in 1956, with only modest changes in personnel and lip service to the need to rout the cult of personality and restore socialist legality. By 1961, however, the previously dynamic economy in Czechoslovakia also began to show the effects of Stalinism. After the economy registered a negative growth rate in that year, party leaders commissioned a team of loyal party economists at the Academy of Science to propose economic reforms. This step, which was followed by the formation of other commissions to examine ways to reform other areas of life, initiated a large-scale process of renewal and rethinking at the elite level. Coupled with growing demands for intellectual freedom on the part of creative intellectuals, particularly writers, it resulted in the elaboration of a new model of socialism that its creators deemed more appropriate to a Western, developed society. The mid-1960s also saw the growth of Slovak dissatisfaction with Slovakia's position in the common state with the Czechs, as well as greater activism on the part of youth and several of the mass organizations.[7]

In late 1967, the reform process spread to the Communist Party itself, and in January 1968 Alexander Dubček replaced Antonín Novotný as head of the statewide party. Despite the persistence in the leadership of a hard-line faction, under Dubček and his supporters, the reform developed an explicitly political aspect. With the end of censorship in March 1968, the movement for change also spread to groups outside the party and its loyal intellectuals. More radical in its demands than those of the reformists within and associated with the party, this mass current kept pressure on Dubček and his colleagues in the party leadership to continue their efforts to create "socialism with a human face," as the model they were elaborating came to be called.

The reformist communist leadership that supported Dubček wanted to pursue reforms within the system. Best expressed in the Action Program adopted by the party in April, these demands did not include an end to the Communist Party's monopoly of power or any effort to renounce membership in the Warsaw Pact or separate Czechoslovakia from the Soviet Union and other socialist countries.[8] However, conservative leaders in East Germany and Poland, as well as the Soviet leadership, became increasingly fearful that the reformist spirit would spread to their countries.

Dubček and his supporters were caught between the need to maintain the slowly growing trust of the population and the need to satisfy their allies that socialism was not under threat. The growth of groups outside the party, including the Club of Engaged Nonparty People (KAN) and Club 231 (a club of former political prisoners), as well as the increasingly radical demands being voiced by some intellectuals,[9] led reformist leaders to consider the use of force to rein in the reform process, even as they attempted to reassure their colleagues in other socialist states.[10] After several meetings with the Soviet leadership in the summer of 1968 failed to produce the desired results, Soviet and other Warsaw Treaty Organization forces invaded Czechoslovakia on August 21, 1968.

After returning to Prague from Moscow, where they had been forcibly taken during the invasion, Dubček and his supporters attempted to preserve the reform course. It became increasingly difficult to do so, particularly with Soviet forces stationed in the country once again, and in April 1969, when Gustáv Husák, also a Slovak leader, replaced Dubček at the head of the party, it was clear that the reform era was over. Husák presided over the effort to restore orthodoxy in a process known at the time as "normalization." An attempt to reverse the reforms in all areas of life, "normalization" involved the reassertion of a clear monopoly of political power by the Communist Party, the restoration of censorship, and the end of economic reform. It was accompanied by a massive personnel purge that removed most of the most talented figures in areas as diverse as culture, education, the economy, and politics from their public and professional positions. The loss of these reformists, estimated to have included from two hundred thousand to five hundred thousand people, and the restoration of party control over the mass organizations and media led to an almost twenty-year period of stagnation. During this time, Czechoslovakia once again became a model satellite. All discussions of reform became taboo, and only small numbers of intellectuals, soon labeled dissidents by the regime, engaged in independent activity.

During this period, the regime relied on a combination of material incentives and coercion to gain the population's compliance. The standard of living improved, and many families acquired summer or weekend cottages. Coercion was used primarily against dissident intellectuals who refused to accept the status quo or were active in the small number of independent groups that developed to protest the regime's disregard for human rights and to support independent activity. Charter 77, formed in response to the regime's signing of the Helsinki Accords and the prosecution of a group of young rock musicians, the Plastic People of the Universe, in 1977, was the most important of these. Founded by Václav Havel and other intellectuals centered mainly in Prague and other large cities in Bohemia and Moravia, Charter 77 was named for the document to which these intellectuals were signatories, which circulated in *samizdat* (unauthorized material reproduced and circulated clandestinely). In the last years of communist rule, in particular, the group came to serve as the center of a growing community of independent activists, and many people who remained in good standing with the official world came to rely on its analyses for alternate information about problems that the regime either did not want to discuss or handled in a clearly biased way.[11] In 1989 and the years immediately following the end of communist rule, Charter 77 exerted an influence disproportionate to its numbers, as its leaders founded Civic Forum, and many of its members moved into prominent positions in public life in the early postcommunist period. In Slovakia, where few intellectuals signed the charter, dissent based on religious grounds was the most prominent form of opposition. Unauthorized pilgrimages to religious shrines drew upward of five hundred thousand people in the late 1980s, and lay Catholic activists organized a candlelight demonstration in Bratislava in December 1988 demanding religious freedom. Some Slovak intellectuals also participated in what came to be called "islands of creative deviation"—that is, groups of people who still held their positions in the official world and used approved organizations as venues for conducting unauthorized, nonconformist activities.

On November 17, 1989, the process that came to be known as the Velvet Revolution was set in motion by police brutality during a peaceful demonstration called to commemorate the death of a student during the period of Nazi occupation. Encouraged by the fall of the Berlin Wall and changes in Hungary and Poland earlier that year, hundreds of thousands of citizens participated in mass demonstrations against the regime. As it became clear that the demonstrators were not going to give up and that the Soviet Union would not intervene to preserve communism in Czechoslovakia, leaders of the Communist

Photo 10.1.   Citizens of Prague, Czechoslovakia, turn out by the thousands in November 1989 to protest communist regime led by Miloš Jakeš. (David Turnley/Corbis)

Party began negotiations with Civic Forum in Prague and Public against Violence in Bratislava—umbrella groups formed by Charter 77 and other dissidents in Prague and members of the opposition in Bratislava to coordinate the mass demonstrations. Within twenty-one days, the rigid, seemingly all-powerful, repressive communist system in Czechoslovakia fell. Many of the most conservative, compromised party members were removed from the federal legislature, and new elections were scheduled for June 1990. The election of former dissident playwright Václav Havel as president of Czechoslovakia on December 31, 1989, by a parliament still dominated by Communist Party members, capped the victory of the so-called Velvet Revolution.

The Transition and the Velvet Divorce

After the end of communism, Czech and Slovak leaders faced many of the same tasks as leaders in other postcommunist states. The top-priority goals were aptly summarized in the election slogans of almost all parties that ran candidates in the June 1990 parliamentary elections: democracy, the market, and a return to Europe. In the political realm, the country's new leaders had to come to terms with the communist past and establish new institutions or reorient the work of existing institutions so that they could function democratically. Other tasks included the recruitment of new leaders to replace the discredited old elite; the repluralization of the political landscape, both in terms of political parties and associational life; and the need to combat the legacy of communism on political values and attitudes and to create a new political culture suitable to a democratic polity.

In the economic realm, the new elites had to enact the legislative basis for the re-creation of private ownership and private enterprise; find a way to privatize state assets, which in Czechoslovakia accounted for over 90 percent of all economic activity at the end of communist rule; encourage the development of new private enterprises; restore economic assets to their rightful owners or their heirs; deal with rising unemployment, poverty, and inequality in a previously very egalitarian society; and address the environmental consequences of the communist pattern of industrialization. With the breakup of the Soviet Union and the Council for Mutual Economic Assistance, they also were required to reorient the country's trade, which had remained heavily centered in the socialist bloc, to the West.

In the area of foreign policy, the new leaders soon reasserted the country's status as a sovereign nation by negotiating the withdrawal of Soviet troops from its territory and began the process of reclaiming their rightful place on the European stage. In the early years after 1989, this process involved discussion about the abolition of NATO as well as the Warsaw Treaty Organization, which was dissolved in 1991. After the breakup of the Soviet Union in 1991, however, Czech and Slovak leaders began a campaign to join existing European and Transatlantic institutions. The EU and NATO were the main targets of these efforts.

The new leadership of the country, as well as its citizens, also had to cope with the social and psychological aspects of the far-reaching changes the transition entailed. In the social realm, these included changes in the social structure, as well as the emergence into the open and exacerbation of old social problems, such as juvenile delinquency, alcoholism, drug abuse, crime, and domestic abuse, as well as new issues, such as human trafficking and organized crime that emerged with the opening of borders and decline in police repression. The widespread dislocations, as well as, in many cases, the positive effects of the transition, including the vastly expanded choices available to citizens, also had negative psychological effects on many members of the population.

Very soon after the end of communism, it became evident that the transition, and particularly the shift to the market, would be more difficult in Slovakia. Because Slovakia had industrialized largely during the communist era, it had more of the "monuments of socialist industry," or very large, inefficient factories that could not compete in market conditions. Slovakia had also become the center of the country's sizable arms industry. The shift to the market, with its emphasis on profit and the ability to compete on the world market, therefore, created much greater economic disruption in Slovakia, where levels of unemployment were significantly higher than in the Czech Lands. In 1993, for example, when 3 percent of the population was unemployed in the Czech Republic, close to 15 percent was unemployed in Slovakia.

The nature of the Czechoslovak federation was another irritant to many Slovaks. Although the adoption of a federal system was one of the few changes discussed during the reform period of 1968 that was implemented in 1969, the provisions that granted Slovakia a great deal of autonomy in managing its own economic as well as cultural and educational affairs were soon rescinded as the country was "normalized." After 1971, the federation functioned largely as a unitary state. Growing Slovak dissatisfaction with Slovakia's position in the common state was reflected in public opinion polls conducted in the early 1990s that showed that some 80 percent of Slovaks were dissatisfied with the federation.[12] Although most Czechs and Slovaks continued to say that they did not want the state to break up, Czech and Slovak leaders were unable to agree on an acceptable division of power between the republic and federal governments. After the June 1992 parliamentary elections led to the victory of the center-right under Václav Klaus in the Czech Lands and the center-left led by Vladimír Mečiar in Slovakia, the two leaders oversaw the process of dissolving the federation. This step formally occurred on January 1, 1993, when the Czechoslovak Federative Republic, as it was called, was replaced by the Czech Republic and the Slovak Republic.

Initially, political and economic developments diverged markedly in the two independent states. Initial expectations that the transition would be smoother in the Czech Republic were borne out by that country's inclusion in the first round of expansion of both NATO and the EU. Vladimír Mečiar's dominance of political life in Slovakia, on the other hand, and the antidemocratic actions of his government, stalled economic reform and resulted in Slovakia's exclusion from the first round of NATO expansion. The victory of Citizens' Campaign 98 (OK'98) in the 1998 parliamentary elections brought a broad coalition of parties favoring reform to office. The government of Prime Minister Mikuláš Dzurinda quickly restarted economic reforms, included representatives of the 460,000-strong Hungarian minority in the government, rescinded anti-Hungarian measures adopted by the Mečiar government, and restored the rule of law and respect for human rights and political liberties. These steps put Slovakia back on track, and the country was admitted to NATO in the second round of expansion and included in the EU's first round of expansion to the postcommunist world in 2004.

As the pages to follow illustrate, both the Czech Republic and Slovakia have largely achieved the major goals, articulated soon after the end of communism, of restoring

Photo 10.2.   Vladimír Mečiar, Václav Havel, and Václav Klaus hold a press conference about the future of the country

democracy and the market and returning to Europe. However, in both, important problems persist in consolidating democracy and dealing with the economic aftermath of communism.

Political Institutions

The legislature elected for a two-year term in Czechoslovakia in June 1990 was to have been a constitutive assembly: its main task was to revise the country's constitution and reform its legal system to be compatible with democratic government and the creation of a market economy. Although the country's new leaders made a great deal of progress in the latter area, their inability to agree on a division of power between the federal and republican governments contributed to the breakup of the state.

The two new states that replaced the federation in January 1993 were both unitary. Their constitutions, adopted in both countries on January 1, 1993, identify them as parliamentary democracies and include provisions guaranteeing their citizens broad political and civil liberties.

In both states, the government is formed based on the results of parliamentary elections and is responsible to the legislature. The Czech Republic has a bicameral legislature. The lower house consists of two hundred members elected for four-year terms on the basis of proportional representation. The upper house, the Senate, created in 1996, consists of eighty-one members elected according to the majority principle for six-year terms. One-third of senators are elected every two years. Slovakia has a unicameral legislature. Its 150 members are elected to four-year terms according to proportional representation.

In addition to governments headed by prime ministers responsible to parliament, both countries also have presidents who serve as head of state. The president is directly elected in Slovakia and, since 2013, in the Czech Republic. Previously, the Czech president was elected by parliament. Officially, the duties of the president are largely ceremonial in both countries. However, in both cases, the office has sometimes been used to counteract or counterbalance actions by the government in ways that go beyond its formal powers. These activities were most evident in Slovakia during the Mečiar period, when President Michal Kováč, formerly a close colleague of Prime Minister Mečiar, came to be seen as an opponent of Mečiar's more authoritarian actions. Václav Havel, who was both the first postcommunist president of the federation and the first president of the independent Czech Republic, exercised influence that far exceeded the powers of his office due to his enormous moral authority and reputation around the world.[13]

The next Czech president, Václav Klaus, a known Euroskeptic, held up Czech ratification of the Lisbon Treaty in October 2009 by refusing to sign without certain EU guarantees. He finally signed on November 3 after the Constitutional Court rejected a challenge from the Civic Democrats, making the Czech Republic the last country to approve the treaty. His successor, Miloš Zeman, the first popularly elected president in the Czech Republic, has tried since his election in 2013 and reelection in 2018, to expand the powers of the office beyond its ceremonial duties. In the 2014 presidential elections in Slovakia, Andrej Kiska (see photo 10.3), a wealthy businessman and philanthropist with no previous political experience, won an upset victory over Robert Fico, the incumbent Prime Minister, with 59.4 percent of the vote in the first round. Fico's election, had it occurred, would have meant that both the majority in parliament and president were

Photo 10.3. Andrej Kiska was elected in 2014 as Slovakia's fourth president. (Corbis)

from the same party, an outcome Slovak voters evidently wanted to avoid. Kiska, who is thought to be a moderate politically, has no affiliation with a political party. He has often taken positions at odds with those of Fico and the government, particularly on immigration and refugee policy.[14]

Political Parties and Movements

After the end of communism, one-party rule by the Communist Party was replaced by a plethora of political parties. The most important of these, initially, were the broad umbrella groups formed in November 1989 to direct the mass demonstrations and negotiate with the government: Civic Forum in the Czech Lands and Public against Violence in Slovakia. Almost immediately, however, other political parties began to form. These included successors to parties that had been active in the interwar period and were banned under communism, new parties with links to parties in the rest of Europe, nationalist or regional parties and movements, and single-issue groups and parties focused on new issues. Several small parties that had been allowed to exist under communism, albeit under the control of the Communist Party, began to act independently. Reformed and unreformed versions of the Communist Party also participated in politics in both regions.[15]

Although they won the June 1990 elections resoundingly, Civic Forum and Public against Violence soon splintered into smaller groups. In the Czech Lands, then finance minister Václav Klaus broke away from Civic Forum in April 1991 to form the Civic Democratic Party. Those who remained in Civic Forum founded the Civic Democratic Movement and the Civic Democratic Alliance, which succeeded in electing candidates to the Federal Assembly in the 1992 elections but were not viable political entities after that. In Slovakia, Vladimír Mečiar, initially part of Public against Violence, broke away in April 1991 to found the Movement for a Democratic Slovakia, which became the most popular party or movement in that republic. Public against Violence was replaced by a variety of other parties on the center-right.

As table 10.1 illustrates, the number of political parties and movements that have fielded candidates has in fact increased in both the Czech Republic and Slovakia since 1990. However, many of these were unable to obtain enough votes to pass the threshold of 3 or 5 percent of the vote required to seat deputies in parliament. Thus, four parties gained enough votes to seat deputies in the federal legislature in the Czech Lands and five in Slovakia in 1990; in 1992, six parties crossed the threshold in the Czech Lands and five in Slovakia. Six parties were represented in the Czech Chamber of Deputies in 1996, five in 1998, and four in 2002. In Slovakia, seven parties seated deputies in parliament in 1994, six in 1998, and seven in 2002. After the 2006 elections, there were once again six parties in the parliament in Slovakia and five in the Czech Chamber of Deputies. In the 2010 elections, eight parties seated deputies in the Czech Chamber of Deputies and six in the Slovak National Council. In the early elections in Slovakia in 2012, six parties seated deputies in the Slovak National Council; in the Czech Republic's early elections in October 2013, seven parties seated deputies in the Chamber of Deputies, including one newly formed party. After the 2016 elections in Slovakia, eight parties held seats in the Slovak parliament. In the Czech Republic, nine parties won enough votes to obtain seats in the parliament in 2017, the highest number since the end of communism.

Although a relatively small and stable number of parties have seated deputies in the legislatures since 1990, the figures in table 10.1 mask an important aspect of politics in the period since 1989. As table 10.2 illustrates, parties continue to appear and disappear with great frequency. Thus, seventeen of the twenty-five parties that competed in the 2002 elections in Slovakia were new or newly formed combinations of previous political groups, as were two of the seven parties that seated deputies. In the Czech Republic, twenty-one of the twenty-five parties that fielded candidates in the 2002 parliamentary elections were either new or reincarnations of previous parties. In the 2006 Czech parliamentary elections, the pattern remained the same, as thirteen of the twenty-six parties that fielded candidates were new. In Slovakia, however, only eight of the twenty-one

Table 10.1. Ratio of the Number of Parties Seating Deputies to the Number of Parties Fielding Candidates by Election

Czechoslovakia Federal Assembly (Chamber of Nations and Chamber of People)

	Czech National Council	Czech Lands	Slovakia	Slovak National Council
1990	0.31 4/13	0.27 4/15 +0.27 4/16	0.29 5/17 +0.29 5/17	0.44 7/16
1992	0.42 8/19	0.30 6/20 +0.30 6/21	0.27 6/22 +0.23 5/22	0.22 5/23

	Czech Republic Chamber of Deputies		Slovakia National Council
1996	0.40 6/15	1994	0.41 7/17
1998	0.42 5/12	1998	0.35 6/17
2002	0.14 4/28	2002	0.28 7/25
2006	0.20 5/25	2006	0.29 6/21
2010	0.31 8/26	2010	0.33 6/18
2013	0.30 7/23	2012	0.23 6/26
2017	0.29 9/31	2016	0.35 8/23

Source: Statistical Office of the Slovak Republic, "Elections and Referenda," http://volby.statistics.sk/index-en.html, Czech Statistical Office, http://www.volby.cz/.

Table 10.2. Number of Parties Fielding Candidates and Number of New Parties in the Czech Republic and Slovakia since Independence

	Czech Republic				Slovakia		
	New Parties	Total Parties	Ratio		New Parties	Total Parties	Ratio
1996	8	15	0.53	1994	12	17	0.71
1998	5	12	0.42	1998	13	17	0.76
2002	21	28	0.75	2002	17	25	0.68
2006	13	25	0.52	2006	8	21	0.38
2010	13	26	0.50	2010	9	18	0.50
2013	10	23	0.43	2012	15	26	0.58
2017	17	31	0.55	2016	12	23	0.52

Source: Statistical Office of the Slovak Republic, "Elections and Referenda," http://volby.statistics.sk/index-en.html, Czech Statistical Office, http://www.volby.cz/.

parties that fielded candidates in 2006 were new. In 2010, there were thirteen new Czech parties out of twenty-five fielding candidates and nine new Slovak parties in a field of eighteen. Fifteen of the twenty-six parties that competed in the Slovak elections of 2012 were newly formed, as were ten of the twenty-six parties that contested the early Czech elections in 2013. In 2016, twelve of twenty-three parties in the Slovak elections were newly formed. Seventeen of the thirty-one parties in the Czech elections were new in 2017, a proportion exceeded only in 2002.

Analysts of politics in both countries have disagreed about how to characterize the political party system that followed the breakup of the initial umbrella organizations. By the mid-1990s, some analysts argued that the proliferation of political parties that followed the demise of these groups was coming to an end and that a simplified party system was emerging. Others argued that, although party labels continued to change, the electorate was sorting itself into two coherent, identifiable large blocs that corresponded in a general way to the left-right division seen in many other European polities.[16] As subsequent elections have demonstrated, events since that time, with few exceptions, have not supported either view. Instead, the party system has continued to be fluid, as voters have generally tended to "throw the rascals out" at each election. As table 10.2 illustrates, both the number of parties and the parties themselves have also tended to change from one election to another. The reelection of a center-right government in Slovakia in the 2002 elections and a center-left government in the Czech Republic in the same year, although both with changes in the composition of the coalition, was unusual not only in those countries but in the postcommunist region as a whole.[17]

In the 2006 parliamentary elections, voters in both countries reverted to the more common pattern of defeating the incumbent government. In Slovakia, the Smer (Direction) movement led by Robert Fico won the largest number of votes, soundly defeating the center-right government of Mikuláš Dzurinda. Fico eventually formed a coalition government with deputies from Vladimír Mečiar's center-left Movement for a Democratic Slovakia and the extreme right-wing Slovak National Party. In the Czech Republic, the center-right Civic Democrats emerged as the strongest party in the June elections, but the minority government they led, which was formed only several months after the election, was a fragile coalition with the Christian Democrats and the Greens that survived four no-confidence votes between 2006 and 2009 but was toppled by a vote of no confidence in March 2009, when the Czech Republic held the presidency of the EU. An interim government led by Jan Fischer, former head of the State Statistical Office, governed the country until early elections in May 2010. Both of the largest parties, the Czech Social Democratic Party and the Civic Democratic Party (ODS), lost votes in the 2010 elections, although the socialists received more votes than any other party (22.08 percent).[18] In the 2013 elections, held after a scandal involving corruption and misuse of government resources led to the resignation of the prime minister and the appointment of a caretaker government, ODS, the dominant party in the three-party coalition formed after the 2010 elections and a constant in the Czech political party scene since its founding in 1991, barely received enough votes to seat deputies in parliament. In parliamentary elections held in October 2017 in the Czech Republic, the ANO party of Andrej Babiš won by far the largest share of the votes, 29.7 percent, followed by ODS with 11.3 percent, the Pirate Party with 10.8 percent, and the Freedom and Direct

Democracy Party with 10.6 percent. The Communist Party's share of the vote dropped to 7.8 percent and that of ANO's coalition partners in the previous government, the Social Democrats and Christian Democrats, to 7.3 percent and 5.8 percent, respectively. Two other parties, TOP 09 and the Mayors and Independents, barely passed the 5 percent threshold with 5.8 percent and 5.2 percent, respectively.

Despite the fact that his party won nearly a third of the vote, Babiš was unable to form a coalition with any other party. On December 13, President Miloš Zeman appointed a fourteen-member minority government consisting solely of ANO members. This government began working without a vote of confidence by parliament, a fact that may well lead to early elections in 2018.

Although Robert Fico's Smer won by far the largest share of the vote (29.14 percent) in the 2010 parliamentary elections in Slovakia, he was unable to form a coalition due to the failure of Mečiar's party to cross the 5 percent threshold necessary to seat deputies and the unwillingness of all parties except the Slovak National Party, which won 11.73 percent of the vote, to form a coalition with him.[19] A center-right coalition consisting of the Slovak Democratic Christian Union-Democratic Party (SDKU-DS), Christian Democratic Movement (KDH), and two new parties, Most-Híd, which broke off from the Hungarian Coalition Party prior to the elections, and the Freedom and Solidarity Party (SaS), a center-right party focused on the need for tax reform, thus formed the new government with Iveta Radičová, a sociologist and longtime civic activist before she joined the SDKU-DS, as prime minister. In the early 2012 elections held after the Radičová government fell in 2011, Smer gained 44.42 percent of the vote, which translated into 83 of the 150 seats in parliament, enabling the party to form a government without forming a coalition. Support for the SDKU-DS fell dramatically to 6.10 percent of the vote, in large part due to the so-called Gorilla corruption scandal, in which former Prime Minister Dzurinda and other top center-right leaders were caught on tape discussing bribes.

Fico's Smer party lost its majority in the 2016 parliamentary elections, although it remained the largest vote-getter with 28.3 percent of the vote. SaS, a center-right party formed in 2010 that was the cause of the fall of the Radičová government, came in second with 12.1 percent of the vote, followed by OCaNO, Ordinary People and Independents with 11.0 percent of the vote. The Slovak National Party gained 8.6 percent of the vote, followed by three parties new to parliament, two of which were formed after the last parliamentary elections, *We Are Family*, with 6.6 percent, #Siet (Network) with 5.6 percent, and the far-right People's Party-Our Slovakia led by Marian Kotleba, with 8.0 percent. Most-Híd (Bridge), the Hungarian-Slovak party that received most of the votes of the Hungarian minority, won 6.5 percent. One of the perennial political forces in Slovak politics, the Christian Democratic Movement, received less than 5 percent of the vote and did not seat deputies in parliament. As Tim Haughton, Darina Malová, and Kevin Deegan-Krause note, although three of the eight parties that entered parliament were new to that body, more voters moved from one established party to another than to new parties.[20] The most shocking result of the election was the fact that a neo-Nazi, far right-wing party, Marian Kotleba's People's Party-Our Slovakia, gained entry to parliament for the first time. Kotleba, who won election as head of one of Slovakia's regions in the 2013 regional elections, benefited from the anti-immigrant mood in the country that Fico sought to exploit, as well as the general dissatisfaction of most citizens with the

Photo 10.4. Former Czech Prime Minister Mirek Topolánek and current Slovak Prime Minister Robert Fico. (Official website of the government of the Slovak Republic, http://www.government.gov.sk)

government and political leaders.[21] In 2017, two of the party's members of parliament were charged with hate speech and the attorney general has sought to ban the party for what he described as attacks on the democratic system. Kotleba's party was also defeated in the regional elections in 2017.

The coalition government formed after the 2016 elections brought together Fico's center-left Smer, and the nationalist Slovak National Party (SNS) with the center-right Most-Híd or Bridge party and #siet, or Network. This coalition, which spans left and right, has to date proved stable, despite initial fears that it would not serve out its mandate.

The election of a far-right-wing party to the Slovak parliament, as well as the presence in the Czech parliament elected in 2013 of the far-right party Dawn, illustrate one of the results of the current system of political parties in both countries. Most political parties in the Czech Republic and Slovakia are weak organizationally, with small memberships and poorly staffed local organizations. The unreformed Communist Party in the Czech Republic and the Christian democratic parties in both countries had larger memberships than most other parties, but their memberships are also relatively small. Levels of party identification, which in more established democracies helps simplify political choices, link citizens to the political system, and moderate conflict, have also remained low. Many citizens do not believe that parties play an essential role in a democratic state, and many continue to hold parties and party leaders in low regard.[22]

In part, these trends reflect the legacy of the communist period. In reaction to the need to be a member of the Communist Party or its youth organization if one wanted to study at university or hold many professional jobs, many people have refused to join any party. Low levels of party membership may also reflect, however, the trend in much of the rest of Europe for parties to change from being membership organizations that influence many aspects of their members' lives to electoral parties more along the lines of US political parties. The lack of willingness to become a member of a party or take part in party-sponsored activities, as well as negative attitudes toward parties, may also reflect citizens' experiences in the postcommunist era. The tendency of parties to come and go, the similarities in the platforms of many parties, and the frequent change in the party affiliation of political figures all make it difficult and costly in terms of time and attention for citizens to affiliate with particular parties. These trends also reinforce citizens' views of parties as vehicles to advance the personal fortunes of their leaders rather than as mechanisms to aggregate interests and pursue broader policy objectives. The lack of strong partisan identification with particular political parties, in turn, makes voters more susceptible to mobilization by anti-system parties, such as those discussed above.

Civil Society

In contrast to the situation in Poland and Hungary, where strong civil societies independent of the government had begun to form prior to the end of communism, there were very few independent groups in Czechoslovakia prior to 1989. Due to heavy repression and the very real threat of imprisonment, removal from jobs, and other forms of retaliation, the number of independent organizations remained very small even after Mikhail Gorbachev's reforms in the Soviet Union began to have some impact in Czechoslovakia. Experts estimated that there were approximately fifteen hundred independent groups in Hungary in the late 1980s.[23] In Czechoslovakia, there were approximately thirty at that time.[24]

Following the end of communism, Czechoslovakia experienced the same resurgence of associations and voluntary organizations that occurred elsewhere in the postcommunist world. As with political parties, some of these groups had ties to groups that had been active in the interwar or immediate post–World War II periods. Some were attached to the newly emerging parties or were branches of international organizations. Still others were new groups designed to further the interests of their members, provide charitable services, or unite citizens with similar hobbies.

Most of these new nongovernmental organizations (NGOs) were funded in the early years after the end of communism by outside sources, and many remained heads without bodies, that is, groups of intellectuals in the major cities with few links to ordinary citizens or members. Domestic philanthropy has increased over time, as has the number of NGOs that no longer rely on foreign funders. Similarly, citizens are more likely to participate in the work of NGOs than in that of partisan political organizations, and the number of citizens who indicate that they participate in the work of such organizations has increased in both the Czech Republic and Slovakia.[25]

The NGO sector was particularly well-organized in Slovakia during the mid-1990s when Vladimír Mečiar dominated partisan politics. A coordinating committee known as the Gremium included representatives of the main sectors of the NGO community and sponsored an annual conference to discuss issues of importance to the sector. The Gremium and activists who had participated in NGO campaigns formed the core of those who organized the OK'98 campaign of civic actions that increased voter turnout sufficiently to oust Mečiar as prime minister in 1998. The impact of this campaign, the first full elaboration of the electoral model of ousting semi-authoritarian leaders in the postcommunist world, was not limited to Slovak politics but served as an inspiration and model for NGO activists in other postcommunist countries.[26]

Once the Dzurinda government was formed, NGO activists articulated their desire to continue to serve as watchdogs of the government and succeeded in passing a freedom-of-information law. With the end of government harassment of NGO activists and the return of respect for democratic procedures, the unity of the sector has diminished. During the 2002 election campaign, individual NGOs sponsored election-related actions. However, there was no repetition of the large-scale NGO campaign to get out the vote that occurred in 1998. Although some NGOs continue to lobby political leaders and monitor their actions, most NGOs have returned to focusing on their particular areas of activity.[27] Others have redirected their activities toward providing assistance to NGOs seeking to promote democracy in other countries.[28] Civil society is still weaker in both the Czech Republic and Slovakia that it is in older European democracies, and many citizens do not trust NGOs, although participation in such groups has increased over time since the end of communism.[29] Citizens also have organized protests over a variety of issues in both countries independently of NGOs such as those that occurred in 2017 in Slovakia to protest corruption in Fico's government and efforts to combat hate speech in the Czech Republic.[30]

In addition to democratically oriented civic groups, antidemocratic, extreme right groups have also formed at various times in the both the Czech Republic and Slovakia since the end of communism. Some of these were short-lived skinhead or extreme right groups that were active mainly on the local level and posed little real threat to the democratic system, although some of their members engaged in sporadic and at times deadly violence against members of the Roma and Hungarian minorities. In recent years, more organized groups have formed, including some affiliated with extreme right political parties, such as Kotleba's party in Slovakia. Members of the latter, who were affiliated with Kotleba's previous political party that was banned for racist and antidemocratic speech and behavior, wore black shirts reminiscent of Nazi uniforms and were vehemently anti-Roma and anti-Jewish. More recently, anti-immigrant sentiment, stoked in part by mainstream political leaders such as Slovak Prime Minister Fico as well as by extremists like Kotleba, whose party was the third largest vote-getter in the 2017 Slovak elections, has led to an increase in support for extremist rallies and actions.[31] The actions of extremist groups have led to the organization of groups and individuals that try to combat the views of extremists among youth and publicly identify extremists online.[32]

In the Czech Republic, anti-system activities have also been evident in the recent past. Ministry of the Interior reports indicate that the total number of such incidents decreased somewhat from 2015 to 2016. The nature of the incidents also changed. As in previous years, more episodes were organized by far-right than by far-left groups. However, in 2016, nearly all such actions reflected anti-immigrant and anti-refugee views.[33] In perhaps the most bizarre episode, Martin Konvicka, a far-right activist who had founded a number of far-right groups, rode a camel into Prague's Old Town Square wearing an Arab headdress and robes in August 2016; he was followed by "fighters" firing mock guns in a simulated Islamic State invasion.[34] The Bloc against Islam, which he led, however, dissolved itself in April 2016.[35]

Political Values and Attitudes

As in many other postcommunist countries, the political attitudes and values of citizens in the Czech Republic and Slovakia continue to reflect a variety of influences. Some of these stem from the precommunist political culture, which contained both democratic and nondemocratic elements in both countries. Others derive from the communist era, and still others have developed in response to the politics and economic policies of the transition since 1989.

The political attitudes of citizens of the Czech Republic and Slovakia differ somewhat from those of citizens in non-postcommunist members of the EU. These differences are most evident in perceptions of and levels of trust in government institutions and in citizens' perceptions of their own political roles. Thus, although citizens' levels of interest in politics in the Czech Republic and Slovakia, as well as in Hungary and Poland, do not differ greatly from those in older EU member states, citizens of postcommunist states have lower levels of trust in government institutions. They also have lower levels of political efficacy or the sense that they can make a difference at either the local or national level if their interests are threatened.[36]

Surveys conducted in 1994 and 2004 in the Czech Republic and Slovakia found that most citizens in both countries supported democracy. They held views of democracy that included protection of individual rights and other political liberties; they also believed that democracy should bring with it a high level of well-being. In the early 1990s, citizens in the Czech Lands were more likely than those in Slovakia to agree with the notion that citizens should be responsible for ensuring their own well-being; they also accepted the idea that a certain level of unemployment was an inevitable element of the shift to the market. As unemployment rates grew in the Czech Republic, however, differences between the two countries in this regard decreased. Popular resistance to the institution of fees for higher education and medical services, as well as to other measures that have decreased the government's responsibility for services and welfare, are further indications of the extent to which citizens internalized the belief common during the communist period that the state owes citizens a great deal of material security.[37]

Early studies of tolerance in the two areas found that levels of anti-Semitism were lower in the Czech Republic than in Slovakia, Poland, and Hungary.[38] However, studies done at that time and more recently have repeatedly documented very high levels of prejudice against the Roma in the Czech Republic as well as in Slovakia.[39] Anti-Islam and anti-refugee attitudes are common among inhabitants in both countries.[40]

The Economic Transition

Shortly after the end of communism, Czechoslovakia's new elites began debating the best way to return to a market economy. Early discussions of a more gradual, or third, way to transform the economy soon gave way, under the direction of the then federal finance minister Václav Klaus, to the decision to move rapidly and decisively to the market. This decision—accompanied by the end of or decreases in government subsidies, a rapid increase in prices, and efforts to privatize the economy, which was almost entirely in state hands—led to a steep drop in production and an increase in unemployment, economic hardship, and poverty. The negative effects of the shift to the market were especially evident in Slovakia.

The country's new leaders used a variety of methods to privatize economic assets. These included auctions, sales to foreign investors, and, most distinctively, the use of vouchers or coupons. Under the latter system, citizens were able to buy vouchers or coupons very inexpensively, which they could then exchange for shares in privatizing companies. This system, which became a sort of parlor game at the time, was designed to compensate for the lack of domestic capital at the end of communism as well as to give most citizens a personal stake in the continuation of market reforms. However, because it was not accompanied by changes in the banking sector or even, until several years later, the adoption of a bankruptcy law, it did little to restructure the economy. As in other postcommunist countries, privatization was also accompanied by massive fraud and corruption.[41]

Political elites also adopted laws to regulate restitution, the return of property that had been seized by the state to its rightful owners or their heirs, and stimulate the development of new private enterprises. The country's trade was also rapidly reoriented to the West, particularly after the collapse of Council for Mutual Economic Assistance and the Soviet Union.

Eventually, the shift to the market created more favorable economic conditions in both the Czech Republic and Slovakia. However, in the period soon after the end of communism, policies designed to achieve this goal created greater hardship in Slovakia. They also affected different groups of the population very differently. Thus, the economic transition created both winners and losers. The former were those who had the education, contacts, and ability to benefit from the new opportunities to increase their skills and qualifications, travel abroad for study or work, practice their occupations free of ideological interference, take the risk of working for a private or international corporation, or found a private business. These were primarily the young, urban, and well educated. For those lacking such skills and opportunities (those who were older, rural, and less educated, as well as families with several or many children and the Roma), the shift to the market and other economic changes brought primarily hardships.

As chapter 3 in this volume on economics indicates, both the Czech and Slovak economies have attracted sizable amounts of foreign investment. In the Slovak case, outside investors began to seriously consider investing in Slovakia after the victory of the liberal opposition in the 1998 elections. Both countries now play an important role in producing many products for the European market, including, most notably, automobiles. After nearly a decade of high growth rates, both countries suffered from the 2008–2009 global economic crisis. Gross domestic product contracted in 2009 by 4.1 percent in the Czech Republic and 4.7 percent in Slovakia, after 2.5 percent growth in the Czech Republic and 6.2 percent growth in Slovakia in 2008.[42] Both economies began to recover in 2010 but grew at slower rates and more unevenly than in the 1990s (see table 10.3).

As planned, Slovakia adopted the euro on January 1, 2009. Despite fears about the impact of this move on more vulnerable parts of the population, most analysts believe that it helped Slovakia weather the global crisis.

Table 10.3. Real GDP Growth in Czech Republic and Slovakia, 2010–2016

	Real GDP Growth (%)	
	Czech Republic	Slovakia
2010	2.3	5.0
2011	2.0	2.8
2012	−0.8	1.7
2013	−0.5	1.5
2014	2.7	2.6
2015	4.5	3.8
2016	2.4	3.3

GDP = gross domestic product
Sources: OECD (2017), "Country Statistical Profile: Slovak Republic," *Country Statistical Profiles: Key Tables from OECD.* http://dx.doi.org/10.1787/csp-svk-table-2017-2-en; and OECD (2017), "Country Statistical Profile: Czech Republic," *Country Statistical Profiles: Key Tables from OECD.* http://dx.doi.org/10.1787/csp-cze-table-2017-2-en.

Social Consequences

In addition to bringing poverty and unemployment to some groups, the shift to the market and the broader transition also had a number of social consequences. First among these was growing inequality. Although inequalities in terms of lifestyles, values, and access to higher education existed under communism,[43] and the communist leadership clearly had many material privileges, Czech and Slovak societies were generally very egalitarian, and those who had greater wealth were fairly circumspect about it. With the return to the market, inequalities increased dramatically. Wage differentials, which had been among the lowest in the communist world, widened significantly, and with the expanded availability of consumer durables and goods, it suddenly became clear to many families that they were not living as well as their neighbors.

Czech and Slovak societies have once again become more complex, as the return of the market led to the emergence of new occupations and groups, particularly in the rapidly expanding service and financial sectors. Restitution and the growth of the private sector also led to the reemergence of certain previously banned social categories, such as capitalists and entrepreneurs. There were also important shifts in the status and prestige, as well as the incomes, of different occupations and groups. At the same time that these changes opened up many new opportunities for some citizens, the situation of members of other groups, such as agricultural workers, unskilled and skilled manual workers, and some members of the party's former apparatus, worsened.

The opening of the borders and decline of tight political and police control also led to the intensification of all forms of social pathology, such as alcoholism, drug use, and abuse within the family, and to the emergence of new issues, such as trafficking in persons, smuggling, and HIV/AIDS. Many of these problems were intensified by the economic transition, as economic hardship took its toll on families.

The end of communism also allowed certain issues, such as ethnic tensions and issues related to sexuality, to emerge into the open and get onto the political agenda. Hungarian activists in Slovakia formed their own political parties and began to make demands for greater respect for minority culture and more attention to minority rights. The positive start to forging new relationships evident in the inclusion of a Hungarian party in the first postcommunist coalition government in Slovakia was interrupted temporarily by Mečiar's government, which enacted a number of laws that, among other things, restricted the right of the Hungarian minority to use its language in official dealings, removed dual-language street signs, and required Hungarian women to add the Slavic suffix *ová* to their last names.

With the victory of the democratically oriented opposition in 1998, the by-now-single Hungarian party was once again included in governing coalitions, and the most offensive legislation of the Mečiar era was reversed. Hungarian leaders continued to press for greater recognition of minority rights but played a constructive role within the coalition government on many issues. The inclusion of the nationalist, anti-Hungarian Slovak National Party in Prime Minister Robert Fico's coalition after the 2006 elections halted the progress made in this regard. There were several isolated incidents of violence by Slovaks against ethnic Hungarians who were speaking Hungarian. The inflammatory rhetoric used by some political leaders at this time heightened tensions within Slovakia and also contributed to worsening relations between Slovakia and Hungary. Ethnic relations and Slovak-Hungarian relations took a turn for the worse in 2009 when a language law was enacted that restricted the use of Hungarian and other non-Slovak languages in official contacts in Slovakia. The government's effort to replace Hungarian geographic names with Slovak names in Hungarian-language textbooks, which Hungarian-language schools refused to use,[44] further angered ethnic Hungarians in Slovakia. The center-right government formed after the 2010 elections, which once again included representatives of a Hungarian party, worked to improve Slovak-Hungarian relations within the country and Slovakia's relations with Hungary. The formation of a political party explicitly designed to cross the ethnic divide, Most-Híd (a party whose name consists of the Slovak and Hungarian words for "bridge") reflects the effort of some Hungarian and Slovak leaders to foster good relations among the two groups.

The status of the Roma community has also become an important issue. Subject to various measures to foster assimilation during the communist era, the Roma continue to face widespread prejudice and discrimination in both the Czech Republic and Slovakia. Education levels among the Roma are very low, and the practice of sending Roma children to special schools for the mentally handicapped remains widespread. Unemployment rates approach 85 percent in many Roma communities. The living conditions of many Roma, who reside in "settlements" on the outskirts of towns and cities, are very poor, as many Roma communities lack running water, electricity, and other public services. Violence against the Roma has also been an ongoing problem in the last twenty-five years. Unlike the Hungarian minority, the Roma have not developed effective political organizations to raise their claims in the political arena. Both the Czech and Slovak governments have adopted programs, in part at the prodding of the EU, to improve the status of the Roma, but serious problems, including overwhelmingly negative public attitudes toward the group, remain in both countries.[45]

Gender issues have also emerged as political issues since 1989. In part because women's equality was an official goal during the communist era, and in part because the uneven pattern of change in women's roles created great stress for women and their families,[46] many Czechs and Slovaks rejected the idea of women's equality after the end of communism. This backlash was reflected in the view that women should emphasize their maternal rather than economic roles, as well as in the reluctance on the part of many women to be actively involved in politics. Although most women continued to be employed, women were more likely than men to lose their jobs in the Czech Republic as a result of the transition. In both countries, they also faced increased competition from men for jobs in areas such as tourism, law, and financial services, which became more attractive under market conditions, and like men, they encountered new pressure to work productively. Given the continued traditional division of labor within the home, the task of dealing with the results of declining social services and the need to stretch family budgets to cover necessities also fell most heavily on women during the early part of the transition.

Women's political representation also declined in the early postcommunist period. Many women appeared to share the view of male leaders, including some former dissidents, who argued that politics was too dirty for women or that women had more important tasks than arguing about political issues. This pattern began to change in the late 1990s, as levels of women's representation increased in both the Czech Republic and Slovakia. However, women are still underrepresented among the political elite, and it is still difficult for women leaders to raise issues of particular concern for women.[47] As a result of the 2010 elections, Iveta Radičová, a former NGO activist and sociologist who has done research on gender issues, became Slovakia's first woman prime minister. She also became the first woman candidate for president to advance to the second round, although she lost to the incumbent.[48] Despite Radičová's position as head of the government, the number of women in the Slovak parliament decreased from 18 to 15.3 percent after the 2010 elections. In the Czech Republic, 22 percent of members of the lower house of parliament were women after the 2010 elections. Women's representation remained at approximately the same level in Slovakia (16 percent) after the 2012 elections and decreased slightly to 19.5 percent in the Czech lower house after the 2013 early elections.[49] In Slovakia, women's percentage of deputies in the legislature increased slightly to 20 percent after the 2016 elections; in the Czech Republic, women's representation returned to its 2010 level of 22 percent after the 2017 elections.[50]

By the mid-1990s, the backlash against even considering or discussing issues related to women's status began to decrease. Social scientists and women's advocates succeeded in getting certain issues related to women's situation onto the political agenda. Women's groups, particularly the small number of such groups that identify themselves as feminist, have also succeeded in establishing links with a few political leaders and have provided background materials as well as position papers on issues such as same-sex partnerships and legislation prohibiting sexual harassment in the workplace. Public discussion of women's issues in the media also increased. The EU accession process accelerated these trends in both countries, as political leaders were forced to adopt certain laws and establish government institutions to address issues related to women's status as part of that process.

Foreign Policy

As noted earlier in this chapter, foreign policy concerns were a major element of the transition in both the Czech Republic and Slovakia. A first step of the new government was to negotiate the withdrawal of Soviet troops from Czechoslovakia. The country's new leaders also sought to reclaim Czechoslovakia's place on the world stage as an independent country once again. Helped by the international stature of then president Václav Havel, Czech and Slovak leaders played an active role in upgrading the status of the Organization for Security and Co-operation in Europe. They also were key players in establishing the Visegrad group of Czechoslovakia, Hungary, and Poland, which sought to coordinate the three countries' efforts to join NATO and the EU and continues to coordinate the initiatives of the Czech Republic, Slovakia, Poland, and Hungary in these organizations now that these countries are members.

After the breakup of the federation, the foreign policies of the newly created Czech and Slovak republics diverged for several years. The Czech Republic maintained its status as a candidate for inclusion in the first round of NATO expansion, a goal it achieved in 1999, and began negotiations for EU accession. Although the Slovak leadership never renounced the goals of joining NATO and the EU, under Mečiar Slovakia fell out of the group of countries included in the first round of NATO expansion and was in danger of being excluded from EU expansion as well. The Mečiar government also sought to increase Slovakia's ties with Russia. After the victory of the opposition in the 1998 elections, Slovakia's foreign policy once again emphasized EU accession and NATO membership. Slovakia was included in the second round of NATO expansion in 2004 and became a member of the EU, along with the Czech Republic and eight other countries, that year.

In 2009, the Czech Republic became the second postcommunist country to hold the presidency of the EU. The country's ability to pursue its three announced priorities—economy, energy, and Europe in the world—was hampered by the fall of the government in March. Although the interim government received praise in some quarters, the Czech presidency received mixed reviews. The fact that President Klaus was the last holdout in signing the Lisbon Treaty further tarnished the country's reputation in the EU.

As members of NATO and the EU, both Slovakia and the Czech Republic at times have faced competing pressures from their European and US allies. These became evident almost immediately after the Czech Republic joined NATO in 1999 in the context of the NATO bombing campaign in Serbia and Kosovo in reaction to Slobodan Milošević's expulsion of most of the Albanian population from Kosovo. The governments of both countries supported this effort, but this step was unpopular with citizens of both.

US actions in Afghanistan and particularly the war in Iraq posed even more starkly the dilemma these countries face in trying to maintain good relations with other EU members and the United States. Both countries sent specialized units to Afghanistan and Iraq. However, as in most of Central and Eastern Europe, citizens in both countries opposed these deployments. Most Czech citizens welcomed the decision in 2009 by the Barack Obama administration to scrap the George W. Bush administration's plans to place a radar station in the Czech Republic as part of a missile defense system as there was widespread popular opposition to the plan, despite the Czech government's approval.

The reaction of both governments to the crisis posed by events in Ukraine in 2013 and by Russia's occupation and annexation of Crimea, fomenting of separatist activities and arming of separatists in eastern Ukraine, and invasion of eastern Ukrainian in 2014 reflected their previous experiences with Russia and the obligations of their existing foreign policy commitments as members of the EU and NATO. The Czech government condemned the use of violence against protestors by the Victor Yanukovych regime and flew many of those wounded to hospitals in the Czech Republic for treatment and rehabilitation. Government spokespersons also condemned the illegal annexation of Crimea and supported EU sanctions, although President Miloš Zeman took a more ambiguous position. In Slovakia—which, unlike the Czech Republic, which has coal, is more dependent on Russia for its energy supplies—Prime Minister Robert Fico has taken a more neutral stance on Crimea and Russian actions in eastern Ukraine. Arguing that they would hurt Slovakia's economy, he urged caution in applying sanctions and opposed additional sanctions against Russia for its actions in Ukraine.

Both governments have been resistant to EU efforts to settle refugees from Syria and other parts of the Middle East in their countries. In 2015, both opposed the EU majority's decision to use quotas to share the burden of resettling refugees. In June 2017, the EU opened infringement proceedings against the Czech Republic, along with Poland and Hungary, over their failure to accept their assigned number of refugees. Poland and Hungary had not accepted any refugees; the Czech Republic initially accepted twelve but later refused to accept additional refugees. These proceedings could eventually result in serious financial penalties for the countries involved. Slovakia joined Hungary in suing the EU over the refugee issue in the European Court of Justice in May 2017. To date, Slovakia has escaped infringement proceedings, in part because although the government continues to oppose quotas, the country has accepted sixteen refugees, some within the last year before the EU started infringement proceedings against Poland, Hungary, and the Czech Republic.[51]

Future Challenges

As the preceding pages have illustrated, both Slovakia and the Czech Republic are among the success stories in the postcommunist world. Although political and economic developments diverged in Slovakia under Mečiar, in the period since 1998, political leaders have successfully achieved many of the objectives set out after the fall of communism in 1989. Thus, both Slovakia and the Czech Republic are now among those countries classified as "free" by Freedom House and other international ranking bodies. Although important problems remain with the party system, as well as with elite and mass political culture, both are widely recognized as functioning liberal democracies.

Both countries' economies have also been among the success stories in the region. Economic growth rates were among the highest in Europe prior to the 2008 crisis in the world economy, and foreign direct investment continues to increase. Privatization was successfully accomplished, and the standard of living has long surpassed its 1989 level in both countries. Although both economies were hurt by the worldwide economic crisis of 2008 and 2009, both have since recovered. Securely anchored in European and transatlantic institutions, both Slovakia and the Czech Republic have also achieved recognition for their roles in supporting pro-democracy movements abroad, particularly in the postcommunist world.

As in other postcommunist, as well as many other developed, Western countries, numerous problems remain in all of these areas. In the political realm, these include the need to develop a stable system of political parties and to increase linkages between political leaders and citizens, as well as between political leaders and the NGO sector. The inclusion of far-right parties in the parliaments of both as the result of recent elections is another worrisome trend that reflects the weaknesses in the party system as well as ongoing issues with both elite and mass political values and attitudes. As anti-Islamic demonstrations and the negative attitudes of citizens to refugees illustrate, both countries also need to continue to foster tolerance as well as a political culture that supports democracy and includes a greater sense of citizens' responsibility to take action to resolve public problems and actively join with others to address common issues. The election of Andrej Babiš in the Czech Republic in 2017 and steps his government has taken to try to limit the number of people involved in policy making as well as the elimination of press conferences after cabinet meetings raise the possibility that the Czech Republic may also experience democratic backsliding, as has the recent reelection of Miloš Zeman.

There is also room for improvement in dealing with corruption in the political and economic arenas in both countries. Both have experienced major political scandals in the recent past that have tainted political life and called into question the competence of political elites. In Slovakia, the Gorilla corruption scandal continues to hamper the development of a strong center-right party. In the Czech Republic, the forced resignation of Prime Minister Petr Nečas after revelations that his chief of staff had improperly used state resources to spy on his estranged wife and about his own role in offering bribes to parliamentary deputies led to a caretaker government for several months and to the near elimination from political life of his party, the Civic Democratic Party, which had been a mainstay of the Czech party system since 1991. Prime Minister Babiš also faced investigation for improper use of EU funds prior to the victory of his party in 2017.

In the economic arena, both governments continue to face regional disparities in growth and unemployment, as well as a host of problems arising from aging and declining populations. They also must address the problem of persistent poverty among certain groups, particularly the Roma, as well as other unresolved issues related to the marginal status of the Roma in both societies. Gender issues are another area requiring greater attention. As their economies continue to grow and the wage differentials compared to more developed EU members that have made both countries attractive to foreign investors change, Czech and Slovak leaders will also need to find other incentives to attract outside capital. They must also deal with the lingering impact of the 2008–2009 economic crisis on their economies.

In the area of foreign policy, leaders in both countries will continue to face the need to balance their relations with the rest of Europe and the United States. They must also find a way to play constructive roles as small countries within the EU as well as in regional groupings and to define their relations with countries to the east.

As this listing of areas indicates, political leaders and citizens face important challenges in both Slovakia and the Czech Republic. Some of these continue to reflect the legacy of communism and its impact on the transition. Others derive from the transition process itself and its unintended or, in some cases, seemingly inevitable consequences. The problems that dominate the political agenda in both Slovakia and the Czech Republic also include those that confront leaders in other developed, Western societies.

Study Questions

1. How were developments in the precommunist and communist periods reflected in the postcommunist period in the Czech Lands and Slovakia?
2. What caused the Velvet Divorce, and what were its consequences?
3. What role did NGOs play in the ouster of Mečiar in Slovakia in 1998?
4. What trends are evident in the party systems in each country?
5. What major challenges face leaders and citizens in each country?

Suggested Readings

Bunce, Valerie J., and Sharon L. Wolchik. *Defeating Authoritarian Leaders in Postcommunist Countries*. New York: Cambridge University Press, 2011.

Fisher, Sharon. *Political Change in Post-Communist Slovakia and Croatia: From Nationalist to Europeanist*. New York: Palgrave Macmillan, 2006.

Guasti, Petra. "Development of Citizen Participation in Central and Eastern Europe after the EU Enlargement and Economic Crises." *Communist and Post-Communist Studies* 49, no. 3 (September 2016): 219–31.

Haughton, Tim, Teresa Novotna, and Kevin Deegan-Krause. "The 2010 Czech and Slovak Parliamentary Elections: Red Cards to the 'Winners.'" *West European Politics* 34 (2011): 394–402.

Innes, Abby. *Czechoslovakia: The Short Goodbye*. New Haven, CT: Yale University Press, 2001.

Krause, Kevin Deegan. "Slovakia's Second Transition." *Journal of Democracy* 14, no. 2 (April 2003): 65–79.

Leff, Carol Skalnik. *The Czech and Slovak Republics: Nation vs. State*. Boulder, CO: Westview Press, 1996.

Skilling, H. Gordon. *Czechoslovakia's Interrupted Revolution*. Princeton, NJ: Princeton University Press, 1976.

Stolarik, M. Mark, ed., *The Czech and Slovak Republics: Twenty Years of Independence*. Budapest: Central University Press, 2016.

Vachudova, Milada Anna. *Europe Undivided: Democracy, Leverage, and Integration after Communism*. Oxford: Oxford University Press, 2005.

Wolchik, Sharon L. *Czechoslovakia in Transition: Politics, Economics, and Society*. London: Pinter, 1991.

Websites

CZECH REPUBLIC

Prague Daily Monitor: http://praguemonitor.com
Prague Post: http://www.praguepost.com

SLOVAKIA

Slovak Spectator: http://spectator.sme.sk
Pozor Blog: http://pozorblog.com

Notes

1. Samuel Harrison Thomson, *Czechoslovakia in European History* (Princeton, NJ: Princeton University Press, 1953).
2. Zora Pryor, "Czechoslovak Economic Development in the Interwar Period," in *A History of the Czechoslovak Republic: 1918–1948*, ed. Victor S. Mamatey and Radomír Luza (Princeton, NJ: Princeton University Press, 1973).
3. Owen V. Johnson, *Slovakia, 1918–1938: Education and the Making of a Nation* (New York: Columbia University Press, 1985).
4. H. Gordon Skilling, "Stalinism and Czechoslovak Political Culture," in *Stalinism: Essays in Historical Interpretation*, ed. Robert C. Tucker (New York: W. W. Norton, 1977).
5. Lucy S. Dawidowicz, *The War against the Jews: 1933–1945* (New York: Bantam Books; Bratislava: Institute for Public Affairs, 1975), 20.
6. See Arthur Koestler, *Darkness at Noon* (New York: Macmillan Press, 1941), for a fictionalized account of the purges.
7. Barbara Jancar, *Czechoslovakia and the Absolute Monopoly of Power: A Study of Political Power in a Communist System* (New York: Praeger Press, 1978); and Golia Golan, *The Czechoslovak Reform Movement: Communism in Crisis, 1962–1968* (Cambridge: Cambridge University Press, 1971).
8. Robin Alison Remington, ed., *Winter in Prague: Documents on Czechoslovak Communism in Crisis* (Cambridge, MA: MIT Press, 1969).
9. Ludvík Vaculík, "2,000 Words to Workers, Farmers, Scientists, Artists and Everyone," in *Winter in Prague: Documents on Czechoslovak Communism in Crisis*, ed. Robin Alison Remington (Cambridge, MA: MIT Press, 1969).
10. Kieran Williams, *The Prague Spring and Its Aftermath: Czechoslovak Politics, 1968–1970* (Cambridge: Cambridge University Press, 1997); and Jaromír Navrátil, ed., *The Prague Spring '68* (Budapest: Central European University Press, 1998).
11. Sharon L. Wolchik, "Czechoslovakia," in *The Columbia History of Eastern Europe in the Twentieth Century*, ed. Joseph Held (New York: Columbia University Press, 1992).
12. Sharon L. Wolchik, "Institutional Factors in the Break-Up of Czechoslovakia," in *Irreconcilable Differences: Explaining Czechoslovakia's Dissolution*, ed. Michael Kraus and Allison Stanger (New York: Rowman & Littlefield, 2000).
13. Sharon L. Wolchik, "The Czech Republic: Havel and the Evolution of the Presidency since 1989," in *Postcommunist Presidents*, ed. Ray Taras (Cambridge: Cambridge University Press, 1997).
14. See Beata Balogová, "Kiska: 'I Am Not One of Those Traditional Politicians,'" *Slovak Spectator*, March 9, 2014; and "Kiska: Attitude to Migration Crisis to Define the Character of Slovakia," September 7, 2015, https://spectator.sme.skc/20060149/kiska-attitude-to-migration-crisis-to-define-the-character-of-slovakia.html.
15. Sharon L. Wolchik, "The Repluralization of Politics in Czechoslovakia," *Communist and Post-communist Studies* 26 (December 1993): 412–31.
16. Tomáš Kostelecký, *Political Parties after Communism: Development in East Central Europe* (Baltimore, MD: Johns Hopkins University Press, 2002).
17. See Martin Bútora, "New Prospects for Alternative Politics," in Zora Bútorová, Olga Gyárfášová, and Grigorij Mesežnikov, eds., *Alternative Politics? The Rise of New Political Parties*

in Central Europe (Bratislava: Institute for Public Affairs, 2013), 11ff; Sarah Engler, "Corruption and Electoral Support for New Political Parties in Central and Eastern Europe," *West European Politics* 39, no. 2 (2016): 278–304; and Oľga Gyárfášová, Miloslav Bahna, and Martin Slosiarik, "Sila nestálosti: volatilita voličov na Slovensku vo voľbách 2016," *Středoevropské politické studie,* 2017, roč. 19, č. 1, s. 1–24. ISSN 1212 7817. https://journals.muni.cz/cepsr/article/view/6861/6357>(APVV-14-0527:.

18. "Volby do Poslanecké sněmovny Parlamentu České republiky konané ve dnech 28.05.–29.05.2010," Volby.cz, http://www.volby.cz/pls/ps2010/ps2?xjazyk=CZ. A center-right coalition, led by Petr Nečas of the ODS and consisting of the ODS and two new parties, TOP 09 (Tradition, Responsibility, and Prosperity) led by Karel Schwarzenberg and VV (Public Affairs), a fiscally conservative party, took office in July 2010.

19. http://www.volbysr.sk/nrsr2010/sr/tab3.html.

20. Tim Haughton, Darina Malová, and Kevin Deegan-Krause, "Slovakia's Newly Elected Parliament Is Dramatically Different and Pretty Much the Same. Here's How," March 9, 2016, www.washingtonpost.com/news/monkey-cage/Slovakia's-newly-elected-parliament-is-dramatically-different-and-pretty-much-the-same-here's-how.

21. Tim Haughton, Darina Malová, and Kevin Deegan-Krause, "Slovakia's Newly Elected Parliament Is Dramatically Different and Pretty Much the Same. Here's How," March 9, 2016, www.washingtonpost.com/news/monkey-cage/Slovakia's-newly-elected-parliament-is-dramatically-different-and-pretty-much-the-same-here's-how.

22. See Institute for Public Opinion Research, "Evaluation of Political Parties and Selected Institutions," June 2017, https://cvvm.soc.cas.cz/en/press-releases/political/politicians-political-institutions/4382-evaluation-of-the-activities-of-political-parties-and-selected-institutions-june-2017; see also Naděžda Čadová, "Důvěra k vybraným institucím veřejného života, březen 2017," https://cvvm.soc.cas.cz/media/com_form2content/documents/c6/a4297/f77/po170410.pdf; Naděžda Čadová, "Názory české veřejnosti na úroveň demokracie a respektovánì lidských práv v ČR – únor 2017," March 28, 2017, https://cvvm.soc.cas.cz/en/press-releases/political/democracy-civic-society/4280-public-opinion-on-the-functioning-of-democracy-and-respect-to-human-rights-in-the-czech-republic-february-2017; and Robert Klobucký and Marianna Mrava, "Všeobecná dôvera v slovenskej populácii je na relatívne nízkej ale stabilizovanej úrovni: tlačová konferencia v rámci projektov APVV-14-0527, APVV-15-0653, 3.2.2017," SAV [elektronický zdroj]. Bratislava: Sociologický ústav SAV, 2017. 3 s. http://www.sociologia.sav.sk/cms/uploaded/2543_attach_TB_Klobucky_Mrva.pdf>.

23. Rudolf Tokes, "Hungary's New Political Elites: Adaptation and Change, 1989–1990," *Problems of Communism* 39 (November–December 1990): 44–65. http://www.unz.org/Pub/Problems of Communism.

24. George Schopflin, Rudolf Tokes, and Ivan Volgyes, "Leadership Change and Crisis in Hungary," *Problems of Communism* 37, no. 5 (September–October 1988): 23–46.

25. Tereza Vajdová, *An Assessment of Czech Civil Society in 2004: After Fifteen Years of Development* (Prague: Civicus, 2005).

26. See Pavol Demeš, "Non-Governmental Organizations and Volunteerism," in *Global Report on Society, Slovakia 2002*, ed. Grigorij Mesežnikov, Miroslav Kollár, and Tom Nicholson (Bratislava: Institute for Public Affairs, 2002); and Valerie J. Bunce and Sharon L. Wolchik, "Favorable Conditions and Electoral Revolutions," *Journal of Democracy* 17, no. 4 (October 2006): 5–18. See also Peter Vandor, Nicole Traxler, Reinhard Millner, and Michael Meyer, eds., *Civil Society in Central and Eastern Europe: Challenges and Opportunities* (Vienna: ERSTE Foundation, 2017).

27. Jana Kadlecová and Katarina Vajdová, "Non-Governmental Organizations and Volunteerism," in *Global Report on Society, Slovakia 2003*, ed. Grigorij Mesežnikov and Miroslav Kollár (Bratislava: Institute for Public Affairs, 2004), 605–23.

28. See Tsveta Petrova, *From Solidarity to Geopolitics* (New York: Cambridge University Press, 2014).

29. See Marc Morje Howard, *The Weakness of Civil Society* (New York: Cambridge University Press, 2003); and Jiří Navrátil and Miroslav Pospíšil, *Two Decades Later, Civic Advocacy in the Czech Republic* (Brno: MUNI Press, 2014).

30. Pavol Frič and Martin Vávra, "Czech Civil Sector Face-to-Face with Freelance Activism," *The International Journal of Sociology and Social Policy* 36, no. 11 (2017): 774–91, http://proxygw.wrlc.org/login?url=https://search-proquest-com.proxygw.wrlc.org/docview/1832070360?accountid=11243. See also Roberto Stefan Foa and Grzegorz Ekiert, "The Weakness of Postcommunist Civil Society Reassessed," *European Journal of Political Research* 56, no. 2 (May 2017): 419–39.

31. "Kotleba accused of extremism, faces losing mandate," https://Spectator.sme.sk/c/20615664/kotleba-accused-of-extremism-faces-losing-mandate.html, July 28, 2017.

32. See www.protinavisti.cz and www.exitSlovensko for examples.

33. See also Vandor et al., Civil Society in Central and Eastern Europe.

34. Ministerstvo vnitra České Republiky, *Report on Extremism in the Territory of the Czech Republic in 2016*, Prague, 2017.

35. www.radio.cz/en/sefin/news, April 25, 2016.

36. Zdenka Vajdová and Jana Stachová, "Politická kultura české populace v regionálním rozměru," *Czech Sociological Review* 41, no. 5 (2005): 881–903; and Zora Bútorová, *Political Culture in Slovakia* (Bratislava: Institute for Public Affairs, 1999).

37. See Sharon Wolchik et al., results of "Citizens Political Attitudes and Values in the Czech Republic and Slovakia," in 1994 and 2004, as reported by STEM, Prague, Czech Republic, FOCUS, and the Institute for Public Affairs, Bratislava, Slovakia.

38. Sharon L. Wolchik, *Czechoslovakia in Transition: Politics, Economics, and Society* (London: Pinter, 1991).

39. Michal Vašečka, Martina Jurásková, and Tom Nicholson, eds., *Global Report on Roma in Slovakia* (Bratislava: Institute for Public Affairs, 2003).

40. Gallup, "Syrian Refugees Not Welcome in Eastern Europe," May 5, 2017, http://www.gallup.com/poll/209828/syrian-refugees-not-welcome-eastern-europe.aspx. See also Michael Colborne, "Surveying Some Surveys: Czechs & Refugees, Immigrants, and Islam," April 27, 2017, https://michaelcolborne.com/2017/04/27/surveying-some-surveys-czechs-refugees-immigrants-and-islam/; and "Survey: European Youth Give Thumbs Up to the EU but Dissent on Immigration," http://www.dw.com/en/survey-european-youth-give-thumbs-up-to-the-eu-but-dissent-on-immigration/a-38047275.

41. Jiří Pehe, *Vytunelování demokracie* (Prague: Academia, 2002).

42. Economist Intelligence Unit, "Country Report: Czech Republic" (London: Economist Intelligence Unit, 2009), 19; and Economist Intelligence Unit, "Country Report: Slovakia" (London: Economist Intelligence Unit, 2009), 18.

43. David Lane, *The End of Inequality? Stratification under State Socialism* (New York: Penguin Books, 1971).

44. Freedom House, "Slovakia," in *Nations in Transit 2009* (Washington, DC: Freedom House, 2009), 494, http://www.freedomhouse.org/report/nations-transit/2009/slovakia#.U9f80lYSAeI.

45. Vašečka, Jurásková, and Nicholson, *Global Report on Roma in Slovakia*; and Freedom House, "Slovakia," 494.

46. Jane S. Jaquette and Sharon L. Wolchik, eds., *Women and Democracy: Latin America and Central and Eastern Europe* (Baltimore, MD: Johns Hopkins University Press, 1998).

47. See also Marilyn Rueschemeyer and Sharon L. Wolchik, eds., *Women in Power in Post-Communist Parliaments* (Bloomington: Indiana University Press, 2009), for the results of interviews with women deputies in six postcommunist parliaments.

48. Sharon Wolchik, "Iveta Radičová, the First Female Prime Minister in Slovakia," in *Women Presidents and Prime Ministers in Post-Transition Democracies*, ed. Veronica Montecinos (New York: Palgrave Macmillan, 2017): 239–58.

49. Inter-Parliamentary Union, "Women in National Parliaments," http://www.ipu.org/wmn-e/classif.htm.

50. Inter-Parliamentary Union, "Women in National Parliaments," http://www.ipu.org/wmn-e/classif.htm; Czech Statistical Office, Volby.cz.

51. "EU Opens Sanctions Procedure against Hungary Poland, and the Czech Republic over Refugees," *Euractiv*, June 13 and 15, 2017, www.euractiv.com/section/justice-home-affairs/eu-opens-sanctions-procedures-against-hungary-poland-and-the-czech-republic-over-refugees.

Map 11.0.   Hungary

CHAPTER 11

Hungary

PATHBREAKER OF POPULIST NATIONALISM

Federigo Argentieri

In the late spring of 1989, a twenty-six-year-old bearded graduate in law spoke in extremely blunt terms to a large crowd in Budapest's Heroes' Square on the occasion of the solemn reburial of Imre Nagy, the leader of the government put in place by the 1956 revolution, and his associates, who had been executed thirty-one years earlier and dumped into mass graves. The speech demanded the immediate withdrawal of Soviet troops from Hungary. This frightened many observers, on grounds that such a request was premature and could have backfired. The speaker was Viktor Orbán, leader of FiDeSz, a party formed the previous year, who became the favorite politician of international public opinion supporting democratic change in the region.

Almost three decades later, on July 22, 2017, at the very end of a speech, the same Viktor Orbán, prime minister of the country since 2010, stated, "27 years ago here in Central Europe we believed that Europe was our future; today we feel that we are the future of Europe."[1] The meaning of this declaration can be understood in light of the events of the previous three years. On July 26, 2014, at the very same summer youth camp in Romania, the neighbor country with the largest Hungarian minority, Orbán had clearly spelled out his political views and plans for Hungary.[2] The words that caused the loudest international echo were, "we have to abandon liberal methods and principles of organizing a society, as well as the liberal way to look at the world." The FiDeSz chief went on explaining that liberalism "holds that we are free to do anything that does not violate another person's freedom . . . Instead the principle should be do not do to others what you would not do to yourself. And we will attempt to found a world we can call the Hungarian society on this theoretical principle, in political thinking, education, in the way we ourselves behave, in our own examples."

In his 2017 speech, Orbán proudly claimed that Hungary had "defended itself—and Europe at the same time—against the migrant flow and invasion." After praising Donald Trump's July 6 speech in Warsaw, he specified in unambiguous terms:

> Certain theories describe the changes now taking place in the Western world and the emergence on the stage of the US president as a struggle in the world political arena between the transnational elite—referred to as "global"—and patriotic national leaders. I believe that this is a meaningful description, and there's much truth in it. If we relate it to ourselves, we can also say that back

in 2010, well before the US presidential election, we were forerunners of this approach, the new patriotic Western politics.

These statements reflect what has commonly been described as democratic backsliding in Hungary, which was one of the leaders in the movement away from communism and considered to be one of the earliest "success stories" in democratization. Hungary's transition out of communism toward democracy began over three decades before 1989 with the 1956 revolution and ended in 2010, the year of the first sweeping electoral victory by FiDeSz. Orbán, in his first two terms, managed the "disintegration of the Third Hungarian Republic"[3] by creating an "illiberal democracy" in what had been one of the most politically stable and—at least until 2008—economically prosperous of the postcommunist states in Central and East Europe.

Historical Background and Communist Experiences

Hungary's history has played a major role in its present. Its triumphs and defeats left a complicated legacy for both the communist rulers and the postcommunist system. Reunified as of 1713 inside the Austrian Empire, Hungarians had far greater cultural independence than the nations that were part of the Ottoman and Russian empires. The Age of Reforms—a set of gradual steps away from the absolute rule of the monarch, initiated in 1825 by Count Széchény—triggered a revolution for freedom and independence in 1848–1849, which failed. Yet, changes in the geopolitical realities of Central Europe subsequently resulted in 1867 in a dual Austro-Hungarian Empire in which Hungarians had separate administrations in every field but military and foreign affairs. As a result, by the end of the nineteenth century, Hungary's economy and culture had blossomed. In the cities, the workers prospered, even as the countryside remained backward and relations with most ethnic and religious minorities remained tense.

All this came to an end when the expansion of the Austro-Hungarian Empire into Bosnia-Herzegovina and its alliance with Germany brought the empire into World War I. As punishment for its defeat, large portions of what had been Hungarian land were occupied by Czechoslovakia and the Balkan states of Romania and Serbia, with the endorsement of Western powers. Meanwhile, a democratic republic was proclaimed in Hungary, which was quickly replaced by the Bolshevik Republic of Councils in the spring and summer of 1919. Bolshevism in Hungary, although it often disregarded Vladimir Lenin's instructions and had a certain cultural liveliness, was still characterized by mostly brutal and chaotic policies, which left communism with a negative image.

The Bolshevik experiment ended in a counterrevolutionary offensive by part of Hungary's new military, led by Admiral Miklós Horthy. As of August 1919, he and his forces had suppressed the Red regime and appointed a new regency government, which encouraged anti-Jewish pogroms because of an infamous equivalence between Bolshevism and Jewishness. To compound the political battles, the Trianon peace treaty, signed in 1920, resulted in Hungary losing not only the areas inhabited by other ethnic groups but also much of its own historic territory: 120,000 square miles and half its population were taken. Over 3 million Hungarians were cut off from Hungary.

These losses, coupled with the toppled Red regime and the debacle of World War I, left Hungarians wary of and at odds with both the Soviets and the West. During the interwar years, students began their classes by chanting, "Nem, nem, soha!" (No, no, never!), meaning that they would never accept the injustice of the Trianon treaty. In domestic politics, a semi-authoritarian system emerged that outlawed the Communist Party and limited voting rights as well as Jews' access to universities,[4] based on the false assumption that automatically linked Jews to communism. As pointed out in a classic essay by István Bibó, one of the most original political thinkers of the region and a main inspiration for the young Viktor Orbán, this policy was part of a more general problem caused by the collapse of prewar Hungary, which ended the successful gradual assimilation of most of the Jewish population into Magyar society by making Jews suddenly appear responsible for all of the catastrophes that had befallen the nation.[5]

After the end of communism in Hungary, this stereotypical anti-Jewish prejudice would pop up anew—not only in the surge of parties of the far right, such as Miép and Jobbik, but also inside pro-government forces. Current Prime Minister Orbán's longtime friend and proud carrier of FiDeSz party card number five, Zsolt Bayer, for instance, in an infamous article published in the daily *Magyar Hirlap* (January 4, 2011), expressed his regret at "all the Jews not having been buried to their necks at Orgovány," the site of one of the most gruesome Horthy-sponsored pogroms carried out in the fall of 1919.[6]

The combination of the Great Depression and Hungarians' interest in reclaiming their territory drew Hungary into the orbit of Adolf Hitler's Germany. After the Munich Agreement and the 1938–1939 dismantling of Czechoslovakia, southern Slovakia and Ruthenia were returned to Hungary. Then, after the Molotov-Ribbentrop Pact, Hungary regained most of Transylvania. In return, Hungary had to not only increase its restrictions on Jews but also participate in the 1941 invasions of Yugoslavia and the Soviet Union.

At the end of World War II, as Hitler's position weakened with the German defeat at Stalingrad and the Allied landing in Italy, Hungary's military and political leader, Admiral Horthy tried to switch sides. Hitler responded by occupying Hungary in March 1944 and replacing Horthy (who was arrested in October 1944) with Ferenc Szálasi, head of the Arrow Cross Party and Hungarian equivalent to the Nazis. More than half a million Jews were deported and killed. At the same time, the Soviets invaded Hungarian territory, which they occupied by April 1945, after a merciless and destructive fight.

The communist takeover of Hungary took almost three years. Winston Churchill and Joseph Stalin first agreed in October 1944 that Hungary would be evenly split between the Soviet sphere of influence and the West. Although Hungary was occupied by the Red Army, the first parliamentary elections in November 1945 were free and fair, but their follow-up was not. The centrist, Christian, anticommunist Independent Smallholders Party won an absolute majority of over 57 percent of the votes, yet was unable to form a government by itself because the Allied Control Commission, dominated by the Soviets, forced it to go into a coalition with three left-of-center parties: the Social Democrats, the Communists, and the National Peasant Party. In February 1946, Smallholder Zoltán Tildy was elected president in what would prove to be democracy's last gasp.

Even as Hungary was establishing a democratic government, albeit in an awkward coalition of anticommunist centrists and left-wing parties, Mátyás Rákosi, head of the Hungarian Communist Party, was engaged in cutting democracy down through what he called "salami tactics" by using the secret police and other pressures to slice off pieces of the noncommunist parties until there was nothing left. The communists first pressured the Smallholders to expel their "right wing." Then, as soon as the Treaty of Paris was signed in 1947 and the Allied Control Commission was dissolved, the main leader of the Smallholders, Béla Kovács, was arrested for "espionage" by the Soviet troops, who had remained in Hungary in order to secure connections with their contingent in Austria. Finally, Prime Minister Ferenc Nagy, who had resisted every attempt to nationalize property, was forced into exile. The social democrats were then given the choice of merging with the communists or facing serious consequences. Some accepted the unification. Others refused and were, at the least, forced out of public life. Some, such as the particularly stubborn Anna Kéthly, were imprisoned. The Hungarian Workers' Party was born of this unification in June 1948, signaling clearly the communists' final victory.

Having successfully taken over the political institutions, the communists openly imposed control over all other sectors of society. The economy was transformed: agriculture was forcibly collectivized, and the rest of the economy was nationalized. A massive industrialization drive shifted the economy from an agricultural to an industrial one. These policies were accompanied by an exodus from the countryside to the cities, and millions of young people suddenly got a chance at education. Religious institutions were attacked. Not only were citizens punished for supporting religion, but also the head of the Hungarian Catholic Church, Cardinal József Mindszenty, was arrested, tried, and sentenced to life imprisonment. Terror even hit the Communist Party's own elite. The show trial and execution of Minister of the Interior László Rajk for being a Titoist agent in 1949 came to symbolize the spiral of terror that lasted until Stalin's death in 1953.

After Stalin's death, the different factions in the Kremlin manipulated Hungarian politics. Control of the state and the party was split between Rákosi, as head of the party, and Imre Nagy, the first communist minister of agriculture, as prime minister. The Soviets pressed the Hungarian leadership to shift from attempts at establishing heavy industry to greater production of consumer goods. Nagy pushed reform further to include a relaxation of the terror and an end to the permanent hunt for "traitors" that had paralyzed Hungarian life since the communist takeover. But as the balance of power shifted from liberals to conservatives in the Kremlin, Nagy was forced out, and Rákosi returned to power.

In 1956, to strengthen the accord with Yugoslavia and follow through on the denunciations of Stalin and his cult of the personality, Nikita Khrushchev, the new Soviet leader, forced more change in Hungary. Rákosi, who had boasted of being "Stalin's best Hungarian disciple," was dismissed from office and went into exile in the Soviet Union. He was replaced as head of the Communist Party by the equally Stalinist Ernő Gerő. At the same time, the verdict against László Rajk was nullified, and his body was publicly reburied. This step, coupled with the example of liberalization in Poland during the Polish October, as well as the constant shifts in leadership, convinced Hungarians that change was possible.

The Hungarian Revolution[7] began with student demonstrations on October 23, 1956. Within a few hours, Soviet tanks entered Budapest and fired on the demonstrators. Three days later, a new government was brought in, with János Kádár as head of the Communist Party and Imre Nagy as prime minister. By this time, though, virtually the entire population was engaged in the struggle for freedom and the effort to create a genuine pluralist democracy. Parties abolished in 1948 resurfaced and were brought into Nagy's executive. The Hungarian Workers' Party dissolved itself and formed a new

Photo 11.1. This statue of Imre Nagy in Budapest was put up in 1996 for the centennial of his birth.

Hungarian Socialist Workers' Party (HSWP), and grassroots national committees and workers' councils mushroomed, declaring their wish to be complementary and not alternative to political parties. After briefly starting to withdraw their troops, the Soviets intervened a second time on November 4 to suppress the revolution, at which point the

Hungarian government, buoyed by the increasingly loud demands of insurgents and the population throughout the country, denounced the Warsaw Pact even as Soviet troops killed thousands of demonstrators, jailed thousands more, and sent many thousands into exile. All of this remained seared in the national memory even though, officially, it was not allowed to be discussed until 1989.

János Kádár agreed to lead a new government with the support of the occupying Soviet troops. When Nagy refused to resign as prime minister, he and other leaders loyal to the revolution were arrested and deported to Romania. In 1958, they were secretly tried in Hungary, sentenced to death, executed the next day, and buried in unmarked graves. Much as the Rajk reburial had opened the floodgates in 1956, the memorial service for and reburial of Nagy and others who had been tried and buried with him in June 1989 triggered the end of communist control and then the dissolution of the HSWP.

In spite of the violence of the revolution's repression, its programs remained on a virtual agenda and were very gradually reintroduced, albeit with many stop-and-go's, from 1962 to 1963 onward; however, only the economic and cultural fields were affected, as politics remained exclusively in the hands of the ruling party. From the mid-1960s on, Hungarians lived with "goulash communism" and its guarantees of satisfactory supplies of food and consumer goods in exchange for the appearance of support for the regime. Whereas other systems actively repressed dissidents and those who questioned the system, Hungary was renowned for the mantra, "He who is not against us is with us."

The repression that accompanied the Soviet occupation and the reestablishment of a one-party system under Kádár's control lasted into the 1960s. In 1963, following negotiations with the United Nations, some surviving freedom fighters and leaders were released from prison, and Kádár moved away from ruling by repression. The New Economic Mechanism (NEM) was introduced in 1968 and brought a real improvement in the Hungarian standard of living and the availability of goods by providing for "profit" to become a motive for state enterprises and for open wage differentiation. Although the central planning process persisted under the NEM, it no longer dictated the details of what was produced and how. Instead, it set priorities and left decisions about production and pay to factory managers. Once collectivization of the agricultural sector was quite ruthlessly completed in 1961, farms were allowed to direct their own production and engage in side businesses. Peasants, along with the urban population, also received cradle-to-grave social welfare benefits. In the process, the NEM recognized a range of unions and professional organizations as players in the policy process. Although Hungary remained a part of the Council for Mutual Economic Assistance (CMEA) and was tied to ruble-based exchange rates and Soviet bloc economic priorities, it opened up to Western investment and became the recipient of sizable loans, which were used almost exclusively to support improved living standards. In the 1970s that investment brought in some Hungarian refugees from 1956 as well as West Europeans who set up factories in Hungary and imported and exported goods. The result was a consumer economy vibrant and varied enough to make Hungary "the happiest barrack in the camp" until the 1980s, when the forward and backward moves in the NEM and the aging of the economy showed in the failings of the consumer sector.

Politically, communism in Hungary from the mid-1960s was consistently less repressive than elsewhere in the bloc. This difference was due in part to the fact that the population was both satisfied with what it had economically and wary of trying for political change after the experience of 1956. In part, it resulted from János Kádár's equally vivid memory of 1956 and his concern with preventing tensions inside the party and between the party and the populace. Dissident groups, far weaker than in Poland, existed without any real repression or mass popular support. After the mid-1960s, Hungary's borders were more open for its own citizens and for émigrés and tourists. Life, for Hungarians, was a trade-off: political silence for comparative economic prosperity.

By mid-1980s, however, the elaborate system of carrots and sticks that had held Hungarian communist rule in place was crumbling. The NEM, which had already suffered a political setback between 1972 and 1977, was now worn down. The annual growth in gross domestic product decreased from 4.8 percent in the 1970s to 1.8 percent between 1980 and 1985 and continued on a rapid downward trajectory.[8] For workers, tensions over wages grew more acute because the instruments being used to manage the economy did not allow employers to raise wages to improve enterprise performance.[9] Thus, Hungarians' real incomes stagnated and began declining, causing savings to decrease.

At the same time, changes in the Kremlin reduced whatever fear remained of Soviet repression. The Soviet occupation troops meant little when Mikhail Gorbachev came to power and made it clear that reform in the Soviet Union would evolve in ways the Hungarians had not dared attempt and that the Soviet Union would no longer rein in its satellites. The rise of Poland's Solidarity movement in the early 1980s inspired Hungarian dissidents to publish journals that challenged historical taboos. Repression of dissidents was not an option: Hungary had signed the Helsinki Final Act in 1975. Perhaps more importantly, it was increasingly indebted to the International Monetary Fund and other Western financial institutions. So its leaders could not risk the kinds of financial sanctions imposed on Poland after the imposition of martial law if they were going to try to keep their economic bargain with the Hungarian people. And dissent involved only a tiny section of the population.

In addition, Kádár himself had aged. Whereas Hungary had changed, he had not. When he did appear in public, his hands shook, and his speeches fell flat. The men who had risen up behind him in the party, Károly Grósz, Imre Pozsgay, and Miklós Németh, began to take the lead in the public eye and behind the scenes. Their postures, though, were increasingly critical of Hungary's status quo and divided over what should come next and how to deal publicly with the past and present. In 1988, Kádár was forced to retire.

The Transition

In large part, the smoothness of the 1989–1990 transition was a result of the distance Hungary had traveled in economic reforms and its limited political liberalization after the repression of the late 1950s, as well as the success of reform movements within the party and of intellectual dissent in the late 1980s. Not surprisingly then, Hungary's transition was the product of ongoing and overlapping discussions and a series of roundtables that involved reform communists and intellectual groups whose roots were framed by Hungarian historical debates.

As the regime's system of carrots and sticks crumbled, intellectuals in and out of the party began to meet and push the old limits. In June 1985, a good part of Hungary's intellectual elite met at Monor to discuss the failings of the system since 1956. In these discussions, which happened with no interference from the party or police, the political divide that had characterized Hungarian thinking from the 1930s reemerged. The "people's nationalists" looked on the peasantry and Christianity as the base of the Hungarian spirit and wanted to find a "third way" between capitalism and communism. The "urbanists" were secular and oriented toward Western democracies and European integration. On the one hand, the people's nationalists pressed for Hungary to intervene to prevent the increasing repression of Hungarians abroad, particularly in Romania, where Nicolae Ceaușescu was engaged in a full-scale assault on Romania's sizable Hungarian minority. The urbanists, on the other hand, emerged as liberal democrats and defenders of human rights at home and sponsored radical pro-market economic reforms along with membership in all of the Euro-Atlantic organizations.

This initial meeting, the crumbling of the economy, and the visible decrease in Soviet power or interest in Central and Eastern Europe triggered the emergence of a plethora of different political groupings that have played a role not only in the transition but also in democratic Hungary. In 1987, the Hungarian Democratic Forum (MDF) formed as a political and cultural movement based on Christian democracy and the traditions of "people's nationalism." Its members were quite willing to tolerate and even compromise with the reformist wing of the HSWP. In 1988, a group of young lawyers founded the Alliance of Young Democrats, or FiDeSz. It was far more outspoken than earlier movements and opposed both the reformist and nonreformist versions of the communist system. Months later, the Committee for an Act of Historical Justice (TIB) emerged, demanding the political, civic, and moral rehabilitation of the veterans of the 1956 revolution and pension benefits for its survivors. Then, a Network of Free Democratic Initiatives appeared and pushed for a reduced role of the state and the protection of individual rights; it later transformed into the Alliance of Free Democrats (SzDSz), the third of the key noncommunist parties in democratic Hungary.

These parties and two associations representing the intelligentsia met between March and June 1989 in what was known as the Opposition Roundtable (ORT). Their ultimate goal was to come to a consensus so that they could be monolithic in their negotiations with the regime before it had a chance to pass reform legislation and take control of the transition. They agreed to negotiate with the Communist Party (HSWP), but only about holding free elections, not about what would follow. In the process, the ORT discussions spilled out and further challenged communist control.

As the opposition crystallized into groups and then political parties, the HSWP began to fall apart. After Kádár was forced to resign, Károly Grósz, a relative conservative, took over. But his was not the only faction in the HSWP. Younger reformers like Miklós Németh and Imre Pozsgay, in alliance with older ones such as Rezső Nyers, struggled within the party. On the outside, the party's position vacillated. Grósz ordered the suppression of the demonstrations on the anniversary of Imre Nagy's execution in June 1988, which had been promoted by all the new organizations. Then, the younger and more liberal leaders began to reconsider the "1956 events," met with opposition leaders, and symbolically removed the Iron Curtain in May 1989 by cutting the barbed-wire fence between Austria and Hungary. As a compromise between the two groups, a "committee of experts" made up of scholars and politicians was established in 1989 to investigate the real causes of the 1956 events. Its report created a major political stir. The Kádárist notion that the 1956 events were a "counterrevolution" was rejected, and the events were designated a "legitimate national uprising."

Preparations began for the reburial of Nagy and the other leaders of the Hungarian Revolution. Kádárist-style rule was clearly in its last days. In the spring, the party divested itself of much of its power, even shifting the responsibility for dealing with the politically explosive reburial to the state. Old parties that had been a part of Hungary's moment of democracy and reemerged briefly in 1956 reappeared only to fade away once the transition had happened. Despite the objections of some in the HSWP and leaders in Bulgaria, Germany, Romania, and Czechoslovakia, the funeral of Imre Nagy was held as a public ceremony in Budapest's Heroes' Square. As more than 250,000 people observed in the square and millions more watched on television, the reform communists stood as honorary pallbearers. New political leaders from the new and old parties gave speeches. The leaders who had survived, including Nagy's press spokesman, Miklós Vásárhelyi, "spoke of justice, national unity, and the opportunity for 'a peaceful transition to a free and democratic society.'" As already mentioned, the then young FiDeSz leader, Viktor Orbán, explicitly demanded the withdrawal of Soviet troops.[10]

With the Communist Party shifting its powers to the state, the history of 1956 rewritten, and the reburial of Nagy complete, there was no stopping the transition. Negotiations between the ORT and the regime began on June 13, 1989 (simultaneously with the semi-free Polish elections). The HSWP agreed to focus only on establishing the rules for free elections and amendments to the communist constitution rather than to try to follow the Polish model of negotiating political, social, and economic issues as well. In exchange, the ORT parties had to agree to a triangular table, with the HSWP's voting power aided by the inclusion of the trade unions as minor players in the negotiations. On October 23, 1989, the Third Hungarian Republic was proclaimed. A week earlier, the communist HSWP had declared its transformation into the Western-style, social democratic Hungarian Socialist Party (HSP) and announced its intention to participate in the forthcoming elections.

The final battle of the transition was over whether to elect the president or the parliament first. For the ex-communists, the best scenario was to hold the presidential election first because their leader, Pozsgay, was still popular for dismantling the Communist Party and was the best-known politician. The Alliance of Free Democrats and FiDeSz refused to agree to this plan and instead organized a referendum on whether to first elect the president or the parliament (whose members would then elect the president). On this issue, the ORT groups split from the Hungarian Democratic Forum, urging abstention rather than changing the roundtable agreement to elect the president and then the parliament. In that referendum, the option of holding the parliamentary elections first won with 50.07 percent. The monolithic opposition started to divide.

Despite these divisions, the period from the end of communism to 2010 saw Hungary make significant progress in establishing a democratic political system. As the section on parties below discusses in greater detail, political parties gravitated toward the center, and government coalitions were generally stable. Hungary also made substantial progress economically and was one of the first countries admitted to NATO in 1999 and to the European Union (EU) in 2004.

FROM 2010 TO THE PRESENT

In 2010, a new phase began, characterized by a stronger emphasis on nationalism and the central role of a charismatic leader, which, along with a catchall economic policy and some gradually increasing authoritarian features, constitute the classic ingredients of populism.[11] In that year, Hungary celebrated the twentieth anniversary of the first democratic election after communism with a remarkable political turnaround. The center-right party FiDeSz won a stunning 68.14 percent of votes—that is, a two-thirds majority—leaving the rival HSP (MSzP), which had been in office since 2002 and between 1994 and 1998, with a meager 15.28 percent, less than one-fourth the FiDeSz score. The other four parties that had gained seats in 1990 disappeared from parliament and were replaced by the far-right Jobbik, with 12.18 percent of the vote, and the new Politics Can Be Different (LMP) environmental party, with 4.15 percent. The victorious party was thus empowered to amend the constitution and immediately started to pass legislation such as granting Magyar citizenship to Hungarians abroad—a move that raised suspicion and concern in neighboring Slovakia and Romania.[12] On June 29, 2010, former Olympic champion Pál Schmitt was elected the fourth president of the Hungarian Republic since 1990, only to resign less than two years later over a plagiarism scandal. He was replaced by János Áder, then a member of the European Parliament and a former speaker of the Hungarian Parliament, who was reelected in March 2017 for another five years[13]: both could be described as FiDeSz loyalists.

In 2011, one year into its two-thirds majority, FiDeSz passed its own new Fundamental Law[14] (all other parliamentary groups voted against it). It subsequently amended it in ways that many commentators viewed as authoritarian,[15] capping it all with a new electoral system that went in the same (i.e., authoritarian) direction. The common element of these changes was the reduction of guarantees related to pluralism and the independence of judiciary, among others.[16]

Viktor Orbán triumphed again in the April 2014 parliamentary elections, securing for the second legislature in a row a supermajority (i.e., two-thirds) of 133 out of 199 available seats for his party, the Alliance of Young Democrats (FiDeSz), and its junior ally, the Christian Democratic People's Party (KDNP). True, the coalition's percentage of the vote was considerably smaller than in 2010, and the opposition forces increased their score, but it all happened in the context of a new electoral law that downsized seats from 386 to 199 and redesigned electoral districts in a way almost admittedly meant to help the incumbents retain a majority. Quite aptly, Princeton professor Kim Lane Scheppele, the most relentless Western critic of Orbán's policies, defined the 2014 elections as "legal but not fair"; the Organization for Security and Co-operation in Europe expressed a similar sentiment.[17] However, the supermajority was lost in February 2015 due to the appointment of a FiDeSz parliamentarian as EU commissioner and the subsequent by-election, won by an independent candidate.[18]

In summer of 2015, massive flows, most escaping the Syrian catastrophe took the "Balkan route" and tried to reach the EU via Turkey, Greece, Serbia, and Hungary rather than the more traditional Libya-Italy-by-sea route of African immigrants. They put the policies of Orbán to a very serious test. His government made it clear that refugees could receive some humanitarian assistance but would be increasingly discouraged from crossing

Hungary. To substantiate this position, orders were given to build a barbed-wire fence along the border with Serbia, which runs for approximately 160 km. Hungary's brand of populist nationalism had followers: in the region (Poland, but also Slovakia and possibly the Czech Republic), in Western Europe (a region where most countries have like-minded parties or movements with parliamentary seats, although none of them is in office as of summer 2017). The main ingredients of this "political recipe" can be condensed as follows:

- an open hostility to "globalization," viewed not as an ineluctable process but as an international attempt at diluting and eventually eliminating national identities;
- an equally explicit hostility to Islam, not as a faith per se but in connection to some of its traditions;
- a rejection of multiculturalism and a defense of national traditions, values, and religion;
- direct opposition to the influx of refugees from Africa and the Middle East toward Europe (or the United States);
- a lukewarm commitment to Euro-Atlantic institutions, particularly the EU; and
- endemic temptations to eliminate, limit, or threaten basic civil rights and more or less open intolerance toward freedom of the press. As the result of these attitudes, the Orbán government has come into conflict with the EU over its refusal to accept refugees as well as over its actions threatening civil and political rights in Hungary.

Photo 11.2. Hungarian wall and national border guards prevent the entrance of Syrian refugees in 2015 from crossing through Hungarian territory. (Website of the Hungarian Government)

Photo 11.3. Hungarian Prime Minister Viktor Orbán speaking at a national conference in 2016. (Website of the Hungarian Government)

Political Institutions

The Roundtable Accords, as they were modified after the referendum, and the old parliament's vote for the president to be directly elected provided for a parliamentary system. After its election in March 1990, the initial center-right parliament revised the transitional constitution so that only a simple majority was needed to pass most laws and the president was elected by the parliament every five years by a two-thirds majority. The single-house parliament was to be elected every four years with a mixed electoral system and was also to select the prime minister. The prime minister was responsible for selecting and guiding the ministers. The president had ceremonial powers and some ability to intervene when there were problems within the system. None of these powers were decisive, however.

Árpád Göncz, elected president by the parliament, created a model for the Hungarian presidency that generated criticism but also secured his reelection in 1995. His model entitled the president, who represents the country, to work behind the scenes to reach consensus among the various political groups. Through this process, Göncz and his successors have tried to avoid identifying with one side or the other. At the same time, Göncz used the ability to approve the removal of such officials as the heads of radio and television to push the parties away from partisanship in these areas. His successor, Ferenc Mádl (elected in 2000), followed this model. László Sólyom, who was president from 2005 to 2010, however, was often criticized for an alleged bias toward FiDeSz.

Dominant coalitions shifted from election to election. Until 2010, all of the cabinets were products of coalitions of centrist parties, and none was controlled by a single party. József Antall, Péter Boross, and Viktor Orbán served as conservative prime ministers. There have been four socialist-sponsored prime ministers since 1990—Gyula Horn, Péter Medgyessy, Ferenc Gyurcsány, and Gordon Bajnai. None of the prime ministers carried out real policy shifts until Orbán's 2010 triumph. A former left-leaning liberal, yet consistently anticommunist, Orbán had astutely moved to the right in 1993 and 1994 on realizing that the death of Antall, founding member of the MDF, had created a huge vacuum on that side of the political spectrum. In his first mandate as leader of a supermajority, he imposed a style of government that left little or no room for collegiality.

The stability of Hungary's political system was clear early on when József Antall, the first postcommunist prime minister, died in office in late 1993. He was immediately replaced by another Hungarian Democratic Forum leader, Péter Boross, who served six months until that parliament's term ended. After the socialist's loss in the 2004 elections to the European Parliament, the HSP shifted its leadership to respond to the public's disaffection. This allowed Ferenc Gyurcsány to become the first prime minister to serve two successive terms until he also resigned in spring 2009, to be replaced by Bajnai.

Although the ministers changed with every election, the upper ranks of the state bureaucracy remained quite stable. Because no effective legislation purged the state of workers from the communist era, they were allowed to remain in their positions if they declared allegiance to the new system. Where changes occurred, they were the result of the government's efforts to make Hungary's overall bureaucracy smaller and more professional. Then, the 2010–2014 legislature, with the FiDeSz supermajority made an effort to ensure political loyalty from all sectors of the state apparatus, thereby attracting severe criticism and frequent accusations of authoritarianism. The Orbán government's reply was to argue that most formerly communist bureaucrats had remained glued to their posts and were inclined to be disloyal toward the new government, thereby requiring serious streamlining in the country's interest. In truth, however, FiDeSz acted as the communist regime in appointing its own loyalists to each and every relevant administrative position of the country. Former dissident and postcommunist mayor of Budapest Gábor Demszky said in Washington, DC, in December 2013 that "the current Hungarian government has created a system that is more repressive than the communist government of the 1980s." When challenged by Anna Stumpf of the Hungarian Embassy, who asked how he could possibly make that comparison, Demszky answered simply, "I have lived in it."[19]

Elections and Political Parties

Elections for the first freely elected parliament since 1945 were scheduled for March 25, 1990, with a runoff on April 8. The electoral system provided for a parliament of 386 seats, of which 176 were to be elected in single-member districts with a French-type, double-ballot, majoritarian system, and 152 were to be selected from party lists for each region using a proportional system. The remaining seats (a minimum of fifty-eight) would be distributed to national party lists to compensate for "extra votes" that were over and above what a candidate needed to get elected or had been cast for losing candidates in the single-member districts. The goal of this redistribution was to keep the parliament truly representative of the overall national vote. At the same time, any party that received less than 4 percent of the vote nationally was disqualified from seating deputies in the parliament. Although the system has been responsive to changes in Hungarian public opinion, until 2010 it was also extremely stable, with governing coalitions shifting regularly from right to left but both sides remaining close to the center and ready to step over ideological divides.

The unquestionable winner of the first election was the MDF, whose president, József Antall, was inaugurated as prime minister in May 1990. Six parties received enough votes to make it into that parliament. Three (MDF, SzDSz, and FiDeSz) were brand-new. They won 277 seats in this first election and would remain the centerpieces of Hungarian politics into the twenty-first century. One (the HSP) could be called both new and old, as it was made up mostly of the reform wing of the old HSWP. The remaining two (the Independent Smallholders Party and the People's Christian Democrats) had existed before the communist period. Together, these two got a total of sixty-five seats. Among these parties, there was a clear consensus about the direction Hungary should take: toward Europe, democracy, and capitalism. The differences had more to do with the details of Hungary's move forward and assessments of the past. These divisions reflected the old Hungarian separation of people's nationalists and urbanists. As Bill Lomax has observed,

> Hungarian parties are, almost without exception, elite groups of intellectuals, often long-standing personal friends more like political clubs than representative institutions. Many of Antall's government ministers went to the same school with him. Most of the Free Democrats were together in the democratic opposition. Several of [FiDeSz]'s leaders studied law together. . . . The political identities and cleavages they do represent are based neither on social interests, nor political programmes, nor structured belief systems. In fact, to the extent that such cleavages do exist in Hungarian politics, they are found to cut across the parties almost equally—each party has its liberals, its nationalists, its conservatives, its social-democrats, its populists, its radicals.[20]

Initially, the leaders of all the parties except FiDeSz were intellectuals from academia and the arts. The leaders and members of FiDeSz, or the Young Democrats, were different. They and their constituents were young people. Most of the party's leaders had studied law together in the 1980s. As a result, until 1993, they were less bound by ideology and more West European in their thinking and presentation.

In 1994, the HSP was the first successor to an old ruling Communist Party of Central and Eastern Europe to be reelected and returned to power with an absolute majority of seats. Yet, in the first of a series of unlikely coalitions, the HSP joined with the Alliance of Free Democrats. Their gains were a reaction to people's initial disappointment with what the transition had brought and also to the weakness in the Hungarian Democratic Forum brought to a head by József Antall's death and the splintering effect of the Hungarian Truth and Life Party led by István Csurka. Like the Polish social democrats, leaders of the HSP talked not of returning to the old communist system but of modernization, economic and political reform, and joining Europe. The Alliance of Free Democrats actually lost votes in 1994, but the Hungarian Democratic Forum lost far more, and the Alliance of Free Democrats was—despite its history of opposition to communism—the largest and most viable partner for the HSP.

In 1998, there was a shift in all the major players' positions and strengths. The Hungarian Democratic Forum had essentially collapsed by 1998. Most of the pre-communist parties could no longer get enough votes to seat deputies in parliament. In the aftermath of Antall's death and the partnership of the Alliance of Free Democrats and HSP (confirmed by their signing of the Democratic Charter in 1991), FiDeSz moved to the right. Its leaders were able, despite the simultaneous success of the extreme rightist Truth and Life Party, to present themselves as the legitimate successors of the declining MDF. The party leader, Viktor Orbán, when he became prime minister, openly claimed Antall's legacy. Their coalition was made up of the Smallholders and the remnants of the MDF. To further their popularity, they also added "Hungarian Civic Party" to their name (it later became "Hungarian Civic Alliance").

Toward the end of the legislature, in late February 2002, Orbán signaled his intentions to profoundly revise recent Hungarian history as told in the communist and postcommunist versions. He inaugurated a statue to Béla Kovács on the fifty-fifth anniversary of his arrest and deportation, as well as Budapest's Terror House Museum, a controversial yet interesting institution intended to equate the Hungarian versions of Nazism and communism and the crimes committed by their proponents. While nobody took issue with the first decision, the second was seriously questioned for its portrayal of historical events.[21]

A few weeks later, the balance shifted back to the coalition of the socialists and the Alliance of Free Democrats after a close race with the Young Democrats and the Democratic Forum Alliance. The two parties were able to govern with a razor-thin majority. However, when the coalition lost in its first elections to the European Parliament and right-wing and Euroskeptic candidates took a number of districts, Péter Medgyessy (who had been a member of the HSWP, a banker in France, and a leader in the private sector in Hungary) resigned. He was replaced by Ferenc Gyurcsány, who had gone on from the Communist Youth Organization to become one of the wealthiest businessmen in Hungary. Under his leadership, the Socialist–Free Democratic Alliance was the first coalition to win two successive elections. This made Gyurcsány the first Hungarian prime minister to serve more than one term, as he led the party to a much clearer victory in 2006.

Until the riots that followed the revelation that Gyurcsány had lied about the status of the Hungarian economy just before the fiftieth-anniversary celebrations of the 1956 Hungarian Revolution, political parties and groups in Hungary were quite restrained and remained very centrist. The closeness of the parties ideologically, their ability to form coalitions, and the low turnout rate in Hungarian elections at all levels since the transition began are all reasons for and demonstrations of Hungarian voters' lack of engagement with particular parties and political battles. In fact, many local government elections have had to be held a second time because less than 50 percent of the population voted in the regular election round. This disengagement changed, at least momentarily, after the Gyurcsány revelation. Budapest and other major cities were rocked by riots by angry and disillusioned voters, which in the long run led to Gyurcsány's resignation in 2009 and the installation of a caretaker government until the next elections. Gyurcsány's resignation, however, did not prevent crushing defeats for the socialists in 2010 and 2014.

Photo 11.4. Riots in Budapest in 2006. (MTI Foto, Olah Tibor)

The Economic Transition

Economic weakness has been the Achilles' heel of Hungarian politics. In the last decade of communism, borrowing money from abroad was the regime's only way to sustain the living standards of its population and keep itself in power. Even with that infusion of foreign loan money, the transition in Hungary was stirred by the stagnation of the economy and its double-digit inflation. The new leaders of Hungary inherited far less debt and a far better economy than their Polish counterparts, but they still faced high popular expectations, a debt of over $20 billion from the Kádár regime's borrowing, and the disaster wrought by the collapse of the CMEA market.

Hungary avoided the Polish "shock therapy" model. Instead, it began by creating a "social market economy" that moved toward private ownership in industries producing consumer goods and providing services. Although legislation allowed for beginning bankruptcy actions against failing enterprises, very few large-scale industries were closed. Instead, foreign investment and ownership were used as tools to get the economy going.

Hungary's transition was complicated by its high debt to the West, the collapse of the Soviet market, and the end of cheap Soviet oil and natural gas supplies. Between 1989 and 1992, Hungary's gross domestic product had collapsed by 18 percent, "a decline comparable only to the worst of the Great Depression of the 1930s."[22] Western banks and governments wrote off much of Hungary's debt when they wrote off the Polish debt as part of a package to help both the Hungarian and Polish economies correct themselves. The International Monetary Fund, European Community, and World Bank also provided large loans.

Only in March 1995 was the Bokros Plan for serious economic reform implemented. This reform program encouraged privatization with monetary incentives and openness to foreign investment. At the same time, state enterprises were allowed to survive, and new private enterprises were established alongside them. The goal was for these private enterprises to edge out the state enterprises. A similar policy governed the reforms in agriculture and social services. The costs of health care and education ballooned as the state continued to provide funds, while the wealthy opted out and provided for themselves by creating private health and educational institutions. By 2005, 80 percent of the Hungarian economy was in private hands. Foreign ownership went from about 4 percent in 1990 to 52.1 percent in 1997.

The reforms all seemed to work in the first decade. The population was satisfied. By 1997, the economy had begun to grow by 4 to 5 percent annually. However, the gains came with real hidden costs; many hard economic moves were avoided, and the economy depended instead on its Kádár-era base and foreign investment. Keeping costly social welfare programs and encouraging foreign investment by allowing profits to go abroad meant that the apparent upward course was far from secure. Government accounting only hid the problem. In 2006, as Gyurcsány's leaked admission to party elites indicated, Hungary's deficit stood at 10 percent. The rhetoric of the ensuing demonstrations and the opposition politicians who led them showed that they had no alternative economic proposal. Rather than deal with the social consequences of how Hungary could best deal with its budget deficit and rationalize its economy, political rhetoric focused on accusations that individuals were communist or anti-Semitic. The promised tax reduction was not to be; taxes actually had to go up to pay for increases in government spending and inflation and to placate foreign investors. The plan for Hungary to adopt the euro in 2010 (which required a deficit below 3 percent) was also called into question as wishful thinking and turned out to be utterly unrealistic. But the anger dissipated when it was clear there were no alternatives to the course Hungary was on.

On winning the elections in 2010, Orbán set the country on a path characterized by strong anti–foreign capital rhetoric (and deeds) and various measures declared to be aimed at enhancing domestic resources as opposed to leaving a peripheral Hungary at the mercy of the global market. According to the pronouncements of FiDeSz, only in this context can the necessary budget cuts be implemented and economic growth encouraged. By late 2013, the results were encouraging on both accounts, which was one of the key factors leading to the 2014 FiDeSz victory.[23] A similar scenario is likely to appear in the wake of the 2018 elections.

Social Consequences

The social consequences in Hungary were no different from those in other countries when they began to transform their economic and political systems. Despite the problems in the Hungarian economy in 1989, Hungarians started the transition with higher expectations because they were accustomed to living better than most in the bloc. However, as Prime Minister Antall detailed after the 1990 elections, the country faced declining health and falling living standards. He stated that Hungarians' life expectancy was the lowest in Europe, that for the past decade the number of deaths had exceeded the number of births, and that because of the polluted environment and the need to work long hours, the health and life expectancy of middle-aged Hungarians were the worst among civilized nations.[24]

The limited economic reforms Hungary undertook at the start of the 1990s left 1 million of Hungary's population of 10.6 million living below the subsistence level and 2 million living at the officially defined social minimum. Those hardest hit were pensioners, families with more than two children, and the unemployed. Homelessness also appeared because factories closed workers' hostels, citizens were unable to pay the increases in their rent, and people came to Budapest in search of jobs. Roma and illegal aliens—largely ethnic Romanians or Hungarians who had "escaped" the more disastrous Romanian economy—added to the numbers of homeless.[25]

In the decade and a half that followed, Hungary's living standards continued to fall. Hungarians, accustomed to rising consumption, have proved less willing than Poles to tolerate a considerable drop in living standards. Also, public opinion has focused on whether consumer goods markets function reasonably well, whether most goods are readily available, and whether there is a "visible" economic crisis. Hence, consumption rose more slowly than incomes, and with real income actually falling, consumption has declined sharply. Increases in consumer prices were exacerbated by subsidy reductions and price liberalization.

While some had prospered during the 1980s, those lacking the skills needed to access the wealth from the "second economy" and those reliant on state incomes did relatively badly. Job opportunities for unskilled or uneducated people diminished throughout this time as a result of a continuing decrease in the number of vacant jobs and the shift in labor demand toward skilled workers.

Hungary became steadily more polarized, and Hungary's ethnic groups, particularly the Roma and illegal aliens, suffered from the economic reforms. While in 1971 Roma males and females had been regularly employed and earned incomes, from the late 1980s onward, they were systematically pushed out of the labor market.[26] By 1993, this trend resulted in shockingly high unemployment figures for the Roma. Less than half of the Roma unemployment rate could be accounted for by factors like Romas' lower educational levels and disadvantageous distribution of labor power. The rest was due to discrimination by employers. Thus, the Roma are generally described as major losers in the economic transition. Although they make up only 5 percent of the total population, approximately 25 percent of the 2 million poor in Hungary are Roma. Moreover, the Roma in Hungary are discriminated against not only by employers but also by state or state-controlled institutions like public education, the National Health Service, the police, and the courts.[27] In addition, between 2008 and 2009, six apparently random but clearly racially motivated assassinations of Roma people illustrated the unresolved situation in which they lived and reawakened fearsome ghosts of the country's past. Zsolt Bayer, one of the first FiDeSz members, in yet another deplorable outburst in the daily *Magyar Hirlap* on January 5, 2013, exactly two years after his anti-Semitic article, commented on a felony allegedly committed by Roma, calling them "animals deserving to be punished" and stirring up another domestic and international scandal. Although some government and FiDeSz officials distanced themselves from him and he subsequently retracted his statement, at least in part, the government left the impression of taking an ambiguous stand on anti-Roma prejudice and violence.

In its struggle to keep up economic growth and deal with its budget deficit, Hungary has essentially ignored the need to reform its social services. According to the Organization for Economic Co-operation and Development country survey for 2005, Hungary needed to take strong measures to prevent "failure in the welfare regime change."[28] The problem is that unpopular political decisions must be made to streamline the public health system, limit disability pensions to the really disabled, make labor mobility more effective, and deal with problems in most other state welfare sectors. No political group wants to deal with these issues directly. Conservatives and liberal-socialists are separated more by rhetoric than by concrete differences in economic and social policy.

Neither the left nor the right has championed the needs of Hungary's poor. Instead, they have talked about "trickle-down economics." In the early years of the transition, the government gave in when faced with demonstrations by those who had suffered from the economic reforms. The most famous of these demonstrations were the so-called Taxi Wars in 1990, when taxi drivers and others blocked the streets of Budapest and roads around the country in response to the government's sudden decision to raise the price of gasoline by 66 percent overnight and the announcement that the price of other energy products would increase in order to deal with shortages caused by decreases in sales by the Soviet Union. In the end, the government backed down.

Until the 2006 demonstrations, other responses to social problems were far smaller and more subdued. Groups have, when they could, taken matters into their own hands. Some self-help and advocacy groups have been organized, and many, like the homeless, have broken the law to provide for themselves.

Foreign Policy and the Clash over CEU

Hungary was a leader in the move toward Europe. It was the first member of the Soviet bloc to become a member of the Council of Europe. On June 4, 1990, the new and free Hungarian parliament marked the seventieth anniversary of the Trianon peace treaty by adopting a resolution that reiterated the acceptance of its existing borders.

Following the dissolution of Yugoslavia, the CMEA, the Warsaw Treaty Organization, and the Soviet Union itself (all of which happened between June 25 and December 25, 1991), Hungary attempted to conduct bilateral negotiations with its old and new neighbors and to march resolutely toward membership in NATO and the EU. Its attempts to deal with its eastern neighbors were far more politically problematic. The state treaty with Ukraine, signed in 1991, caused major repercussions in domestic politics. A faction within the MDF, led by the playwright István Csurka, openly rejected the agreement on borders and walked out of that party, eventually forming a new group called the Hungarian Truth and Life Party.[29] As the 2013–2014 "Revolution of Dignity" or Euromaidan unfolded in Ukraine, Hungary's main eastern neighbor, Orbán took an ambivalent stance on the events, focusing more on the never-threatened status of the Magyar minority rather than on the evident similarity with 1956, thereby "freeing the Hungarian Left of their most important political burden."[30] In the subsequent four years, the FiDeSz government, albeit not questioning the EU sanctions imposed on Russia, appeared to be a lot more concerned with keeping good relations with Putin than about the multiple violations of international law committed against its Eastern neighbor.[31]

After the 1991 agreement with Ukraine, further treaties were signed with Croatia and Slovenia (1992), Slovakia (1995), and Romania (1996), all dealing with principles of good neighborliness, respect of the borders, and the rights of minorities. These treaties settled Hungarian affairs to the east and left Hungary open to move toward the EU.

The process of gaining EU membership began with the signing of an association agreement with the EU in 1994, followed by the transformation of the former Soviet base of Taszár in southwestern Hungary into a NATO logistical base in 1996 and receipt of full NATO membership in March 1999, on the eve of the Kosovo War. As relations between the United States and parts of the EU deteriorated in 2003 because of the invasion of Iraq, Hungary cautiously supported the George W. Bush administration, while making the point that good relations with all EU members were a priority. In May 2004, full EU membership was achieved.

Ever since 2010, but especially after the double electoral victory of 2014 (Hungarian and European elections), FiDeSz leaders have more or less openly challenged several EU directives, especially in the domain of refugees policy. By mid-2015 the so-called Dublin agreement (whereby refugees into the EU had to remain in the first member country they reached) was declared obsolete and a more even distribution according to each country's size, economy, and so on was envisaged. However, Hungary along with the other Visegrád countries (Poland, Slovakia, and the Czech Republic) rejected this approach and stated that it would not accept anything not decided by its domestic legislation.

The following year, a major confrontation occurred, which had developed rather silently over the previous years, until it became public in the spring of 2017 between Viktor Orbán and his government on one side, and George Soros and his institutions, particularly Budapest's Central European University or CEU on the other side.

George Soros, a native of Budapest who survived the Holocaust, immigrated in 1947 to the United Kingdom, where he became a disciple of Karl Popper, the philosopher of open society and fallibility of social theories. Ten years later, he became a US citizen and amassed a fortune in finance. In the early 1980s, he met Miklós Vásárhelyi, a veteran of the 1956 revolution who had obtained permission to spend an academic year at the Columbia school of journalism. Soros decided to appoint him to head a cultural foundation, which he wanted to establish in Hungary. Having obtained permission from the communist regime, the Soros Foundation was inaugurated in 1984. A few years later, as the regime change approached, the Soros Foundation generously subsidized various cultural and social groups and individuals, including almost the entire leadership of FiDeSz. Viktor Orbán himself was awarded a scholarship to pursue an MA at Pembroke College, Oxford, during the 1988–1989 academic year.

After the regime change, between 1991 and 1995, Soros established the Central European University as a US-accredited institution of graduate studies, awarding degrees that were also recognized in Hungary, along with other research institutes like the Open Society Archives. Additionally, and especially after 2010, Soros established and funded several NGOs in Hungary and elsewhere. Those in Hungary clashed openly with the Hungarian government during the 2015 summer crisis. Soros' activism was all the more evident as the center-left opposition appeared unable to offer serious alternatives to the government's position.

In early April 2017, an amendment to Hungary's higher education law was passed in Parliament that decreed that any non-European university wishing to award degrees in Hungary needed to have a campus in its place of origin, and "set an impossibly tight deadline for establishing an American campus, ensuring that the CEU would no longer be able to accept new students by the beginning of 2018."[32] Despite several mass demonstrations, involving up to eighty thousand participants, and vehement protests from academics and universities from all over the world, the amendment was confirmed by President Áder's signature and became effective. George Soros reacted in a Brussels speech on June 1 by echoing the title of an academic book published by the CEU Press and calling Hungary "a Mafia State,"[33] to which Orbán replied the next day stating that "Soros' network . . . operates in a mafia style."[34] Thus, the stage is set for a continuing tug-of-war, the outcome of which is not yet predictable.

Despite more outbursts of anti-Semitism against Soros, not openly supported but tolerated by FiDeSz, Orbán scored a success in July 2017 by hosting an official visit of Benjamin Netanyahu, the Israeli prime minister, which appeared to close—at least for the time being—the issue of anti-Semitism in Hungary, with a solemn promise made to protect the country's Jewish population.[35]

Conclusion

The remarkable unity displayed by the Hungarians in 1956 and 1989 did not last after the end of communism. Yet, although the two traditional political factions (i.e., people's nationalists and secular liberals) have railed at each other rhetorically, it was in 2010 that the Hungarian parties began to move far from the center in their actual policy goals. The economy appears to have recovered from the huge burden of moving from goulash communism (which in the long run proved a major liability) to capitalism, but the upheavals in 2006 over revelations of the economy's true problems were more about being misled than about the financial restraints that had to be imposed. For Hungary, joining the EU has been a decided benefit. Clearly, there is no interest in turning back or slowing Hungary's move forward. And yet, the Orbán government's legislation—while taking full advantage of the benefits of membership—has repeatedly challenged various EU institutions, particularly regarding civil liberties, resulting in numerous warnings and admonishments but no substantial consequences yet. The truth of the matter is that, as long as the European People's Party—the EU's grouping of conservative and Christian democratic parties of which FiDeSz is a member—and its most relevant leader, German chancellor Angela Merkel, refuse to oppose Orbán and his choices, things are unlikely to change. Despite his renunciation of "liberal" democracy in his speech in Romania in 2014, Orbán will most probably stay in power until the opposition proves capable of rallying a majority of Hungarians behind it.

Study Questions

1. Why are the Jewish and Roma questions so relevant in Hungarian politics?
2. What are the main reasons for Orbán's continued support by a majority of Hungarians?
3. To what extent can Hungary be called a parliamentary democracy and a state based on the rule of law?

4. Is Orbán proving more successful in economic policy than his socialist predecessors?
5. How should the Hungarian center-left opposition act in order to increase its future chances of electoral victory?

Suggested Readings

Berend, Iván T., *The Hungarian Economic Reforms 1953–1988*. Cambridge: Cambridge University Press, 1990.

Braun, Aurel, and Zoltan Barany, eds. *Dilemmas of Transition: The Hungarian Experience*. Lanham, MD: Rowman & Littlefield, 1998.

De Nevers, Renée. *Comrades No More: The Seeds of Change in Eastern Europe*. Cambridge, MA: MIT Press, 2003.

Barát, Erzsébet. "Populist Discourses in the Hungarian Public Sphere: From Right to Left (and Beyond)?" *Journal of Language and Politics* 16, no. 4 (June 12, 2017): 535–50.

Fábián, Katalin. *Contemporary Women's Movements in Hungary: Globalization, Democracy, and Gender Equality*. Washington, DC: Woodrow Wilson Center Press; Baltimore, MD: Johns Hopkins University Press, 2009.

Gati, Charles. *Failed Illusions*. Stanford, CA: Stanford University Press, 2006.

Guy, Will, ed. *From Victimhood to Citizenship: The Path of Roma Integration*. Budapest: Kossuth, 2013.

Gyuricza, Péter. *The Media War II—Evolution of the Media in Hungary 2010–2013*. North Charleston, SC: CreateSpace, 2014.

The Media War in Hungary I—Media and Power in Hungary from 1989–2009. 2nd ed. North Charleston, SC: CreateSpace, 2014.

Herman, Lise Esther. "Re-Evaluating the Post-Communist Success Story: Party Elite Loyalty, Citizen Mobilization and the Erosion of Hungarian Democracy," *European Political Science Review: EPSR* 8, no. 2 (May 2016): 251–84.

Janos, Andrew C. *East Central Europe in the Modern World*. Stanford, CA: Stanford University Press, 2000.

Király, Béla K., and Bozóki András, eds. *Lawful Revolution in Hungary, 1989–1994*. Boulder, CO, and New York: Social Science Monographs and Columbia University Press, 1995.

Umut Korkut, *Liberalization Challenges in Hungary—Elitism, Progressivism, and Populism*. New York: Palgrave MacMillan, 2012.

Körösényi, András. *Government and Politics in Hungary*. Budapest: Central European University, 2000.

Körösényi, András, Tóth Csaba, and Török Gábor. *The Hungarian Political System*. Budapest: Hungarian Center for Democracy Studies Foundation, 2009.

Krasztev, Péter, and Jon Van Til, eds. *The Hungarian Patient—Social Opposition to an Illiberal Democracy*. Budapest and New York: CEU Press, 2015.

Kun, J. C. *Hungarian Foreign Policy: The Experience of a New Democracy*. Washington Papers 160. Westport, CT: Praeger, 1993.

Lendvai, Paul. *Hungary: Between Democracy and Authoritarianism*. London: Hurst, 2012.

Lomax, Bill. "The Strange Death of Civil Society in Post-Communist Hungary," *Journal of Communist Studies and Transition Politics* 13 (1997): 41–63.

Bálint Magyar, *Post-Communist Mafia State—The Case of Hungary*. Budapest, New York: CEU Press, 2016.

Morlang, Diana. "Hungary: Socialists Building Capitalism." In *The Left Transformed in Post-Communist Societies*, edited by Jane Curry and Joan Urban, 61–98. Lanham, MD: Rowman & Littlefield, 2003.

Pittaway, Mark. *The Workers' State: Industrial Labor and the Making of Socialist Hungary, 1944–1958*. Pittsburgh, PA: University of Pittsburgh Press, 2012.

Sárközy, Tamás. *Magyarország kormányzása 1978–2012* [*The Governing of Hungary, 1978–2012*]. Budapest: Park, 2012.

Schmidt, Mária, and László Tóth Gy. *Transition with Contradictions: The Case of Hungary, 1990–1998*. Budapest: Kairosz, 1999.

Tokes, Rudolf. *Hungary's Negotiated Revolution: Economic Reform, Social Change, and Political Succession*. Cambridge: Cambridge University Press, 1996.

Volgyes, Ivan. *Hungary—A Nation of Contradictions*. Boulder, CO: Westview Press, 1982.

Websites

Politics.hu: http://www.politics.hu

Hungarian Spectrum: http://hungarianspectrum.wordpress.com

National Széchényi Library, 1956 Institute and Oral History Archive: http://www.rev.hu

Notes

1. https://visegradpost.com/en/2017/07/24/full-speech-of-v-orban-will-europe-belong-to-europeans/.

2. http://budapestbeacon.com/public-policy/full-text-of-viktor-orbans-speech-at-baile-tusnad-tusnadfurdo-of-26-july-2014/10592.

3. Bálint Magyar, *Post-Communist Mafia State—The Case of Hungary* (Budapest, New York: CEU Press, 2016), 15–16. The First Republic is considered to have been the period between late October 1918 until late March 1919; the second was proclaimed in February 1946, ending in August 1947 or May 1949, depending on points of view; the third was inaugurated on October 23, 1989.

4. Andrew Janos, *The Politics of Backwardness in Hungary: 1825–1945* (Princeton, NJ: Princeton University Press, 1982), 176–82.

5. I. Bibó, *Democracy, Revolution, Self-Determination* (Highland Lakes, NY: Atlantic Research, 1991), 155–322. See also Paul Lendvai's observations in *Hungary: Between Democracy and Authoritarianism* (London: Hurst, 2012), 53–65.

6. See a rough translation of the article in Eva S. Balogh, "Zsolt Bayer Vents against Hungarian Jews and the Foreign Press," Hungarian Spectrum, 2011, https://hungarianspectrum.wordpress.com/2011/01/05/zsolt_bayer_vents_against_hungarian_jews_and_the_foreign_press. Neither Orbán nor any other FiDeSz official ever said anything to the effect of distancing him- or herself from, let alone against, Bayer—apparently (and interestingly) of Jewish origin himself—on this occasion or when he dismissed Imre Kertész, the 2002 Nobel laureate in literature, as a "non-Hungarian author," a definition that Kertész subsequently endorsed on moving to Berlin. Even more interestingly, in late June 2013, the Constitutional Court, renamed Curia, despite its reputation as a government tool, ruled that the accusations of anti-Semitism made by the liberal Klubrádió (see http://www.klubradio.hu/index.php?id=215) against Bayer, following which the latter had filed a libel suit, were legitimate. In the summer of 2014, two contradictory nominations happened. In July, a man called Péter Szentmihályi Szabó, a notorious anti-Semite with no diplomatic record, was appointed to be Hungary's ambassador to Italy. Following loud protest in both countries and internationally (and some embarrassment inside of FiDeSz), he decided to withdraw from the scene. On August 20, 2014, the recently restored Order of Saint Stephen, the highest Hungarian

state decoration, was bestowed on Kertész, who shared the honor with Ernő Rubik, inventor of the famous cube. It is difficult to not see here a deliberate "stick-and-carrot" approach by the Orbán government, which is trying to appease Jobbik, the center-left opposition, and international public opinion. See Hungary around the Clock, "Fidesz Members Worried by Italy Ambassador Nomination," Politics.hu, July 25, 2014, http://www.politics.hu/20140725/fidesz-members-worried-by-italy-ambassador-nomination; MTI, "Contested Appointee Declines Ambassador to Italy Role," Politics.hu, July 25, 2014, http://www.politics.hu/20140725/contested-appointee-declines-ambassador-to-italy-role; MTI; "Jobbik Protests Planned State Award to Kertész," Politics. hu, August 25, 2014, http://www.politics.hu/20140815/jobbik-protests-planned-state-award-to-kertesz; MTI; and "Kertész, Rubik Presented High State Award," Politics.hu, August 20, 2014, http://www.politics.hu/20140820/kertesz-rubik-presented-high-state-award.

7 For a database of the Hungarian Revolution and all the actors involved, see "The 1956 Revolution," National Széchényi Library, 1956 Institute and Oral History Archive, http://www.rev.hu/history_of_56/naviga/index.htm.

8. Iván T. Berend, *The Hungarian Economic Reforms 1953–1988* (Cambridge: Cambridge University Press, 1990), 246–58.

9. Berend, *Hungarian Economic Reforms*, 246–58.

10. Rudolf Tokes, *Hungary's Negotiated Revolution* (Cambridge: Cambridge University Press, 1996), 330.

11 Ghiţa Ionescu and Ernst Gellner, eds., *Populism: Its Meaning and National Characteristics* (London: Weidenfeld & Nicholson, 1970); Yves Mény and Yves Surel, *Democracies and the Populist Challenge* (New York: Palgrave, 2002); and the more recent work by Jan-Werner Mueller, *What Is Populism?*, Philadelphia: University of Pennsylvania Press, 2016.

12. See Eva S. Balogh, "Fidesz Gathering in Front of Parliament," *Hungarian Spectrum*, May 2010, http://hungarianspectrum.wordpress.com/2010/05.

13. See http://presidential-power.com/?p=6294.

14. See the text in English at "The Fundamental Law of Hungary (25 April 2011)," Website of the Hungarian Government, http://www.kormany.hu/download/e/02/00000/The%20New%20Fundamental%20Law%20of%20Hungary.pdf; and the main drafter's viewpoint at Max Harden, "The New Hungarian Constitution," John Cabot University, http://news.johncabot.edu/2012/02/20/jozsef-szajer-new-hungarian-constitution/.

15. For a complete description and honest discussion of the amendments, see "Hungary: Constitutional Amendments Adopted," Library of Congress, http://www.loc.gov/lawweb/servlet/lloc_news?disp3_l205403520_text.

16. See K. L. Scheppele's article, "Hungary and the End of Politics," *The Nation*, May 26, 2014, https://www.thenation.com/article/hungary-and-end-politics/.

17. See, respectively, Paul Krugman, "Legal but Not Fair (Hungary)," *New York Times*, April 13, 2014, https://krugman.blogs.nytimes.com/2014/04/13/legal-but-not-fair-hungary/; and International Election Observation Mission, Hungary—Parliamentary Elections, April 6, 2014, "Statement of Preliminary Findings and Conclusions," Organization for Security and Co-operation in Europe, http://www.osce.org/odihr/elections/117205?download=true.

18. http://www.politics.hu/20150222/government-loses-parliamentary-supermajority-as-fidesz-candidate-beaten-in-veszprem-by-election/.

19. Scheppele, "Hungary and the End of Politics."

20. Bill Lomax, "From Death to Resurrection: The Metamorphosis of Power in Eastern Europe," *Critique* 25 (1993): 68.

21. Béla Kovács (1908–1959) had been, in 1930, one of the founders of the Independent Smallholders Party, a political force characterized by a strong pro–land reform and antidictatorial

stand. He led it to the November 1945 electoral triumph (57 percent of the votes), only to be arrested and deported to a forced-labor camp in the USSR, where he remained until after the twentieth Congress of the Communist Party of the Soviet Union in 1956. During the revolution later that year, he briefly resumed his position and stated that "the land and the factories shouldn't be turned back to their old owners," a position unpopular with FiDeSz, eager to emphasize solely his anticommunist relevance. As for the Terror House Museum, established in the infamous building on Andrássy Avenue that played an important role under both the Nazi and Stalinist regimes, several observers pointed to the fact that only one hall is devoted to Nazism and the Arrow Cross, and many more treat the communist regime in all its variants, which is acceptable in terms of years in power but not victims. However, Socialist-led executives from 2002 to 2010 did not alter the structure of the museum, which has since become one of the cultural attractions of Budapest.

22. Eva Ehrlich and Gabor Revesz, "Coming in from the Cold: Hungary's Economy in the 20th Century," *Hungarian Quarterly* 41, no. 157 (Spring 2000): 18.

23. "Economic Survey of Hungary 2014," OECD, http://www.oecd.org/economy/economic-survey-hungary.htm.

24. Karoly Okolicsanyi, "Prime Minister Presents New Government's Program," *Report on Eastern Europe* (June 18, 1990): 21.

25. Paul Marer, *Economic Transformation, 1990–1998*, in *Dilemmas of Transition—The Hungarian Experience*, ed. Aurel Braun and Zoltan Barany (Lanham, MD: Rowman and Littlefield, 1998), 165–68.

26. Project on Ethnic Relations, *Roma in Hungary: Government Policies, Minority Expectations, and the International Community* (Princeton, NJ: Project on Ethnic Relations, 2000), 16.

27. Angéla Koczé, *Political Empowerment or Political Incarceration of Romani? The Hungarian Version of the Politics of Dispossession*, in *The Hungarian Patient—Social Opposition to an Illiberal Democracy*, ed. Péter Krasztev and Jon Van Til (Budapest, New York: CEU Press, 2015).

28. *A jóléti rendszerváltás csődje—Gyurcsány-kormány első* éve [*The Failure of Welfare Regime Change—Gyurcsány's Government's First Year*] (Budapest: Századvég, 2005). This is the third volume of a yearbook on the activity of the executive, sponsored by FiDeSz.

29. Over the 2000–2010 decade, Csurka's party was gradually replaced by another one called Jobbik, which actually is more outspoken in its extreme rightist approaches and the related racist features, including a more explicit reference to Hungary's past fascist-type ideas and rulers; after winning three seats at the 2009 European elections, Jobbik gained forty-seven parliamentary seats at the April 2010 vote and became the third-largest party of the country, just below the socialist MSzP. Such a position was maintained in 2014, placing Jobbik again long after FiDeSz and just below the fragmented galaxy of center-left parties and electoral alliances.

30. "Hungary's Reaction to Ukraine Crisis Illustrates Tensions within Fidesz's Foreign Policy Discourse," Politics.hu, March 21, 2014, http://www.politics.hu/20140321/hungarys-reaction-to-ukraine-crisis-illustrates-tensions-within-fideszs-foreign-policy-discourse.

31. In his previously mentioned Romania speech of July 2014, held a few days after the shooting of Malaysia's MH17 airplane, Orbán called it "an act of terrorism," without further comments. See note 9 above.

32. Jan-Werner Müller, "Hungary: The War on Education," *The New York Review of Books*, May 20, 2017.

33. https://www.georgesoros.com/essays/remarks-delivered-at-the-brussels-economic-forum/.

34. http://www.miniszterelnok.hu/soross-network-operates-like-the-mafia/.

35. http://abcnews.go.com/International/wireStory/hungary-jewish-group-israels-soros-ads-48679427. Also, http://www.jpost.com/Israel-News/Politics-And-Diplomacy/Why-do-the-Hungarians-and-Netanyahu-want-each-other-499996.

Map 12.0. The Baltic States

CHAPTER 12

The Baltic Countries

FACING NEW CHALLENGES IN POLITICS, SOCIETY, AND SECURITY

Daina S. Eglitis

The Baltic countries of Latvia, Lithuania, and Estonia together have a population of only 7 million, but they are playing an outsized role in contemporary global politics. Since their exit from the USSR in 1991, the three countries have engaged in a determined effort to shed their Soviet past and establish a firmly "European" identity, as well as prosperity, democracy, and security. Today, they are members of the European Union (EU), the North Atlantic Treaty Organization (NATO), and the Eurozone. At the same time, their proximity to the Russian Federation and the presence of large Russian-speaking populations continue to underpin regional political and military tensions. Western concern over Russia's aggressive stance toward the Baltics has recently led to the stationing of NATO troops in the three countries in one of the biggest European deployments since the end of the Cold War. The Baltics are small but significant players in the contentious post-Soviet space where Western institutions vie with Russian interests for power and influence.

Located on the Baltic Sea to the west of the Russian Federation and east of Scandinavia, the Baltic countries survived a tumultuous twentieth century, at the dawn of which Latvia and Estonia were provinces of the Russian Empire, and Lithuania was divided between Germany and Russia. The Baltic countries also experienced the turmoil of revolution in Russia, beginning in 1905 and continuing through the end of the empire and the beginning of Bolshevik rule. Following World War I, the Baltic countries were among the progeny of an era that brought into being a host of small states, and all three became independent. Independence was, however, short-lived, and the nonaggression pact between Adolf Hitler's Germany and Joseph Stalin's Soviet Union sealed their political fate as victims of more powerful neighbors. By the end of World War II, during which the Baltic countries lost a substantial proportion of their populations to war, deportation, genocide, and the flight of refugees, all three were occupied republics of the USSR.

Nearly half a century later, the ascent of Mikhail Gorbachev created unprecedented opportunities for open discussion and dissent. The Baltics were among the first republics to take advantage of new freedoms and to demand change. The collapse of the Eastern bloc and, subsequently, the USSR, opened the door to the reestablishment of independence in Latvia, Lithuania, and Estonia. The twenty-first century has witnessed the birth of new democratic states in the post-Soviet space, but global and regional politics have brought difficult choices and dramatic challenges to the Baltics, who again find themselves caught between the powers to the east and west.

Early-Twentieth-Century History

The Baltic countries had just two decades of experience with independence when they regained autonomous statehood in 1991. In all three cases, independence was declared for the first time in 1918, though formal recognition by the international community came later. The Soviet Union recognized the independence of the former provinces in separate peace treaties concluded between February and August 1920. Between 1921 and 1922, the international community extended its acceptance of the new states and welcomed them into the League of Nations.

This first period of independence was a time of dramatic transformations. Emerging from World War I (1914–1918), the Baltics had to overcome the burdens of decimated populations and devastated economies. For example, Latvia's population plummeted from 2.5 million in the prewar period to just 1.58 million in 1920. Estonia and Lithuania also lost substantial proportions of their populations to fighting and refugee flight. Agriculture, a key economic sector, was deeply damaged by the war, and farmlands lay virtually fallow. The nascent industrial sector, which had taken root in the Latvian and Estonian territories, was in ruins, as most heavy equipment had been moved to the Russian interior during the war. The economic foundations for the new states were tenuous.

The Baltics undertook massive land reforms focused on the transfer of land from private estates concentrated largely in the hands of Baltic Germans to the landless peasantry, who had tilled the soil for generations but never owned the land. One goal of reform was to create a rural economy based on small family farms. There was also an interest in transferring more rural land to indigenous populations: in Latvia, most private land was in the hands of non-Latvians. Fear in the government of Bolshevik sympathies among the rural peasantry compounded the perceived urgency of reform. Land reform was relatively successful in meeting its goals. In Latvia, by 1925 over 70 percent of rural dwellers, many of them Latvians, were landowners. Though the states regulated some sectors of their economies, the trajectories in all three pointed toward the creation of capitalist economies rooted in private ownership, agriculture, and entrepreneurship.

Political pioneers in the Baltics laid the foundations for democratic states, putting in place the constitutional and institutional building blocks of parliamentary democracies with universal suffrage (they were among the first European states to guarantee voting rights for women), equality before the law, and guarantees for minority rights. The parliamentary systems were characterized by weak executive powers (Estonia, in fact, had no head of state separate from the legislative branch) and, following the constitutional model of Weimar Germany, proportional representation in the legislature based on party lists. One intention of the parliamentary system was to guard against authoritarianism. Paradoxically, the fragmented legislatures that emerged from this system contributed to the later rise of authoritarian governments.

The Baltic governments suffered instability, in part because parliaments were populated by a multitude of small parties characterized by a spectrum of narrow interests. Governments were short-lived, and political alliances were ever shifting. By 1926, Lithuania was under an authoritarian presidential regime, led by Antanas Smetona. In Estonia and Latvia, democratic parliamentary systems lasted longer but were also plagued by political problems rendered more acute by a worldwide economic depression. In Estonia, between 1919 and 1933, the average duration of governments was eight months, and in early 1934, Konstantin Päts rose to rule by presidential decree. Later that year, Latvia's parliament was also dismissed and its political parties dissolved by President Kārlis Ulmanis.[1]

While the regimes of Smetona, Päts, and Ulmanis severely limited political opposition, they succeeded in establishing stability that benefited the economy, including private business and agriculture, which had responded poorly to political unpredictability. Cultural life and education for titular populations flourished. However, the nationalist sentiment embraced by the regimes adversely affected opportunities for minority populations to fully realize their aspirations. In Latvia, the slogan "Latvia for Latvians" was manifested in policies that marginalized the interests of minority populations, including Jews, Russians, and Germans, in areas like the economy, education, and culture.

Although the Baltics sought to remain neutral in the face of growing tensions in Europe, the world around them was erupting in violence. Germany had embarked on the decimation of its Jewish population, and the Third Reich cast a menacing shadow over its regional neighbors. Stalin's regime in the Soviet Union had already engineered a devastating famine in the republic of Ukraine and conducted murderous purges of enemies real and perceived throughout the USSR. The partnering of these powers against the Baltics sealed their fate: the Molotov-Ribbentrop Pact, signed by Germany and the Soviet Union in August 1939, contained a "secret protocol" (the existence of which the Soviets denied until the glasnost era) that divided the Baltic countries (as well as Poland, Romania, and Finland) into spheres of influence: Latvia and Estonia were ceded to the USSR, Lithuania to Germany (though later Lithuania would be claimed by the Soviets). Notably, even today, Russia, the USSR's legatee, denies that an occupation took place, arguing that the Baltics voluntarily joined the USSR in 1940.

War and Occupation in the Baltic Countries

Between September and October 1939, Estonia, Latvia, and Lithuania were forced to accept the terms of mutual-assistance treaties with the USSR. The treaties permitted the stationing of Soviet troops on the Baltic countries' territories, and tanks rolled across their borders with no resistance: this capitulation in the face of the Soviet threat remains an object of historical debate, as many have wondered if resistance could have prevented a half-century-long occupation.

In July 1940, new governments, "elected" from a slate of regime-approved candidates in compulsory voting, requested admission to the USSR. This electoral farce took place against a bloody backdrop: the violence that had been limited during the initial occupation exploded into mass arrests in the summer of 1940 and reached its pinnacle on the night of June 14, 1941, with the deportation to Siberia of, it is estimated, more than twelve thousand Estonians, fifteen thousand Latvians, and thirty-four thousand Lithuanians, as well as members of minority populations like Jews and Poles.[2]

In late June 1941, the German army attacked the USSR by land and air, occupying the Baltic territories in a matter of weeks. As the Soviet Army retreated, tens of thousands evacuated, including Communist Party functionaries and managers of defense-related industrial enterprises, along with many of their workers. Among those fleeing the Nazi onslaught were also Baltic Jews. An estimated fifteen thousand Latvian Jews fled ahead of occupation, but another seventy thousand, whether by chance or choice, remained behind. By the end of 1941, much of Latvia's Jewish population had been murdered by the Germans and their Latvian collaborators, including over twenty-five thousand in the Rumbula Massacre that followed the clearing of the Riga Ghetto in late November and early December of 1941.[3] The Holocaust in all three Baltic territories was dramatic and brutal: by the time the Soviet Army returned to reoccupy the Baltics in 1944, an estimated 90 percent of Lithuania's Jewish population, which numbered about 250,000 in 1941, had been killed, as had nearly all of Estonia's small population of 4,500 Jews.[4] Few survivors of the Baltics' historical population of Jews remain today.

The postwar years of Soviet occupation (1944–1990) cannot be uniformly characterized. The Stalin era represented a stranglehold of social control and fear. The collectivization of agriculture gained momentum in the late 1940s and was nearly complete by 1952. Collectivization in the Baltics was slow, in part because there was rural resistance by farmers who sought to retain their land and autonomy. This resistance was broken by a new round of deportations in 1949, in which about one hundred thousand rural dwellers, including women and children, were deported from the Baltic republics.[5]

Violent repression and public fear declined with Stalin's death in 1953. Although the persecution of individual dissidents continued under his successor, Nikita Khrushchev, most of the population, if willing to abide by Soviet norms and laws, could live in relative normalcy. Cultural and social life was still controlled, though less stringently restricted than before.

In terms of economic life, the Baltics were considered among the "prosperous" Soviet republics and known for a generally higher standard of living. This made them a magnet for migration from other republics, further shifting the demographics and driving the titular population, particularly in Latvia and Estonia, closer to minority status.[6] One consequence of this development was linguistic: whereas most Balts spoke fluent Russian, few Russians learned the republics' languages. The 1970 census in the Latvian Soviet Socialist Republic, for instance, showed that over half of Latvians (and a higher proportion in younger generations) spoke Russian, but fewer than a fifth of ethnic Russians could speak Latvian.[7]

In 1964, Leonid Brezhnev came to power. His regime continued to exercise stringent social control, and in the 1970s he initiated a concentrated campaign against nationalism: as in Khrushchev's time, the goal was to create *Homo sovieticus*, the Soviet man, exorcised of his bourgeois inclinations toward ethnic allegiances. Episodes of dissent were few and far between, though they arose periodically in the Baltics. The public self-immolation in 1972 of Romas Kalanta, a Lithuanian student, sparked demonstrations in Kaunas.

Most opposition, however, remained small and contained, though apparently there was enough concern about simmering discontent that Khrushchev's short-lived successor, Yuri Andropov, a former KGB chief, cracked down on dissent, real and perceived.

Discontent in the Baltics was centered in the indigenous populations, whose older members retained the living memory of independence. These populations also feared demographic marginalization. All three countries, but particularly Latvia and Estonia, had below-replacement fertility rates and aging populations. Latvia and Estonia also had large Russian-speaking populations, whose numbers had risen again in a wave of immigration in the 1970s. Soviet population data showed Latvians approaching the 50 percent mark in their republic, a proportional downward slide that showed few signs of abating. The fear of ethnic extinction would become an important issue in the mobilization of civil society in the Gorbachev era.

In the Baltic countries, mobilization of independent civil society and, ultimately, the path to independence proceeded along similar lines. Prior to 1987, independent mass demonstrations were forbidden in the USSR, and a culture of fear wrought by decades of repression made such collective action unlikely. Whereas individual and small group dissident activities dotted the Soviet historical map, most citizens were docile, unwilling or unable to openly oppose the regime. Gorbachev's ascent to power in the Soviet Union and his adoption of a policy of glasnost, with the accompanying possibilities for freer expression, opened the door to Baltic social movements that evolved from small demonstrations of discontent to massive manifestations of open opposition to the state and regime, the economic, environmental, and ethnic policies of the USSR, and the refusal of the Soviet government to recognize the illegal occupation of the three countries in 1940.

Early opposition focused on the preservation of folk culture and the environment, issues that were less politically sensitive than secession from the USSR or Soviet distortions of history. At the same time, the elevation of issues of nature and culture was profoundly symbolic. In Latvia, early civic activism centered on a hydroelectric station (HES) proposed for the Daugava, a river central in Latvian history, folktales, and poems: it has been called Latvia's "river of destiny." Opponents of the HES argued that its construction would damage the river and flood surrounding arable lands. The response to an article on the topic published in a progressive weekly newspaper, *Literature and Art*, in 1986 was tremendous: thousands of Latvians wrote to the newspaper to voice their criticism of the project. In early 1987, construction of the HES was halted by the USSR Council of Ministers. The voices of civil society, long suppressed, had achieved a significant victory, setting the stage for the coming years of opposition.[8]

In neighboring Lithuania, as in the other Baltic countries, indigenous elites played an important role in the early construction of independent civil society. In Lithuania, an important part of the active elite included scientists. Widespread discussion and, eventually, opposition focused on the Ignalina Atomic Energy Station (AES), built in the 1970s just eighty miles from Vilnius, the capital city of the republic. Some scientists and other activists questioned the environmental and safety standards of the AES. The disaster at Chernobyl in Ukraine in 1986 rendered these questions even more critical, though widespread public activism around Ignalina did not begin until 1988. Leaders of the nascent opposition appealed to the public with science and symbols: the Lithuanian nation was rooted in the earth, and Ignalina posed a threat to both nature and nation. While opponents could not speak overtly against the Soviet government in 1988, environmental issues provided a platform for civil society to gain a foothold.[9]

Civil Society and the Transition from Communism

By 1989, the opposition was openly asking questions about historic distortions, demographic issues, and autonomy for the republics. There was quiet but persistent discussion of secession from the USSR. Symbolic restoration of independent nationhood was already under way, as the interwar flags flew over demonstrations and Balts began publicly celebrating pre-Soviet national holidays. Demonstrations grew to the tens and then hundreds of thousands. The largest demonstration, the Baltic Way, took place on August 23, 1989, the fiftieth anniversary of the Molotov-Ribbentrop Pact. On this day, nearly one million Balts joined hands across the three countries, forming a human chain stretching from Vilnius in the south, through Riga, to Tallinn in the north. At the same time, opposition was becoming institutionalized, and changes in some political structures of the USSR and the republics offered new opportunities for challenging the Soviet system from within.

Competitive elections began in the Baltic countries before those countries regained independence in 1991. In early 1990, the Soviet government permitted partially open elections, and opposition groups in the Baltics fielded candidates for the Supreme Soviets of their respective republics. In Lithuania, which had the distinction of hosting the first multiparty elections in the history of the USSR, pro-independence candidates carried the election. In Latvia and Estonia, which held their elections later, the results were mixed but tilted toward pro-independence candidates. Ethnic Latvians and Estonians overwhelmingly favored these candidates, but a notable proportion of Russian-speaking residents also selected pro-independence candidates.[10]

The legislative activities in the three republics were important, but the speed at which changes were taking place meant that legislative change, especially within existing Soviet-era political structures, would trail the initiatives of civil society. The opposition, already demanding independence, was further radicalized by events in Lithuania and Latvia in January 1991. In that month, conservative Soviet forces sought to take over the Vilnius television tower, which was defended by thousands of Lithuanians. In the violence that followed, Soviet forces killed fifteen protesters and injured hundreds: the graphic images of Lithuanians crushed beneath the treads of a Soviet tank received global coverage and signaled a new turn in the political climate, as Gorbachev sought to distance himself from both the Vilnius killings and the deaths of five civilians that occurred when Soviet special forces attacked buildings belonging to the Ministry of the Interior in Latvia.

In a widespread rejection of the evolutionary change offered by Gorbachev or the regressive course embraced by conservative elements, the Baltic countries voted in February and March 1991 in referenda on independence. In February, fully 90 percent of participants in Lithuania (who were required to be eighteen years of age or older and permanent residents, a category that essentially excluded only Soviet military forces stationed in the republic) voted for independence. In March, 78 and 74 percent of inhabitants of Estonia and Latvia, respectively, voted in the affirmative.

The hard-line coup attempt that took place in Moscow in August 1991 did not substantially change the Baltic course, which pointed toward independence. The failed coup effectively destroyed the remaining legitimacy of the Soviet Communist Party, and the Soviet Union itself was rendered little more than a shell of a country. These developments brought independence more rapidly than most people had expected: on September 6, 1991, the USSR recognized the Baltic countries as independent entities, and less than two weeks later they were admitted to the United Nations.

Institutional Structures and Electoral Systems in the Baltics

Latvia, Lithuania, and Estonia built their early postcommunist political institutions based on the assumption that independence was being "restored" rather than "established" in 1991. Consequently, constitutions, electoral systems, judicial structures, and other key political institutions were initially renewed rather than constructed from scratch. Although the tension between those who wished to follow a more conservative and nationalistic path of restoration (rhetorically constructed in Latvia as the "renewal of the First Republic of Latvia") and those who wished to construct a historically grounded but modern and "European" state (articulated as the creation of the "Second Republic of Latvia") would grow as time passed, all three states were initially inclined to ground themselves in the foundation of the independent past.[11]

Restoration of independence included the renewal of prewar constitutions, which underscored the legal continuity of institutions. In Estonia, the new constitution of 1992 was based on the constitution of 1938. In Latvia, the 1922 constitution was restored in 1993. In Lithuania, the 1938 constitution was temporarily accepted, but the leadership of the country opted ultimately to write a new constitution, as the prewar document, despite its symbolic importance, was declared authoritarian and not well suited to the country.[12]

There is also some continuity with the electoral systems of the past in the Baltics. In the postcommunist period, Latvia's one-hundred-member Saeima (parliament) has been elected through a system of proportional representation with a 5 percent threshold. In the interwar period, this electoral system brought a multitude of small parties into the Saeima. Political fragmentation in the legislature was a justification for President Ulmanis's 1933 assumption of authoritarian leadership in a coup. Indeed, the 1995 election in Latvia produced a parliament with nine parties, none of which earned more than 16 percent of the vote. In both 2011 and 2014, thirteen parties competed, though just five and six, respectively, earned seats in the legislature. In both elections, the single party oriented toward Latvia's Russian-speaking population earned the highest number of seats, but governing coalitions were formed by Latvian-dominated parties that had earned fewer seats.

In Lithuania, the Seimas (parliament) is elected through a mix of proportional representation and direct constituency voting. The voting is split across two nonconsecutive days: the first 70 of 141 seats are elected through open-list proportional representation; the remaining 71 are filled through voting in single-member districts. Estonia's Riigikogu is also a unicameral body; its 101 seats are filled using a complex proportional representation system (the d'Hondt method).

Lithuanian and Estonian legislatures have also been characterized by the presence of a multitude of parties. Lithuania's most recent elections (2012 and 2016) produced bodies with, respectively, eight and ten parties (and some independent legislators). Estonia's first elections of the new millennium (2003 and 2007) saw the seating of six parties each; in 2011, just four parties were seated, but in 2015, the figure rose again to six.

Another historical continuity between the interwar and new states is the relatively short life span of governments. In the interwar parliamentary period, short-lived governments characterized the three countries. The new states have inherited this dubious legacy: in Latvia, between 1990 (when the Latvian legislature declared its independence from Soviet control) and 2016, there were fourteen different prime ministers (several of whom served more than once). Beginning with the first postcommunist parliamentary elections in 1993, there have been nineteen coalition governments, several of them weak minority coalitions: the average government coalition has lasted less than one year in power. The large number of parties and coalitions competing for legislative seats and the low threshold required for winning places create optimal conditions for shifting allegiances and alliances, though recent governments have been among the most enduring in the postcommunist period.

Political Leadership

All three Baltic countries have a titular head of state with limited powers. The president is elected by the parliament by secret ballot for a term of five years in Estonia and four in Latvia. In Lithuania, the president is elected by popular vote. The prime minister has greater power over policy, though the presidency has offered leaders a powerful bully pulpit for the pursuit of political goals.

Notably, Estonia had no presidency during most of the first independence period: from 1918 to 1938, the parliament governed alone. Revisions to the 1938 constitution, however, brought the office into being. While largely a ceremonial position, postcommunist occupants of the presidency have had significant public profiles, drawing largely positive global attention to the small country. In 2016, Estonia's parliament elected the country's first woman president, Kersti Kaljulaid.

The Latvian president has the power to dissolve the legislature and to convene and preside over extraordinary sessions of the cabinet, though a good deal of the president's power rests on his or her ability to set a public agenda with a visible presence in the media and society, as Latvia's second postcommunist president, Vaira Vīķe-Freiberga, did during her tenure (1999–2007). Her strong support of Latvia's entrance into the EU and the NATO helped solidify societal support for membership.

Vīķe-Freiberga's successor, President Valdis Zatlers, used his presidential powers to dissolve the parliament. In May 2011, just days before the Saeima was scheduled to vote for a president, Zatlers responded with this dramatic action to the legislative body's failure to permit the search of a legislator's home on suspicion of corruption. Although Zatlers was not subsequently reelected to a second term by the Saeima, in a required referendum on the action a large majority of voters supported his dissolution of the body. Zatlers was succeeded by Andris Bērziņš, who served one term as president. Former minister of defense Raimonds Vējonis was elected by the parliament in 2015.

Photo 12.1.   Kersti Kaljulaid, Estonian president, May 6, 2017.

As noted above, Lithuania differs from its neighbors in that it chooses a president through a popular vote. Lithuania's current president (and first woman president) is Dalia Grybauskaite, who was elected in 2009 with over 69 percent of the vote. She was reelected with 58 percent of the vote in 2014 in a second round of voting after earning under

50 percent in the first round. Recently, Grybauskaite has been a strong voice in the region against Russian aggression, saying in a 2014 interview that Russian president Vladimir Putin's tactics were similar to those employed by Stalin and Hitler: "(Putin) uses nationality as a pretext to conquer territory with military means. That's exactly what Stalin and Hitler did."[13] As the perception of Russian threat has grown in the Baltics, the position of the presidents as public faces and diplomatic representatives of their respective countries has, arguably, become more critical for maintaining alliances and security.

Postcommunist Political Culture, Parties, and Elections

Political parties in the Baltic countries are still at an early stage of development. While parties put forth candidates for election, candidates also run on lists associated with political organizations that are not formally political parties. Even most of the parties themselves are not political parties as that institution is understood in the West: they are not mass organizations with broad memberships, and few residents are official members of any party. Some "parties" are financed by private businesses. In Latvia, due to the lack of party-subsidy legislation, which offers state subsidies to parties winning a minimum percentage of votes, some parties have been the financial "projects" of local oligarchs rather than representative political organizations. Among other problems, the low and shifting support of individual parties translates into an unstable political party system. As political scientists Daunis Auers and Andres Kasekamp note, "A remarkable feature of the Latvian political party system is that, until 2006, all national elections were won

Photo 12.2.   Lithuanian strikes. (European Trade Committee for Education)

by a party which had not existed at the time of the previous national elections. Though the Estonian political party system can be characterized as more consolidated, it was only in 2007 that an Estonian prime minster and his party were re-elected."[14] In Estonia, the March 2011 national election was the first in which no new parties participated. In the 2015, however, three new parties joined the list of candidates; one succeeded in earning seats in the legislature.

The fortunes of political parties have also shifted dramatically, sometimes owing to corruption or loss of popularity of leading politicians, and sometimes due to changing societal priorities. Lithuania's 2016 election, for instance, lifted a small, centrist party, the Lithuanian Peasant and Greens Union, from a single seat in parliament to a stunning 54-seat victory in the 141 member Seimas. The party's preeminent issue was emigration: specifically, how to stanch the flow of Lithuanians leaving the country. Since Lithuania joined the EU in 2004, it has lost an estimated five hundred thousand citizens. In 1990, just before the end of communism, Lithuania's population stood at about 3.7 million; today it is around 2.9 million. Concern about population loss is shared by many Lithuanians, who point to labor shortages in some sectors and a dropping university population as precursors to a demographic crisis.

While parties are likely to evolve in the direction of a West European model, most continue to be ephemeral entities, reflecting short-term political and financial interests and charismatic personalities as much as clear political ideologies. Lack of confidence in or identification with parties may be linked to declines in electoral participation. Voter participation in elections has declined markedly since the early years of independence. More than 91 percent of eligible voters cast ballots in Latvia's first postcommunist elections in 1993. In the next elections in 1995, just over 72 percent of citizens opted to participate; in subsequent elections (1998 and 2002), the proportion of participants held steady at about 71 percent, then dropped below 63 percent in 2006. It has since continued to fall, remaining steady at 59 percent in the 2011 and 2014 elections. Lithuanian participation has been still lower: in 2016, just over 50 percent of voters participated in the first phase of national elections (which filled 70 of 141 seats in the legislature), and 38 percent took part in the second phase (which filled the remaining 71 seats).

Like its Baltic neighbors, Estonia experienced low rates of voting after the initial activism of the early 1990s: while nearly 70 percent voted in parliamentary elections in 1995, only about 58 percent of eligible voters participated in 1999 and 2003. In 2007, however, Estonia instituted an innovative internet-based voting option and remains the only country in the world with full online e-voting available. In the 2011 elections, about 15 percent of Estonian citizens voted in advance via the internet; in 2015, the figure rose to 33 percent. This may account for a rise in participation: about 64 percent of eligible voters cast ballots, a small increase from 62 percent in 2011. Estonia is also one of the few countries in the world that permits legal residents (including noncitizens) to vote in local elections.

While many residents have chosen not to vote, others have not been eligible to participate. In Estonia and Latvia, automatic citizenship was granted first to citizens of the interwar republics and their descendants. These laws had the effect of creating a substantial population of stateless persons (mostly ethnic Russians) who were citizens of neither the renewed countries nor the defunct USSR. While both Latvia and Estonia offered legal residency, neither was eager to introduce a large number of Soviet-era migrants into the pool of potential voters. In Lithuania, citizenship was granted more broadly, as that country had a far lower proportion of non-Lithuanians living in the territory than did Latvia or Estonia. The body of citizenry in Estonia and Latvia has grown as well, however. Whereas in 1992, just 68 percent of residents in Estonia held citizenship, by 2012, the figure was 84 percent; most of this change was driven by high levels of naturalization in the 1990s, though some was also the result of noncitizen emigration. Today, the roughly 330,000 ethnic Russians in Estonia are nearly evenly divided between those that hold Estonian citizenship, those that hold Russian Federation citizenship, and those that hold the "gray passport" offered to resident aliens in the country. In Latvia, in 2000, just over three-quarters of residents were citizens. By 2016, noncitizens constituted about 12 percent of the population; most others are citizens and a tiny proportion is made up of foreign nationals. Some legal residents eligible for citizenship have opted not to pursue it, while others remain ineligible due to, for example, their lack of language proficiency or failure to meet residency requirements.

Economic Transition

The Baltic countries have undergone substantial economic changes in the transformation from command to free market economies. From a comparative perspective, the Baltics fared better in the first decade and a half than other former Soviet republics, though perhaps not as well as Central and East European states like Hungary and the Czech Republic. Growth rates in the Baltics largely met or exceeded expectations, with the

Photo 12.3.   Lithuanian president Dalia Grybauskaitė, with Obama on February 15, 2016. (*The Baltic Times*)

exception of a crisis in 1998, when the crash of the Russian ruble damaged neighboring economies. One hallmark of the Baltics' transformation was the speed with which they privatized formerly state-owned industries. In Latvia and Estonia, privatization at the ten-year mark of independence was almost complete, with most formerly state-owned small and medium-size enterprises fully privatized.

Another key dimension of the construction of an economic and social order rooted in private property was the restitution to prewar owners of the urban and rural properties taken from them when Soviet occupiers nationalized property and drove many members of the "ownership class" out of their countries. This move was symbolically significant because it "righted" a perceived Soviet wrong: in the early postcommunist period, nearly any action seen as undoing what the communists had done was likely to find a sympathetic constituency. Restitution was also intended to restore the grid of private property that existed in the interwar period and reestablish an ownership society, the basis of restored capitalism.

The advent of free markets and the spread of ownership, investment, and entrepreneurship fueled powerful growth in the Baltics.[15] In the early years of the new millennium, the economies of all three states were characterized by dynamic development and a rapid rise in gross domestic product (GDP), which translated into rising wages, consumption, and living standards for the new middle class. Perhaps ominously, these welcome developments were accompanied by 2007 by a steep rise in housing prices, widespread and profligate use of credit, and high inflation.

Baltic economic expansion came to an abrupt and dramatic halt in late 2008, as key economic indicators turned downward and the Baltics, like much of the globe, slid into recession. Lithuania had experienced strong GDP growth in the new millennium: this economic indicator rose from 3.3 percent in 2000 to a stunning 9.8 percent in 2007. It turned down precipitously in 2008, falling to 2.8 percent before crashing in 2009 and dropping to –18.1 percent. Latvia followed a similar trajectory, reaching a real GDP growth rate of 12.2 percent in 2006 before tumbling to –18 percent in 2009. Estonia's fall from the heights was smaller but still deep: its real GDP growth fell to –13.7 percent in 2009.[16]

Arguably, the severity of human distress in the crisis period was exacerbated by the significant stratification already present when the Baltic economies were flourishing. Even in this period of prosperity, the rising tide failed to lift all boats: macroeconomic policies did little to alleviate economic distress at the bottom of the ladder. In Latvia, for instance, the measured "poverty risk" grew from 16 percent in 1996 to 23 percent in 2006, though it declined to 21 percent in 2007. Notably, this measure is relative rather than absolute: according to Eurostat, which compiles social and economic indicators on European states, the indicator "is defined as the share of persons with an equivalized disposable income below the risk-of-poverty threshold, which is set at 60 per cent of the national median equivalized disposable income (after social transfers)." As such, it reflects the position of the lowest earners relative to the median. As the median rose in the years of prosperity, absolute poverty may not have risen, but the gap between the worst off and the middle and upper classes grew.[17]

The proportion of Baltic populations "at risk of poverty" has remained high in the decade following the economic crisis. In Latvia, for instance, the proportion of inhabitants at risk in 2015 was 27.3 percent before social transfers (like child allowances, unemployment, or pensions) and 22.5 percent after social transfers. Eurostat employs a second measure of deprivation as well, the "at risk of poverty and social exclusion" indicator, which encompasses income poverty, severe material deprivation, and presence in a household with low work intensity. By this measure, in 2015, over 30 percent of Latvia's population, 24 percent of Estonia's population, and 29 percent of Lithuania's population were at risk.[18]

Perhaps paradoxically, while Baltic indicators of deprivation have been among the most acute in the EU, these countries have also experienced high rates of postcrisis growth. In Latvia, the fall in GDP approached 20 percent in 2009, but the rebound brought Latvia the fastest-growing economy in Europe by 2013. Estonia too roared back with the Estonian economy experiencing robust growth of 2.9 percent, powered in part by an entrepreneurial and creative high-technology sector. Lithuania came back more slowly but also registered growth of nearly 3 percent in 2012. Notably, economic recovery in the Baltics was largely been built on austerity measures pushed through by national governments and advocated by the EU and International Monetary Fund. These measures temporarily pushed up unemployment and shrank wages in the large public sector. More recently, unemployment has fallen and wages are on the rise, growing closer to the EU average. At the same time, however, prices are also on the rise, underscoring the challenge for the Baltics of ensuring access to necessities for those segments of the population who have been left behind by prosperity.

All three Baltic countries are members of the Eurozone: Estonia became a member in 2011, Latvia in 2014, and Lithuania in 2015. The Maastricht Treaty, which set the rules of the Eurozone, has a host of requirements for aspirants, including the demand that countries achieve a budget deficit equivalent to about 3 percent of GDP and maintain low inflation. While the governments of all three countries were strongly oriented toward Eurozone membership, public attitudes toward the change in currency ranged from enthusiasm to ambivalence to fear. A 2016 Eurobarometer survey found dramatic differences by country in public attitudes toward the Euro. Asked whether the Euro was good for their own country, 64 percent of Estonia's respondents said yes and just 14 percent said no. By contrast, 42 percent of Lithuania's residents agreed that the Euro was good for their country, while 45 percent asserted that it was not. Latvia's respondents fell in between: 56 percent suggested the common currency was good for the country and 29 percent said it was not.[19]

While official data are helpful in understanding the economies of the Baltics, it is notable that all three have substantial "shadow economies." The most significant part of the "shadow economy," by one estimate, is constituted by unreported business income and unreported wages paid to employees (sometimes called "envelope" wages). In 2016, the "shadow economy" comprised about 20 percent of GDP in Latvia, 16.5 percent in Lithuania, and 15 percent in Estonia, representing a potentially significant loss of tax revenue to these states.[20]

Social Transition

Communism embraced an ideology of equality. Capitalism, by contrast, embraces an ideology of competition. In the period of Soviet communism, all citizens were theoretically equal: women and men, Russians and non-Russians, professionals and laborers. In reality, the situation was more complex.

Although well represented in the workforce, women tended to occupy positions with less prestige and authority. They also carried the double burden of paid work and primary, if not sole, responsibility for domestic work. Some observers suggested that women bore a "triple burden," the third being that they were usually the ones to wait in long lines for groceries or other goods.

In addition, despite ostensible ethnic equality, some Soviet citizens, to paraphrase George Orwell's *Animal Farm*, were "more equal than others." Russian was the lingua franca of the USSR, and all nationalities were expected to learn the language. Russians were often given priority in acquiring housing while others waited many years for an apartment.

In the capitalist and democratic context of postcommunism, there have been both changes and continuities in the forms of inequality experienced in the Baltics. In terms of gender, women are legally equal to men and have comparable opportunities to gain educational training. In fact, women are more likely than men to be highly educated, and they make up the majority of students in most institutions of higher education. At the same time, women still suffer a gender wage gap and are less likely to occupy positions of power and authority, particularly in business and politics (although Latvia was home to Central and Eastern Europe's first female president, Vaira Vīķe-Freiberga, and in 2017, both Estonia and Lithuania had female presidents).[21]

Although women are well represented in the paid labor force, the early postcommunist period in particular saw a push from some conservative political organizations for women to return to home and hearth in order to ensure the creation of new Latvians, Estonians, and Lithuanians. In the demographic and social context of the Baltics, issues of family formation are widely deemed to be of public importance: none of the countries has replacement rate fertility (defined as a total fertility rate, or TFR, of 2.1): in 2016, the TFR in all three was 1.6. All have lost population through declining birth rates, as well as emigration.[22] Perhaps predictably, the three countries have pro-natalist policies and programs of social support for parents.

The sands of ethnic equality have also shifted in the Baltics. Whereas in the Soviet period, Russians were the "most equal" of all legally equal nationalities, in the postcommunist Baltics, legal equality is extended to all, but the titular nationalities have asserted dominance through citizenship, language, and educational policies.

Although the Baltic countries have not experienced serious political violence and day-to-day relations between ethnic groups are peaceful, recent years have seen manifestations of tensions over these issues. A constitutional referendum to make Russian an official second language in Latvia was held in February 2012. The referendum was the result of a petition drive, organized largely by ethnic Russians, which successfully gathered enough signatures to prompt the vote. Notably, the referendum saw voter turnout much higher than that of recent parliamentary elections: fully 70 percent of eligible voters opted to participate. The effort to make Russian an official second language failed, with only 25 percent of voters supporting the constitutional change. While some observers feared a backlash after the failure, negative reactions were largely limited to the Russian-language press, which had supported the measure.

On the one hand, interethnic relations have been and will continue to be influenced by state policies and actions: laws about language, education, and equal access to opportunities will contribute to the integration or alienation of Russian speakers in the Baltics. On the other hand, social and economic factors not controlled by the state influence the issue of Russian speakers' acquiring titular languages and ethnic relations. In Latvia, the rate of ethnic intermarriage is high: many families are mixed, and children learn both languages and bridge two cultures. As well, the practical imperative of profit making in capitalism has induced young people and other would-be entrepreneurs to learn multiple languages in order to serve customers more effectively. In sum, while ethnic tensions are present in the Baltics, macro- and micro-level forces help maintain equilibrium and reduce potential for the ethnic conflict that has devastated areas like former Yugoslavia.

Civil Society

Public opinion polling suggests that trust in political institutions, particularly parliament and political parties, among the masses has been low in the past decade and a half. Little of this discontent, however, has been reflected in public activism: after the end of several years of civil society activism in the opposition period, some observers lamented the "death of civil society."

All, however, has not been quiet. In Latvia, anger at government corruption was manifested in 2007 in large public protest actions not seen since the late years of anti-Soviet protest. In November 2007, an estimated eight to ten thousand people gathered in central Riga to protest rampant graft, an action that contributed to the resignation that month of the sitting prime minister. Public anger was sharpened by the economic crisis in the region, and another large antigovernment demonstration in January 2009 ended with violence. While ten thousand protesters gathered in Riga's city center to speak against economic mismanagement and to demand early elections, riots involving several hundred demonstrators followed the peaceful action.

Most protest actions across the Baltics, however, have been small and nonviolent. Among groups engaging in regular demonstrations are farmers, who have struggled to compete with agricultural products flowing into the Baltic marketplace from other EU states. For instance, in September 2016, the Central Union of Estonian Farmers arranged ten thousand bottles of milk in a public square in Tallinn to draw attention to the plight of farmers and rural areas. This demonstration followed on a year earlier in which 101 tractors were parked in front of the Riigikogu, the Estonian legislature. University students have also been vocal in their demands for state support of higher education: government threats to reduce subsidies for tuition, for example, attracted about one thousand students to the Latvian Cabinet of Ministers building to protest in October 2016.

Most activity in Baltic civil society takes place in the sphere of nongovernmental organizations (NGOs), which are plentiful across the region and embrace issues ranging from environmental protection to worker rights to internet freedoms. NGOs focused on women's issues date back to the early 1990s, though only recently have some prominent NGOs expanded their issue range to include support for victims of domestic violence, an issue long subject to public silence.

Contemporary civil society in the Baltics also includes some new groups of actors, including sexual minorities, whose social marginality dates back to the Soviet era. In the summer of 2004, the first gay-pride march took place in Estonia, followed a year later by a similar event in Latvia. Lithuanian activists held the first gay-pride march in 2012. The marches have taken place annually, though they have generated some resistance from both police, who have suggested that they cannot guarantee the safety of the marchers, and conservatives, who have aggressively opposed them. While the Baltic countries largely mirror their Scandinavian neighbors in liberal attitudes toward practices such as nonmarital cohabitation and childbearing, these societies continue to be conservative in their attitudes toward sexual minorities.

Foreign Policy and Security

After a half-century as citizens of the Soviet Union, many in the Baltics embraced the slogan "Back to Europe." Having regained independent statehood in 1991, the Baltic countries sought seats in the United Nations, and all three became members in September of that year, an important symbolic step that signaled international acceptance of the states. The accession of the Baltic countries to the EU in May 2004 represents another

Photo 12.4.   Raimonds Vējonis, Latvian president. (Latvia.eu)

important symbolic and substantive step. In terms of symbolism, the EU's expansion signals the first time since the historical Hanseatic League that nearly the entire Baltic Sea region is part of a single economic and political bloc. In terms of modernity, it brings a geographic part of Europe back into economic and political Europe.[23]

In March 2004, another major foreign policy goal was realized: the Baltic countries became members of the NATO. NATO membership represents an important symbolic link to Europe and, critically for the Balts, provides through Article 5 a commitment of member states to mutual defense. Even before formally joining NATO, the Baltics deployed small contingents of soldiers and specialists to Western missions, joining, for instance, the "coalition of the willing" for service in Iraq in 2003. Baltic troops have also served with Operation Enduring Freedom in Afghanistan, in which 9 Estonians, 4 Latvians, and 1 Lithuanian have lost their lives and a total of 116 have been wounded in action.

Whereas the Baltics have cultivated close relations with many Western neighbors, relations with Russia have been tense. Despite cooperation in some areas of mutual interest, including trade relations, there are significant points of conflict that range from disputes over history to divergent claims about the treatment of ethnic Russians in the Baltics to tensions over NATO's presence on Russia's borders.

It is notable that dominant Baltic and Russian (previously Soviet) historical narratives about World War II differ markedly. In brief, whereas the former highlight Soviet occupation and oppression, the latter embrace the story of a heroic Red Army liberating Europe (including the Baltics) from the deadly grip of Nazism.[24] In early 2007, the Estonian government decided to relocate the Bronze Soldier, a monument to the "Soviet liberators" erected during the communist period, from central Tallinn to a more remote location. While Estonian nationalists supported the decision, seeing the soldier as an affront to the suffering of Estonians under the Soviet regime, the removal of the monument sparked two nights of rioting and looting, mostly by young Russians, in the capital. At least eleven hundred persons were detained in the worst collective violence of the independence period. Russia also took a public stand against the Estonian state's decision to remove the soldier, calling the act, among other things, "blasphemous." Estonians, in return, accused the Russian media of stoking unrest with allegations that the monument had been destroyed (it was moved but not damaged).

Shortly after the dispute over the Bronze Soldier, Estonia experienced a massive cyberattack, which effectively disabled the entire Internet structure of the country, paralyzing financial, government, media, and even personal transactions (mobile phone networks were temporarily frozen as well). As a state that has taken pride in establishing one of the world's first e-governments, where much of the business of the state is conducted electronically, the attack was deeply damaging. NATO responded by sending cyberterrorism experts to Estonia to study the attack and assist in recovery.

Estonia and a host of Western observers accused Russia of being behind the attacks based on both timing and technical evidence. Notably, in 2013, Lithuania also experienced a distributed denial-of-service (DDOS) cyberattack, which, though not as serious as that experienced by Estonia, slowed internet traffic considerably and rendered some Lithuania-based pages temporarily unavailable to the outside world. This DDOS followed an article published by the Lithuanian DELFI news portal that alleged Russian vote buying at the popular continental music festival Eurovision. As the next section shows, the internet has become an increasingly potent weapon wielded by the Russian state against its Baltic neighbors.

Clearly, Baltic security can no longer be understood only in terms of borders, troops, and Western alliances. At the same time, Russian military activities continue to cause concern in the Baltics, particularly in the wake of the Russian annexation of Crimea in 2014 and the ongoing conflict in Eastern Ukraine. Since that time, NATO has stepped up its presence in the Baltics considerably. In early 2017, the alliance had plans to add battalions of 800 to 1,200 troops to each of the three countries, as well as Poland. They join dozens of US Special Operations troops on the ground to support training efforts. NATO has also prepositioned artillery, armored vehicles, and tanks in Poland for rapid deployment to the Baltics if needed. While Baltic defense budgets are modest in comparison to most Western countries, they have grown robustly in the wake of rising threats: by one estimate, spending of the three countries on defensive military equipment grew from $210 million in 2014 to $390 million in 2016. Baltic armies are small (Estonia's numbers at about six thousand), but with increased defense spending, the support of NATO allies, and even nascent efforts to build insurgent capabilities in some military troops, Latvia, Lithuania, and Estonia hope to deter Russian aggression on their soil.

Significant Political Developments

In the aftermath of the US presidential campaign of 2016, followers of American politics became familiar with the term "fake news." At the time of this writing, US congressional representatives, investigators, and media outlets were confronting the dramatic possibility that Russia had interfered in the election with a campaign of disinformation that intentionally and purposefully introduced fake news into the US media environment. The US is not the first country to experience Russian disinformation: the Baltics have struggled with the problem for many years, though it has grown particularly acute recently.

Evidence gathered by Baltic governments and outside investigators strongly suggests that Russia is behind a spectrum of fake news stories that have circulated in the Baltics. Though promptly debunked, the speed of disinformation often outpaces the efforts of the governments and mainstream media outlets, and the fake news makes its way into social media and public consciousness. Among false stories that have circulated are the following: German NATO soldiers dispatched to support Lithuanian security raped a teenaged girl in that country; after the election, US president Donald Trump dressed down the Baltic presidents, telling them to "shut up"; the Lithuanian government contaminated a ship with a chemical weapon that killed five people; the Baltics are failed states with struggling economies; and Baltic populations are racist and will not tolerate nonwhite NATO soldiers. Perhaps the most common theme in the disinformation campaigns, however, is the longstanding narrative that the Baltic countries are illegitimate and hold no claim to national independence and existence. While the intended audiences of disinformation campaigns vary, the target population of the story that these countries and governments are not legitimate is the large Russian-speaking population of the region, most of whom reside in Latvia and Estonia. The parallels to propaganda efforts in the Crimea, which Russia annexed from Ukraine, have raised concerns about Russia's military intentions in the Baltics. Lithuania, which shares a border with the heavily militarized Russian territory of Kaliningrad, has expressed alarm about Russia's deployment of nuclear-capable missiles and the upgrading of military readiness in that area.

Estonia has taken an aggressive position on both Russian cyber hacking and disinformation. In 2010, the government introduced a defense strategy that includes "psychological defense," which encompasses the preservation of "common values associated with social cohesion and a sense of security," in part through focused efforts to counter Russian propaganda messages, particularly those aimed at the Russian-speaking population. To this end, Estonia also launched a domestic Russian-language news channel to offer an alternative source of information. The Latvian state has also stepped up efforts to counter disinformation, sponsoring public service announcements that point out fake news, as well as developing lessons on media literacy for schools.

What Makes the Case Interesting?

The evolution of postcommunist states and societies has followed some similar patterns across the region. The Baltics are not alone in their effort to chart a path toward democratic and capitalist development; nor are they unique in encountering both internal and external obstacles. The Baltic countries have frequently led the region in both dramatic economic growth and devastating economic crises, which have created some of the most stratified societies in the EU. At the same time, Baltic entrepreneurship, particularly Estonian innovation in the high-technology sector, has been robust and remains a promising foundation for the development of an economically secure middle class.

Unlike their neighbors in Central Europe, the Baltics carry legacies of the Soviet occupation, including large Russian-speaking populations, which have had a profound effect on citizenship policies, debates over education and language, electoral politics, and, most recently, foreign and security policy. The evolution of the relationship—and conflict—with Russia renders the Baltics a potentially important, though volatile, test of Russia's willingness to challenge Western Europe, the United States, and NATO.

Conclusion

The outlook for the Baltic countries of Latvia, Lithuania, and Estonia cannot be uniformly or easily characterized. On the one hand, the Baltics have achieved many of the important goals they set in the early postcommunist period. The basic mechanisms of democracy and free markets have been put in place, membership in those European organizations that ideally bring them closer to security (NATO) and prosperity (EU) has been achieved, and the countries are recognized as postcommunist success stories without the violence and upheavals that have cast a shadow over transition in some other states in the region.

On the other hand, the Baltic countries face both internal and external challenges. Even in the years of prosperity that preceded the recent economic crisis, all three countries experienced a dramatic rise in social stratification, as a segment of the population expanded its human capital, wealth, and power, while other groups were left powerless and poor. The global and local economic crisis brought acute threats to stability and prosperity in these countries, but recovery has also been robust and sustained in recent years. Other challenges to maintaining stable and prosperous states and societies lie in addressing substantial socioeconomic stratification, corruption, public health threats, demographic declines, and aging populations.

Externally, the Baltics continue to seek their footing in the global economy, which presents particular challenges to small states with educated and mobile populations. Relations with Russia, as that country attempts to assert its influence over smaller neighbors, are likely to remain tense. Baltic attention to maintaining stable ethnic relations internally may help to mitigate tension, though it is unlikely to solve the larger problems of the fragile relationship. Responsive, democratic governments and institutions, combined with the active voices of civil society, are the best hope to address societal problems and to foster the positive future progress of three small countries that have experienced dramatic changes and challenges.

Study Questions

1. The Baltic states are commonly presented as a single entity in published works on the region. Based on your reading of the chapter, is this justified? Do the commonalties outweigh the differences in history and contemporary experiences?
2. A half-century of occupation denied residents of the Baltic countries the opportunity to freely choose candidates in democratic elections. In the postcommunist period, high rates of political engagement in early elections have been followed by falling rates of voter participation. What factors cited in the chapter could account for the decline in voting? How has Estonia addressed the problem of low voter turnout?
3. Based on the discussion of security issues in the chapter and your knowledge of contemporary news events, how would you assess the level of military and other security threats to the Baltic countries from neighboring Russia? What defensive options are available to the Baltic countries if these threats are realized?
4. Compared to other countries about which you have read, what advantages do the Baltic countries appear to have in terms of successful political, economic, and social development? What disadvantages can you identify?

Suggested Readings

Auers, Daunis. *Comparative Politics and Government of the Baltic States: Estonia, Latvia, and Lithuania in the 21st Century*. London: Palgrave Macmillan, 2015.

Beresniova, Christina. *Holocaust Education in Lithuania: Community, Conflict, and the Making of Civil Society*. Lanham, MD: Lexington Books, 2017.

Buttar, Prit. *Between Giants: The Battle for the Baltics in World War II*. New York: Osprey, 2013.

Eglitis, Daina, and Laura Ardava. "Challenges of a Post-Communist Presidency: Vaira Vīke-Freiberga and the Leadership of Latvia." In *Women Presidents and Prime Ministers in Post-Transition Democracies*, edited by Veronica Montecinos. New York: Palgrave, 2017.

Lieven, Anatol. *The Baltic Revolution: Estonia, Latvia, Lithuania and the Path to Independence*. New Haven, CT: Yale University Press, 1993.

Lumans, Valdis. *Latvia in World War II*. New York: Fordham University Press, 2006.

Misiunas, Romuald, and Rein Taagepera. *The Baltic States: Years of Dependence, 1940–1990*. Berkeley: University of California Press, 1993.

Purs, Aldis. *Baltic Facades: Estonia, Latvia, and Lithuania since 1945*. London: Reaktion Books, 2012.

Weiss-Wendt, Anton. 2009. *Murder without Hatred: Estonians and the Holocaust*. Syracuse, NY: Syracuse University Press.

Websites

Baltic Times: http://www.baltictimes.com (a long-standing English-language newspaper that offers both up-to-the-minute news and analytical and investigative reporting)

Baltic Course: http://www.baltic-course.com (English-language media platform offering news on the Baltics, focusing primarily on business and economics)

Latvian Institute: http://www.latvia.eu (English-language website based in Latvia providing contemporary information on social, cultural, and political life in Latvia and links to further sources)

Riga Ghetto Museum: http://www.rgm.lv/?lang=en (English, Latvian, and Russian-language website featuring information on victims, rescuers, and significant places of the Holocaust in Latvia)

Notes

1. David Kirby, *The Baltic World, 1772–1993: Europe's Northern Periphery in an Age of Change* (New York: Longman, 1995), 317–28.

2. Walter C. Clemens Jr., *Baltic Independence and Russian Empire* (New York: St. Martin's Press, 1991), 53.

3. U.S. Holocaust Memorial Museum, *Holocaust Encyclopedia*, "Riga." Retrieved from https://www.ushmm.org/wlc/en/article.php?ModuleId=10005463.

4. U.S. Holocaust Memorial Museum, *Holocaust Encyclopedia*, "Lithuania." Retrieved from https://www.ushmm.org/wlc/en/article.php?ModuleId=10005444.

5. Kevin O'Connor, *The History of the Baltic States* (Westport, CT: Greenwood Press, 2003), 126.

6. Alan Palmer, *The Baltic: A New History of the Region and Its People* (New York: Overlook Press, 2005), 380–81.

7. For broad examination of interethnic relations with a focus on the Baltic republics, see Rasma Karklins, *Ethnic Relations in the U.S.S.R.: The Perspective from below* (New York: Routledge, 1988). On the glasnost-era discourse about Russian knowledge of the Baltic languages, see Clemens, *Baltic Independence and Russian Empire*, 78–82.

8. Daina S. Eglitis, *Imagining the Nation: History, Modernity, and Revolution in Latvia* (University Park: Pennsylvania State University Press, 2002), 34–36.

9. For an interesting discussion of the impact of environmental activism in opposition movements, see Jane I. Dawson, *Eco-Nationalism: Anti-Nuclear Activism in Russia, Lithuania, and Ukraine* (Durham, NC: Duke University Press, 1996).

10. For a comprehensive discussion of the opposition and early postcommunist periods, see Anatol Lieven, *The Baltic Revolution: Estonia, Latvia, Lithuania and the Path to Independence* (New Haven, CT: Yale University Press, 1993).

11. The tension between political currents favoring the past as a model for transformation and those favoring Western Europe as a model is discussed in Eglitis, *Imagining the Nation*.

12. Thomas Lane, *Lithuania: Stepping Westward* (New York: Routledge, 2002), 132.

13. Quoted in Michelle Martin, "Lithuanian President Compares Putin to Hitler and Stalin." Reuters. June 22, 2014. Retrieved from http://uk.reuters.com/article/ukraine-crisis-lithuania-idUKL6N0P30FB20140622.

14. Daunis Auers and Andres Kasekamp, "Explaining the Electoral Failure of Extreme-Right Parties in Estonia and Latvia," *Journal of Contemporary European Studies* 17, no. 2 (August 2009): 251.

15. For a discussion of the "radical" neoliberal economics embraced by the Baltics in early postcommunism, see Dorothy Bohle and Bela Greskovits, "Neoliberalism, Embedded Neoliberalism, and Neocorporatism: Towards Transnational Capitalism in Central-Eastern Europe," *West European Politics* 30 (2007): 443–66.

16. Updated economic data and forecasts for the region are available at the European Bank for Reconstruction and Development website: http://www.ebrd.com.

17. Daina S. Eglitis and Tana Lace, "Stratification and the Poverty of Progress in Post-Communist Latvian Capitalism," *Acta Sociologica* 52, no. 4 (December 2009): 329–49.

18. Eurostat data is updated regularly. Data on the risk of poverty and social exclusion for 2015 can be found at http://ec.europa.eu/eurostat/statistics-explained/index.php/People_at_risk_of_poverty_or_social_exclusion.

19. The European Commission provides public opinion data on a variety of topics, including attitudes to the Euro in the Eurozone. Data can be accessed at http://ec.europa.eu/COMMFrontOffice/publicopinion/index.cfm/Survey/getSurveyDetail/instruments/FLASH/surveyKy/2104.

20. The "shadow economy index" is published by the Stockholm School of Economics in Riga: http://www.sseriga.edu/en/centres/csb/shadow-economy-index-for-baltics/.

21. Akvile Motiejunaite, *Female Employment, Gender Roles, and Attitudes: The Baltic Countries in a Broader Context* (Stockholm: Stockholm University, 2008).

22. Updates on total fertility rates in these countries and around the world are published annually by the Population Reference Bureau. Figures for 2016 are available here: http://www.prb.org/Publications/Datasheets/2016/2016-world-population-data-sheet.aspx.

23. For a review of Baltic foreign policies, particularly those related to Russia and the European Union, see Eiki Berg and Piret Ehin, eds., *Identity and Foreign Policy: Baltic-Russian Relations and European Integration* (New York: Routledge, 2016).

24. For a broad-ranging examination of issues of collective memory and history in the region, including the dispute over the Bronze Soldier in Estonia, see "Contested and Shared Places of Memory, History and Politics in North Eastern Europe," special issue of *Journal of Baltic Studies* 39, no. 4 (December 2008).

Map 13.0.   Bulgaria

CHAPTER 13

Bulgaria

PROGRESS AND DEVELOPMENT

Janusz Bugajski

In the last twenty-four years, Bulgaria successfully conducted two historic transformations: from a centrally controlled communist system to a pluralistic market-oriented democracy and from the closest ally of the Soviet Union in the former Warsaw Pact to a full member of the North Atlantic Treaty Organization (NATO). This dual transformation was neither consistent nor predictable. For much of the early and mid-1990s, the postcommunist Bulgarian socialists ruled. They resisted full-blown capitalism and a close alliance with the West largely in an effort to preserve their political and economic positions and maintain their traditional ties with Moscow. Sofia's turn toward Western institutions and economic models accelerated after 1998, when a reformist coalition government was elected. Bulgaria became a member of NATO in 2004 and of the European Union (EU) in 2007.

Precommunist Bulgaria

Bulgaria emerged as an independent state from the Ottoman Empire in several stages. In 1878, following the Russo-Turkish War, the Treaty of San Stefano created a large Bulgarian state stretching from the Danube to the Aegean and including most of present-day Macedonia. The Treaty of Berlin in July 1878 reduced this territory at the insistence of the great powers because of fears of Russian dominance throughout the Balkans. Bulgaria subsequently included the region between the Danube and the Balkan Mountains. The area between the Balkan Mountains in the north and the Rhodope Mountains in the south formed the autonomous Ottoman province of Eastern Rumelia. These border readjustments and Bulgaria's reversion to a semiautonomous Ottoman principality under a German ruler created widespread resentment. However, in 1879, Sofia adopted the progressive Turnovo Constitution that guaranteed individual rights, and in the following two decades, a number of political parties were established, including the National Liberal Party and the Bulgarian Agrarian Union.

The country proclaimed its full independence from Turkey in 1908 after several popular revolts, including the Ilinden uprising in August 1903, centered in the Macedonian and Thracian regions. Bulgaria's territorial claims contributed to fueling two Balkan wars in 1912 and 1913. In the first, the new Balkan states combined their forces to drive the Ottoman armies out of the region. In the second, Bulgaria was unsuccessful in its military campaign against Serbia and Greece and once again lost territories in Macedonia and Thrace to its two neighbors. The result left a lasting sense of injustice in Sofia with regard to Bulgaria's rightful frontiers. Sofia retained only a small slice of Pirin Macedonia and a sector of the Thracian coastline. During World War I, Bulgaria allied itself with Germany and Austria, but with the defeat of the Central Powers, it was forced to accept a harsh peace treaty at Neuilly in November 1919 and lost all access to the Aegean Sea.

For most of the interwar period, Bulgaria witnessed political turmoil and economic crisis, particularly after the overthrow of the Agrarian government led by Aleksandur Stamboliyski in 1923. Following a military coup d'état supported by political rivals and nationalist Macedonian activists, Stamboliyski and other Agrarian leaders were murdered. After a decade of political instability and conflict, another coup in May 1934 led by military officers resulted in the formation of a personalistic regime under King Boris III. During World War II, Sofia imposed a royal dictatorship and capitalized on the German occupation of Yugoslavia and Greece to forge an alliance with Berlin to regain parts of Macedonia and Thrace. Sofia also repossessed the region of southern Dobruja from Romania. King Boris died in August 1943. For the rest of the war, the country was ruled by a regency, as Boris's successor, Simeon, was only six years old. Bulgaria's territorial advances, including access to the Aegean coastline, were again reversed at the close of World War II, as Sofia found itself once more on the losing side.

Communist Experience

Communist forces, with Soviet military and political assistance, seized power in Bulgaria in September 1944 during the closing stages of World War II. At the end of 1947, they eliminated all organized political and social opposition. They then held falsified elections to legitimize their assumption of absolute power. Former Moscow-directed Communist International (Comintern) agent Georgi Dimitrov returned to Bulgaria from exile and assumed leadership of the Communist Party and the state. A new Stalinist "Dimitrov" constitution was passed in December 1947 that replicated the Soviet prototype. The communist regime, under Soviet supervision, began to place tight restrictions on cultural and political life, conducted a full-scale drive toward state control over the economy, and pursued agricultural collectivization among the peasantry.

Dimitrov died in July 1949 and was replaced by Vulko Chervenkov, another hardline Stalinist. Chervenkov, in turn, was replaced by Todor Zhivkov in April 1956 during the slow process of de-Stalinization. However, Zhivkov and his Communist Party maintained tight control over the country for the next thirty-four years, until the collapse of the centralized system. Zhivkov's absolute loyalty to Moscow and his ability to thwart any organized domestic opposition to Leninist rule earned him the complete support of the Soviet leadership. There is even evidence that the Bulgarian regime sought to join the USSR as the sixteenth republic. Bulgaria was thus considered to be Moscow's closest and most loyal ally in the entire Soviet bloc.

Transition from Communism

Following a wave of public protests and increasing political pressures against the communist regime, on November 10, 1989, the Bulgarian Communist Party (BCP) Central Committee announced the resignation of Todor Zhivkov as secretary-general and his replacement by foreign minister Petar Mladenov. The new leader promised sweeping political and economic changes to transform Bulgaria into a "modern democratic state." The BCP organized pro-Mladenov rallies, depicting itself as the initiator of progressive reforms, scapegoating the Zhivkov leadership for all of the country's maladies, and trying to deny the reformist initiative to the emerging, but still embryonic, democratic opposition movement.

As head of the BCP, Mladenov held meetings with dissident activists in mid-November 1989 and pledged to implement substantive democratic reforms and legalize all types of independent groups and activities. The BCP's subordinate bodies, including the Komsomol youth association, were allowed to be more critical in an attempt to deflate some of the opposition's demands. Reshuffles were conducted in the BCP's governing Politburo and Central Committee, and Mladenov declared himself in favor of free general elections. Following massive public protests in Sofia, the regime dropped the BCP's "guiding force" role from the constitution and promised to curtail the repressive role of the security services. These steps paved the way for the creation of a multiparty system. While the BCP endeavored to maintain its political initiative, dozens of new political groups were forming during this time.

Some reform communists demanded the resignation of the entire BCP Central Committee as divisions deepened with the emergence of the Alternative Socialist Association as a faction within the party. In early December 1989, a preparatory meeting was held between BCP officials and representatives of some independent groups. Mladenov promised that the authorities would hold a constructive dialogue with all groups "supporting socialism." In order to incorporate leading opposition elements in some workable coalition and to prevent destructive splits within the party, the BCP initiated roundtable discussions with officially sponsored organizations and some of the newly formed opposition groups in January 1990.[1]

The regime continued to be treated with mistrust by most of the opposition, which refused to enter the Government of National Consensus proposed by the communists. At its Extraordinary Congress, held in early February 1990, the BCP selected Alexander Lilov as its new secretary-general and replaced the Central Committee with a smaller Supreme Party Council and the ruling Politburo with a new presidency. BCP leaders also initiated steps to separate the party from the state (which they had fully controlled), and the party itself was renamed the Bulgarian Socialist Party (BSP) to distance it from its totalitarian past.

The National Assembly (parliament), controlled by the BSP, elected Andrey Lukanov as the new prime minister. Lukanov attempted to form a more broadly based coalition government, but the initiative was rejected by the Union of Democratic Forces (UDF), which had grown into the chief democratic opposition alliance. The new cabinet became an all-communist body as the BSP's former communist-era coalition partner, the Agrarian People's Union, refused to join the Lukanov government and purged itself of compromised older leaders. In addition, reformist BSP intellectuals established an Alternative Socialist Party and cast serious doubts on the BSP's ability to democratize. Meanwhile, the UDF organized public demonstrations to protest the slow progress in the roundtable negotiations and the limitations on the democratic transition.

By mid-March 1990, the BSP and UDF had reached an agreement on the transition to a democratic system and the scheduling of competitive national elections. The BSP won the parliamentary elections held on June 10 and 17, 1990, with 47.15 percent of the vote, giving the party 211 of the 400 parliamentary seats. The UDF obtained a disappointing 36.20 percent (144 seats). The Agrarian People's Union took 8 percent (sixteen seats), and the Turkish party, Movement for Rights and Freedoms (MRF), garnered 6 percent of the vote (twenty-three seats). The UDF accused the regime of ballot rigging and maintaining a monopoly over the media. The opposition had insufficient time to organize an effective election campaign and scored particularly poorly in rural areas where the communist-socialist apparatus remained largely intact.

In April 1990, parliament formally created the office of the president but limited its authority to security matters and ceremonial functions by giving the president no veto power over parliamentary legislation. On July 6, 1990, Mladenov resigned as acting president, and the BSP threw its support behind Zheliu Zhelev as the country's new head of state. When the UDF refused to form a coalition to ensure a two-thirds parliamentary majority, the Lukanov government was stalemated. The BSP-led Lukanov government resigned at the end of November 1990 and was replaced a month later by a coalition headed by Prime Minister Dimitur Popov that included the BSP, the UDF, the Agrarians, and independents.

Political Institutions

The unicameral National Assembly also became a constitutional assembly that drafted Bulgaria's new democratic constitution. The document defined Bulgaria as a parliamentary democracy and a unitary state and prohibited any form of territorial autonomy or the creation of political parties founded on an "ethnic, racial, or religious" basis. Parliament was given legislative supremacy; the president had the right to veto legislation passed by the National Assembly. This constitution was eventually adopted in July 1991 despite opposition from some UDF factions. The National Assembly is elected every four years by a popular ballot, and the majority party or a coalition that consists of a parliamentary majority forms the new government. The president of Bulgaria is elected in a general election every five years. According to the constitution, his or her role is more ceremonial and symbolic than substantive in terms of decision-making, but he serves as commander-in-chief at time of war. Any amendments to the constitution require a three-fourths majority in parliament. However, a completely new constitution would need to be adopted by a newly elected Grand National Assembly. Bulgaria's local government consists of twenty-eight provinces named after the provincial capitals, with the national capital itself forming a separate province. The provinces are further subdivided into a total of 264 municipalities, which are the main units of local government.

Parties and Elections

Prior to the October 1991 elections, the UDF split because its largest coalition partners, the Social Democratic Party and the Agrarian National Union "Nikola Petkov," were refused a more prominent voice on the UDF Council or a greater number of candidates on the UDF electoral list. In addition, it was divided between advocates of a moderate line toward the BSP (the "light blues") and a majority demanding far-reaching de-communization and a settling of scores with the repressive communist leadership (the "dark blues"). The light blues withdrew from the union and formed the UDF-Liberals. The dark blues became known as the UDF-Movement and inherited the coalition's organizational network and media outlets.

In the October 1991 elections, the UDF-Movement narrowly won a plurality of votes despite declining support for the BSP. The UDF received 34.36 percent of the vote (110 of 240 parliamentary seats). The BSP gained 33.14 percent, claiming 106 seats. The only other party to clear the 4 percent threshold and gain parliamentary seats was the Turkish-based MRF. Not surprisingly, the parliament became highly polarized, and the UDF had to form a coalition government with the MRF, headed by Prime Minister Filip Dimitrov, who was installed in office in November 1991.

A top priority of the UDF-MRF administration was de-communization in all public institutions and the elimination of subversive activities by secret service officers who were trying to obstruct market reform. This task proved difficult because of the entrenched interests that pervaded most state bodies and enterprises. The National Assembly passed a law to confiscate communist property. The prosecution of former communist officials was intensified. About fifty prominent figures were indicted, including Todor Zhivkov. Former members of the defunct communist structures depicted the de-communization campaign as a witch hunt that undermined economic progress and failed to do anything for ordinary citizens. The UDF leadership asserted that without the ouster of communist officials and the elimination of special interests, which were undermining the Bulgarian economy, the market reform program would not succeed.

The Dimitrov government gave qualified support for Zheliu Zhelev in the first direct presidential ballot in January 1992. Zhelev was a sociologist who had been expelled from the Communist Party in the late 1980s for organizing a group to support political reform. The president was pressured to accept as his running mate prominent Bulgarian writer Blaga Dimitrova from the UDF-Movement in return for the party's endorsement. Zhelev received only 45 percent of the votes in the first round of balloting and 53 percent in the second round against the BSP candidate Velko Vulkanov. There was incessant hostility between the UDF administration and President Zhelev, who represented a more moderate policy line toward the socialists. Both the government and parliament criticized Zhelev for appointing ex-communists, and both institutions tried to further undercut the president's powers.

By the summer of 1992, the Dimitrov government faced internal splits over such issues as the return of the monarchy, the leadership of the Bulgarian Orthodox Church, and the pace of economic reform. The MRF was particularly disturbed: the decline in the economy seriously affected the Turkish rural population since the land reforms implemented favored former Bulgarian owners, and the state was slow to redistribute property to minorities from the state land fund. MRF leader Ahmed Dogan called for a change of policy, but when this failed in October 1992, the MRF parliamentary delegation joined with the BSP in a vote of no confidence in the UDF government. This motion was supported by Zhelev, who accused Dimitrov of undermining the presidency and alienating the population.

Prime Minister Dimitrov resigned on October 28, 1992. His cabinet was replaced by an "expert" government headed by the socialist Lyuben Berov that survived until September 2, 1994. It came under mounting criticism for rampant corruption and ties to clandestine business interests. As a result, it was replaced by a caretaker administration under Reneta Indzhova on October 17, 1994, that was to hold power until early general elections were held.

The BSP returned to power in the elections of December 18, 1994, winning 43.5 percent of the popular vote and 125 parliamentary seats. This time, only five parties were able to cross the 4 percent threshold to gain parliamentary representation, compared to the seven parties that entered parliament after the June 1990 elections. BSP leader Zhan Videnov, known as a hard-liner and an anti-reformer, became the new prime minister.[2] Two allied parties, the Bulgarian Agrarian People's Union "Alexander Stamboliyski" and the Political Club Ecoglasnost, which were on the same list as the BSP in the elections, joined the government coalition. The popular swing toward the BSP was confirmed during local elections in October 1994, when socialist candidates received 41 percent of the votes and the UDF only 25 percent.

The UDF had suffered substantial losses in these elections, gaining only sixty-nine parliamentary seats. The party's defeat was blamed largely on the preelection economic downturn and on internal squabbling that made a coherent and determined policy line impossible. Following their defeat, the UDF leadership resigned en masse. In early 1995, Ivan Kostov, a liberal reformer and former professor at Sofia Technical University, was elected to replace Filip Dimitrov as UDF leader. He moved to better coordinate the UDF, undercut the independence of its constituent parties and factions, and improve relations with the MRF and other opposition formations.

During its term in office, the socialist administration under Videnov's leadership, which took power after the December 1994 elections, was accused of maintaining secret connections with business conglomerates siphoning off state funds for the benefit of the old communist apparatus. Failure to follow through on reform measures also led to a rapid downturn of the economy that seriously affected living standards. Policy differences between reformists and conservatives became insurmountable, and the opposition frequently called for votes of no confidence in the administration.

The slow progress of the BSP during 1995 and 1996 in implementing reforms, as well as its mishandling of the economy, led to a host of financial, social, and economic problems. These reached crisis proportions by the mid-1990s. Meanwhile, the UDF gradually began to regain its popular support by promoting a pro-reform and pro-Western agenda. The UDF had several splits, but it remained the most credible center-right force in Bulgarian politics throughout the 1990s. It operated as a broad anti-communist movement from its inception, with support drawn mostly from among the young, educated, entrepreneurial, and urban populations.

The year 1996 proved to be a watershed in Bulgaria. The country experienced serious economic difficulties caused by the absence of systematic market reforms, widespread corruption, and even outright theft by government officials. Pressures increased for an early parliamentary ballot that could dislodge the former communists from power. However, the BSP and its coalition partners maintained a secure parliamentary majority despite growing pressures from the major opposition bloc, the UDF. The political scene remained polarized between these two formations. Their ideological differences were evident in all major issues affecting Bulgarian society. The socialists were determined to maintain the economic status quo and stalled the mass privatization program, leading to an even more serious economic decline. Moreover, the government was opposed to NATO membership and strengthened its relations with Russia, despite criticisms from the opposition.

Rifts were also evident within the Socialist Party between the harder-line members linked to Prime Minister Zhan Videnov and reformist elements critical of government policy. These divisions widened after the assassination of former Prime Minister Andrey Lukanov at the beginning of October 1996. Lukanov had become an outspoken critic of official resistance to reform. Allegedly, he also possessed information on corruption at the highest levels of government that he reportedly planned to make public.[3] Observers contended that Lukanov himself was deeply involved in corruption, and his killing resembled a gangland assassination.

The presidential elections further undermined the socialist administration. UDF candidate Petar Stoyanov gained an overwhelming percentage of votes (44 percent) over the socialist Ivan Marazov (27 percent) in the first round of voting on October 27, 1996. Stoyanov was elected president in the second-round runoff on November 3, 1996, with 59.7 percent of the vote to Marazov's 40.3 percent.[4] Although the post of president was primarily ceremonial, the result emboldened the opposition to push for a no-confidence vote in the socialist government.

During 1996, Bulgaria faced a major financial crisis. Its hard-currency reserves plummeted, and there were growing doubts that Sofia could meet its critical foreign debt payments. The government continued to prop up obsolete and uncompetitive state-owned industries. Moreover, the former communist apparatus still controlled and exploited much of the economy through shady "economic groups," in which corruption was believed to be rampant. An ambitious mass-privatization program remained stalled in parliament because of powerful vested interests. As the financial crisis deepened and the currency collapsed, prices soared dramatically. Bread shortages were reported in various parts of the country, and analysts warned of severe food and fuel shortages during the winter months. Bulgaria was in the midst of a banking crisis and entered a period of hyperinflation, which surpassed 2,000 percent on an annual basis in March 1997.[5]

Large sectors of the public were angry about the rapid decline in their living standards and the reports of widespread corruption among government officials. Following several months of protests and public demonstrations, the increasingly isolated socialist government of Prime Minister Videnov resigned in December 1996. The newly inaugurated President Stoyanov called for early parliamentary elections in April 1997 and appointed the mayor of Sofia, the popular and charismatic reformer Stefan Sofianski, as caretaker prime minister.

The UDF participated in the presidential elections in October and November 1996 and in the April 1997 parliamentary elections as part of a broader coalition, the UDF. Its chief allies in the coalition included the Democratic Party and the Agrarian

People's Union, which formed the People's Union alliance. The Agrarian People's Union, originally a founder of the UDF in 1989 under the name Agrarian People's Union "Nikola Petkov," was one of about twenty groups claiming to be the successors of the pre-communist Agrarians. Most of them were right-of-center formations.

The UDF won the April 1997 election overwhelmingly with 52 percent of the vote, gaining 137 of 240 parliamentary seats; the BSP only got 22 percent of the vote and 58 seats. Ivan Kostov, the UDF leader, was appointed prime minister. The composition of his cabinet reflected Bulgaria's commitment to intensive economic and political reforms and included pro-Western liberal reformers. The new administration benefited from broad public support even though the impact of the planned economic reforms was painful for workers in state industries.

The key priorities of the UDF-led coalition government were stabilizing the economy, combating crime and corruption, and pursuing Euro-Atlantic integration. The UDF-dominated legislature passed a number of important measures to root out the corruption that had become endemic among state officials and industrial managers. A new law passed in September 1997 prohibited members of the former communist apparatus from obtaining high positions in the civil service for a period of five years. Parliament also approved the opening up of secret police files to determine which top officials had collaborated with the communist-era security services and engaged in repressive acts. This move indicated that the authorities favored openness and transparency in government operations. Investigations into large-scale corruption were also initiated since some former socialist officials were believed to have embezzled millions of dollars from state funds.

The authorities were determined to pursue a radical economic reform program to avert a major financial crisis. In consultation with the International Monetary Fund (IMF), Sofia launched a far-reaching "stabilization program" that lifted most price controls, pegged the national currency to the German mark, and established a currency board to control government spending. As a result, the inflation rate decreased dramatically. Parliament also approved a new budget that cut state spending and reduced the subsidies on unprofitable industries. An extensive privatization program was launched that had an impact on the majority of state-owned enterprises. The possibility for social unrest remained since living standards declined sharply as a result of the government's austerity measures and budgetary discipline.

The new government was also determined to pursue Bulgaria's integration into various Euro-Atlantic institutions. President Stoyanov declared that Bulgaria was seeking membership in NATO and was willing to undertake the necessary reforms of its military structure. The previous socialist administration had been ambiguous about alliance membership and preferred a policy of neutrality and close relations with Russia. The new pro-NATO policy dismayed Bulgaria's traditional ally Russia. As a result, relations between Sofia and Moscow grew tense. Bulgaria's interior minister also accused Moscow of racketeering because of its manipulation of gas prices and control over Bulgarian energy supplies.

The parliamentary majority held by the UDF ensured that the socialist opposition did not seriously challenge the reform program. Stoyanov remained very popular despite the painful austerity program imposed by the UDF authorities. However, the local elections in October 1999 were a setback for the UDF, which only narrowly defeated the socialists in a majority of Bulgarian municipalities. Growing public frustration with layoffs and state spending cuts resulted in a decreased voter turnout of some 50 percent. However, the UDF retained control of the two major cities, Sofia and Plovdiv. Despite the progress achieved by the UDF in securing macroeconomic stability and fulfilling the criteria for international loans, the living standards of the majority of citizens actually stagnated or fell after the elections, especially among pensioners, rural workers, and blue-collar employees, angering the population.

The Bulgarian political scene changed dramatically in April 2001 with the return of the exiled King Simeon II. The ex-monarch, deposed by the communists after World War II, formed his own political group, styled as the National Movement Simeon II (NMS). This center-right organization drew support away from both the UDF and the opposition socialists. In the parliamentary elections held on June 17, 2001, the NMS scored a landslide victory, gaining 42.73 percent of the vote and 120 seats in the 240-seat legislature. The UDF finished a distant second with 18.17 percent and fifty-one seats. Two other parties passed the electoral threshold: the Socialist Party captured 17.14 percent of the vote and forty-eight seats; the Turkish minority-based MRF garnered 7.45 percent and twenty-one seats.

Simeon II thus became the first monarch to return to power in postcommunist Central and Eastern Europe, although he made no attempt to re-create the monarchy. His party captured the protest vote of impoverished elements of the Bulgarian population, and his selection of young Western-educated professionals as parliamentarians and ministers increased public support for him and his party. The king himself did not run in the elections and, at first, did not even put himself forward as prime minister. He also denied that there were any plans to restore the monarchy and pointed out that the country had far more pressing issues to contend with, such as unemployment, poverty, and corruption.

Critics charged that the NMS message was too populist and insufficiently specific on economic policies. NMS leaders countered that they would continue with the reform program launched by the UDF while paying more attention to combating corruption, attracting foreign investment, reforming the judicial system, and creating new employment opportunities. Moreover, Simeon underscored his government's commitment to the EU and NATO integration.

The NMS triumph jettisoned what had essentially become a two-party system. However, the victors indicated they were intent on creating a coalition government to achieve broader political consensus and ensure effective government during a difficult reform process. The Bulgarian public seemed to reject the continued polarization of public life by voting for this movement that pledged to unify the nation. The MRF was the first party to offer its cooperation, indicating a valuable opportunity for involving the sizable Turkish population in the governing process. In mid-July 2001, Simeon agreed to assume the post of prime minister and proceeded to form a new cabinet.

The NMS electoral base proved diverse. The party's ministers were a mixture of young bankers with Western experience, older Bulgarian lawyers, and representatives of local business groups. However, the NMS government's failure to meet unrealistic popular expectations led to a progressive drop in support for the government and its programs, as well as increasing divisions within the NMS itself. By late 2003, 11 members of parliament (MPs) had defected from the NMS's initial parliamentary contingent of 120; ten of them formed the National Ideal of Unity faction to the left of the NMS. The New Time group of twenty-two MPs on the NMS's right also became largely independent. NMS candidates performed poorly in local elections in October 2003, especially as the movement lacked any significant local structures. Although it declared its intention to transform itself into a political party, the NMS lacked cohesion and was principally based on the personality of its leader.

Following its defeat in the 2001 elections, the UDF disintegrated. In fact, by 2004 the center-right splintered into several rival formations, most with weak organizational structures but with charismatic leaders. Some activists were concerned that this development would exclude them from parliament or enable the socialists to form a workable governing coalition. Mayor of Sofia and former caretaker Prime Minister Stefan Sofianski broke away from the UDF in late 2001 after failing to persuade his colleagues to form a coalition with the NMS. He founded a separate party, the Union of Free Democrats. Although the party was small, Sofianski benefited from high ratings on a national level. Ivan Kostov resigned as the UDF's leader and created the Democrats for a Strong Bulgaria (DSB) in May 2004, pulling some supporters away from the UDF. Other center-right groupings included the Bulgarian Agrarian People's Union, the St. George's Day Movement (Gergyovden), and the New Time.[6]

The appointment of Nadezhda Mihailova, the former foreign minister, as UDF caretaker leader in March 2002 provoked intense criticism and did not improve the UDF's popularity ratings. The UDF's performance in the local elections in October 2003 was disappointing for the party. Mihailova came under increasing attack from Kostov and other UDF leaders at that time. UDF's public support had dropped even further by the 2005 elections.

In 2005, the Bulgarian electorate followed its pattern of always voting out the ruling coalition. This time it was motivated by disappointment that the NMS had not managed to transform the economy enough to benefit the older and less educated part of the population or achieve its promises to control both corruption and organized crime. Beyond this, the "kingmaker" MRF gained from the emergence of a far-right, anticommunist, xenophobic party, Ataka, which ultimately got 8.75 percent of the vote. Its attacks stimulated MRF voters to go to the polls, allowing the MRF to do far better than had been expected.

This time, both the UDF and the NMS lost to the Coalition for Bulgaria, which centered on the BSP, the successor to the BCP. Its victory was marginal; with only 34.17 percent of the vote for the BSP and 14.17 percent for the MRF, the two could not form a majority coalition. The BSP, therefore, had to reach out to the NMS (22.8 percent) to join forces for a three-party center-left coalition. This process was facilitated by the BSP's campaign commitment to continuing the economic reforms and maintaining a centrist posture to keep Bulgaria turned toward the West. The resulting government was peopled by men and women in their thirties and forties, with Sergey Stanishev, the thirty-nine-year-old BSP leader, as prime minister. The three deputy prime ministers represented the three coalition partners. Financial issues were given to a former member of the UDF. The minister of European affairs, charged with moving Bulgaria toward its 2007 entry into the EU, continued on from the NMS movement.

Despite all these political splits, by the early 2000s, Bulgaria had developed a relatively stable democratic system with a functioning market economy. The country had held several free and democratic elections, and the political transition between governing parties had been smooth and trouble free. The policies of all the major political forces had

Photo 13.1. Ultranationalist party Union Attack members demonstrate against a loudspeaker at a mosque in Sofia. (Nadya Kotseva/Sofia Photo Agency)

been pro-reform and pro-NATO, and even the postcommunist Socialist Party developed a Western and pro-NATO orientation after losing power in 1997.

Most of the BSP social base consisted of pensioners, peasants, some of the technical intelligentsia, and Bulgarians in ethnically mixed areas who veered toward nationalism. The party itself incorporated a spectrum of political trends, from Marxist dogmatists to social democrats. The more market-oriented social democrats began to prevail in the late 1990s after the party's credibility was undermined by the 1996–1997 economic collapse. Georgi Parvanov, elected BSP leader in 1996, pursued a policy of economic reform, social democracy, and pro-Westernism, including support for NATO membership. His position was buttressed by his victory in the presidential ballot in 2001. Perceived as a young reformist at the time, Sergey Stanishev was elected to be his successor as Socialist Party leader in December 2001.

During 2003 and 2004, the BSP increased its popularity largely in reaction to falling public support for the incumbent NMS-led government as a result of hard-hitting reforms. This fact was demonstrated in its performance in the 2003 municipal elections. However, the party also has experienced internal divisions. It has endeavored to consolidate its popularity by broadening its appeal among younger citizens. Most of the BSP's political partners are small, center-left formations with limited public support, including the Bulgarian Social Democratic Party and the United Labor Bloc. A relatively successful center-left formation in the late 1990s called Euroleft formed as a breakaway group from the BSP. It entered parliament in 1997 but failed to gain seats in 2001 and subsequently disappeared from the political scene.

Photo 13.2.   Georgi Parvanov was elected president in 2001. (Website of the president of the Republic of Bulgaria, http://www.president.bg)

Bulgaria has come a long way in its transformation process, as demonstrated by its accession into NATO and the EU in 2007. However, economic development, structural reform, judicial effectiveness, and public trust continue to be undermined by official corruption and organized cross-border criminality.[7] Political corruption deepened in 2008 and 2009 involving cases bordering on state capture, flagrant instances of conflict of interest, and the use of public resources for personal benefit. Although corruption among business decreased by 50 percent after Bulgaria's EU accession, procurement of public funds, and particularly EU funding for a number of development projects, became the new target for corruption schemes. As a result, the European Commission withdrew millions of euros allocated to agriculture and administrative modernization in Bulgaria. The impunity of high-level corruption and organized crime earned Bulgaria the label of "the most corrupt EU country."[8]

Bulgarian parliamentary elections on July 5, 2009, revolved around tackling official corruption and controlling the economic recession. Because of widespread dissatisfaction with the ruling socialists and public outrage with misappropriation of EU funds, the elections were comfortably won by the center-right Citizens for the European Development of Bulgaria (GERB), which received 39.7 percent of the vote. The BSP slipped to 17.7 percent; the Turkish MRF gained 14.4 percent, the ultranationalist

Ataka, 9.4 percent, the center-right Blue Coalition (led by the UDF), 6.8 percent, and the rightist Order, Lawfulness, and Justice (RZS), 4.1 percent. GERB gained 116 out of 240 parliamentary seats, followed by BSP (40), MRF (38), Ataka (21), the Blue Coalition (15), and RZS (10). Boyko Borisov, a former chief secretary of the Interior Ministry and former mayor of Sofia, became prime minister on July 27, 2009.

The GERB government undertook measures to combat corruption and organized crime and restore confidence in Bulgaria's ability to manage EU funds. Shortly after taking office, Borisov's government adopted a fifty-seven-point plan to implement the EU's recommendations to reform law enforcement and the judiciary. The EU unblocked €156 million in preaccession agriculture funds due to the new government's initial efforts to implement EU recommendations. Specialized police operations against organized criminal groups eliminated the most notorious ones, and a number of high-profile criminal bosses were imprisoned. However, little improvement was observed in reform of the judicial system. Media freedom also declined with the few remaining independent news outlets subjected to political pressure. Concentrated media ownership by interrelated oligarchic structures raised EU criticism.[9]

In the midst of Europe's financial crisis, the Borisov government managed to maintain financial stability and largely preserve the country's fiscal reserves. Austerity measures helped keep the budget deficit low—it was 0.8 percent of gross domestic product (GDP) in 2012.

The government revised three major Russian energy projects signed by the previous socialist-led coalition: the Burgas-Alexandropulos oil pipeline with a 51 percent Russian share, the second nuclear power plant at Belene with Russian-built reactors, and the South Stream natural gas pipeline with 50 percent Russian ownership. The government scrapped the first two projects, backing only South Stream. The GERB-controlled parliament adopted an indefinite moratorium on shale gas exploration and extraction under pressure from green groups and lobbyists for Russian energy interests in Bulgaria.[10]

Increased electricity prices provoked massive public protests in January and February 2013, forcing the government to resign on February 20. On March 13, President Rosen Plevneliev appointed a caretaker government headed by career diplomat Marin Raykov. Parliamentary elections took place on May 12, 2013, with only four political parties passing the threshold. GERB won the elections with 30.54 percent of the vote, gaining 97 of the 240 seats in parliament, but it was unable to form a government without a coalition partner. The elections produced a hung parliament, with BSP and its junior partner, MRF, together gaining exactly half the seats in the National Assembly. BSP received 26.61 percent of the vote and eighty-four parliamentary seats, MRF took 11.31 percent and thirty-six seats, and Ataka received 7.30 percent and twenty-three seats. Ataka declared it would not enter into coalition with GERB and refrained from formally entering into a coalition with BSP and MRF. However, the ultranationalists eventually sided with the socialist-led coalition and helped it form a government. For the first time, none of the traditional center-right parties instrumental in Bulgaria's democratic transition made it to parliament, including the UDF and DSB.

On May 29, the Socialist Party, in coalition with the ethnic Turkish MRF, formed a government supported by Ataka. Two weeks later, parliament provoked public outrage with the appointment of controversial media mogul Delyan Peevski, an MP from the Turkish party, as chairman of the State Agency for National Security. Peevski's name has been linked to corruption and shady business interests.[11] A wave of public protests continued even after the appointment was revoked, with thousands of demonstrators demanding the government's resignation. Daily demonstrations took place in Sofia during the summer and fall of 2013 as Bulgaria entered a period of political turmoil with a government that had little credibility. An October 2013 opinion poll showed that only 23 percent of citizens trusted the government, and 76 percent wanted early elections.[12] President Plevneliev expressed support for the protestors and called for early elections. But the government survived, and as the crisis in Ukraine began in late 2013, security concerns preoccupied the politicians and the public, along with preparations for the May 2014 elections for the European Parliament. The MRF nominated Delyan Peevski as its leading candidate for the European Parliament, sparking new controversies.[13]

Six coalitions and very few independent candidates competed in the election for the European Parliament on May 25, 2014, which also served as a litmus test for the early parliamentary election scheduled in the fall. Although the turnout was still low, the GERB party led again and had a chance to win the subsequent national elections. GERB gained six seats in the Bulgarian delegation of seventeen members in the European Parliament, followed by the leftist Coalition for Bulgaria with four seats, MRF and the new populist formation "Bulgaria without Censorship" each won two seats, and the center-right Reformist Bloc (RB) remained with only one seat. As the second candidate in the MRF party list, Delyan Peevski was elected member of the European Parliament but quit his mandate under public pressure over allegations of corruption.[14] This, however, did not end the controversy surrounding the failed appointment of Peevski as national security agency chief the year before. His name came up again in dealings surrounding the collapse of the Corporate Commercial Bank in mid-2014, which had caused the biggest financial crisis in Bulgaria since 1996, costing clients and the state millions in losses.[15]

The following three years saw three elections and four governments with the public becoming increasingly frustrated with the governing coalition. Support for the individual political parties fragmented. And, Russian interference in politics grew—through trolling, propaganda, fake news promulgation, and various methods of political influence. The public protests that started in May 2013 continued for months. They intensified when the Constitutional Court allowed Delyan Peevski to return to his duties as member of Parliament in September 2013, although his appointment, however brief, as the head of the National Security Council, required resignation from parliament.[16] This was not the only reason for the massive protest wave that swept Sofia and many big cities for months. People demanded change because the government of Plamen Oresharski was not working to end the culture of corruption in Bulgarian politics. The government's attempt to push the Russian South Stream natural gas project through, over EU objections and despite the sanctions against Russia for its aggression in Ukraine, also caused the withdrawal of support from coalition member MRF.

It was clear that the Socialist Party would not be able to form another cabinet given the hung parliament. The Turkish party publicly disagreed with the Socialists over South Stream and its parliamentary group refused to support an amendment to the Energy Act to exempt Bulgarian territorial waters from the requirements of EU's Third Energy

Package. The split was exacerbated when it became public that Gazprom operatives had been the ones who concocted the draft amendment. Officially, the MRF said it was leaving the ruling coalition because of the Socialists' poor performance in the European parliamentary elections. The real reasons were the clearly pro-Russian policies of the Socialist Party: the South Stream project that put Sofia in conflict with the European Commission and the Socialists' muted reaction to Moscow's intervention in Ukraine. This was consistent with the party's long stance as an outspoken critic of any attempt to change Bulgaria's European orientation to a pro-Russia one because of the Turks experience of ethnic discrimination under Communism and their support for the protections for ethnic minorities afforded by the EU.[17]

In August 2014, President Rosen Plevneliev appointed a caretaker government led by Georgi Bliznashki. He then organized a snap parliamentary election in October 2014. Eight parties gained seats in parliament, but none had a majority. The National Assembly was fragmented to the extent that any new government had to depend on some unstable coalition. GERB won 32.7 percent of the vote, followed by BSP with 15.3 percent, the MRF with 14.8 percent, center-right RB with 8.9 percent, the nationalist Patriotic Front (PF) with 7.3 percent, Bulgaria without Censorship with 5.7 percent, Attack with 4.5 percent, and the leftist Alternative for Bulgarian Revival (ABV) led by the former president Georgi Parvanov had just over 4 percent.[18] The result was inconclusive and disappointing for all major players, but it demonstrated the level of public confusion and disillusionment with the political establishment.

After a month of negotiations, GERB reached a deal with the RB, PF, and ABV to form the next Bulgarian cabinet. GERB and the RB sealed the coalition agreement when the PF committed to support their alliance and ABV sent former foreign minister, Ivaylo Kalfin to the cabinet thereby ensuring the support of another eleven MPs. This meant the government was able to count on a parliamentary majority of 137 (out of 240) lawmakers.[19]

One of the major decisions the new government was supposed to make was whether to continue with the Russia-led South Stream gas pipeline project or risk further "infringement procedures" and the loss of $12 billion assistance from the EU between 2014 and 2020. The choice was clear but, before Borisov made any official statements, Russian president Putin canceled the project in December 2014. He announced a new undertaking—the Turkish Stream project from Russia to Turkey, supposedly connecting through Greece to Italy and bypassing Bulgaria.

Bulgaria's president, Rosen Plevneliev (January 2012–January 2017), was particularly critical of Russia's annexation of Crimea, its actions in eastern Ukraine, and the "hybrid war" launched on Bulgaria and the Balkans.[20] He spoke openly about the security challenges to Bulgaria stemming from Russia's assertive behavior in the region. As a result, he was often criticized by Russian politicians and subjected to numerous media attacks.[21] The GERB leadership was concerned that his candidacy for a second mandate might not receive enough public support, because of the fierce opposition of pro-Russian circles in the country. Former GERB prime minister, Boyko Borisov was also courting various Russophile organizations and nationalist formations; associations of former military officers (some armed and functioning as a militia); the Bulgarian Orthodox Church; the sizable Russian energy lobby; and politicians with business links to Moscow.

In 2016, President Plevneliev announced that he would not run for reelection. GERB nominated the speaker of the parliament Tsetska Tsacheva, but she lost to the candidate of the Socialist Party Rumen Radev, former air force commander, in the second round of elections on November 13, 2016. Radev has expressed aspirations to develop closer relations with Moscow and opposed EU sanctions against Russia.[22] Once in office, he started lobbying Brussels for the removal of those sanctions.[23]

During the presidential election campaign, Borisov indicated he would resign if his party's candidate did not win. Tensions were already threatening coalition unity as one of the main parties in the RB—Democrats for Strong Bulgaria—split from RB and left the government in early 2016. Subsequently, ABV also departed from the ruling coalition as its leader was preparing to run in the upcoming presidential election in November.[24] Eventually, Borisov delivered on his promise to resign and another parliamentary election was scheduled that would bring the seventh government to power since the beginning of 2013. The election held on March 26, 2017, produced a result that promises further governmental and parliamentary instability. GERB won the plurality of the vote and gained 95 out of 240 seats with close to 33 percent support, followed by BSP with 27 percent, the nationalist United Patriots (UP) with just over 9 percent, and ethnic Turkish MRF with almost 9 percent. A new populist formation, Volya, gained 4 percent and twelve seats in the national assembly. For the first time, Bulgarian nationalists surpassed the Turkish party and also, for the first time, were included in the governing coalition. None of the traditional center-right parties made it to parliament, as they remained divided and ran separately. Borisov formed a coalition with the three nationalist parties comprising the UP and the external support of Volya. The UP is a loose coalition of three nationalist parties: Ataka, VMRO-Bulgarian National Movement, and National Front for Salvation of Bulgaria (NFSB). They express anti-Turkish, anti-Roma, pro-Russian, Eurosceptic, and anti-NATO views and hold anti-immigration stands. At the same time, they demand increased social spending. A prominent representative of the nationalist coalition— Krasimir Karakachanov—became a defense minister, who will have to represent Bulgaria at NATO, despite the ideological views of his party.[25] Nevertheless, GERB's pro-European and pro-NATO policy is hardly in danger in the hands of those ministers, because keeping their high positions seems to be more important to them than promoting their ideological views.

Economic Transition

By the end of the 1990s, Bulgaria had made steady progress in stabilizing its economy under the center-right government of UDF elected in 1997. UDF came to power after a devastating financial collapse in 1996, caused to a large extent by the previous governments' gradual approach to privatization that focused on restructuring unprofitable companies before selling them. The UDF administration focused instead on privatizing major state-owned enterprises and proved successful in stabilizing the banking sector and reforming social security, health care, and the pension system. Major economic reforms were implemented largely under the auspices of the IMF. These included price liberalization, reduction of tariffs, a balanced state budget, liquidation of unprofitable companies, privatization, removal of state subsidies, a simple taxation system without preferential treatment for any social sector, and the deregulation of the energy and telecommunications sectors.

The Bulgarian economy was stabilized at a macroeconomic level under the UDF government in the late 1990s when it introduced an effective currency board system to control state spending. This currency board is still in place as of 2017. When the NMS government came to power in 2001, it maintained its commitment to privatization, economic growth, and attracting foreign investment. The country registered a steady growth in GDP in the early 2000s, reaching a nearly 5 percent growth rate in 2002, 4.2 percent in 2003, 5.8 percent in 2004, and 4.3 percent in 2005. Agriculture has been steadily declining in Bulgaria in terms of overall economic growth, from just under 17 percent of GDP in 1999 to under 12 percent in 2003 and 9.3 percent in 2005. The service sector contributed some 58 percent of GDP and industry about 29 percent. Fruits, livestock, tobacco, vegetables, and wine continued to be among Bulgaria's chief exports, while imports mainly included machinery, equipment, technology, mineral fuels, and processed goods. Bulgaria's national debt continued to climb and stood at $13.7 billion in 2003 and €14.5 billion ($17.5 billion) at the close of 2005, an indication the economy continued to be at least partially reliant on borrowing from overseas sources. Nevertheless, the government was able to meet its debt-repayment requirements on schedule.

During the 1990s, Bulgaria diversified its trade and became less reliant on the former Soviet bloc. Trade with the EU increased steadily, especially with Italy, Germany, and Greece. Bulgaria's exports to the ten new EU member states increased by 10.5 percent in the first quarter of 2004, while imports from these countries grew 29.4 percent. As Bulgaria wanted to join the EU, it increasingly geared its economy toward compatibility with the European market and sought investments from Western countries.

The rate of foreign direct investment (FDI) steadily increased during the term of the center-right governments after 1997 as Western business felt more confident in Bulgaria's institutional, fiscal, and social stability. Anticorruption measures were implemented, although Western businesses and the EU pressured Sofia to pursue more comprehensive judicial and administrative reform to increase investor confidence. According to data from the Bulgarian National Bank (BNB), between 2000 and 2003 Bulgaria attracted around $3 billion in direct business investment from abroad, which was about half of the total investment attracted for the previous eleven years. In 2003 alone, foreign investment was estimated to be $1.32 billion, or 7 percent of the country's GDP. FDI inflows in 2005 reached $3 billion and continued to climb until the global economic downturn in 2008.

Most of the measures adopted by the NMS government after it came to power in 2001 were aimed at supporting specific business sectors. These measures involved the introduction of tax preferences and concessions in public procurement and increased subsidies for agriculture, tobacco growing, and certain state-owned enterprises. At the same time, in order to maintain fiscal discipline, public spending in 2002 was reduced to 39 percent of GDP, compared to 40 percent in 1998 and 44 percent in 2000. The percentage rose after 2007 as Bulgaria began to make its first contributions to the EU budget.[26]

The privatization process has accelerated since 2003, when just over a half of state-owned assets were privatized. It included a number of large enterprises, including the

Bulgarian Telecommunications Company; the tobacco-industrial complex, Bulgartabac; seven electric-power distribution companies; and thirty-six hydroelectric power plants have been sold. The privatization program was implemented in three ways: capital market offerings, centralized public auctions, and cash privatization. Among the bigger enterprises offered for sale were the Pleven oil and gas prospecting company; the Energoremont companies for power facility repairs in Ruse, Bobov Dol, Varna, and Sofia; and the Maritsa 3 thermal power plant in Dimitrovgrad.

The restitution of land and other assets to property owners or their relatives dispossessed by communist nationalization and collectivization proved complicated. Many of the private holdings acquired by farmers after 1990 were small and required owners to band together in some form of cooperative in order to afford mechanized equipment or irrigation. Compensation notes and vouchers were issued in the restitution process to owners who could not recover their actual property for a variety of reasons.

Although the Bulgarian economy continued to grow until 2008, income distribution remained a serious problem. Several parts of the population have not felt any improvement in their living standards. The most deprived groups are those who live in rural communities, ethnic minorities, and unemployed citizens. Large sectors of the population continue to experience low standards of living, long-term unemployment, and low salaries, while the extent of foreign investment has been limited compared to that in other postcommunist states such as Poland or Hungary.[27] The unemployment rate remained high throughout the transition. It stood at 16.3 percent of the total workforce by the end of the 1990s and climbed to 17.6 percent in 2002 before falling to 10 percent in 2005 and rising again during the economic recession in 2008 and 2009. The reasons are common for most postcommunist states: closure of old loss-making enterprises, unstable business environment in a fragile market economy, and slow development of new businesses, which are mostly small- or medium-sized. In 2009, the booming construction market in Bulgaria collapsed, seriously impacting unemployment rates. The labor market is also relatively rigid; bureaucratic restraints make hiring and firing very costly. In addition, privatization, enterprise restructuring, and military downsizing have left many people jobless.

Faced with the challenge of high unemployment, the government implemented various reforms aimed at removing some bureaucratic restraints, encouraging labor market flexibility, and funding a variety of retraining programs for job seekers. These reforms proved relatively successful and, coupled with significant infrastructure spending after Bulgaria joined the EU, significantly decreased jobless rates. Unemployment fluctuated between 9 and 13.3 percent in the period 2010–2014, but started to steadily decline in 2015, reaching 7.6 percent in April 2017.

After the government reforms, the job market improved with steady 5 to 6 percent economic growth between 2003 and 2008 and increased foreign investment in this period. Urban unemployment is drastically lower than in rural areas. In 2012, the difference between employment rates in rural and urban regions stood at 12.8 percent, according to Eurostat. In 2016, this difference was halved, as the unemployment rate in urban areas was 6.3 percent and in rural regions 12.4 percent. EU regional development funds and various government and private initiatives are intended to further remedy the situation.

According to a report by the National Statistical Institute (NSI) released in June 2004, the total average personal income in April 2004 reached 157 leva ($96.86) per month, while the average income per household per month totaled 406.47 leva ($250.60). Average personal income increased steadily during the 2000s and kept pace with the inflation rate until the global recession began to impact the Bulgarian economy at the end of the decade. In the first quarter of 2017, the average monthly salary in Bulgaria reached €516 ($589), with the highest salaries of €1,000 ($1,162.98) in the IT sector. Income for people living in regions away from the three biggest cities was about €300 ($348.89). Despite average income increase in the last few years, the poverty level has increased, with 22 percent living below the poverty line in 2014, compared to 18 .4 percent in 2005.[28]

The IMF registered an 11.7 percent fall in Bulgaria's GDP in 2009, bringing it to –5.5 percent. GDP growth returned to barely positive levels in 2010 (0.4 percent) and remained insignificant in 2011 (1.6 percent) and 2012 (0.2 percent). However, economists and EU governments applauded the fiscal restraint shown by the government of Prime Minister Borisov, elected in 2009 on a promise to combat corruption, a problem that led the EU to freeze $1.56 billion (€1.34 billion) in aid to Bulgaria in 2008. Under his administration, Bulgaria's economy avoided emergency financing and the double-digit economic contractions seen in Latvia, Lithuania, and Estonia.

After 2012, the economy started slowly growing again to 1.3 percent in 2013, 2.4 percent in 2014, and 3.6 percent in 2016.[29] According to the European Commission, the positive outlook will continue in the near future, with real GDP expected to grow by 2.9 percent in 2017 and marginally decline in 2018. Domestic demand will continue to be the main growth driver over the forecast horizon and unemployment will continue decreasing. Bulgaria achieved a balanced budget in 2016 mainly due to higher tax revenues and reduced public investment, but a deficit of 0.4 percent of GDP is forecast in 2017. Risks to the growth outlook are broadly balanced, according to the European Commission.[30]

Civil Society

A host of independent groups appeared in the early 1990s, ranging from environmental movements to consumer organizations and public policy institutes.[31] A new nongovernmental organization (NGO) law adopted in 2000 introduced the concept of public benefit organizations. This legislation created special financial and tax incentives for NGOs because they were seen as complementary to the state in dealing with important social issues. Parliament also formed the Civil Society Committee, a special standing committee to promote the development of civil society. It provides NGOs with an opportunity to publicly present their issues. However, because of the diversity of civil society, not all of its members' important issues are presented at this forum. To increase its legitimacy, the Civil Society Committee has created its own consultative body, the Public Council, with NGO representatives from different fields of expertise and diverse geographic regions to more effectively promote its agenda in parliament.

In some areas, the NGO-government partnership has developed fruitfully, especially in terms of providing social services at the local level. Often, municipalities contract with

NGOs to be independent providers of social services. NGOs are allowed to perform a few health activities in the areas of mental health and health education.

In September 2013, after a summer of massive public protests, President Rosen Plevneliev established a Civil Society Forum. He stated at the opening of the Forum that, "Civil society came on stage, attracted the spotlight, and now sets the agenda of the institutions". It had, as he noted, drawn attention to issues such as corruption, mafia, monopolies, oligarchs, inefficient judicial system, and unfair state. While the young people who joined the Protest Network in the summer of 2013 boosted the political role of civil society in Bulgaria, the NGOs have now fewer sources of funding than they did in the 1990s. Despite the marked activation of citizen's groups, especially in promoting judicial reform and rejecting corruption, Bulgaria's ranking on civil society by Freedom House has been slightly downgraded, citing vigilante group attacks on refugees in 2016 and the endorsement they received from some politicians and media outlets.[32]

Social Impact

In an attempt to bridge the poverty gap, the government undertook a series of initiatives and social welfare programs. It increased the subsidies for agriculture, tobacco growing, and state-owned enterprises. The ratio of subsidies as a portion of GDP increased from 2.1 percent in 1998 to 2.4 percent in 2002; social and welfare spending increased from 11 percent of GDP in 1998 to 14.6 percent in 2002.[33] However, simultaneously under IMF requirements, Bulgaria needed to balance the state budget. Doing so was difficult without increasing the tax burden on besieged small and medium enterprises, which make up the majority of the economy. Instead of increasing such taxes, the authorities have tried to broaden the tax base and make tax collection more effective. Although the government faced difficulties in meeting the IMF's budgetary targets in some years, in 2003 it registered a budgetary surplus, which remained in place until 2009 when a budgetary deficit of –0.9 percent was registered. The budgetary deficit was –3.9 percent in 2010, dropped slightly to –2.1 percent in 2011, and decreased further to –1.9 in 2012. Bulgaria, though, ended 2016 with a fiscal surplus of 1.6 percent of the GDP, compared with a budget shortfall of 2.8 percent in 2015.[34]

An ongoing problem for Bulgaria, as for several other Central and East European countries, is a steady decline in the population, especially as many of the most economically productive, skilled, and educated younger generation have emigrated to find more lucrative employment in Western Europe and the United States. Officials estimate that approximately fifty thousand citizens have emigrated annually since 1995; according to official data, some 850,000 people have left Bulgaria since the early 1990s. Out of a population of 8.7 million in the early 1990s, the total declined to 7.28 million by 2012, when the annual growth rate stood at –0.8 percent. Birthrates have fluctuated but generally remained low. There were nine births per thousand people in 2000, only 8.4 births per thousand by 2003, and 9.2 births per thousand in 2012. After a peak of 81,000 births in 2009, the number of new births fell to 62,000 in 2012, the lowest since the end of World War II. In 2016, the birth rate remained low with 64,984 live births or a birth rate of 9.1 per thousand people. The demographic crisis continued to deepen due to immigration and the high death rate, which was 14.32 per thousand in 2012, but increased to

15.4 per thousand in 2016. The population decreased almost 52,000 that year, reaching the historic low of 7,101,859.[35]

About 85 percent of Bulgaria's population of approximately 7.2 million is Slavic Bulgarian. The country's three largest minorities are the Turks, at about 9 percent of the population, the Roma, estimated at around 4 percent, and the Pomaks, or Slavic Muslims, who make up less than 1 percent of the population. Under the communist regime, during the 1980s, there was a policy of forced assimilation directed primarily at the ethnic Turkish minority, which led to a mass exodus to neighboring Turkey. Since the collapse of communism, Bulgaria has not suffered through any significant ethnic conflicts. After Todor Zhivkov's oust, Bulgarian officials made strenuous efforts to improve the country's minority policies and to repair the damage suffered by ethnic Turks during the repressive government campaigns of the 1980s. During Zhivkov's assimilation campaign, for instance, Turks had to "Bulgarize" by adopting Slavic names—typically, a Slavic suffix was added to a Muslim name, and after 1984, the Turks were forced to choose an entirely new name from a list of acceptable Bulgarian names—and give up many of their national customs. Over three hundred thousand Turks fled the country fearing even more severe repression. Their properties were confiscated by the state or sold at low prices to Bulgarians. About half this number of Turks returned to Bulgaria after the democratic changes, but many faced problems in reclaiming their houses and other possessions. In the following decade, many immigrated to Turkey for economic reasons. But when Bulgaria joined the EU in 2007, the country became attractive for younger generations of Bulgarian Turks living in Turkey to return, start businesses, and take advantage of the expanded trade opportunities with Europe.

During the summer of 1989, at the height of the Turkish exodus from Bulgaria to Turkey, the bulk of the Pomak (Slavic Muslim) population opposed efforts at forcible integration, and some sought to emigrate. The Pomaks, ethnic Bulgarians who had converted to Islam during the Ottoman occupation, are a small group estimated to be anywhere between seventy thousand and four hundred thousand people. Most of them do not self-identify as Bulgarian Muslims or Pomaks. The authorities proved reluctant to allow them to leave the country and denied passports to people residing in predominantly Pomak regions. These policies resulted in several substantial Pomak protests. Pomak regions suffered steep economic decline with the closure of local industries. Observers feared that economic problems would intensify political tensions. Bulgarian officials warned that unemployment and economic deprivations in regions with ethnically and religiously mixed groups were alarmingly high, and minorities complained about increasing discrimination in employment. After 1989, many Pomaks adopted a Turkish identity or demanded Turkish-language education, viewing it as advantageous to associate with a stronger and more influential minority.

The ethnic repression of its communist regime was one of the first parts of its past that Bulgaria jettisoned. In December 1989, the BSP (then still named the BCP) renounced forcible assimilation, allowing Muslims the freedom to choose their own names, practice Islam, observe traditional customs, and speak their native language. In January 1990, the National Assembly recommended the adoption of a special statute for minority rights. With Sofia's policy reversal, thousands of ethnic Turks returned to Bulgaria and faced new problems of adjustment. Most had lost their jobs and sold their houses for less than their true value. On their return, they demanded appropriate reparations. Ahmed Dogan, the political leader of Bulgaria's Turks, demanded a legal resolution that would restore property to victims of the exodus. Turkish deputies in parliament eventually introduced a law that was adopted in July 1992. It stipulated that all Turks were to be given back their property by April 1993 for the low price at which it had been sold. Those who proved unable to buy back their former homes would be given low-interest loans toward the purchase of alternative housing.[36]

In March 1990, the country's major political forces agreed to pass a Bulgarian Citizens' Names Law that allowed all victims of forcible assimilation to return to their old names. New birth certificates were issued, and the process of changing names was simplified from a judicial process to a straightforward administrative measure. The process was complicated and costly only for those Muslims who did not act before December 31, 1990.[37]

The issue of minority rights, particularly language use, education, and access to the mass media, generated some controversy. According to the 1991 constitution, Bulgarian was to be the sole official language. Under the Zhivkov regime, ethnic Turks were forbidden to use their mother tongue officially. The legacy of language discrimination persisted in a variety of forms. For example, parliament was reluctant to implement Turkish-language programs in secondary schools for fear of ultranationalist reactions.[38] The problem was solved in 1991 with the adoption of the new Bulgarian constitution, which guaranteed ethnic minorities the right to study and use their language. The Bulgarian parliament promised to implement a state-controlled Turkish program in all public schools with a significant minority enrollment. Bulgaria's nationalist opposition claimed that these programs were unconstitutional, so parliament issued assurances that they would not jeopardize the "unity of the Bulgarian nation."[39]

The Bulgarian constitution adopted in 1991 prohibits the creation of political parties based on "ethnic, racial, or religious lines" and organizations that "seek the violent usurpation of power."[40] Although intended to protect the Bulgarian state, these stipulations were frequently cited in efforts by nationalists to undermine the rights of minorities. Nationalist organizations capitalized on Bulgarian fears of alleged Turkish subversion and applied pressure on government organs to outlaw ethnic-based associations on the grounds that they were politically motivated and therefore "anti-state."

Even with the regime's repudiation of the old communist-era ways, the Turks have had a hard time advocating for themselves. The main Turkish organization, the MRF, was singled out for attention. In August 1991, the Sofia City Court decided that a political party formed by the MRF was unconstitutional because it was ethnically based. As a result, it could not participate in any elections. The MRF, in turn, claimed that it was not an entirely ethnic party and harbored no separatist ambitions. In September 1991, the Supreme Court barred the Rights and Freedoms Party (the political wing of the MRF) from participation in general elections on the grounds that it propounded an exclusivist ethnic and religious platform.[41] Nonetheless, the MRF itself and various Turkish cultural and social organizations were not prohibited from functioning, and the MRF legally competed in the second general elections in October 1991. It gained twenty-four parliamentary seats, with 7.55 percent of the popular vote, making it the third strongest party in Bulgaria and a coalition partner for the UDF. On April 21, 1992, the Constitutional Court rejected a petition by ninety-three MPs, mostly associated with BSP, to declare the MRF unconstitutional, opening the way for modern politics in Bulgaria.[42] For almost two decades, the MRF would play the role of a "balancer of power" in virtually all Bulgarian parliaments and governments, until 2009 when Bulgarian nationalist movements started assuming that role. By that time, corruption scandals and controversial appointments discredited the party, but it still retained a measure of voter support and a parliamentary presence.

In some respects, Macedonian groups have been more persecuted than either Turks or Pomaks. The Bulgarian government, together with most Bulgarian political parties, has refused to accept Macedonians as a legitimate minority. Instead, they have defined them as Slavic Bulgarians with the same language and history as the rest of the country. They persist in this policy even though the Council of Europe and some human rights groups have criticized Sofia for its alleged political discrimination against the Macedonian minority.[43] For instance, according to Bulgarian leaders, a Macedonian minority did not exist in the Pirin region in western Bulgaria despite the activities of local radicals who wanted some form of regional autonomy or even unification with the independent state of Macedonia. An openly Macedonian organization styled as Ilinden was established in the Pirin area and applied for official registration only to be turned down in July 1990 by a district court.

Protests by Ilinden supporters were suppressed, and Bulgaria's Supreme Court ruled that Ilinden violated the unity of the Bulgarian nation. Ilinden's statutes promoted the recognition of a sovereign Macedonian minority, a fact that evidently served as evidence that the organization intended to achieve "a united Macedonian state." Ilinden was ordered to disband but persisted in a covert fashion, claiming that the decisions of the Bulgarian courts were in violation of international law.[44] In November 1998, the local court in Blagoevgrad reversed its earlier decision and allowed the registration of a Macedonian organization, OMO "Ilinden"–Pirin, with its headquarters in Blagoevgrad.[45]

Nationalist pro-Macedonian groupings were active in Bulgaria in the 1990s and called for closer social, economic, and political links with Macedonia that they hoped would culminate in eventual reabsorption of this former Yugoslav republic by Bulgaria. At the same time, some autonomist Macedonian organizations became active in western Bulgaria, amid suspicions that they were funded by Belgrade and by some militant groups in the Republic of Macedonia to sow discord within Bulgaria and press for the separation of the Pirin region from the Bulgarian state.

Although Bulgaria addressed its most pervasive ethnic problems during the 1990s and early 2000s, the treatment and position of the large Roma minority remains a problem. Bulgarian officials claim the country's policies have been guided by the Human Rights Charter and the Bulgarian constitution. Clearly, they were in part a response to the tragic treatment of the Turkish population at the end of the communist era. Just as clearly, the outside pressures and aid by international human rights organizations and the European institutions Bulgaria wished to join have influenced the Bulgarian government to develop more coherent legislation that balances concerns over national security and state integrity with full respect for minority rights and ethnic aspirations.

The social and economic position of the large Roma minority and the persistent prejudice and discrimination against it remain major problems. The Roma themselves are split on what they want and need. Unlike the Turks in Bulgaria, whose leaders perceived the gravest threat as coming from forcible assimilation, Romani spokesmen have been particularly opposed to the segregation and marginalization of the Roma population.

Many representatives of the Roma have opposed separate schooling for Roma children because it results in inferior education, insufficient exposure to the Bulgarian language, and stymied career advancement. On the other side, some Roma leaders are pressing for a revival of Romani culture, education, and ethnic identity, fearing gradual assimilation by either the Bulgarian or Turkish communities. In addition, the law on political parties, which prohibited the registration of organizations established according to ethnic or religious criteria, worked to the detriment of Romani self-organization. After all, even though the Roma clearly do not represent a threat to Bulgaria's "territorial integrity" and the "unity of the nation" or "incite national, ethnic, and religious hostilities," they are barred from forming electoral associations.[46] But their ethnic traditions and migrant lifestyles make it impossible for them to fit into other parties, which, at best, do not advocate for Romani interests.

A few populist and nationalist groupings have been formed to advocate for "Bulgarian" national interests. Shortly after it was established, Ataka managed to win twenty-one seats in the June 2005 parliamentary elections and tried to mobilize anti-Roma sentiments in Bulgarian society. The party gained twenty-three seats during the 2013 parliamentary elections and supported the Socialist-led coalition with the MRF, although it did not formally join the government. Its program has been opposed by the majority of parliamentary deputies, but as the "kingmaker" in the government coalition, it had a significant impact on official policy.

For two decades after the fall of Communism, the Bulgarian nationalist formations were not significant political players—including the Nationwide Committee for the Defense of National Interests and various parties working together as the Internal Macedonian Revolutionary Organization (IMRO). IMRO has campaigned for Bulgarian "national interests" on issues such as the rights of Bulgarian minorities abroad. It has attracted some support in a few regions and posts in local government, but rarely won seats in parliament. IMRO and Gergyovden stood together for parliament in 2001, narrowly missing the 4 percent threshold. However, that changed with the influx of refugees from the Middle East, as public fear gave impetus to Bulgarian nationalism. As a result, for the first time, Bulgarian nationalist organizations became part of the government. While Bulgaria avoided serious interethnic clashes in early 1990s by including the Turkish party, the MRF, in mainstream politics, the country is now facing the prospect of rising nationalist sentiments and populist attitudes as a result of identity politics. In fact, anti-Roma demonstrations started shortly after the new government was sworn in.[47]

Foreign Policy

After the end of World War II, Bulgaria became part of the Soviet bloc. Its security revolved around membership in the Warsaw Pact, dominated by the Soviet Union, which ensured communist rule in each of the Central and East European countries. Bulgaria was largely isolated from the West and even from its Balkan neighbors, such as the Yugoslavs. Its economy was tied to the Moscow-centered Council for Mutual Economic Assistance. Since the collapse of the Soviet bloc, Bulgaria has made substantial progress in developing relations with all of its Balkan neighbors. It has also succeeded in joining NATO and became a member of the EU in 2007.

Bulgaria was one of the few countries to recognize Macedonia immediately after the republic declared its independence from Yugoslavia in early 1992. At the same time, the Bulgarian authorities were not willing to recognize the existence of a separate Macedonian nation and refused to recognize the Macedonian ethnic minority within Bulgaria. Sofia and Skopje ended a period of political deadlock concerning Bulgaria's recognition of a separate Macedonian language with the signing of a joint declaration and a number of accords on February 22, 1999. Bulgarian Prime Minister Ivan Kostov and his Macedonian counterpart, Ljubčo Georgievski, signed an agreement to settle the language dispute and to open the way to normalize relations. The joint declaration, signed in both Bulgarian and Macedonian, stipulated that the two countries would not undertake, incite, or support unfriendly activities against each other, including making territorial claims or applying pressure to ensure minority rights. Seven other bilateral agreements were signed at the same time to promote cooperation, trade, and investment.

Bulgaria has played a leading role in a number of regional cooperation formats, including the multinational South-Eastern Europe Brigade (SEEBRIG), headquartered in the city of Plovdiv, which promoted military interoperability between participating states. Sofia has participated in the regional security initiative South-Eastern Europe Defense Ministerial (SEDM). Following the ouster of Serbian president Slobodan Milošević in October 2000, Bulgaria has also contributed to democratic developments in Serbia by assisting NGOs and local authorities in Serbia.

The crisis in Yugoslavia posed one of the most difficult foreign policy problems for postcommunist Bulgaria. Bulgaria's relations with Yugoslavia deteriorated under the Milošević regime in the 1990s, and NATO's war with Serbia worsened these relations. Sofia was outspoken about the culpability of Milošević in Balkan instability and supported NATO in its efforts to restore security to Kosovo despite some opposition to this policy inside the country. Bulgaria suffered from a loss of trade as a result of the Yugoslav wars, primarily because of United Nations sanctions on Yugoslavia and the blockage of traffic along the Danube River. Sofia has continued to develop good relations with both Greece and Turkey by balancing its ties with the two Balkan rivals. However, the financial collapse in Greece in 2014 has created tensions with Athens, particularly as a result of labor strikes that blocked the southern border crossing for many days. The government has also been active in developing regional initiatives to enhance security and cooperation across Balkan borders.

In its relations with Russia, Bulgaria has had to deal with significant pressures from Moscow. Moscow considers the Black Sea states of Bulgaria and Romania strategically significant for several reasons. Traditionally, Russia sought to keep open the Bosporus Strait between the Black Sea and the Mediterranean for its navy and raw materials. This goal was accomplished in the late nineteenth century at the expense of the independence of all states in the region, including Bulgaria and Serbia, which became Russian quasi-protectorates. Continuing influence over these countries is critical for several reasons. First, it projects Russian political and economic ambitions throughout southeastern Europe and keeps the Black Sea itself as a zone of Russian dominance. Second, Bulgaria and Romania can provide the infrastructure and energy linkage between Europe and the Caucasus and Caspian regions. And third, Bulgaria is viewed as a historical ally that can help restore Russia's outreach.

In the early 1990s, politicians in Moscow hoped they could draw Bulgaria into a closer political orbit through membership in the CIS or in alliance with the pro-Russian quadrilateral inner core of the Commonwealth (Russia, Belarus, Kazakhstan, Kyrgyzstan). These proposals by President Boris Yeltsin were viewed with dismay in Sofia, leading President Zheliu Zhelev to declare them an "insult to Bulgarian sovereignty and national dignity."[48] Moscow concluded a bilateral treaty with Bulgaria during Yeltsin's visit to Sofia in August 1992. Nevertheless, relations did not develop smoothly, and there was no agreement on the repayment of Russia's debt to Bulgaria, which stood at $38.5 million by the end of 2004. Russia vowed to repay the bulk of this debt in military equipment and other goods. Trade between the two countries declined, largely as a result of disputes over the price of Russian gas sold to Bulgaria. The disintegration of the Soviet bloc raised the question how Sofia could protect its independence and promote economic development while maintaining balanced relations with Moscow.[49] Bulgaria elected a pro-NATO reformist government in April 1997, and its progress toward NATO entry generated political tensions with Moscow.

President Vladimir Putin's policy proved more focused and politically active than Yeltsin's. It relied on Russian businesses to sponsor public relations campaigns aimed at redirecting Bulgaria's national strategy toward Moscow. However, Russian leaders were perturbed once again when they "lost" Bulgaria in the parliamentary election victory of the King Simeon movement in June 2001. This result prevented the Bulgarian socialists from regaining power and potentially redirecting the country toward Moscow, as they had in the mid-1990s.

Despite Bulgaria's NATO entry, Putin repeatedly sought to revive the Russian-Bulgarian relationship. During a visit to Bulgaria in March 2003 to mark Bulgaria's liberation from the Ottoman Empire and the 125th anniversary of the Russo-Turkish War, Putin stressed that Russo-Bulgarian collaboration would "significantly contribute to the development of a prosperous and self-determining Europe."[50]

Under the socialist administration (2005–2009), relations between Sofia and Moscow improved, and Bulgaria agreed to several large-scale economic contracts with Russian energy companies. However, in the fall of 2009, Bulgaria's newly elected center-right government began to review several projects with Russia, including the South Stream natural gas pipeline, intended to transit Russian gas under the Black Sea to the Balkans, the construction of the Belene nuclear power plant, and participation in a trans-Balkan oil pipeline between the Bulgarian port of Burgas and the Greek port of Alexandroupolis. Borisov stated that the government would give priority to the EU-sponsored Nabucco pipeline project due to bring Caspian gas to Europe via the Balkans and reduce dependence on Russia. Nabucco then was canceled in 2013 when the Shah Deniz Consortium that was extracting natural gas in Azerbaijan decided to build the Trans-Adriatic Pipeline (TAP) through Greece and Albania and ending in Italy instead. Regarding Belene, Sofia sought a clearer and more transparent financing structure because of soaring costs and dwindling budget revenues. Eventually, the government scrapped the project for lack of economic feasibility and inability to attract a major Western investment. Sofia also quit the Burgas-Alexandroupolis oil pipeline in December 2011 but signed an investment agreement with Russia for the construction of South Stream. Since the project's cancellation in 2014, Bulgaria has tried to negotiate an increase of the previously negotiated small volumes of future gas deliveries from Azerbaijan with the Shah Denis Consortium.

Relations with Russia became extremely complicated and divisive after the annexation of Crimea and Russia's aggression in eastern Ukraine. Officially, Sofia endorsed the EU sanctions against Moscow, but Russian influence within society grew through penetration of the information space by trolls and fake news. So, Bulgarian society was torn between loyalty to the EU and to NATO on the one hand and a historic affinity for Russia reinforced by dependence on Russian energy sources. As the government took a strong stand supporting the territorial integrity of Ukraine, the Ataka party leadership called for a veto of the sanctions and recognition of the disputed March 2014 referendum in Crimea. Moreover, holding the balance of power in the Bulgarian parliament, Ataka threatened to topple the government if it supported further sanctions against Moscow. Party members transformed themselves from Bulgarian nationalists to pro-Russian nationalists, sending over twenty representatives to help the ethnic Russians in Crimea. The public debate about events in Ukraine has raised questions concerning the extent to which Bulgaria remains a reliable EU and NATO member.[51]

An opinion poll in 2014 showed that 22 percent of the Bulgarians would like to join the Russian-led Eurasian Economic Union and 40 percent wanted to stay in the EU. The opinion poll revealed that the strongest supporters of Bulgaria's rapprochement with Russia were backers of Ataka (38 percent), the BSP (34 percent) and its splinter ABV, created by former president Georgi Parvanov (34 percent).[52]

Bulgarian president Plevneliev has stated on numerous occasions that Russia is a threat to Bulgarian security. The original report prepared for the NATO summit at Wales in September 2014 clearly stated that Moscow's ambitions to restore Russia's influence along its flanks and establish itself as a pole of power was a serious danger to Bulgaria and the security of the NATO alliance. Among the risks stemming from Russia's behavior are "the new hybrid war, combining conventional methods with insurgency, cyber and informational war, as well as actions in violation of international law." The report stated that "Russian propaganda, spread especially through Bulgarian political and economic entities, media outlets, and non-governmental organizations represents an evident informational war that undermines the integrity of state institutions and sovereignty, and attacks directly the national democratic values, spirit and will."[53] The report's language was subsequently softened at the request of the interim prime minister, but Plevneliev spoke openly on this topic to Bulgarian and foreign audiences.

President Plevneliev's staunch opposition to Russia's "hybrid war" in Bulgaria has been replaced by a more Russia-friendly attitude by the new president, Rumen Radev, elected in November 2016 on the Socialist Party ticket. Radev has spoken in favor of lifting the EU sanctions against Russia for the annexation of Crimea.[54]

Bulgaria considers itself a partner and ally of the United States. There is overall agreement on major decisions related to Bulgaria's contribution to NATO and the anti-terrorist campaign. As a nonpermanent member of the UN Security Council during the 2002–2003 period, Bulgaria supported US positions more consistently than several of the United States' West European NATO allies. The center-right government of the NMS (2001–2005) backed Washington in the Iraq War despite verbal criticism by socialist president Georgi Parvanov and the socialist opposition in parliament. Although the socialists are supportive of NATO membership, some of their leaders have also maintained close links with Russian authorities, who seek to diminish the United States' global role.

To join NATO, Bulgaria had to transform its military and its weaponry to fit NATO standards and consolidate democratic civilian control over the armed forces. The government restated its commitment to downsizing and modernizing the armed forces in line with its Defense Plan 2004. The Bulgarian army became fully professional in January 2008, two years ahead of the government's schedule. According to the Development Program of the Bulgarian Armed Forces of 2010, Bulgaria was to have 27,000 standing troops by end of 2014, consisting of 14,310 troops in the land forces, 6,750 in the air force, 3,510 in the navy, and 2,420 in the joint command.[55]

There was comprehensive political and public support for Bulgaria's NATO membership, despite the country's financial constraints, with a firm commitment to allocate approximately 3 percent of GDP to defense spending over the coming years. The government calculated that the benefits of NATO membership, in terms of military modernization, downsizing, and international interoperability, outweighed the high costs of maintaining an obsolete military structure. As of 2017, however, Bulgaria is still far behind in achieving the minimum defense spending of 2 percent of GDP required by NATO. In 2016, its defense budget was 1.4 percent of GDP, but it is supposed to grow to 2 percent by 2024.[56] There is a high level of protection of classified information in compliance with NATO standards, and the government has tightened controls over the export of possible dual-use weapons and technologies.

Bulgaria supported US and NATO military operations in both word and deed. It granted airspace for the NATO Allied Force operation in Serbia in March through June 1999. Bulgaria played an important role in avoiding a possible crisis in relations between NATO and Russia in June 1999 by denying Russian forces overflight rights during NATO's intervention in Kosovo. Sofia facilitated NATO's actions when Kosovo-bound forces were allowed through. Bulgaria also participated in two NATO-led peacekeeping operations: in Stabilization Force (SFOR) in Bosnia-Herzegovina and in Kosovo Force (KFOR).

In the US-led antiterrorist and anti-rogue-state campaign since September 11, 2001, Bulgaria has allowed air, land, and sea transit to coalition forces and temporary deployment of US aircraft for refueling and cargo-lifting purposes in both the Afghanistan and Iraq operations. It has allocated military units to the International Security Assistance Force (ISAF) in Afghanistan and dispatched an anti–nuclear, biological, and chemical unit to Iraq. Bulgaria sent a total of 485 soldiers to Iraq between 2003 and 2008 and maintained a larger contingent in Afghanistan as part of ISAF, with the highest number of 681 in 2012. By 2016, it was reduced to only eighty soldiers and in October 2016, Prime Minister Borisov said that Bulgaria would withdraw its contingent entirely.[57]

Bulgaria has consistently supported the US position on the Iraqi question in the UN Security Council and dispatched a contingent of troops to the country after the American-led military invasion. Although several Bulgarian soldiers died in Iraq, Sofia remained steadfast in its involvement in the peace-enforcement coalition.

Bulgaria signed a defense cooperation agreement with the United States in 2006. It has welcomed the construction of small US bases on Bulgarian soil that could be valuable for America's strategic access to areas of potential crisis in the Middle East. Cooperation between the two countries expanded as Russia threatened the security of the Black Sea after annexing Crimea in 2014. In February 2017, the United States deployed a small contingent of 120 troops to the US-Bulgarian military base at Novo Selo in the eastern part of Bulgaria as part of Operation Atlantic Resolve, aimed at showing Moscow Washington's commitment to its allies.[58]

Photo 13.3.   Kristalina Georgieva, currently UN Commissioner for International Cooperation, Humanitarian Aid, and Crisis Response. (*Kapital Weekly*, Bulgaria)

In April 2005, Bulgaria signed an accession treaty with the EU; it became a full EU member on January 1, 2007. The government had successfully completed the implementation of all thirty-one chapters of the EU's voluminous *acquis communautaire*, which stipulated the reforms that needed to be enacted in various areas of the economy and administrative structure for Bulgaria to meet EU standards. Brussels also included a clause in the treaty that could have led to a delay in Bulgaria's entry if the remaining reforms in the judicial system and in combating corruption were not implemented.

EU membership itself closed an important chapter in Bulgaria's post–Cold War history, as it signaled that the country had successfully completed its transformation from a communist dictatorship to a capitalist democracy. However, following EU entry, some turbulence has been evident in Bulgaria's relations with several West European partners over its relations with Washington. Sofia and other Central and East European capitals seek to strengthen the transatlantic link within the EU. At the same time, they are subject to increasing pressures from Brussels and various West European capitals to coordinate their policies more closely with the EU's emerging security and foreign policy, even if the latter is sometimes at odds with Washington. For instance, tensions were evident during the George W. Bush administration when Sofia supported US policy in Iraq despite opposition from several large EU members.

Bulgaria found itself at odds with the EU over the prospective Russian-led South Stream natural gas pipeline. In December 2013, the EU Energy Commission pronounced illegal all contracts signed between six EU members and Gazprom regarding the construction of the pipeline. The contracts fell short of complying with the EU's Third Energy Package on competitiveness. As the EU Energy Commission took the lead in renegotiating the contracts with Moscow, the Bulgarian parliament decided to amend the Energy Act in order to try to bypass the provisions of the Third Energy Package. The EU warned Bulgaria that such actions would lead to a heavy infringement procedure against the country.[59] Bulgaria suspended the project in mid-2014. This ultimately led to its cancelation by Russian president Putin later that year and his blaming Sofia for the demise of South Stream.

Emerging Challenges

It will take many years for Bulgaria to achieve the economic level of its West European partners, but EU membership also means access to the union's structural funds, which will help to develop the country's economy. The government will seek to attract greater volumes of investment from Western Europe and to reverse the outflow of the most educated sectors of society. It will also plan to recover from the impact of the global recession.

The Bulgarian position is complicated by the fact that the EU itself has been undergoing major challenges deriving from the refugee crisis, terrorism threats, Brexit, Russian interference in elections and internal politics, and the growth of populist and nationalist parties. Like other new democracies, Bulgaria wants the EU to become a united and effective organization. At the same time, it wants to maintain close relations with the United States and maintain a prominent role for the NATO alliance in international security. For this to happen, though, Bulgaria must develop its infrastructure and halt the illegal drug trade that traverses the country. It must also prepare its economy and legal structures to meet EU standards. Persistent problems with the rule of law, corruption, and media freedom undermine Bulgaria's position within the EU.

Bulgaria is particularly affected by the crisis in Ukraine as Russian military planes fly near the Bulgaria's eastern borders, raising security alarms, and Russia continues to militarize the Black Sea. The country may request a heavier NATO military presence on its soil if provocations persist. Potential disruptions of Russian gas supplies may also have a devastating impact on Bulgaria, as the country has no alternative gas supplies and very limited gas storage capacity.

The main challenge for Bulgaria is the prolonged political crisis that the country entered with the resignation of Boyko Borisov's government in February 2013. The next government of an unstable Socialist-led coalition survived for only a year, giving way to an interim government, followed by yet another electoral cycle in 2014. It was followed by two more parliamentary elections until Borisov formed yet another government in May 2017. The aftermath was seven governments, three parliamentary elections, plus a regular presidential election, in the short period of some four years. As a result of these developments, Bulgarian nationalist parties became part of the government for the first time in twenty-eight years of the transition. The traditional center-right parties that were the carriers of change in Bulgarian society since 1989 failed to pass the threshold in the 2017 parliamentary election and remained outside of parliament, for the first time. The fractured political party system that undermines public trust, nationalist and populist politics, continuing pervasive corruption, and the lack of an efficient judicial system will be the main reasons for economic stagnation and a high rate of immigration among young Bulgarians in the future.

Study Questions

1. Why did communism collapse in Bulgaria?
2. What are the key components in the construction of a democratic system in Bulgaria?
3. How did Bulgaria qualify for NATO and EU membership?
4. How important and extensive are ethnic minority rights in Bulgaria?
5. Why did the traditional center-right coalition lose its place in parliament in 2013?
6. What are the major characteristics of Bulgarian nationalism, and why is it rising?

Suggested Readings

Anguelov, Zlatko. *Communism and the Remorse of an Innocent Victimizer.* College Station: Texas A&M University Press, 2002.

Bell, John D., ed. *Bulgaria in Transition: Politics, Economics, Society, and Culture after Communism.* Boulder, CO: Westview Press, 1998.

Bell, John D. *The Bulgarian Communist Party from Blagoev to Zhivkov.* Stanford, CA: Hoover Institution Press, 1986.

Bugajski, Janusz, and Assenova, Margarita. *Eurasian Disunion: Russia's Vulnerable Flanks,* Washington, DC: Jamestown Foundation, 2016.

Crampton, R. J. *A Concise History of Bulgaria*. New York: Cambridge University Press, 2005.

Ganev, Venelin I. *Preying on the State: The Transformation of Bulgaria after 1989*. Ithaca, NY: Cornell University Press, 2007.

Ghodsee, Kristen R. *Muslim Lives in Eastern Europe: Gender, Ethnicity and the Transformation of Islam in Postsocialist Bulgaria*. Princeton, NJ: Princeton University Press, 2010.

Groueff, Stephane. *Crown of Thorns: The Reign of King Boris III of Bulgaria, 1918–1943*. Lanham, MD: Madison Books, 1987.

Katsikas, Stefanos. *Bulgaria and Europe: Shifting Identities*. Cambridge: Cambridge University Press, 2012.

Leviev-Sawyer, Clive. *Bulgaria: Politics and Protests in the 21st Century*. Sofia: Riva. 2015.

Marushiakova, Elena, and Vesselin Popov. 1997. *Gypsies (Roma) in Bulgaria*. Frankfurt am Main: Peter Lang, 1993.

Neuburger, Mary. *The Orient Within: Muslim Minorities and the Negotiation of Nationhood in Modern Bulgaria*. Ithaca, NY: Cornell University Press, 2004.

Perry, Charles M., Dimitris Keridis, and Monica R. P. d'Assunção Carlos. *Bulgaria in Europe: Charting a Path toward Reform and Integration*. Dulles, VA: Potomac Books, 2006.

Websites

Bulgarian government portal: http://www.government.bg/fce/index.shtml?s=001&p=0023
Bulgarian National Statistical Institute: http://www.nsi.bg/Index_e.htm
Center for Liberal Strategies: http://www.cls-sofia.org
Embassy of the Republic of Bulgaria in the United States: http://www.bulgaria-embassy.org
European Commission in Bulgaria: http://ec.europa.eu/bulgaria/index_bg.htm
European Foreign Policy Council in Bulgaria: http://ecfr.eu/sofia
National Assembly: http://www.parliament.bg
Major English-Language Bulgarian Media
Bulgarian News Agency: http://www.bta.bg/en/home/index
Sofia Echo: http://www.sofiaecho.com
Sofia News Agency: http://www.novinite.com
News Websites
Investor.bg: http://www.investor.bg
Mediapool.bg: http://www.mediapool.bg
Major Print Media
24 Hours Daily: http://www.24chasa.bg
Dnevnik Daily: http://www.dnevnik.bg
Kapital Weekly: http://www.capital.bg
Sega Daily: http://www.segabg.com
Standart Daily: http://www.standartnews.com
Trud Daily: http://www.trud.bg

Notes

1. For a valuable account of postcommunist Bulgaria, see John D. Bell, "Democratization and Political Participation in 'Postcommunist' Bulgaria," in *Politics, Power, and the Struggle for Democracy in South-East Europe*, ed. Karen Dawisha and Bruce Parrott, 353–402 (Cambridge: Cambridge University Press, 1997).

2. Stefan Krause, "Socialists at the Helm," *Transition* 1, no. 4 (March 1995): 33–36.

3. Ivo Georgiev, "Indecisive Socialist Party Stumbles into Crisis," *Transition* 2, no. 26 (December 1996): 26–28.

4. Stefan Krause, "United Opposition Triumphs in Presidential Elections," *Transition* 2, no. 26 (December 1996): 20–23.

5. Anne-Mary Gulde, "The Role of the Currency Board in Bulgaria's Stabilization," *Finance and Development Magazine*, IMF, December 1999, http://www.imf.org/external/pubs/ft/fandd/1999/09/gulde.htm.

6. For an overview of the center-right, see Dilyana Tsenova, "SDS to Have Golden Moment in 40th Parliament," *24 Chasa* (April 2004).

7. Center for the Study of Democracy, *Corruption, Contraband, and Organized Crime in Southeast Europe* (Sofia: Center for the Study of Democracy, 2003); *Corruption Assessment Report, 2003* (Sofia: Coalition, 2000, 2004); *On the Eve of EU Accession: Anti-Corruption Reforms in Bulgaria* (Sofia: Center for the Study of Democracy, 2006); and *Anti-Corruption Reforms in Bulgaria: Key Results and Risks* (Sofia: Center for the Study of Democracy, 2007).

8. Center for the Study of Democracy, *Crime without Punishment: Countering Corruption and Organized Crime in Bulgaria* (Sofia: Center for the Study of Democracy, 2009).

9. "Bulgarian Media Ownership Trends Worrying, German Ambassador Says," *Sofia News Agency*, October 2, 2013, http://www.novinite.com/articles/154145/Bulgarian+Media+Ownership+Trends+Worrying,+Says+German+Ambassador; and "A Few Media Magnates Create 'a State within the State,'" Dnevnik Daily, October 2, 2013, http://www.dnevnik.bg/analizi/2013/10/02/2152421_niakolko_mediini_magnati_si_suzdavat_durjava_v_durjava.

10. For more information, see *Eurasia Daily Monitor* reporting on Bulgaria from 2011 to 2014 by Margarita Assenova at http://www.jamestown.org/programs/edm, or articles by the author on the Jamestown Foundation website at http://www.jamestown.org/articles-by-author/?no_cache=1&tx_cablanttnewsstaffrelation_pi1%5Bauthor%5D=651.

11. "Who Is the New Chairman of the NSC Delyan Peevski?," *Capital Daily*, June 14, 2013, http://www.capital.bg/politika_i_ikonomika/bulgaria/2013/06/14/2081416_koi_e_noviiat_predsedatel_na_dans_delian_peevski; and Margarita Assenova, "Is Organized Crime Taking over the Bulgarian State?" *Jamestown Foundation Blog*, June 14, 2013, http://jamestownfoundation.blogspot.com/2013/06/is-organized-crime-taking-over.html.

12. "'Alpha Research': The Delitimization of the Institutions and a Sense of Instability in the Beginning of the Political Season," *Dnevnik Daily*, October 2, 2013, http://www.dnevnik.bg/analizi/2013/10/02/2152409_alfa_risurch_delegitimaciia_na_instituciite_i/?ref=substory.

13. "DPS: Delyan Peevski Is Most Suitable for MEP," *Sofia News Agency*, April 9, 2014, http://www.novinite.com/articles/159652/DPS%3A+Delyan+Peevski+Is+Most+Suitable+For+MEP.

14. **"Делян Пеевски Няма да е Евродепутат"** (Delyan Peevski will not be a Euro deputy), *Capital.com*, May 26, 2014, http://www.capital.bg/politika_i_ikonomika/bulgaria/2014/05/26/2308123_delian_peevski_niama_da_e_evrodeputat/.

15. Frances Coppola, "Bulgaria's Failed Corpbank: The Former Owner's Story," *Forbes.com*, October 5, 2015, https://www.forbes.com/sites/francescoppola/2015/10/05/bulgarias-failed-corpbank-the-former-owners-story/#6d60311b50d7.

16. "Конституционният Съд Остави Пеевски Депутат, След Като Не Взе Решение," (Constitutional Court Leaves Peevski as MP after Failing to Reach Decision), *Dnevnik.com*, October 8, 2013, http://www.dnevnik.bg/bulgaria/2013/10/08/2156480_konstitucionniiat_sud_ostavi_peevski_deputat_sled_kato/#.

17. Margarita Assenova, "Bulgaria Suspends South Stream as the Ruling Coalition Falls Apart," *Eurasia Daily Monitor*, June 9, 2014, https://jamestown.org/program/bulgaria-suspends-south-stream-as-the-ruling-coalition-falls-apart/.

18. Bulgarian Electoral Commission, http://results.cik.bg/pi2014/rezultati/index.html.

19. "Bulgarian MPs Approve New Cabinet, Ministers Sworn In," *Novinite.com*, November 7, 2014, http://www.novinite.com/articles/164611/Bulgarian+MPs+Approve+New+Cabinet%2C+Ministers+Sworn+In.

20. Ukraine Today TV, September 26, 2014, https://www.youtube.com/watch?v=rLTdt3vxjgc.

21. "Олигарсите и Зависимите Медии Разпространяват Руска Пропаганда в Цяла Европа," Interview of Rosen Plevneliev for BBC, *Terminal3.com*, November 5, 2016, http://terminal3.bg/oligarsite-i-zavisimite-medii-razprostranqvat-ruska-propaganda-v-evropa/;   and "Плевнелиев: Срещу Мен Воюваха Мрежи на ДС, Руски Тролове и Политици от Петата Колона," *Dnevnik.bg*, January 20, 2017, http://www.dnevnik.bg/bulgaria/2017/01/20/2903699_plevneliev_sreshtu_men_vojuvaha_mreji_na_ds_ruski/.

22. "Russia Is Preying on Bulgaria's Next President," *Politico*, November 5, 2016, http://www.politico.eu/article/russia-is-preying-on-bulgarias-next-president-tsetska-tsacheva-rumen-radev/.

23. "Sanctions 'Hurt' Russia and the EU, Says Bulgaria President Rumen Radev," *Euronews*, February 16, 2017, http://www.euronews.com/2017/02/16/sanctions-hurt-russia-and-the-eu-says-bulgaria-president-rumen-radev.

24. "Президентска Република, но с Мен за Президент," (Presidential Republic, but with Me as President), *Capital.bg*, May 16, 2016, http://www.capital.bg/politika_i_ikonomika/redakcionni_komentari/2016/05/16/2760659_prezidentska_republika_no_s_men_za_prezident/.

25. Nina Barzachka, "Analysis | Bulgaria's Government Will Include Far-Right Nationalist Parties for the First Time," *Washington Post*, April 25, 2017, https://www.washingtonpost.com/news/monkey-cage/wp/2017/04/25/bulgarias-government-will-include-nationalist-parties-on-the-far-right-heres-why-and-what-this-means/.

26. For useful economic statistics, see "Economic Structure: Annual Indicators," Economist Intelligence Unit, Country Report Subscription, October 1, 2006.

27. For more details, see Institute for Regional and International Studies, *Country Report: Bulgaria, State of Democracy, Roadmap for Reforms, 2001* (Sofia: Institute for Regional and International Studies, 2002).

28. World Bank, http://data.worldbank.org/country/bulgaria.

29. Bulgaria Economic Outlook, *FocusEconomics.com*, http://www.focus-economics.com/countries/bulgaria.

30. European Commission, Economic Forecast for Bulgaria, https://ec.europa.eu/info/business-economy-euro/economic-performance-and-forecasts/economic-performance-country/bulgaria/economic-forecast-bulgaria_en.

31. For more details, see Luben Panov, "NGOs and the State in Bulgaria: Towards Greater Cooperation," *Social Economy and Law Journal* (Winter 2003–Spring 2004): 42–43.

32. Nations in Transit 2017, *Freedom House*, https://freedomhouse.org/report/nations-transit/2017/bulgaria.

33. Krassen Stanchev, "Bulgarian Economic Policy Is Not Rightist," A study by the Institute for Market Economics, *Kapital Weekly*, July 19, 2003.

34. "Bulgaria Ends 2016 with Budget Surplus of 1.6 pct of GDP," *Reuters*, January 25, 2017, http://www.reuters.com/article/bulgaria-budget-idUSL5N1FF2LU.

35. National Statistical Institute, Population in 2016, http://www.nsi.bg/sites/default/files/files/pressreleases/Population2016_en_722R06L.pdf.

36. Stephen Ashley, "Migration from Bulgaria," Radio Free Europe/Radio Liberty (RFE/RL) Research Institute, *Report on Eastern Europe*, December 1, 1989; Stephen Ashley, "Ethnic Unrest during January," RFE/RL, *Report on Eastern Europe* 1, no. 6 (February 9, 1990); and Kjell Engelbrekt, "The Movement for Rights and Freedoms," RFE/RL, *Report on Eastern Europe* 2, no. 22 (May 31, 1991).

37. For a discussion of cultural assimilation and the Name Change Law, see "Minority Problems Persist: Elections Set for June," in *News from Helsinki Watch*, "News from Bulgaria," March 1990. On the new law on names, see "Deep Tensions Continue in Turkish Provinces, despite Some Human Rights Improvements," in *News from Helsinki Watch*, "News from Bulgaria," August 1990.

38. Goran Ahren, "Helsinki Committee on Turkish Bulgarians: Continued Political Oppression," *Dagens Nyheter* (Stockholm), December 24, 1989, *JPRS-EER-90-009*, January 24, 1990.

39. Mitko Krumov, "New Deputies Yuriy Borisov and Vasil Kostov Replace Dobri Dzhurov and Georgi Velichkov Who Resigned," *Duma* (Sofia), January 10, 1991, *FBIS-EEU-91-013*, January 18, 1991. For a discussion of the major strikes in Kardzhali, see Bulgarian News Agency (BTA), February 26, 1991, *FBIS-EEU-91-038*, February 26, 1991.

40. Constitution of the Republic of Bulgaria, adopted July 12, 1991.

41. "Second Yilmaz Letter Is Unprecedented and Greatly Alarms Nationwide Committee of Defense of National Interests," *Duma* (Sofia), August 30, 1991, *FBIS-EEU-91–172*, September 5, 1991; and Kjell Engelbrekt, "The Movement for Rights and Freedoms to Compete in Elections," RFE/RL, *Report on Eastern Europe* 2, no. 91 (October 4, 1991).

42. Venelin I. Ganev, "History, Politics and the Constitution: Ethnic Conflict and Constitutional Adjudication in Postcommunist Bulgaria," *Slavic Review* 63, no. 1 (Spring 2004): 66–89.

43. See the January 2004 report on Bulgaria on the website of the Council of Europe's Committee against Racism and Intolerance, http://hudoc.ecri.coe.int/XMLEcri/ENGLISH/Cycle_03/03_CbC_eng/BGR-CbC-III-2004-2-ENG.pdf.

44. See Duncan M. Perry, "The Macedonian Question Revitalized," RFE/RL, *Report on Eastern Europe* 1, no. 24 (August 24, 1990); Evgeni Gavrilov, *Duma* (Sofia), November 14, 1990, *FBIS-EEU-90-223*, November 19, 1990; and Bulgarian News Agency (BTA), September 23, 1991, *FBIS-EEU-91-185*, September 24, 1991.

45. *State Gazette* (Sofia), February 23, 1999, and March 14, 1999; and Bulgarian News Agency (BTA), November 3, 1998.

46. See Helsinki Watch, *Destroying Ethnic Identity: The Gypsies of Bulgaria* (New York: Human Rights Watch, 1991).

47. Mariya Cheresheva, "Bulgarian 'Migrant Hunter' Held after Anti-Roma Rally," *Balkaninsight.com*, July 3, 2017, https://www.balkaninsight.com/en/article/migrant-hunter-arrested-after-anti-roma-rally-in-bulgaria-07-03-2017.

48. President Zhelev quoted in Bulgarian News Agency (BTA), April 2, 1996. Bulgaria's Foreign Ministry called Yeltsin's "invitation" to Bulgaria "a cause for concern." Leaders of the opposition UDF claimed that Russia's ultimate aim was the restoration of the Soviet Union, in which Bulgaria would be a constituent element. In 1963, Bulgaria's Communist Party leader had offered to make Bulgaria the sixteenth republic of the USSR; the Kremlin seemed to believe that such offers were still valid. The incident mobilized the pro-NATO opposition against the Russian-oriented socialist government led by Prime Minister Zhan Videnov and backfired against Moscow's policy.

49. Ognyan Minchev, "Bulgaria and Russia," in *Bulgaria for NATO* (Sofia: Institute for Regional and International Studies, 2002). Even though Bulgarian-Russian friendship has a long pedigree, relations have also been marked by conflicts, as Russia's tsars demanded that the newly liberated Bulgarian state in the late nineteenth century demonstrate "total economic and political dependence on Russia" (120).

50. "Putin Expresses Aspirations for Russia and Bulgaria Together in a Self-Determining Europe," Mediapool.bg, March 3, 2003. Mediapool is an influential electronic news portal in Bulgaria.

51. "Bulgarian Nationalists May Topple Government over Russia Sanctions," *Reuters*, April 1, 2014.

52. "22% of Bulgarians Want to Join Russia's 'Eurasian Union,'" *EURACTIV.com*, May 15, 2014, https://www.euractiv.com/section/elections/news/22-of-bulgarians-want-to-join-russia-s-eurasian-union/.

53. "Defence Ministry: Bulgaria Subject to Russian Information War," *Sofia News Agency,* August 26, 2014, http://www.novinite.com/articles/162925/Defence+Ministry%3A+Bulgaria+ Subject+To+Russian+Information+War.

54. Tsvetelia Tsolova, "Bulgarian Vote Shows Russia Winning Hearts on EU's Eastern Flank," *Reuters,* November 11, 2016, http://www.reuters.com/article/us-bulgaria-election-russia-idUSKBN13611H.

55. *White Paper on Defense and the Armed Forces of the Republic of Bulgaria,* Ministry of Defense of Bulgaria, October 2010, http://www.md.government.bg/en/doc/misc/20101130_WP_EN.pdf.

56. Slav Okov and Elizabeth Konstantinova, "Bulgaria May Get Saab Jets in Its Biggest Defense Deal in Decades," *Bloomberg.com,* April 26, 2017, https://www.bloomberg.com/news/articles/ 2017-04-26/bulgaria-may-get-saab-jets-in-biggest-defense-tender-in-decades.

57. "Bulgaria Warns of Troop Withdrawal from Afghanistan over Refugee Crisis," *1tvnews.af,* October 3, 2016, http://1tvnews.af/en/news/afghanistan/25189-bulgaria-warns-of-troop-withdrawal-from-afghanistan-over-refugee-crisis.

58. "U.S. Troops Deploy in Bulgaria as Mattis Meets NATO in Brussels," *Reuters,* February 15, 2017, http://www.reuters.com/article/us-nato-defence-usa-bulgaria-idUSKBN15U23R.

59. Margarita Assenova, "Bulgaria: The Cost of Resuscitating South Stream," *Eurasia Daily Monitor* 11, no. 65 (April 7, 2014), http://www.jamestown.org/single/?tx_ttnews%5Bswords%5D= 8fd5893941d69d0be3f378576261ae3e&tx_ttnews%5Ball_the_words%5D=bulgaria%20 nabucco&tx_ttnews%5Bpointer%5D=2&tx_ttnews%5Btt_news%5D=42193&tx_ttnews%5B backPid%5D=7&cHash=4501a453bdd9d08a5f33cb661caa8560#.U9gPuFYSAeI.

CHAPTER 14

Romania since 1989

OLD DILEMMAS, PRESENT CHALLENGES, FUTURE UNCERTAINTIES

Monica Ciobanu

The lengthy and essentially uneven process of creating modern Romania began over 150 years ago when a new national state was formed in 1859 by the great powers. This was followed at the conclusion of World War I by the Versailles Treaty that awarded Romania territory annexed from the defeated powers and doubled the country's size. After a brief experience with democracy during the interwar period, in World War II, Romania fell for a time under a pro-Nazi dictatorship. Since 1944, it found itself in the hands of Soviet-occupying forces, until their withdrawal in 1958. Under Soviet tutelage,

Map 14.0. Romania

373

the Romanian Communist Party (RCP) established a repressive communist regime that ruled Romania until 1989 when, almost without warning, it was overthrown in an internal revolution. Integrated first into the North Atlantic Treaty Organization (NATO) in 2004 and then into European Union (EU) membership in 2007, Romania appeared to have recovered itself and has since seemed set upon a path toward a genuine and stable modernization that would, as many have hoped, become irreversible.

However, both internal and external current developments indicate that Romania still faces the legacies of its recent and more distant past. At the same time, its future in the region remains uncertain due to major shifts in the international arena. The 2016 parliamentary elections that returned the leftist Social Democratic Party (PSD), the heir to the RCP, to power resulted almost immediately in widespread popular protests against the attempt of the new government to reverse hard-fought reforms to establish the rule of law and an independent judiciary after more than two decades of cronyism, corruption, and uncertain democratization. Similarly, the current crisis facing the EU because of the United Kingdom's decision to leave in June 2016, in the context of the rise of right-wing populist and anti-EU parties both in former communist and West European countries, could potentially exacerbate existing divisions in Romania and its political elites over the future direction of the country. Russia's overtly aggressive expansionist foreign policy in the region since the annexation of Crimea in 2014 and its simultaneous ongoing military involvement in Ukraine could play an equally destabilizing role as Romania finds itself next door to a protracted political and military conflict. In addition, the victory of Donald Trump in the November 2016 presidential election in the United States, who on numerous occasions has expressed reservations about NATO to which Romania was formally admitted in 2004, has only served to increase its anxiety about its geopolitical security.

Given this complicated and apparently unfavorable combination of internal and external circumstances, where does Romania find itself? Is it likely after the only bloody revolution in Central and Eastern Europe in 1989, after difficult battles to join the EU and NATO and a lengthy effort to persuade the world that Romania is "European" and not "Balkan," that the slow but still progressive movement toward a Western-style model of society and government could be reversed? Is it still possible to sink back in the "gray area" of postcommunist Europe? Or is the new vibrant civic engagement that has resurfaced among the better educated and those more attuned to the global liberal values of modern life in the post-1989 generation a reason for optimism? How different is Romania today than it was in 1989? This chapter addresses these questions by examining and comparing the political institutions, civil society, and economic transition during the pre-EU accession years and post-2007 political and socioeconomic developments. To establish a context for this analysis, a brief look at precommunist and communist history as well as at the 1989 revolutionary exit from communism and its immediate aftermath will be useful.

Precommunist History

It was not until the middle of the nineteenth century that any national project of political unification developed among Romanians living in the principalities of Wallachia and Moldova, which were also known as the Danubian principalities. This project was embraced and promoted by the political and cultural elite of the time on the basis of a deepening sentiment of nationalism. From 1717 to 1831, Moldova and Wallachia had been economically and financially exploited by the Ottoman Empire under conditions of economic monopoly and a governing class, the *Phanariots*, who were drawn primarily from the Greek quarter of Constantinople and appointed by the Porte. As chief administrators, they were considered princes. This period of history is significant, for, until now, Romanians have generally blamed the legacies of the Phanariot era and Turkish rule for an institutional culture of patronage and clientelism. But historically, the Phanariot class was in fact ethnically diverse and included Albanians, Bulgarians, and Romanians, as well as Greeks who were assimilated to a native aristocracy.[1] What is particularly important, however, is that during the eighteenth century, these territories were the target of geopolitical ambition among the principal neighboring powers—Russia, Austria, and Turkey—that fought each other on and over Romanian soil. There was then no significant middle class while the last decades of the century were frequently characterized by corruption, injustice, and oppression. At the same time, other Romanians living within the Hapsburg Empire in Transylvania were subject to assimilation but exposed to other and different types of political and cultural influences.[2]

National awakening and the rediscovery of the Latin roots of Romanians came quite suddenly.[3] European ideologies of nationalism and bourgeois liberalism became influential through children of aristocracy who were exposed to French culture and the ideas of the French Revolution. Since the nineteenth century and through the interwar years, France was to become an important political ally and the Romanian elite continued to express strong ties to French culture. By the early 1800s, Europe generally and Russia in particular became sympathetic and supportive of the national struggles for independence among Christian populations in the Balkan Peninsula (Albanians, Bulgarians, Croats, Serbs, Slovenians, as well as Romanians). It was under these circumstances that the great powers met in Paris in 1858 and gave their blessing to the unification of the two principalities. The Old Kingdom was ruled from 1859 until 1866 by an elected prince, Alexandru Ioan Cuza. He was eventually overthrown and a well-orchestrated plot installed a German prince and former Prussian army officer, Karlvon Hohenzollern, to replace him, who ruled the country for almost half a century (as a prince from 1866 until 1881 and then as King Karl I after 1881 until his death in 1914). In his reign, Romania became independent from Turkey in 1877 and embarked on the road to modernization. Once the monarchy was consolidated and had become well-respected (a process that continued under Karl's I successor, Ferdinand I [1914–1927]), German influence clearly came to coexist with an already well-established French culture.

But only after 1918, at the end of World War I, and as agreed to at the Paris Peace Conference, did genuine Romanian "national unification" occur. Additional territory was awarded to Romania: Transylvania, the Banat, and Bukovina from Austria-Hungary; Bessarabia from revolutionary Russia; and Southern Dobruja from Bulgaria. This new state, whose territory was significantly enlarged, faced major challenges. In the first place, it had to integrate the ethnic and religious minorities inherited from newly incorporated territories. By 1930, census data showed that out of a total population of 18,057,028, with a Romanian ethnic majority of almost 72 percent, other minorities including Hungarians, Germans, Jews, Russians, and Bulgarians were now significantly represented within the overall population.[4] These groups had been incorporated with different prior political and other experiences and had no necessary allegiance to a state that defined itself in national terms and was disinclined to grant any of them cultural autonomy. Second, as a predominantly agrarian country—almost three-quarters of the population worked in agriculture— multiple reforms needed to be simultaneously undertaken. Land redistribution, industrialization, urbanization, and, last but not least, educational reform to increase the general level of literacy were all pressing needs that could not be easily fulfilled.

Although modernization of the state was not fully achieved at this time, the country made reasonable economic progress. But in the interwar period, especially significant was an extraordinary flowering of the arts and literature. Bucharest, the capital, was commonly referred to as the Little Paris (*micul Paris*), attesting to its cultural eminence. A constitutional monarchy was established in the 1923 constitution and King Ferdinand managed to maintain some balance in a relatively peaceful alteration in power of what were then the two main political parties represented by the National Peasant Party (PNȚ) and the National Liberal Party (PNL). This, despite a good deal of political fraud and corruption, ensured relative stability throughout the 1920s. Yet, this apparently stable parliamentary system was short-lived and Romania's increasingly imperfect democracy in the 1930s was threatened by the rising influence of a xenophobic ultranationalist and Christian Iron Guard movement among increasing members of the rural population, the rural clergy, and even some well-known intellectuals.[5] It is important to note that during the interwar period, the economy remained predominantly agrarian and dominated by small landowners. Politically, the brief authoritarian monarchy of Carol II (1938–1940) was unable to insulate the country from the turmoil of World War II and from the consequences of the emerging conflict between the Soviet Union and Nazi Germany over the domination of Eastern Europe and the Balkans. The 1939 Non-Aggression Treaty between Germany and the Soviet Union (the Ribbentrop–Molotov Pact) contained a secret protocol that ceded Bessarabia, northern Bukovina, and the Hertza region to the Soviet Union. This was followed by two other treaties between the Axis Powers: the Vienna and Craiova Treaties signed in August and September 1940. As a result, Romania ceded the northern territory of Transylvania to what had become occupied Hungary and Southern Dobruja to fascist Bulgaria. Romania during the war became an ally of Nazi Germany under the dictatorship of General Ion Antonescu. Until the present time, Antonescu continues to provoke controversial disputes among historians and others. While some regard him as a hero and patriot, others associate him with a criminal fascist regime.[6] But it is chiefly the Holocaust visited on the Jewish population during Antonescu's government, which led to the deaths of between 250,000 and 400,000 Jews, that produces the strongest emotional reactions among Romanians today.[7] In respect to wartime relations, it was the Axis defeat at Stalingrad in 1943 and the significant losses suffered by Romanian troops on the Eastern front that raised major internal doubts about the country's military alliance with Hitler. Given Antonescu's reluctance to submit to what he viewed as extremely disadvantageous Allied terms in early 1944, Romania's secession from the Axis was ultimately accomplished only through a coup d'etat organized by King Michael (Carol II's son) on August 23, 1944. Eight days later, Soviet troops entered Bucharest.

However, the royal coup and the weakness of the RCP made the communist takeover difficult for the Soviet occupation. At the time, the RCP counted barely one thousand members. Because of its perceived anti-national orientation, the party had been banned shortly after its creation in 1921 and forced to operate clandestinely. But with the now direct involvement of the Soviet Union, democratic institutions were quickly dismantled. The country embarked on a process of communization through a combination of terror and draconian legislation. Finally, King Michael was forced to abdicate in 1947. As a result of this interconnected series of events, the Romanian Popular Republic (RPR) was created on December 30, 1947, and the communist regime was established at one stroke. Communism, its ideological interpretation, and regime in its several guises would significantly impact all major aspects of the society until its collapse in December 1989.

The Communist Experience

By 1948, the communization and Sovietization of the country was already well advanced under the leadership of the Romanian Workers' Party (*Partidul Muncitoresc Român* [PMR]), as the Communist Party had named itself after 1945. In July 1965, it once again became the RCP. The foundation of the communist legal system had been laid and newly established People's Tribunals quickly began prosecuting and punishing class enemies and traitors. Intensive communization targeting the collectivization of agriculture and the dismantling of private property was forcefully pursued through both terror and repressive legislation. Unlike Yugoslavia and Poland, which had abandoned collectivization in 1953 and 1956, respectively, the PMR renounced collectivization in 1962.[8] It rapidly became a repressive regime that required the creation of a special department within the Ministry of Internal Affairs (MAI)—a General Directory of People's Security or simply Securitate— as an essential mechanism of social and political control. Securitate was set up in 1948 with the help of the Soviet People's Commissariat for Internal Affairs, then known as the NKVD. For almost two decades, until the release of the last political prisoners in 1964, Securitate pursued a gulag-style strategy of repression on a massive scale.[9] Parallel with, and in addition to, the collectivization of agriculture, the regime initiated a rapid program of industrialization and urbanization that, however, signally failed to ensure a minimal standard of living for a newly emerging industrial working class.[10]

But by 1958, when a purely ethnic Romanian faction of the party led by Secretary Gheorghe Gheorghiu-Dej emerged victorious from a power struggle with Ana Pauker and Vasile Luca, who then led what was known as the "Moscow faction," it appeared that a more independent national communism was set to emerge. After the withdrawal of Soviet troops in 1958, Dej issued what become known as a "declaration of independence" that criticized the USSR's hegemony in the Soviet bloc and proclaimed Romania's independence. From the early 1960s on, history began to be rewritten; Russian language studies were abolished as a requirement in the school curricula and bourgeois intellectuals and professional cadres willing to serve the socialist regime were rehabilitated. The same independent line was pursued in the economic area, especially after 1962 when the PMR simply refused to accept the relegation of Romania to the status of agricultural supplier to the Eastern bloc. However, this nativization of communism (similarly introduced at the time by Polish and East German communists to legitimize themselves as national regimes) did not lend itself to a program of genuine de-Stalinization. To the contrary, Dej successfully managed to avoid any relaxation of the system after Nikita Khrushchev's 1956 secret speech. By the time of his death in 1965, Dej had become the undisputed leader of the party and his carefully constructed cult of personality well established.[11]

This quasi-independent nationalist line and the increasing role of the party leader as the supreme leader of both country and state continued under Nicolae Ceauşescu, Dej's successor. Ceauşescu came to power in 1967 after a brief period of collective leadership. He attempted to restore socialist legality, which had become arbitrary and discriminatory, by denouncing his predecessor in a fashion similar to Khrushchev's denunciation of Stalin and promised that such routine abuses would no longer take place. He also introduced several populist measures intended to improve the standard of living, including price reductions on consumer goods and improvement in state housing facilities. A brief period of cultural liberalization that was to end in 1972 also attracted some support among intellectuals. But it was his strongly nationalist stance on foreign policy during the late 1960s and early 1970s distancing Romania from the USSR that endeared Ceauşescu to the West and boosted his popularity in the country. A public speech given in 1968 when Czechoslovakia was invaded by the Soviet Union and other members of the Warsaw Pact represented the zenith of his popularity. Seen as a maverick within the Soviet camp, Ceauşescu became the darling of Western governments. He and his wife, Elena, were invited to tour Western capitals and enjoyed state visits to Britain and other countries. In turn, major political figures from the capitalist world visited Romania. Richard Nixon's 1969 state visit, for example, was the first by an American president to any communist country. But Ceauşescu never threatened to take Romania out of the Soviet bloc. Rather, he forged a carefully balanced position between East and West, supporting the Soviet Union on most foreign policy issues but always holding out a welcoming hand to the capitalist West.[12]

However, repression, manipulation, the cult of personality, and xenophobic nationalism were to be Ceauşescu's tools to ensure his complete domination over the RCP, institutions of the state (especially after 1974 when he became the president of the republic), and over the whole society in general. Through sustained propaganda and the complete subordination of the mass media, the identification between the state, RCP, proletariat, nation, and Ceauşescu himself was fully accomplished by the 1980s. The secret police and the upper echelons of the party were also made subordinate to Ceauşescu. Through physical and psychological coercion and the widespread use of informers and collaborators, Securitate preempted any attempt at opposition or revolt.[13] Top positions in the party and state were filled with family members or loyalists close to Ceauşescu, eliminating the possibility of a reformist faction emerging within the party. The regime became—as scholars of Romanian communism called it—no less than "dynastic socialism" or "national Stalinism."[14] Moreover, Romanians also found that they must endure the severities of an "economy of shortages" after Ceauşescu decided to repay Western debt at the cost of drastically reducing the standard of living. Slowly, Ceauşescu lost international support. In 1988, the US government decided to withdraw its "most favored nations" status in response to human rights violations. At the same time, Soviet economic and political reforms of glasnost and perestroika promoted by Mikhail Gorbachev placed Ceauşescu and the regime in an increasingly vulnerable position.

By 1989, Romania had become the most repressive, isolated, and deprived country among all socialist countries in Central and Eastern Europe, perhaps with the exception of Albania. In the late 1980s, poorly lit streets and long queues of people waiting outside grocery stores for food and other basic commodities were an ever-present part of the daily routine. In addition, strict rules limiting contact with foreigners and the annual registration of typewriters with the police preempted the mergence of organized opposition movements or of any *samizdat* publications. The state's intrusion in the private sphere, as a result of harsh policies governing reproduction and abortion, was equally repressive.[15] Ceauşescu also continued the process of "Romanization" initiated by Dej, which particularly targeted the Hungarian minority in Transylvania through assimilation policies. In 1968, he abolished the Magyar (Hungarian) Autonomous Region. This was replaced by the county system (judet). As the economy of shortages worsened, Hungarians became the scapegoats of the regime. The country seemed almost immune from the political upheavals and changes occurring elsewhere in the region as well as in the Soviet Union. Although acts of protest and dissidence had somewhat increased during the last few years of the regime, they remained disparate, isolated, and ineffective.

The Transition from Communism

During 1989, communist regimes quickly collapsed. In February, after the communist government in Poland initiated negotiations with the opposition represented by the working-class Solidarity movement, similar developments following slightly different trajectories occurred in Hungary and Bulgaria. They were peaceful and followed a round-table model or a negotiated transition.[16] Although street demonstrations triggered the fall of the regime in East Germany and Czechoslovakia, the willingness of the ruling party to compromise avoided any bloodshed. In sharp contrast in Romania, there was no organized opposition movement or any strong reformist faction within the RCP willing to negotiate the terms and conditions of a democratic transition. In consequence, the popular uprising that had begun on December 15, 1989, in the western city of Timişoara and which spread through the country and, in particular, into the largest cities, turned into a bloody affair that led to street fighting and a significant number of deaths. The demise of communism thus followed the typical path of a classical revolution: flag-waving demonstrations in the streets and calls for the army to join them. As in other cases of violent regime change, the dictator and his wife were summarily executed on December 24, following a trial by a military tribunal of doubtful legality.[17] Several days earlier, after Ceauşescu's unsuccessful attempt to flee Bucharest on December 21, all state institutions had immediately collapsed.

Senior party officials took advantage of this sudden legal vacuum and ongoing street fighting to oust Ceauşescu and seize power for themselves. Lower-ranking members of the *nomenklatura* together with some Securitate elements led by Ion Iliescu (a well-known communist who was marginalized by Ceauşescu and was alleged to have close ties with Gorbachev), quickly organized themselves as a provisional political body symbolically styled as the National Salvation Front (NSF). Despite initial promises, the NSF quickly

Photo 14.1.   Bucharest's youth celebrate the flight of Nicolae Ceaușescu in December 1989. (Dan Dusleag)

began reproducing the organizing apparatus of the RCP and announced its intentions to run in what would be the May 1990 elections. This prompted important dissidents such as Ana Blandiana, Doina Cornea, Mircea Dinescu, and Radu Filipescu to leave the Front. NSF leaders (including Iliescu himself) then began employing tactics of manipulation and promoted a nationalist-populist rhetoric suspiciously reminiscent of the previous era.[18] Thus, the events of December 1989 have been referred to as a coup d'état, or a stolen revolution, by some. This ambiguity or ambivalence regarding whether it had really been a revolution continued to linger during the next two decades and led to acute tensions among politicians and the public alike.[19]

Photo 14.2. Poor technology and infrastructure are rendering Romania's coal-mining industry obsolete. (John Gledhill)

The Founding Elections and Political Institutions

The chaotic political climate following the events of December 1989, dominated by the increasing power of the NSF and the legacies of Ceaușescu's dynastic socialism, have influenced both the founding elections in May 1990 and the design of a new constitution. The immediate aftermath of the revolution was characterized by a general climate of intolerance and incivility among political actors and destabilizing street violence.

The government that ascended to power after the 1990 elections was composed largely of former members of the party *nomenklatura*, although many were functionaries who had at some point fallen out of favor with Ceaușescu. The NSF polled 66 percent of the votes for the Chamber of Deputies and 67 percent for the Senate. The Democratic Alliance of Hungarians in Romania (DAHR), founded in December to represent the interests of the Hungarian minority, was a distant second behind the NSF with little more than 7 percent in both chambers. The newly emerging political opposition was represented by the reestablished prewar historical parties the National Peasant Party, now renamed the National Peasant Christian-Democratic Party (PNȚCD), and the PNL. In both cases, these were senior party members who survived communist jails and political repression and became the natural leaders of the two parties. They looked back, as might be expected, to the interwar political system as a model for postcommunist democracy.[20] The most vocal and well respected among them was Corneliu Coposu, a lawyer by training who had spent almost eighteen years in prison. Until his death in 1995, Coposu played an instrumental role in the creation of the anti-communist democratic opposition.[21] Both parties, however, performed modestly in these elections: the PNL obtained 6–7 percent in the two houses and PNȚCD a little under 3 percent. Ion Iliescu became the uncontested president having won the first round with 85 percent of the votes, followed far behind by Radu Câmpeanu of PNL and Ion Rațiu of PNȚCD.

In order to offset the image of continuity with the past that NSF appointments would create, President Iliescu appointed Petre Roman—a young, French-educated college professor—to the position of prime minister. Although Roman showed some interest in reform, Iliescu was ambivalent about the nature of the new system that was about to be constructed. Indeed, his early rhetoric referred to the need for "original democracy" in Romania—a system somehow different from the liberal democracies developing in the rest of postcommunist Europe. As he saw it, the new regime would be a type of "one-party democracy," a "form of political pluralism . . . [based on] maintaining and consolidating the national consensus."[22] In fact, during the early postrevolutionary period, the secret services that had inherited the institutional mantle of the communist-era secret police, the Securitate, showed themselves quite willing to employ violence in furthering Iliescu's goal of realizing this newly minted "original democracy." Specifically, when anti-Iliescu and anti-Front demonstrations in Bucharest turned contentious in June 1990, the new secret services used the situation as a pretext for mobilizing an opposition of some sixteen thousand civilians. Those mobilized—mainly coal miners from Transylvania—were brought into Bucharest and then encouraged to set upon any groups that had expressed political opposition to Iliescu and the Front. The office headquarters of opposition parties were sacked and pro-democracy advocates were beaten and arrested. Scenes of street violence in Bucharest shocked observers, who had hoped that the end of the Ceaușescu dictatorship would lead to more "civilized" forms of political life. For the next several years, however, those hopes proved largely illusory. The miners returned later in 1991 to oust the prime minister, Petre Roman, who had already emerged as a rival to Iliescu.[23]

This violence, which unfolded in the aftermath of the controversial May elections, overshadowed discussions taking place in the parliament respecting the passage of a new constitution. Some criticism was expressed by the Hungarian party of a declaration that Romania was a national unitary state and by some leaders of the historical parties concerning the impossibility of restoring a constitutional monarchy. But the constitution was later approved as a result of the December 1991 referendum in which a substantial 30 percent of the electorate did not participate. However, the ratification represented a major victory for the NSF as a political force invested with revolutionary legitimacy.[24]

According to the constitution of December 1991, revised in 2003, Romania was to be a semi-presidential representative democracy with a bicameral parliament consisting of a Senate and a Chamber of Deputies, each with four-year terms. The Chamber of Deputies, the lower house, was to hold 333 seats, of which 315 would be filled through proportional representation with an additional 18 allocated to ethnic minorities whose parties fail to pass the electoral threshold (3 percent for individual parties, 8 percent for coalitions). The Senate was to be a 137-member body. The president was to share executive power with the prime minister and his government and was to be directly elected to a five-year term through a two-round majoritarian ballot. This constitutional arrangement posed and continues to provoke significant challenges for Romanian democracy as well as serious tensions for other representative institutions. In the first place, the strong semi-presidential prerogatives granted the head of state to have the effect of constantly putting the office of presidency at odds with that of prime minister.[25] Second, the legislative role of the parliament has been constantly undermined by the ability of the executive to pass emergency ordinances with impunity.[26]

Elections and Political Parties (1992–2007)

The first decade of the democratic transition was characterized by extreme confrontational rhetoric between the two main political actors represented by former communists gathered around the heirs of the NSF and the historical parties PNL and PNȚCD who were in coalition with other anti-communist groups. These sharp divisions between the two poles, which persisted through the 1992, 1996, and 2000 elections, were primarily rooted in disagreements over the country's communist and precommunist past and, to a much lesser extent, over programs or policies that would normally distinguish left and right. In this vein, former communists appealed to the memories of the good years of communism (the 1970s) and to the fears of the industrial working class and rural electorate over the capitalist dismantling of the socialist welfare system. On their part, the anti-communist opposition parties attempted to revive the precommunist era as a "golden" historical epoch. Some even attempted to promote the possibility of restoring the monarchy.[27] At the same time, following in the footsteps of the RCP, the Democratic NSF (the DNSF, which was Iliescu's faction of the NSF that had won the 1992 elections) pursued patrimonial practices in its government, but with a much-reduced mandate. The new government and its prime minister, Nicolae Văcăroiu, followed its predecessor by introducing a bare minimum of reforms. Indeed, Văcăroiu's government seemed primarily interested in ensuring that the basic structures of power remained in the hands of the ex-communist elite that had successfully come to dominate Romania's postcommunist system. Ninety-six percent of the members of his government, for example, were former Communist Party members.[28] The DNSF's democratic credentials were further undermined by its choice of allies that it pursued in order to ensure a parliamentary majority from 1992 to 1996. These allies consisted of the xenophobic nationalist Greater Romania Party (PRM) led by the poet and journalist Corneliu Vadim Tudor. He was best known for his bombastic style, as a sycophant of the communist regime and one of the main proponents of Ceauşescu's cult of personality.[29] The nationalist Party of National Unity Support (PUNR) and former hard-line communists organized as the Socialist Party of Labor (PSM) made up the other two components of this tripartite coalition.

Despite the political advantage of the ex-communists and their ability to transform themselves into an economic oligarchy by monopolizing state institutions and the privatization of state enterprises for their own benefit, the self-proclaimed democratic opposition dominated by the two historical parties set up a new coalition in 1991 calling itself the Democratic Convention of Romania (CDR). Although not initially driven by a coherent ideology but by the desire to remove Iliescu and his party from power, the coalition grew in strength in the years to follow. By 1995, under the leadership of university president Emil Constantinescu and the unifying slogan "We can only succeed together," the CDR had developed into a credible and strong political alternative. In the 1996 elections, it promulgated and ran under a program with the catchy title "Contract with Romania." It emphasized specifically the need for serious economic reform and a real competitive market economy, as well as the introduction of a genuine anti-corruption campaign. These promises attracted a large number of diverse civic associations and political organizations and the CDR was able to gather more than ten other parties into its ranks. Notable was the presence of the reformist faction of the NSF led by former Prime Minister Petre Roman under the banner of the Democratic Party (PD).The Party of Civic Alliance (PAC), made of humanist intellectuals and former dissidents, the Association of Former Political Prisoners (AFDPR), and the DAHR representing the Hungarian minority were other key elements of this nascent opposition. Confirmation of a turn in Romania's political tide came with the victory of the Democratic Convention in the parliamentary elections of 1996 and Constantinescu's assumption of the presidency displacing Iliescu, who had held the office since the revolution.[30] The Convention garnered 30 percent of the vote in the lower house of parliament, while Iliescu's Front (now renamed the PSD in Romania, PSDR) came in second with only 22 percent. The Convention then entered into a coalition with other anti-Iliescu parties and formed a new government under Prime Minister Victor Ciorbea.

Yet, it was the heterogeneous composition of the Convention that was its main weakness. The politicians, who made it up and were brought together by circumstances, were not up to coping with the challenges of governing in the face of a systemically corrupt bureaucracy and in a structurally weak economy. Constantinescu himself was unable to prevent the inevitable divisions and subsequent disintegration of the coalition. He lacked both the charisma and the moral credentials of his predecessor, Coposu, whose legacy the Convention had rallied to win the elections. The withdrawal of the PD and, later, the Liberals from the coalition placed the country in an uneasy, if not untenable, position. Despite these setbacks, however, the EU decided in 1999 to open negotiations for Romania's accession. But by 2000, the PNȚCD as the last remaining major party in the Convention could no longer sustain a credible governing political alternative. This disappointing end led Constantinescu to refuse to run for a second term and he acknowledged defeat at the hands of corrupt politicians and the meddling of the secret services.

It was in this unstable political climate that the ex-communists, now handily renamed the PSD of Romania, resumed to power. The Social Democrats took 36 percent of the vote in the lower house while Iliescu regained the presidency only in the second round of the election after a dramatic first round in which Tudor accumulated almost a third of the vote. In fact, the 2000 elections produced a major realignment of the political spectrum as the xenophobic PRM ran second by securing a fifth of the mandate in the lower house. The PRM's behavior during the campaign and its obvious resemblance to an anti-system party in refusing to follow any ordinary rules of civility and legality, compounded by Tudor's extreme xenophobic messages, triggered immediate and serious concerns. At the time the international community faced possible war in Kosovo and fears of now a second Yugoslav disaster were uppermost in the Western media. These several concerns prompted anti-communist groups to endorse Iliescu in the second round of presidential elections. But it was primarily Tudor's forceful anti-corruption message that attracted voters increasingly disenchanted by weak and corrupt politicians. If nothing else, it was a protest vote.[31] In fact, the success of Tudor and his party luminaries was short-lived, as the PRM was able to gain no more than 13 percent of the vote in the November 2004 parliamentary elections and failed to pass the electoral threshold of 5 percent in the subsequent 2008 elections.

In the next four years, however, it appeared that Romania was finally moving toward democratic consolidation and a party system that resembled that of a European state in which there is a clear, reasonable distinction between left and right based on distinctive electoral platforms. Once the PNȚCD disappeared as a principal actor in 2000, it seemed that destructive political antagonism had ceased to play a significant role in political life. Some hopeful signs were also emerging from social democrats, now more vocal in the PSD, which was more open to styling itself a modern European socialist party committed to European integration. Its alliance with the Hungarian party further added to its credibility, and the PSD government of Adrian Năstase came to be seen as a more reliable partner for the EU and also, not least, for the International Monetary Fund. A closer look at the PSD's practices and its implementation of the anti-corruption measures under the guidance of the EU shows that the reformation of former communists was still, at most, cosmetic. The party continued to monopolize regional and local administration through corrupt officials known as "local barons."[32] The work of the National Anticorruption Prosecutor Office (a body set up in 2002) was severely undermined by the governing executive and suffered from heavy political interference. Anticorruption legislation was unable to reform nepotistic and patrimonial-type state institutions and promote a semblance of transparency and accountability among elected officials. For example, the minister for European integration herself, Hildegard Puvak, attempted to evade disclosure of her assets as required by prevailing law. Despite the rapid introduction of new laws and a serious attempt at creating checks and balances, the EU nonetheless signaled the country's lack of preparedness for admission in 2007 (the date agreed to in 1999).[33]

This lackluster ability of the PSD to address corruption and the concerns expressed by the EU provided the center-right parties with an opportunity to establish themselves as a strong political alternative. In 2003, the Democrats and Liberals established a new electoral approach under the coalition banner "Truth and Justice Alliance." The success of the alliance in the 2004 elections and the remarkable victory of its presidential candidate Traian Băsescu in the second round of voting against the heavily favored Adrian Năstase can largely be attributed to two main factors. In the first place, the Alliance and Băsescu engaged in a virulent attack against corrupt PSD practices and aligned themselves in turn toward liberalism, as had been promoted with great Western acclaim during the Ukrainian Orange Revolution in 2004. Second, in contrast to the somewhat arrogant and elitist Năstase (as he was perceived by many PSD supporters and Iliescu himself), Băsescu (a former navy captain before 1989, a member of the PD and mayor of Bucharest at the time) proved to be a shrewd and effective politician driven by populist instincts and capable of appealing to large and diverse constituencies. His blunt admission of his connection to the communist elite and willingness to accept this as simply a problematic aspect of Romanian democracy turned out to be the decisive moment during the second presidential runoff and ensured him a vote margin of 250,000 over Năstase.[34] Unlike the previous legislature that had been dominated by the PSD, the new parliament was almost evenly divided between two blocs of almost equal strength. Băsescu's win, however, drew smaller parties into the alliance, which allowed for the formation of a coalition government led by the chairman of the PNL, Călin Popescu Tăriceanu.

The creation of the Alliance government seemed to mark a clear generational shift in Romanian politics, as young ministers were appointed to important portfolios such as foreign affairs and justice. Most significantly, perhaps, the social democrats removed

Iliescu as party leader, and replaced him with the younger Mircea Geoană. This, and the results of the elections, led some political analysts to argue that "Romania has successfully completed the first phase of the transformation from an electoral to a liberal democracy."[35] Momentum also began to gather in favor of punishing those who had ties with the communist regime. In 2006, new legislation led to the opening of communist-era secret service files of members of parliament for public scrutiny. Several leading figures from the Social Democratic, Liberal, and Conservative parties were disgraced after their records showed collaboration with Securitate. The whole question of the communist era, in fact, became one of the central issues of Băsescu's presidency. After commissioning a blue-ribbon panel of historians and other intellectuals to investigate the nature of the communist era, Băsescu publicly denounced the communist system as "an illegitimate and criminal regime." However, during an official session to discuss it held on January 18, 2007, both the PSD and PRM virulently attacked the report and refused to endorse it.[36] That stance—and the threat of possible lustration legislation—caused the parliament to seek to oust Băsescu later in the year, an attempt that failed after a national referendum yielded strong public support for the president.

By cultivating a double image as both a "man of the people" and a statesman of international standing, Băsescu was able to generate widespread popular support during the first years of his presidency. That support received a further boost in 2007, when he oversaw Romania's accession to the EU. From 2004 until 2006, the anti-corruption campaign was accelerated under the direction of the minister of justice, Monica Macovei, and moved from lesser cases of bribery and corruption among public servants and the judiciary to examining the conduct of top officials. The latter especially involved former prime minister and speaker of the house Adrian Năstase that ultimately was to lead to his resignation. Băsescu's support with the Romanian public, however, was in sharp contrast to the growing discontent at his leadership within the Truth and Justice Alliance, as the Liberal Prime Minister Tăriceanu struggled with President Băsescu for preeminence in Romania's semi-presidential system. The inclusion in the coalition of the controversial Dan Voiculescu, a media mogul and former Securitate informer, also undermined popular trust in the government. In April 2007, that struggle came to a head when the Liberals announced their intention to withdraw from the alliance so that they might form a minority government with the Hungarian Democratic Union of Romania. But after a long-fought battle and fifteen years of protracted attempts at consolidated democratization, Romania finally was to become part of the EU. Does this mean that accession marks a turning point to a stable liberal democracy inaugurating an irreversible process? We will address this issue in the following section by providing an analysis of postaccession political developments.

Democracy in a Postaccession Era: Living Beyond Expectations

Since 2007, Romania has held three parliamentary elections, in 2008, 2012, and 2016, and two presidential contests, in 2009 and 2014. As a result of the 2003 constitutional revision, which extended the presidential term from four to five years, the legislative and presidential elections have been decoupled. Contrary to expectations, this electoral change has not led to any depersonalization of politics or to any improvement in the performance of political parties. Instead, parliamentary election turnout has declined and the presidential race has become the primary focus of a highly divided electorate. This political polarization, taken together with the fragmentation of party politics, continuing clientelistic practices that cross party lines, the lack of both a genuine democratic left and a solidly articulated civic liberal pole, and ongoing tensions between the executive and the president have simply resulted in persistent political instability. From 2008 to 2012 under President Băsescu, Romania has had three governments, and between 2012 and 2015 three acting prime ministers. Under PSD president Victor Ponta, no less than three governments were formed. But the most serious source of concern among outside EU officials was the PSD's attempts to undermine democratic institutions and anti-corruption reforms in the aftermath of the 2012 parliamentary elections. In 2012, an unreformed PSD with a new leadership, whose practices were reminiscent of the 1990s, made an unexpected electoral comeback. A similar situation occurred after the 2016 elections. However, in both instances, a combination of external pressure and civic activism prevented the possibility of an authoritarian restoration emerging. This continuing political uncertainty was described by Paul Sum and Ronald King as a case of "triage democratization"(while there was no overt authoritarian backsliding): "[R]eform is conducted in partial and piece-meal fashion . . .(m)inimum standards are met to comply just enough with visible pressures."[37]

Earlier, the 2008 elections had been conducted under a new electoral system based on a system of single majority representation under a new law, no. 35/2008. It resulted in an almost evenly divided legislature. Traian Băsescu's Democratic Liberal Party (PDL—as it was renamed in December 2007 after the unification with a splinter of the PNL)ran second with 314 seats in the lower house behind the PSD that allied itself with the Conservative Party of Dan Voiculescu. The Conservatives had won just one extra seat.[38] Despite long-term animosities between the two, they formed a "grand coalition" led by PDL leader Emil Boc. But in September 2009, the PSD withdrew and a Boc minority government was ousted in a no-confidence vote and replaced with a new government also led by Boc and including the PNL and the Hungarian party. The 2009 presidential elections took place in this unstable climate, but the outcome of Băsescu's reelection was rather precarious. He won against PSD candidate Mircea Geoană in the second runoff with the narrowest of margins (less than 1 percent). It was actually the vote of expatriate Romanians living abroad that tipped the balance in Băsescu's favor. During his second term, he continued to govern as what he called a "player president," which seemed to contradict the constitutional requirement that the president be above party politics. Always direct, Băsescu frequently and bluntly expressed public criticism of the political class and especially his PSD opponents as "unclean." Analysts also pointed out that in citing the needs of the anti-corruption campaign, Băsescu overstepped his authority by subordinating state institutions (including the secret services) to the presidency. His enemies did not wait long to retaliate, and a newly created alliance, the Social Liberal Union (USL) consisting of the PSD(led by Ponta since 2010) and the PNL, orchestrated a second impeachment in 2012. Although the two parties represent different ideologies (the PSD is a member of the Socialist

International and the PNL of the Liberal International), they quickly joined forces against Băsescu, their common enemy. But Băsescu, never an easy target, survived this attack and retained the presidency.[39]

However, massive and sometimes violent street protests against austerity measures initiated by the Boc government in 2010, which had been triggered by the global economic recession, led to its collapse. After the short-lived government of Mihai Răzvan Ungureanu, the USL took over in 2012, and Băsescu's sworn enemy Ponta became prime minister. But Ponta's rise to power was problematic first because of his strong affiliation with the local barons of the PSD, and especially with Năstase, and his tainted reputation stemming from ongoing criminal investigations into tax evasion and plagiarism in his doctoral dissertation (which had actually been supervised by Năstase himself!). As it turned out, fears of Ponta's attempts to derail democratic reforms were well grounded. In the 2012 elections, the USL had won an absolute majority and secured more than 60 percent of the votes in the lower house. This extraordinary victory can be explained by three factors: (a) Boc, again prime minister, found he was unable to sell the austerity measures to the public;(b)corruption scandals had involved some prominent PDL officials; and (c)the virulent and manipulative campaign launched by media outlets (mostly Antena 1 owned by Voiculescu) against the PDL and Băsescu. In fact, the PDL (now part of a new alliance—the Right Romania Alliance—with some smaller center-right parties) came in a distant second with barely 17 percent of the votes. The biggest winner in these elections was the newly formed People's Party-Dan Diaconescu (PP-DD) in 2011, which was third, with 14 percent. The PP-DD conducted a populist campaign led by a controversial but well-known TV presenter Dan Diaconescu who was eventually convicted for extortion in 2015, his party disappearing with him. Once Ponta became the head of the government, however, he quickly and unsurprisingly moved toward dismantling democratic institutions by illegally removing the two speakers of the house, as well as replacing the ombudsman, and attempted to alter the referendum law that preserved Băsescu in the office as president. In the end, a sharp rebuke from high-level officials in the EU and in the US state department prevented the country's slide into authoritarianism.[40]

The USL coalition broke up in February 2014 after the PSD blocked the PNL appointment of Klaus Iohannis (an ethnic German and the successful mayor of Sibiu serving four terms there and a politician of stainless reputation) as deputy prime minister. In consequence, Ponta's political decline came quickly. After winning the presidency of the PNL, Iohannis became the undisputed presidential candidate of a center-right coalition that brought together liberals and what was left of the PDL, which was now estranged from Băsescu. As Romania marked the twenty-fifth anniversary of the end of the communist dictatorship, Iohannis's defeat of Ponta in the presidential elections was perceived by many as an event that finally marked a crucial breakthrough with the lingering legacies of the old regime. The outcome of this contested election was settled in the second round when a far higher proportion of voters was mobilized through social media (similar to an earlier mobilization protesting Băsescu's impeachment) that called on the government to facilitate the diasporas' right to vote. Many expatriate Romanians had been disenfranchised and endured long queues in front of Romanian embassies in European countries. It is estimated that 90 percent of Romanians living abroad, representing almost 339,000 voters, endorsed Iohannis. Iohannis's support was among city residents and younger middle-class voters.[41] As Tom Gallgher put it, these elections reflect deep divisions between a traditional provincial electorate living in poorly underdeveloped areas and a modern urban electorate supported by a civic-oriented diaspora.[42] It would appear that a president who enunciates less and eschews verbal polemics (distinguishing him from his predecessor) may have or actually has inaugurated a new style of leadership. The following year, Ponta suffered another blow forcing him to resign after large-scale protests were held rallying under the slogan "Corruption Kills." Ponta was at the time facing charges of tax evasion and money laundering. This general and growing dissatisfaction with the political class was made even worse by an incident leading to many deaths in a nightclub fire. The cause was a failure to enforce safety regulations to which authorities had been slow to respond, forcing the resignation of the government. A new government dominated by technocrats and led by former EU agricultural commissioner Dacian Cioloș was appointed in its place.

However, in the 2016 legislative elections, the PNL was unable to capitalize on the reformist record of the Cioloș government and the PSD made yet again a major comeback by winning a comfortable 45 percent of the votes, this time under the leadership of Liviu Dragnea. Dragnea is currently serving a suspended sentence for electoral fraud involving the 2012 impeachment referendum. In the absence of strong leadership, the PNL was second with only 20 percent of the votes. The surprise of the elections was the unexpected performance of the Union for the Salvation of Romania (USR) organized the same year by newcomers to politics committed to rooting out corruption. It won a substantial 9 percent of the votes. Three other parties passed the electoral threshold: the Democratic Alliance of Hungarians, the Democratic Alliance of Liberals and Democrats (ALDE) founded in 2015 and the People's Movement Party (PMP) led by Băsescu. As allies, PSD and ALDE promoted an anti-EU populist campaign promising Romanians that they would take back the country. Such a nationalistic anti-foreign campaign (targeting Iohannis himself and the Hungarian-American billionaire and philanthropist George Soros) resonated remarkably well in the current international political context dominated by the rise of fascist, populist, and anti-EU movements. Political analysts also pointed out that the fragmentation of the liberal right, the lack of charismatic leadership within the PNL, and Iohannis's preferred style or approach of taking a back seat also contributed to the PSD's success.[43] Given that a 2001 law prevents anyone convicted of a crime from becoming a minister (which included Dragnea himself), the appointment of a new prime minister turned out to be problematic. Eventually, a new government was appointed in January 2017 under the premiership of Sorin Grindeanu, a former minister of telecommunications in the Ponta government. Fears that Grindeanu's appointment was just a cover-up for a puppet government run by Dragnea proved to be correct. Grindeanu attempted to pass two controversial emergency ordinances secretly without parliamentary debate and without the president's signature, both aimed at undermining the work of the Anticorruption Directorate (DNA).[44] A proposal for an amnesty for those serving prison terms of less than five years and halving the sentence for those over sixty would serve very well both Voiculescu and Dragnea himself. In response to this, in the beginning of February 2017, large crowds (estimated at totaling five hundred thousand) took to the streets in many cities under the banners "Resist" and "Corruption Kills." Again, as in 2014, civic activism and international pressure responded to this arrant attempt to ram through such a self-serving decree conceived so obviously in secret.[45] But six months after the PSD government was appointed, a nonconfidence vote resulted in

Grindeanu's ousting by his own party and his replacement with a new prime minister, Mihai Tudose. Tudose is mostly known as a former economy minister who was once accused of plagiarism.[46] Political analysts explained Grindeanu's forced resignation as an indication of Dragnea's and other PSD moguls' dissatisfaction with his failure to relax the anti-corruption legislation.

ECONOMIC TRANSITION

After the first decade of the democratic transition, which has been characterized by endemic corruption, mismanagement, and populist policies, the Romanian economy seemed to experience unprecedented growth. According to the World Bank, when negotiations for EU accession began in 2000 and until 2009 (the beginning of the global economic recession), the gross domestic product (GDP) per capita income grew from 27 percent of the EU average to 48 percent.[47] However, when Romania officially entered recession, it experienced a significant decline over the next five years. The economy picked up again in 2013 and solid GDP growth peaked at 4.9 percent in 2016.[48] But despite this recovery and the fact that Romania is to be one of the fastest growing EU economies, GDP per capita still lags behind the Czech Republic, Hungary, Poland, the Slovak Republic, and the Baltic countries.[49]

The main challenges facing the economy today include income inequality, endemic poverty (both estimated as among the highest in the EU), and a serious workforce crisis in the labor market. The latter is the result of two main factors. First, an overall demographic decline (from almost 23 million in 1989 to 19,760,000 as of January 2016) has resulted in an increased aging population. Second, the migration of 3 million Romanians, estimated by the UN as in the top twenty countries with the largest diaspora, has contributed to a significant loss of young and qualified workers.[50] A brief overview of the state of the economy before 1989, the slow reforms undertaken throughout the 1990s, and issues of corruption shed better light on current economic issues and future prospects for the country.

Under Ceauşescu, the Romanian economy essentially ground to a halt. Enormous industrial enterprises, constructed in the 1970s, generated more pollution than products. Oil refining and coal mining, two of the mainstays of the economy, contracted. Agricultural production, burdened by outdated technology and a collectivized system that provided few incentives for individual farmers, declined. Although the economy had become ossified by the late 1980s, Romania did have one relative advantage, however, over a number of neighboring transition states. Throughout the 1980s, Ceauşescu was obsessed with the eradication of Romania's foreign debt. Imports were cut drastically and radical austerity programs were introduced in order to allow for the export of Romanian foodstuffs. Although the social repercussions of this step were severe, Romania did manage to begin its transition to a market economy with no foreign debt. Furthermore, the state had large foreign reserves and was the only country in the region that was already a member of the International Monetary Fund.

These seemingly structural advantages, however, did not lead to an improvement in the overall economy in the aftermath of December 1989. Instead, the NSF and its heirs' socioeconomic policies were guided by political self-interest. In 1990, populist measures of raising salaries and shortening the workweek accounted for a 22 percent decline in worker productivity.[51] Heavy industry, especially the branches of mining, chemical, metallurgy, and petroleum, experienced massive and rapid decline after December 1989. From 1990 to 2001, the labor force occupied in industry was halved. This deindustrialization did not result in any economic modernization based in an economy of services. In the 1990s, a reverse migration to rural areas contributed to a reagrarianization of the economy leading to an economy of subsistence. This was the result of a sharp increase in urban unemployment and, beginning in 1991, the restitution of agricultural land to original property holders and their heirs primarily in the form of small plots.[52] Iliescu consistently argued that he felt a responsibility to Romanians to avoid applying shock therapy reforms that had been initiated in other Central European countries. Yet, few moves were made to encourage large-scale privatization. In reality, Iliescu and his party attempted to forestall large-scale unemployment that could turn the population against them and undermine the party's legitimacy.

The election of the center-right Convention government in November 1996 was accompanied by an immediate increase in the level and kind of structural reforms, many of which were introduced under pressure from international financial institutions. Some observers described this new reform program as Romania's own version of shock therapy, since the Convention's program of rapid reform saw the adoption of more than a hundred pieces of privatization and liberalization legislation during 1997 alone.[53] But in 1999, the government's plan to shut down 140 mines in the Hunedoara region of Transylvania resulted once again in the violent descent of miners on Bucharest in angry reaction.

As noted earlier, the Romania economy began an upward trend after 2000, and between 2006 and 2008, it became one of the fastest growing economies in Europe, registering annual growth rates of around 8 percent and extremely large year-on-year increases in average real wages (as much as 17 percent in 2007).[54] In its regular reports on the Romanian economy, the World Bank attributed these positive indicators to the country's increased integration with the world economy and its willingness to exploit comparative advantages in the production of textiles, clothing, furniture, automobiles, midlevel technologies, and information services.[55] The Economist Intelligence Unit, however, located the immediate impetus to growth somewhat closer to home—in the rapid expansion of easy credit and a commensurate increase in domestic consumer demand and spending, which grew by 13 percent in 2007.[56] As conditions improved, conspicuous consumption became fashionable in Romania as those who had long borne the burden of languishing as one of Europe's poorest states chose to celebrate this apparent growth with increased spending.

But this sudden increase in the standard of living and increased consumption was stalled by the 2008 world financial crisis and subsequent recession. Economic mismanagement and loose fiscal and wage policies found the country unprepared to cope with such a crisis. As a result, in 2009, the International Monetary Fund, the EU, and the International Bank for Reconstruction and Development put together a loan of €19.5 billion ($22.92 billion). In exchange, the government was forced to pursue harsh austerity measures that led to a deep 25 percent cut in public employee wages and reduction of jobs. As the value of the leu fell and foreign investments dropped to a low of €1.6 billion ($1.88 billion) in 2012, many found themselves once again in difficulty.[57] Romanians living abroad now found themselves (yet again) important contributors to the country's

GDP in the shape of remittances, which provided a significant economic boost. But more recent economic growth and optimistic predictions for 2017 should still be regarded with caution. Among serious weaknesses and concerns regarding the Romanian economy, the World Bank lists the following: nonperforming loans in the banking sector, persistent poverty among a third of the population, the need for better-skilled workforce, and political instability in combination with corruption.[58]

In fact, it is the latter—corruption—that was, and has remained, one of the major challenges to economic stability. Despite numerous efforts to implement anti-corruption laws and institutional mechanisms during the preaccession years, the EU continued to closely monitor Romania's progress in this area. In 2007, the Cooperation and Verification Mechanism was set up to address the shortcomings in the judicial reforms and the fight against corruption.[59] As of this writing, recent social unrest has been triggered by popular dissatisfaction, with the government's attempts to undermine the independence of the judiciary and interfere with its investigations of public officials. The annual corruption index conducted by Transparency International in 2016 ranks Romania as the fifth most corrupt country in the EU, after Bulgaria, Greece, Italy, and at the same level as Hungary. On a global corruption scale, the country ranks 57th of 176 countries, that is, in the bottom third.[60]

The underlying causes of corruption are multiple and both cultural and institutional factors should be considered when analyzing the Romanian case. In the first place, the country's history going back to Ottoman rule and the history of the Orthodox Church, and then more recently in the Ceauşescu years (characterized as they were by an economy of shortages and a barter economy), shaped a state organized along deeply patrimonial lines. Thus, the state is and always has been seen by both public officials and citizens as a source of personal gain and enrichment. Corruption is deeply ingrained in everyday life and manifests itself at all levels. Twenty-eight years after the December 1989 revolution, many still feel and acknowledge the need to bribe medical staff, school teachers, and local authorities in order to receive services or benefits to which they are otherwise fully and legally entitled.[61] At the same time, the reemergence and continued reproduction of political elites after 1989 meant that those who benefited from the shadowy system developed under Ceauşescu would have little interest in reforming it.

The transfer of power in 1996 saw certain anti-corruption programs introduced. Yet, the real impetus for reform has come from the EU, which has been harsh in its criticism since the beginning of the accession talks. With the carrot of EU membership dangling before the country, real efforts were made to curtail corruption before Romania finally joined the EU in January 2007. In 2000, the Law on Preventing, Detecting, and Punishing Acts of Corruption was introduced to provide for the creation of a National Section for Combating Corruption and Organized Crime under the direction of the general prosecutor's office. A 2003 law brought Romania further into conformity with EU norms by increasing freedom of information and clarifying the kinds of acts that actually constitute corruption. Through public awareness campaigns, the Coalition for a Clean Parliament (an alliance representing civil society) played an important role in exerting control over corrupt politicians. Civil rights activist Monica Macovei, who in 2004 was appointed justice minister by the Truth and Justice Alliance, made corruption her number one priority. Despite the stir of real interest upon the appointment of Macovei, the prosecution of high-level corruption cases has slowed since she was removed from her post in April 2007. Political instability within the Alliance and corruption allegations against some of its members further weakened the work of the anti-corruption agencies.

However, the crusade gained new momentum after 2013, when a young prosecutor, Laura Codruţa Kövesi, was appointed head of the National Anticorruption Directorate (DNA, as it was renamed in 2006). DNA focuses on a high-level graft involving more than €10,000 and reports, and is subordinated to the Highest Court of Cassation. The year 2015 represented a high peak in DNA's endeavors as it brought indictments against the then Prime Minister Ponta, five other ministers, and twenty-one members of parliament. The following year, DNA continued to pursue corrupt officials at both national and local levels.[62] A recent study undertaken by the think tank Romanian Academic Society shows half of the cases involving local officials involve the misuse of EU funds.[63] Politicians and business people exploit loopholes in the legislation, while some are actually able to reduce their sentences by publishing ghostwritten books or plagiarized works while serving time in prison. As indicated earlier, the current government is trying to introduce legislation in order to protect the PSD and its members as well as other corrupt politicians. Kövesi, for her pains, is the object of both praise and vilification. Younger people and anti-corruption protesters together with EU officials praise her work and stand behind her.[64] But PSD supporters and officials accuse Kövesi of using DNA as a means to curtail freedoms and civil liberties in alliance with the secret services (SRI) and President Iohannis. As the Grindeanu government continues to threaten her removal, the struggle between the justice system and the political class remains an open and unresolved chapter in the history of post-EU accession.

Civil Society

As we have seen, the peaceful collapse of communist regimes in 1989 in Central and Eastern Europe was the result of negotiations between the elements of communist parties and representatives of civil society organizations or intellectual dissidents. The latter influenced the terms of the transition and ensured that some form of institutional power sharing was implemented. This role was played in Poland by the leaders of the Solidarity movement (working-class unions), neo-Marxist intellectual dissent, youth movements and interest organizations in Hungary, ecological movements in Bulgaria, intellectuals centered on Charter 77, and the dissident writer and future president Václav Havel in Czechoslovakia. Regarding the latter, it is important to emphasize that although intellectuals and artists in the Czech Lands and in Slovakia still held jobs in the official world, they participated in nonconformist activities under the radar of the regime. In contrast, Ceauşescu's repressive and nationalist Stalinism suppressed any possibility for independent groups and associations to organize. Revolts of the miners in 1977, attempts to establish independent unions in 1979, and strikes of workers from the industrial city of Braşov in 1987 were all squashed by Securitate. And neither could a *samizdat* culture develop, since typewriters were required to be registered with the police. Although some dissidents did manage to express criticism of the regime through Radio Free Europe or Voice of America, most writers and artists chose to use an encoded language as a form of protest. It is then not surprising that, in this absence of organized opposition, the Romanian revolution did not follow a peaceful, pacted transition.[65]

However, after December 1989, intellectuals were swift to organize themselves under the banner the "Group for Social Dialogue," a month later, in January. Together with other organizations represented by former political prisoners, student groups, and intellectuals from Timişoara, they were to be major players in demonstrations in Bucharest's University Square in 1990. They were also instrumental in promoting the "Proclamation of Timişoara" in March—a document that called for lustration laws against former communist officials, liberal reforms, and European integration. But in the context of the populist anti-intellectual rhetoric promoted by Iliescu and the NSF, and given that the RCP was still a mass party in December 1989, the Proclamation failed to resonate with most of the population.[66] Many feared a witch hunt against former party members and losing their social welfare security. In fact, throughout the 1990s and early 2000s, labor unions representing various sectors of the economy (mining, transportation, power plants) engaged in numerous strikes over these issues and became increasingly militant.[67] A serious rift emerged as a result between anti-communist groups and the labor unions. This polarization affecting the growth of civil society across class lines inhibited the development of any vital civic culture that should have been intrinsic to the institutionalization of democracy.

By 2008, more than forty-three thousand nongovernmental organizations (NGOs) representing diverse agendas and interests (including social support for street children and advocacy on issues of domestic violence, corruption, and environment) had been registered. But many of these groups were either inactive or highly dependent on external funding. Analysis of Romanian civil society suggested concern regarding the potential negative impact of the termination of European funds after EU accession on the ability of NGOs to sustain themselves as proactive and self-sufficient.[68] However, it seems that this pessimistic view has been, in part, counteracted by new types of protest that have vigorously emerged since 2012. As Toma Burean and Gabriel Bădescu point out, "[T]he profile of protests in Romania witnessed a significant shift from workers strikes for higher wages and better jobs . . . to social movements in which young urban educated citizens mobilize with the help of social networks for issues that are linked to the quality of democracy."[69] For example, in January 2012, the protest against government attempts to introduce measures for the privatization of the health care system was transformed into a wider anti-political movement. The same year, civil society action against the Roşia Montana mining project led to the resignation of the government. This project, which was developed by a Canadian company in cooperation with a Romanian state-owned enterprise, involved the use of a technology that degraded much of a mountainous area in Transylvania and displaced one local community. Local and national environmental NGOs joined forces with transnational organizations including Greenpeace and Mining Watch.[70] These and the later 2015 large-scale protests "Corruption Kills" involved the participation of younger educated people who mobilized through social media like Facebook and Twitter. This new generation of protesters was an impressive presence in the aftermath of the 2016 parliamentary elections when the ruling PSD tried (yet again) to derail the reform of state institutions. The demonstrations extended over more than two months and gathered as many as five hundred thousand protesters throughout the country while also engaging Romanian expatriates from abroad. What is interesting about these protests is that they combined the symbolism of the December 1989 revolution (a Romanian flag with a hole in it cutting away the hammer and sickle) with novel forms of expression that illustrate the concerns of an entirely new generation who grew up after 1989. Slogans such as "We don't want to be a nation of slaves" or "We don't want to emigrate" seem to indicate a generational shift and a commitment to breaking with a corrupt state system that had not at all been eliminated in 1989.[71]

The current political crisis involving the political establishment in general and the ruling PSD in particular could only exacerbate further this social and generational polarization. It remains to be seen, however, whether in any foreseeable future these new forms of social movement will result in a new relationship between state and society and between political institutions and citizens.

Photo 14.3. The street sign reads, "Romania: That'll do." (Ian Barbu)

Foreign Policy

In foreign relations, Romania has become much more strongly oriented toward the West, especially after joining NATO in 2004 during the second wave of enlargement and the EU in 2007. As discussed earlier, accession was a difficult process because of concerns about corruption, the economy, and political reform. In fact, the Cooperation and Verification Mechanisms put in place by the EU after 2007 in order to monitor Romania and also Bulgaria for progress on reforming the justice system and tackling corruption is still utilized ten years after accession as a pressure mechanism. In the last five years, Brussels has exerted ongoing pressure on Romania to address these shortcomings and during the 2012 and early 2017 political crises has vigorously reacted to political attempts to derail the course of democratization.

As for Romania's contribution to NATO, the United States seized the opportunity early on during the Constantinescu presidency to press for a "strategic partnership" between Bucharest and Washington that was signed in 1997. Romania is the second largest country (after Poland) in Central and Eastern Europe, and its geographic location on the Black Sea gives it access to an increasingly significant Eurasian waterway. Moreover, the country's problematic history with Russia and its own desire to legitimize itself as a Western country committed it to such a military alliance with the United States. It participated substantially in multinational operations, for example in Afghanistan, Iraq, Libya, and Kosovo. In 2010, the Supreme Council of National Defense signed an agreement of participation for the development of a US ballistic antimissile system. This was followed a year later by the ratification of an agreement regarding its deployment in Romania. The agreement was implemented in May 2016 when a missile defense was established and activated in southern Romania in Deveselu. It cost $800 million. This became the sixth of several joint-use facilities such as the airbase at Mihail Kogălniceanu on the Black Sea that is currently used as a transit base for the US military. Although US officials have often reiterated that the Deveselu system is not targeted against Russia's strategic missile capabilities but is rather designed to protect against potential missile attacks from states such as Iran, Moscow has been quick to react. Officials from the Russian Ministry of Foreign Affairs claim that the Deveselu base is integral to NATO's attempt to contain Russia and simply raises the temperature further in an already overheated situation.[72]

But general anxiety over Romanian border security has become much more evident after 2012 when Russia annexed Crimea. The issue of Moldova's sovereignty reemerged and security was again questioned after Vladimir Putin supported Russian separatist actions in eastern Ukraine and potentially in Transnistria.[73] However, Romania is not alone in its concern for this geopolitical instability further to the east. A general feeling of insecurity is shared in most countries in the region, especially in the Baltic countries, Poland, the Czech Republic, Ukraine obviously, and some Balkan nations. In 2015, a meeting was held in Bucharest to discuss the possibility of a Central European Intermarium (an alliance of states from Central and southeast Europe that originated after World War I) to counteract Russian aggression. More recently, the new US president, Donald Trump, has questioned several times the viability and utility of NATO and this has further increased the feeling of uncertainty.[74] However, some countries in which more right-wing and pro-Moscow governments have been elected (including Hungary,

Moldova, Bulgaria, and Montenegro) could quite possibly switch their pro-NATO and EU allegiances.

Since 1989, relations with Moldova have been characterized not only by national-istic enthusiasm (chiefly used by politicians for electoral gain) but also by a degree of ambivalence among those Romanians primarily concerned with economic problems and their relationship with the EU. Nevertheless, both Băsescu and Iohannis have expressed support for Moldova's economic and cultural integration with the West. But relations were certainly strained after the election of the pro-Russian head of the Socialist Party, Igor Dodon, who won the presidency in the November 2016 elections on an anti-EU and pro-Moscow ticket. During the elections, he also claimed that Romania should respect the sovereignty of Moldova and accept that the two countries have distinctive histories and cultural identities. In fact, after his election, Dodon removed the EU flag from the presidential webpage, and replaced "Romanian language" with "Moldovan language" (although Moldovan is a Romanian dialect). He also revoked Băsescu's Moldovan citi-zenship, who was known for his pro-unification views only recently acquired before his election.[75] It still remains to be seen to what extent this rhetoric will impact relations between the two countries.

A positive outcome of EU integration has been improved relationships with Hungary, which had been tense throughout much of the communist period when Ceaușescu had encouraged the settlement of ethnic Romanians in Transylvania and a number of Hungarian cultural sites and villages were destroyed. But in 1996, the two signed an agreement affirming their interstate relations. However, some lingering questions over historical borders and ethnic minorities, which had from time to time been raised by nationalist politicians, were not completely resolved. By 2012, relations reached a new low when the use of the Szekler flag in the Hungarian-majority county of Covasna was challenged by the Romanian authorities. Early in 2017, Hungarian authorities expressed their desire to improve bilateral relations with Romania.[76] Ultimately, the future of this relationship as well as other major challenges in foreign affairs discussed above will, to a larger extent, be influenced by forthcoming developments in the EU and, of course, by the still uncertain relationship between the United States and Russia, and, as part of that, the United States and NATO. As Romania is scheduled to assume the rotating presidency of the EU in 2019, the country seems destined (as it was in the nineteenth century) to be caught between the competing interests of its neighbors and those of the world powers.

Current Issue and Future Challenges

Belonging to a Latin country surrounded by Slavic enclaves and historically situated at the crossroads between three competing empires—the Ottoman, Russian, and Hapsburg (later Austro-Hungarian) Empires—Romanians have always defined themselves as both victims of history and as a unique people. This sense of exceptionalism was amplified by its communist experience, especially during the last decade of Ceaușescu's regime, and after 1989 by its need to navigate between the sometimes-divergent foreign policies of Brussels and Washington. However, if we consider the territorial gains in 1918 and the immediate benefits following EU accession (in terms of both economic growth and labor mobility), Romanians should consider themselves as fortunate winners rather than losers. In fact, thanks to the EU and NATO, Romania has avoided the ethnic wars that ravaged Yugoslavia and now may threaten to break up Ukraine.

It is certainly true that postaccession has not led to a cleansing of the political class and its corrupt patrimonial state, but these problems have also manifested themselves in varying degrees throughout the region in the last decade. The end of the Washington neoliberal consensus, increased economic and social inequalities, the global economic crisis of 2008, and the recent refugee crisis in Europe have found fertile ground for right-wing populism, xenophobia and anti-EU ideologies, political parties, and other actors. In this current context, Romania faces common challenges as do its neighbors and all other European countries. It will be up to the society to challenge the still corrupt and unaccountable political establishment and very much up to its leaders to pursue smart and coherent diplomacy in an increasingly complex and volatile world. Given the country's recent social movements involving educated and liberal youth and a civic-oriented diaspora, we can look at this half-full side of the glass and hope for the best.

Study Questions

1. To what extent has Romania's precommunist and communist history influenced the post-1989 transition to democracy?
2. How do you explain Romania's violent revolutionary scenario in December 1989?
3. To what extent is Romanian politics of continuity comparable with the appearance of rupture and change?
4. Describe the similarities and differences between Romania and other postcommunist countries in East and Central Europe.
5. How would you assess Romania's future prospects in the EU and NATO?

Suggested Readings

Clark, Roland. *Holy Legionary Youth: Fascist Activism in Interwar Romania.* Ithaca and London, NY: Cornell University Press, 2015.

Deletant, Dennis. *Ceauşescu and the Securitate: Coercion and Dissent in Romania, 1965–1989.* London: Hurst, 1995.

Gallagher, Tom. *Modern Romania: The End of Communism, the Failure of Democratic Reform, and the Theft of a Nation.* New York: NYU Press, 2008.

Georgescu, Vlad. *The Romanians: A History,* edited by Matei Călinescu. Columbus: Ohio State University Press, 1991

King, Charles. The Moldovans: Romania, Russia and the Politics of Culture. Stanford, CA: Hoover Institution Press, 2000.

King, Ronald. F., and Paul E. Sum eds. *Romania under Băsescu: Aspirations, Achievements, and Frustrations during His First Presidential Term.* Plymouth, UK: Lexington Books, 2011.

Kligman, Gail. *The Politics of Duplicity: Controlling Reproduction in Ceauşescu's Romania.* Berkeley: University of California Press, 1998.

Kligman, Gail, and Katherine Verdery *Peasants under Siege: The Collectivization of Romanian Agriculture, 1949–1962.* Princeton, NJ: Princeton University Press, 2011.

Livezeanu, Irina. *Cultural Politics in Greater Romania: Regionalism, Nation Building & Ethnic Struggle, 1918–1930*. Ithaca, NY, and London: Cornell University Press, 1995.

Siani-Davies, Peter. *The Romanian Revolution of 1989*. Ithaca, NY: Cornell University Press, 2005.

Stan, Lavinia. *Transitional Justice in Post-Communist Romania: The Politics of Memory*. Cambridge: Cambridge University Press, 2013.

Stan, Lavinia, and Diane Vancea, eds. *Post-Communist Romania at 25: Linking Past, Present and Future*. Lanham, MD: Lexington Books, 2015.

Tismăneanu, Vladimir. *Stalinism for All Seasons: A Political History of Communism*. Berkeley: University of California Press, 2003.

Verdery, Katherine. *The Vanishing Hectare: Property and Value in Postsocialist Transylvania*. Ithaca, NY: Cornell University Press, 2003.

Notes

I would like to acknowledge the chapter authored by Charles King and John Gledhill in a previous edition of this volume as a model. However, this present chapter was significantly expanded and revised from the earlier version.

1. See Neagu Djuvara, *A Brief Illustrated History of Romanians* (Bucharest: Humanitas, 2014).

2. See Vlad Gerorgescu, *The Romanians: A History*, ed. Matei Călinescu (Columbus: Ohio State University Press, 1991); and Irina Livezeanu, *Cultural Politics in Greater Romania* (Ithaca, NY: Cornell University Press, 1995).

3. After the Cyrillic script was replaced by the Latin alphabet in 1863, the Romanian language became instrumental in the construction of national identity.

4. See Georgescu, *The Romanians*, 189–90.

5. See Roland Clark, *Holy Legionary Youth: Fascist Activism in Interwar Romania* (Ithaca, NY, and London: Cornell University Press, 2015).

6. For the controversies regarding the Holocaust, see Irina Livezeanu, "The Romanian Holocaust: Family Quarrels," *East European Politics and Societies* 16, no. 3(2003): 934–47; and Michael Shafir, "Memory, Memorials, and Membership," in *Romania since 1989: Politics, Economy and Society*, ed. Henry F. Carey (Lanham, MD: Lexington Books, 2004).

7. See Radu Ioanid, *The Holocaust in Romania* (Chicago, IL: Ivan Dee, 2000).

8. See Gail Kligman and Katherine Verdery, *Peasants under Siege: The Collectivization of Romanian Agriculture, 1949–1962* (Princeton, NJ: Princeton University Press, 2011).

9. See Dennis Deletant, *Communist Terror in Romania: Gheorghiu-Dej and the Police State, 1948–1965* (London: Hurst, 1999).

10. See Stelian Tănase, *Elite și Societate: Guvernarea Gheorghe Gheorghiu-Dej, 1948–1965* (Bucharest: Humanitas, 1998).

11. For an overview of Romanian communism see Vladimir Tismăneanu, *Stalinism for All Seasons: A Political History of Communism* (Berkeley: University of California Press, 2003); and Dennis Deletant, *Romania under Communist Rule* (Iași, Romania: Center for European Studies, 1999).

12. For Romania under Ceaușescu see Michael Shafir, *Romania: Politics, Economics and Society: Political Stagnation and Simulated Change* (Boulder, CO: Lynne Rienner, 1985); and Katherine Verdery, *Identity and Cultural Politics in Ceaușescu's Romania* (Berkeley: University of California Press, 1991).

13. For the secret police under Ceaușescu see Dennis Deletant, *Ceaușescu and the Securitate: Coercion and Dissent in Romania, 1965–1989* (London: Hurst, 1995).

14. See Vlad Georgescu, "Romania in the 1980s: The Legacy of Dynastic Socialism," *East European Politics and Societies* 2, no. 1 (1987); and Tismăneanu, *Stalinism for All Seasons*.

15. See Gail Kligman, "Political Demography: The Banning of Abortion in Ceauşescu's Romania," in *Conceiving the New World Order: The Global Politics of Reproduction*, eds. Faye Ginsberg and Rayna Rapp (Berkeley: University of California Press, 1995), 234–55.

16. See John Elster, ed., *The Roundtable Talks and the Breakdown of Communism* (Chicago, IL: University of Chicago Press, 1996).

17. See Peter Siani-Davies, *The Romanian Revolution of 1989* (Ithaca and Cornell, NY: Cornell University Press, 2005).

18. On the early postrevolutionary years, see Vladimir Tismăneanu and Matei Călinescu, "The 1989 Revolution and Romania's Future," *Problems of Communism* 40, no. 1 (January–April 1991):42–59; and Daniel Nelson, ed., *Romania after Tyranny* (Boulder, CO: Westview Press, 1992).

19. For how the events of 1989 are remembered in Romania see Bogdan Murgescu, ed., *Revoluţia Română din Decembrie 1989: Istorie şi Memorie* (Iaşi: Polirom, 2007); see also the well-acclaimed movie directed by Corneliu Porumboiu, *12:08 East of Bucharest*, 2006.

20. See Tismăneanu and Călinescu, "The 1989 Revolution and Romania's Future."

21. For Corneliu Coposu, see Tudor Călin Zarojanu, *Viaţa lui Corneliu Coposu* (Bucharest: Editura Maşina de Scris, 2005).

22. Quoted in Georgeta Pourchot, "Mass Media and Democracy in Romania: Lessons from the Past, Prospects for the Future," in *Romania in Transition*, ed. Lavinia Stan (Aldershot, UK: Dartmouth, 1997), 70.

23. For an account of these events (*mineriadă*), see Mihnea Berindei, Ariadna Combeş, and Anne Planche, *Mineriada: 13–15 iunie 1990. Realitatea unei Puteri Neocomuniste* (Bucharest: Humanitas, 2010).

24. See Dinu Pietraru, *Romania: The Stolen Constitution* (New York: New School for Social Research, 1996), unpublished dissertation.

25. See Lavinia Stan and Diane Vancea, "House of Cards: The Presidency from Iliescu to Băsescu," in *Post-Communist Romania at 25: Linking Past, Present and Future*, eds. Lavinia Stan and Diane Vancea (Lanham, MD: Lexington Books, 2015), 193–218.

26. See Dimitris Papadimitriou and David Phinnemore, *Romania and the European Union: From Marginalization to Membership* (London and New York: Routledge Press, 2008), 81.

27. See Vladimir Pasti, *The Challenge of Transition* (Boulder, CO: East European Monographs, 1997).

28. Sorina Soare, "La construction du systéme partisan roumain entre sorties et entrées imprévues," *Studia politică* 4, no. 1 (2004): 92.

29. See Michael Shafir, "The Greater Romania Party and the 2000 Elections in Romania: A Retrospective Analysis," *RFE/RL East European Perspectives* (August 22, 2001).

30. See Dan Pavel and Iulia Huiu, *Nu Putem Reuşi decît Împreună: O Istorie Analitică a Convenţiei Democratice* (Bucharest: Polirom, 2003).

31. For the 2000 elections, see Monica Ciobanu, "Problems of Democratic Consolidation in Eastern Europe: The Case of Romania in Comparative Perspective," *RFE/RL East European Perspectives* (August 16 and 17, 2003), 5; for the PRM and the 2000 elections, see Michael Shafir, "The Greater Romania Party and the 2000 Elections in Romania. A Retrospective Analysis," *RFE/RL/East European Perspectives* 3, nos. 15, 16 (2001).

32. See Tom Gallagher, *Theft of a Nation: Romania since Communism* (London: Hurst, 2005).

33. See Monica Ciobanu, "Romanian's Travails with Democracy and Accession to the European Union," *Europe-Asia Studies* 58, no. 8 (December 2007):1429–50.

34. For the 2004 elections, see Monica Ciobanu and Michael Shafir, "2004 Romanian Elections: A Test for Democratic Consolidation?" *RFE/RL/East European Perspectives* 7, no. 3 (April 2005).

35. Peter Gross and Vladimir Tismăneanu, "The End of Postcommunism in Romania," *Journal of Democracy* 16, no. 2 (April 2005):146–62.

36. For the final version of the report, see Vladimir Tismăneanu, Dorin Dobrincu, Cristian Vasile, eds., *Raport Final: Comisia Prezidenţială pentru Analiza Dictaturii Comuniste din România* (Bucharest: Humanitas, 2007).

37. Ronald F. King and Paul E. Sum, "Introduction: Triage Democratization," in *Romania under Băsescu: Aspirations, Achievements, and Frustrations during His First Presidential Term*, eds. Ronald F. King and Paul E. Sum (Plymouth, UK: Lexington Books, 2011), 7.

38. See Lavinia Stan and Diane Vancea, "Old Wine in New Bottles: The Romanian Elections of 2008," *Problems of Post-Communism* 56, no. 5 (2009): 47–61.

39. See Dan Bilefski, "Romania's President Survives Ouster Bid in Low-Turnout Vote," *New York Times*, July 30, 2012.

40. See Tom Gallagher, "Unsocial Democrats: The PSDs Negative Role in Romanian Democracy," in *Post-Communist Romania at 25*, eds. Lavinia Stan and Diane Vancea, 171–91.

41. For the 2014 presidential elections, see Sergiu Gherghina, "The Romanian Presidential Elections, November 2014," *Electoral Studies* 38 (2015):109–315.

42. See Gallagher, "Unsocial Democrats," 183–85.

43. See "De ce a cistigat PSD? Explicatiile lui Cristian Tudor Popescu," December 11, 2016, available at www.digi24/ro/stiri/actualitate/politica/alegeri-parlamentare-2014-de-ce-a-cistigat-psd-explicatia-lui-cristian-tudor-popescu, accessed on April 21, 2017; and Cristian Preda, "De ce a cistigat PSD maimult ca niciodata," 22, December 12, 2016, available at revista22online.ro/70258801/de-ce-a-castigat-psd-mai-mult-ca-niciodata.html (accessed April 19, 2017).

44. See Luciana-Alexandra Ghica, "A Not So Fresh Chapter of a Tragi-Dramedy Unfolding: Newly Appointed Romanian Government Faces Old Scandals," *Party Systems & Government Observatory*, January 6, 2016, available at https://whogoverns.eu/a-not-so-fresh-chapter-of-a-tragi-dramedy-unfolding-newly-appointed (accessed April 7, 2017).

45. See "Romanian Protesters Call for Government to Go," *Transitions Online*, February 13, 2017, available at http://www.tol.org/client/article/26695-romanian-protesters-call-for-government-to-go.htm (accessed February, 14, 2017); and Raluca Abăseacă, "Resist: Citizens Are Back on the Streets in Romania," available at https://www.opendemocracy.net/can-europe-make-it/raluca-ab-seac/rezist-citizens-arre-back (accessed March 9, 2017).

46. See "Eight Things You Should Know about Romania's New Prime Minister," *Euronews*, June 27, 2017, available at www.euronews.com/2017/06/27/eight-things-you-should-know-about-romanias-new-prime-minister (accessed July 13, 2017).

47. See Document of the World Bank, Report no. 84830-RO, "Country Partnership Strategy (CPS) for Romania for the Period 2014–2017," April 28, 2014, available at www.documents.worldbank.org/curated/en/801961468096541262/pdf (accessed April 27, 2017).

48. See European Commission, Commission Staff Working Document, "Country Report Romania 2017," Brussels, 22.2.2017, SWD (2017) 88 final, available at www.ec.europa.eu/info/sites/info/files/2017-european-semeter-country-report-romania-en.pdf (accessed April 26, 2017).

49. See IMF World Economic Outlook (October 2016), February 27, 2017, available at www.statisticstime.com/economy/european-country-by-gdp.per-capita-php (accessed April 27, 2017).

50. See Institutul Naţional de Statistică, available at www.insse.ro/cms/sites/default/files/field/publicatii/populatia-romaniei-dupa-domiciliu-la-1-iul-2016-v.pdf (accessed April 28, 2017); also Rodica Milena Zaharia, ed., *Relaţia dintre fenomenul migraţiei legale şi piaţa muncii din România* (Bucharest: Institutul European din România, 2016).

51. See Wally Bacon, "Economic Reform," in *Romania since 1989: Politics, Economics and Society*, ed. Henry F. Carey (Lanham, MD: Lexington Books, 2004), 376.

52. Dumitru Sandu, *Spaţiul Social al Tranziţiei* (Iaşi: Polirom, 1999).

53. Organisation for Economic Co-operation and Development, *OECD Economic Surveys 1997–1998: Romania* (Paris: OECD, 1998), 22.

54. Economist Intelligence Unit (EIU), *Romania: Country Profile 2009* (London: The Economist Intelligence Unit), 17, 20.

55. World Bank Country Memorandum, *Romania: Restructuring for EU Integration—The Policy Agenda* (Washington, DC: World Bank, June 2004), 6.

56. EIU, *Romania*, 17.

57. "Five Years under Economic Crisis. What Happened to the Romanian Economy during This Time," *Antena 3*, September 18, 2013, available at www.antena3.ro/en/romania/five-years-under-economic-crisis (accessed April 28, 2017).

58. See Document of the World Bank Report, "Country Partnership Strategy (CPS) for Romania for the Period 2014–2017."

59. For the latest report on Romania, see European Commission, Brussels, 25.1.2017, COM (2017) 44 final, "Report from the Commission to the European Parliament and the Council," available at www.ec.europe.en/info/sites/info/files/com-2017-44_en1.pdf(accessed April 29, 2017).

60. See www.transparency.org.news/feature/corruption_perceptions_index_2016#table (accessed April 29, 2017).

61. For a cultural argument, see Alina Mungiu-Pippidi, "Crime and Corruption after Communism: Breaking Free at Last, Tales of Corruption from the Post-Communist Balkans," *East European Constitutional Review* 6, no. 4 (Fall 1997); for the most recent public perceptions, see Palko Ranesz, "In Romania, Corruption's Tentacles Grip Daily Life," *New York Times*, February 9, 2017, available at www.nytimes.com/2017/02/09/world/europe/romania-corruption-coruptie-guvern-justitie.html (accessed April 29, 2017).

62. See Ministerul Public, Direcţia Naţională Anticorupţie, "Raport de Activitate 2016," available at www.pna.ro/object2.jsp?id=285(accessed April 22, 2017).

63. See www.romaniacurata.ro/harta-coruptiei/?=despre(accessed April 29, 2017).

64. See "Bringing in the Scalps: The Woman Leading War on Corruption," *The Guardian*, November 5, 2015, available at www.theguardian.com/world/2015/nov/04/woman-leading-war-on-corruption-romania (accessed April 29, 2017).

65. See Cristina Petrescu, *From Robin Hood to Don Quixote: Resistance and Dissent in Communist Romania* (Bucharest: Editura Enciclopedică, 2013).

66. For the politics of memory after 1989, see Lavinia Stan, *Transitional Justice in Post-Communist Romania: The Politics of Memory* (Cambridge: Cambridge University Press, 2013).

67. See Thomas J. Keil and Jacqueline J. Neil, "The State and Labor Conflict in Postrevolutionary Romania," *Radical History Review* 82 (2002): 9–36.

68. See Paul E. Sum, "Civil Society under Băsescu: Continuity, Change, and Sustainability," in *Romania under Băsescu*, eds. King and Sum, 181–202.

69. See Toma Burean and Gabriel Badescu, "Voices of Discontent: Student Protest Participation," *Communist and Post-Communist Studies* 47 (2014): 385.

70. See Lucian Vesalon and Remus Creţan, "<Cyanide kills!> Environmental Movements and the Construction of Environmental Risk at Roşia Montană, Romania," *Area* 45, no. 5 (2013): 443–51.

71. See endnote 45 and also Anna Adi and Darren G., Lilleker, *# Resist-Romania's 2017 Anti-Corruption Protests: Causes, Development and Implications* (Berlin: Quadriga University of Applied Sciences, 2017).

72. See Diana Robu, "Moment istoric la Deveselu: Scutul antirachea e operational, Rusia se simte amenintata," May 12, 2016, available at www.ziare.com/stiru/antirachetistorica/moment-istoric-se-inaugureaza-scutul-antiracheta-de-la-deveselu-1421482 (accessed on May 5, 2017); also, for Romania's foreign policy, see Romanian Ministry of Foreign Affairs, *Key Policy Area*, available at www.mae/ro/en/taxonomy/term/558/2 (accessed May 5, 2017).

73. On the history of the Moldovan question, see Charles King, *The Moldovans: Romania, Russia and the Politics of Culture* (Stanford, CA: Hoover Institution Press, 2000).

74. See Linda Kinstler, "What Trump Means for Central and Eastern Europe," *The Atlantic*, November 28, 2016, available at www.theatlantic.com/internaitonal/archive/2016/11/trump-putin-nato (accessed May 5, 2017).

75. See "Razboiul rece al lui Dodon cu Romania," January 13, 2017, available at www.ziare.com/igor-dodon/presedinte-republica-moldova-razboiul-rece-al-lui-dodon-cu-romania-144970 (accessed May 5, 2017).

76. See "Nemeth Zsolt despre relatiile romano-ungare: Ultimii cinci ani au decurs in ger; Ungaria doreste redeschiderea lor," April 22, 2017, available at www.agerpres.ro/politica/2017/22/nemeth-zsolt-despre-relatiile-romano-ungare (accessed May 5, 2017).

Map 15.0. Albania

CHAPTER 15

Albania

AT A DEMOCRATIC CROSSROAD

Elez Biberaj

Since the demise of its communist regime in the early 1990s, Albania has undergone a profound political, economic, and social transformation. It has held nine parliamentary elections, with power alternating between major political parties. Democratic norms have largely been embraced, democracy is widely seen as the ideal political system, and the protection of human rights and the separation of powers are enshrined in the constitution. The implementation of reforms has resulted in solid economic growth rates, major infrastructure improvements, and a reduction in poverty. Albania has also witnessed the emergence of diverse and dynamic media outlets. While the level of civic engagement is not very high, civil society is gaining prominence in shaping national debate and, in some cases, impacting government policy decisions.

Albania's foreign policy positions have been broadly consistent with key US and European Union (EU) interests in the Balkans and further afar. With its strategic partnership with the United States, membership in NATO, and, since 2014, as a candidate for EU membership, Albania is clearly anchored in the West. Albanians have accepted the narrative that emphasizes their nation's historical connections to European, democratic values. Albania has emerged as a strong proponent of Balkan cooperation and reconciliation, and its regional salience has increased significantly.

Domestically, after a series of contested elections and postelection disputes that resulted in political gridlock and set the tiny southeast European country apart from its neighbors, Albania conducted parliamentary elections in June 2017, whose results were certified by domestic and international observers and accepted by the major players. The Socialist Party won a second mandate, securing 74 of the 140 assembly seats. The landslide victory will give Prime Minister Edi Rama the ability to accelerate the implementation of comprehensive economic, political, and judicial reforms that are expected to overhaul an entrenched and corrupt justice system, jumpstart the economy, and pave the way for the opening of accession talks with the EU.

But despite these significant gains, Albania faces daunting social and economic challenges, and much about the quality of its democracy is tentative and fragile. Freedom House rates Albania as partly free.[1] More than any other country in southeastern Europe, Albania suffers from weak governance, ineffective institutions, and a failure to fully embrace the rule of law, and its shift to democracy has been slow and more challenging.

It is part of the cluster of former communist countries that are beset by democratic deficits and classified as "hybrid regimes."[2] While rated higher on democracy indices than authoritarian regimes, such as those of Russia and other former Soviet republics, Albania is characterized by semidemocratic political arrangements and superficial checks and balances. If Albania is to fully achieve its democratic potential, its leaders will have to take decisive measures to create an inclusive political process, establish the rule of law, and ensure effective and accountable governance.

Political Background

Albania's overriding objective historically has been to preserve its independence and territorial integrity from its more powerful neighbors. Although one of the most ethnically homogeneous countries in the region, it has long lacked national cohesion. Its political development has been obstructed by regional, tribal, and religious differences. At several points in its troubled history and as recently as 1997, it came close to being classified as a "failed state." Albania had a short-lived experiment with a multiparty system in the 1920s. But virtually all of its history has been one of repressive governments that were not responsive to the needs of the population and displayed little sense of accountability or transparency.

Albanians, the descendants of the Illyrians, are considered the oldest inhabitants of the Balkans. Albania has a long history of invasions, foreign occupation, and territorial losses, and Albanian nationalism is steeped in a deep sense of injustice. Turks overran the country in 1478, following the death of Gjergj Kastriot Skenderbeu, the leader of a twenty-five-year resistance to the Ottomans. For the next five centuries, the country remained under Ottoman occupation. And in the seventeenth century, the majority of Albania's population converted to Islam. Albania gained its independence in 1912 during the Balkan wars. When the international community recognized its independence in 1913, some 40 percent of the Albanian-speaking population and half of its territory, including Kosovo and Çameria, remained outside its borders. Since then, Albania has been unique because more Albanians lived outside its borders than inside, and Albanian-speaking populations border Albania on almost all sides. This mismatch between state and national/ethnic borders severely hindered the country's political and economic development and complicated its ties with its neighbors. After the country gained its independence, Albanian politics was dominated by forces and parties whose main objectives were focused on its sovereignty and independence and on regaining Kosovo. The internal organization of the Albanian polity was far less clear. Western political ideas were slow to penetrate, as few Albanians had been educated in the West. The country also lacked a well-developed middle class imbued with democratic ideals, and most of the emerging political, cultural, and military elites had been educated in Turkey rather than in the more democratic societies of Western Europe. The semifeudal Albanian society was characterized by widespread authoritarian tendencies.

In the early 1920s, Albania witnessed the emergence of several parties, the most important of which were the People's Party, led by Fan S. Noli, a Harvard-educated Orthodox clergyman, and the Progressive Party, led by Ahmet Zogu, a chieftain from central Albania. This experiment with a multiparty system was short-lived. The country's main forces could not agree on much. After a period of political instability, Ahmet Zogu took power by force in December 1924. After restoring order and eliminating his political enemies, Zogu in 1928 declared himself king. His exact title was "King of the Albanians," making it clear that Albania had not given up on liberating Kosovo. The king instituted significant social, political, and economic changes and laid the foundations of a modern state. His rule was interrupted in April 1939 when Italy invaded Albania. For the next six years, Albania remained under Italian and/or German rule.[3]

Communist Experience and Transition to Democracy

Albania's communist history was unique: the state was ruled by one of the most repressive, Stalinist leaders for a longer period than any other Central or East European country.[4] The main pillars of Enver Hoxha's regime were the military and the secret police, the Sigurimi. Through a continuous reign of terror and purges, Hoxha's regime succeeded in eliminating all traces of open opposition to its rule.[5] Purges eventually extended to the top echelons of the Communist Party, leading to the demise of even its most prominent leaders, including in 1981 Mehmet Shehu, who had been prime minister for three decades. Hoxha also skillfully exploited disagreements within the communist bloc to consolidate his power and ensure the survival of his regime. He first allied Albania with Yugoslavia. He then took advantage of Josip Broz Tito's break with Joseph Stalin to align himself with Moscow. When Soviet leader Nikita Khrushchev's de-Stalinization policy in the middle to late 1950s threatened his tenure in office, he switched alliances and sided with Mao Zedong's China, at the time the most dogmatic communist regime. And finally, when China moved toward a rapprochement with the United States, Tirana broke with Beijing and embarked on a policy of self-reliance. This move had very serious repercussions for the country's political and economic development. Private property was abolished, and the country was prohibited by law from seeking foreign assistance, including loans and credits.

As most other communist countries experimented with economic and political reforms, Albania became progressively more repressive and isolated. In the late 1960s, Hoxha launched his own version of the Chinese Cultural Revolution to extend the Communist Party's control over all aspects of life and to eliminate any center of potential power that could threaten its primacy. All religious institutions were closed down, and Albania became the world's first official atheist state. Many mosques and churches, some dating back centuries, were destroyed. Imams and priests were imprisoned or executed. The intelligentsia, long distrusted by Hoxha, came under severe attack. Prominent intellectuals were chastised for ideological deformations. Intellectuals also were ordered to live in the countryside for extended periods. The party launched a well-coordinated campaign for the emancipation of women. By the mid-1980s, women had made significant strides in securing equal social and political rights and held important posts in the party and the government. Whereas the trend in most other socialist countries was toward increased liberalization and a decrease in the party's tight grip on society, in Albania the opposite occurred. By the time Ramiz Alia became party leader following Hoxha's death in April 1985, Albania faced a serious economic crisis and a dispirited and apathetic population.

Alia had been among the youngest members of the postwar communist elite. He skillfully survived Hoxha's violent purges. From the very beginning of his reign in 1985, he came under pressure from both the conservative and the more liberal elements of the party. In an attempt to institute some changes in the country's highly centralized economic system, he loosened the party's grip on the cultural sector and took measures to end Albania's international isolation. At the same time, he was determined to preserve the party's leading role. This process of controlled reforms could not keep up with internal demands for changes, fueled by the end of the 1980s by a seriously deteriorating economic situation and the revolutions in other Central and East European countries.

Albania was the last communist domino to fall. In December 1990, a year after the downfall of Romania's regime, Alia's government was forced to sanction the creation of noncommunist political parties. The Communist Party won the first multiparty elections in March 1991. Alia was elected to a five-year term as president, and a new government was formed, led by Prime Minister Fatos Nano, a thirty-nine-year-old economist. Nano's government, however, was short-lived. He was forced to resign in June 1991, paving the way for the creation of a broad coalition government dominated by noncommunists. Early elections were held in March 1992, and the opposition Democratic Party won an overwhelming victory, capturing 92 seats in the 140-seat parliament. Alia then resigned as president and was succeeded by the Democratic Party's leader, Sali Berisha.

Political Institutions

Immediately following the demise of the communist regime in 1990 and 1991, the newly created Democratic Party and other opposition forces pushed for a radical transformation of the country's political institutions, demanding a modern, democratic constitution. The communists, who held the necessary two-thirds majority in parliament, tried to preserve as much as possible of the old order. However, under strong pressure from the opposition and the international community, they were forced to compromise. The parliament rejected a draft constitution submitted by Alia that retained many of the features of the 1976 constitution and granted substantial powers to the president. Instead, it approved the Law on the Main Constitutional Provisions. The constitutional law endorsed political pluralism and a multiparty system and guaranteed human rights. The document defined Albania as a parliamentary republic and limited the powers of the country's president.

Following the Democratic Party's landslide victory in the March 1992 elections, the Law on the Main Constitutional Provisions was completely revamped, and a new constitutional order was created with checks and balances, safeguards for fundamental rights and freedoms, and judicial review. The democrats argued that the new president needed expanded powers to deal with the serious problems facing Albania. The parliament thus amended the April 1991 law, granting extensive powers to the presidency. Although Albania was defined as a parliamentary republic, the constitutional provisions granted the president broad authority, including the capacity to appoint the prime minister and, from his nominations, other members of the cabinet. The document also granted the president the power, after consultations with the prime minister and speaker of the parliament, to dissolve the legislature if it was unable to exercise its own functions. While the prime minister was granted a leading role in the government, the president was empowered, in special instances, to chair meetings of the Council of Ministers and to set the agenda. The parliament was vested with substantial powers, including electing the president, determining the basic orientation of the country's domestic and foreign policy, and approving the government's programs.

The 1991 Law on the Main Constitutional Provisions had not contained separate chapters on the judiciary and the protection of fundamental human rights. So, in April 1992, the parliament adopted a chapter on the organization of the judiciary and the Constitutional Court, which provided for judicial independence and created a bipartite system, composed of the regular court system headed by a Supreme Court and a separate Constitutional Court. A year later, the parliament adopted the Charter on Fundamental Human Rights and Freedoms, which contained guarantees of the freedoms of speech, religion, conscience, press, assembly, and association, as well as assurances on the due process of law.

The unicameral People's Assembly consists of 140 deputies who serve a four-year term. The parliament is the highest institution. It elects the president, the prime minister, and members of cabinet. The most recent constitution was adopted by a national referendum in 1998 and was amended in 2008. The president is the head of state and serves a five-year term. Initially, the president was to be elected by a three-fifths vote. Amendments approved in 2008 stipulate that the president is selected by a simple majority of votes if, in the first three rounds of voting, a candidate cannot secure a three-fifths majority. Although the presidency is largely ceremonial, the constitution does make the president the commander in chief of the armed forces and chairman of the National Security Commission.

Albania's postcommunist justice system was similar to that of other European countries and consisted of a Constitutional Court, a Supreme Court, and appeals and district courts. The president appointed, with the consent of the parliament, the nine members of the Constitutional Court, which interprets the constitution, determines the constitutionality of laws, and resolves disputes between different branches of government and between national and local authorities. The Supreme Court, the country's highest court of appeal, was composed of eleven members appointed by the president with the consent of parliament. The judicial system was overseen by a fifteen-member High Council of Justice chaired by the president.

In July 2016, after intense US and EU pressure, the parliament passed a comprehensive package of constitutional amendments aimed at fundamentally reforming the justice system. The package, and the related legislation enacted subsequently, included the restructuring of the High Council of Justice; the establishment of a special prosecutor's office and special courts to tackle corruption, organized crime, and crimes by high-level officials; and a vetting body that will reevaluate the backgrounds and assets of all currently serving judges, prosecutors, and legal advisors. The High Council of Justice was replaced by a High Judicial Council, composed of eleven members—six judges appointed by their peers and five lay members elected by parliament. While the president had chaired the High Council of Justice, the chair of the High Judicial Council will be elected from among its lay members, thus making the council less prone to political influence. A High

Prosecutorial Council, also composed of eleven members, will propose to parliament the candidate for the position of general prosecutor and will have the responsibility to take disciplinary actions against corrupt and inefficient prosecutors.[6]

Although the constitutional provisions provided for a parliamentary republic, during Berisha's tenure as president (1992–1997), Albania developed a hybrid presidential-parliamentary system. Not unlike his counterparts in other transitional countries, such as Russia's Boris Yeltsin and Poland's Lech Wałęsa, the Albanian president amassed enormous powers, exercised broad decision-making powers, and eclipsed the prime minister and the cabinet.

The 1991 constitutional law was intended to be in force for a limited period until a new constitution was promulgated. However, strong disagreements between the ruling Democratic Party and the opposition Socialist Party, the successor to the Communist Party, on the institutional alternatives and the specific powers of each branch of government prevented the adoption of a new constitution. The democrats argued that Albania needed strong executive leadership. The socialists, on the other hand, advocated reducing the president's powers, essentially confining the head of state to a merely ceremonial role. In an attempt to break the constitutional deadlock, Berisha bypassed the parliament and submitted a draft constitution to a national referendum in November 1994. His efforts failed, as Albanian voters rejected the draft. He then resigned as president after the socialists won the June 1997 elections held in the wake of popular unrest sparked by the collapse of pyramid schemes. In 1998, the socialist-controlled parliament adopted a new constitution, which apportioned the largest share of political power to the prime minister and the cabinet.[7]

Berisha's successor, Rexhep Meidani, served during very challenging times as Albania was engulfed in widespread civil unrest, the Democratic Party's boycott of institutions, and the 1999 war in Kosovo. Because Meidani was so closely associated with the Socialist Party and faced with the hostility and unwillingness of Berisha to work with him, he was never able to play the role of a unifying figure. By the end of his tenure, he did not have sufficient support within his own Socialist Party to run for a second term. After his plans to become president failed, Socialist Party chairman Fatos Nano, in a rare example of cooperation between the ruling party and the opposition, agreed to a compromise candidate proposed by Berisha, Alfred Moisiu, who was elected president on June 24, 2002. A career military man and the son of famous World War II commander Spiro Moisiu, he had held senior positions in the communist regime but was supported by the Democratic Party from the very beginning. In the early 1990s, he served as deputy defense minister and subsequently headed the North Atlantic Association that promoted Albania's membership in NATO.

Following the Democratic Party's return to power in 2005, Moisiu clashed repeatedly with Prime Minister Berisha. He vetoed several laws approved by the parliament and, in October 2006, rejected the legislature's recommendation to dismiss Prosecutor General Theodhori Sollaku, whom the democrats accused of having failed to prosecute high-profile corruption cases and of having links with criminal groups. This step led to a dysfunctional relationship with Berisha, the speaker of the parliament Josefina Topalli, and other Democratic Party officials.[8]

As the end of Moisiu's tenure approached in July 2007, the ruling Democratic Party and the opposition Socialist Party engaged in a prolonged and tense political struggle over the next presidential election. It had been widely believed that Berisha and Nano had reached an understanding in 2002 that, since the democrats had proposed Moisiu for president, the socialists would select his successor. Following his resignation as chairman of the Socialist Party when Berisha won in the 2005 election, Nano openly campaigned for president. Berisha sought to work with the opposition to find a consensus candidate but, in return, demanded that the socialists support the dismissal of Prosecutor General Sollaku. Edi Rama, Nano's successor as Socialist Party chairman, was interested neither in supporting Nano's candidacy for president nor in working with Berisha on finding a consensus candidate. Emboldened by his party's good showing in the local elections in February 2007, Rama wanted to block the election of the president—the democrats lacked the necessary eighty-four votes to elect their own candidate—and force the country to hold early parliamentary elections.

Having failed in his efforts to find a compromise with the socialists, Berisha named Bamir Topi as the Democratic Party's candidate for president. Topi, the number two person in the Democratic Party and leader of the party's parliamentary group, was a surprise choice because he was seen as too important for a ceremonial post. After three rounds of voting, when it appeared that parliament would not be able to elect the president and there would have to be new elections, Nano, disappointed that Rama did not support his bid to become president, convinced six of his supporters in parliament to vote for Topi. The fifty-year-old Topi had been elected to parliament in 1996 and served as minister of agriculture in 1996 and 1997. He developed a good reputation as a moderate and was able to represent the Democratic Party successfully in difficult negotiations with the socialists. Topi's election averted the potential crisis of early elections and was a major boost for the governing coalition.

In early 2008, parliament, on the basis of a consensus reached by the democrats and socialists, approved a package of reforms including important constitutional changes in the way the president was elected, the establishment of a system of proportional representation based on regions for electing members of parliament, and limiting the prosecutor general to a fixed five-year term of office instead of an unlimited one.[9] While the two big parties hailed the constitutional changes, small parties were fiercely critical, arguing that the new rules would make it very difficult for them to win national representation. President Topi, who evidently had not been consulted by his own party, was also strongly critical of the new measures. He showed his displeasure by vetoing several laws passed by parliament. As a result, his relations with the democrats were severely strained.

In June 2012, Bujar Nishani, a close Berisha ally, was elected president. The international community had exerted considerable pressure on both sides to elect a consensus candidate. However, Rama refused to propose a candidate or endorse the nomination of Xhezair Zaganjori, a respected member of the Constitutional Court. Nishani was elected with a simple majority in the fourth round of voting. A founding member of the Democratic Party, Nishani had held senior positions in Berisha's cabinet, first as minister of justice and then as minister of internal affairs. The socialists criticized Nishani's election, claiming that he was too closely associated with the democrats to play the role of a nonpartisan head of state. Following the socialists' landslide victory in June 2013, Prime Minister Rama made every effort to marginalize Nishani.[10] The president came under increased criticism, with senior government officials maintaining limited contacts with him.

In April 2017, in an unexpected move and with the democrats boycotting parliament, the two coalition partners, the Socialist Party and the Socialist Movement for Integration

Photo 15.1. Current Albanian president Ilir Meta elected in 2017, after serving as prime minister from 1999 to 2002. Also chairman of the parliament from 2013 to 2017. (Institution of the President of the Republic of Albania)

(SMI), elected Ilir Meta, chairman of the SMI and speaker of parliament, as the country's seventh president since the collapse of the communist regime. He resigned as chairman of his party and was replaced by his wife Monika Kryemadhi. Meta's election came at a time of increased tensions within the governing coalition, as the SMI had publicly clashed with Rama on important issues, including the approval of judicial reforms. Rama's endorsement of Meta's election masked what had become a tumultuous relationship. The prime minister had become increasingly disenchanted with Meta's hesitation to renew their coalition and the latter's flirting with the democrats. There was a widespread belief that Rama offered Meta the ceremonial post of the president in an effort to remove him from the active political scene. Born in 1969, Meta participated in the student demonstrations that led to the collapse of the communist regime in 1990. He soon joined the youth wing of the Socialist Party and was elected to parliament in 1992. An ambitious politician, he moved rapidly to the top ranks of the party, becoming prime minister in 1999 and then again after the 2001 parliamentary elections. His career as prime minister, however, was cut short because of his troubled relationship with the party's chairman Fatos Nano. In 2004, he broke with the socialists, creating the SMI. Although his party won only four seats in the 2009 elections, Meta entered into a coalition with Berisha's democrats. Four years later, he switched alliances, entering into a coalition with the Socialist Party. An astute politician, Meta is known for his lavish lifestyle and many consider him as one of the country's most corrupt politicians.[11] None of Albania's postcommunist presidents have been able to live up to their constitutional role as a unifying force above party politics and to be a voice of moral authority.

Elections and Political Parties

Since the end of communism, Albania has held nine multiparty parliamentary elections: in March 1991, March 1992, May 1996, June 1997, May 2001, July 2005, June 2009, June 2013, and June 2017. Most of the elections have been problematic and contested by the losing party. While it has made significant progress and every election has represented a qualitative step forward, Albania's difficulty in holding elections in full accordance with international standards has adversely impacted its democratic development and integration into the EU.

The electoral system was changed on numerous occasions. Before 2008, the electoral code combined single-member electoral districts with proportional representation. Under that system, one hundred members of parliament were elected by direct popular vote in districts, and the remaining forty seats were allocated based on the political parties' shares of national votes. The threshold was 2.5 percent. In 2008, the Democratic Party and the Socialist Party agreed to revise the electoral code, addressing several recommendations offered by the Office for Democratic Institutions and Human Rights of the Organization for Security and Co-operation in Europe (OSCE) and the Council of Europe's European Commission for Democracy through Law (Venice Commission) to alleviate abuses and shortcomings under the previous electoral law. The old system tended to favor the smaller parties. The new electoral law, approved by parliament in early 2009, provides for a regional proportional system with 140 members of parliament elected in twelve regional constituencies corresponding to the country's administrative regions. The law sets a 3 percent threshold for political parties and a 5 percent threshold for coalitions. The law favors big parties and grants special rights to the chairpersons of political parties, allowing them to run on their party's lists in each of the twelve electoral districts simultaneously.[12] The democrats and the socialists maintained that the new electoral system would ensure a more stable government by producing clear majorities and reducing the inflated presence of small political parties. However, smaller parties across the political spectrum fiercely objected to the new electoral code, arguing that the regional proportional system would favor the two largest parties.

Although there are more than thirty political parties across the political spectrum and most of them field candidates in national and local elections, Albanian politics has been dominated by the country's two major political forces—the center-right Democratic Party and the Socialist Party, the successor to the Albanian Communist Party. These two have tended to view elections in terms of a zero-sum game, often disregarding democratic norms, manipulating electoral procedures, intimidating the judiciary and the media, and contesting unfavorable results. The two big parties have alternated power: the democrats governed from 1992 to 1997 and from 2005 to 2013 and the socialists from 1997 to 2005 and since 2013. Both have largely governed in a partisan and nontransparent fashion. Despite occasional calls to work constructively with each other, the democrats and the socialists have generally failed to find much common ground. When in opposition, each party has done its best to make life as difficult as possible for the government.

The Albanian electorate continues to be polarized around strong Democratic Party and Socialist Party positions. The two dominant parties claim to reflect competing strains of public opinion and hold contrasting views of Albania's future. However, a close analysis of their platforms reveals that they have become largely indistinguishable. Indeed, in recent years, the ideological gap between them has narrowed. There are no deep philosophical differences, and their approach to most issues is pragmatic and nonideological.

The Democratic Party, led by Sali Berisha, came to power in 1992. From 1992 to 1996, Berisha's government was viewed as one of the most progressive in the region. During this period, Berisha had a virtual free ride from an admiring West. He moved swiftly to fill the political vacuum created during the turmoil following the sanctioning of political pluralism. The immediate priority of the new government was to arrest the nation's economic decline, restore law and order, begin the difficult task of institution building, and reintegrate the country into the international community after decades of isolation. Albania witnessed rapid and significant institutional and legislative transformations. Berisha was able to secure substantial foreign assistance—Albania became the largest recipient of Western aid on a per capita basis in Central and Eastern Europe. Outside aid helped Albania institute radical economic reforms and an ambitious mass-privatization program. By 1996, Albania had emerged from the ruins of a totally state-owned economy as a market economy, with the private sector accounting for more than 65 percent of GDP and about 70 percent of the national wealth.

By the mid-1990s, Berisha's almost universal popularity had eroded as he turned increasingly autocratic. He showed no qualms about jailing Socialist Party leader Fatos Nano on what many saw as dubious corruption charges, imposed restrictions on basic political actions, introduced a restrictive media law, and allowed corruption and pyramid schemes to flourish. The wind shifted markedly against him after the flawed elections in 1996. These elections were followed by a falling out between Berisha and the international community, including the United States, his key foreign backer. Berisha resorted to increasingly repressive measures against his opponents (particularly the socialists), restricting freedom of the press and becoming less and less tolerant of dissent within his own Democratic Party.

The political crisis was compounded by rising economic problems, which were caused by the mushrooming of pyramid schemes. The collapse of those firms in 1997 sparked an armed revolt. State institutions folded, and the police and armed forces disintegrated. In March 1997, the government reached an accord with the opposition, agreeing to form a national unity government and hold early elections. Under a state of emergency, Albania held early elections in June 1997. The democrats suffered a humiliating defeat, and the socialists were swept back into power. Berisha resigned as president and was succeeded by the Socialist Party's general secretary, Rexhep Meidani. Nano, who had escaped from prison during the March unrest and was subsequently pardoned by Berisha, became prime minister.

During the next eight years (1997–2005), the Socialist Party held a monopoly on political power nationally and locally. Within a relatively short period, the socialist-led government rebuilt the country's police and armed forces and restored law and order in most parts of the country. Albania adopted a new constitution through a national referendum, enacted important legal reforms, and experienced significant economic growth. However, socialist rule was characterized by political instability, a lack of cooperation between the government and the opposition, and a dramatic rise in corruption and organized crime activities. The Socialist Party was also consumed with personal strife between

Nano and Ilir Meta, the former head of the party's youth organization and a rising star in the Socialist Party. Nano was forced to resign as prime minister following the assassination of student leader and close Berisha associate Azem Hajdari in September 1998. His successor, Pandeli Majko, was in turn forced to resign under pressure from the Socialist Party chairman after only one year in office, paving the way in November 1999 for Meta to become prime minister.

Nano and Meta reached a temporary truce on the eve of the June 2001 parliamentary elections, the first elections after the tumultuous events of 1997. The Socialist Party won seventy-three seats, while its allies—the Social Democratic Party, the Union for Human Rights Party, the Agrarian Party, and the Democratic Alliance—secured thirteen seats. The democrats and their allies garnered forty-six seats. The elections were seriously flawed: five rounds of voting were required to complete the process. In October, the OSCE election observation mission issued its final report, expressing concern about the government's interference in the election process and noting serious irregularities, police intimidation, Socialist Party manipulation, and dubious decisions by the Central Electoral Commission. The report, however, was unusually restrained in its criticism and largely dismissive of opposition complaints.[13]

Meta was reconfirmed as prime minister. However, he was unable to show any political resolve to undertake pressing domestic reforms or improve relations with the opposition. He faced an immediate and open challenge from Nano, which destabilized the government, paralyzed the state administration, and eventually delegitimized the ruling coalition. Resorting to press leaks, political pressure, and petty harassment, Nano launched a devastating campaign against Meta driven by two main considerations. First, although he was the party leader and had organized and led the electoral campaign, Meta had largely excluded Nano and his closest allies from the spoils of victory. Second, Meta refused to endorse Nano's candidacy for president. Nano focused his campaign on corruption, raising questions about Meta's role in the privatization of large, strategic state assets and portraying his administration as geared toward powerful, entrenched interests. As prime minister, Meta had displayed authoritarian tendencies, amassed too much power, and become very arrogant, alienating significant groups within the party. Unable to resist Nano's onslaught, Meta resigned in January 2002. Pandeli Majko, his predecessor who had served as prime minister from 1998 to 1999, succeeded him.

The Democratic Party made great efforts to seek partisan advantages from the string of scandals that befell the socialists. In an attempt to improve his image, Berisha expressed readiness for a compromise with the socialists and willingness to work with the government. The democrats ended their disruptive street tactics, expanded their international contacts, and returned to parliament. Under pressure from the international community and faced with a serious challenge from Meta's faction and the opposition, Nano reached out to Berisha. The two agreed to recommend Alfred Moisiu as a consensus candidate for president. Following Moisiu's election as president, Majko resigned, paving the way for Nano to return to the post of prime minister. Meta was appointed deputy prime minister and foreign minister. But Nano's thaw with both Berisha and Meta was short-lived. Rancorous skirmishes followed partial elections in Elbasan, with the democrats accusing the socialists of rigging the voting. Disagreements over changes in the electoral code and property issues brought parliamentary proceedings to a standstill. Meta, on the other hand, found himself largely marginalized in Nano's government and resigned in 2003. After several years of acrimony, in September 2004, Meta and his closest associates broke away from the Socialist Party and formed the SMI. The split, amid rising disenchantment with socialist rule, was a very significant factor in the Socialist Party's defeat in the 2005 parliamentary elections.

Democratic Party Rule (2005–2013)

The Democratic Party remained the most important opposition force because the post-1997 efforts of other parties and forces to supplant it as the only viable alternative to the Socialist Party had failed. The democrats had made great efforts to exploit opportunities created by the splits within the Socialist Party and the rising disenchantment with socialist rule. In the 2003 local elections, the Democratic Party expanded its base of support, winning in socialist strongholds in the south. Berisha launched a charm offensive aimed at improving his image and relations with the international community. He took measures to open up his party and worked hard to form a broad coalition, similar to the one in 1992.

The Democratic Party won fifty-six seats. Other parties that made it into parliament were the Republican Party, with eleven seats; the New Democratic Party, four seats; the Agrarian and Environmentalist Party, four seats; the Christian Democratic Party, two seats; the Union for Human Rights Party, two seats; and the Liberal Democratic Union, one seat. In addition, one independent candidate won a seat. On the left, the Socialist Party won forty-two seats; the Social Democratic Party, seven seats; the Democratic Alliance, three seats; and the Party of Social Democracy, two seats. Meta's SMI secured only five seats. The socialists were driven out of power. Nano resigned as chairman of the Socialist Party and was replaced by Edi Rama, the mayor of Tirana.

The election results represented an astonishing comeback not only for Berisha personally—in the wake of Albania's implosion on his watch in 1997, most observers had discounted him—but also for his Democratic Party after it had fallen from grace with Albanian voters. The democrats formed a coalition government with six other parties, and Berisha became prime minister. Berisha's government laid out an aggressive agenda to combat the economic crisis, improve the business environment, fight corruption and organized crime, and speed up Albania's integration into NATO and the EU. During the next four years, the government made significant progress in its efforts to create a stable political environment with functional democratic institutions. Albania experienced strong economic growth, averaging an annual real GDP growth of 7 percent. Poverty and unemployment were reduced, and pensions and wages in the public sector increased. Perhaps the government's greatest achievement was Albania's membership in NATO. Berisha termed Albania's attainment of this strategic objective as the most important event since independence. However, membership in the EU, Tirana's other major foreign policy objective, eluded Albania because of the poisonous relationship between the government and the opposition and the slow progress in implementing reforms aimed at strengthening the judicial system, enforcing property rights, fighting corruption, and respecting media freedom.[14]

The next parliamentary elections, held in June 2009, showed that the Albanian electorate remained deeply and closely divided between the two major political parties. The democrats won 68 out of 140 seats, three more than their socialist opponents; Ilir Meta's SMI won four seats; two parties allied with the democrats and one allied with the socialists won one seat each. Though the Democratic Party emerged with most parliamentary seats, it fell short of the majority required to form the government. In an abrupt about-face, Berisha entered into a coalition agreement with the SMI, denying the socialists the chance to form the new government. Berisha's coalition with Meta came as a surprise. They were archenemies, and on the eve of the elections, Berisha had ruled out the possibility of entering into a coalition with either Meta or Rama.[15] Meta had been one of Berisha's fiercest critics, at one point calling him "the most dangerous enemy of the Albanian state."[16] Although the coalition caused some rumblings within both the Democratic Party and the SMI, the two leaders had no difficulty justifying it to their electorates. Given the narrow margin of his victory, Berisha had limited options, and without Meta's support, he could not form the new government. Meta, for his part, was bitter that Rama had bluntly rejected his repeated offers for a preelection coalition and had made every effort to marginalize the SMI. Meta became deputy prime minister and foreign minister. His party received two other posts: the Ministry of Health and the powerful Ministry of Economy, Trade, and Energy. In addition, Meta's party got to name its own to 20 percent of all senior posts in the administration. Berisha's new coalition government pledged to continue the implementation of market reforms and to pursue an aggressive campaign against corruption and organized crime, as well as other reforms aimed at improving Albania's chances for EU integration.

Following the elections, relations between the government and the opposition were marked by constant tensions. Rama refused to accept the results, although international observers had deemed them sufficiently credible.[17] The socialists boycotted the parliament and resorted to threats, ultimatums, and disruptive actions in pursuit of their demands. They shunned government calls for cooperation and stymied efforts to pass important legislation. Rama heightened his antigovernment rhetoric and organized protests in several cities demanding that the ballot boxes be opened in several districts where the socialists had alleged irregularities. The democrats maintained an uncompromising attitude and refused to reach out to the opposition.

The dispute over the elections led to a long political impasse, diverted attention from pressing economic and social challenges, stalled progress on key reforms, and tarnished Albania's image and democratic credentials. While there was a wide consensus on the importance and potential benefits of Albania's integration into the EU, Albanian leaders permitted short-term political considerations to trump the country's EU integration.

Whereas the Democratic Party's first term was marked by significant progress, its second term (2009–2013) was characterized by sluggish economic growth, prolonged political gridlock, and the inability to implement significant political and economic reforms, strengthen the rule of law, or effectively fight corruption and organized crime. Despite the government's anti-corruption strategy, corruption continued to worsen, as reflected in reports by Transparency International. In 2011, Albania was ranked in 95th place, but two years later it dropped to 116th position out of 177 countries and territories.[18] Senior government officials and politicians were reputed to have used their positions to build huge private fortunes, but no senior official was prosecuted. Berisha's inability to significantly reduce corruption dimmed public confidence in his government.

Ilir Meta's trial on corruption charges—based on a video released by his former deputy, Dritan Prifti, which purported to show Meta discussing bribe taking—eroded the coalition's popularity. His case became a source of acute embarrassment and cast an unflattering light not only on Meta and his party but also on Berisha's government. The socialists made Meta the focus of their corruption criticism, and the violence that erupted in January 2011, in which four opposition supporters were killed in clashes with police forces, was sparked by popular anger at Meta. The socialists vehemently criticized Meta's acquittal in early 2012. There was a widespread perception that Meta had escaped prosecution because of the government's undue influence over the courts.

Following Meta's acquittal, Berisha struggled to keep the coalition intact. Jockeying, increased competition among coalition partners, and politicking in the run-up to the June 2013 elections significantly impacted the government's reform and legislative agendas. Meta undermined the coalition by adopting positions on major issues that were likely to improve his party's election prospects. Finally, in April 2013, Meta quit the coalition and signed an election alliance with the Socialist Party, virtually sealing the Democratic Party's election defeat.

The Socialists Return to Power (2013–)

The June 2013 parliamentary elections, which resulted in a landslide victory for the Socialist Party–led coalition and the defeat of the Democratic Party, ushered in a major political realignment. These were perhaps the most credible and peaceful elections since 1992 and improved Albania's democratic reputation and its EU membership prospects. The Democratic Party–led Alliance for Employment, Well-Being, and Integration had some twenty-five parties in its coalition, including the Republican Party, the Movement for National Development, and the Party for Justice Integration and Unity. In addition to the SMI, the Socialist Party–led Alliance for a European Albania grouped together more than thirty-five parties, including the Social Democratic Party, the Union for Human Rights Party, and other parties spanning the country's political spectrum.

The democrats presented a report of accomplishments during their eight years of rule but no credible road map detailing the direction in which they intended to take the country. There was no question that between 2005 and 2013, Albania had made progress on many fronts. But after eight years in power, the ruling party had experienced a significant erosion of popularity. Many blamed the government for the post-2009 election gridlock and slow progress toward EU integration. In addition, the ruling party faced growing economic hardships, its inability to address the corruption issue decisively, and increased social discontent. The socialists made very ambitious election pledges, focusing their campaign on accusations of poor governance, mismanagement, corruption, and the democratic stranglehold on institutional power. They advocated government-supported social programs, rapid economic development, job creation, and tax reform.

The socialist-led coalition won a landslide victory, gaining 83 out of 140 seats; the socialists won 66 seats, only one more than four years earlier; and the democratic-led coalition received 57 seats. Meta's Movement for Socialist Integration emerged as the unexpected big winner with sixteen seats, a fourfold increase from the 2009 elections. In September 2013, Rama became prime minister and formed the new government. Out of nineteen ministerships, Meta's party received five. Meta took the post of the speaker of parliament. The government had a clear mandate and the political capital to advance its political and economic agenda. Moreover, the defection of a deputy from the democratic-led coalition gave the socialists the three-fifths of votes in the parliament required to enact important legislation, including constitutional changes. Rama unveiled his government's program, promising a different governing model from that of Berisha. He articulated an ambitious agenda: accelerating EU integration, fighting corruption, improving the efficiency of the public administration, strengthening the independence of the judiciary, reducing public debt, addressing economic problems, replacing the flat income tax of 10 percent with a progressive tax system, and creating three hundred thousand jobs within the next four years.[19]

The Democratic Party, which suffered a humiliating defeat and lost badly even in previously secure constituencies, was not in a position to contest the results of the elections, which were certified by international observers. Berisha, the unchallenged democratic leader for over two decades, accepted responsibility for the defeat and resigned as party chairman. Lulzim Basha, the incumbent mayor of Tirana who had previously served as minister of transportation and public works, minister of foreign affairs, and minister of internal affairs, succeeded Berisha.

The 2013 elections created expectations of change, hope, and reform. With the exception of the first democratically elected government in March 1992, no other government has had such a sweeping mandate for change and therefore the opportunity to implement fundamental political and economic reforms. Rama had made many promises during his high-pitched election campaign to strengthen institutional capacity to implement needed reforms, but the record of his first mandate was mixed. While the government succeeded in stabilizing the financial sector, reducing unemployment, and accelerating economic growth, Albania, as the European Commission underscored in its annual progress report released in November 2016, still needed to do more to establish the rule of law, reform the public administration, implement judicial reforms, and effectively combat corruption and organized crime.[20]

The EU, in close coordination with the United States, had made it clear that it would not begin membership negotiations until Albania agreed to implement key judicial reforms. But the approval of judicial reforms was a prolonged and torturous process. While declaratively expressing support for the reforms, Albanian leaders in practice engaged in endless maneuvering and grandstanding. Instead of seeking a consensus with the opposition, Rama portrayed the reforms as necessary to rid the system of corrupt judges and prosecutors named by the previous administration. The democrats, for their part, accused the prime minister of attempting to capture the justice system. Disagreements over judicial reforms also exposed cracks within the governing coalition. Despite occasional flare-ups, the coalition had worked relatively well and Rama and Meta had successfully managed their disagreements and policy disputes. But disagreements over judicial reforms led to a significant erosion of their relationship. Meta insisted that the reforms could be approved only by consensus, even threatening to resign as speaker of parliament if the socialists attempted to pass the reforms unilaterally.

It was only after intense pressure from the EU and the United States that Albania's parliament in July 2016 passed a comprehensive package of constitutional amendments aimed at fundamentally reforming the justice system. The package, and the related legislation enacted subsequently, included the restructuring of judicial institutions, the establishment of a special prosecutor's office and special courts to tackle corruption, organized crime and crimes by high-level officials, and the establishment of independent bodies that will assess the professional and personal suitability of some eight hundred judges, prosecutors, and legal advisors.

Rama's government displayed little political will to combat high-level corruption, drug trafficking, and organized crime. Corruption had become ingrained across all levels of government and society. Transparency International ranked Albania as one of the most corrupt countries in Europe.[21] Albania's drug trafficking problem also increased and the country risked becoming Europe's epicenter of the illegal drugs trade. A US Department of State report in March 2017 identified Albania as a key transit country for narcotics distribution throughout Europe and "a base of operations for regional organized crime organizations." The report listed Albania as a major money-laundering country.[22] The government had used the police raid in summer 2014 in the southern village of Lazarat as an indication of its commitment to fight drug trafficking. While the crackdown on Lazarat was characterized as a success, soon afterward cannabis cultivation and trafficking operations spread across the country, turning Albania into the main supplier of cannabis to the EU. By mid-2016, some 2.4 million cannabis seeds were planted across Albania and tons of marijuana worth billions of dollars were shipped to Italy and Greece.[23] During a visit to Tirana in February 2017, Italy's top organized crime prosecutor, Franco Roberti, said marijuana shipments from Albania had increased threefold within a year.[24] The opposition accused Rama and his minister of internal affairs, Saimir Tahiri, of colluding with organized crime figures and drug traffickers. In January 2017, Rama fired Ylli Manjani, the minister of justice from the SMI, reportedly after he made similar accusations about links between government officials and organized crime groups.[25] Despite numerous reports of links of high government and Socialist Party officials with criminal groups and major drug traffickers, and that police and customs officials were implicated in organizing illegal drug traffic, the government failed to take effective measures.[26] The most egregious example involved Klement Balili, a local official and a businessman in the southern city of Saranda, dubbed as "the Escobar of the Balkans." In May 2016, Greek authorities issued an arrest warrant, accusing Balili of heading a major drug trafficking ring. Despite Greek and US pressure, the Albanian police refused to execute the warrant and Balili went into hiding. He was believed to have close links with senior government officials. Meta had attended the inauguration of a hotel, Santa Quaranta, run by Balili's family.[27] Human trafficking also remained a huge issue. According to the State Department, Albania was a source, transit, and destination for trafficking in persons and the Albanian government did not meet the minimum standards for the elimination of human trafficking.[28]

Rama had failed to take advantage of what could have been a watershed moment and institute a radical course correction. Enjoying a comfortable majority, the prime minister did not make serious efforts to reach out to the opposition and did not shy from making efforts to circumscribe institutional checks and balances that his party had advocated before coming to power. Instead of seeking to reverse the acrimony and dysfunction that had characterized the relationship between the two parties, Rama displayed a penchant for inflammatory statements and pursued a confrontational strategy.

Concomitantly, the opposition Democratic Party, preoccupied with recovering from its election defeat, displayed little political will to engage with the government on vitally important issues. Lulzim Basha, Berisha's successor, struggled to create his own political profile, consolidate his position, and keep together the various party factions. He resorted to the traditional role of Albanian opposition leaders, that of a harsh critic engaging in a gloom-and-doom talk and resorting to some of the same destructive tactics that Rama had employed before the 2013 election. His ambiguous position on the enactment of judicial reforms damaged his relationship with Western embassies in Tirana and left the impression that democrats opposed the reforms. In February 2017, Basha announced a boycott of parliament and said that the Democratic Party would not participate in the June 18 parliamentary elections unless Rama resigned and a technical government was formed to prepare the ground for fair and free elections. He said that the socialists had failed to agree to electoral reforms recommended by OSCE/OSCE's Office for Democratic Institutions and Human Rights (ODIHR) after the parliamentary elections in 2013. Basha blamed Rama for the "cannibalization" of Albania and expressed concern that the socialists would use illicit proceeds from drug trafficking to manipulate the upcoming parliamentary elections. Basha's supporters raised a huge tent in front of the prime minister's office and blocked the main boulevard. The Democratic Party action increased political tensions and also exposed serious cracks in the governing coalition. While Rama rejected Basha's demands out of hand, Meta urged a compromise. His public statements and attempts to reach out to the democrats underscored the widening gap between the two coalition partners.

Both the EU and the United States dispatched senior envoys to Tirana to mediate the crisis. Basha was told in no uncertain terms that the international community would recognize the elections even if the Democratic Party refused to take part. Finally, on May 18, 2017, in a face-to-face meeting Rama and Basha struck a deal, ending the three-month opposition boycott. Rama agreed to postpone elections by a week and to make significant changes in the cabinet. Candidates proposed by Basha replaced the deputy prime minister and six ministers, including the ministers of internal affairs and justice. The chairman of the Central Election Commission was also replaced. The agreement stipulated that political parties would run on their own in the elections, thus excluding the possibility of preelection coalitions.[29] Opposition lawmakers returned to parliament and on June 17 voted to approve a bill that will establish bodies to evaluate the background of judges and prosecutors.[30] In addition, the two sides pledged to cooperate in the postelection period to enact constitutional and electoral changes and advance Albania's accession to the EU.

The agreement received a rapturous welcome and prompted a resurgence of hope. Before the deal, Albania seemed on the verge of a major political upheaval. The agreement had an immediate impact in lowering tensions. But as details of the deal became public, the two leaders were criticized for lack of transparency and exclusion of other political parties. Rama and Basha had showed total disregard for the views of other parties or for their own inner circles. Meta was clearly disappointed and offended that he had been marginalized by Rama and expressed concern that the leaders of the two largest political parties were coordinating their activities to defeat the SMI. As he had done when he broke with Berisha in 2013, Meta lost no time in distancing his party from Rama, blaming the socialists for the failures of the coalition government, although his party had held important cabinet posts. The two former partners now engaged in open warfare. Other, smaller parties also criticized the agreement, expressing grave concern that the deal did not offer the smaller parties an opportunity to join preelection coalitions, thus seriously restricting their chances of entering the parliament. Some of the provisions of the agreement were also criticized for being inconsistent with the electoral law by prohibiting contestants from forming preelection coalitions, obligating private television stations to provide free time to parties running in the election, and replacing the chairman of the Central Electoral Commission by bypassing legally prescribed procedures.[31]

The Rama-Basha agreement ensured one of the most peaceful election campaigns since the collapse of the communist regime, void of any serious irregularities and violence. Although 18 political parties fielded candidates for the 140 seats in parliament, the Socialist Party, the Democratic Party, and the Socialist Movement for Integration fiercely contested the elections. The three major parties made almost identical promises and their platforms reflected no clear distinctions. This was also one of the most personalized campaigns Albania had witnessed, with Rama, Basha, and Meta personally leading their parties' electoral efforts.

Rama highlighted the reforms that had been introduced but acknowledged that the coalition government had not achieved all its objectives. He pledged to fully implement the justice reforms that were enacted, modernize the economy, radically reform the public administration, and combat pervasive corruption. But to complete the fundamental reforms needed to pave the way for Albania's membership in the EU, Rama insisted that the Socialist Party needed an outright majority. Excluding the possibility of a postelection coalition with the SMI, Rama campaigned hard to secure seventy-one seats, a sufficient number of seats to govern alone. He complained that the SMI had extorted too high a prize for joining the coalition and accused his former ally of having obstructed the government's reforms. He also said he was in favor of a bipolar political system, claiming that the smaller parties had made governing more difficult, thus causing political instability.[32] Basha focused his campaign on the economy, pledging to accelerate economic growth, reduce the high rate of unemployment, fight corruption, and implement judicial reforms. However, the democrats' campaign was plagued by leadership divisions, lack of organization, and inability to mobilize its support base. Instead of taking measures to placate his internal critics and unite his party, Basha moved to consolidate his power by carrying out a sweeping purge of his opponents. Basha's agreement with Rama and the compilation of the list of candidates without any meaningful consultations demonstrated his flouting of democratic norms and exacerbated already deep-seated antagonisms within the top echelons of his party. He excluded prominent democrats from the list of candidates for parliament, such as Josefina Topalli, Eduard Selami, Arben Imami, Ridvan Bode, and Astrit Patozi. And the three-month protest and delay in starting the campaign put the Democratic Party at a stark disadvantage with the Socialist Party and the SMI. With Basha's stewardship publicly questioned by senior party members, the democrats entered the campaign demoralized and unsure of the direction into which the leadership was taking them.

Both Rama and Basha aimed their attacks against the SMI, which in the last two elections had played the role of kingmaker. Meta launched a well-coordinated campaign and mobilized young activists throughout the country. He portrayed his party as an alternative to the other two parties, blaming them for the many problems facing the country. Contrary to the spirit of the law, president-elect Meta personally led his party's campaign, traveling throughout the country and waging a fierce campaign, focusing on discrediting Rama. The two former allies engaged in vitriolic personal accusations and recriminations over who was responsible for the coalition government's shortcomings.

The Socialist Party won a landslide victory, capturing 74 of the 120 parliament seats (48.33 percent)—nine seats more than four years ago. Rama secured a mandate to continue his quest for fundamental reforms aimed at finally paving the way for Albania's integration into the EU. The Democratic Party suffered its second consecutive defeat, securing only forty-three seats (28.81 percent)—seven seats less than in the 2013 elections. Meta's SMI saw an increase in its electorate, winning nineteen seats (14.28 percent)—three more seats than in the previous election. Only two other parties secured seats in the parliament: The Party for Justice, Integration and Unity won three seats, and the Social Democratic Party one seat.[33] The latter two were likely to align themselves with the Socialist Party, giving Rama a comfortable majority of seventy-eight seats. Both the Democratic Party and the SMI claimed the elections were manipulated and that the socialists had used "drug money" and criminal gangs to buy votes and intimidate voters. International observers acknowledged that there were cases of vote-buying, political intimidation, and irregularities.[34] Basha came under harsh criticism for the election defeat and his high-handed approach. The Democratic Party faces formidable challenges and will need time to reform and rehabilitate itself with the Albanian electorate.

Economic and Social Transition

Albania has carried out fundamental reforms aimed at establishing a functioning market economy. These have resulted in solid growth rates, infrastructure improvements, reduction in poverty, and an overhaul of the financial sector. Between 1998 and 2008, Albania averaged an annual real GDP growth of 7 percent. Between 2002 and 2008, poverty declined by one-third, from 25.4 to 12.4 percent. Berisha's government made significant efforts in improving governance and in reducing poverty and unemployment. In the public sector, wages in real terms increased by 36.5 percent between 2005 and 2008. Berisha launched a huge public infrastructure program, the most important project being the highway linking Albania's port city of Durrës with Kosovo; it was Albania's largest and most ambitious project since the fall of communism. The government also made great efforts to improve the country's business climate, establishing a one-stop-shop registration system that reduced the time and money required to open a business, introducing a 10 percent flat tax rate on personal and corporate income, and implementing a series of measures to increase tax revenues. The 2008 global economic crisis, however, impacted Albania, causing a decrease in exports, a significant decline in remittances from Albanians abroad, and lower foreign investments. Real GDP growth slowed to 1.6 percent in 2012, from 3 percent in 2011, and to 0.9 percent in 2013. Public debt soared, reaching

60 percent of GDP, and the budget deficit widened to 6 percent of GDP. Moreover, corruption remained pervasive. Transparency International ranked Albania 85th out of 180 countries in its 2008 Corruption Perceptions Index; a year later, Albania was ranked ten places lower; and in 2013, it listed Albania as the most corrupt country in Europe.

During his first mandate, Rama adopted a broad-based reform program aimed at reaching macroeconomic and fiscal sustainability, stabilizing the financial sector, accelerating economic growth, improving tax collection, addressing major problems in the energy sector, and improving the investment climate. The government made progress in improving the budget balance, fighting the informal economy, and reducing unemployment. Economic growth accelerated, with real GDP growing by 2.8 percent in 2015 and 3.1 percent in 2016. After several years of contraction, investments grew significantly. But despite the progress, Albania continued to face formidable economic challenges. Public debt relative to GDP stood at more than 70 percent, the current account deficit remained high at 11.3 percent of GDP, and the informal economy was estimated to account for more than a third of GDP. The unemployment rate had declined but still remained high: 15.9 percent in 2016.[35]

Despite the significant economic and social transformations, Albania remains one of the poorest countries in Europe. According to the World Bank, one out of three Albanians is poor. Some five hundred thousand Albanians live in extreme poverty, subsisting on less than $1 per day. Albania has yet to move from consumption-based to investment- and export-led growth to encourage foreign direct investments. The climate for foreign investments remains problematic, with officials favoring local, politically connected companies. Foreign investments are hindered by "uneven enforcement of legislation, cumbersome bureaucracy, and a lack of transparency."[36] More than a million-and-a-half Albanians have emigrated, with those between the ages of 20 and 40 emigrating in the largest numbers. As a result, Albania has experienced a major brain drain. The remittances of emigrants, estimated at close to $1 billion annually, are an important factor in the country's stability, but such a high emigration flow also has significant political, social, demographic, and economic ramifications.

Despite the apparent prosperity of Albania's major cities—Tirana, Durrës, and Vlore—much of the rest of the country remains poor and overwhelmingly agrarian. The rural areas are characterized by economic stagnation and endemic poverty, with the population relying mostly on the informal economic sector and with poor access to education and health services. In central and south Albania, there has been significant progress and social change. The north has experienced less social and economic development. If these regional disparities are not addressed, growing resentment will likely provide a fertile breeding ground for political demagogues.[37] Albania's main challenges over the midterm are the strengthening of state institutions (particularly the judiciary), developing infrastructure, fortifying the banking system, and taking further measures to encourage foreign investments.

Civil Society and the Media

A vibrant civil society has already developed. Numerous nongovernmental organizations—women's organizations, human rights organizations, environmental groups, professional associations, and policy institutes—operate freely, engaging in a wide range of activities.

They have had some success in influencing policy and enhancing government account-ability, transparency, and openness by engaging policy makers on various topics of public interest, offering policy recommendations, and staging protests. Following widespread protests organized by the Alliance against the Import of Waste, in October 2016 President Nishani vetoed a bill allowing waste imports for recycling purposes. Civil society activists joined their efforts to prevent the construction of hydropower plants on the Vjosa and Valbona rivers.[38] The Coalition of Domestic Observers, an election watchdog organiza-tion, has played an important role in working to enhance the transparency of the electoral process and—through its monitoring reports—raising awareness about irregularities and corruptive practices.

While in the past many nongovernmental organizations were closely linked with the government and political parties, in recent years they have achieved a degree of indepen-dence, which has increased their effectiveness. As the economy improved, nongovern-mental organizations were able to secure domestic funding and are now less dependent on foreign donors. The National Council for Civil Society, established in November 2016, is expected to result in increased cooperation and coordination between civil society and the government.

Since the demise of communism, the media in Albania have undergone dramatic changes. From a totally government-controlled media, Albania has seen the emergence of diverse and dynamic media outlets. There are more than seventy-five television stations, over one hundred radio stations, and twenty daily newspapers. Social media have come to play a major role. The government, political parties, and civil society groups and organizations widely use social media tools for their messaging.

However, the Albanian media have made slow progress in becoming a functioning fourth estate and rank low among trusted institutions. Most media outlets are associated with the government or a particular political party or politician, thus failing to effectively promote public accountability and vigorous political debate. While various Albanian governments have cast themselves as champions of press freedom, they have often resorted to various instruments of pressure on the media, including denying advertisements and putting pressure on owners and their businesses. Prominent businessmen, closely allied with the government or opposition political parties, have bought key newspapers and television stations that serve as major news sources for the population. Influence over key nationwide television channels has given Rama an effective means of ensuring that his government's line is promoted and his desired message disseminated to a wide audience. Many journalists, vulnerable to political and economic pressures, engage in widespread self-censorship and lack professionalism and ethics. If truly free media are to take hold, local journalists must take a stronger position in defending their rights. Closely related to this is the need for local journalists to adhere to professional journalism standards. In most cases, there is no firewall between government officials and owners, on the one hand, and reporters, on the other, to ensure editorial integrity and independence.

Foreign Policy

Under the communist regime, Albania had pursued a maverick policy, with high costs for the country's development and international standing. After its break with China in the mid-1970s, Albania embarked on an isolationist policy, almost totally cutting itself off from the outside world and maintaining contacts with only a limited number of countries. With the collapse of the communist government, Albania moved rapidly to end its international isolation, restoring ties with the United States; joining the OSCE, the International Monetary Fund, and the World Bank; and reaching out to neighboring countries. Tirana forged a special relationship with the United States, which openly supported the Democratic Party in the 1992 elections; developed extensive ties with Italy and Greece; and embarked on a policy of integration into Euro-Atlantic institutions. Tirana pursued a constructive policy vis-à-vis ethnic Albanians in Kosovo and was among the first to recognize the independence of Macedonia. Ties with Italy and Greece improved, although periodic crises over Tirana's treatment of the ethnic Greek minority characterized its relationship with Athens.

The downfall of Berisha's government in 1997 had no significant impact on the country's foreign policy. Initially, Fatos Nano displayed an ambivalent attitude toward the United States, his predecessor Berisha's strongest international benefactor, and showed a preference for Italy and Greece. Eventually, he became a strong proponent of Albania's strategic partnership with the United States. His successors, Majko and Meta, pursued similar policies.

Despite government changes in Tirana, the goal of integration into Euro-Atlantic institutions has remained constant and enjoys overwhelming popular support. While Albanian politics has been characterized by fragmentation and politicization, the prospect of integration has served as an important stimulus for political and economic reforms. Albania was the first former communist country to seek membership in NATO. With the outbreak of the conflict in former Yugoslavia in the early 1990s, Albania developed close relations with the alliance and in 1994 joined NATO's Partnership for Peace program. Albania played an important role in NATO's strategy of preventing the expansion of the Yugoslav conflict, placing its air and port facilities at the alliance's disposal. The war in Kosovo in 1999 provided an unprecedented opportunity for Albania to appear on the world stage. Albania hosted NATO troops and played a major role in the alliance's strategy of ending the ethnic cleansing of Albanians in Kosovo. A staunch supporter of NATO's engagements, Tirana deployed troops in Afghanistan and Iraq as part of the American-led multinational forces in those countries.

Aspirations to join the EU have been closely related to Albania's NATO membership. In 2009, Albania submitted its membership application, but until 2014 the European Commission ruled that Albania had not made sufficient progress to be granted candidate status. The adoption of a series of key electoral, judicial, and public administration reforms in 2012 and 2013 stipulated by the EU as required to achieve candidate status, as well as the conduct of orderly elections in June 2013, significantly improved Albania's EU prospects. In its annual progress report in October 2013, the European Commission concluded that Albania had made significant progress and recommended it be granted candidate status on the understanding that it will continue to take action in the fight against organized crime and corruption.[39] In June 2014, the European Commission, acknowledging that Rama's government had demonstrated a commitment in the fight against organized crime and corruption, granted Albania EU candidacy status. Following the June 2017 elections, Rama expressed the hope that accession talks would begin by the end of the year. But despite reassuring statements from Brussels,[40] there were uncertainties regarding EU enlargement, with many fearing that EU expansion may have ended with Croatia's admission in 2013. After Brexit and given the political polarization, governance issues, and economic and social problems faced by the Balkan countries, there was little appetite in Brussels for another round of EU enlargement. But if the EU closes its doors to the Balkans, that would likely lead to increased political tensions, economic problems, democratic backsliding, and growing Russian and perhaps Turkish influence in Albania and the region.

The hallmark of Albania's foreign policy has been the development of a strategic partnership with the United States. Washington played a major role in assisting Albania in fostering its democratic institutions and furthering economic growth and was the driving force behind Albania's accession to NATO and Kosovo's independence. Albania, for its part, has been a staunch ally of the United States, supporting American actions in both Afghanistan and Iraq. Rama's administration was very supportive of the US policy of combatting violent religious extremism and terrorism, and promoting regional stability and cooperation in southeastern Europe. With the emergence of the Islamic State of Iraq and Syria (ISIS) terrorist group, there were increased signs of Islamic radicalization in Albania and Kosovo. The two predominantly Muslim countries as well as Bosnia had become a focus for ISIS efforts to recruit foreign fighters. Reportedly, several hundred residents, mainly youth, from Albania and Kosovo had joined radical Islamic groups fighting in Syria and Iraq.[41] Working closely with US authorities, the Albanian government intensified its efforts to deal with threats emanating from activists who had become prey to ISIS propaganda, counter ISIS propaganda targeting vulnerable youths, and address the root causes of radicalization. Albania also joined the US-led, seventy-two-member Global Coalition to Defeat ISIS.

As was the case during Berisha's administration, Rama's first term as prime minister did not witness a significant expansion of Tirana's relations with Moscow, mainly because of Albania's close ties with the United States and Russia's strong support for Serbia's position on Kosovo. Russia's growing assertiveness and attempts to hinder the integration of Balkan countries into Euro-Atlantic institutions caused consternation in Tirana. Albanian officials urged a strong and coordinated Western response to Russia's aggression against Ukraine, bellicose posture toward its Eastern European neighbors, and its malign influence in the Balkans. With the uncertainty regarding President Donald Trump's foreign policy toward the Balkans and the EU facing formidable challenges in the wake of the Brexit vote, Russia was assiduously courting Serbia, Bosnia's Republika Srpska, and Macedonia, using political and cultural influence and news media obfuscation. At the same time, the Kremlin made concerted efforts to prevent Montenegro's accession to NATO, going so far as to support a coup attempt in October 2016. In an interview with *The Telegraph* in February 2017, Rama expressed concern that the Balkans could easily slip under Russian influence if the new US administration ignored the region.[42] Although Washington's attention had clearly shifted to other, more important areas, Under Secretary of Political Affairs Thomas A. Shannon reaffirmed the close relationship between Albania and the United States during Foreign Minister Ditmir Bushati's visit to Washington in April 2017.[43]

Albania has been decidedly in favor of increased regional cooperation, deepening its political, economic, and cultural ties with all its neighbors—Greece, Italy, Bosnia, Croatia, Macedonia, Montenegro, and Kosovo. The Albanian government was widely praised for its significant contribution to stability at what was one of Europe's most acute flash points. Rama also pursued a diplomatic rapprochement with Serbia—at a time when Belgrade was waging a fierce, worldwide diplomatic campaign to prevent other nations from recognizing Kosovo's independence. While both sides expressed their desire to improve relations, there was limited substantive improvement in economic and political relations. Efforts to forge closer ties continued to be hampered by mutual suspicions and disagreements over Kosovo.

Rama expressed early interest in closer ties with Turkey. Unlike Berisha, who was wary of growing Turkish influence in the region, Rama after coming to power in 2013 embraced Turkish leader Recep Erdogan, characterizing Turkey as a key strategic partner—a term hereto used only for the United States and the EU. Officials and pro-government media positively portrayed the relationship, while critics maintained that Rama's tilt toward Ankara undermined Albania's Euro-Atlantic orientation. In an unusual move on the eve of the June 2017 parliamentary elections, Erdogan publicly endorsed Rama.[44] While Albania and Kosovo appear to be specific targets of Ankara's policy, the Turkish government has also pursued closer and friendly relations with Serbia, Macedonia, and Bosnia in an attempt to increase its overall influence in the Balkans. But despite Rama's close relationship with Erdogan, on most important international issues Tirana took a pro-EU and pro-US rather than pro-Turkish positions.

The declaration of Kosovo's independence in February 2008 was perhaps one of the most momentous events in the Albanian nation's contemporary history and led to a massive expression of pan-Albanian sentiments throughout the Balkans. Kosovo's independence, along with Albania's membership in NATO and the increasing empowerment of Albanians in Macedonia and Montenegro, gives Albanians throughout the region a new sense of confidence and unprecedented security. Long known as the underdogs in the Balkans, the Albanians have never been in a more favorable geopolitical position. The relationship between Albanians in Albania and Albanians in the countries of former Yugoslavia has undergone significant transformations. Albanian communities have not only restored old ties but are also fostering new types of community relations. These developments have led some observers to raise questions about Albanians' long-term plans and nationalist aspirations.

Undoubtedly, Kosovo's independence has revived the idea of the national unification of Albanians. However, with the exception of a few extremists, Albanians, in general, and their leaders, in particular, have maintained a healthy balance between realism and idealism on the unification issue. Albanians have pursued a pragmatic and rational approach and realize that the benefits of continuing with their current pro-Western agenda of Euro-Atlantic integration and intensified regional cooperation far outweigh the perceived benefits of pursuing political unification and change in current state borders. Unification seems to be overshadowed by other, more urgent challenges, such as the strengthening of governance and democratic institutions in Albania, the consolidation of Kosovo's statehood, and securing a greater share of power for Albanians in Macedonia and protection for Albanian minorities in southern Serbia and Montenegro.

National unification has not been a dominant theme in the Albanian public discourse. Kosovo was not a salient issue in Albania's June 2017 elections. To the extent that the idea of unification is present in Albania, it is advocated by diverse individuals and groups that currently do not seem to enjoy much popular support and therefore are not likely to be in a position to mobilize masses in pursuit of the unification objective.

Official Tirana has been eager to please the United States and the EU and has not taken any independent stand on Kosovo. Instead, the leadership's goal has been engagement with neighbors, giving priority to the interests of the state of Albania over those of the wider Albanian "nation." Even in the case of Serbia, Tirana has repeatedly approached Belgrade with a readiness to expand ties and explore areas of common interest, without in any way contesting Serbia's objectionable policies and actions vis-à-vis Kosovo. Moreover, Albanian elites in Kosovo and Macedonia have different priorities and tend to take independent action and Tirana's leaders have little clout in Pristina. Albanians in Kosovo, in particular, see themselves as equal to their brethren in Albania. With the erosion of the Serbian threat after 1999, Kosovar elites and the population at large are less enthusiastic than in the past about reunification with Albania. Arguably, Kosovar leaders have a strong motivation and self-interest in the consolidation of a separate Kosovar state. They cannot expect to play the same prominent role in a "Greater Albania." Finally, the Kosovars rightly fear that any move toward reunification would lead to the partition of Kosovo.

The downfall of communism, Kosovo's independence, the rapid advances in information technology, and the erosion of government control over information have, however, transformed the relationship among Albanians in the region, restoring old ties and fostering new types of community relations. Officials in Albania, Kosovo, and western Macedonia do not speak with one political voice; nor do they have one national platform. Yet a remarkable consensus has emerged between decision makers and political actors in Tirana, Pristina, and Tetova. Albanians have publicly rejected unification while subtly coordinating policies and strengthening cooperation in all fields, particularly economic and cultural ties. Since Kosovo's independence, the Balkans have witnessed the emergence of an Albanian "space"—with open borders and a free trade zone but lacking a political center and joint state and government institutions.

The spectacular celebration of Albania's one hundredth anniversary of independence in November 2012 throughout Albania, Kosovo, Macedonia, Montenegro, and southern Serbia was associated with a sudden and dramatic increase in nationalistic rhetoric. The centennial celebrations kicked off in Skopje, the capital of Macedonia. In a speech at the event, which was attended by senior Albanian leaders from Albania and Kosovo, Berisha said that while Albanians were committed to EU integration, their dream was national unification. He invoked the historical Albanian narrative and raised the specter of the unification of all Albanians into one state, adding, "From Skopje, I call on the Albanians to work, every minute, every hour, every day, every week, every month and every year for their union."[45]

This nationalist rhetoric triggered a harsh international response. Berisha was accused of using nationalism to channel popular discontent away from the failures of his government to deal with domestic problems. He was forced to temper his nationalist rhetoric following international criticism that this rhetoric threatened US and EU security objectives of regional cooperation promotion. Although Rama, too, had taken an increasingly pan-Albanian position, organizing an exhibition of historical Albanian national flags and traveling to Kosovo, Macedonia, and southern Serbia on the eve of the centennial of Albania's independence, he was quick to denounce Berisha, accusing him of damaging Albania's relations with its strategic partners. While criticizing Berisha for advocating what he termed "primitive nationalism," the Socialist Party leader called for the deepening of cooperation between Albania and Kosovo, including a unified educational system, a customs union, and joint projects for the development of energy and tourism.[46] But once in power, Rama, too, engaged in nationalistic rhetoric and pressed for closer coordination of policies between Tirana and Pristina. The two governments held several joint cabinet meetings and agreed on a series of measures aimed at increasing cooperation in all areas. Both sides were careful to assure neighboring countries that they had nothing to fear from closer Tirana-Pristina ties.[47] In an interview in April 2017, Rama raised the prospect of Albania's unification with Kosova in the event the EU rejected them.[48] His statement drew widespread international condemnation. Donald Lu, the US ambassador to Albania, criticized Rama's remarks, adding that Washington was "against careless talk of unification. It undermines the stability of the region and the European path of both countries."[49]

Conclusion

The postcommunist period has proved that there are deep-seated obstacles to Albania's democratization—lack of a democratic culture, the legacy of the totalitarian nature of Enver Hoxha's regime, and economic and social underdevelopment. But without diminishing the importance of these factors in its slow and painful transition, Albania's democratic underperformance has been a direct function of the choices and decisions made by its governing elites. Missed opportunities, misguided policies, mistakes, and failures have transcended democratic and socialist administrations.

Albania is at a critical juncture. While it has achieved an impressive level of democratic maturity and economic and social development, it faces a number of highly complex challenges that will test the leadership skills of its current leaders and determine whether Albania can indeed fully consolidate its democracy. With his landslide reelection in 2017, Prime Minister Rama is well positioned to address some of the most serious barriers to a more rapid pace of his country's economic development and democratization. Arguably, Rama's key challenge remains the economy and corruption, which appears ingrained across all levels of government and society. Albania still ranks among the poorest countries in the region, stricken with poverty, high unemployment, and limited economic opportunities. Many Albanians have lost hope and apparently do not believe they are in a position to influence policy decisions that affect their vital interests or shape their country's future. While it has one of the highest birth rates in Europe, Albania's population has been declining because of the high rate of emigration. In 2017, Albania's population was estimated at 2.9 million—the same as it was in 1989—and by 2050 is expected to decline to 2.6 million.[50] Since the early 1990s, a million-and-a-half Albanians have fled in search of a better life to Western Europe and the United States. Albania is losing many young, educated citizens—the most vital part of the population—and arguably has experienced a higher brain drain than any other country in southeastern Europe. According to a Gallup survey released in June 2017, some 56 percent of Albanians would like to emigrate, a dramatic increase from 2012, when 36 percent of respondents expressed a desire to migrate. Out of 156 countries polled, Albania ranked in the third place, after Sierra Leone and Haiti.[51]

Pervasive corruption, perpetual illegality, and the failure to strengthen rule of law present an existential threat to Albania's democracy. Holding public or administrative office has become the best path to riches. The country's wealth and access to power are concentrated in the hands of a small group and the gulf between the rulers and the ruled is very high. The justice system is viewed as one of the most corrupt institutions in Albania. Corruption and the lack of the rule of law are best reflected by the brazen way in which government officials vie to influence court decisions. Rarely are elected or appointed officials sanctioned for abuse of power, corruption, and other misdeeds. It should therefore come as no surprise that, despite the approval of comprehensive judicial reforms in 2016, the public is skeptical of Rama's anti-corruption campaign and prospects for the full implementation of the reforms. With growing economic hardships and increased social discontent, the government faces the risk of a serious public backlash. Rama will have to take decisive and immediate steps to address the corruption issue and deliver on the Albanians' aspirations for greater political, social, and economic opportunity. Given his comfortable majority in the new parliament, the Socialist leader will not be able to blame the democrats or his former coalition partner, the SMI, if the government fails to deliver on its promises.

Albanian politics remains highly divisive and confrontational, and political polarization is a significant impediment to the realization of Albania's full democratic potential. The country's major political forces have largely refused to engage in the give-and-take that is normally associated with a democratic order, their overriding objective being to gain and keep power. To this end, they have often engaged in questionable democratic practices—failure to embrace the rule of law, distributing public goods on a preferential basis, rewriting the rules from one election to another, and exerting pressure on independent institutions and civil society groups. While in opposition or during electoral campaigns, Albanian politicians tend to portray themselves as inspiring leaders, reformers, and consensus builders who have embraced fundamental political and economic reforms aimed at transforming Albania into a functioning democratic polity. But once in power, they soon veer off the democratic path, circumscribing the institutional checks and balances that they had earlier advocated, engaging in undemocratic behavior to consolidate their positions, and attempting to capture the state for economic gain. And every incoming administration has engaged in widespread purges of the state administration. While there is a widespread acceptance that political power can legitimately be acquired solely from the ballot box, too much drama surrounds Albanian elections. They are viewed as a life-or-death struggle, rather than a contest between political platforms. It is incumbent on the ruling socialists to find ways to break the mind-set that views politics in terms of a zero-sum game. The costs of the dysfunctional relationship between major political actors have been high, undermining the country's political stability, leading to poor governance, and inhibiting the speed of EU integration.

At the beginning of his second term, Rama pledged to seek a wide consensus and work closely with the opposition to implement fundamental reforms that could have a longer lifespan than an administration's term in office.[52] It remains to be seen if Rama is truly committed to a positive course correction and has the political will to address some of the most glaring shortcomings and deficiencies that have hampered Albania's ability to attain its democratic potential. During his first mandate as prime minister, Rama displayed authoritarian tendencies and did little to replace party patronage and sectarianism with meritocracy in government employment. Emboldened in June 2017 by having secured a solid majority in parliament and facing few political and institutional constraints, Rama might be tempted to maximize his power by marginalizing the opposition, isolating the president, and using the recently enacted reforms to exert control over public institutions. But any attempt by Rama to govern outside the confines of democratic institutions would lead to unaccountable governance, a serious degradation of already weak institutions, and steer the country away from a more democratic path.

Albania's foreign policy will probably remain constant and will continue to be heavily driven by Tirana's long-standing priorities of strengthening its strategic partnership with the United States, membership in the EU, and improved regional cooperation through advocacy of greater political, economic, security, and cultural links. The United States and the EU have considered Albania an important part of their vision for southeastern Europe: the spread of democracy, the establishment of a multiethnic society, protection of minority rights, and the promotion of peaceful conflict resolution. Washington and Brussels have pursued a common strategy and have devoted enormous resources aimed at advancing Albania's democratization. The international community, preoccupied as it is with many and much more pressing issues than Albania, is less likely to be forthcoming if Tirana's leaders are perceived as corrupt and divisive and their commitment to democracy is questionable. Thus, Albanian leaders should be aware of the dangers of "Albania fatigue."

But while the international community can provide valuable assistance and support, in the final analysis it is up to Albania's leading political forces to create inclusive political and economic systems that provide opportunity for all, build a future that sustains democracy, increases transparency and accountability, and promotes sustainable growth policies. For Albania to achieve these objectives, the country's leaders will have to put aside their narrow interests and take responsibility for tackling the myriad uncertainties and daunting challenges that their country is likely to face in the near and midterm.

Study Questions

1. What was the nature of Albania's communist system, and how did it contrast with that of other communist states in Central and Eastern Europe?
2. What challenges has Albania faced in its transition from a Communist Party state to a multiparty system and market economy?
3. What role did Albania play during the conflict in former Yugoslavia in the mid-1990s?
4. When did Albania join NATO?
5. What are the main objectives of Albania's foreign policy?
6. Why is corruption so pervasive and how has Albania attempted to combat it?
7. Has Albania been able to establish the rule of law?
8. What is the media situation in Albania?
9. How do Albania's democratic credentials compare with those of the other neighboring countries?

Suggested Readings

Abrahams, Fred C. *Modern Albania: From Dictatorship to Democracy in Europe*. New York: New York University Press, 2015.

Biberaj, Elez. *Albania in Transition: The Rocky Road to Democracy.* Boulder, CO: Westview Press, 1998.

Fischer, Bernd J. *Albania at War, 1939–1945.* West Lafayette, IN: Purdue University Press, 1999.

Fevziu, Blendi. *Enver Hoxha: The Iron Fist of Albania.* London: I.B. Tauris, 2016.

Gjonça, Arjan. *Communism, Health, and Lifestyle: The Paradox of Mortality Transition in Albania, 1950–1990.* Westport, CT: Greenwood Press, 2001.

Kola, Paulin. *The Myth of Greater Albania.* New York: New York University Press, 2003.

Schwandner-Sievers, Stephanie, and Bernd J. Fischer, eds. *Albanian Identities: Myth and History.* Bloomington: Indiana University Press, 2002.

Vickers, Miranda, and James Pettifer. *Albania: From Anarchy to a Balkan Identity.* New York: New York University Press, 1997.

United Nations Development Program. *Human Development Report: Albania 2016.* Tirana: United Nations Development Program, 2016.

World Bank Group. *Country Partnership Framework for Albania, 2015–2019.* Tirana: World Bank Group, 2015.

Websites

Balkan Web: http://www.balkanweb.com/indexi.php

Freedom House: http://www.freedomhouse.org

National Democratic Institute, "Albania": http://www.ndi.org/albania

World Bank, "Albania": http://www.worldbank.org/en/country/albania

Zëri i Amerikës: http://www.zeriamerikes.com (Voice of America)

Notes

1. Besfort Lamallari, "Albania," in Freedom House, *Nations in Transit 2017: The False Promise of Populism* (Washington, DC: Freedom House, 2017), 4, https://freedomhouse.org/sites/default/files/NIT2017_Albania.pdf.

2. The Economist Intelligence Unit classifies Albania as a "hybrid regime," a category that includes Bosnia, Macedonia, and Montenegro. Its 2016 Democracy Index ranks Albania 81st out of 167 countries. See Economist Intelligence Unit, *Country Report: Albania* (London: Economist Intelligence Unit, 1st quarter 2017), 11.

3. Stavro Skendi, *The Albanian National Awakening, 1878–1912* (Princeton, NJ: Princeton University Press, 1967); Edwin E. Jacques, *The Albanians: An Ethnic History from Prehistoric Times to the Present* (Jefferson, NC: McFarland & Co., 1995); Miranda Vickers, *The Albanians: A Modern History* (London: I.B. Tauris, 1995); Bernd J. Fischer, *King Zog and the Struggle for Stability in Albania* (Boulder, CO: East European Monographs, distributed by Columbia University Press, 1984); and Bernd J. Fischer, *Albania at War, 1939–1945* (West Lafayette, IN: Purdue University Press, 1999).

4. Nicholas C. Pano, *The People's Republic of Albania* (Baltimore, MD: Johns Hopkins Press, 1968); Elez Biberaj, *Albania and China: A Study of an Unequal Alliance* (Boulder, CO: Westview Press, 1986); Elez Biberaj, *Albania: A Socialist Maverick* (Boulder, CO: Westview Press, 1990); William E. Griffith, *Albania and the Sino-Soviet Rift* (Cambridge, MA: MIT Press, 1963); Arshi Pipa, *Albanian Stalinism: Ideo-political Aspects* (Boulder, CO: East European Monographs, distributed by Columbia University Press, 1990); Peter R. Prifti, *Socialist Albania since 1944* (Cambridge,

MA: MIT Press, 1978); and Anton Logoreci, *The Albanians: Europe's Forgotten Survivors* (London: Victor Gollancz, 1977).

5. Blendi Fevziu, *Enver Hoxha: The Iron Fist of Albania* (London: I.B. Tauris, 2016).

6. European Commission, *Albania 2016 Report* (Brussels: European Commission, November 2016), 13–16, https://ec.europa.eu/neighbourhood-enlargement/sites/near/files/pdf/key_documents/2016/20161109_report_albania.pdf.

7. Elez Biberaj, *Albania in Transition: The Rocky Road to Democracy* (Boulder, CO: Westview Press, 1998); Miranda Vickers and James Pettifer, *Albania: From Anarchy to a Balkan Identity* (New York: New York University Press, 1997); and Fred C. Abrahams, *Modern Albania: From Dictatorship to Democracy in Europe* (New York: New York University Press, 2015).

8. Alfred S. Moisiu, *Midis Nanos dhe Berishës* [*Between Nano and Berisha*], vol. 3 (Tirana: Toena, 2009).

9. *Gazeta shqiptare*, April 22, 2008, 2.

10. In one of his first actions as prime minister in September 2013, Rama signed an executive order replacing the president's picture from all state institutions with that of Ismail Qemali, who declared Albania's independence on November 28, 1912, and served as the country's first president.

11. During a visit to the United States in 2015, Meta made headlines with his angry and arrogant answers during a live interview on the Voice of America's Albanian Service television newscast. Asked if he was concerned about accusations of corruption and the life of luxury while many Albanians live in poverty, Meta replied very angrily: "What luxury? . . . I don't even own a car because the state provides it for me." He suggested that the VOA reporter "should study journalism from scratch." The interview was conducted by VOA's reporter Ardita Dunellari. https://www.zeriamerikes.com/a/ilir-meta-voa-zeri-amerikes/3028446.html.

12. *The Electoral Code of the Republic of Albania* (Tirana, 2009), http://www.refworld.org/pdfid/4c1f93e32.pdf. See also the European Commission for Democracy through Law (Venice Commission), "Joint Opinion on the Electoral Code of the Republic of Albania," Opinion No. 513/2009, Strasbourg/Warsaw, March 13, 2009. For a critical assessment of the electoral code, see Claude Moniquet, "Albania: The Adoption of a New Electoral Code Compromises Possibilities for Holding Free Elections," European Strategic Intelligence and Security Center, Background Note, December 17, 2008, http://www.esisc.org/publications/analyses/albanie-ladoption-du-nouveau-code-electoral.

13. See OSCE Office for Democratic Institutions and Human Rights, "Republic of Albania: Parliamentary Elections, 28 June 2009," Warsaw, October 11, 2001, http://www.osce.org/odihr/elections/albania/38598?download=true.

14. Commission of the European Communities, *Albania 2009 Progress Report* (Brussels: Commission of the European Communities, October 2009).

15. *Koha Jonë*, June 25, 2009, 2–3.

16. *Albania* (Tirana), April 26, 2008, 4.

17. OSCE Office for Democratic Institutions and Human Rights, "Republic of Albania: Parliamentary Elections, 28 June 2009," Final Report, Warsaw, September 14, 2009, 1, http://www.osce.org/odihr/elections/albania/38598?download=true.

18. "Corruption Perceptions Index 2013," Transparency International, http://www.transparency.org/cpi2013/results. See also Marsida Nence, "Corruption, Albania's Biggest Challenge for Integration in E.U.," Portal on Central Eastern and Balkan Europe (PECOB), December 2013, http://www.pecob.eu/Corruption-Albania-biggest-challenge-integration-E-U.

19. Alliance for a European Albania, *Programi i qeverisë, 2013–2017* (Tirana: Alliance for a European Albania, 2013).

20. European Commission, *Albania 2016 Report* (Brussels: European Commission, November 2016), https://ec.europa.eu/neighbourhood-enlargement/sites/near/files/pdf/key_documents/2016/20161109_report_albania.pdf.

21. Transparency International, *Corruption Perceptions Index 2016*, https://www.transparency.org/news/feature/corruption_perceptions_index_2016#table.

22. United States Department of State, Bureau for International Narcotics and Law Enforcement Affairs, *International Narcotics Control Strategy Report*, vol. II (Washington, DC: Bureau for International Narcotics and Law Enforcement Affairs, March 2017), 29.

23. Besfort Lamallari, "Albania," in Freedom House, *Nations in Transit 2017: The False Promise of Populism* (Washington, DC: Freedom House, 2017), 4, https://freedomhouse.org/sites/default/files/NIT2017_Albania.pdf.

24. Armand Mero, "Italian Prosecutor Raises Concern about Marijuana Traffic from Albania," *Voice of America*, February 23, 2017, https://www.voanews.com/a/italian-prosecutor-raises-concern-marijuana-traffic-from-albania/3737930.html.

25. Beata Stur, "From Cannabis to Corruption in Albania," *New Europe* (Brussels), April 10, 2017, https://www.neweurope.eu/article/cannabis-corruption-albania/.

26. Luke Coffey, "History Repeating Itself as Balkan Woes Threaten U.S. Security," *Washington Times*, April 11, 2017, A5. See also David Clark, "EU Cannot Ignore Albania's Descent into Disorder," *Financial Times*, May 12, 2017, https://www.ft.com/content/7350d242-36fd-11e7-99bd-13beb0903fa3.

27. The US ambassador to Albania, Donald Lu, publicly complained about the Balili case, saying the failure to arrest him represented a major failure of the police and justice system: "U.S. law enforcement has been telling the prosecutor General's Office to arrest Balili. For seven months, I have encouraged the police, the Minister of Interior, the Minister of Justice and the Prosecutor General to arrest him. If Albania cannot catch Klement Balili, how will it go after other big fish? Who will want to work with Albania? Who will believe this is a serious country in the fight against drug trafficking?" The ambassador added that "the United States has told Albania that our future cooperation on anti-narcotics is conditioned upon Albania arresting and prosecuting big fish, including Klement Balili." See "Remarks by Ambassador Donald Lu at the Advocate of the People Conference," US Embassy in Albania, December 14, 2016, https://al.usembassy.gov/remarks-ambassador-donald-lu-advocate-people-conference/.

28. US Department of State, *Trafficking in Persons Report June 2017* (Washington, DC: US Department of State, 2017), 58–60.

29. The text of the agreement was published on the Socialist Party's and the Democratic Party's websites, http://ps.al/te-reja/marreveshje-politike-18-maj-2017 and https://demokratet.al/marreveshja-politike-18-maj-2017/. See also *Washington Post*, May 19, 2017, A13.

30. *Panorama* (Tirana), June 18, 2017, 4–5.

31. Organization for Security and Cooperation in Europe, *Albania, Parliamentary Elections, 25 June 2017: Statement of Preliminary Findings and Conclusions* (Tirana: Organization for Security and Cooperation in Europe, June 26, 2017), http://www.osce.org/odihr/elections/albania/325491?download=true.

32. See Prime Minister Edi Rama's interview with Lutfi Dervishi, *RTSh*, June 23, 2017. https://rtsh.al/lajme/rama-ne-perballe-dy-parti-jane-pak-tre-shume/.

33. ATA in English (Tirana), 1256 GMT, June 28, 2017.

34. Organization for Security and Cooperation in Europe, *Albania, Parliamentary Elections, 25 June 2017: Statement of Preliminary Findings and Conclusions* (Tirana: Organization for Security and Cooperation in Europe, June 26, 2017), http://www.osce.org/odihr/elections/albania/325491?download=true.

35. European Commission, *Albania 2016 Report* (Brussels: European Commission, November 2016), 26–30, https://ec.europa.eu/neighbourhood-enlargement/sites/near/files/pdf/key_documents/2016/20161109_report_albania.pdf. See also European Bank for Reconstruction and Development, *Strategy for Albania* (London: European Bank for Reconstruction and Development, January 2016); and International Monetary Fund, *Albania*, Country Report No. 17/64 (Washington, DC: International Monetary Fund, February 2017).

36. US Department of State, *Investment Climate Statements for 2017* (Albania: US Department of State, July 2017), 4, https://www.state.gov/e/eb/rls/othr/ics/investmentclimatestatements/index.htm#wrapper.

37. See World Bank, *Albania: World Bank Group Partnership Program Snapshot* (Washington, DC: World Bank, October 2013); World Bank Group, *Country Partnership Framework for Albania, 2015–2019* (Tirana: World Bank Group, 2015); and United Nations Development Program, *Human Development Report: Albania 2016* (Tirana: United Nations Development Program, 2016).

38. Besfort Lamallari, "Albania," in Freedom House, *Nations in Transit 2017: The False Promise of Populism* (Washington, DC: Freedom House, 2017), 5–6, https://freedomhouse.org/sites/default/files/NIT2017_Albania.pdf.

39. European Commission, *Key Findings of the 2013 Progress Report on Albania* (Brussels: European Commission, October 16, 2013), http://europa.eu/rapid/press-release_MEMO-13-888_en.htm; and European Commission, *Albania 2013 Progress Report* (Brussels: European Commission, October 2013), http://ec.europa.eu/enlargement/pdf/key_documents/2013/package/al_rapport_2013.pdf.

40. At a summit meeting in Trieste in July 2017, European Union leaders assured their Western Balkan counterparts that the EU was still committed to the Balkans despite the fact the enlargement process is on hold until 2019. "EU Seeks to Assure Balkans at Summit, despite Own Problems," *Washington Post*, July 12, 2017, https://www.washingtonpost.com/business/eu-seeks-to-assure-balkans-at-summit-despite-own-problems/2017/07/12/e80e47e2-6707-11e7-94ab-5b1f0ff459df_story.html?utm_term=.07aecd100c75. A Gallup poll released at the time of the Trieste's summit found that majorities in four of six Balkan countries see huge benefits in joining the EU, with residents in Kosovo and Albania exhibiting the highest level of approval, 84 percent and 80 percent, respectively. Zacc Ritter and Galina Zapryanova, "Many in Western Balkans See Benefit in Joining EU," *Gallup*, July 12, 2017, http://www.gallup.com/poll/213899/western-balkans-benefit-joining.aspx?version=print.

41. Adrian Shtuni, "Ethnic Albanian Foreign Fighters in Iraq and Syria," *CTC Sentinel*, 8, no. 4, April 2015, 11–14, https://ctc.usma.edu/v2/wp-content/uploads/2015/04/CTCSentinel-Vol8Issue49.pdf.

42. Thomas Harding, "Don't Abandon Us to the Russians, Pleads Albanian Leader, Fearing US Will Walk Away," *Telegraph*, February 24, 2017, http://www.telegraph.co.uk/news/2017/02/24/dont-abandon-us-russians-pleads-albanian-leader-fearing-us-will/. Rama was apprehensive about his government's relations with the Trump administration. During the US presidential election, Rama had made unflattering remarks about Donald Trump, which the opposition democrats attempted to exploit on the eve of the June 2017 elections. In an interview with the CNN in April 2016, Rama characterized Trump's campaign rhetoric as "really frightening," adding that his victory would not only harm America but also the democratic world. "Albanian PM: Trump Nomination Would Harm America," *CNN*, April 13, 2016, http://www.cnn.com/videos/business/2016/04/13/albanian-prime-minister-edi-rama-intv-qmb.cnn. Following Trump's election, Rama backtracked on his comments. Two weeks before the June 25, 2017, elections, Basha interrupted his campaign to attend an event in the United States with President Trump. Upon his return to Tirana, the Democratic Party chairman published a picture with the US president, saying he had held "an extraordinary" meeting with Trump. "Basha Publishes Photo from 'Extraordinary Meeting' with Trump," *Tirana Times*, June 16, 2017, http://www.tiranatimes.com/?p=132869.

43. Media Note, Office of the Spokesperson, US Department of State, "Under Secretary Shannon's Meeting with Albanian Foreign Minister Bushati," April 20, 2017, https://www.state. gov/r/pa/prs/ps/2017/04/270374.htm#.WPlT9F6FAMA.facebook.

44. Sokol Balla, "Interview with Turkish President Erdogan," *Top Channel*, June 19, 2017, http://m.top-channel.tv/lajme/artikull.php?id=357816&fundit.

45. *Panorama*, November 26, 2012; and *Gazeta shqiptare*, November 26, 2013.

46. Edit Rama, "Nationalist's Cries: Government's Offer," *Shekulli* (Tirana), December 29, 2012, 9.

47. See joint article by the two foreign ministers, Ditmir Bushati and Enver Hoxhaj, "Strategic Partnership: A Model of Regional Cooperation," *Shqip* (Tirana), January 14, 2014, 8.

48. Andrew Macdowall, "Albanian Prime Minister: EU Faces 'Nightmare' If Balkan Hopes Fade," *Politico*, April 18, 2017, http://www.politico.eu/article/albania-prime-minister-edi-rama-eu-faces-nightmare-if-balkans-denied/.

49. Fatjona Mejdini, "US Ambassador Calls Rama's Pan-Albanian Talk 'Careless,'" *Balkan Insight*, April 21, 2017, http://www.balkaninsight.com/en/article/us-condemns-albanian-pm-statement-over-unification-with-kosovo-04-21-2017.

50. United Nations, Department of Economic and Social Affairs, *World Population Prospects: The 2017 Revision* (New York: United Nations, Department of Economic and Social Affairs, 2017), 23, https://www.un.org/development/desa/publications/world-population-prospects-the-2017-revision.html. According to the most recent census, conducted in October 2011, Albania had a residential population of 2,831,741, a decline of about 8 percent compared to the 2001 census (3,069,275 residents). Some 83 percent (2,312,356) declared themselves Albanian, 0.87 percent (24,243) Greek, 0.3 percent (8,301) Roma, 0.3 percent (8,266) Aromanian, and 0.2 percent (5,512) Macedonian; 14 percent (390,938) of respondents refused to declare their nationality. In terms of religious affiliation, Muslims accounted for 56.70 percent (1,587,608) of the population, Bektashi 2.09 percent (58,628), Catholics 10.03 percent (280,921), and Orthodox 6.75 percent (188,992). Some 386,024 respondents (13.79 percent) refused to declare their religious affiliation. See the Institute of Statistics, *Population and Housing Census in Albania*, part 1 (Tirana: Institute of Statistics, 2012), 14, 71, http://www.instat.gov.al/media/177354/main_results__population_and_housing_census_2011.pdf.

51. Neli Esipova, Julie Ray, and Anita Pugliese, "Number of Potential Migrants Worldwide Tops 700 Million," Gallup, June 8, 2017, http://www.gallup.com/poll/211883/number-potential-migrants-worldwide-tops-700-million.aspx?g_source=Albania%2c+migrants+survey+2016&g_medium=search&g_campaign=tiles. According to the poll, other Balkan countries had a significantly lower share of potential migrants than Albania: Bosnia, 36 percent; and Kosovo and Macedonia, 34 percent each.

52. *Gazeta shqip*, July 6, 2017, http://gazeta-shqip.com/lajme/2017/07/06/rama-na-votuan-se-besojne-qe-meritojme-te-provohemi-te-vetem-ne-timon/.

Map 16.0.   Former Yugoslavia and Its Successors

CHAPTER 16

Former Yugoslavia and Its Successors

Mark Baskin and Paula Pickering

It is impossible to compress the story of the Socialist Federal Republic of Yugoslavia (SFRY) and its successor states into a neat and simple story of transition. Its succession twists and turns through pathways of war, reconstruction, and reconstitution into national states—a process not yet completed. In this contentious tale, observers sharply differ on the sources of dissolution, the causes of war, and the current state and future prospects of the post-Yugoslav governments.[1]

The tragedies that occurred are all the more painful since it seemed, in 1990, that the SFRY was on the verge of joining the European Community. It had long ago done away with many of the overtly repressive trappings of Central and East European socialism. Since the 1950s, Yugoslav leaders had been experimenting with liberalizing economic and political reforms, and Yugoslavia had been broadly integrated into international economic, political, and cultural developments. Yugoslavia's socialist regime was more open, transparent, and accepting of non-Marxist ideologies than any in Central and Eastern Europe. And since the 1960s, its citizens had massively enjoyed the opportunities to travel, study, and work abroad.[2] Literature and culture forbidden in the East, from George Orwell's *1984* to punk rock and neoliberal economics, were long prominent on the Yugoslav market.

By 1989, Yugoslav efforts to find a "third way" between Western capitalism and Soviet socialism had clearly run into a dead end. A burgeoning civil society, a business-oriented prime minister, and the popular Slovenian cry, "Europa Zdaj!" (Europe Now!), appeared to move Yugoslavia toward an evolving Europe. But Yugoslavia's other republics and provinces did not share Slovenia's relatively smooth ascension to the European Union (EU), and most have remained outside the "European home."

This chapter explores the causes and consequences of the SFRY's demise. It suggests that the agenda for the dissolution of multinational Yugoslavia was set by a series of incomplete economic and political reforms that left Yugoslavia without the institutional resilience to overcome increasing interregional differences. The national revivals that swept unevenly across Yugoslavia in the 1980s enabled the rise of the uniquely talented leader Slobodan Milošević, who advanced Serbian interests in the name of preserving Yugoslavia. The wars of Yugoslav succession were the outcome of unequal bargaining in the absence of compelling central authority, the failure of ambitious republican leaders to find a basis for future common existence, and the initial disinterest of Europe and the United States. Yugoslavia's violent dissolution led to a delayed international intervention, settlements that have helped to define the newly independent states, the prominence of international agencies in domestic developments, and transitions that have lasted far longer than foreseen in the early 1990s.

Precommunist History

The heterogeneous cultural, social, and political precommunist traditions in the lands of former Yugoslavia stem from their location amid the divisions in Europe between the Eastern and Western Roman Empires; Eastern Orthodoxy, Western Catholicism, and Islam; the Ottoman Empire, the Republic of Venice, and the Hapsburg Monarchy; and the Warsaw Pact and the North Atlantic Treaty Organization (NATO).[3]

Many national leaders who emerged in the 1990s focused on the historical antecedents to the post-Yugoslav national states. The medieval Croatian, Serbian, and Bosnian states were relatively brief preludes to their integration into larger, imperial state structures. An agreement with the Hungarian throne in 1102 led to a separate but unequal existence for Croatia within the Kingdom of Hungary until 1918, which put it under the Hapsburg Monarchy after 1526. The battle on a Kosovo field in 1389 between Serbian and Ottoman forces led to the ultimate end of medieval Serbia in 1459. By the time Serbian power again controlled this area in the early part of the twentieth century, Serbs were greatly outnumbered by Albanians in Kosovo. The Ottoman forces conquered independent Bosnia in 1463 and Herzegovina in 1483. The Slovenes lost their political independence in the eighth century and were incorporated into the Hapsburg Monarchy by the four-teenth century. Macedonia did not enjoy independence during the medieval era and fell under Byzantine, Bulgarian, Ottoman, and Serbian rule in the period before World War I. The departure of the Serbian state northward after 1389 enabled the development of a Montenegrin state, where the bishops of the Orthodox Church became rulers after 1516.

The legacies of imperial rule continue to be felt in these lands. The Ottomans imposed a centrally controlled regime of land tenure, tax collection, and native religious rights that gave extensive autonomy to religious communities. Large-scale conversions to Islam took place among only Bosnians and Albanians, but the forced conversion of young boys to Islam for the Ottoman officer corps remains a potent anti-Islamic symbol. The Ottomans twice advanced to the gates of Vienna and the Hapsburg court and administra-tion: in 1529 and 1682. In response to the Ottoman threats, the Hapsburgs established a military border populated largely by Orthodox Serbs on the Croatian side of Bosnia-Herzegovina. The aspirations of the Hapsburg Monarchy in the eighteenth century to impose enlightened absolutism and bureaucratic uniformity did not succeed in providing a unifying link within the empire—especially as the Croatian lands did not constitute a single administrative entity in the pre-Yugoslav period. Similarly, Ottoman efforts at internal reform throughout the nineteenth century did not provide a basis for reviving the authority of the center in these far-flung parts of the empire. By the eve of World War I, the Austro-Hungarian Dual Monarchy was neither a vital nor an authoritative state, and in the First Balkan War in 1912, the Ottoman Empire had been pushed out of the Balkans by an alliance consisting of Bulgaria, Greece, Serbia, and Montenegro.

This imperial decline was attended by the spread of ideas of the Enlightenment, the Romantic Movement, and Napoleonic Revolution of the early nineteenth century, which led, among the peoples of former Yugoslavia, to the emergence of modern national movements rooted in the language and culture of the common people. As discussed below, contending notions of the Yugoslav state combined with the uneven appearance of national movements in the nineteenth century. Serbia was the first state to emerge in a series of uprisings against the Ottomans that began in 1804 and culminated in formal independence at the Congress of Berlin in 1878. It gained experience in administration, in exercising influence in the region, and in its difficult relations with the government of the Hapsburg Dual Monarchy. The small state of Montenegro also gained international recognition in 1878 in Berlin as a separate government under Russian tutelage. Independence movements in different parts of Croatia and Slovenia were constrained by their relative weakness within the Hapsburg state and by a shifting set of goals rooted in some form of pan-south-Slav federalism, liberalism, integral nationalism, and an enhanced position within the Hapsburg Monarchy. At the Congress of Berlin, the Dual Monarchy took over the administration of Bosnia and, to great Serbian protest, formally annexed it in 1908. In the First Balkan War, the Ottomans lost both Kosovo to Serbia and Macedonia to a larger coalition. But the Second Balkan War in 1913 saw Serbia annex a great deal of Macedonia from Bulgaria. The end of World War I created conditions for the formation of a common state for Serbs, Croats, Slovenes, Bosnian Muslims, and Montenegrins that would also house significant numbers of Albanians, Hungarians, Turks, Italians, and others.

The decline of the Ottomans and the Hapsburgs set an agenda that did not favor the emergence of democratic institutions following World War I because of many unanswered questions in economic development, administration, cultural policy, and foreign policy. In his magisterial *The Yugoslav National Question*, Ivo Banac suggests, "The national question permeated every aspect of Yugoslavia's public life after 1918. It was reflected in the internal, external, social, economic, and even cultural affairs. It was solved by democrats and autocrats, kings and Communists. It was solved by day and unsolved by night. Some days were particularly bright for building, some nights particularly dark for destroying. One horn of the dilemma was that a single solution could not satisfy all sides. Was the other that a firm citadel could be maintained only by human sacrifice?"[4]

The Communist Experience

The felicitous title of Dennison Rusinow's superb *The Yugoslav Experiment* effectively captures socialist Yugoslavia's policy of permanent political improvisation.[5] The communist-led Partisans' seizure of power during World War II, with minimal assistance from the Soviet Union, began a search for a governing formula that would combine an efficient and equitable strategy of economic development with an approach to governance balanced between the leadership of a Leninist party and the broad inclusion of mass organizations. The communists' capacity to mobilize mass and external support during World War II provided the new regime, led by Josip Broz Tito, with the resilience, absent in other Central and East European socialist regimes, to resist the domination of its internal political and policy agendas by the Soviet Union. This toughness was essential for the experiments in governance that were conducted in an unusual international environment and that addressed economic decision-making and organization and the evolution of national communities within the Yugoslav federation.

In the first element of the experiment, socialist Yugoslavia found itself in a unique international environment in which it was a member of neither the Warsaw Treaty Organization nor NATO, where it was viewed as a communist country by the West and as a capitalist country by the Soviet bloc. Joseph Stalin's expulsion of Yugoslavia from the Communist Information Bureau, or Cominform, in 1948 provided a context to search for a legitimizing formula that would leave Yugoslavia both independent and socialist.[6] Military spending increased from the necessity to maintain a Yugoslav National Army (JNA) that could deter attack. While the top officer corps was ethnically balanced, the middle and noncommissioned officer corps were dominated by Serbs and Montenegrins—a matter of great significance, as most Yugoslav military assets fell to the Serbs during the wars of succession in the 1990s.

By the early 1960s, the Yugoslav government under Tito had adopted an "open" foreign policy between the two Cold War blocs and the newly independent countries in the developing world in which it came to play a prominent role in the movement of nonaligned countries.[7] Tito's Yugoslavia actively pursued an independent political course within the United Nations. It simultaneously traded extensively with communist-bloc countries and developed relations with multilateral financial institutions, such as the International Monetary Fund. It opened its borders so that by the early 1970s, over 1 million Yugoslav citizens lived and worked abroad. From the early 1950s, in other words, an increasingly diverse set of foreign relationships helped maintain Yugoslav independence and came to shape the character of internal policy choices.[8] However, by the fall of the Berlin Wall in 1989, Yugoslavia had ceased to represent a daring experiment that commanded Western and Soviet support.

The second element of the experiment lay in a strategy of economic development that was socialist but non-Soviet. Abandoning central planning early on, Yugoslav leaders adopted "self-management" decision-making within firms as the regime's central economic symbol. From the early 1950s onward, Yugoslav leaders engaged in a series of partial economic reforms that fell short of creating a market economy similar to those in Europe or North America. These reforms included the de-collectivization of agriculture; the decentralization of economic decision-making; the establishment of workers' councils in firms; liberalization of foreign trade; banking reforms; the creation of a fund for the development of underdeveloped regions; efforts to simulate or create financial, commodity, and labor markets; efforts to remove the party from everyday decision-making in the economy; the redesign of the economy in the mid-1970s into a "contractual economy"; and a policy of liberalizing "shock therapy" in 1990.[9]

The reforms did not work very well over the medium term, mainly because they neither fully embraced the implications of liberalizing reforms that would lead to significant privatization of economic assets nor ensured that the economy would remain "socialist." They did not provide stable economic growth based on a productive agriculture. Instead of narrowing intra-Yugoslav inequality, they were associated with increased economic inequality across and within republics. They appeared to increase Yugoslav dependence on the international economy and led to significantly increasing unemployment and the wholesale departure of labor to jobs in the West. They also continued political meddling in production. By 1990, Yugoslav debt to Western banks had grown to $20 billion. Unemployment reached 15.9 percent and in the least developed region, Kosovo, was 38.4 percent.[10] At one point in 1989, inflation had grown to 1,750 percent. In the best of political times, the Yugoslav government might have overcome these difficulties, but by 1991 it was the worst of times.

The final element of the experiment lay in political reforms embodied in large-scale efforts to define new constitutional orders in 1946, 1954, 1963, and 1974. Among other things, these constitutions attempted to devolve power away from the Communist Party of Yugoslavia to mass organizations that were more sensitive to diverse popular aspirations. Signs of this devolution included renaming the party the League of Communists of Yugoslavia (LCY) at its Sixth Congress in 1952, taking the party out of a command position in the mid-1960s by investing more authority in the regional organizations, and purging the hard-line secret police. The LCY leadership attempted to enhance the authority of nonparty governmental and administrative institutions but stopped short of divorcing the party from power. The purges of liberal party leaders throughout Yugoslavia in the early 1970s led to the re-Leninization of party organizations, which became incubators of the fractious nationalism they were meant to eliminate. This party-led regionalism provided the context for the end of the Yugoslav experiment in brotherhood and unity, the dissolution of the state, and war.

The idea of brotherhood and unity was central to the Yugoslav experiment. Yugoslavia, in reality, was a heterogeneous collection of Muslims, Eastern Orthodox, and Catholics; Serbs, Croats, Slovenes, Bosniacs,[11] Macedonians, and Montenegrins; and Albanians, Hungarians, Italians, Slovaks, Czechs, Turks, and others. Their modern national movements began at different times throughout the nineteenth century and enjoyed different degrees of success. The idea of creating some sort of state of South Slavs, or Yugoslavia, was also in the mix. But even the nineteenth century saw tensions between the idea of creating an overarching common identity and that of a Yugoslav identity that would merely bind together national groups sharing a common political space. This tension characterized political debates between centralizing "unitarists" and decentralizing "federalists" in both royalist and socialist Yugoslavia. And there was nothing inevitable about the creation of the Kingdom of Serbs, Croats, and Slovenes at the end of World War I, an entity that became known as Yugoslavia in 1929. Its Serbian royal dictatorship tried to push a common cultural Yugoslav identity that was in practice Serb-dominated. Serb-Croat political conflicts wracked the country right up until its dismemberment by the Nazis in 1941 into puppet regimes in Slovenia, Croatia, and Serbia and the annexation of Kosovo, Macedonia, and parts of Croatia by neighboring countries with their own claims to these regions. The communist-led Partisans won the civil war that took place during World War II in good measure because the symbol of Yugoslav "brotherhood and unity" was a supranational appeal to reason and survival.

To recognize and balance national interests, the SFRY was a federation of six republics: Serbia, Croatia, Montenegro, Slovenia, Macedonia, and Bosnia-Herzegovina. Bosnia-Herzegovina, the only republic without a titular nation, was a "community of Moslems, Croats, and Serbs."[12] There were two autonomous provinces within Serbia: Vojvodina, which was home to large numbers of Hungarians, and Kosovo, which had been predominantly Albanian since the end of World War II.[13] Croatia's population was 12 percent Serb in 1991. Many Serbs in Croatia lived in compact settlements in areas that comprised the Hapsburg military border from the sixteenth century, and others lived in large urban settlements. The Serbs were the SFRY's most dispersed nationality; more Serbs than any other ethnic group lived outside their nominal republic.

Successive constitutions defined a series of increasingly complex power-sharing arrangements between federal, republican, and regional governments that came to resemble consociational institutions theorized to build stable democracies in culturally plural societies.[14] By 1974, the pattern of representation in all federal-level decision-making bodies was carefully allotted to individuals from each republic (with attention paid to the intrarepublican nationality composition of such delegations) in order to ensure the formal picture of federal multinationalism. There was an intricate pattern of interrepublican decision-making, wherein republican and provincial representatives in state and government institutions held a virtual veto over each stage of federal decision-making.[15] The ethnic key guided all federal-level institutions. The presidency, parliamentary delegations, and cabinets included representatives of all republics and autonomous provinces. Under the 1974 constitution, the republics became the SFRY's most significant centers of power. But decentralization of politics left the LCY as "the one ring to bind them all," in Rusinow's phrase, despite the party's loss of political coherence.

Tito also tried to ensure that the country would remain unified by establishing a collective state presidency in 1971. Thus, each republic seat had a member to serve as part of the collective head of state. The president of the collective state presidency, who was Tito until his death, rotated among the republics and provinces each May, according to a predetermined arrangement.

With Tito's death in 1980, the fragility of this house of cards became increasingly apparent. As the winds of change began sweeping through socialist Europe, official Yugoslav politics remained committed to the methods of economic and political half reforms of the earlier socialist era. The bankruptcy of politics-as-usual could be seen in the suppression of demonstrations calling for republican status in Kosovo, in trumped-up show trials of Bosnian Muslims for ostensibly advocating an Islamic republic, and in a series of other public "political cases" meant to demonstrate the strength of the political center against disloyal enemies. But the absence of an authoritative political center was exposed in the failure of successive federal governments to identify an effective strategy of economic development and in the failure of republican oligarchs to agree on amendments to the 1974 constitution. The loss of a central vision was clearest in the failure of the Yugoslav presidency to act with any independent authority and the minor role relegated to federal Prime Minister Ante Marković in the political drama of succession. The torch had passed to republican leaders who were unable to reach agreement on a constructive course forward.

Most ominously, this political impasse led to the rise of Slobodan Milošević in Serbian politics in a 1987 coup against his political patron, Ivan Stambolić. Milošević revolutionized Yugoslav politics as the first party leader to depart from a convoluted and ideological public language to simple and direct rhetoric comprehensible to the broad masses. He explicitly integrated Serbian national goals into an "antibureaucratic revolution" that was supposed to preserve socialist Yugoslavia but provided an Orwellian tinge to his accumulation of greater power. Aside from taking over the Serbian media, Milošević employed techniques of mass mobilization to make credible threats against the socialist governments in Slovenia and Croatia after he had put his loyal minions in power in Kosovo, Vojvodina, and Montenegro, thereby giving him political control over four of the eight Yugoslav political units. This tactic made him the single most influential political force in late socialist Yugoslavia. He remained the commanding force in Serbian politics until his electoral defeat in autumn 2000 and arrest by the International Criminal Tribunal for the former Yugoslavia (ICTY)—a decade after the first window of democratic transition closed.[16]

The silver lining to this political cloud might have been the opening up of civil society throughout Yugoslavia in the middle and late 1980s. This involved publicly confronting previously suppressed conflicts and official excesses and beginning the process of reconciliation. In theory, a new democratic politics would be inclusive and strive to integrate all citizens and groups into a series of nested political communities that began locally and grew outward to the federation. In practice, it opened a Pandora's box and sometimes resulted in such inflammatory programs as the Serbian Academy of Sciences' "Memorandum" of 1986, which gave a cogent critique of economic mismanagement alongside a nationalist program aimed at protecting Serbs throughout Yugoslavia. The increasing openness of Yugoslav society meant that former officials and political prisoners could gather at meetings of the Association for Yugoslav Democratic Initiative to search for common ground for the future. It meant the return of *gastarbeiteri*, or Yugoslav guest workers who had been working abroad, and the entry of political émigrés into a rapidly evolving political mainstream. It meant coming to terms with the transnational character of ethnopolitical communities in the 1980s and 1990s—whether in the selection of a US citizen, Milan Panić, as the Serbian prime minister in 1992, the prominent role played by overseas Croats in Croatian domestic politics in the 1990s, or the substantial support of Albanian émigré communities for political and military action in Kosovo.

Greater pluralism combined with mounting economic problems to deepen the antagonism between political and economic development strategies pursued in the more economically developed regions (Slovenia and Croatia) and those regions that were less economically developed.[17] Slovenian and Croatian elites favored a looser, asymmetrical federation together with liberal political and economic reforms. Serbian leaders countered with reforms calling for a recentralization of the state and political system together with a streamlined self-management system. Each plan suited the self-interest of the regionally rooted elites who proposed it. Forces for compromise—federal Prime Minister Ante Marković and leaders of the less developed and ethnically diverse republics of Bosnia and Macedonia—were easily drowned out. Already disgruntled over having to foot what they considered more than their fair share of the bill for central government and economic development in poorer regions of the country, leaders in Slovenia and Croatia in the late 1980s balked when asked to contribute to Serbia's strong-arm tactics over restive Kosovo. Fearing they would lose the battle with Belgrade over reform of Yugoslavia, the Slovenian party elite in 1989 saw the benefit of "giving in" to the increasing demands of republic youth and intellectuals for pluralism and sovereignty. The pursuit of liberal reform was more contentious in Croatia, where 12 percent of the population was Serb, and reformers only gained the upper hand at the end of 1989.

By 1989, the pressure for comprehensive change was great. The federal LCY ceased to exist in January 1990 when the Slovene and Croat delegations walked out of the Fourteenth Extraordinary Congress of the LCY after the Serbian bloc rejected all Slovene motions—for example, to confederalize the party, ban the use of torture, and provide clearer guarantees of the right of dissociation—without any meaningful discussion. Most former republican LCY organizations soon morphed into social democratic parties (SDPs).[18] This development did not auger a happy outcome for the intense interrepublican political bargaining about Yugoslavia's future architecture. For the first time since World War II, nationalist ideas were viewed as legitimate, and nationalist "enemies" of socialism became centrally important actors in Yugoslav politics. By 1991, few political or institutional constraints were commonly accepted throughout Yugoslavia. There was also a sense that the window of political opportunity would not remain open long. The Serbian government viewed itself as the protector of Serbs throughout former Yugoslavia, and Croatian president Franjo Tudjman would soon make the error of trying to extend the Croatian state into Bosnia.

State Formation and War

The Yugoslav government barely paused at the precipice of dissolution and war in 1990 and 1991. As detailed below, republic-level elections throughout the federation in 1990 selected leaderships accountable to ethnically based republican constituencies. These leaders failed to reach consensus on the shape of a democratic Yugoslav federation. Slovenian and Croatian leaders held well-orchestrated referenda on independence and began transforming their reserve forces into armies. European mediators failed to prevent a war at this "hour of Europe," and the US government was not sufficiently interested to act.[19] While the underlying causes of the wars of Yugoslav succession remain in sharp dispute, most scholars have rejected simplistic explanations that conjure up centuries of ethnic enmity in favor of more complex explanations in which ambitious elites exacerbated ethnic tensions and dramatically increased the potential for violence.

On the eve of war, the SFRY's economy was in decline and the legitimacy of its socialist institutions in disrepair to the increasing frustration of ordinary citizens. With no authoritative political center, the emergence of politicized ethnicity that exacerbated unresolved grievances from World War II allowed little room for compromise among elites. Against this background, the newly elected republican leaderships in 1990 failed to resolve their differences in negotiations and used a "crisis frame" of interethnic relations that led to war in mid-1991.[20] Five interconnected armed conflicts took place that still cast long shadows on developments in all seven successor states. It has been difficult to establish precise figures, but an estimate of people killed during the entire conflict is somewhat under 150,000; over 4.5 million people were displaced at some point in the conflicts. By mid-2017, the UN High Commissioner for Refugees estimated that some 83,716 refugees remained in exile and that 317,957 internally displaced persons were still seeking durable solutions by returning home.[21]

SLOVENIA

The Slovene government declared independence on June 25, 1991, following careful preparations for defense that effectively stymied an ill-prepared JNA offensive. By June 30, Serbian leaders ordered the JNA to prepare to abandon Slovenia. There were eight military and five civilian deaths among the Slovenes, and thirty-nine members of the JNA died. Slovenian independence was formally acknowledged on July 18.[22] Slovenia subsequently entered the EU in 2004 together with nine other countries, became the first new member to adopt the euro as its currency in 2007, and was invited to become a member of the Organization for Economic Co-operation and Development in October 2010.[23]

CROATIA

The Croatian government declared independence on June 26, 1991. Following the initially artful invitation to the leader of the Serb Democratic Party to become a vice president in the Croatian government in spring 1990, the Tudjman government awkwardly began firing Serb administrators, teachers and police throughout Croatia in the name of achieving ethnic balance in official employment. Armed conflict began in 1990 with a series of skirmishes and the Serbs' consolidation of control in the illegally constituted Serb Autonomous Regions with the aid of JNA officers and arms by mid-March 1991. Croatian Serbs largely boycotted the Croatian referendum on independence. The war featured sieges of Croatia's Danubian city of Vukovar and the Adriatic city of Dubrovnik. Former US secretary of state and UN negotiator Cyrus Vance devised a plan that allowed 13,500 UN troops to deploy to oversee the reintegration of the one-third of the republic's territory controlled by Serbs into Croatia.[24] An estimated twenty thousand people died during the war. Despite European Community concerns over the Croatian government's treatment of its Serb minority, Germany recognized Croatia's independence in early 1992; the United States and other European governments soon followed.

International negotiators from the United Nations, the European Community, the United States, and Russia presided over three years of inconclusive negotiations between the Croatian government and rebel Serbs, who repeatedly refused to begin talks concerning the reintegration of Serb-held territory into Croatia in accordance with the Vance Plan. The Croatian government launched two offensives to regain control of most Serb-held territory in May and August 1995, after which approximately three hundred thousand Serbs fled Croatia.[25] As part of the larger process of ending the war in Bosnia-Herzegovina, the UN Transitional Administration in Eastern Slavonia (UNTAES) mediated the formal return of territory by early 1998. The Organization for Security and Co-operation in Europe (OSCE) later remained to monitor aspects of policing, media, and the return of refugees. The Croatian government's reassertion of control over its entire territory by 1998 was a turning point that removed the issue of Serb occupation and enabled the emergence of more normal political bargaining and political reform that ultimately led to Croatia's membership in the EU, as discussed below.

BOSNIA-HERZEGOVINA

By autumn 1991, a delicately balanced coalition government among Muslim, Serb, and Croat parties broke down with disputes over power sharing and Bosnia's relationship to rump Yugoslavia, the departure of the Serb Democratic Party delegation led by Radovan Karadžić, and the formation of multiple Serb Autonomous Regions with JNA support.

Croatian president Tudjman had already discussed the partition of Bosnia-Herzegovina with Serbian president Slobodan Milošević by March 1991, in an initiative that would betray Croatia's image as a victim of aggression, strengthen the hand of radically nationalist Croats in Herzegovina, and establish the "territorial integrity of the Croat nation in its historic and natural borders" in a way that would expand the Tudjman government's influence in Bosnia.[26]

The Bosnian government's declaration of independence was recognized by several Western governments on April 6, 1992, while both the Bosnian Serb and the Serbian leadership in Belgrade rejected independence. Initial Serb military campaigns in 1992 rapidly led to the capture of about 60 percent of Bosnia's territory, gains that remained basically intact until the fighting ended in autumn 1995. In an attempt to destroy Bosnia's complex social geography and control territory, the Serb military engaged in ethnic cleansing[27] and created prison camps. The radical Croatian Defense Council (HVO) subsequently launched offensives in Herzegovina and central Bosnia. Radicalized by foreign Muslim volunteers, a Muslim brigade in central Bosnia also committed crimes, while both Serb and Croat forces destroyed Islamic cultural monuments.[28] The war in Bosnia generated 2.5 million refugees and internally displaced persons, well over half of the prewar population.

The international community proved ineffective at ending the war. The UN Security Council passed over one hundred normative acts that established an arms embargo that de facto favored the well-armed Bosnian Serb Army against the poorly equipped Army of the Republic of Bosnia-Herzegovina and that addressed daily crises in the provision of humanitarian assistance and protection of civilians. Concurrently, international negotiators from the European Community, United Nations, United States, and others drafted a series of peace plans but took few steps to compel the parties to reach agreement and did not intervene in support of the elected Bosnian government headed by Alija Izetbegović. Under a Chapter VI mandate, the UN Security Council deployed twenty-six thousand lightly armed troops in the UN Protection Force (UNPROFOR), which were scattered throughout Bosnia-Herzegovina in support of humanitarian assistance, to help build confidence among the parties and in six "safe areas" for civilians. But these troops were neither sufficiently armed nor empowered to compel compliance with the UN mandate and were, in effect, at the mercy of the strongest party on the ground—the Bosnian Serb Army. International negotiators succeeded in compelling Croat forces in Herzegovina and the Bosnian government to cooperate against Serb forces by forming the Federation of Bosnia and Herzegovina in early 1994. By mid-1995, Serb forces became increasingly assertive, culminating in their conquest of Srebrenica in the largest single post–World War II European massacre. Soon afterward, NATO air intervention and a Bosniac-Croat offensive ended the fighting and culminated in the US-led negotiations in Dayton, Ohio, in November 1995. The most respected, though still contentious, estimate holds that just over 97,100 people died in the conflict.[29]

The US-led negotiations in Dayton resulted in peace accords that created a Bosnia that largely recognized the "facts" created on the ground by the war, particularly the violent creation of ethnic "homelands."[30] Dayton Bosnia consists of an unwieldy configuration of two entities: Republika Srpska (RS; 49 percent) and the Bosniac-Croat Federation (51 percent), each initially with its own police and army, though the army was eventually unified. The RS is relatively centralized, while the federation is composed of ten cantons with substantial autonomy. Two cantons are explicitly mixed, three are dominated by Croats, and five are dominated by Bosniacs. A large NATO military implementation force and complex civilian intervention began in early 1996, and its work is continued by a considerably smaller multinational force led by the EU.[31] Under the authority of the fifty-five-member Peace Implementation Council (PIC), the High Representative for Bosnia and Herzegovina has overseen efforts to implement the Dayton Peace Accords by the United Nations, the EU, the OSCE, the World Bank, and a host of nongovernmental organizations (NGOs). The High Representative won extraordinary powers at a meeting of the Peace Implementation Committee in Bonn in December 1997, which has enabled him to override Bosnian institutions to pass legislation and remove domestic officials from office. Since 2006, the PIC has aspired to close the Office of the High Representative in an effort to stand Bosnian institutions on their own feet to "take responsibility for the peace process and the problems that the country faces," but the failure to settle all of the war's outstanding issues has not permitted this to take place.[32]

KOSOVO

Kosovo has long been an apple of discord between Serbs and Albanians. It served both as the center of the medieval Serbian state and as the birthplace of the modern Albanian national movement in the nineteenth century. In the period immediately after World War II, the Serbian-dominated secret police imposed a harsh anti-Albanian order in Kosovo; in the 1950s, the situation was so bad that many Albanians declared themselves Turks and emigrated to Turkey. The pendulum swung in the other direction after the fall of secret police chief Aleksandar Ranković in 1966; by 1974, Kosovo had become almost an equal member of the federation, and Albanians were the largest ethnic group in the province. But beginning with demonstrations in 1981, the pendulum again began swinging back against Albanian interests. Between 1988 and 1990, the Serbian government forced the province's two top leaders to resign, forced the federal assembly to reducing the province's autonomy, suppressed the provincial assembly and the executive council, terminated Albanian-language instruction in the schools, and caused over one hundred thousand Kosovar Albanians to lose their jobs in the administrative, education, and health sectors. This led to large-scale Albanian emigration from Kosovo efforts to resettle Serbs (including refugees from Croatia) there.[33]

In response to these developments, the Democratic League of Kosovo (LDK), which was headed by Ibrahim Rugova, spearheaded a peaceful movement for autonomy and then independence. In parallel elections, the LDK won the broad support of Albanians in Kosovo and Rugova was elected president. It established a parallel administration in education and health care that was widely used and supported by Albanians. However, Rugova did not win a place at any international negotiating table beyond that of observer, partly because international negotiators viewed Milošević as essential to ending conflicts in Croatia and Bosnia-Herzegovina. This failure created the conditions for a more militant phase of the national movement when the Kosovo Liberation Army (KLA) took the initiative in support of independence for Kosovo. Beginning with violent assaults against Serbian police stations in December 1997, the KLA began operations, which elicited increasingly harsh responses from Serbian forces. International efforts to establish an OSCE Verification Mission in the autumn of 1998 did not succeed in deterring further violence. The failure of the Rambouillet negotiations in France in early 1999 led to more intense ethnic cleansing of Albanians from Kosovo and a seventy-seven-day NATO air campaign against Serbia and Serb positions in Kosovo. The campaign ended with a Military-Technical Agreement between the International Security Force and the Governments of the Federal Republic of Yugoslavia and Serbia on June 9 and with UN Security Council Resolution 1244 on June 10, which created an interim administration for Kosovo that was meant to provide a framework for a broader political settlement.

From June 1999 through February 2008, the UN Mission in Kosovo cooperated with newly evolving domestic institutions and the NATO-led Kosovo Force to oversee the establishment of political and administrative institutions in Kosovo. From the initial establishment of the Joint Interim Administrative Structure in late 1999 through the passage of a constitutional framework in mid-2001, elections to local government in October 2000, and creation of the Assembly of Kosovo in November 2001, the United Nations oversaw efforts to establish security and judicial institutions, administration, and services and to regulate economic activity and trade. Beginning in November 2005, former president of Finland Martti Ahtisaari led negotiations among all relevant stakeholders that led to the Final Comprehensive Proposal for a Kosovo Status Settlement in March 2007 as a basis for negotiations among the political leaderships in Serbia and Kosovo.

The parties failed to reach an agreement over Kosovo's future status. It was believed that some leaders sought to partition Kosovo so that several northern municipalities, including industrially developed Mitrovica, would be exchanged for Albanian majority municipalities—Preševo, Medvedje, and Bujanovac—in southeastern Serbia. Influential international officials stepped in to block this potential deal and Kosovar Albanian leaders have subsequently insisted that Kosovo retain its prewar administrative borders. Consequently, on February 17, 2008, the Kosovo Assembly declared Kosovo "an independent and sovereign state" that would "be a democratic, secular and multiethnic republic, guided by the principles of non-discrimination and equal protection under the law."[34] Following a period of "supervised independence" guided by the International Civilian Office that ended in September 2012, a substantial international presence remains in Kosovo, including the European rule of law mission called EULEX, the Kosovo Force, and a number of other multilateral aid missions and influential bilateral diplomatic missions.

By early 2017, over 111 governments had recognized Kosovo's independence, but this number excludes important powers such as Russia and China and European governments such as Spain, Slovakia, and Romania. This partially reflects the diplomatic efforts of the Serbian government, which formally objected to Kosovo's independence before the International Court of Justice.[35] In spring 2013, Serbian Prime Minister Ivica Dačić and Kosovo Prime Minister Hashim Thaqi concluded two years of EU-facilitated meetings with an agreement to establish an association of Kosovo Serb municipalities, to integrate Serbian police and judicial structures into Kosovo, and to prepare for local elections.[36]

By mid-2017, Kosovo remained in this "half-way house" to full international sovereignty. The Kosovo government signed a Stabilization and Association Agreement (SAA) with the EU in October 2015 but has yet to approve the border demarcation with Montenegro. Authorities in Serbia and Kosovo continue to meet routinely for technical talks in Brussels, although the "practical implementation of dialogue agreements" proceeds slowly, as is seen in creating an Association/Community of Serb Majority Municipalities in Kosovo.[37] These difficulties are compounded by an ongoing series of incidents that "poison the waters," including successful Serbian lobbying against Kosovo membership in UNESCO, a Serbian train arriving in northern Kosovo with the phrase "Kosovo is Serbia" in many languages, a Kosovo declaration to transform the Kosovo Security Force into an armed professional military force, demands of Serbian authorities to extradite former and current Prime Minister Ramush Haradinaj to Serbia for trial, and many others.[38]

MACEDONIA

Enduring Bulgarian, Greek, and Serbian claims to Macedonia have been less significant in destabilizing Macedonia than have internal disputes among Macedonian parties and between Macedonians and Albanians.[39] Yet, the government of Greece has consistently objected to "Macedonia's 'appropriation' of a name and symbols it deem[s] exclusively Hellenic" since 1990. As a result, Greece has obstructed Macedonian accession to European institutions and has accepted its UN membership only as the "Former Yugoslav Republic of Macedonia."[40]

Albanians constitute 25 percent of the population of Macedonia and mainly live in the area in the northwest bordering on Kosovo and Albania and in the capital, Skopje.[41] A "policy of half-hearted, half-reluctant ethnic cohabitation" in a series of multiethnic coalition governments since the early 1990s helped maintain a fragile peace but did not provide a basis for integrating the two groups into a common community.[42] Nor did the policies of the UN Preventive Deployment Force, the European Community, or the OSCE in the mid-1990s lead to political integration. Albanian guerillas supported by Kosovar irregulars engaged in skirmishes in 2001 in northwestern Macedonia with Macedonian forces. After several months, international diplomats brokered the Ohrid Agreement, which provides for constitutional amendments and reforms to improve the status of Albanians while maintaining the unity of the state. NATO briefly deployed in Macedonia to collect weapons, and an OSCE mission remains in place. Since 2001, EU and US diplomats have mediated political disputes that have repeatedly stymied progress in developing effective and inclusive democratic governance.

MONTENEGRO

The declaration of Montenegrin independence on June 3, 2006, was another significant act in the post-Yugoslav drama of succession. Through 1996, the Montenegrin government largely supported Yugoslav war aims, and Montenegrin soldiers actively participated in the siege of Dubrovnik and surrounding areas in October 1991. In 1992, Montenegro joined Serbia in a truncated Federal Republic of Yugoslavia, which on February 4, 2004, devolved into the State Union of Serbia and Montenegro; on May 21, 2006, Montenegro won full independence in a referendum, with a relatively narrow vote of 55.5 percent of voters supporting independence and 44.5 percent opposing it. This was the culmination of a process of alienation between Serbia and Montenegro and an internal divide in Montenegro over relations with Serbia that began in 1991.[43] Elections in 1997 and

1998 put a reform wing of the former League of Communists led by Milo Đukanović firmly in power. And with the adoption of the German mark as the parallel currency and abolishing of visas for foreigners in 1999, the Montenegrin government staked out its future claim to independence. The Montenegrin government dramatically departed from Serbian policy in its recognition of Kosovo's independence in October 2008. The European Council endorsed the opening of accession negotiations with the Montenegrin government in June 2012. It has completed some "important work on alignment and preparation for the implementation with the EU *acquis communitaire*."[44] Montenegro also became a member of NATO in June 2017 against strong internal opposition and objections from the Russian government—following general speculation that the Russian government was involved in an attempted coup d'etat in Montenegro in October 2016 on the heels of elections (see below).[45]

In sum, the SFRY violently dissolved into seven small countries following the first democratic elections in 1990, and the aftershocks of this dissolution have not yet fully ended. A mid-size country of 21 million citizens had been subdivided into seven countries with populations ranging from 625,000 to just over 7 million citizens. The failure of the international community to act in a timely fashion in the late 1980s and early 1990s contributed to the uncertainty that permitted stronger anti-Yugoslav forces to undermine efforts at the peaceful construction of a normal political system. The wars of Yugoslav succession made the transition from socialism in the countries of former Yugoslavia significantly more complicated than transitions in Central and Eastern Europe. Each successor state has followed its own trajectory toward a degree of twenty-first-century-style sovereignty. The wars' legacies become clearer after surveying transformation of elites and institutions, party politics, transitional justice, civil society, attitudes toward politics, and economic development.

Political Transitions and Political Institutions

The chaotic political transition and the wars of Yugoslav succession have left a deep imprint on the patterns of elite transformation and development of political institutions in the successor states. Old and new leaderships easily blended together. Former communists, such as Serbian president Milošević and Croatian president Tudjman, became nationalist leaders in the new regimes, and former SFRY finance minister and president of the National Assembly Kiro Gligorov became the first president of Macedonia. Many former democratic dissidents also became nationalist leaders and ideologues. Some former nationalists became liberal, democratic human rights advocates. Returning political émigrés blended effectively with former communists in nationalist parties. Among the older generation, former communists work easily with former nationalist "enemies." Younger, able, and politically nimble politicians and administrators rose quickly to prominence in all governments. A careful examination of elite transformation in Croatia, Serbia, Bosnia-Herzegovina, and Kosovo would show how nationalist leaders employed the wars to deepen their hold on power and expand political machines that limited interparty electoral competition. The wars thus delayed political democratization and economic liberalization.

The international community also contributed to this delay. The command systems that were established during the wars facilitated alliances between external agencies and the warring parties at the expense of the citizens for whom the assistance was intended. For example, in Bosnia-Herzegovina, the warring parties took a cut of all humanitarian aid intended for civilians as part of their war effort.[46] After peace agreements were negotiated with the wars' protagonists, "peace-building" international agencies tacitly helped to buttress the authority of corrupt leaders who were resisting democratization simply by treating them as legitimate leaders, for example. The peace accords in Kosovo and Bosnia-Herzegovina did not settle disputes about power sharing or sovereignty, or provide a clear road map to stable and democratic institutions. The failure to resolve open issues peacefully—for example, the status of Kosovo, the capture of indicted war criminals, the return of refugees and displaced persons—ensured that recalcitrant leaders would selectively implement only those elements of the peace accords that suited their own narrow agendas. Finally, many important domestic functions were taken over by international officials from the United Nations, OSCE, Office of the High Representative, and EU. These often inexperienced officials generally spoke none of the languages and knew little about the region. As a result, their actions have often made the transition even more difficult.

By 2006, all former Yugoslav republics had adopted proportional representation (PR) electoral systems. All could be described as parliamentary democracies, except for Bosnia and Kosovo, and Macedonia, which are characterized as hybrid regimes.[47] However, most did not start the postcommunist period that way. Domestic and international forces helped alter the distribution of power between the president and the parliament, as well as the electoral systems of the former Yugoslav states. For example, as democratic groups gained strength in Croatia and Serbia, they weakened their countries' presidencies by building up and increasing the independence of nonpresidential political institutions. In Croatia, they also jettisoned the single-member district system and adopted the more representative PR system.

Institutional engineering was most elaborate in those regions of former Yugoslavia that experienced significant international intervention. There, international diplomats compelled the adoption seats for minorities. The pull of the EU also encouraged dedicated seats for minorities in Montenegro and Slovenia, though the latter reserves seats only for its indigenous minorities. Germany helped convince Croatia also to reserve seats for minorities. In addition, Croatia and Macedonia reserved seats for representatives chosen by their diasporas.[48] Electoral engineers also adopted laws on gender quotas in all former Yugoslav countries to ensure the representation of women in political offices.[49] Despite all the attention to crafting political institutions in Bosnia and Kosovo, these domestic institutions currently share power with unelected international officials who exercise executive authority. Both of these practices considerably complicate the search for effective governance for all citizens in these newly independent countries.

Elections and Political Parties

The countries of former Yugoslavia share characteristics of their Central and East European neighbors, including weak party systems, a rather amorphous ideological spectrum, party fragmentation, inconsistent commitment to programs, and problems with internal party democracy.[50] Former Yugoslav governments are riddled with personalistic parties that rely primarily on patronage networks to govern. Taken together with the frequent formation of new parties and disappearance of other parties, these characteristics have significantly undermined parties' capacity to aggregate interests effectively. Bosnia-Herzegovina, Macedonia, and Kosovo have been subjected to intensive international involvement in domestic politics and also feature entrenched ethnic party systems, both of which undermine party responsiveness to the interests of ordinary citizens. Valerie Bunce suggests that the victory of a liberal, anticommunist opposition in the first multiparty election permits a decisive break with the authoritarian past and a launching of a liberal program. In contrast, the victory of an ethnically exclusive opposition can obviate democratization and lead to challenges to state boundaries.[51] Communist parties can also adopt nationalist agendas in order to maintain their hold on power.

By the criteria outlined above, only Slovenia experienced a relatively smooth democratic transition and process of state formation in its first post-Yugoslav election, the founding parliamentary election. The noncommunist coalition Democratic Opposition of Slovenia (DEMOS) won. The leader of the reformed Communist Party won the presidency. This new government enacted pluralist and market reforms and declared Slovenia's independence from Yugoslavia. After the movement-based DEMOS disintegrated, the fragmented party system appeared to consolidate into four strong parties: the left-oriented Social Democrats, the moderate-left Liberal Democracy of Slovenia, the center-right Slovenian Democratic Party, and the Christian Democratic Party. Broad agreement among Slovenia's elite that their future was tied to European and Euro-Atlantic institutions helped the country achieve early membership in the EU and NATO. In addition, the absence of substantial minorities allowed Slovenia's significant illiberal forces to remain relatively harmless during its march into Europe.[52] The heavy impact of the 2008 global recession, 2011 Eurozone crisis, and domestic austerity policies generated conditions for a vote of no confidence in September 2011, the formation of two new political parties, and the holding of the first early elections in the postcommunist period in December 2011. Antiestablishment sentiment contributed to the victory of a party with a vague, anti-corruption, and pro-liberalization platform formed only the month prior to the July 2014 parliamentary elections—the Miro Cerer Party, which leads a five-party coalition government.[53] Former Prime Minister Jansa of Slovenian Democratic Party campaigned in 2014 from jail, where he was serving a sentence for bribery. These developments have exposed the turbulence in Slovenia's party system and governance.[54]

By contrast to developments in Slovenia, the first post-Yugoslav elections in Croatia and Serbia enabled nationalist parties to advance ethnic agendas rather than build consensus and undermine democratization with hybrid systems at home. Only at the end of these conflicts could opposition coalitions overcome internal bickering to win elections in second transitions and initiate reform programs that contributed to more normal political competition, albeit within the weak party systems described above.

In Serbia, Milošević weathered several waves of antiregime demonstrations in the 1990s and intraparty conflict and remade the League of Communists of Serbia into an authoritarian nationalist party with its own satellite, the United Yugoslav Left, headed by Milošević's wife. In the founding election in 1990, his Socialist Party of Serbia (SPS) ensured that it would dominate the parliament. The SPS's program appealed to socialist conformists as well as to Serbs who had criticized Tito's "weakening of Serb interests" in Yugoslavia in the 1980s.[55] The party was strongest outside Belgrade and in the Serbian heartland. Milošević used existing structures to retain power, acquire wealth, distribute patronage to his family and allies among his criminalized support structure,[56] and manage "Serb" territories outside Serbia. War and a monopoly over politics, effective propaganda through government-directed media, and control of the security forces allowed Milošević to demobilize political opposition and eliminate political alternatives.[57]

With the end of the fighting in Kosovo, the SPS could no longer label oppositionists as traitors. Ordinary Serbs increasingly attributed their worsening circumstances to the SPS's poor governance. Milošević's supporters among the criminal class had become independent of his patronage. The leaders of the liberal opposition finally set aside personal antagonism to unite, and the youth organization Otpor (Resistance) effectively led civic mobilization. These forces overturned Milošević's plans to rig the 2000 presidential elections and helped secure the victory of Vojislav Koštunica, who was supported by an eighteen-party opposition coalition, the Democratic Opposition of Serbia (DOS). The DOS coalition convincingly won the December 2000 parliamentary elections, selecting the Democratic Party's (DS) Zoran Đinđić as prime minister. However, differences

Photo 16.1. Funeral procession for Serbian Prime Minister Zoran Đinđić, who was assassinated by Serbian radicals in 2003. Đinđić had made many enemies for his pro-Western stance, reformist economic policies, and clampdown on organized crime. He also had Slobodan Milošević arrested and handed over to the International Criminal Tribunal for the Former Yugoslavia at The Hague. (Website of the Serbian Government, http://www.srbija.gov.rs)

between Koštunica and Đinđić over a bargaining strategy with the West led to the disintegration of the coalition. Soon thereafter, war profiteers assassinated Đinđić in response to his intention to reform the security sector and cooperate more closely with the ICTY.

In the 2003 and 2007 parliamentary elections, Vojislav Šešelj's extremist Serb Radical Party (SRS) received more votes than any other party, gaining support from dissatisfaction with incumbents, sacrifices connected to economic reform, and resentment of Western demands for closer Serbian cooperation with the ICTY and for the relinquishment of Kosovo. However, pressure from the West led Koštunica to form center-right coalitions after both elections that denied the SRS a formal role.[58] But SRS influence was felt in the National Assembly's quickly drafted constitution that was unanimously adopted in September 2006. Prime Minister Koštunica struggled to balance demands within his broad coalition: the government's liberal partners, G17 Plus, and the DS pushed for reforms needed to resume talks with the EU on an SAA, while their powerful and populist supporters remained resentful of EU pressure on Serbia. With the formation of a government and closer cooperation with the ICTY in capturing high-profile indictees, the EU resumed SAA talks with Belgrade in June 2007.

New elections were held within a year. In the first presidential elections since the dissolution of Serbia's state union with Montenegro, President Tadić narrowly won reelection in January 2008 over SRS candidate Tomislav Nikolić. In May 2008 parliamentary elections, the DS-led "For a European Serbia" narrowly won the election and formed a coalition government with DS, G17 Plus, the leftist coalition led by the SPS—for the first time since 2000—and parties of national minorities: Hungarians, Bosniacs, and Albanians. Under Ivica Dačić, the SPS has been exploring membership in the Socialist International as a European party.

In September 2008, because of differences with ICTY-indicted leader Vojislav Šešelj over EU membership, Tomislav Nikolić led a bloc of twenty members of parliament out of the SRS to form the considerably more moderate Serbian Progressive Party (SNS). The SNS quickly established its credibility in opposition to the government dominated by President Tadić by appealing to Serbs in small towns outside the capital and reaching out to Serbia's key international partners abroad. This strategy paid off in the elections held in spring 2012. Nikolić defeated President Tadić in the second round of voting, and the SNS's "Let's Get Serbia Moving" coalition defeated the DS's "Choice for a Better Life" coalition in parliamentary elections, then formed a coalition with Dačić's SPS, which placed third in the voting. Since late 2013, these partisan realignments have led formerly important smaller parties, such as the Liberal Democratic Party, G17 Plus, and Democratic Party of Serbia, to fade even further into the background of serious political contention and to the continuing rise of the SNS.

In elections held in 2014 and 2016, the SNS continued strengthening its position as the dominant political force in Serbia. In 2014, the SNS-led coalition, "The Future We Believe In" won just over 48 percent of the votes and a majority of seats in the National Assembly. It formed a coalition government with Dačić's SPS-led coalition, which won the second most seats. SNS leader Aleksandar Vučić served as prime minister and SPS leader Dačić served as first deputy prime minister and foreign minister. Riding a wave of popularity, the SNS again called new elections in 2016 and its "Serbia Is Winning" coalition again won an absolute majority and formed a government together with the

SPS: Vučić served as prime minister and Dačić was again first deputy prime minister and foreign minister.

It appears that President Aleksandar Vučić is building an unassailable position in Serbian politics recalling that of Milošević in the 1990s. He successfully manages relations among key domestic parties and personalities, authoritatively oversees the fortunes of Serbian political forces in Kosovo, and effectively balances off the key EU, US and Russian outreach to Serbia. In the 2017 presidential elections, he won an absolute majority of votes on the first round of voting and then appointed the nonparty technocrat Ana Barbić as the first female, openly gay prime minister in late June 2017.[59]

It was noteworthy that the leading candidates and parties in the 2012 presidential and parliamentary elections, for the first time in the postcommunist period, all pledged to support Serbia's integration into the EU, while Vučić and other Serbian leaders continue to cultivate warm relations with Russia.[60] Although the Serbian government has not committed to formal recognition of the independence of Kosovo, the European Council granted Serbia candidate country status in March 2012. Aside from its progress in developing a market economy and parliamentary democracy, the European Commission (EC) report noted the Serbian government's cooperation with the ICTY and agreements with the government of Kosovo as part of its process of dialogue. The commission further reports that Serbia continues to participate constructively in regional initiatives with Croatia aimed at reconciliation and cooperation and is "committed to the implementation of the agreements in the EU-facilitated dialogue."[61] In retrospect, this naively hopeful assessment emerges either from "best-case scenario" planning or from the willingness to set a very low bar for Serbian accession to the EU.

In Croatia, the nationalist movement was led by the Croatian Democratic Union (HDZ) under the leadership of former Partisan general and later political dissident Franjo Tudjman with substantial support from political émigrés. The HDZ won power in 1990 on the basis of its anticommunist expression of Croatian identity. It was viewed as the most serious alternative to the atheistic socialism of the ex-communists or the Party of Democratic Change (later renamed the SDP).[62] A majoritarian electoral system turned the HDZ's 46 percent of the popular vote into 67.5 percent of the seats in parliament. The losing Coalition of National Accord, composed of former communists and liberals, fragmented and formed a series of smaller parties. A majority of Serb SDP members chose to leave the evolving Croatian SDP. Regional parties in Istria have demonstrated considerable staying power. The war began in 1990 and 1991 with the refusal of the Serb Democratic Party (SDS) leadership to join the broad governing compact led by HDZ in 1990, which strengthened exclusivist tendencies within the HDZ as the most serious defender of Croatia against Serb aggressors. As long as Serbs occupied Croatian territory, Tudjman's HDZ monopolized power in Croatia. It supported moderate Serb groups in Croatia in a demonstration of political openness, but its monopoly of power enabled the HDZ political and administrative elite to engage in corrupt practices.

With the return of all Serb-held territory and changes in electoral laws, the diverse opposition to the HDZ made significant electoral gains on platforms of good governance and political change. After President Tudjman's death in the run-up to elections in early 2000, a moderate six-party opposition coalition headed by the SDP won control of parliament. Its governing program included accession to the EU, cutting the purse strings of the hard-line HDZ in Bosnia, and cooperation with the ICTY. However, a governing coalition whose connecting bond lay mainly in beating the HDZ would not prove authoritative itself. Its inability to improve economic performance and its cooperation with The Hague's efforts to capture Croatian generals for trial led to its defeat in elections in 2004 by a more compact and reformed version of the HDZ. Following its loss of power in 2000, the HDZ had splintered and adapted its own electoral appeal to pursue integration into the EU. Its increased cooperation with the ICTY in 2006 helped convince EU leaders to begin talks on accession. The HDZ won another close election in late 2007 and formed a government with support from a broad range of parties, including those representing national minorities. It included one deputy prime minister from the Independent Democratic Serbian Party (SDSS), committed to proportional Serb presence in public institutions, and encouraged the return of Serbian refugees to Croatia.[63] However, Prime Minister Ivo Sanader resigned under a cloud in July 2009 in favor of Jadranka Kosor, the first woman to serve as prime minister in Croatia since its independence in 1990.[64] Sanader was sentenced to ten years in prison for accepting bribes in 2011 and is the highest official to serve time for corruption in Central and Eastern Europe since 1990. This assuaged EU fears that Croatia would ignore corruption and enabled the HDZ to reconfigure itself over the medium term.

Kosor's government was short-lived. In January 2010, SDP candidate Ivo Josipović was elected as the third president of Croatia since 1990. The SDP-led Kukuriku (Cock-a-Doodle-Do) coalition claimed victory over the HDZ-led coalition with 80 of the 151 seats in the Sabor and with the support of the eight seats set aside for ethnic minorities. Kukuriku's campaign focused on corruption scandals, high unemployment, and the poor economic performance of the previous HDZ government. Following this defeat, HDZ leadership passed from Kosor to Tomislav Karamarko, the rightist former minister of the interior and director of security and intelligence, who appeared to be leading a party that was both resurgent and moving to the right at the end of 2013.

This resurgence has led to the precarious political ascendance of the HDZ once again in Croatian politics. In early 2015, HDZ's Kolinda Grabar-Kitanović beat incumbent SDP president Josipović in the second round of a very close election, but this did not spell a clear political victory for the Croatian right under a HDZ umbrella. New parties of outsiders have appeared, especially "Most" or the Bridge of Independent Lists and Živi Zid (the Human Wall).

In elections held in Fall 2015, the HDZ-led coalition narrowly outpolled the SDP-led coalition and formed a government with the centrist Most party on condition that HDZ leader Karamarko serve as deputy prime minister to the nonpartisan, Croatian-Canadian businessman Tihomir Orešković. In addition, a group of small, right-wing parties joined the government and made demands for lustration of former communists and changes in cultural, media, and education policy that reopened broad ideological and cultural divisions within the ruling coalition and in Croatia, more generally.[65]

This government was riddled with internal fissures among the junior coalition partner, Most, and all other parties. With news of his conflict of interests over his official position and his wife's business, Deputy Prime Minister Karamarko resigned from both the government and the HDZ party leadership. This led to the dissolution of the parliament and new elections in September 2016. Under the more moderate Andrej Plenković, the HDZ-led coalition again won a narrow victory. Plenković formed a government with Most and with support from parties representing minorities, and without the radical right parties from the previous government. But there are still problems. In April 2017, Prime Minister Plenković sacked three ministers from Most for their failure to support the government in a no-confidence vote initiated by the opposition SDP. This led HDZ to further moderate its positions and seek allies among the opposition HNS (Croatian National Party) and other small, centrist parties that had been allied with the leftist SDS in recent elections.[66]

Croatia joined the EU formally on July 1, 2013. On the one hand, Brussels did not greet this accession with the same fanfare displayed at the 2004 induction of eight former socialist states. On the other hand, the Croatian public appeared unenthusiastic about the EU: less than 21 percent of Croatian voters participated in the July 1 elections to the European Parliament won by the opposition HDZ. In elections held on May 25, 2014, a turnout of 25 percent of Croatian voters elected to the European Parliament six from the HDZ coalition, four from the Kukuruku coalition, and one from the Croatian Sustainable Development Party. Further, the EU threatened, in the fall of 2013, to sanction Croatia for passing a law three days before joining the EU that limits the execution of European arrest warrants to crimes committed after August 2002.[67]

Early on, leaders in Bosnia-Herzegovina and Macedonia sensed that the disintegration of Yugoslavia could lead to the dissolution of their own republics and they sought compromises among competing political forces to fend off powerful and covetous neighbors. Ethnic party systems came from a combination of electoral rules, social structure, and anticommunist sentiment. With the rejection of their compromise proposals for Yugoslavia's future, Macedonian and Bosnian leaders pursued independence. In both countries, external interventions drastically rewrote domestic political rules.

A 1990 court decision striking down Bosnia-Herzegovina's ban on ethnic parties and an electoral rule mandating that election results not deviate more than 15 percent from the ethnic distribution in the census contributed to the victory of the ethnically based Muslim Party of Democratic Action (SDA) and Bosnian branches of the HDZ and SDS in the founding elections. During the campaign, all three party leaders committed to protecting ethnic interests and to interethnic cooperation.[68] Although twice jailed in socialist Yugoslavia (in 1946 and 1983) for Islamic activities, SDA leader and president of Bosnia-Herzegovina Alija Izetbegović continued Yugoslavia's socialist practice that Bosnia is a state of three constituent peoples and others, the latter representing a residual category for those citizens not declaring themselves Bosniac, Serb, or Croat. However, interparty cooperation deteriorated over the formula for the ethnic distribution of positions within the government. A majority of Bosnian citizens supported the referendum on independence, although Serbs boycotted the vote. Leaders in Serbia and Croatia egged on and armed their coethnic parties in Bosnia on the pretext that radical Muslims dominated the republic.

Ethnic cleansing, international intervention, and institutional engineering created a break with the Yugoslav tradition of brotherhood and unity. The Dayton Accords included an unwieldy constitution with ineffective state institutions that easily became dominated by the ethnically based SDA, HDZ, and SDS in the name of institutionalizing power sharing.[69] Electoralism—or the idea that holding elections will jump-start the democratic process—has enabled the wartime protagonists to buy into the new system, strengthen patronage networks, and increase interethnic tensions in Bosnia.[70] Since ethnically based parties rarely win votes from other ethnic groups, party leaders have strong incentives to make radical appeals to ensure greater turnout of their own group.[71] Nonetheless, nationalists won increasingly narrow victories until the 2000 elections, when international officials convinced diverse social democratic forces to unite behind the SDP-led Coalition for Change. The coalition's efforts at comprehensive reform failed due to internal bickering and opposition from nationalist groups. The leading Bosniac, Croat, and Serb parties in the mid-2000s reaffirmed their divergent objectives, which strengthened political deadlock in national-level politics and scuttled domestic initiatives in late 2008 and EU–US initiatives in October 2009 for constitutional changes to create a more functional state and advance Bosnia's accession to the EU.

In the federation, the Party for Bosnia-Herzegovina has advocated for a more unified Bosnian state and has challenged the RS's right to exist. Croat parties continue to advocate for increased Croatian collective rights. An expert group supported by the US embassy in spring 2013 formulated 188 recommendations to reconfigure and trim the cumbersome federation structure.[72] Major political leaders reacted coolly to the recommendations, apparently from fear of damaging their patronage networks. Leaders from virtually all major political parties have confronted credible allegations of corruption.[73]

Since 2006, the RS's governing Party of Independent Social Democrats (SNSD) has shown little interest in the central government or in international officials. Instead, it has sought to enhance the RS's already substantial autonomy, holding a referendum on the republic's "statehood" day, and threatening referenda against state judicial institutions and on secession, which is not permitted under the Dayton constitution. In the run up to the 2016 national elections, the Bosnia-Herzegovina state's Constitutional Court ruled that RS legislation establishing the republic's "statehood" day on an Orthodox holiday discriminated against non-Serb citizens of the republic and was unconstitutional and won support for this from international officials. RS president and SNSD leader Dodik defied the ruling and held the referendum.[74] As result, the US Treasury in January 2017 sanctioned Dodik for obstructing implementation of the Dayton Peace Agreement, but this has not compelled Dodik to moderate his rhetoric or his actions.[75]

Increasingly, divisive politics in the two entities and efforts to enhance RS autonomy have further weakened national-level governance. Following the 2010 parliamentary elections, it took sixteen months for the SDP to form a central government. Beginning in 2012, the EU declared that Bosnia's progress on the EU agenda had stalled because of failure to agree on functional state institutions; to amend the constitution to meet the European Court of Human Rights' ruling that individuals other than Bosniacs, Serbs, or Croats can run for the presidency and House of Peoples; and to strengthen the justice sector.[76] An SDA-led coalition with Croat politician Ivo Komsic's Democratic Front, the Serb Alliance for Changes, and HDZ has governed since the 2014 parliamentary elections. Bosnia's presidency presented a formal application for EU membership in February 2016, although Bosnian officials have made little effort to adopt and implement reforms needed to make substantial progress in the EU accession process.

International intervention has generally failed to build effective and self-sustaining domestic political institutions in Bosnia, and the aid and leverage exerted through the EU accession process have not deepened democratic reform.[77] Nor have international officials pursued a consistent strategy: they failed to act against ethnic extremists in the period just after Dayton and then significantly employed executive powers to override Bosnian institutions to pass legislation and remove domestic officials. In the period from December 1997 through September 2013, the High Representative employed this tool 923 times, a rate of almost five decisions per month. In the period from 1999 through 2005, the High Representative made 728 decisions at a rate of almost nine decisions per month.[78] This employment of executive authority was constrained after 2006 in response to internal disagreements within the PIC, the diminishing utility of international executive authority, and increasing calls for giving real authority to Bosnian officials. The self-interested policies of powerful domestic leaders and declining external interest in Bosnia have revived pessimism over Bosnia's viability and fears that the withdrawal of international forces could lead to violence.[79]

In Macedonia, nationalists and reformed communists (soon to form the Social Democratic Union of Macedonia [SDSM]) split the vote during the founding elections. Although the nationalist Internal Macedonian Revolutionary Organization (later called the VMRO-DPMNE) won the most parliamentary seats in 1990, its government fell in a vote of no confidence in 1991. The reformed communists then formed a four-party coalition government. The party's leader, Kiro Gligorov, was elected president by the parliament and served as a bridge between the communist past and pluralist future. The coalition supported interethnic cooperation by including four Albanian cabinet ministers in the government.[80]

All coalition governments have been multiethnic. The Ohrid Framework Agreement, which ended the fighting in 2001, provided Macedonians with incentives to form an inclusive government and power-sharing arrangements, albeit far less rigid ones than in Bosnia. After the first postconflict election, SDSM formed a multiethnic coalition government committed to the agreement. However, VMRO-DPMNE won the next several national elections. They initially continued SDSM-initiated reforms required for EU accession and NATO membership. However, in 2008, VMRO-DPMNE initially reached out to its traditional coalition partner, the Democratic Party of Albanians, which won fewer votes than its rival Democratic Union for Integration (DUI). DUI won US and European support and was ultimately included in the coalition government. Notwithstanding Western demands for a rerun of the 2008 elections in competitive Albanian-dominated municipalities experiencing violence on Election Day, observers viewed the largely peaceful elections as a step toward EU membership.

Macedonia faces serious problems with organized crime, ethnic separation, corruption, and economic development that cannot be so nimbly resolved. Greece scuttled Macedonia's membership bid for NATO in 2008 and has undermined progress toward EU membership. The stalled EU accession process and VMRO-DPMNE's ten-year grip on power (it and DUI also won the 2011 and 2014 elections) have laid the foundation for increasing and credible accusations of institutionalized corruption. In 2011, small opposition parties joined the boycott that protested what SDSM characterized as "undemocratic rule" following arrests of executives from the largest independent television station, A1 TV. The 2011 elections were held under a controversial new electoral law pushed through by VMRO-DPMNE that allowed the Macedonian diaspora to vote for 3 of the 123 seats in parliament. The 2014 elections for president and the parliament were criticized for inadequately separating party and state activities.[81]

The political crisis deepened after the opposition released illegal recordings of wiretapped telephone conversations between top government officials, which contained suggestions of high-level crimes. In June 2015, EU and US mediators brokered an agreement on an interim government that included the opposition, the resignation of Prime Minister Gruevski in January 2016, reforms for April 2016 elections, and a Special Prosecutor's Office to investigate criminal allegations contained in the wiretaps. Despite VMRO-DPMNE obstruction, the investigations led to indictments of former officials in late 2016.[82] In the December 2016 elections, the SDSM-led coalition gained two fewer seats than the VMRO-DPMNE-led coalition but formed a multiethnic coalition government excluding VMRO-DPMNE. Macedonia's president, a member of VMRO-DPMNE, only gave SDSM leader Zoran Zaev the mandate to form the government in May 2017.

The president had alleged that Zaev "endanger[ed] the country's sovereignty" by accepting demands of Macedonian Albanian parties for inclusion in a ruling coalition that focused on greater language and economic rights for the Albanian community.[83] During this standoff, VMRO-DPMNE supporters stormed the parliament and injured ten members of parliament belonging to the new majority. This crisis was primarily generated by an intraethnic Macedonian struggle for power, with the ruling VMRO-DPMNE leadership using state resources, allied social groups, and ethnically divisive rhetoric to cling to power. Further, Macedonia's Albanian parties played into Macedonian nationalist fantasies when they exacerbated interethnic tensions with demands for greater Albanian rights at a meeting with Albanian officials in Tirana. These troubling developments illustrate the vulnerability of Macedonia's political system to democratic backtracking and intra- and interethnic conflict.

Analyses of the accomplishments of the Ohrid Framework Agreement have been mixed, though significantly more positive than analyses of the Dayton Accords in Bosnia. One scholar argues that it has "been able to remove some of the obvious inequalities of the system," meaningfully including Albanians in the state. However, it has been "unable to address the systemic problems," which include ethnic divisions in politics, segregation in education, party patronage in the public sector, and neglect of smaller minorities.[84] The EC has nonetheless recommended several times that the European Council move Macedonia to the next stage in the accession process by opening negotiations, in hope that this would consolidate reforms and facilitate resolution of the dispute over the name "Macedonia" between Greece and Macedonia.[85]

Politics in Montenegro remains personalistic. The Democratic Party of Socialists (DPS) has dominated Montenegrin politics and government since it emerged from the League of Communists in 1991, and Milo Đukanović has led the party since 1997 on a platform of increasing autonomy from a Serbian-dominated Yugoslavia. Đukanović has served as president or prime minister with short breaks from 2006 to 2008 and 2010 to 2012. In elections in 2012, the DPS fell short of an absolute majority and formed a multiethnic coalition government. DPS president Filip Vujanovic was reelected in April 2013 to serve his third term in office.

Montenegrin politics has since become especially quarrelsome—as seen in the absence of transparency in its preparations for EU accession, in controversies and scandals related to the establishment of the Agency for the Prevention of Corruption, in splits in established parties and the establishment of new parties, and in disagreements within

Photo 16.2. July 2006 rally in Macedonia held by the then ruling coalition led by the Social Democratic Alliance of Macedonia during the parliamentary elections campaign. (Paula Pickering)

the ruling coalition on economic and political issues.[86] A clear victor did not emerge in October 2016 elections amidst allegations that the government was authoritarian and corrupt, and that the opposition received Russian funding. The DPS again formed a government with participation of minority parties and in which Đukanović formally stepped aside as prime minister in favor of long-time deputy Duško Marković.[87] These developments have led to greater political polarization in the republic. By mid-2017, two leaders of the opposition have been stripped of parliamentary immunity and indicted for alleged participation in the coup attempt and thirty-nine members of the opposition have boycotted the parliament for several months in response to these developments. Notwithstanding the underlying dynamics of these developments, the EU Commission reports that "important work on alignment and preparation for the implementation of the *acquis* has taken place."[88]

Public life in Kosovo remains dominated by wartime personalities. Since 2001, the late president Ibrahim Rugova's LDK has steadily lost ground to parties that emerged from the KLA, including former prime minister Hashim Thaqi's Democratic Party (PDK) and Ramush Haradinaj's Alliance for the Future of Kosovo (AAK). The PDK had appeared to succeed in establishing its credibility throughout Kosovo while pursuing European integration, negotiations with the government of Serbia, and governing with minority parties. The PDK headed all governments between 2008 and 2014.

In the June 2014 parliamentary elections, the PDK won a plurality of votes but was initially unable to form a government. Three opposition parties, LDK, AAK, and the Initiative for Kosovo or NISMA, created a postelection coalition that could have formed a majority government with the eventual support of the leftist Vetevendosje or Self-Determination. Following two months of deadlock, President Atifete Jahjaga sought the opinion of the Constitutional Court. It *de facto* supported PDK by ruling that the party or coalition that is certified by the Kosovo Central Election Commission before elections and that won a majority or plurality of votes in the elections will have the first opportunity to nominate a prime minister and parliamentary speaker. LDK subsequently abandoned the opposition coalition and a government was formed with LDK leader Isa Mustafa as prime minister and former prime minister Thaqi as foreign minister.

Political life has not yet fully settled into a pattern of "normal" bargaining and competition. First, the only ethnically Albanian party with a distinctive policy platform is Vetevendosje. It stands against corruption, believes that Kosovo institutions should not be wholly dependent on the leadership of international officials, and favors unification with Albania. The other parties all vaguely support declarations in the "Euro-Atlantic Agenda" with support from diplomatic and international officials. Second, the SNS from Belgrade continues to play an important role in Kosovo's policy making through its influence on the "Serbian List" party that dominates Serb politics within Kosovo and through its continued subsidies to public employees in Serb communities.

Third, the government dragged its feet on legislation considered an important part of Kosovo's "Euro-Atlantic Agenda" despite pressure from the EU and other diplomatic missions to Kosovo. These include the approval of the Specialist Chambers and Specialist Prosecutors' Office (see below), the demarcation of the border with Montenegro, and the establishment of the Association/Community of Serb Majority Municipalities. Here, the opposition has employed unconventional tactics to block implementation of these EU-brokered agreements with Serbia. In addition to demonstrations that have deteriorated into violence, Vetevendosje members of parliament have released tear gas in parliament to halt proceedings that would enable progress on the "Euro-Atlantic Agenda." These frequently used tactics slowed down routine policy making and attracted loud criticism by the influential diplomatic community in Pristina. With the end of President Jahjaga's mandate, former prime minister Hashim Thaqi's election as president in the National Assembly illustrated this dynamic: members of the opposition released tear gas in the parliament and were thus banned from participation; demonstrators outside the parliament threw stones; and Thaqi became president with a simple majority of votes on the third round of voting after failing to win the two-thirds majority that is necessary in the first two rounds of voting.

Following many months of increasing tensions among PDK and LDK in the governing coalition, the government fell in May 2017 to a vote of no-confidence after it promised to pass legislation approving the demarcation of the border with Montenegro. In the elections, PDK headed a "war wing" coalition of former guerilla-led parties with AAK and NISMA. LDK formed a coalition with newer parties and Vetevendosje ran as "outsiders" who have never sullied themselves with power. Vetevendosje doubled its support—from 13 percent to 26 percent of the vote over the results from 2014—but fell short of the PDK-led "war wing" coalition's approximately 31 percent and thirty-nine seats in parliament when sixty-one seats is the minimum number required to form a government. Following three months of negotiation, the "war wing" formed a broad coalition government led by AAK leader Haradinaj that commands a narrow one-vote majority in parliament. The coalition includes all minority parties as well as the small party led by businessman-politician Bexhet Pacolli. This government could face difficulties in addressing basic issues related to rule of law, corruption, organized crime, minority rights, negotiations with Serbia, and economic and political reform in order to demonstrate domestically and externally a commitment to strengthening the stable, democratic, and normal state desired by ordinary citizens of Kosovo.[89]

In sum, there is uneven progress in the development and institutionalization of party systems across former Yugoslavia. In Slovenia and Croatia, movement parties that won the founding elections have dissipated and given way to party systems with solid conservative and SDPs and sets of parties with amorphous programs somewhere in the middle. The inclusion of minority parties in governing coalitions in Croatia, Macedonia, Serbia, Montenegro, and Kosovo is a positive sign that partly comes from EU pressure and that can enable these "catchall coalition" parties to divide the spoils.

Bosnia-Herzegovina's rigid power sharing further entrenches its ethnic party system and encourages dysfunctional governance. The emergence of outsider parties in Slovenia, Croatia, Kosovo, and Montenegro reflects popular dissatisfaction with the status quo. The unfinished character of the second transitions means that these countries' political parties have not completely outgrown the zero-sum, constitutional dilemmas, or moved more fully into interest-driven politics. Regional parties and the emergence of outsider parties have demonstrated their influence, both in facilitating the formation of coalition governments and reflecting growing discontent among voters with the mainstream parties that have dominated post-Yugoslav politics.

Transitional Justice

The establishment of rule of law and justice systems has been significantly impeded by the wars, extended political transitions in the Yugoslav successor states, and domination of political life by individual personalities and parties. To be sure, there has been ample external assistance for development of legal codes in accordance with international norms and practice; physical reconstruction of courts, prisons, and police services; and training in the full repertoire of policing, case management, and good judicial practice. International deployments focusing on police and the rule of law have provided substantial numbers of international professionals to assist the governments of Bosnia-Herzegovina, Kosovo, and Macedonia in the relatively early stages of legal system development, especially in areas of interethnic and domestic war crimes. The governments of Croatia, Macedonia, Montenegro, and Serbia have received less assistance, and international officials have not had any executive authority in these states. Overall, this assistance has led to progress in formally developing legal systems and codes that are in accordance with international norms, although domestic practice often falls short.

There has been progress in addressing the grave crimes of the war. With some hesitation, the deepest and longest of which was exhibited by Serbia, all governments in the region have responded to external demands to cooperate with the ICTY. Domestic Courts in Croatia, Serbia, Bosnia, and Kosovo have been adjudicating war crimes cases, although these domestic courts have not always operated very effectively. International officials continue to contribute substantially to these issues in Kosovo. In 2014, a EULEX (European Rule of Law) investigative task force found evidence to substantiate allegations of KLA war crimes, including organ harvesting, made in a 2010 report issued by Council of Europe rapporteur Dick Marty. The Kosovo Assembly voted in August 2015 to amend the constitution and establish the "Kosovo Specialist Chambers and Specialist Prosecutors Office" as part of the Kosovo judicial system with a seat in The Hague and with international judges, prosecutors, and staff. It has a mandate "over certain crimes against humanity, war crimes and other crimes under Kosovo law, which allegedly occurred between 1 January 1998 and 31 December 2000."[90] Opposition political parties requested that the Constitutional Court annul the amendments that enabled the new court to be established, saying they violated Kosovo's sovereignty.

The issue of war crimes remains highly divisive: amid routine commentary on the biased and political nature of the international court, governments in Croatia and Serbia have only reluctantly cooperated with the ICTY. Further, several relatively short sentences, deaths of prominent indictees during trial (e.g., Milošević), delayed acquittals, and reversals of convictions, as well as the clear conditionality of cooperation with the ICTY for accession to the EU—which has affected Serb, Croat, Bosniac, and Kosovar Albanian indictees—have strengthened a sense that these war crimes trials are not contributing to strengthening norms of rule of law and objectivity of the legal system. In addition, the contradiction between official compliance with the ICTY and official support for the defense of coethnic indictees and lack of support for mechanisms (educational programs or truth commissions) that engage the region's populations in a serious discussion of responsibility for past crimes hinder movement toward reconciliation. Given these political dynamics, the polarized reaction to ICTY's conviction in 2016 of wartime Bosnian Serb political leader Radovan Karadžić (in 2016) and Ratko Mladić (in 2017) for genocide and crimes against humanity was not surprising.[91]

There has also been some progress in high-profile corruption cases, as with former Croatian Prime Minister Sanader and several "tycoons" in Serbia. But domestic civil society organizations have pointed out that these high-profile cases have drawn attention to the more systematic corruption and sweetheart privatization deals from the 1990s for which few people have been held accountable and that these corrupt patronage systems remain intact. In Bosnia-Herzegovina, Macedonia, Kosovo, and Montenegro, governments have become enmeshed in corrupt iron triangles between political leaders, pliant bureaucracies, and large firms. In the best of cases, for example, Croatia, corruption cases find their way through the system. Kosovo's strong anti-corruption legislation, full range of institutions against corruption, and a good number of indictments have not changed the popular perception of widespread corruption in public institutions.[92]

It is also the case that minorities in all of these countries, including Slovenia, face a very uneven legal playing field in supporting their claims and winning protection and security. For example, the Slovene government views inhabitants from former Yugoslavia not as minorities but as "economic migrants" who have had difficulties in regularizing their status despite the fact many of them have long lived and worked in Slovenia.[93]

Civil Society

It is often held that voluntary organizations produce social capital that will strengthen democratization in the successor states. However, the actual impact of such organizations depends partly on the type of social capital they build and the rootedness of the organizations in local society. Advocacy organizations that link citizens to policy makers can help hold political leaders accountable. Those groups that disperse authority horizontally, rather than concentrate it, are best at cultivating the repeated interdependent interaction that builds interpersonal trust. Groups that look outward, beyond the interests of their own members toward benefiting the larger community, are better at solving broader social problems than those that focus only inward. Finally, those groups that link together people of different cultural backgrounds are better at helping integrate a diverse society than those that bring together and provide social support only to those of the same cultural background.[94]

The developments described in this chapter leave little doubt that many civil society organizations in the region are monoethnic. Voluntary associations that focus on strengthening bonds within single ethnic groups contributed to conflict in Yugoslavia's multiethnic republics. For example, many religious leaders' direct participation in exclusivist nationalist appeals in the 1990s undermines the capacity of religious organizations to facilitate reconciliation and moderation.[95] Some monoethnic local organizations, which were linked to nationalist parties, crowded out a range of moderate groups that opposed violence.[96] Other organizations are inward looking, hierarchically structured, and willing to use violence to realize their exclusivist goals. These included wartime paramilitary groups whose leaders were indicted by the ICTY.[97]

Some local, multiethnic organizations that grew out of the war produce social capital that bridges ethnic divisions. Medica Zenica, for example, is a voluntary organization formed by local women residents of all backgrounds in Zenica, Bosnia, to aid female victims of the war.[98] Other groups include displaced persons, veterans, and families of missing persons. Victims' groups in Bosnia and Kosovo can adopt different strategies: either to return as minorities to their homes in their places of origin or to rebuild new lives in areas where they are among the ethnic majority. Veterans associations, which are split along ethnic lines and are inward looking, resent their marginalization in the postconflict period and tend to support nationalist parties.[99]

Western agencies have assisted the NGOs that supposedly support democratization and transitional justice but overlook groups that emerge from local traditions of informal mutual-help networks rooted in everyday life, such as in the neighborhood and the workplace.[100] Donors have favored NGOs that engage in advocacy—even where they have shallow roots in society—and whose formation is driven largely by donors' needs. A recent study of civil society in the Western Balkans found that civic organizations remain heavily dependent on foreign donors.[101] It is encouraging that leaders of advocacy groups, such as legal aid and human rights groups, have made progress in forming networks to monitor and influence government. Some examples of NGO effort to affect policy include the following: Bosnian NGOs ensured that Serbs, Croats, and Bosniacs are all legally constituent peoples throughout the country and successfully advocated for the adoption of a law on the direct election of mayors; Serbian NGOs contributed to the Law on Associations in Serbia; and Kosovar NGOs led a successful campaign for an open-list, proportional electoral system and have also participated in government-led initiatives related to reconciliation and rule of law.[102] In general, however, NGOs tend to be sidelined in discussions of politically sensitive policies.[103] In diverse societies, nationalist leaders tend to use conflict to discourage the formation of civic organizations that unite diverse peoples around common interests and thus help keep intercommunal peace.[104]

The long-term character of building tolerant civil societies in Yugoslavia's successor states may be clearer to many local activists and some international implementers on the ground than to donor agencies that demand immediate results. Multiple studies concluded that many NGOs in southeastern Europe "have weak links with their communities" because of their orientation toward international donors.[105] Citizens remain disaffected and often view local NGOs as promoters of Western agendas and sources of funding for opportunistic leaders. A nationally representative survey in 2009 in Bosnia found that only 17.8 percent of the respondents reported participating in a nonparty organization.[106] In an example that fuels citizens' skepticism about NGOs, a 2013 investigative report on seven years of contracts awarded by Serbia's Ministry of Youth revealed that the party controlling the ministry awards the largest projects to organizations headed by fellow party members.[107] A different study conducted in Serbia found that many citizens were skeptical of local NGOs because they were perceived to work on issues that are unimportant, narrowly focused, or imported, rather than on issues that resonated with citizens' priorities and values, including socioeconomic needs and community welfare.[108]

To be sure, some domestic activists have made progress in strengthening organizations that embrace civility and democratic principles. A new generation of young, urban, highly educated, and well-trained activists who played a role in the electoral revolutions or have worked with international NGOs is striving constructively to hold elected leaders accountable.[109] However, they often lack active support from citizens. And the successor states' civil societies remain dominated by organizations that promote narrow group interests rather than focusing on crosscutting problems, such as social integration or political accountability. International donors could be more successful in cultivating broad-based habits of civic participation by working in partnership with domestic groups that are well rooted in local communities and adopting goals and timelines that respond to local needs and capacities.

Citizens and Politics

As in most postcommunist systems, the significant gap between elites and ordinary citizens that persists in the Yugoslav successor states is a legacy of the one-party system, of relatively weak party systems, and of corruption. Neither the wars nor the repeated political crises within the Yugoslav successor states were initiated wholly from grass-roots sentiments. The willingness of citizens to participate in politics has varied according to timing, political context, and economic situation. Citizens quickly discerned the self-serving behavior of political elites working in the new political institutions. In all countries, voter turnout for parliamentary elections declined from high rates in 1990 to stable but moderate rates two decades later, slipping from 84.5 percent in 1990 to 52.6 percent in 2016 in Croatia; from 71.5 percent in 1990 to 56.1 percent in 2016 for

Serbia; from 80 percent in 1990 to 54.1 percent in 2014 in Bosnia; and from 78 percent in 1990 to 66.8 percent in 2016 in Macedonia. Across the region, youth are substantially less likely than other age groups to vote.[110]

Elections for the president of Serbia were invalidated three times when less than 50 percent of voters bothered to turn out in 2002 and 2003. Only amending the law allowed the elections to succeed. The heavy hand of the Office of the High Representative in Bosnia-Herzegovina has further depressed citizens' reported efficacy. Of those who did not vote in the last elections, 43 percent explained that they stayed home on Election Day because "Bosnia and Herzegovina's politicians cannot change anything."[111] It appears that these modest levels of participation result from a general perception that parties do not offer meaningful political alternatives, are not responsive to citizens' concerns, or have little power compared to the High Representative. Citizens across much of the former Yugoslavia share the first two perceptions.

Levels of participation in political activities beyond voting in the former Yugoslav states are roughly the same as the modest level of political participation for the Central and East European region as a whole. As elsewhere in East-Central Europe, citizen mistrust of political organizations is widespread in the Yugoslav successor states and also leads to low levels of membership in and attachment to political parties.

During wartime, exclusivist leaders succeeded in deflecting the effect of citizen-initiated protests for liberalization that had become common in the late 1980s through 1991 in Slovenia, Croatia, and Serbia. We saw above that Milošević used demonstrations of unemployed and embittered Serbs to change republic and provincial leaderships. Large nonviolent demonstrations for political reform in Belgrade in 1991 and peace in Sarajevo in 1992 were met with violence by the JNA and SDS snipers, respectively. The Tudjman and Milošević governments easily deflected antiwar protests by committed activists—often women—and could enlist rural-based and nationalist "victims groups" in support of national goals. But from the mid-1990s onward, antiauthoritarian protests in Zagreb and Belgrade grew larger and bolder. An estimated one hundred thousand people protested their leaders' attempts to silence popular opposition radio stations in Croatia, for example.[112] In Serbia, the youth organization *Otpor* took advantage of low-key US aid and a weakened SPS to mobilize citizens successfully against Milošević in the fall of 2000. A relatively high percentage of respondents in Serbia reported participating in such demonstrations. In Bosnia and post-Milošević Serbia, citizens are more willing to engage in protests that involve economic rather than political issues.[113]

Nationalist protests continue to take place in Croatia, Macedonia, Kosovo, and Bosnia, sometimes with the assistance of ruling parties and the tacit support of local police. Developments that threaten entrenched nationalist leaders—returning refugees and internally displaced people, the normalization of relations in the divided communities of Mostar (Bosnia) and Mitrovica (Kosovo), campaign rallies by minorities, and (re)construction of religious institutions—have sometimes drawn violent responses, particularly through the mid-2000s. Two days of cross-Kosovo violence in March 2004 that saw Albanian extremists attack Serbs and Roma, as well as UN and NATO forces, were the most significant incidence of this. Soccer matches between ethnically based teams or with teams from outside the Balkans can also become explosive. Through 2017, intraethnic political competition for the spoils of political office was occasionally violent in Serbia, Kosovo, Bosnia, and Macedonia.

Frustration with formally organized groups has led progressive young people to be active in more informal and less hierarchical ways. For example, citizens frustrated by poor governance and economic conditions have engaged in plenums, sit-ins, and protests (in Slovenia, Croatia, Serbia, Macedonia, Bosnia-Herzegovina, Kosovo); efforts to help victims of flooding in 2014 (in Bosnia-Herzegovina, Serbia); and antidevelopment protests (in Belgrade and Zagreb).[114] In June 2013, Bosnian citizens launched weeks of spontaneous protests in major cities against the Bosnian parliament's unwillingness to pass legislation on obtaining personal identification numbers needed for access to health care and travel.[115] This was followed by mass protests and plenums in ten cities in February 2014 against unresponsive and corrupt cantonal and some local governments in the federation. These plenums made similar demands throughout, including the formation of new governments of experts without political affiliation, audits of the salaries and benefits of public officials, and audits of privatization, and succeeded in compelling the resignation of multiple cantonal governments. [116] The most recent burst of social mobilizations occurred in April 2017, among progressive youth opposed to the rule of newly elected Serbian president Vučić. Like the plenums in Bosnia-Herzegovina, participants in Serbia focused on horizontal processes, participation, and dialogue.[117] These movement tactics have succeeded in mobilizing and giving voice to significant numbers of citizens for short periods of time. But participants' unwillingness to coalesce around leadership, prioritize feasible demands, and develop organizational structures have undermined their sustainability and their effectiveness in bringing about political and economic reform.

Political Values and Attitudes toward Politics

Some political scientists hold that the nations of former Yugoslavia tend to have "subject" political cultures, [118] in which citizens sit back and expect the government to provide for them—as part of the socialist legacy. However, recent research suggests that citizens are rationally disaffected with a political system whose parties present them with few meaningful choices, especially when patronage networks do not deliver benefits to ordinary citizens.[119] In deeply divided societies with ethnic party systems, citizens have few options other than voting for ethnically exclusive parties. Only 19 percent of Bosnian respondents in a nationally representative survey believed that only monoethnic parties could protect their vital interests.[120] Citizens also avoid involvement in politics, which is viewed as dirty. Some citizens believe that political parties contribute to ethnic tension.[121] However, this perception does not fully immunize them from parties' hate speech. For example, even though participants in focus groups among voting-aged youth in Kosovo said they opposed politicians who use hate speech, a quarter of these participants expressed anger toward the fictional target of hate speech in three different experimental scenarios.[122]

Surveys indicate that citizens in most Yugoslav successor countries lack confidence in their political institutions (see table 16.1). This finding runs counter to the expressed aspiration for a democratic political system. The percentage of respondents who agreed "though democracy has its problems, it is the best political system" ranged from a high of 96 percent in Croatia to a low of 81 percent in Macedonia,[123] findings consistent with opinions across postcommunist Europe. When asked to identify elements of democracy they considered extremely important, citizens from Serbia, Vojvodina, Kosovo, Croatia,

Table 16.1. Levels of Trust in Political and Social Institutions (Percentage)

	Political Parties	National Assembly	Judicial Institutions	Police	Army
Bosnia	15.8	18.9	22.0	60.0	54.0
Croatia	13.0	24.0	29.0	56.0	68.0
Kosovo	13.4	20.0	19.6	50.0	NA
Macedonia	18.0	27.0	24.0	41.0	53.0
Montenegro	24.0	40.0	47.0	54.0	65.0
Serbia	11.0	27.0	36.0	44.0	65.0
Slovenia	6.0	14.0	21.0	66.0	72.0

Sources: For public opinion data in Croatia, Macedonia, Montenegro, Serbia, and Slovenia, answers refer to those respondents who "tend to trust" the specific institutions. "Standard Eurobarometer 86: Public Opinion in the European Union, Autumn 2016, Annex," European Commission, December 2016, http://ec.europa.eu/commfrontoffice/publicopinion/index.cfm/Survey/getSurveyDetail/yearFrom/1974/yearTo/2016/surveyKy/2137 (accessed June 14, 2017). For public opinion in Kosovo, answers refer to those respondents who expressed 6–10 on a 0–10 scale (with 0 corresponding to no trust at all and 10 corresponding to complete trust) in the specific institutions: European Social Survey Dataset: ESS6-2012, ed.2.3, Norwegian Social Science Data Services, 2012, http://www.europeansocialsurvey.org/data/download.html?r=6. Kosovo does not have a national army. For public opinion in Bosnia, answers refer to those respondents who expressed some or a lot of confidence in the specific institutions. Bosnian data on confidence in political parties and the national government (rather than the national assembly): Gallup, "Balkan Monitor: Insights and Perceptions: Voices of the Balkans," 2010. Bosnian data on confidence in the police and army: Gallup, "Balkan Monitor 2012." Bosnian data on trust in judicial institutions: Regional Cooperation Council Secretariat, "Balkan Barometer 2015: Public Opinion Survey Analytical Report," Sarajevo, 2015, http://www.rcc.int/docs_archive (accessed April 28, 2017).

Bosnia, and Macedonia all ranked "a justice system treating everybody equally," "economic prosperity in the country," and "a government that guarantees meeting the basic economic needs of all the citizens" as their top three associations with democracy.[124] These priorities reflect concern about arbitrary rule, the absence of prosperity, and the prevalence of corruption. They also indicate an enduring preference for the state to provide for basic needs. The low priority given to political elements of democracy, such as civil liberties and political pluralism, is consistent with the views of citizens in Romania and Bulgaria.[125] When asked in 2012 whether they were satisfied with the way democracy works in their country, only 20 percent of respondents in Slovenia and 22 percent of respondents in Kosovo answered yes.[126] This dissatisfaction across the region may partly reflect the respondents' even lower levels of satisfaction with their economies. Throughout the successor states, citizens consistently identify unemployment or lack of new jobs as the most important problem facing their countries.[127] Poverty and corruption vie for second place, with opinions about the latter contributing to dissatisfaction with judicial institutions and the functioning of the political system.

Citizens express moderate-to-low levels of tolerance for other ethnic groups. As expected in areas experiencing interethnic brutality, levels of tolerance toward other ethnic groups worsened during and in the immediate wake of violence. Tolerance has not been restored to prewar levels, and ethnically motivated crimes continue.[128] Nationalist demonstrations against the use of the Cyrillic alphabet on signs in Vukovar, Croatia, in 2013 highlight the enduring psychological wounds of war.[129] Consistent with prewar patterns in the region, Kosovo displays the lowest levels of ethnic tolerance. Only 20 percent of Kosovar Serbs and 29 percent of Kosovar Albanians say that they would agree to live on the same street with each other.[130] Although Bosnia experienced much higher levels of violence than Macedonia, Bosnian citizens express higher levels of tolerance than do Macedonian citizens. In 2007, only 8 percent of Bosnian respondents in a nationally representative sample survey expressed unwillingness to live next door to someone of another religion, whereas 12 percent of Macedonian respondents expressed such unwillingness.[131]

In response to policies primarily formulated by a dominant national group, ethnic minorities express significantly less pride in the nationality of their state and trust in political institutions than do members of the predominant group.[132] Economically marginalized and disillusioned youth across ethnonational and religious backgrounds are also more intolerant and susceptible to extremism.[133] A 2016 study in Serbia concluded that social isolation, a lack of economic possibilities for youth, and the role of regional and global politics contribute to radicalization of youth, which leaves young people in Southern Serbia particularly vulnerable to extremism.[134]

As the memory of mass violence recedes, ethnic tolerance among citizens in Bosnia, Croatia, and Macedonia has increased somewhat, which suggests that interethnic relations have made greater progress at the grassroots than at the elite level. A survey conducted in Bosnia in 2016 found that fewer respondents, regardless of ethnicity, expressed support for "separation into ethnic territories" as a way to improve ethnic relations in 2016 than in 2005, with youth being the age cohort least likely to support ethnic separation.[135]

The extent to which political values vary according to socioeconomic status depends partly on the political environment. For example, in the immediate wake of Milošević's ouster, voters in Serbia with some university education overwhelmingly (65 percent) supported the DOS opposition coalition, while only 5 percent supported SPS in 2001.[136] With the breakup of DOS, the difficult economic transition, and disputes with the EU over war crimes and Kosovo, there appeared no strong correlation between values and socioeconomic status by 2004.[137] However, generational differences in values are still reported, with young Bosnians expressing relatively liberal views.[138] Surveys also reveal that urbanites resent rural residents—even within the same ethnonational group—who have fled their villages for cities because of violence and poverty in a manner that reflects the region's traditional urban–rural divide[139]

The transformation of values into support for democratic principles and processes is necessary for democratic institutions to take root and to prevent a reversion to authoritarianism. In particular, tolerance toward other ethnic groups is essential for transition toward more normal political competition and stable states that promote regional stability. The bad news is that the strongest political forces have rarely supported tolerance. The good news is that citizens express levels of confidence in new political institutions and values that are largely consistent with the rest of Central and Eastern Europe. They are broadly supportive of democratic ideas but lack confidence in those political institutions that have often failed to function effectively, be responsive, or consistently deliver benefits to ordinary citizens.

Economic Transition and Social Change

Wars in Croatia, Bosnia, Serbia, and Kosovo both strengthened corruption and inhibited foreign investment. The economies suffered physical destruction of infrastructure and productive capacity, as well as the emigration of young, highly educated, and skilled

Table 16.2. Increasingly Divergent Economies in 2015

	GNI per Capita, (current US$)	Real GDP Growth Rate (percentage change on previous year volume)	Foreign Direct Investment, Net Inflows, (percentage of GDP)	Unemployment (as percentage of labor force)	Share of Youth Not in Education, Employment, or Training (as percentage of youth)
Bosnia	4,670	3.1	1.81	26.3	27.7
Croatia	12,760	2.2	0.33	16.3	18.5
Kosovo	3,960	4.1	5.36	32.9	31.4
Macedonia	5,140	3.8	2.94	26.1	24.7
Montenegro	7,220	3.4	17.55	17.5	16.5
Serbia	5,540	0.8	6.31	17.7	19.9
Slovenia	22,250	2.3	3.93	9.0	9.5

Sources: For Gross National Income (GNI) per capita, "GNI per Capita, Atlas Method (Current US$)": Foreign Direct Investment, Net Inflows (as percentage of GDP), Unemployment (as percentage of labor force (all countries except Kosovo); and Share of Youth Not in Employment, Education or Training (NEET) (as percentage of youth 15–24 or 29): World Bank, World Development Indicators Database, last updated June 1, 2017, http://data.worldbank.org/indicator/NY.GNP.PCAP.CD. For Real Gross Domestic Product (GDP) Growth Rate (percentage change on previous year volume): European Commission, Eurostat database, http://ec.europa.eu/eurostat/data/database (accessed June 15, 2017). For Kosovo's Unemployment Rate: Kosovo Agency of Statistics, Results of the Kosovo 2015 Labour Force Survey, June 2016, http://ask.rks-gov.net/media/1687/results-of-the-kosovo-2015-labour-force-survey.pdf.

labor. Serbia suffered under sanctions throughout the decade for its support of the Serb war effort in Bosnia. Macedonia suffered from a Greek boycott of its economy in the early 1990s and from the cutoff of Yugoslav markets that had been easily available before 1990. The wars dramatically slowed the economic development of all successor states, particularly in the first half of the 1990s. In a period of increasing unemployment, these economies uniformly experienced great inflation and decreasing production and gross domestic product (GDP).

The wars also significantly curtailed already decreasing interrepublican trade. Those countries with more advanced economies—Slovenia and Croatia—more easily integrated into the European and global economy than did the less developed republics (see table 16.2). But even Slovenia privatized its banking sector slowly.[140] For Serbia, Montenegro, Bosnia, and Macedonia, trade tends to be split among former Yugoslav successors and the EU. Deepened political commitment to integration with the EU has accelerated the economic reforms and improved the economic performance—albeit to varying degrees—of those countries still seeking entry into the EU. At the same time, EU-backed austerity policies have produced hardship and resentment among the poorest and most vulnerable segments of society.

The wars in Bosnia, Croatia, and Kosovo provided fertile soil for the development of gray economies and corruption—especially with the golden goose of international reconstruction aid. Corruption significantly hampers economic development and democratization in all successor states but Slovenia. In terms of Freedom House's measure of corruption from 1 (least corrupt) to 7 (most corrupt), Slovenia scores 2.5, Croatia and Serbia score 4.25, Macedonia and Montenegro score 4.75, Bosnia scores

5.00, and Kosovo brings up the rear at 5.75.[141] Of the postcommunist states, only the non-Baltic countries of the former Soviet Union score worse. Leadership circles around Serbian president Milošević and Croatian president Tudjman were especially prone to personalizing the public trust, practices that have traveled through the successor states.[142] Estimates of the size of Bosnia's gray economy in 2005 ranged from 30 to 40 percent of unadjusted, official GDP.[143] Control over the gray market has also enabled the leading nationalist parties in Bosnia to maintain power and undermine implementation of the Dayton Accords. Attempts to prosecute war profiteers in Serbia cost Zoran Đinđić his life. Criminal networks among Macedonia's Albanians contributed to armed violence in 2001.[144] These phenomena are linked to transnational trafficking networks in people and commodities that will not be easily eradicated.

The wars significantly slowed economic reform and the privatization of property that led to uneven postwar economic growth. The social implications of the wars and uneven growth are no less severe. A higher percentage of women than men are unemployed. Young adults are unemployed at higher levels than other age cohorts. Even today, the countries of the region, with the exception of Slovenia, suffer from high unemployment rates. An important indicator of economic hardship felt by young people, the share of youth "Not in Employment, Education or Training" (NEET) (as percentage of youth aged fifteen to twenty-four), reveals intense hardship experienced by youth in Kosovo, Bosnia-Herzegovina, and Macedonia, where these figures are approximately 33, 26, and 26 percent, respectively (table 16.2, last column). This fact leads young and educated labor to emigrate, a brain drain that impairs future economic development. An average of 37 percent of youth in the region expressed a desire to leave their countries, mainly because of perceptions of poor economic opportunities.[145] In Kosovo, Bosnia, and Croatia, unemployment is higher for minorities than for majorities. Substantial poverty in Bosnia, Serbia, Montenegro, and Kosovo has led to social atomization, political demobilization, and potential susceptibility to radicalism.[146] In these countries, high unemployment and underemployment, coupled with severe cutbacks in the social safety net, results in many citizens living from day to day. Bosnia and Kosovo, in particular, have not yet embarked on the process of substantial reform and modernization.

International agencies initially attempted to address these problems in the postconflict countries as part of larger peace accords. They have donated over $14 billion to the Bosnian economy since the signing of the Dayton Accords, and donors' conferences have generated substantial income for Croatia and Kosovo. Although this aid contributed initially to the repair and reconstruction of housing and infrastructure, it was not framed in properly functioning legal frameworks, was unevenly distributed, and was denied to those groups—especially in RS and among the Serb community in Kosovo—that did not explicitly support the implementation of the peace accords. The EU accession process has attempted to promote market reforms, but the implementation of reforms has been uneven, and vulnerable citizens feel left out. The global recession that began in 2008 hampered efforts of the region's governments to attract sufficient investment to help diminish unemployment and improve standards of living. The combination of the 2008 recession and Eurozone crisis hit Slovenia particularly hard.[147] Overall, a European Bank for Reconstruction and Development report argues that the Western Balkans, which suffered a decline in economic activity, weathered the crisis better than expected because of "mature policies by governments and strong financial support from international organizations, and the continued commitment of privately owned foreign companies and banks to the region."[148] The region is expected to achieve small average annual growth rates in 2017, partly due to low commodity prices. Croatia's economy in 2015 grew for the first time in seven years on the back of a good tourist season, a strengthening of external demand, and reduction in oil prices.[149]

Demographically, ethnic cleansing campaigns, urbanization, postwar ethnic engineering by nationalists, and brain drain have dramatically reduced areas of coexistence and created increasingly ethnically dominant territories within each of the postconflict countries of the former Yugoslavia. For example, according to a contested 2011 census, Kosovo is approximately 90 percent Albanian, and Serbs are now substantially concentrated in northern Kosovo adjacent to Serbia and in other enclaves throughout Kosovo. In Bosnia, a still-contested census conducted in 2013 indicated that Bosniacs made up 50.11 percent of the Bosnian population and that 92.11 percent of all Bosnian Serbs lived in RS, while 91.39 percent of Bosnian Croats and 88.23 percent of Bosniacs lived in the federation.[150]

Critical Issues

There is no shortage of critical issues facing governments in Yugoslavia's successor states. First, the governments of all post-Yugoslav successor states either aspire to EU membership or hope to maintain good standing in the EU.[151] EU membership encourages democratic practices and open economies but is not a simple end point that will ensure democratic consolidation. Domestic advocacy groups and EU sanctions for backtracking can encourage the governments of Slovenia and Croatia to continue to strengthen rule of law, reduce corruption, and genuinely treat citizens equally regardless of ethnicity or other status. However, although accession to the EU requires demonstrating a break with past autarkic and undemocratic practices, this leverage over domestic political behavior of states once they become members is weakened.

The other successor states face even higher thresholds for addressing these issues as they seek entry from the outer circle of potential EU membership. The government of Serbia has made substantial progress in its cooperation with the ICTY but has not fully demonstrated its commitment to abandoning its "nonaligned" stance between Russia and the EU. Serbia still must substantially tackle obstacles to the rule of law and press freedom, eradicate public corruption and organized crime, undertake economic reform in order to expand employment, find durable solutions for internally displaced persons and refugees, and comply with EU demands over relations with Kosovo.[152] These are no small tasks in a government increasingly dominated by a single personality. Nor is it clear that Serbia will be able to maintain its middle ground between the EU and Russian interests in the Balkans as is seen in Serbian support to Montenegro amidst the alleged Russian support for the attempted coup in Montenegro.[153]

Other governments must still resolve the basic issues of political status and the constitutional order. The continued implementation of the Ohrid Agreement and strengthening of an independent judiciary could help create a better functioning political system in Macedonia that can prepare itself for EU membership. But for this desirable scenario to play out, its political leaders must agree to move beyond narrow partisan and personal interests. Bosnia-Herzegovina has a far longer way to go to demonstrate its readiness for EU membership. Good governance there remains crippled by ineffective international efforts to integrate RS at the same time that RS institutions function more effectively than do the more complex ones in the federation. Bosniac, Croat, and Serb political leaders have proved unwilling to cooperate in governing in cantonal, entity, and state-level institutions. Macedonian and Bosnian governments have not reduced party patronage or partisan polarization. Nor has either government made much progress in addressing organized crime, corruption, ethnic separation, and economic development.

A final settlement of differences among the governments of Kosovo and Serbia is not imminent. Recent elections in Serbia and Kosovo can help to reboot recent EU-brokered agreements and provide a basis for building confidence for conventional social, economic, and political development in both countries. Both governments must overcome increasing domestic opposition to continuing this open-ended dialogue along its current trajectory and ensure that the dialogue between Serbia and Kosovo can lead to full normalization of relations. They both face difficult tests: Kosovo authorities must take steps to conclude the demarcation of its border with Montenegro and ensure that Serbian cultural and historical interests are fully recognized in Kosovo, while the Serbian government must influence Kosovo's Serbs to view the Association/Community of Serb Majority Municipalities as an integral part of Kosovo institutions rather than an autonomous entity resembling RS. Clearly, improving relations among Serbia, Montenegro, and Kosovo could help "normalize" politics in all three countries and strengthen their efforts to join the EU.

There are limits to the capacity of the EU accession process to support democratization and facilitate the emergence of fully "normal" politics and policy making in the post-Yugoslav successor governments. The EU's preaccession process helped induce meaningful reform in Croatia, but this has not stopped expressions of Croatian intolerance to Serbs in Croatia or the renewed glorification of the World War II Ustaši regime.[154] The EU integration process also initially spurred some positive reforms in Macedonia and Serbia but this "carrot" has been much less successful in Bosnia. Scholars have convincingly argued that the EU accession process works best in encouraging meaningful reforms among applicant countries that have already resolved fundamental state-building issues and with domestic leaders whose commitment to reform also brings personal political benefits.[155] The record of EU accession in spurring self-sustaining reforms must also be judged by new member Croatia's decision to limit the execution of European arrest warrants.

Serbia, Bosnia, Montenegro, and Kosovo will endure an extended wait in the EU outer ring. And the EU's own internal problems are likely to further blunt its capacity to play a powerful, constructive role in these governments. As the EU copes with Brexit, antiestablishment parties, and economic and migration crises, EU expansion will be on hold in the near term, which will weaken the modest leverage of the EU accession process over democratic reforms in post-Yugoslav governments. But further EU and US disengagement from the post-Yugoslav region is unlikely to promote deeper rule of law and democratic reforms or policies advancing the long and challenging process of reconciliation. In the past, Western inattention and ham-fisted "liberal imperial" policies,[156] have granted powerful and malevolent forces disproportionate influence over the region's political, economic, and social developments.

"Local ownership" of government that is financed by international donors provides no Rosetta stone for good governance in the Yugoslav successor states. A generation of leaders who have enjoyed support of the diplomatic and donor community have learned to accumulate power through a combination of public fealty to the Euro-Atlantic agenda of reform and inclusion, substantial patronage to political machines, and populist appeals to mass electorates. Western disengagement could ensure mainly that the populist political machines would either seek less principled external supporters or risk economic stagnation, political instability, and social unrest. In such circumstances, the post-Yugoslav governments will not be able to settle outstanding differences with their neighbors, strengthen democratic development, and resist potential predations of regionally resurgent powers of Russia and Turkey at the same time.

Yugoslavia's successor states remain at a crossroads; they undoubtedly have made tremendous progress since the dark days of the 1990s but continue to face multiple challenges in building tolerant societies and effective and democratically accountable institutions at the same time that they continue their transition to market economies. The successor governments must find ways to increase employment for their citizens and build cooperation and economies of scale with governments and businesses in the region. These difficult challenges are complicated by unconstructive conflicts among political and ethnic factions, often acting from narrow self-interest. The failure to sustain economic growth could open the door to increasing action by radical nationalist groups, as well as to religious extremists, some of whom have links to ISIS and other radical Islamist groups abroad.

Domestic leaders bear the greater burden of addressing these problems of governance. Yet, durable solutions to these constitutional problems will require constructive assistance from the international community, the same community that neither acted to preserve Yugoslavia nor intervened to end aggression. International agencies have overseen and abetted the often flawed implementation of peace accords throughout the region. Particularly in those countries with substantial international deployments—Bosnia-Herzegovina, Macedonia, and Kosovo—international missions and powerful embassies have often failed to advance economic development and strengthen good governance. They have typically favored short-term objectives of stability over long-term objectives of capacity building in political and technical affairs. This is seen in external political support to corrupt leaderships who undermine democratic processes in the name of "continuity" and in assisting in budget and financial backing to domestic officials who fail to meet key benchmarks in good governance. This strategy strengthens dependence on international organizations while it erodes social and political resilience.[157] It may prevent a short-term return to war, but it contributes little to building accountable and democratic governments. So the international community's greatest test will consist of learning from its earlier mistakes and adapting to evolving domestic political dynamics in order to more adroitly assist governments in the successor states in managing the transition from war to sustainable and democratic peace.

Study Questions

1. What external and internal factors contributed to the violent disintegration of Yugoslavia?
2. What external and internal factors explain differences in the timing and pace of the democratization of the governments of the Yugoslav successor states?
3. What key social, economic, and political issues face the governments of the Yugoslav successor states?
4. How are relationships between political elites and ordinary citizens in the former Yugoslav states similar, and how do they differ during the postsocialist period?
5. How effectively has international intervention into the countries of former Yugoslavia promoted inclusive and stable democratization? Why?

Suggested Readings

Bieber, Florian. *Post-War Bosnia: Ethnicity, Inequality and Public Sector Governance*. New York: Palgrave, 2006.

———, ed. "Unconditional Conditionality? The Impact of EU Conditionality in the Western Balkans." Special issue of *Europe-Asia Studies* 63, no. 10 (2011): 1775–1946.

Brown, Keith, ed. *Transacting Transition: The Micropolitics of Democracy Assistance in the Former Yugoslavia*. Bloomfield, CT: Kumarian Press, 2006.

Burg, Steven L., and Paul S. Shoup. *The War in Bosnia-Herzegovina*. Armonk, NY: M. E. Sharpe, 1999.

Cohen, Lenard, and John Lampe. *Embracing Democracy in the Western Balkans*. Washington, DC: Woodrow Wilson Center Press, 2011.

Dauphinee, Elizabeth. *The Politics of Exile*. New York: Routledge, 2013.

Dawisha, Karen, and Bruce Parrott, eds. *Politics, Power, and the Struggle for Democracy in South-East Europe*. Cambridge: Cambridge University Press, 1997.

Donais, Tim. *The Political Economy of Peacebuilding in Post-Dayton Bosnia*. New York: Frank Cass, 2005.

Gagnon, V. P. *The Myth of Ethnic War: Serbia and Croatia in the 1990s*. Ithaca, NY: Cornell University Press, 2004.

Greeberg, Jessica. *After the Revolution: Youth, Democracy, and the Politics of Disappointment in Serbia*. Stanford, CA: Stanford University Press, 2014.

Hromadzic, Azra. *Citizens of an Empty Nation: Youth and State-Making in Postwar Bosnia-Herzegovina*. Philadelphia: University of Pennsylvania Press, 2015.

Judah, Tim. *Kosovo: War and Revenge*. New Haven, CT: Yale University Press, 2000.

Lampe, John. *Yugoslavia as History: Twice There Was a Country*. 2nd ed. Cambridge: Cambridge University Press, 2000.

Naimark, Norman, and Holly Case, eds. *Yugoslavia and Its Historians: Understanding the Balkan Wars of the 1990s*. Stanford, CA: Stanford University Press, 2003.

Petersen, Roger D. *Western Intervention in the Balkans: The Strategic Use of Emotion in Conflict*. Cambridge: Cambridge University Press, 2011.

Ramet, Sabrina Petra. *Balkan Babel: The Disintegration of Yugoslavia from the Death of Tito to the Fall of Milošević*. 4th ed. Boulder, CO: Westview Press, 2002.

Skendaj, Elton. *Creating Kosovo: International Oversight and the Making of Ethical Institutions.* Washington, DC: Woodrow Wilson Center Press and Ithaca, NY: Cornell University Press, 2014.

Subotic, Jelena. *Hijacked Justice: Dealing with the Past in the Balkans.* Ithaca, NY: Cornell University Press, 2009.

Woodward, Susan. *Balkan Tragedy.* Washington, DC: Brookings Institution, 1996.

Websites

Balkan Investigative Reporting Network (BIRN): http://birn.eu.com

European Commission, "Enlargement Package 2013: Strategy and Progress Reports": http://ec.europa.eu/enlargement/countries/strategy-and-progress-report/index_en.htm

European Stability Initiative: http://www.esiweb.org

International Crisis Group, "Balkans": http://www.crisisgroup.org/en/regions/europe/balkans.aspx

United Nations Secretary General, "Reports Submitted by/Transmitted by the Secretary-General to the Security Council": http://www.un.org/en/sc/documents/sgreports

Bosnia-Herzegovina

Government: http://www.vladars.net/eng/Pages/default.aspx; http://www.fbihvlada.gov.ba/

Office of the High Representative: http://www.ohr.int

Organization for Security and Co-operation in Europe, Mission to Bosnia and Herzegovina: http://www.oscebih.org/Default.aspx?id=0&lang=EN

Parliament: http://www.parliament.ba

United Nations Development Programme in Bosnia and Herzegovina: http://www.ba.undp.org/bosnia_and_herzegovina/en/home.html

USAID, "Bosnia and Herzegovina": http://www.usaid.gov/where-we-work/europe-and-eurasia/bosnia

World Bank, "Bosnia and Herzegovina": http://www.worldbank.org/en/country/bosniaandherzegovina

Croatia

Government: https://vlada.gov.hr

Parliament: http://www.sabor.hr/English

United Nations Development Programme in Croatia: http://www.hr.undp.org/croatia/en/home.html

World Bank, "Croatia": http://www.worldbank.org/en/country/croatia

Kosovo

EULEX Kosovo: http://www.eulex-kosovo.eu/en/front

Government: https://www.rks-gov.net/en-US/Pages/Fillimi.aspx

Kosovo Force (KFOR): http://www.aco.nato.int/kfor.aspx

Organization for Security and Co-operation in Europe, Mission to Kosovo: http://www.osce.org/kosovo

Parliament: http://www.kuvendikosoves.org/?cid=2,1

United Nations Development Programme in Kosovo: http://www.ks.undp.org/kosovo/en/home.
html

USAID, "Kosovo": http://transition.usaid.gov/kosovo/eng

World Bank, "Kosovo": http://www.worldbank.org/en/country/kosovo

Macedonia

Government: http://www.vlada.mk/?language=en-gb

Organization for Security and Co-operation in Europe, Mission to Macedonia: http://www.osce.
org/skopje

Parliament: http://www.sobranie.mk/en

USAID, "Macedonia": http://www.usaid.gov/where-we-work/europe-and-eurasia/macedonia

World Bank, "Macedonia": http://www.worldbank.org/en/country/macedonia

Montenegro

Government: http://www.gov.me/en/homepage

Organization for Security and Co-operation in Europe, Mission to Montenegro: http://www.osce.
org/montenegro

Parliament: http://www.skupstina.me/index.php/en/

United Nations Development Programme in Montenegro: http://www.me.undp.org/montenegro/
en/home.html

USAID, "Montenegro": http://www.usaid.gov/where-we-work/europe-and-eurasia/montenegro

World Bank, "Montenegro": http://www.worldbank.org/en/country/montenegro

Serbia

B-92: http://www.b92.net/eng

Government: http://www.srbija.gov.rs/?change_lang=en

Organization for Security and Co-operation in Europe, Mission to Serbia: http://www.osce.org/
serbia

Parliament: http://www.parlament.gov.rs/national-assembly.467.html

United Nations Development Programme in Serbia: http://www.rs.undp.org/serbia/en/home.html

USAID, "Serbia": http://www.usaid.gov/where-we-work/europe-and-eurasia/serbia

World Bank, "Serbia": http://www.worldbank.org/en/country/serbia

Slovenia

Government: http://www.vlada.si/en

Parliament: http://www.slovenia.si/slovenia/state/parliament-the-national-assembly

World Bank, "Slovenia": http://data.worldbank.org/country/slovenia?view=chart

Notes

1. To get a sense of differences, see essays by Sabrina Ramet, *Thinking about Yugoslavia: Scholarly Debates on the Western Balkans and the Wars in Bosnia and Kosovo* (Cambridge: Cambridge University Press, 2005); Gale Stokes et al., "Instant History: Understanding the Wars of Yugoslav Succession," *Slavic Review* 55, no. 1 (1996): 136–60; Sarah Kent, "Writing the Yugoslav Wars," *American Historical Review* 102, no. 4 (1997): 1085–114; and Ivo Banac, "Historiography of the Countries of Eastern Europe: Yugoslavia," *American Historical Review* 97, no. 4 (1992): 1084–102.

2. William Zimmerman, *Open Borders, Non-Alignment and the Political Evolution of Yugoslavia* (Princeton, NJ: Princeton University Press, 1986).

3. It is impossible to do justice to the diverse cultural, social, economic, and political background of the lands of former Yugoslavia in so short a space. For a general introduction, see Ivo Banac, *The Yugoslav National Question* (Ithaca, NY: Cornell University Press, 1984); Barbara Jelavich, *History of the Balkans*, 2 vols. (New York: Cambridge University Press, 1983); Charles Jelavich and Barbara Jelavich, *The Establishment of the Balkan National States, 1804–1920* (Seattle: University of Washington Press, 1977); Joseph Rothschild, *East Central Europe between the Two World Wars* (Seattle: University of Washington Press, 1974); Jozo Tomasevich, *Peasants, Politics and Economic Change* (Stanford, CA: Stanford University Press, 1955); John Lampe, *Yugoslavia as History: Twice There Was a Country*, 2nd ed. (Cambridge: Cambridge University Press, 2000); Gale Stokes, *Three Eras of Political Change in Eastern Europe* (New York: Oxford University Press, 1997); and Mark Mazower, *The Balkans: A Short History* (New York: Random House, 2002).

4. Banac, *The Yugoslav National Question*, 415–16.

5. Dennison Rusinow, *The Yugoslav Experiment, 1948–1974* (Berkeley: University of California Press, 1978).

6. See Ivo Banac, *With Stalin against Tito: Cominform Splits in Yugoslav Communism* (Ithaca, NY: Cornell University Press, 1988).

7. See Zimmerman, *Open Borders*; and Alvin Z. Rubinstein, *Yugoslavia and the Nonaligned World* (Princeton, NJ: Princeton University Press, 1970).

8. Zimmerman nicely makes this argument. See also Susan Woodward, *Socialist Unemployment: The Political Economy of Yugoslavia, 1945–1990* (Princeton, NJ: Princeton University Press, 1995).

9. Woodward, *Socialist Unemployment*; and Lampe, *Yugoslavia as History*.

10. Woodward, *Socialist Unemployment*, 384.

11. The term "Bosniac" is used to describe the Slavic Muslims who live mainly in Bosnia-Herzegovina, but also in Serbia, Montenegro, and Kosovo. They had been known as Muslims in a national sense since 1971, but the Congress of Bosniac Intellectuals officially adopted "Bosniac" as the name for the people in 1993, and it has been generally accepted among all Slavic Muslims. See Mustafa Imamović, *Istorija Bošnjaka* (Sarajevo: Preporod, 1998); Francine Friedman, *The Bosnian Muslims: Denial of a Nation* (Boulder, CO: Westview Press, 1995); and Banac, *The Yugoslav National Question*.

12. Radivoj Papic, "Sta je to 'Zajednistvo,'" *Komunist*, September 14, 1972, as cited in Mark Baskin, "National in Form, National in Content: Some Consequences of Consociationalism in Yugoslavia" (paper prepared for delivery at the American Political Science Association, August 30 to September 2, 1984).

13. Kosovo became an "autonomous province," in 1974 enjoying almost all of the perquisites of republican status, but with fewer representatives in the state presidency and without the formal right to secede. It had earlier been an "autonomous region" within Serbia. See Mark Baskin, "Crisis in Kosovo," *Problems of Communism* 32, no. 2 (March–April 1983): 61–74.

14. Arend Lijphart, *Democracy in Plural Societies* (New Haven, CT: Yale University Press, 1980); Paul Shoup, *Yugoslav Communism and the National Question* (New York: Columbia University Press, 1968); Pedro Ramet, *Nationalism and Federalism in Yugoslavia, 1963–1983* (Bloomington: Indiana University Press, 1984); and Steven Burg, *Conflict and Cohesion in Socialist Yugoslavia: Political Decision Making since 1966* (Princeton, NJ: Princeton University Press, 1983).

15. Burg, *Conflict and Cohesion*, 346.

16. Lenard J. Cohen, *Serpent and Bosom: The Rise and Fall of Slobodan Milošević* (Boulder, CO: Westview Press, 2001).

17. Lenard J. Cohen, *Broken Bonds: Yugoslavia's Disintegration and Balkan Politics in Transition*, 2nd ed. (Boulder, CO: Westview Press, 1995), 47. See also Dijana Plještina, *Regional Development in Communist Yugoslavia* (Boulder, CO: Westview Press, 1992).

18. Lampe, *Yugoslavia as History*, 354–55; and Sabrina Petra Ramet, *Balkan Babel: The Disintegration of Yugoslavia from the Death of Tito to the Fall of Milošević*, 4th ed. (Boulder, CO: Westview Press, 2002), 54–55.

19. Jacque Poos, Luxembourg's foreign minister at the time of Luxembourg's presidency of the European Community Council of Ministers in 1991, famously declared that "this is the hour of Europe" during his shuttle diplomacy between Belgrade, Zagreb, Ljubljana, and Brioni. See International Commission on the Balkans, *Unfinished Peace: Report of the International Commission on the Balkans* (Washington, DC: Carnegie Endowment for International Peace, 1996), 56; and Dan Smith, "Europe's Peacebuilding Hour? Past Failures, Future Challenges," *Journal of International Affairs* 55, no. 2 (spring 2002): 441–60, quote on 442.

20. Lenard Cohen, "Prelates and Politicians in Bosnia: The Role of Religion in Nationalist Mobilisation," *Nationalities Papers* 25 (September 1997): 481–99; Ramet, *Thinking about Yugoslavia*; V. P. Gagnon, *The Myth of Ethnic War: Serbia and Croatia in the 1990s* (Ithaca, NY: Cornell University Press, 2004); Ramet, *Balkan Babel*; Cohen, *Broken Bonds*; and Anthony Oberschall, "The Manipulation of Ethnicity: From Ethnic Cooperation to Violence and War in Yugoslavia," *Ethnic and Racial Studies* 23, no. 6 (2000): 994–95.

21. Estimates are taken from the UNHCR Population Statistics Reference Database.

22. Lampe, *Yugoslavia as History*, 370.

23. "The 2004 Enlargement: The Challenge of a 25-Member EU," European Union, http://europa.eu/legislation_summaries/enlargement/2004_and_2007_enlargement/e50017_en.htm; "Slovenia Joins the Euro Area," European Commission, http://ec.europa.eu/economy_finance/articles/euro/slovenia_joins_the_euro_area_en.htm; and "Accession: Estonia, Israel and Slovenia Invited to Join OECD," OECD, http://www.oecd.org/estonia/accessionestoniaisraelandslovenia invitedtojoinoecd.htm.

24. For basic information on the UN Protection Force (UNPROFOR), see "Former Yugoslavia—UNPROFOR," United Nations, http://www.un.org/Depts/dpko/dpko/co_mission/unprof_p.htm.

25. An estimated nine hundred Serbs were killed in the Croatian offensive against Serb-held Krajina in 1995. See "Croatia: Three Years since Operations Flash and Storm—Three Years of Justice and Dignity Denied," Amnesty International, EUR 64/05/98, August 4, 1998, http://www.amnesty.org/ar/library/asset/EUR64/005/1998/fr/c416cce8-d9d6-11dd-af2b-b1f6023af0c5/eur640051998en.pdf (accessed August 4, 2007).

26. Quoted in Branka Magaš, "Franjo Tudjman, an Obituary," *Independent*, December 13, 1999, reprinted in *Bosnia Report* (December 1999–February 2000), at http://www.bosnia.org.uk/bosrep/decfeb00/tudjman.cfm.

27. Ethnic cleansing is a campaign in which authorities, acting according to a premeditated plan, capture or consolidate control over territory by forcibly displacing or killing members of opposing ethnic groups. Human Rights Watch/Helsinki, *Bosnia and Herzegovina: Politics of*

Revenge—the Misuse of Authority in Bihac, Cazin, and Velika Kladua (New York: Human Rights Watch/Helsinki, 1997), 6.

28. For example, the HVO destroyed the beautiful sixteenth-century bridge that united east and west Mostar, and Serb forces destroyed the Ferhadija Mosque in Banja Luka, the largest in Europe, among the many objects.

29. Mirsad Tokača, *Bosanske knjige mrtvih: Ljudski gubici u Bosni i Hercegovini 1991–1995* (Sarajevo: Istraživačko Dokumentacioni Centar, 2012).

30. Gerard Toal and Carl Dahlman, *Bosnia Remade: Ethnic Cleansing and Its Reversal* (Oxford: Oxford University Press, 2011), 140.

31. For information on Operation EUFOR ALTHEA, see the European Military Force (EUFOR) website at http://www.euforbih.org; information on the NATO-led Stabilization Force can be found at http://www.nato.int/sfor/index.htm and http://www.nato.int/sfor/organisation/mission.htm (accessed August 19, 2014).

32. See "The Mandate of the OHR," Office of the High Representative, February 16, 2012, http://www.ohr.int/ohr-info/gen-info/default.asp?content_id=38612 (accessed September 22, 2013).

33. See, e.g., Tim Judah, *Kosovo: War and Revenge* (New Haven, CT: Yale University Press, 2000).

34. For the declaration of independence, see "Full Text: Kosovo Declaration," BBC News, February 17, 2008, http://news.bbc.co.uk/2/hi/europe/7249677.stm. On developments in Kosovo from 1999 to 2008, see, e.g., Mark Baskin, *Developing Local Democracy in Kosovo* (Stockholm: IDEA, 2005), http://www.idea.int/publications/dem_kosovo/index.cfm; and Conflict Security and Development Group, *Kosovo Report* (London: International Policy Institute, 2003), http://ipi.sspp.kcl.ac.uk/rep005/index.html. See also Tim Judah, *Kosovo: What Everyone Needs to Know* (Oxford: Oxford University Press, 2008).

35. The ICJ ruled in July 2010 that Kosovo's declaration of independence did not violate international law. See the opinions at "Kosovo in International Court of Justice," Ministry of Foreign Affairs, Republic of Kosovo, http://www.mfa-ks.net/?page=2,61 (accessed September 22, 2013).

36. See UN Security Council, "Report of the Secretary General on the United Nations Interim Administration Mission in Kosovo," S/2013/444, July 26, 2013. Among the other issues are integrated border management, multiethnic policing, energy and telecommunications, the exchange of liaison officers, freedom of movement, civil registry, cadastral records, and acceptance of university diplomas. See "Serbia and Kosovo Reach Landmark Deal," European External Action Service, http://eeas.europa.eu/top_stories/2013/190413__eu-facilitated_dialogue_en.htm; "Serbia and Kosovo: The Path to Normalisation," International Crisis Group, February 19, 2003, http://www.crisisgroup.org/en/regions/europe/balkans/kosovo/223-serbia-and-kosovo-the-path-to-normalisation.aspx; and "The Implementation of Kosovo-Serbia Political Dialogue," Policy Paper No. 4/13, KIPRED, July 2013, http://www.kipred.org/advCms/?id=5,1,1,1,e,299. Both governments have shown commitment to this process; see, e.g., "PM Strongly Condemns Killing of EULEX Member," *B-92*, September 19, 2013, http://www.b92.net/eng/news/politics.php?yyyy=2013&mm=09&dd=19&nav_id=87721.

37. "Report of the Secretary General on the United Nations Interim Administration Mission in Kosovo" S/2017/387, May 3, 2017, http://www.un.org/ga/search/view_doc.asp?symbol=S/2017/387.

38. "Report of the Secretary General on the United Nations Interim Administration Mission in Kosovo" and the SG report of February 6, 2017.

39. See, e.g., Banac, *The Yugoslav National Question*, 307–28.

40. "Macedonia's Name: Why the Dispute Matters and How to Resolve It," Report No. 122, International Crisis Group Balkans, December 10, 2001, http://www.crisisgroup.org/~/media/Files/europe/Macedonia%2014.pdf, 12–13. See also "Macedonia's Name: Breaking the Deadlock,"

Europe Briefing No. 52, International Crisis Group, January 12, 2009, http://www.crisisgroup.org/ ~/media/Files/europe/b52_macedonias_name___breaking_the_deadlock.pdf.

41. Republika Makedonija Državni zavod za statistika, *Popis 2002* (Skopje: Republic of Macedonia State Statistical Office, December 1, 2003), http://www.stat.gov.mk/PrikaziPoslednaPublikacija_en.aspx?id=54.

42. See, e.g., "Macedonia: Not Out of the Woods Yet," International Crisis Group, February 25, 2005, http://www.crisisgroup.org/home/index.cfm?id-3295&l-1.

43. See Florian Bieber, "Montenegrin Politics since the Disintegration of Yugoslavia," in *Montenegro in Transition: Problems in Identity and Statehood*, ed. Florian Bieber (Baden-Baden: Nomos Verlagsgesellschaft, 2003), 11–42; and "Montenegro's Independence Drive," International Crisis Group, December 7, 2005, http://www.crisisgroup.org/en/regions/europe/balkans/montenegro/169-montenegros-independence-drive.aspx.

44. European Commission, Montenegro 2016 Report, SWD (2016) 360 final, https:// ec.europa.eu/neighbourhood-enlargement/sites/near/files/pdf/key_documents/2016/20161109_report_montenegro.pdf.

45. "David Bronstrom, "Russia Threatens Retaliation as Montenegro Becomes 29th NATO Member." *Guardian*, June 5, 2017, http://www.reuters.com/article/us-usa-nato-montenegro-idUSKBN18W2WS; and Damir Marusić, "Did Moscow Botch a Coup in Montenegro?" *American Interest*, October 30, 2016, https://www.the-american-interest.com/2016/10/30/did-moscow-botch-a-coup-in-montenegro/.

46. Mary Kaldor, *New and Old Wars: Organized Violence in a Global Era* (Palo Alto, CA: Stanford University Press, 1999).

47. Freedom House, *Nations in Transit 2017: The False Promise of Populism,* https://freedomhouse. org/report/nations-transit/nations-transit-2017.

48. Mirjana Kasapovic, "Voting Rights, Electoral Systems, and Political Representation of Diaspora in Croatia," *East European Politics and Societies and Cultures* 26, no. 4 (2012): 777–91.

49. International Institute for Democracy and Electoral Assistance, "Gender Quotas Database," http://www.idea.int/data-tools/data/gender-quotas/country-overview.

50. Center for Research and Policy Making, *Analysis of Internal Party Democracy in Macedonia* (Skopje: Konrad-Adenauer-Stiftung, 2013), http://www.crpm.org.mk; and Georgi Karasimeonov, ed., *Organization Structures and Internal Party Democracy in South Eastern Europe* (Sofia: Goetex Press, 2005).

51. Valerie Bunce, "The Political Economy of Postsocialism," *Slavic Review* 58 (Winter 1999): 756–93. See also Vernon Bogdanov, "Founding Elections and Regime Change," *Electoral Studies* 1 (1990): 288–94; and Valerie Bunce, "Rethinking Recent Democratization: Lessons from the Postcommunist Experience," *World Politics* 55, no. 2 (January 2003): 189.

52. Sabrina Petra Ramet, "Democratization in Slovenia—the Second Stage," in *Politics, Power, and the Struggle for Democracy in South-East Europe*, ed. Karen Dawisha and Bruce Parrott, 189–217 (Cambridge: Cambridge University Press, 1997); and Patrick Hyder Patterson, "On the Edge of Reason: The Boundaries of Balkanism in Slovenian, Austrian, and Italian Discourse," *Slavic Review* 62, no. 1 (Spring 2003): 110–41.

53. Alenka Krašovec and Lars Johannsen, "Recent Developments in Democracy in Slovenia," *Problems of Post-Communism* 63, nos. 5–6 (2016): 313–22, doi:10.1080/10758216.2016.1169932.

54. See, e.g., Peter Spiegel, "The Day after: Digging Deeper into Slovenia," *Financial Times* Brussels blog, May 30, 2013, http://blogs.ft.com/brusselsblog/2013/05/the-day-after-digging-deeper-into-slovenia.

55. Eric Gordy, *The Culture of Power in Serbia* (University Park: Pennsylvania State University Press, 1999).

56. Gagnon, *The Myth of Ethnic War*, 92.

57. Gagnon, *The Myth of Ethnic War*; and Gordy, *The Culture of Power*.

58. Vladimir Matić, *Serbia at the Crossroads Again* (Washington, DC: US Institute of Peace, 2004). Many observers regard Koštunica's DSS as merely more savvy, not less nationalistic, than SRS. See International Crisis Group, *Serbia's New Government: Turning from Europe* (Belgrade and Brussels: International Crisis Group, May 2007).

59. https://www.theguardian.com/world/2017/jun/15/serbia-gains-its-first-female-and-gay-prime-minister-ana-brnabic.

60. See the commentary by Prime Minister Ivica Dačić in the *Financial Times*, http://blogs.ft.com/beyond-brics/2013/09/17/guest-post-no-time-to-rest-as-serbia-moves-towards-europe; and "Vučić Delivers Victory Day Message to Russia in Russian", *B-92*, May 8, 2017, http://www.b92.net/eng/news/politics.php?yyyy=2017&mm=05&dd=08&nav_id=101211.

61. "European Commission Opinion on Serbia's Application for Membership of the European Union," Brussels, 12.10.2011 COM(2011) 668 final, European Commission, http://ec.europa.eu/enlargement/pdf/key_documents/2011/package/sr_rapport_2011_en.pdf; and "European Commission, Serbia 2016 Report," Brussels, November 11, 2016 SWD(2016) 361 final.

62. Ivan Šiber, "The Impact of Nationalism, Values, and Ideological Orientations on Multi-Party Elections in Croatia," in *The Tragedy of Yugoslavia: The Failure of Democratic Transformation*, ed. Jim Seroka and Vukašin Pavlović, 141–71 (Armonk, NY: M. E. Sharpe, 1992); Mirjana Kasapovics, "Demokratska konsolidacija i izborna politika u Hrvatskoj 1990–2000," in *Hrvatska politika 1990–2000*, ed. Mirjana Kasapovics, 15–40 (Zagreb: Fakultet političkih znanosti, 2001); and Paula M. Pickering and Mark Baskin, "What Is to Be Done: Succession from the League of Communists of Croatia," *Communist and Post-Communist Studies* 41 (2008): 521–40.

63. Miljenko Antics and Maja Dodic Gruics, "The Parliamentary Election in Croatia, November 2007," *Electoral Studies* 27 (2008): 755.

64. Sanadar was ultimately sentenced to ten years in prison for accepting bribes in 2011. This relatively severe penalty for the highest-ranking executive in East Central Europe to be convicted of corruption since 1990 helped to quiet concerns that Croatia was soft on corruption on the eve of its accession to the EU.

65. Andrija Henjak, "Croatia," *Nations in Transit 2017*, Freedom House, 2017, https://freedomhouse.org/report/nations-transit/2017/croatia.

66. Sven Mikelić, "HDZ Embraces Opponents to Remain in Croatia Government," *Balkan Insight*, June 14, 2017, http://www.balkaninsight.com/en/article/hdz-embraces-opponents-to-remain-in-croatia-govt-06-13-2017.

67. "Perkovic Case Puts Croatia, EU in Conflict," *Southeast European Times*, September 25, 2013, http://www.setimes.com/cocoon/setimes/xhtml/en_GB/features/setimes/features/2013/09/25/feature-01.

68. *The 1990 Elections in the Republics of Yugoslavia* (Washington, DC: International Republican Institute for International Affairs, 1991); and Suad Arnautovics, *Izbori u Bosni i Hercegovini 1990* (Sarajevo: Promocult, 1996).

69. "Opinion on the Constitutional Situation in Bosnia and Herzegovina and the Powers of the High Representative," European Commission for Democracy through Law, March 2005, http://www.venice.coe.int/webforms/documents/?pdf=CDL(2005)021-e.

70. Sumantra Bose, *Bosnia after Dayton: Nationalist Partition and International Intervention* (Oxford: Oxford University Press, 2002), 117.

71. Donald L. Horowitz, *Ethnic Groups in Conflict*, 2nd ed. (Berkeley: University of California Press, 2000); and Paul Mitchell, "Party Competition in an Ethnic Dual Party System," *Ethnic and Racial Studies* 18 (October 1995): 773–96.

72. Daria Sito-Sucic, "Bosnian Experts Present U.S.-Backed Plan for Reform," *Reuters*, May 15, 2013.

73. The includes the leader of the second most popular party among Bosniacs and coalition partner with SDA in the Federation Parliament, Alliance for a Better Future, who was indicted in January 2016 for pressuring a witness to give false testimony in a drug trafficking case. See "Bosnia and Herzegovina: Radoncic Eager to Testify at Kelmendi Trial," *Organized Crime and Corruption Reporting Project*, https://www.occrp.org/en/daily/4823-bosnia-and-herzegovina-radoncic-eager-to-testify-at-kelmendi-trial, accessed December 28, 2017.

74. RS officials declared that citizens overwhelmingly approved of the referendum on establishing the RS "statehood day," which a subsequent amendment had superficially declared "secular." However, state election officials' lack of cooperation and independent observers' unwillingness to monitor mean that the referendum results are not possible to verify. Minority groups substantially boycotted the referendum. Even more worrisome for the viability of Bosnia, the RS celebration of "statehood" day in January 2017 included the participation of a Bosnian army unit based in the RS, over the objections of the army command. See Srecko Latal, "Sabre-Rattling over Serb 'Statehood Day' Shakes Bosnia," *BIRN*, January 10, 2017, http://www.balkaninsight.com/en/article/new-warmongering-shakes-bosnia-over-serb-statehood-day--01-10-2017#sthash.lileIOCi.dpuf.

75. Danijel Kovacevic and Eleanor Rose, "Bosnian Serb Leader Calls US Ambassador 'Enemy'," *Balkan Transitional Justice,* January 18, 2017, http://www.balkaninsight.com/en/article/dodik-unrepentant-after-us-sanctions-announced-01-18-2017.

76. CEC, "Bosnian and Herzegovina 2012 Progress Report," COM(2012) 600 final, Brussels, European Commission, October 10, 2012, http://ec.europa.eu/enlargement/pdf/key_documents/2012/package/ba_rapport_2012_en.pdf.

77. Elizabeth Cousens, "Missed Opportunities to Overcompensation: Implementing the Dayton Agreement on Bosnia," in *Ending Civil Wars: The Implementation of Peace Agreements*, ed. Stephen Stedman, Donald Rothchild, and Elizabeth M. Cousens, 531–66 (Boulder, CO: Lynne Rienner, 2002).

78. See "High Representative's Decisions by Topic," Office of the High Representative, http://www.ohr.int/decisions/archive.asp.

79. Patrice McMahon and Jon Western, "Bosnia on the Brink," *Foreign Affairs* 88, no. 5 (September–October 2009): 69–83.

80. Duncan Perry, "The Republic of Macedonia: Finding Its Way," in *Politics, Power, and the Struggle for Democracy in South-East Europe*, ed. Karen Dawisha and Bruce Parrott, 235 (Cambridge: Cambridge University Press, 1997).

81. OSCE, *The Former Yugoslav Republic of Macedonia Presidential and Early Parliamentary Elections 13 and 27 April 2014, OSCE/ODIHR Election Observation Mission Final Report* (Warsaw: OSCE/Office of Democratic Institutions and Human Rights, July 15, 2014), http://www.osce.org/odihr/elections/fyrom/121306.

82. Meri Jordanovska and Sinisa Jakov Marusic, "Pro-Govt Media Inflame Nationalist Hysteria in Macedonia," *BIRN* Skopje, March 15, 2017, http://www.balkaninsight.com/en/article/macedonia-s-propaganda-war-spreads-nationalist-hysteria-03-15-2017#sthash.oSi7aIcj.dpuf.

83. Sinisa Jakov Marusic, "Zaev Wins Mandate to Form Macedonia's Next Govt," *BIRN* Skopje, May 17, 2017, http://www.balkaninsight.com/en/article/zaev-recieves-mandate-to-form-new-macedonian-govt--05-17-2017#sthash.z5tj16UR.dpuf.

84. Florian Bieber, "Assessing the Ohrid Framework Agreement," in *One Decade after the Ohrid Framework Agreement: Lessons (to Be) Learned from the Macedonian Experience*, ed. Marija Risteska and Zhidas Daskalovski, 22 (Skopje: Friedrich Ebert Stiftung and Centre for Research and Policy Making in Macedonia, 2011).

85. CEC, "Enlargement Strategy and Main Challenges 2012–2013," COM (2012) 600 final, 35.

86. Jelena Džankić and Jovana Marović, "Montenegro," in *Nations in Transit 2014*, Freedom House, https://freedomhouse.org/report/nations-transit/2014/montenegro; and Jovana Marović,

"Montenegro," in *Nations in Transit 2016*, Freedom House, https://freedomhouse.org/report/nations-transit/2016/montenegro.

87. Dušica Tomović, "Losers and Activists File Charges about Montenegrin Election," *Balkan Insight*, October 18, 2016, http://www.balkaninsight.com/en/article/losers-and-activists-file-charges-about-montenegro-election-10-17-2016 and Dušica Tomović; and "Bosniac Party Holds Key for Montenegro's Next Government," *Balkan Insight*, http://www.balkaninsight.com/en/article/bosniak-party-holds-key-for-montenegro-s-next-govt-11-22-2016-1.

88. "Montenegro 2016 Report," SWD (2016) 361 final, Brussels, European Commission, November 9, 2016, https://ec.europa.eu/neighbourhood-enlargement/sites/near/files/pdf/key_documents/2016/20161109_report_montenegro.pdf, 6.

89. Preparim Isufi and Taulant Osmani, "Staying Power of Kosovo's New Government Is Doutbed," *Balkan Insight*, September 6, 2017, http://www.balkaninsight.com/en/article/staying-power-of-kosovo-s-new-government-doubted-09-06-2017. In addition, the European Union's Special Investigative Task Force (SITF) is continuing to explore allegations that senior officials were involved in organ trafficking. See Julian Borger, "Senior Kosovo Figures Face Prosecution for Crimes against Humanity," *Guardian*, July 29, 2014, http://www.theguardian.com/world/2014/jul/29/senior-political-figures-kosovo-prosecution-crimes-humanity; and "Statement by the Chief Prosecutor of the Special Investigative Task Force (SITF) on Investigative Findings," SITF, July 29, 2014, http://www.sitf.eu/index.php/en.

90. For information on the chambers, see https://www.scp-ks.org/en.

91. Eric Gordy, "Was the Karadzic Verdict a Just Reckoning?" *Balkan Insight*, March 28, 2016, http://www.balkaninsight.com/en/article/q-and-a-on-the-karadzic-verdict-03-27-2016#sthash.v92ZuDNL.dpuf.

92. Krenar Gashi, "Kosovo," in *Nations in Transit 2017*, Freedom House, https://freedomhouse.org/report/nations-transit/2017/kosovo, 10.

93. "Slovenia Overview," *World Directory of Minorities and Indigenous Peoples*, Minority Rights Group International, http://www.minorityrights.org/?lid=5168; and Alenka Kuhelj, "Rise of Xenophobic Nationalism in Europe: A Case of Slovenia," *Communist and Post-Communist Studies* 44 (2011): 271–82.

94. Robert D. Putnam, ed., *Democracies in Flux: The Evolution of Social Capital in Contemporary Society* (New York: Oxford University Press, 2002).

95. Cohen, "Prelates and Politicians in Bosnia."

96. Oberschall, "The Manipulation of Ethnicity," 994–95; and Patrizia Poggi et al., *Bosnia and Herzegovina: Local Level Institutions and Social Capital Study*, vol. 1 (Washington, DC: World Bank, 2002).

97. Other groups—the Croatian Defense Forces (HOS) in Croatia, Muslim gangs operating in Sarajevo in 1992, the Kosovo Liberation Army in Kosovo, and the Albanian National Liberation Army and Macedonian Lions in Macedonia—have similar elements.

98. Cynthia Cockburn, *The Space between Us: Negotiating Gender and National Identities in Conflict* (London: Zed Books, 1998).

99. Poggi et al., *Bosnia and Herzegovina*, 83; and Bose, *Bosnia after Dayton*, 127.

100. On NGOs, see Paul Stubbs, *Displaced Promises: Forced Migration, Refuge and Return in Croatia and Bosnia-Herzegovina* (Uppsala: Life and Peace Institute, 1999). On good neighborly relations, see Tone Bringa, *Being Muslim the Bosnian Way* (Princeton, NJ: Princeton University Press, 1995). On work, see Paula M. Pickering, "Generating Social Capital for Bridging Ethnic Divisions in the Balkans," *Ethnic and Racial Studies* 29, no. 1 (2006): 79–103; David Chandler, *Faking Democracy after Dayton* (London: Pluto Press, 2000); and Sevima Sali-Terzic, "Civil Society," in *Policies of International Support to South-Eastern European Countries: Lessons (Not) Learnt from Bosnia and Herzegovina*, ed. Žarko Papić (Sarajevo: Open Society Institute, 2001), 138–59.

101. Ivana Howard, "Unfinished Business: Civil Society," in *Unfinished Business: The Western Balkans and the International Community*, ed. Vedran Džihić and Daniel Hamilton (Washington, DC: Center for Transatlantic Relations, 2012), 38–39.

102. For the example of Kosovo, see Elton Skendaj, *Creating Kosovo: International Oversight and the Making of Ethical Institutions* (Washington, DC: Woodrow Wilson and Ithaca, NY: Cornell University Press, 2014), chap. 5.

103. Howard, "Unfinished Business," 40.

104. Ashutosh Varshney, *Ethnic Conflict and Civic Life: Hindus and Muslims in India* (New Haven, CT: Yale University Press, 2001).

105. Jennifer Stuart, ed., *The 2002 NGO Sustainability Index* (Washington, DC: US Agency for International Development, 2003); and Howard, "Unfinished Business," 40.

106. Cynthia Nixon, *The Ties That Bind: Social Capital in Bosnia and Herzegovina* (Sarajevo: UN Development Programme Mission to Bosnia-Herzegovina, Human Development Report, 2009).

107. Aleksandar Djordjevic, "Party Ties Help NGOs Win Key Serbian Ministerial Deals," *Balkan Insight*, September 6, 2013, http://www.balkaninsight.com/en/article/party-ties-help-ngos-win-key-ministerial-deals (accessed September 14, 2013).

108. Sladjana Danković and Paula M. Pickering, "Public Scepticism of Civil Society Organisations: Norms, Citizen Priorities, and Local Groups in Post-Socialist Serbia," *East European Politics* 33, no. 2 (2017): 210–32.

109. See, e.g., the Civil Society Organization, Open Parliament in Serbia at http://www.otvoreniparlament.rs.

110 Statistical analysis of nationally representative sample data from Slovenia, Croatia, Serbia, Bosnia-Herzegovina, Macedonia, Montenegro, and Kosovo indicates that respondents aged eighteen to twenty-four are 32 percent less likely than those fifty-five or older. About 44 percent of respondents aged eighteen to twenty-four reported voting in the most recent elections. Data from European Bank for Reconstruction and Development, "Life in Transition Survey II: After the Crisis," 2010, datafile, http://www.ebrd.com/what-we-do/economic-research-and-data/data/lits.html.

111. UN Development Programme (UNDP), *Early Warning System in Bosnia-Herzegovina* IV (2004), 52. Hard copy is on file with the author and available on request.

112. Lenard J. Cohen, "Embattled Democracy: Post-Communist Croatia in Transition," in *Politics, Power, and the Struggle for Democracy in South-East Europe*, ed. Karen Dawisha and Bruce Parrott (Cambridge: Cambridge University Press, 1997), 112.

113. UNDP, *Early Warning System in Bosnia-Herzegovina*, 70; UNDP, *Early Warning System Report, FYR Macedonia*, November 2004, 20, http://www.undp.org.mk/default.asp?where-publications (accessed October 30, 2005); Mirjana Kasapović et al., *Hrvatska Politika, 1990–2000* (Zagreb: Fakultet političkih znanosti Sveučilišta u Zagrebu, 2001), 301, 336; and International Institute for Democracy and Electoral Analysis (IDEA), "Survey Results: South Eastern Europe: New Means for Regional Analysis," IDEA, 2002, http://archive.idea.int/balkans/survey_detailed.cfm.

114. Tijana Morača, "Between Defiance and Compliance: A New Civil Society in the Post-Yugoslav Space?" *Osservatorio balcani e caucaso*, Occasional paper 2, August 2016, www.balcanicaucaso.org (accessed December 20, 2016).

115. Bedrana Kaletović, "Struggle Continues over Personal ID Numbers in BiH," *Southeast European Times*, July 15, 2013, http://www.setimes.com/cocoon/setimes/xhtml/en_GB/features/setimes/features/2013/07/25/feature-03 (accessed September 14, 2013).

116. Elvira M. Jukić, "Plenum in Bosnian Capital Finalises Demands," *Balkan Insight*, February 29, 2014; and Završeni Protesti u bh gradovim," *Al Jazeera Balkans*, February 10, 2014, http://balkans.aljazeera.net/vijesti/zavrseni-protesti-u-bh-gradovima.

117. Filip Rudic, "Serbia Protesters Mull Ways to Coordinate Rallies," *BIRN*, Belgrade, April 20, 2017.

118. Gabriel Almond and Sidney Verba, *The Civic Culture* (Princeton, NJ: Princeton University Press, 1978).

119. Marc Hooghe and Ellen Quintelier, "Political Participation in European Countries: The Effect of Authoritarian Rule, Corruption, Lack of Good Governance and Economic Downturn," *Comparative European Politics* 12, no. 2 (2014): 209–32.

120. UNDP, *Early Warning System in Bosnia-Herzegovina*, 180.

121. UNDP, *Early Warning System in Bosnia-Herzegovina*, 70; and UNDP, *Early Warning System Report, FYR Macedonia*, 30.

122. International Foundation for Electoral Systems, "The Influence of Political Hate Speech as a Tool on Youth of Kosovo," 2016, 1, https://www.ifes.org/sites/default/files/2016_ifes_the_influence_of_political_hate_speech_as_a_tool_on_youth_of_k.eng_.pdf.

123. European Values Study Group and World Values Survey Association, *European and World Values Surveys Integrated Data File*, 1999–2002, Release 1 (Computer file), 2nd ICPSR version, 2004.

124. IDEA, "Survey Results," http://archive.idea.int/balkans/survey_detailed.cfm. The total survey sample, which includes Romania and Bulgaria, is ten thousand.

125. IDEA, "Survey Results," http://archive.idea.int/balkans/survey_detailed.cfm. The other extremely important elements to have in a society in order to call it democratic include "at least two strong political parties competing in elections; a government that guarantees economic equality of its citizens; the freedom to criticize the government; and equal representation of men and women in elected positions."

126. "European Social Survey Data," ESS6-2012, ed. 2.3, Norwegian Social Science Data Services, http://nesstar.ess.nsd.uib.no/webview.

127. International IDEA, "Survey Results." Numerous other studies corroborate these concerns, including Kasapović's *Hrvatska politika* and UN in Serbia, *The Serbia We Want: Post-2015 National Consultations in Serbia, Final Report* (Belgrade: UN Development Programme, July 13, 2013).

128. Paula M. Pickering, *Peacebuilding in the Balkans: The View from the Ground Floor* (Ithaca, NY: Cornell University Press, 2007); and Zan Strabac, "Social Distance and Ethnic Hierarchies in Croatia," in *The Aftermath of War: Experiences and Social Attitudes in the Western Balkans*, eds. Albert Simkus and Kristen Ringdal (London: Routledge, 2012), 165–66.

129. "Croatian Anti-Cyrillic Protests Continue in Vukovar," *Balkan Insight*, September 4, 2013, http://www.balkaninsight.com/en/article/vukovar-protests-continued-violence-stopped; and Sven Milekić, "Croatia Fascist Slogan Threatens to Topple Govt," *Balkan Insight*, August 20, 2017, http://www.balkaninsight.com/en/article/croatia-fascist-slogan-threatens-to-topple-govt--08-30-2017?utm_source=Balkan+Transitional+Justice+Daily+Newsletter+-+NEW&utm_campaign=276cb797a4-RSS_EMAIL_CAMPAIGN&utm_medium=email&utm_term=0_a1d9e93e97-276cb797a4-319755853.

130. "Public Pulse Report 6," UN Development Programme–Kosovo, Pristina, August 2013, 18–19.

131. Prism and Paula M. Pickering, *Back from the Brink in Bosnia*, database, 2007; and Centre for Research and Policy Making and Paula M. Pickering, *Back from the Brink in Macedonia*, database, 2006. Surveys during the socialist period revealed greater levels of interethnic tolerance in Bosnia than in Macedonia. See Bjiljana Bačević et al., eds., *Jugoslavija na kriznoj prekretnici* (Belgrade: Institut društvenih nauka, 1991). Despite low levels of interethnic tolerance, groups in Macedonia are more resigned to coexisting in the same state than are groups in Bosnia.

132. European Values Study Group and World Values Survey Association, *European and World Values Surveys*.

133. Rodolfo Toe, "Incomplete Analysis Hinders Anti-Extremism in the Balkans," *BIRN*, Sarajevo, March 30, 2016, http://www.balkaninsight.com/en/article/incomplete-analysis-hinders-anti-extremism-in-the-balkans-03-30-2016#sthash.DqVxOYld.dpuf (accessed January 15, 2017).

134. Center for Free Elections and Democracy, "Survey of the Drivers of Youth Radicalism and Violent Extremism in Serbia," Belgrade, November 2016, 5, 10, http://www.rs.undp.org/content/serbia/en/home/library/crisis_prevention_and_recovery/istra_ivanje-o-pokretaima-radikalizma-i-nasilnog-ekstremizma-meu.html (accessed April 19, 2017).

135. Gerard Toal and John O'Loughlin, "20 Years after Dayton, Here's What Bosnians Think about Being Divided by Ethnicity," *Washington Post*, Monkey Cage, 2, February 2016, https://www.washingtonpost.com/news/monkey-cage/wp/2016/02/02/20-years-after-dayton-heres-what-bosnians-think-about-being-divided-by-ethnicity/?utm_term=.2f082c3976fa (accessed January 20, 2017). O'Loughlin and Toal's 2005 survey indicated that 93.2 percent believed that sizeable improvement in economic prosperity would improve interethnic relations. See John O'Loughlin and Gerard Toal, "Accounting for Separatist Sentiment in Bosnia-Herzegovina and the North Caucasus of Russia: A Comparative Analysis of Survey Responses," *Ethnic and Racial Studies* 23, no. 4 (2009): 591–615.

136. European Values Study Group and World Values Survey Association, *European and World Values Surveys*.

137. Matić, *Serbia at the Crossroads*, 17.

138. OSCE Democratization Department, *Public Opinion Research* (Sarajevo: OSCE Mission to Bosnia and Herzegovina, May 2004), http://www.oscebih.org/documents/741-eng.pdf.

139. Anis Dani et al., *A Social Assessment of Bosnia and Herzegovina* (Washington, DC: World Bank, Europe and Central Asia Region, Environmentally and Socially Sustainable Development Unit, ECSSD, April 1999).

140. Harriet Alexander, "Slovenia: The Next Crisis for the EU?" *Telegraph*, September 14, 2013, http://www.telegraph.co.uk/news/worldnews/europe/slovenia/10309237/Slovenia-The-next-crisis-for-the-EU.html.

141. *Nations in Transit 2017*, Freedom House, https://freedomhouse.org/report/nit-2017-table-country-scores. The corruption score includes a measure of government implementation of anti-corruption measures, laws, and public perceptions.

142. Gagnon, *The Myth of Ethnic War*; and Cohen, *Serpent and Bosom*, 90.

143. *Bosnia-Herzegovina: Selected Economic Issues*, IMF Country Report 5/198 (Washington, DC: International Monetary Fund, June 2005).

144. Robert Hislope, "Organized Crime in a Disorganized State: How Corruption Contributed to Macedonia's Mini-War," *Problems of Post-Communism* 49, no. 3 (May–June 2002): 33–41.

145. MDG, *Voices of Youth: Survey on Youth in BiH Quantitative Research Findings* (Sarajevo: MDG Achievement Fund, February 2012); and Gallup, *Gallup Balkan Monitor: The Impact on Migration, 2009*, http://wbc-inco.net/object/document/7162/attach/Gallup_Balkan_Monitor-Focus_On_Migration.pdf.

146. Poggi et al., *Bosnia and Herzegovina*, appendix; Gordy, *The Culture of Power*, chap. 5; and Center for Free Elections and Democracy, "Survey of the Drivers of Youth Radicalism and Violent Extremism in Serbia," November 2016, 5, http://www.rs.undp.org/content/serbia/en/home/library/crisis_prevention_and_recovery/istra_ivanje-o-pokretaima-radikalizma-i-nasilnog-ekstremizma-meu.html.

147. Dylan Matthews, "Move over, Cyprus. Slovenia Is the New Tiny Country You Should Worry about," *Washington Post*, March 24, 2013.

148. Peter Sanfey, "South Eastern Europe: Lessons from the Global Economic Crisis," Working Paper No. 113, European Bank for Reconstruction and Development, February 2010, http://www.ebrd.com/downloads/research/economics/workingpapers/wp0113.pdf.

149. European Bank for Reconstruction and Development, *Transition Report 2016–17: Transition for All, Equal Opportunities in an Unequal World*, 2017, 86, http://www.ebrd.com/transition-report.

150. Agencia za statistiku BiH, *Popis 2013*, http://www.popis.gov.ba/.

151. The EU publishes annual reports on the progress made by the governments toward meeting the conditions. For example, see "Enlargement," European Commission, http://ec.europa.eu/enlargement/index_en.htm and http://ec.europa.eu/enlargement/countries/strategy-and-progress-report/index_en.htm.

152. Marja Živanović, "Election Win 'Toughens Vučić's Grip on Serbia'", *Balkan Insight*, April 3, 2017, http://www.balkaninsight.com/en/article/vucic-s-victory-means-serious-changes-in-serbian-politics-analysts-04-02-2017.

153. Dejan Anastasjević, "Serbia Should Beware of Russians Bearing Gifts," *Balkan Insight*, June 20, 2017, http://www.balkaninsight.com/en/blog/serbia-should-beware-of-russians-bearing-gifts-06-19-2017.

154. Sven Mikelić, Far Right NGO to Honor Ustaša Commander, *BalkanInsight*, June 26, 2017 http://www.balkaninsight.com/en/article/obscure-croatian-ngo-announces-ustasa-commander-plaque-06-26-2017.

155. Florian Bieber, "Building Impossible States? State-Building Strategies and EU Membership in the Western Balkans," in "Unconditional Conditionality? The Impact of EU Conditionality in the Western Balkans," special issue of *Europe-Asia Studies* 63, no 10 (2011): 783–802.

156. Marcus Cox, "Bosnia and Herzegovina: The Limits of Liberal Imperialism," in *Building States to Build Peace*, ed. Charles T. Call (Boulder, CO: Lynne Rienner, 2008), 249–71.

157. Jens Narten, "Dilemmas of Promoting 'Local Ownership': The Case of Kosovo," in *The Dilemmas of Statebuilding*, ed. Roland Paris and Timothy D. Sisk (New York: Routledge, 2009), 252–79.

Map 17.0. Ukraine

CHAPTER 17

Ukraine

THE END OF POST-SOVIETISM AND "BROTHERLY FRIENDSHIP"

Taras Kuzio

In addition to dealing with the tasks that leaders and citizens in the other countries in this volume faced after the end of communism, Ukraine has had its territory invaded by a neighboring state that illegally occupied and annexed Crimea and fomented and supports an ongoing war in the country's east. These acts by Russia have complicated efforts to establish a well-functioning democracy and prosperous market economy in Ukraine.

Ukraine was the second republic in the USSR with the largest republican communist party, a major military–industrial complex, and strategically important economy. In the USSR, Ukrainian national communists and a variety of opposition and dissident groups made Ukrainians into a perennial thorn in Moscow's side with Soviet leader Nikita Khrushchev revealing that his tyrannical predecessor Joseph Stalin had wanted to ethnically cleanse all of them but there was no place to send them all. Left- and right-wing Ukrainian nationalists had failed in their national liberation struggles after the Russian Revolution and in the 1940s, but Ukraine's popularly endorsed referendum on independence led to the largely peaceful disintegration of the USSR in 1991.

With autonomist and pro-independence feelings always strong and Soviet Ukraine a founding member of the United Nations, national identity has always been at the heart of Ukraine's domestic and foreign policies. Identity and border questions have beguiled Ukraine's relations with its powerful Polish and Russian neighbors who both refused (and continue to refuse in Russia's case) to accept the fact that Ukrainians are a separate people with a right to sovereign statehood. Ukraine's age-old conflicts with Poland were resolved in the 1940s by Stalin who ordered deportations of Poles and Ukrainians and enforced a new Polish-Ukrainian border. In Ukraine's east, conflict with Russia over borders and Ukrainian identity dominated diplomatic relations under President Borys Yeltsyn while his successor, Vladimir Putin, turned to military aggression and territorial expansionism, plunging Europe into its worst crisis since World War II. Relations between Russia and Ukraine, the core of the Russian and Soviet empires, would no longer be the same.

Western analysis of the Russian-Ukrainian crisis and war often focus on other questions such as geopolitical rivalries and the Committee of State Security (KGB) origins of Putin's militocratic political system (a regime dominated by the intelligence agencies and military) and in doing so fail to understand how the sources of Putin's military aggression against Ukraine, and information and cyber warfare against the West, lie in Russia's love–hate inferiority complex vis-à-vis the West and its inability to accept Ukrainians as a separate people with a sovereign right to determine their own destiny.

Precommunist and Communist Ukraine and Their Legacy in Contemporary Ukraine

Ukraine entered the twentieth century divided between three states. In the eighteenth century, the tsarist Russian Empire annexed Central, Southern, and Eastern Ukraine. Volhynia in Western Ukraine was also part of that empire. Galicia and Transcarpathia were within the Austrian and Hungarian components of the Austro-Hungarian Empire, respectively. Northern Bukovina was part of the Austrian region of that empire.

Between 1917 and 1920, western and eastern Ukrainians made various attempts to create an independent state, all of which failed. Ukraine declared independence from tsarist Russia on January 22, 1918, and united with Western Ukraine a year later. In 1920 and 1921, Ukrainian lands were divided up between four states. The largest portion of Ukrainian territory that had belonged to tsarist Russia became the Ukrainian Soviet Socialist Republic (SSR). Galicia and Volhynia were transferred to newly independent Poland, and northern Bukovina went to Romania. Transcarpathia went first to the newly constituted Czechoslovakia and then was annexed by the USSR and joined to Soviet Ukraine.

In the Soviet era, Ukraine's territory was enlarged on two occasions. The first occurred at the end of World War II with the annexation of Western Ukraine (becoming the three Galician *oblasts* of Lviv, Ivano-Frankivsk, and Ternopil, and two Volhynian *oblasts* of Volyn and Rivne) from Poland, Transcarpathia from Czechoslovakia, and northern Bukovina (renamed Chernivtsi *oblast*) from Romania. The second enlargement occurred in 1954 when Crimea was transferred from the Russian Soviet Federative Socialist Republic (RSFSR) to the Ukrainian SSR.

Ironically, therefore, the Soviet regime united territories with ethnic Ukrainian majorities into one state (with the exception of Crimea, where Ukrainians were in a minority). The successor state to the Ukrainian SSR that declared independence from the USSR on August 24, 1991, had western borders that had been resolved by Stalin over a half century earlier but in 2014 had to fight to defend its southern and eastern borders in the face of Russian aggression.

Soviet nationality policies bequeathed two important legacies for post-Soviet Ukraine. First, under Soviet rule, the non-Russian republics were designated as homelands for non-Russian peoples, whose Communist leaders, in return, were expected to keep separatist and anti-Soviet nationalism in check in strategically important republics such as Ukraine. Soviet nationality policies also included as a central tenet a policy of Russification by encouraging Russians to settle, and Russian to be used, in non-Russian territories. This policy led to the growth of large numbers of ethnic Ukrainians who spoke Russian as well as Ukrainians who were bilingual in Russian and Ukrainian. A large number of ethnic Russians came to live in Eastern and Southern Ukraine, and many ex-military personnel retired in Crimea, together with the Black Sea Fleet. The Donbas and Crimea in particular resembled mini Soviet Unions with strong regional identities, Soviet nostalgia, and 30 to 40 percent backing for separatism.

In the 1920s, Soviet policies of indigenization (*korenizatsia*) supported the Ukrainianization of education, media, and cultural life in Ukraine. Indigenization in the 1920s led to the migration of Ukrainian-speaking peasants to growing urban centers that became home to industry. State institutions and educational facilities provided a Ukrainian language and cultural framework, and in urban centers, increasing numbers of people came to speak Ukrainian.

Soviet dictator Stalin deemed the continuation of indigenization to be too dangerous, fearing that it would eventually lead to political demands, such as independence, propelled by a growing differentiation of Ukrainians from Russians. Stalin thus reversed early Soviet nationality policies in three areas. First, the Ukrainian Autocephalous (i.e., independent from Russian) Orthodox Church was destroyed. Second, there were widespread purges, arrests, imprisonments, and executions of the Ukrainian intelligentsia, nationalists, and national communists. Poles were also heavily repressed in Soviet Ukraine. Third, Russification replaced indigenization policies, and there was a return to Russian imperial-nationalist historiography propelled by a new Stalinist ideology of national bolshevism. From the mid-1930s, eastern Ukrainian urban centers, although including increasingly large ethnic Ukrainian majorities, came to be dominated by the Russian language and Soviet/Russian culture, especially in the Donbas region.

The most devastating example of the reversal of Ukrainianization policies was the 1933 artificial famine (*holodomor* or terror famine) that claimed 4 to 5 million lives in Ukraine and the Ukrainian-populated region of Kuban in the North Caucasian region of the RSFSR. Historian Timothy Snyder describes the *holodomor* as genocide,[1] a view that opinion polls show is also upheld by the majority of Ukrainians. The Ukrainian nationally conscious peasantry based in private small holding farms (which were common in Ukraine but not in Russia where communal farming was dominant) was decimated. The *holodomor* only became publicly discussed and researched as a "blank spot" in the USSR in the late 1980s as the result of Soviet leader Mikhail Gorbachev's policy of glasnost.

A fifth of Ukraine's current population comes from seven *oblasts* that historically existed outside tsarist Russia or the USSR. Four of these western Ukrainian *oblasts* (in Galicia and northern Bukovina) underwent nation-building under Austrian rule prior to 1918. After its incorporation into the USSR, nation-building in Western Ukraine was ironically further facilitated by the actions of the Soviet regime; populations in urban centers in Western Ukraine became Ukrainian after the genocide of the Jews and the transfer of Poles to the "recovered (former German) territories" in communist Poland. Industrialization and urbanization of Lviv (Lemberg in Austrian, Lwów in Polish) and Western Ukraine further increased the numbers of Ukrainians who came to dominate the region's urban centers.

Transcarpathia also underwent Ukrainian nation-building after its incorporation into the USSR. As a consequence of Hungarian assimilationist policies, the region had always been the least Ukrainian nationally conscious of any western Ukrainian region and by the late 1930s, two orientations competed for the allegiance of its eastern Slavic population: Ukrainian and Rusyn, the adherents of the latter claiming that theirs was a separate and fourth eastern Slavic nationality. After 1945, Soviet nationality policies automatically designated all of the Ukrainian-Rusyn inhabitants of Transcarpathia as Ukrainians.

Paradoxically, Soviet nationality policies also reinforced loyalty to the republics, and non-Russians came increasingly to look on their republics as their homelands and the borders of those republics as sacrosanct. In post-Soviet Ukraine, separatism never became a major security threat in Eastern Ukraine; in Crimea, it was influential only in the first half of the 1990s and following the overthrow of Viktor Yanukovych in 2014, when a Russian invasion force supported it both covertly and overtly. In both instances, separatism only mobilized when it had external military support.

Thus, the Soviet Union pursued contradictory policies in Ukraine. The modernization of Ukraine ensured that its urban centers came to be dominated by ethnic Ukrainians, as seen in the capital city of Kyiv, where the seventeen-day Orange Revolution in 2004 and four-month Euromaidan in 2013–2014 had overwhelming support and where pro-Russian leaders and parties have always received minimal support. In the post-Stalin era, ethnic Ukrainians came to dominate the Communist Party in the Ukrainian SSR and during periods of liberalization, such as the 1960s and second half of the 1980s, when national communists dominated the party's leadership. Nevertheless, the bulk of the republic's largest urban and industrial centers in Eastern and Southern Ukraine became Russophone or bilingually Ukrainian-Russian, rather than linguistically Ukrainian.

Regional divisions complicated national integration but were often exaggerated by Russians and Western experts. These were starkly evident in the differing degrees of support for Viktor Yushchenko and his opponent, Yanukovych, in western-central and eastern-southern regions, respectively, in the 2004 elections during the Orange Revolution. A similar regional breakdown was evident between Yulia Tymoshenko and Yanukovych in the 2010 elections.

At the same time, nation-building was transitioning from the west to the center (by the Orange Revolution) and to east (by the Euromaidan)—especially among young people who have no nostalgia for the Soviet Union. In 1994, Leonid Kuchma was elected president after winning Eastern and Central Ukraine and a decade later Yushchenko won by winning Western and Central Ukraine. In the late 1980s, Western Ukraine, the region incorporated into Soviet Ukraine by Stalin, took its revenge and propelled Ukraine to independence. By the Orange Revolution, the swing region of Central Ukraine had aligned with the west. Another decade later, Ukrainian national identity had spread to the east and south as Putin's aggression forced Russian speakers and those holding dual Ukrainian-Russian identities to choose which side of the fence they sat on. The three triggers of this spread of Ukrainian identity over a quarter of a century of Ukrainian independence were Gorbachev's liberalization (late 1980s), the Orange Revolution (2004), and the Euromaidan Revolution of Dignity and Putin's aggression (2014).

The End of Soviet Rule and Ukrainian Independence

Ukrainians took the risks of protesting, even in the Soviet era, and Ukrainian prisoners of conscience were the largest ethnic group proportionate to their share of the population in the Soviet gulag, or system of forced-labor prison camps. Following this tradition, Ukraine was home to a relatively large number of dissident movements in the post Stalin period. These included the Ukrainian Helsinki Group in the 1970s and 1980s. As in other non-Russian republics, Ukrainian dissidents promoted both national and democratic rights. Ukrainian dissident and opposition movements closely cooperated with Jewish refuseniks, Zionists, Russian liberal dissidents and with Baltic, Georgian, and Armenian nationalists. Some groups (primarily based in Western Ukraine) called for Ukraine's separation from the USSR; others (more often based in Central and Eastern Ukraine) demanded the transformation of the USSR into a loose confederation of sovereign republics.

In 1990 and 1991, the Communist Party within the Ukrainian SSR divided three ways into the Democratic Platform (close to the opposition and dominating the leadership of the *Komsomol* [All-Union Leninist Young Communist League]), sovereign (i.e., national) communists, and pro-Moscow imperial communists. The latter became discredited after they supported the hard-line coup d'état by Soviet national Bolsheviks and Russian nationalists in August 1991. Sovereign communists coalesced around parliamentary speaker Leonid Kravchuk after semi-free elections to Soviet Ukraine's hitherto redundant Supreme Soviet in March 1990. For the first time, a noncommunist opposition, dominated by the Ukrainian Popular Movement for Restructuring (known as *Rukh* or "Movement"), the core of what would be the democratic bloc, obtained a quarter of the seats within the Supreme Soviet (or Rada).

Moderate *Rukh* and nationalist radicals began increasingly to demand Ukrainian independence in 1989–1990 and on July 16, 1990, succeeded in having the Supreme Soviet adopt a Declaration of Sovereignty. Through a combination of pressure from Rukh and sovereign communists, the Ukrainian SSR declared independence on August 24, 1991, after the hard-line coup collapsed in Moscow. All shades of Ukrainian political life (*Rukh*, radical nationalists, liberal communists in the Democratic Platform, and national communists) supported the drive to independence in fall 1991. This movement toward independence was crowned by a December 1, 1991, referendum on independence that received overwhelming support from 92 percent of Ukrainians, including those in Crimea and the Donbas. A week later Ukraine, Belarus, and Russia signed an agreement to transform the USSR into the Commonwealth of Independent States (CIS), and the USSR ceased to exist on December 26, 1991.

The Orange Revolution and the Euromaidan Revolution of Dignity

The Orange Revolution came in response to the authorities' blatantly attempting to rig the presidential elections in 2004, while the, later, Euromaidan took place outside an election cycle and exploded in response to Yanukovych's turning away from European integration after years of wide-scale abuse of office during his presidency. In the lead up to the Orange Revolution, the Yushchenko team had a program, alternative candidates, and a process for change in 2004. The Euromaidan, however, was a spontaneous response to Yanukovych's decision, so it had, initially, no leadership, alternative, or process for making change. As is clear from the choice of orange as an optimistic and neutral color to attract a broad constituency of voters, rather than using the national colors of the blue and yellow flag, the Orange Revolution was intended to be inclusionary. Participants in the Euromaidan, however, carried a wide array of Ukrainian national (blue and yellow), nationalist (red and black), and party flags and did not produce their own colors and symbols.

After leading a successful government and being unceremoniously removed by oligarchs and communists from power in April 2001, Yushchenko led Our Ukraine to victory in the March 2002 election and became the united opposition alternative to Yanukovych, the authorities' candidate in the 2004 election. Yushchenko's opponent, Prime Minister Yanukovych, was widely viewed as authoritarian and uncouth and, because of his record of being in prison twice, two-thirds of Ukrainians believed he was morally unfit to be president.

Two factors provided momentum for civil society prior to the Orange Revolution. First, the Kuchmagate crisis, which began on November 28, 2000, after excerpts of tapes made illicitly in the president's office by Mykola Melnychenko, an officer of the Directorate on State Security (the Ukrainian equivalent of the US Secret Service), were released during a parliamentary session. Kuchma was heard on the tape ordering Interior Minister Yuriy Kravchenko to "deal with" independent journalist Georgiy Gongadze, who had been kidnapped on September 16, 2000, and whose decapitated body was found on November 2, 2000, near Kyiv. The second trigger came from the mounting criticism of anti-corruption policies from oligarchs close to Kuchma who were threatened by anti-corruption measures undertaken by the 2000–2001 Yushchenko government. Deputy Prime Minister Tymoshenko had reorganized the energy sector and targeted distribution companies owned by leading oligarch groups, which returned billions of dollars to the government budget that were used to pay wage and pension arrears. The Kuchmagate crisis and anti-corruption government policies led to an April 2001 vote of no confidence in the Yushchenko government, pushing him into the opposition, where he never was truly comfortable.

The Kuchmagate crisis mobilized the largest opposition movement since the late Soviet era into the "Ukraine without Kuchma" movement, based in Kyiv and dominated by the center-left Socialist Party of Ukraine (SPU) and Bloc of Yulia Tymoshenko (BYuT). The anti-Kuchma protests in 2000 and 2001 were followed by "Arise, Ukraine!" protests in 2002 and 2003 just ahead of the Orange Revolution. The organization of these protests became an important source of experience for youth and election-observer non-governmental organizations (NGOs) as well as for the political parties that empowered them for the 2004 elections and the Orange Revolution.

In that 2004 election, civil society had to organize outside the normal channels because state-administrative resources were massively deployed in support of Yanukovych. The state and oligarch-controlled mass media, particularly television, gave widespread positive coverage to Yanukovych while covering Yushchenko largely in negative terms as a US satrap (his wife is American-Ukrainian) and a Russophobe "fascist."

Yanukovych used official and underground election campaign teams. The official campaign was headed by the chairman of the National Bank Serhiy Tihipko; the shadow campaign was led by Yanukovych's longtime ally, Andriy Kluyev, and Russian "political technologists." They were behind the use of dirty tricks against Yushchenko. The most dramatic of these was his poisoning with dioxin in September 2004. This removed him from the campaign trail for a month. As secretary of the National Security and Defense Council (RNBO), Kluyev would then be behind police violence during the Euromaidan (specifically ordering the Berkut to brutally attack students on the night of November 30, 2013, after Yanukovych had returned from Vilnius very angry at his reception in Lithuania and wanted to see blood). As Yanukovych's chief of staff in his final month in power, Kluyev fled with him into hiding in Russia.

Photo 17.1.   In what would come to be known as the Orange Revolution, protesters take to the streets in Kyiv to protest fraudulent presidential election results in 2004. (This photo was taken through joint efforts of the UNIAN news agency [http://www.unian.net] and the International Renaissance Foundation/George Soros Foundation in Ukraine [http://www.irf.kiev.ua].)

On October 31, 2004, when Yushchenko won the first round of the election, the Yanukovych camp ratcheted up its efforts to deliver him the election in the second round by using more blatant fraud, whatever the actual vote. The Committee of Voters of Ukraine, a respected NGO, calculated that 2.8 million votes were fraudulently added to Yanukovych's tally in round two. Fraud was especially blatant in Donetsk and Luhansk, Yanukovych's home base.

The Ukrainian parliament and the Supreme Court overturned the fraudulent election results that declared Yanukovych elected in round two. Roundtable negotiations brokered by Poland, Lithuania, and the EU led to a compromise; the election law was revised so that many of the fraudulent acts committed in round two could not be repeated. The Supreme Court ordered a repeat election held on December 26, 2004. After winning by 8 percent in the rerun of round two, Yushchenko was inaugurated on January 23, 2005, as Ukraine's third president.

Yushchenko's election victory came about as a consequence of a very broad political alliance that included center-leftists (SPU, BYuT), free-market liberals (Party of Industrialists and Entrepreneurs), center-right national democrats (Our Ukraine), and nationalists (Congress of Ukrainian Nationalists). The divisions within this election alliance over political and institutional policies included support for parliamentary or presidential systems, whether to launch criminal investigations of former regime officials

Photo 17.2. Yushchenko and Yanukovych after Yushchenko won the rerun of the second round of the 2004 Ukrainian election, following the fraud in the second round triggered the Orange Revolution. Two years later, Yanukovych's party won enough votes to dominate the parliament and make him prime minister from 2006 to 2007. In 2010, he won the presidential election. (This photo was taken through joint efforts of the UNIAN news agency [http://www.unian.net] and the International Renaissance Foundation/George Soros Foundation in Ukraine [http://www.irf.kiev.ua].)

on charges of corruption and election fraud, the degree of reprivatization to be undertaken, which economic reforms were needed, whether to pursue land privatization, and NATO membership.

Tymoshenko, who had partnered with Yushchenko in the presidential campaign and the Orange coalition, became prime minister in February 2005. Divisions over economic policies brought about an oil crisis, continuing concerns over populist economic policies that focused on social issues, and a decline in the growth of the gross domestic product (GDP) by half. In September 2005, Yushchenko dismissed Tymoshenko's government and replaced her with loyalist and oligarch-friendly Yuriy Yekhanurov, whose government lasted until after the March 2006 elections. His government was replaced in August by a government led again by Yanukovych, who was to be the first prime minister to benefit from enhanced powers in the parliamentary constitution.

For political scientists, the Euromaidan, which is what the protests that occurred in Ukraine in 2014 are commonly called, was puzzling as it took place outside an election cycle when earlier democratic revolutions had taken place. The Euromaidan was a civil society–driven revolution—rather than one led by political leaders and election candidates as in the Orange Revolution—and was different because there was bloodshed, giving it a large pantheon of martyrs. The Euromaidan exploded spontaneously in November 2013 in protest at Yanukovych's abrupt decision to drop European integration. The passage of antidemocratic legislation on "Black Thursday" (January 16, 2014) and his refusal to compromise and negotiate with the opposition led to two explosions of violence that left over one hundred dead and more than one thousand wounded protesters.

Public outrage had been fueled by four years of attacks on democracy and ethnic Ukrainian national identity and the lawlessness rampant in the courts, police, and Security Service of Ukraine (SBU) and among the lawmakers from the ruling Party of Regions. Ukrainians felt their rulers were treating them with visible contempt as a conquered population and that there was no accountability or limit to what could be stolen. The Constitutional Court was stacked with the president's cronies, and parliament had been turned into a rubber-stamp body through which legislation was railroaded without the votes.

While the standard of living of most Ukrainians was in decline, a small clique of oligarchs and the president's "Family" (a cabal of his family members and loyalists from his home region) had continued to amass fortunes through rigged government tenders. Together, these factors provided a combustible protest mood that united students, middle-class professionals, businesspeople, nationalists, farmers, and workers. The Euromaidan was anti-Soviet, nationalist, and pro-democratic at the same time—much like the protest movements in the late 1980s—and supported Ukraine's European integration.

In 2010–2013, Putin and his hoped to be satrap in Ukraine, President Yanukovych, set off a chain of events that led to the biggest crisis in Europe since World War II and to the West's worst relations with Russia since the onset of détente a half century ago. Yanukovych, one of the leaders of the Donetsk clan defeated by two democratic revolutions, created a mafia state that bankrupted Ukraine, ordered the massacre of innocent protestors and committed treason when inviting in Russian occupation forces into Crimea. Public protests against Putin's bribing of Yanukovych to drop the signing of the EU Association agreement (not coincidentally on the anniversary of the Orange Revolution which he believes stole the election from him) would have largely remained peaceful but the culture of the thuggish Donetsk clan and Party of Regions led them to use police brutality. Kyiv, though, is not Donetsk, and Ukraine is not Russia. Police brutality against young people radicalized them by greatly expanding their numbers and transforming the protests into a broader struggle against Yanukovych's Sovietophile and pro-Russian domestic and foreign policies. Yanukovych's thuggish behavior and unwillingness to compromise by replacing government ministers culminated in the kidnapping, torture, and murder of protestors, which in turn mobilized young nationalists to take the fight back to the police on the streets. On January 22, again not coincidentally on another anniversary, this time Ukraine's 1918 declaration of independence, five unarmed protestors were murdered by snipers.

The Euromaidan lasted for nearly three months, far longer than the seventeen days of the Orange Revolution, and took place outside an election cycle. Violence throughout the Euromaidan was a product of a more thuggish regime and the fact that in contrast to the situation in 2004 when Kuchma had been leaving office, in 2014, Yanukovych was clinging to power at all costs with the support of a more assertive Putin who intervened more forcefully than he had a decade earlier. Yanukovych was forced to flee after the murders of protestors when his security forces deserted him and the parliamentary faction of the Party of Regions denounced the killings, opening the path for the coming to power of the opposition.

The coming to power of Euromaidan revolutionaries spurred parliament to adopt four decommunization laws in May 2015: (1) changes in the commemoration of the victory over Nazism from the Great Patriotic War (1941–1945) to World War II (1939–1945) on May 8 rather than 9, (2) condemning communist and Nazi totalitarianism in Ukraine and banning their symbols, (3) granting access to Soviet-era archives, and (4) the most controversial, conferring status and commemorating the memory of "fighters for the independence of Ukraine."[2] One aspect of this was the changing of the names of streets and towns, such as Dnipropetrovsk to Dnipro. 1,000 villages, towns and cities were renamed and thousands of monuments and plaques from the Soviet era were removed, including 2,500 monuments of Vladimir Lenin and other Communist leaders, following the pulling down of a Lenin monument in Kyiv in December 2013 during the Euromaidan Revolution of Dignity. This final phase of de-communization comes over a quarter of century after the first Lenin monument was pulled down in August 1990 in the western Ukrainian city of Chervonohrad, the first toppling in the USSR. De-communization gradually spread from Western to Central Ukraine by the Orange Revolution and from the 2014 Euromaidan, had moved to Eastern and Southern Ukraine (with the largest Lenin monument pulled down in Kharkiv in September 2014) making Ukraine Lenin-free. Ukraine's de-communization radically contrasts with the Sovetization and re-Stalinization of Russia under Putin.[3]

Crimea and War in the East

In March 2014, Crimea was formally annexed by Russia in a land grab unseen in Europe since the 1930s. Ukrainian forces in the Crimea did not put up a fight, unlike in the Donbas, because they were outnumbered by Russian forces based there and those invading, there was limited local pro-Ukrainian support, and Kyiv was in turmoil during regime change, which undermined policy making. Ukrainian polls have reflected a high degree of support for maintaining the country's inherited borders, including in Crimea where there was never over 50 percent backing for separatism, which makes it highly likely the March 2014 referendum was falsified when it claimed 97 percent support for union with Russia.

The Donbas never had autonomy in Ukraine, and the Party of Regions (despite its false name) centralized Ukraine even more during Yanukovych's presidency. The region's population has an ethnic Ukrainian majority, although the region is also Russian speaking and exhibits (similar to the Crimea) a strong Soviet and regional identity. Donbas anger at the removal of Yanukovych became violent because of four factors. The first was Russian penetration of Ukraine's SBU and other security forces enabling Russian intelligence agents to be on the ground in Eastern Ukraine during the Euromaidan. Russia supplied anti-riot equipment and FSB (Federal Security Service) advisers to Yanukovych during the Euromaidan, although Russia's domestic security service is active throughout the former USSR.

The second was the attitudes of Donetsk oligarchs who sought to use local protests to pressure Kyiv and provide themselves with immunity in the event of regime change. The most powerful oligarch, Rinat Akhmetov, could have used his influence within the security forces, which were controlled by the Party of Regions, and brought his workers and coalminers on the streets (as he did months later in Mariupol). But, Akhmetov did not and preferred to bide his time. The third factor was the wholesale defection and disintegration of the Donetsk, Luhansk, and Crimean security forces. This took place in no other region of Ukraine. The fourth factor was Russian special forces spetznaz special forces led by Igor ("Strelkov" [Shooter]) Girkin and the provision of military training and equipment to pro-Russian proxies in the Donbas. On August 24, 2014 (again on an anniversary, this time on the date when Ukraine declared independence in 1991), sensing the likely defeat of pro-Russian proxies, Russian troops invaded Eastern Ukraine. Ukrainian forces were heavily defeated at Ilovaysk; over 400 troops were killed, 158 were missing, nearly 500 were wounded, and hundreds were captured. A second Russian invasion took place in February 2015 at Debaltseve after Russia signed the Minsk-2 Peace Accords. In both invasions, Russian forces removed insignia from their uniforms and military vehicles to provide a claim of deniability of a Russian invasion.

In 2014, Russia justified its invasion of and annexation of Crimea by claiming that Russians and Russian speakers were threatened by "fascists" who had come to power. International human rights organizations found no evidence of any threats, reflected in the fact that the overwhelming majority of Ukraine's Russian speakers backed Kyiv in opposing Russian military aggression. In contrast, Russian occupation forces in Crimea have repressed and murdered Ukrainian and Tatar activists, religious leaders, and journalists and closed their institutions.

Elected in May 2014, Petro Poroshenko, an oligarch, had to deal with a bankrupt country, a demoralized and gutted army, war, the loss of economically important territory, and nearly 2 million Internally Displaced Persons (IDPs) and refugees. Poroshenko's options for dealing with the conflict in the Donbas (composed of Donetsk and Luhansk *oblasts* [regions]) were better than opposing Russian annexation of Crimea. Ukraine's armed forces and Ministry of Interior National Guard, coupled with large numbers of patriotic volunteers, launched the anti-terrorist operation (ATO) in April 2014 and by the summer were defeating Russia's proxies in the Donbas, giving Putin the choice of

Photo 17.3. Petro Poroshenko was elected president in 2014 after the Euromaidan and the defection of Viktor Yanukovych. (Euromaidan Press)

accepting defeat or using his forces to invade and give direct (no longer covert) backing to separatists. He chose the latter. Putin's "Russian spring" had two goals. The first was to take control of the intellectual city of Eastern Ukraine, Kharkiv, and the major port city of Odessa, the "jewels" of Eastern-Southern Ukraine. The second was to drive his armed forces and proxies southwest along Southern Ukraine toward Odessa to establish *NovoRossiya* (New Russia), the tsarist name he used for Eastern and Southern Ukraine, to provide a land bridge to Crimea. Both of Putin's goals in Eastern-Southern Ukraine failed abysmally because they found limited support among Ukraine's Russian speakers and the security forces remained loyal to Kyiv. Even in the Donbas, Ukrainian forces recaptured half to two-thirds of the region.

The so-called Donetsk Peoples Republic (DNR) and Luhansk Peoples Republic (LNR) continue to exist propped up by six to ten thousand Russian occupation forces and larger numbers of troops based just across the border and through Russian financial subsidies. The ceasefire was recognition of stalemate whereby neither side had won by achieving its objective—defeat of the separatists (Poroshenko) or establishing a "New Russia" state inside Ukraine (Putin). Russian forces and their proxies continue daily attacks that are aimed at wearing Ukrainian willpower down and that have killed hundreds of civilians and soldiers since Minsk 2. Unlike Crimea (or Georgia's South Ossetian and Abkhazian provinces), the continuing Donbas war therefore cannot be defined as a frozen conflict and is best understood as a low-intensity conflict that will continue for many years to come. We can safely assume that Putin is president for life and as long as he rules Russia there will be continued military aggression against Eastern Ukraine and Russian forces will continue to occupy Crimea.

Western sanctions remain in place over Crimea and the conflict in the Donbas until Putin implements the Minsk Accords and this is highly unlikely. Between Minsk 1 and 2, Russia integrated Donbas separatist units into a thirty-five-thousand-strong army with modern weaponry that is larger than the armed forces of half of NATO's members. The July 2014 shooting down of a Malaysian airliner by Russian troops working alongside the separatists killed three hundred innocent people and crew, which woke the EU up to the reality of Russia's military aggression in Eastern Ukraine and led to tougher sanctions.

Although the United States and the United Kingdom had provided security assurances to Ukraine in the 1994 Budapest Memorandum in exchange for Ukraine's giving up the world's third-largest nuclear weapon stockpile, these assurances proved worthless as a third "guarantor," Russia, annexed one region of Ukraine and invaded another. The absurdity of the peace negotiations was not only that they were held in Minsk, capital of the Russian satellite state of Belarus, but also that the United States and the United Kingdom took no part in them and an aggressor state (Russia) did.

Institutions, Political Parties, and Elections

On the same day as the referendum on independence in December 1991, parliamentary speaker and senior leader of the Soviet Ukrainian Communist Party (KPU) Kravchuk was elected in Ukraine's first presidential election, winning in the first round with 61.59 percent while the national democratic reformers grouped in *Rukh* supported the former political prisoner Vyacheslav Chornovil, who obtained a quarter of the vote. The main competition in the 1994 election was between two wings of the pre-1991 national communist camp: former Prime Minister Kuchma and incumbent Kravchuk, who was defeated by 52.1 to 45.1 percent. Not until 2014 would another presidential candidate—Poroshenko—win in the first round.

The Ukrainian parliament continued to be dominated by former communists until the March 1994 elections. Then the results reflected the negative impact of economic reform and delays in the adoption of a post-Soviet constitution. Nationalist and centrist democrats won the 2004 presidential elections after the Orange Revolution and again in 2014 when Ukraine elected its first pro-European parliament, the first without a sizable pro-Russian lobby.

During the Kravchuk presidency (December 1991–July 1994), Ukraine's political landscape continued to be dominated by three groups. The KPU returned, after being banned from August 1991 to October 1993, as a new political party led by Petro Symonenko. Since it was required to register as a new Communist Party, it legally had no connection to the pre–August 1991 party and no claim to Communist Party assets nationalized by the Ukrainian state after the party was banned. The newly registered KPU attracted less than 5 percent of the members of the pre-1991 Communist Party in Ukraine, which, at its peak in 1985, had 3.5 million members and was the largest republican Communist Party in the USSR (the Russian SFSR did not possess its own republican Communist Party). The post-1993 membership of the KPU has never exceeded 150,000 members.

Its high point of influence had been in the 1990s, when it was ostensibly the main opposition to the ruling authorities but in fact it always acted as a satellite party of big business centrists. In the 1994–1998 and 1998–2002 parliaments, the KPU had the largest factions, with 135 and 123 deputies, respectively. In the October–November 1999 presidential election, KPU leader Symonenko came in second in a field of thirteen candidates and then faced incumbent Kuchma in round two. Kuchma, who received votes from throughout Ukraine, defeated Symonenko by a large margin, and the KPU's fortunes declined.

In June 1996, Ukraine was the last former Soviet republic to adopt a presidential constitution in which the government is dominated by and can be dismissed by the president, who is elected in a national vote. After the Orange Revolution, a compromise package was agreed on and voted through by parliament on December 8, 2004. The reformed constitution transformed Ukraine from a presidential into a parliamentary system, also referred to as a semipresidential system because the executive is divided between the president and government, in which the government was responsible to a parliamentary coalition and the president was elected in a national vote rather than by parliament. The president continued to control foreign and defense policy, the RNBO, the SBU, and the general prosecutor's office and also appointed regional governors in consultation with the government.

In April 2004, the election law was changed so that all 450 seats in the Ukrainian parliament were contested in a proportional system with a lower 3 percent threshold for a longer five-year term. This election system was used in the March 2006 and the preterm September 2007 elections. The election law was changed again for the 2012 elections, returning Ukraine to the mixed system used in 1998 and 2002, in which half of seats were elected proportionally under a 5 percent threshold and the other half in first-past-the-post single-mandate districts. Preterm parliamentary elections in October 2014 continued to use this mixed system. The 2019 elections are likely to be held using a fully proportional law but with open lists that would enable voters and members to control who was being elected from political parties. Elected officials and businesspeople traditionally have aligned with the authorities, enabling the Party of Regions, when it held the presidency, to establish a parliamentary majority.

In the 2002–2006 parliament, the KPU faction was halved to sixty-six deputies and the KPU declined rapidly following the end of the Kuchma era, as many voters transferred their allegiance to the Party of Regions with the KPU becoming a satellite party. In the 2006 and 2007 elections, the KPU obtained only 3.66 and 5.39 percent, respectively, of the vote. In 2012, some former communist voters returned from the Party of Regions, and it again came in fourth, with 13 percent. After the Euromaidan, the KPU came under legal scrutiny because its local leaders in the Donbas supported separatism and its popularity plummeted. As a result, the party failed to enter parliament in the 2014 elections, and by refusing to replace its communist symbols (which are illegal under decommunization laws). The KPU cannot participate in elections. Thoroughly discredited, it now will be impossible for the Party of Regions and KPU to revive themselves into serious political forces.

The SPU, led by Oleksandr Moroz, became the only left-wing alternative to the KPU after its formation in October 1991. The SPU is a left-wing social democratic party committed to democratization and Ukrainian statehood but largely opposed to economic reform, especially land reform. The SPU was one of two Ukrainian members of the Socialist International until it was expelled in July 2011 for deserting its "orange" allies and cooperating with the Party of Regions. By the late 1990s, the SPU's membership grew to one hundred thousand, and its electoral support overtook that of the communists, surpassing them in the 2004 presidential and 2006 parliamentary elections. In 2004, Moroz came in third with 5.82 percent of the vote, followed by Symonenko with 4.97 percent. The SPU achieved fourth place in the 2006 elections with 5.69 percent and thirty-three seats, followed by the KPU with 3.66 percent and twenty-one deputies.

The SPU's fortunes declined after it defected from the Orange parliamentary coalition in summer 2006 and joined the Party of Regions and KPU in the Anti-Crisis coalition. The preterm September 2007 and 2010 presidential elections marginalized the SPU as a political force. Moroz, in refusing to step down as leader of the party, took the party down with him: in Ukraine, political leaders treat parties as their private property and refuse to resign following election defeats. In the 2012 elections, the SPU continued its slide into oblivion, coming in tenth with 0.45 percent of the vote, and in 2014 Moroz did not stand as a presidential candidate.

On the right, a plethora of national democratic parties emerged from *Rukh*. As in the Soviet era, these parties and movements combined national and democratic demands, such as affirmative action for the Ukrainian language, making them popular primarily in Ukrainian-speaking regions of Western and Central Ukraine. The 2002 elections proved to be a watershed for national democrats when Our Ukraine, with 23.57 percent of the vote, won a plurality and beat the KPU into second place. But after many voters defected to the BYuT, Our Ukraine fared poorly in the March 2006 and September 2007 elections, coming in third with 13.95 and 14.15 percent of the vote, respectively, and then becoming marginalized after Yushchenko left office in 2010. In the 2006, 2007, and 2012 parliamentary elections, a pattern emerged whereby BYuT—which included the Tymoshenko-led *Batkivshchina* (Fatherland) party, the Social Democratic Party of Ukraine, and the Reforms and Order Party—took second place with between 24 and 31 percent of the vote; and Our Ukraine and the Ukrainian Democratic Alliance for

Reforms (UDAR) came in third, with a total of 14 percent. In effect, national democratic and liberal voters who did not wish to support Tymoshenko backed Our Ukraine and UDAR and also voted for the candidacies of Tihipko and Arseniy Yatsenyuk in 2010. UDAR's leader, Vitali Klitschko, did not run for president in 2014, dropping out in favor of Poroshenko; instead, he ran for and won the election for Kyiv city mayor.

Centrist-liberal and social democratic parties emerged in Ukraine in the late Soviet and early post-Soviet era from two primary sources. The first was the *Komsomol*, whose members, as the youth elite of the Soviet Communist Party, used their connections to enter newly formed cooperatives under Gorbachev and formed the "yuppie" New Ukrainian generation heading banks and new businesses in the 1990s. A second source was so-called centrist parties which emerged in Crimea, Donetsk, and Odessa, the most violent cities and regions during Ukraine's 1990s transition to a market economy. In Donetsk, a nexus of criminal figures, emerging tycoons, and former leaders of large Soviet plants (so-called "Red Directors") played a major role. Violence and assassinations of senior criminal and business leaders were dramatic elements of politics in Odessa, Crimea, and Donetsk throughout the 1990s, the most famous of which were the murders of crime boss Akhat Bragin in the Donetsk football stadium in 1995 and that of Yevhen Shcherban, then Ukraine's wealthiest oligarch, in the city's airport in 1996.

Oligarch Akhmetov, who established a very close political and business alliance with Yanukovych, whom he lobbied for the position of regional governor, replaced Shcherban as Ukraine's wealthiest oligarch. Up to the 2014 crisis, Akhmetov ranked in the top fifty wealthiest persons in the world purchasing luxury properties throughout Europe. The breakthrough for the Donetsk clan came following the appointment of Yanukovych as regional governor in 1997, after which competing criminal groups and political leaders were eliminated, removed, and forced to unite into the Donetsk clan. As a result, violence abated from 1999 to 2000, and the victorious criminal groups, new tycoons, "Red Directors," and regional elites could launch the Party of Regions in 2000–2001. In return for de facto regional autonomy to pursue political consolidation and capital accumulation, the Donetsk clan, which had established a local monopoly of power in all facets of life, supported Kuchma in the 1999 and 2002 elections and, in return, was rewarded with the positions of prime minister and presidential candidate in 2002 and 2004, respectively. Yanukovych was a serial election "fraudster," abusing state administrative resources as Donetsk regional governor (1999, 2002), prime minister (2004), and president (2010, 2012) even as he denied there had been election fraud in 2004 despite overwhelming evidence to the contrary.

The Party of Regions, which emerged from the nexus forged in the violent and criminal Donetsk region, had three attributes that were visible during the Euromaidan and Donbas separatist conflict. First, it was far more authoritarian than former *Komsomol*-led centrist parties active during Kuchma's presidency. Second, with a more leftist populist ideology, it could readily co-opt the KPU, with whom it shared home bases in Donetsk and Crimea. Third, its regional Sovietized culture facilitated an alliance with Russian nationalist-separatists in Crimea whom President Kuchma had fought and marginalized. These three characteristics meant the Yanukovych presidency and Party of Regions posed a greater threat to Ukraine's democracy and statehood than any other group in three ways. First, violence came naturally to them as seen through the imprisonment of opposition leaders, extensive use of violence in the Euromaidan, and widespread human rights abuses during the Donbas separatist conflict.[4] Second, corruption was rapacious, as witnessed by the creation of a mafia state under Yanukovych and luxurious palaces, such as Yanukovich's *Mezhyhirya*, which were opened to the public after his overthrow. The Ukrainian prosecutor's office estimated the Yanukovych team had stolen upward of $100 billion during his four-year presidency, a virtual kleptocracy—nearly enough to trigger a national financial collapse on its own. Third, they were hostile to ethnic Ukrainian national identity, adopted Putin's line on sensitive historical issues such as the *holodomor*, opposed to NATO membership, and lukewarm on EU integration—all of which inflamed patriotic and nationalist sentiment.

The Party of Regions was launched through a merger of five political parties ("Red Director" Labor Party, Party of Regional Revival, Poroshenko's Party of Solidarity, former Kyiv mayor Leonid Chernovetskyi's Party of Beautiful Ukraine, and the Party of Ukrainian Pensioners). In the March 2002 elections, the Party of Regions joined the Party of Industrialists and Entrepreneurs, the Agrarians, the People's Democratic Party (NDP), and Labor Ukraine in the pro-presidential For a United Ukraine (ZYU). With 11.77 percent of the vote, ZYU came in third in the proportional half of the elections but was able to control half of parliament by adding a large number of deputies elected in majoritarian single-mandate districts. In the 2006 elections, the Party of Regions received a plurality with 32.14 percent and 186 seats; it was the only former pro-Kuchma party that succeeded in entering parliament in the next two elections. The Party of Regions won 34.37 percent in the 2007 elections but obtained fewer votes and eleven fewer seats than in the 2006 elections. In the 2012 elections, the Party of Regions again won a first-place plurality with 30 percent but established a parliamentary majority with the support of single-mandate deputies.

Yanukovych pressured the Constitutional Court to return Ukraine to a presidential system to increase his monopoly of power. Then, as one of its first acts, the Euromaidan opposition leadership overturned the Constitutional Court's 2010 decision and reinstated the 2004 parliamentary constitution, because Yanukovych's kleptocratic presidency had thoroughly discredited presidential authoritarianism.

The Party of Regions did not remain a formidable political machine following Russia's annexation of Crimea and military aggression, as well as the ouster of Yanukovych and criminal charges against government and party leaders. The meager vote (3 percent) for its candidate Mykhaylo Dobkin in the 2014 presidential elections represented a major defeat and undoubtedly influenced its decision to not put forward candidates and participate in that year's parliamentary elections.

Ukraine's electoral map changed in the October 2014 preterm parliamentary elections when it elected its first parliament that was pro-European. The OSCE, EU, and United States declared these elections as having been free and fair. Political forces taking the top three places included the Poroshenko bloc; Prime Minister Yatsenyuk's *Narodnyy Front* (Popular Front) that emerged after Tymoshenko was released from jail and would not relinquish her leadership position, so Yatsenyuk split from *Batkivshchina*; and Lviv mayor Andriy Sadovyy's *Samopomych* (Self Reliance) that, together with Tymoshenko's Fatherland party, came in last. These four factions control 63 percent of seats. Yatsenyuk was able to continue as head of government after his hastily created new Popular Front received nearly the same vote as the Poroshenko bloc. It was replaced in April 2016 by Volodymyr Hroysman, an ally of Poroshenko from his home base of Vynnytsya. A new political force elected to the Ukrainian parliament in this election was Sadovyy's

Samopomych, which attracted middle-class businesspersons and professionals in Western and Central Ukraine. In this election, new faces—journalists, civil society leaders, and military commanders—were elected inside most established political forces.

Although Russian television continues to overwhelmingly portray Ukraine as a country run by "fascists," the two nationalist parties (*Svoboda* [Freedom] and *Pravyy Sektor* [Right Sector]) did not enter parliament. In fact, support for the extreme right in Ukraine is one of the lowest in Europe. Ukraine's nationalists are decidedly pro-European, unlike their counterparts throughout the EU, and elected in single-mandate districts joined the pro-European coalition giving it a constitutional majority of over two-thirds of the seats.

Two of the three parties in the former Yanukovych regime failed to enter parliament. The KPU had long ago given up being a party of the downtrodden proletariat and become a satellite of the party of wealthy tycoons. Former deputy Prime Minister Tihipko's Strong Ukraine also failed to cross the 5 percent threshold that had been hastily revived after the party had earlier united with the Party of Regions in 2012. In the second round of the 2010 elections, Tihipko had aligned his party with Yanukovych over Tymoshenko and his reputation was ruined. Yanukovych's flight from Ukraine in 2014, followed by Putin's military invasions, led to the disintegration of the Party of Region's monopolization of power in Russian-speaking Eastern and Southern Ukraine. Crimea and Donbas were the Party of Regions' two main strongholds, and voting took place in only thirteen out of thirty-two election districts in the Donbas controlled by Kyiv. Separatist insurgents threatened anybody attempting to vote in areas under their control. Reconstituted as the so-called Opposition Bloc but still led by the same discredited personalities, the old-new force came in fourth place. The Radical Party that came in fifth is a populist protest party funded by Ukraine's gas lobby, created to take votes from Tymoshenko and nationalist parties.

Civil Society

Civil society's most visible moments have been the two mass demonstrations that lasted weeks and months in the main square in Kyiv: the Orange Revolution in 2004 and the Euromaidan from November 2013 to February 2014. Dissident groups had always been more active in Western Ukraine in the Soviet era and had mobilized support for reforms and opposition to Soviet rule in the late 1980s. In independent Ukraine, western Ukrainians continued to be very active in the "Ukraine without Kuchma" and "Arise Ukraine!" protests of 2000–2004 and provided a large proportion of the protestors during the Orange Revolution. Although this was influenced by US, Canadian, and European support for democratization and civil society, the decisive factor triggering this mass action was the close connection of high levels of ethnic Ukrainian identity, high levels of participation in civil society, and political work and support for integration into Europe. Western discussions have largely ignored the importance of national identity and of how Ukrainian identity has moved eastward through nation- and state-building in independent Ukraine.[5]

The coming to power of the opposition in Ukraine was like in Romania, Bulgaria, and Slovakia, late in coming as the former communist elites had retained power in the late 1980s and early 1990s. In Central and Eastern Europe, the opposition came to power in the second half of the 1990s but in Ukraine this had to wait until 2004 when Yushchenko defeated outgoing President Kuchma's chosen successor, Yanukovych. This was only possible because Yushchenko received support from Western and Central Ukraine, the diffusion of the tactics and training from Serbia and Georgia that had experienced democratic revolutions in 2000 and 2003, respectively; the provision of Western assistance to Ukraine's civil society; and the emergence of the internet. Indeed, the Orange Revolution was described as the world's first "internet revolution."[6]

A decade later, Ukrainian society and civil society were more politically mature and no longer placed trust in the leader to fulfill his or her promises. After the Orange Revolution, civil society and protestors had gone home placing their faith in the "new tsar" Yushchenko to implement his election promises, a political culture that continues to have deep roots in Russia and other former Soviet republics. The Euromaidan benefitted from advances in social media (Facebook and Twitter had not existed in 2004) and indeed the first protests were organized by a Facebook entry written by well-known journalist Mustafa Nayem.[7] Protestors organized themselves through a myriad of NGOs, journalists, women's volunteers, youth groups, local councilors, nationalist organizations, and middle-class businesspersons. They shunned the opposition who, unlike in the Orange Revolution, had no leadership role. Political maturity and civic development, the continued spread of Ukrainian identity through nation- and state-building, and a long period of Western assistance all brought dividends. While western and central Ukrainians had supported the Orange Revolution, the Euromaidan received support nationally (the exceptions being Crimea and the Donbas), as seen by the presence of eastern Ukrainians who were among those murdered. The protestors were able to withstand daily attacks by police special forces; kidnappings, torture, and killings by vigilantes; and a cold winter through collective solidarity, a high degree of voluntarism and determination. This clearly contrasted with protestors organized by President Yanukovych and the Party of Regions who were usually paid and often disinterested, using the opportunity for tourism in Kyiv.

The high degree of voluntarism and dedication of self-defense units in the Euromaidan was beneficial to defending Ukraine after the Euromaidan. Members of self-defense units and nationalist groups volunteered to fight Russian military aggression in Eastern Ukraine and by summer 2014 there were forty volunteer battalions. Without their patriotism, the Ukrainian army, then in a shamble after being deliberately run down and corporate raided by President Yanukovych, could not have halted Putin's aggression.[8] These volunteer battalions had been integrated into the army and National Guard by 2015. Women's volunteer groups, many of which emerged from the Euromaidan, have been crucial to Ukraine's war effort by collecting supplies (uniforms, boots, body armor, night vision goggles, fresh water, food, medicines, sleeping bags, etc.,) and transporting them to troops on the front lines.

Elections from 2006 to 2014

Out of the multitude of parties and blocs that stood in elections in 2006, 2007, 2012, and 2014, only five or six crossed the 3 to 5 percent threshold in each election. The 2006 elections brought three Orange parties to parliament (Our Ukraine, BYuT, and SPU), but the SPU. The 2007 elections brought Our Ukraine, BYuT, and two opposition political forces into parliament, with the Party of Regions the key winner, electing 186 deputies, a threefold increase in its support.

In the 2006 elections, BYuT also scored a remarkable success, tripling its support and becoming the second-largest faction, with 129 deputies. In the 2007 elections, it dramatically increased its vote to 30.71 percent, and in 2012, when blocs were banned from participating, *Batkivshchina* (by then merged with the Viktor Pynzenyk's Reform and Order and Yatsenyuk's Front for Change parties) received 25.54 percent.

Our Ukraine and Our Ukraine–People's Self-Defense (NUNS) received third place in the 2006 and 2007 preterm elections. Our Ukraine/NUNS center-right niche in Ukrainian politics was taken by UDAR (*udar* means "punch" in Ukrainian), led by international boxing champion Vitali Klitschko. Protesting Yanukovych's policies against Ukrainian national identity and the 2012 language law, some national democratic (Orange) voters backed the *Svoboda* party, which became the first nationalist party to enter parliament.

The 2007 elections returned a slim Orange coalition that eventually agreed to put forward Tymoshenko as prime minister but faced two major obstacles. The first was opposition from Yushchenko, who—as in 2005—sought to undermine the government at every turn. Second, from fall 2008, Ukraine was one of the five countries in Europe most affected by the global financial crisis. In September 2008, the coalition collapsed after NUNS voted to withdraw and four months later a new Orange coalition was established by BYuT, NUNS, and the Volodymyr Lytvyn bloc, with Lytvyn offered the position of parliamentary speaker.

In the 2014 elections, the largest vote went to the Poroshenko bloc, an alliance of the president's third Solidarity party and UDAR, that included the largest number of candidates with ties to the *ancien régime*, Yatsenyuk's Popular Front, *Batkivshchina*, and *Samopomych*. All of these political forces included Euromaidan activists, middle-class businesspersons, well-known independent journalists (such as *Ukrayinska Pravda's* [Ukrainian Truth] Serhiy Leshchenko), and military and National Guard commanders.

The January 17, 2010, presidential elections in many ways repeated the 2004 elections, with Yanukovych facing a main Orange opponent, this time Tymoshenko. These two candidates remained unchallenged and made it easily into the second round with 35 and 25 percent of the vote, respectively. In the second round, Tymoshenko greatly expanded her voter base from 25 to 45 percent by including a large number of negative votes against Yanukovych. But this proved insufficient, and she was defeated by 3.48 percent. Yanukovych became the first sitting Ukrainian president not to receive 50 percent of the vote and not win in a majority of Ukrainian regions.

In the first round of the 2010 elections, Yatsenyuk received 7 percent of the vote, pushed into fourth place by Tihipko, who polled 13 percent. Together, the combined Yatsenyuk-Tihipko 20 percent of the vote for third and fourth place represented a new middle-class voting phenomenon in Ukrainian elections that became an important factor in providing resources and supporters for the Euromaidan. Tihipko and Yatsenyuk voters were urban professionals and businesspeople who disliked the second-round choice because it represented the old guard of Ukrainian politics. A large number of Ukraine's urban middle class refused to back Tymoshenko, who received far fewer votes than

Photo 17.4.   Euromaidan demonstrators after the protestors had been attacked by the *Berkut militsiya* special forces. (Taras Kuzio)

Yushchenko had in 2004. Yushchenko's call to vote against both candidates in round two assisted Yanukovych in winning power as it was only listened to by Orange voters.

The next presidential elections were planned for 2015 but the Euromaidan and Yanukovych's flight from Kyiv to Russia brought them forward. In late February 2014, after the Party of Regions disintegrated, the opposition quickly took control of parliament and began to rule the country, introducing reforms backed by a new IMF agreement and with Western diplomatic support from the G7, and set preterm elections. The new government was led by Prime Minister Yatsenyuk and included a wide range of civil society activists.

The May 2014 preterm presidential election campaign was shorter, relations between candidates were less antagonistic, and the mood, following the state of the economy and finances and Russian annexation of Crimea, was more somber. A third of the Donbas, controlled by pro-Russian separatists, could not participate. Pro-European candidates and parties dominated both the May and October 2014 presidential and parliamentary elections with the only pro-Russian force to enter parliament being the Opposition bloc, successor to the Party of Regions.

The Economic Transition

Between 1989 and 1999, Ukraine's GDP collapsed by more than half, the deepest economic recession in the former USSR. The shadow (unofficial) economy has averaged 40 percent (official figure) to 50 percent (World Bank figure) of total economic activity,[9] a factor that further reduced income to the state budget, facilitated corruption, and encouraged ties between business and corrupt figures and criminal structures. Ukraine's economy began to grow in 2000 during the Yushchenko government with a 5.9 percent GDP increase, followed by 9.1 percent the next year, 4.8 percent in 2002, and 8.5 percent in 2003. The 12 percent growth in GDP in 2004 was therefore exceptional rather than the norm. Economic growth was also high in 2006–2007 after a dip in 2005. The Ukrainian economy never fully recovered from the 2008 global financial crisis, and by the end of 2013, following four years of mismanagement under Prime Minister Azarov and President Yanukovych and rampant asset stripping, it came close to default.

Ukraine did go through three rapid periods of economic reform that established and consolidated a market economy, the first between 1994 and 1996 after Kuchma was elected and signed an agreement with the IMF, the second in 2000 and 2001 during the Yushchenko government, and the third after the Euromaidan Revolution under the Yatsenyuk government. Typically, following a country's signing of IMF agreements, government policies have been successful in stabilizing the crisis but then the economy has stagnated because of weak commitment to structural reforms. Until the Euromaidan, Ukraine was, in fact, stuck at the crossroads in what economists described as a "partially reformed equilibrium,"[10] where elites received advantages from the still opaque nature of the economy and business and politics remain closely interwoven.[11] A major opportunity to reduce the power of oligarchs and improve the rule of law was missed during the Yushchenko presidency. As a result, the country turned into a kleptocratic mafia state under President Yanukovych.

According to the conservative Heritage Foundation 2017 rankings of economic freedom, Ukraine is in the bottom tier of countries alongside Belarus, Tajikistan, and Turkmenistan; they define Ukraine as a "repressed economy."[12] The Ukrainian economy is still only three-quarters the size of the Soviet Ukrainian economy in 1989 because heavy industry, predominantly based in the east, has declined while small and medium businesses dominate the economy in the west and center.

Frequent changes of government have been a major problem that plagued Ukraine's economic policies. Economic reform under the first postcommunist president, Kravchuk, was never a priority; instead, he adopted nationalist protectionist policies directed against Russia. These policies proved to be disastrous: in 1993, the country experienced hyperinflation and further economic collapse. Miners' strikes and social unrest deepened and led to preterm presidential elections. Kravchuk's successor, Kuchma, introduced economic reform policies to stabilize the domestic economy after the IMF and World Bank began to provide assistance to Ukraine for the first time. This was in return for a pledge to pursue reforms and relinquish nuclear weapons. However, on the whole, Kuchma's economic policies were similar to his policies in politics and foreign policy in that they lacked any clear direction. Privatization was undertaken in fits and starts from 1994, but it primarily benefited a small group of businessmen with good relations with the president, who became tycoons and oligarchs. The absence of structural reforms dragged out the transition from 1995 until 2000 when Ukraine's economic growth resumed. A small- and medium-sized business class did develop, but not to the same extent as in Central and Eastern Europe, where this sector became the driving force of the postcommunist transitions. Ukraine's corruption, overregulation, and unfriendly business climate also discouraged large amounts of foreign investment from entering the country.

Only three of Ukraine's postcommunist governments, led by Prime Ministers Yushchenko (December 1999–April 2001), Tymoshenko (December 2007–March 2010), and Yatsenyuk (February 2014–April 2016), were truly committed to reform and fighting corruption. Economic reforms, in particular privatization, coupled with a widespread tolerance of corruption, facilitated the rise of an oligarch class that has survived and prospered due to close personal, economic, and corrupt ties to the president.[13] Ukraine introduced its independent currency, the *hryvnya*, in 1996 when Yushchenko was chairman of the National Bank. However, when Yuriy Yekhanurov became prime minister, he ended all speculation on reprivatization by calling a meeting of Ukraine's oligarchs to mend relations between the government and Ukraine's major businessmen, whom he described as Ukraine's "national bourgeoisie." Following the Orange Revolution and Ukraine's recognition as a market economy, Ukraine received high levels of foreign direct investment (FDI) but this was the exception to the rule as the country has received very low volumes of FDI since 1991.

Instead of experiencing real social change, Ukraine became known as the "blackmail state,"[14] where corruption was tolerated and even encouraged by the president, even as it was diligently recorded by the law enforcement bodies. If the corrupt elites remained politically loyal to national leaders, their files were not acted on by the general prosecutor's office. Political loyalty, therefore, was exchanged for rents obtained through corruption and insider privatization.

Corruption has remained a major problem in Ukraine that has contributed to a very poor business environment, holding back economic growth and foreign investment. There have been some notable improvements since the Euromaidan. New institutions have been established such as the National Anti-Corruption Bureau. The ProZorro system has been introduced for transparency in the competition for the awarding of government contracts and e-declarations for state officials to declare their incomes and assets. But, there has been little progress in criminal convictions for abuse of office, which continues to create a climate of weak accountability for elites. Western donors and governments and civil society are pushing for the establishment of a special anti-corruption court to deal with high-level cases during the reform of the judicial system, which will be established in 2018.

Each year Transparency International, the anti-corruption watchdog, has shown that Ukraine has a persistently high level of corruption and, of the fifteen former Soviet republics, ranks fifth from the bottom, alongside four Central Asian states. Members of Putin's Eurasian Union—Russia, Belarus, Armenia, Kazakhstan, and Kyrgyzstan—have lower levels of corruption than a country seeking European integration—Ukraine. One important reason for the high level of corruption in Ukraine is that the media freedom and civil society activism found in democracies coexist alongside Soviet-era institutions (the general prosecutor's office, SBU) that remain under the president's control. The general prosecutor's office, which Western governments have long sought to reform, is one of the biggest criminal rackets in Ukraine, as is evident in the flamboyant wealth of its prosecutors. Criminal cases are closed in exchange for bribes rather than being investigated and brought to trial. The Ukrainian public is highly politicized and receives a huge flow of information about elite abuses of office from an independent media but does not see criminal convictions. This generates poor public perceptions of the state's fight against corruption. Authoritarian regimes in the CIS have no media freedom and therefore the public does not have access to the types of information about elite abuses of office that is freely available in Ukraine.

In the last quarter of a century, over $100 billion has been sent to EU countries (particularly Cyprus, United Kingdom, Austria, and Latvia), Switzerland, and offshore tax havens, such as the Virgin Islands, Panama, Monaco, and Lichtenstein, from sources in Ukraine. The leak of the Panama Papers in spring 2016 shed a spotlight on how Ukrainian elites, including President Poroshenko, were placing their money offshore in opaque tax havens such as Panama.

A major source of corruption in Ukraine through to the post-Euromaidan reforms has been the energy sector. Yushchenko continued to maintain close relations with Ukraine's oligarchs, many of whom saw him as an ally against the Party of Regions and BYuT. Gas tycoon Dmitri Firtash, behind a host of opaque gas intermediaries (Eural-Trans Gas [2002–2004], *RosUkrEnergo* (RUE) [2004–2009], *OstChem* [2010–]), provided an alternative source of funds for Yanukovych and the Party of Regions. Firtash was detained in Vienna in March 2014 at the request of the United States to stand trial on corruption charges.[15] Although the Vienna court initially ruled against his deportation, an appeal by the US government won the case. Firtash is also being sought by the Spanish authorities for collaborating with Russian organized crime on money laundering. Firtash has always been a Russian agent of influence in Ukraine and has admitted long-term ties to Russian mafia boss Semyon Mogilevych with whom he cooperated in the energy sector.[16]

Ukraine's energy dependency on Russia has been a threat to Ukrainian national security. Pursuing Russia-friendly policies did not lead to lower gas prices as Moscow always used energy as a source of pressure. President Yanukovych fulfilled all of the domestic and foreign policy demands laid out in Russian president Medvedev's 2009 open letter to Yushchenko; nevertheless, Russia charged Ukraine the highest gas price in Europe. The disintegration of the pro-Russian political camp, heavily tied to Firtash and the gas lobby, coupled with Russia's military aggression has led to Ukraine ending its dependency on Russia gas. Ukraine has ended the supply of electricity to Russian-occupied Crimea. Russia had never succeeded in establishing a consortium that it controlled over Ukraine's gas pipelines. New legislation adopted in summer 2014 opened up Western investment in the pipelines while at the same time blocking Russian investment and control.

Until the Euromaidan, Ukraine's dependency had been two pronged. Not only was Ukraine dependent upon Russia for its energy supplies but Russia was also dependent on Ukrainian pipelines for the export of 60 percent of its gas and on gas storage in western Ukraine for delivery to European customers in winter. The January 2006 gas contract, following a gas crisis that affected gas supplies to Europe, was contested by BYuT and the then opposition Party of Regions in a parliamentary vote of no confidence in the Yekhanurov government, but the contract was backed by President Yushchenko and Our Ukraine. The contract permitted the opaque RUE to be given the right to transit Central Asian gas through Russia and Ukraine to Europe. A second, longer gas crisis affected Europe in January 2009. On this occasion, the government was better prepared with stored gas that ensured Ukraine could survive a gas blockade by Russia. The ten-year gas contract signed between Prime Ministers Tymoshenko and Putin outlined a two-year shift to European prices, which had collapsed during the global crisis, and the removal of the RUE gas intermediary. The contract was condemned by Yanukovych (then an ally of Firtash) and his Party of Regions allies who backed the creation of a parliamentary investigative committee. The committee's findings and other sources were used as the basis for criminal charges of abuse of office that led to Tymoshenko's imprisonment in May 2011.

The election of Yanukovych returned Ukraine's energy policy to that of the Kuchma era, when Ukraine sought gas subsidies in exchange for granting Russia geopolitical advantages. On April 27, 2010, the Ukrainian parliament railroaded a twenty-five-year extension of the Sevastopol base for the Black Sea Fleet from 2017, when the twenty-year "temporary" lease was set to expire, in exchange for a 30 percent "discount" on Russian gas. The "discount" was flawed as it was based on the pricing formula used in the 2009 gas contract. More importantly, although Yanukovych gave many concessions to Russia in 2010, there was never any willingness by Putin to change the terms of the 2009 gas contract to reduce the price Ukraine paid, which was the highest in Europe.

Social Problems

Ukraine inherited a large number of social problems from the Soviet Union that were exacerbated during the transition to a market economy. From 1991, Ukraine's population declined from 51.6 to 45.2 million, as the death rate exceeded the birthrate and as a reflection of the deteriorating socioeconomic conditions and out-migration. Ukraine now has the fourth worst death rate in Europe at 14.4 per thousand inhabitants, which is higher than its birthrate of 9.7 per thousand inhabitants. Every tenth Ukrainian dies before reaching the age of thirty-five because of health problems. Ukrainian men have a relatively short life span of sixty-three years, compared to women, with seventy-three (with a Ukrainian average of 69.5 compared to 78.6 in the EU). With 86.3 men for every 100 women, Ukraine has the sixth-lowest ratio of men to women among all countries in the world. The life expectancy difference of ten years between Ukrainian men and women is the fifth biggest among all countries in the world, highlighting the impact of lifestyle choices among Ukrainian men. The average worldwide gender life expectancy gap is 4.5 years, and the average worldwide male to female ratio is 101.8 men for every 100 women. A 2001 UN projection of future population trends calculated that Ukraine's population would continue to decline by as much as 40 percent by the middle of the twenty-first century. Ukrainian demographic experts believe the UN projection of a population decline to 33 million by 2050 is too low and project a figure of 36 million.[17] The decline in the Soviet health-care system that began even before the Soviet Union's collapse coupled with alcoholism, widespread tobacco smoking, drug use, and poor diet are the leading cause of death from all causes. The low quality of health care has also led to an increase in the number of epidemic diseases.

Ukraine's consumption of alcohol is high at tenth in the world but below EU members Belgium, Croatia, Lithuania, Romania, and Bulgaria and the former Soviet republics of Russia, Belarus, and Moldova. Ukrainians drink on average 8 liters of alcohol a year, putting them at third in the world in the consumption of vodka after Russia (which comes in first with 13.9 liters) and Belarus (second with 11.3 liters). Ukraine also has one of the highest road-fatality death rates in Europe, with twenty deaths on average each day, as the result of alcohol use and also poorly maintained roads, poor driving habits, and poor vehicle maintenance.[18]

One factor that could contribute to Ukraine's further population decline is the AIDS epidemic. The former USSR is second to Africa in its rate of growth. Ukraine has the second largest HIV epidemic in Europe and Central Asia with 220,000 HIV-positive people.

Ukrainians also drink the most polluted water in Europe. In a ranking of forty-five Ukrainian cities, those in the bottom half are primarily in Eastern and Southern Ukraine, and those in the top half are mainly in less industrialized Central and Western Ukraine.

Ukrainian coal mines are the second most dangerous in the world after China's, leading to nearly four thousand deaths from accidents since 1991. The Donbas conflict has severely damaged the region's outdated coal-mining industry, and much of it has closed down.

With 13 million Ukrainians living below the official poverty line, Ukraine is the second poorest country in Europe after Moldova. The World Bank estimates that over half of Ukrainians live in poverty.[19] The two factors that have contributed to high levels of poverty are reforms that have increased prices, such as those for household utilities, and thereby reduced standards of living and the war with Russia that has led to Ukraine being ranked eighth in the world for the number of IDP's.

This is the second time since Ukraine became independent that there have been internally displaced people. The first was in 1986 following the Chornobyl nuclear accident when 116,000 people were evacuated from the town of Pripyat north of Kyiv. By the end of 2016, there were 1,785,740 registered IDPs of which 1,100,000 were women and 700,000 men. Approximately 1,026,177 have been displaced as a consequence of Putin's military aggression in Eastern Ukraine: 1,003,824 from the Donbas and 22,353 from Crimea (many of whom are Tatars fleeing political persecution). An additional 271,000 Ukrainians have fled to Russia where they are refugees, giving a total of over 2 million people who have been displaced and affected by Putin's military aggression. The difference in number between those registered as IDPs and those displaced is because some Ukrainians who continue to live in the DNR and LNR travel to Ukrainian-controlled areas to collect their pensions and other state benefits. The gender difference is accounted for by the unwillingness of some men to register in order to not be drafted into the army or because men have remained in the war zone to protect property or look after elderly relatives.

Under the Soviet regime, women were theoretically accorded equality with men and allowed to enter many areas of traditional male employment, but usually for lower pay and at the bottom of the social spectrum. The progressive nature of Soviet propaganda clashed with conservative realities about women and homosexuality, banned from 1933 to 1991 in the USSR. Meanwhile, women continued to remain subservient in the home and were regarded not as equals but as limited to traditional roles as housewives and mothers.

Women's rights have expanded since Ukraine became independent but there remains a long way to go to achieve gender equality. In the late 1980s and first half of the 1990s, some women became active in national democratic groups, such as *Rukh*, and formed offshoot NGOs, many funded by Western governments and international endowments. Nevertheless, national democratic groups continue to regard women in traditional nationalist terms as "guardians of the hearth" (*Berehynya*) and protectors of the family and nation. Gender equality was not on their political agenda.

Francesca Ebel writes, "Displays of hyper masculinity and sexist prejudice towards women dominate the Ukrainian political scene."[20] Women Euromaidan activists elected to parliament in 2014 are leading the reforms to allow children into parliament, the installation of baby changing rooms, maternity leave for parliamentary deputies, and a 30 percent female quota for party candidates. Even with these new rules, the view that politics remains the preserve of men continues to be widespread, and the kinds of provisions claimed by women deputies are not options for most Ukrainian women. Nevertheless, the 2014 elections increased the proportion of women in parliament to twelve percent, only seven less than the US and ten percent lower than the international average. An equal opportunities caucus includes 53 members of parliament (40 women, 13 men) from four factions.

Sexism has been generally prevalent within big business-backed centrist parties, such as the Party of Regions. Yanukovych refused to debate Tymoshenko on Ukrainian television in the 2010 elections saying, "women should go to the kitchen" and not dabble in politics. Prime Minister Nikolai Azarov and leader of the Party of Regions was blunter when he said, "Some say our government is too large; others that there are no women." He continued, "There's no one to look at during cabinet sessions: they're all boring faces. With all respect to women, conducting reforms is not women's business."[21]

Discrimination against homosexuality has been promoted by Ukraine's extreme right, as in many European counties, but also by the Party of Regions, the KPU, and Viktor Medvedchuk's Ukrainian Way, which are allies of Putin's promotion of "conservative" values and its virulent hostility to homosexuality. The Party of Regions and its Crimean Russian nationalist allies submitted anti-homosexual legislation in the 2012–2014 parliament. Homophobia among Euromaidan parties has not been prevalent and in November 2015, the Ukrainian parliament adopted legislation banning gender and sexual orientation discrimination in the workplace. The law was one of the many requirements to receive an EU visa-free regime and showed a willingness to be influenced by EU norms. Nevertheless, same-sex marriage continues to remain a taboo subject for a broad range of political forces, including pro-Western parliamentary groups.

Regional Diversity and Interethnic Relations

Ukraine inherited a wide diversity of regions. This regionalism was compounded by weak historic traditions of statehood and a population divided between those holding an exclusively ethnic Ukrainian (primarily Ukrainophone) identity and those with multiple Ukrainian-Russian (primarily Russophone) identities.[22] This division was also complicated by the attempts at nation- and state-building during a severe socioeconomic crisis in the 1990s. Despite these issues, Ukraine experienced harmonious interethnic relations until 2014, and its separatist challenge in Crimea in the 1990s was resolved peacefully—unlike in Moldova, Georgia, Russia, and Azerbaijan. Under President Kuchma, centrist parties did not attempt to mobilize Russian speakers against Ukrainian speakers. This changed after the Orange Revolution when the Party of Regions monopolized Eastern and Southern Ukraine and used inflammatory language to pit Russian against Ukrainian speakers and drew on Soviet-style rhetoric that described their Orange opponents as "fascists." The Party of Regions slogan for 2015 presidential elections was launched in 2013 as "To Europe without fascists!" This divisive election campaigning was introduced by US political consultant Paul Manafort who worked for the Party of Regions and Yanukovych from 2004 to 2015. In 2016, he headed Donald Trump's election campaign and in October of the following year the FBI indicted him with money laundering and tax evasion and he together with other Trump advisers is included in the special investigation into Russia's interference in the US elections.

Ukraine's Jewish population, which is Russian speaking, backed the Euromaidan and has supported Ukraine in the face of Russian aggression. A Jewish self-protection company of volunteers was created in the Euromaidan, and one of its members was killed by a *Berkut* sniper. Jewish-Ukrainian oligarch Ihor Kolomoyskyi, governor of Dnipropetrovsk bordering Donetsk, funded volunteer battalions to prevent separatist forces from taking over in 2014–2015. The Jewish population in the DNR and LNR quickly fled to Ukrainian-controlled areas as Russian proxy forces revived Soviet-era "anti-Zionist" (in reality always anti-Semitic) propaganda and demanded that Jews register.

In the USSR, the myth of the Great Patriotic War ignored Stalin's collaboration with the Nazis in 1939–1941 and its historiography never mentioned the huge Jewish losses at the hands of Nazi death squads. In September 2016, the seventy-fifth anniversary of the Nazi massacre of Jews, Soviet prisoners of war (POWs), and Ukrainian nationalists at Baby Yar near Kyiv was commemorated in the presence of the Israeli and Ukrainian presidents.

Russia's annexation of the Crimea and its military support for proxies in Eastern Ukraine have led to the growth of patriotism among different groups of Ukrainians. At a time of conflict, invasion, and war, people are under pressure to take sides and can no longer sit on the fence, and a majority of Ukrainians who previously preferred to declare they had a dual Ukrainian-Russian identity have increasingly adopted a Ukrainian civic identity. There has been a near fourfold decline of ethnic Russians in Ukraine. In the 1989 Soviet census, 22 percent of Ukraine's population declared they were Russian; in the 2001 census, this figure declined to 17 percent. In surveys since 2014, only 6 percent of Ukrainian citizens declare themselves to be ethnic Russians. This process is not completely new but the war has certainly speeded it up.

Kuchma and Ukraine's first defense minister Kostyantyn Morozov were registered as "Russians" in the USSR but became Ukrainians after 1991.

Western Ukrainians never had illusions about Russia. Ukrainians with dual identities and Russian speakers were the most affected by the war due to the proximity of their region to the fighting and because they viewed Russia's aggression as a personal betrayal. The growth of Ukrainian patriotism was especially noticeable in Kharkiv and Odessa where young Ukrainians defeated pro-Russian separatists who failed to ignite civil strife and create local "people's republics" in the spring of 2014.[23]

Regionalism in Ukraine is not ethnically driven, and separatism remained muted, except in Crimea in the first half of the 1990s and since the Euromaidan Revolution—in both cases supported by Russia. The Eastern and Southern regions of Ukraine are overwhelmingly Russophone, while the Western and Central regions of the country are primarily Ukrainophone, but the majority of Ukrainians are bilingual, especially in the electoral swing region of Central Ukraine. The central issue facing Ukraine is reconciling regional diversity between mutually exclusive Ukrainian and multiple Ukrainian-Russian identities through civic national integration and rebuilding relations between the Central and Eastern Ukraine.[24]

Crimea was a unique region because it had an ethnic Russian majority and most Ukrainians were Russified and held a Soviet and regional identity. In 2014, there was little opposition to Russia's annexation—unlike in the Donbas where Kyiv received some local support. Crimean elites sought to revive the status of autonomous republic after a Crimean referendum overwhelmingly approved the decision in January 1991. Relations between Crimea and the rest of Ukraine were strained between 1992 and 1995 over the delegation of powers to Crimea. Two of Crimea's three political forces—centrists and the KPU—supported the maximum delegation of powers to Crimea but opposed separatism. Only Russian nationalist-separatists advocated Crimea's separation from Ukraine and union with Russia. Russian nationalist-separatist Yuriy Meshkov won the newly created Crimean presidency in

January 1994, and his allies took control of the Crimean Supreme Soviet, but this influence proved short-lived. In March 1995, Kuchma issued a presidential decree abolishing the Crimean presidency, an event that, together with infighting within the Russian nationalist coalition, progressively marginalized Russian nationalist-separatists. The KPU and centrists in Crimea were able to reach agreement with Kyiv on the parameters of a new Crimean constitution adopted in October by the Crimean parliament and ratified in December 1998 by the Ukrainian parliament. The constitution recognized Crimea as part of Ukraine. In 1998 and 1999, both houses of the Russian parliament also recognized Ukraine's borders after Crimea had adopted its constitution. This treaty and the Budapest Memorandum (see next section) were ignored and flouted by Russia when it annexed Crimea.

The Crimean question was reopened in 2005–2006, when the Party of Regions signed a cooperation agreement with Putin's United Russia party and an alliance with Crimean Russian nationalists in regional elections. After being marginalized for a decade, Russian nationalists in Crimea received an infusion of life when the Party of Regions allied with the Russia bloc and the Russian Community of Crimea in the 2006 Crimean elections. The US embassy in Kyiv reported, "Regions had given the Russia bloc undue political prominence in 2006 by forming a single Crimean electoral list, providing them with slots in the Crimean Rada they would not have won on their own."[25] These Russian nationalists, who went on to lead Russia's annexation of the Crimea, were led by Sergei Aksyonov, an organized crime leader in the 1990s with the nickname "Goblin."[26] Self-proclaimed Crimean Prime Minister Aksyonov, leader of the extreme right Party of Russian Unity (which had only three out of one hundred seats in the Crimean parliament), received backing from the eighty-two deputies in the Party of Regions faction in the Crimean parliament. Russian Unity merged with President Putins United Russia party ahead of the Crimea's 2014 election to the Russian parliament.

From 1991 until the eve of Crimea's annexation, Russia supported separatism and covert operations in Crimea and Odessa with policies similar to those pursued in South Ossetia and Abkhazia, such as distributing Russian passports. This reached a crescendo in summer 2009 when two Russian diplomats were expelled, leading to a Russian storm of protest and President Dmitri Medvedev's undiplomatic open letter to Yushchenko.[27] The Party of Regions and Crimean Russian nationalists organized protests against Ukrainian exercises with NATO, derailing the exercises for the first time since Ukraine joined the Partnership for Peace program in 1994. In fall 2008, the Party of Regions, KPU, and Crimean Russian nationalists backed two resolutions recognizing the independence of South Ossetia and Abkhazia, which failed in the Ukrainian parliament but were adopted by the Crimean Supreme Soviet. These were the only signs of support for Russia's aggression against Georgia throughout the CIS outside Russia itself.

Russia's invasion and annexation of Crimea came as a shock to Eastern Ukrainians who viewed it as a neighbor, supposedly friendly and with whom there were treaties. Many Ukrainians saw Russia as kicking Ukraine when it was down and weak. Ukrainians, irrespective of the fact that Putin denied responsibility for the war in the Donbas, have blamed Russian leaders for the conflict. Anti-Russian views are no longer found only in Western Ukraine, although they are directed against Russian leaders and not the Russian people. The direction of Ukrainian anger at Russian leaders and the state—rather than the Russian people—is a reflection of the growth of patriotism rather than ethnic nationalism in Ukraine. Three quarters of Ukrainians hold negative views of Putin, the State

Duma, and Russian government; 93 percent in the west and center; and 50 to 60 percent in the south, east, and Donbas. Only 16 percent of Ukrainians view the conflict in Eastern Ukraine as a civil war between Ukrainian and Russian speakers while 60 percent see it as due to Russian-backed separatism or as a Russian-Ukrainian war. Eighty two percent view the two separatist Donbas enclaves as "terrorist organizations" and only 9 percent believe they represent the population they control.[28]

Interethnic relations in Crimea were complicated because of strained relations between eastern Slavs and Muslim Tatars, who began returning from their forced exile in Central Asia in the late 1980s and now number 15 percent of the Crimean population. The 2001 Ukrainian census showed the progressive decline of ethnic Russians in Crimea to 58 percent, down from 65 percent in the 1989 Soviet census, due to out-migration of Russians and in-migration of Tatars.

The two separatist enclaves have taken a very different trajectory from that of the rest of Ukraine by following Russia's path of re-Sovietization and re-Stalinization. Education, history writing, and state policies contain high doses of nostalgia for the USSR, which is seen as reincarnated in Putin's Russia. There are similar sentiments in Crimea. A Crimean resident said that Crimea joining Russia was "a return to the Soviet Union. Our generation was, is and will always be in the USSR. We will die in the Soviet Union." Those who remain nostalgic for the USSR in Crimea and the DNR and LNR support Putin's Eurasian Union and have no interest in European integration.

Foreign and Security Policy

Ukraine under Kravchuk placed greater emphasis on nation- and state-building and the security of the state, principally vis-à-vis Russia, than on economic and political reform. This influenced Ukraine's slow nuclear disarmament until 1996 and weak cooperation with transatlantic structures. From the mid-1990s, relations between the West and Ukraine improved dramatically following the elections of Kuchma and in the United States, Bill Clinton. When Kuchma was elected president in 1994, he initially supported reforms and agreed to denuclearize Ukraine. In December 1994, Ukraine signed the Nuclear Non-Proliferation Treaty (NPT), which paved the way for denuclearization between 1994 and 1996. In return for nuclear disarmament, the United States, United Kingdom, and Russia signed the Budapest Memorandum providing security assurances for Ukraine's territorial integrity and sovereignty—assurances that Russia tore up when it occupied Crimea. The United Kingdom and United States did very little relatively to back up their security commitments under the Budapest Memorandum; they rejected the sending of defensive military weapons and did not participate in the Minsk peace process. President Trump has not blocked (unlike his predecessor Barak Obama) the sending of military assistance to Ukraine which including Javelin anti-tank weapons, will begin arriving in 2018.

In the second half of the 1990s, the United States sought to support Ukraine both bilaterally in a "strategic partnership" and multilaterally through NATO as a "keystone" of European security. During the Clinton administration, Ukraine became the third-largest recipient of US assistance.[29] The election of Kuchma on a moderate pro-Russian platform failed to change Russia's negative attitudes to Ukrainian statehood, and Ukraine therefore turned westward becoming the most active CIS state within NATO's Partnership for Peace program.

In July 2002, Ukraine officially declared its intention to seek NATO membership, but the government did little to pursue this objective, and NATO was not ready to take in CIS states. NATO membership could have been possible in 2005 and 2006 when it was supported by the George W. Bush administration, which had sought to obtain a MAP (Membership Action Plan) for Ukraine at the November 2006 Riga summit. Ukraine's drive to NATO was undermined by Yushchenko's intense rivalry with Tymoshenko and infighting in the Orange camp. From 2007 to 2008, opposition from Germany and other West European countries to NATO enlargement grew, and Ukraine and Georgia were not invited into MAPs at the April 2008 Bucharest summit. Membership for Ukraine and Georgia has not been a major policy issue for NATO since Bucharest and is unlikely in the short term.

Kuchma was neither pro nor anti-Russian, but at the same time he supported close security cooperation with NATO and recognized that Russia could be a threat to Ukraine's territorial integrity, twin beliefs that Yanukovych never upheld (even though both were Eastern Ukrainians). Yanukovych and the Party of Regions always opposed NATO membership. They cited low levels of popular support for NATO membership that had declined from a third in the 1990s to 20 percent in the Yushchenko era, with especially low levels of support in Eastern-Southern Ukraine. Ukraine's cooperation with NATO plummeted during Yanukovych's presidency when he adhered to Russian demands to seek nonbloc status and renounce the goal of NATO membership. Yanukovych extended the Sevastopol Black Sea Fleet base agreement from twenty years in the 1997 interstate treaty to 2042–2047.

The occupation of Crimea and Russia's proxy war in the Donbas have dramatically increased support for NATO membership; 69 percent of Ukrainians would vote positively in a referendum on joining NATO according to surveys conducted by the well-known Ukrainian NGO, Democratic Initiatives.[30] In December 2014, Ukraine's newly elected parliament voted to replace Yanukovych's 2010 "nonbloc" foreign policy program with the program that existed previously, whose goal was transatlantic and European integration. In June 2017, Ukraine's parliament returned the country's foreign policy to the goal of seeking NATO membership.

Ukraine's cooperation with NATO assisted in reforming and democratizing the armed forces, which paid dividends when they refused to intervene against protesters in the Orange and Euromaidan Revolutions. Public trust in the military was always relatively high and has grown in response to Russian aggression.[31]

Public trust in the Soviet-era *Militsiya* (Ministry of Internal Affairs), which survived through to 2014, was already at rock bottom and fell even lower after *Berkut* violence and murders of protestors on the Euromaidan. Beginning in July 2015, the United States and Canada assisted in reforming Ukraine's Soviet-era *Militsiya* into a European-style police force. The bloated Ministry of Interior is in the process of being cut from 300,000 to 160,000. In fall-winter 2015, the National Police force that replaced the former Soviet *Militsiya* included six departments: Criminal, Narcotics, Cyber, Economic, Patrol Police (incorporating traffic police), and Police Security. The notorious *Berkut* riot police, who were the snipers on the Euromaidan, were replaced by a Rapid Operational Response Unit (KORD). Ministry of Interior Internal Troops became a paramilitary National Guard. Public trust in the police is growing and far higher than for the former Soviet-era *Militsiya*.[32]

The EU has never considered Ukraine or any other CIS state to be potential future members. The partnership and cooperation agreement signed by Ukraine and the EU in 1994 and ratified four years later was an amorphous agreement and never included membership prospects. A three-year action plan with the EU signed in 2005 as part of the European Neighborhood Policy was completed in 2007 and 2008. In fall 2008, after the Tymoshenko government took Ukraine into the World Trade Organization (WTO), Ukraine began negotiating the Deep and Comprehensive Free Trade Agreement (DCFTA) as one of the components of the association agreement. Negotiations for the association agreement were completed in fall 2011—in the same year as Tymoshenko was sentenced on trumped up charges. The EU postponed the initialing of the agreement (signifying a completion of negotiations) from December 2011 until March 2012 and then froze the next two stages of signing and ratification while negotiations continued toward Ukraine fulfilling a host of criteria, including releasing political prisoners. The next two stages—the European Council's signing of the association agreement and its recommendation to the European Parliament and the twenty-eight member states to ratify it in their parliaments—only went ahead after the Euromaidan.[33]

The Eastern Partnership unveiled in 2009 by Sweden and Poland reached out to six CIS (former Soviet) states on the EU's eastern border of whom only three—Georgia, Moldova, and Ukraine—pursued European association agreements. The association agreement and DCFTA provided paths for European integration without membership. The EU was offering what has been described as "enlargement-lite,"[34] that is, integration without membership. Pro-enlargement members of the EU, such as Poland, Sweden, and the United Kingdom, viewed the Eastern Partnership as a stepping-stone to full membership while Germany, Netherlands, and Italy strongly opposed offering membership to Ukraine.

While the "stick" was represented by the difficult and painful reforms Ukraine had to undertake, the two "carrots" were visa-free travel to the EU and access to the EU market. Countries can only be inside one customs union and Georgia; Moldova's and Ukraine's membership of the EU Customs Union rules out their integration into Putin's CIS Customs Union/Eurasian Economic Union. The Euromaidan leadership that came to power after Yanukovych and his cronies fled to Russia signed the political component of the association agreement in March 2014 and the DCFTA in June. The European and Ukrainian parliaments simultaneously ratified the association agreement in September 2014.

Critical Challenges

Ukraine faces three critical challenges: national integration, deepening the rule of law and fighting corruption, and European integration. These three challenges have become both easier and more difficult since 2014. They have become easier through the implosion of the pro-Russian camp because of Yanukovych's kleptocratic and murderous behavior and Putin's aggression, Ukraine's election of its most pro-European parliament, the growth of patriotism and national integration, positive steps toward the rule of law and fighting corruption, and Ukraine's signing of an association agreement, DCFTA, and visa-free regime with the EU. On the negative side, Putin's aggression has annexed Ukrainian territory, including valuable economic and energy assets; destroyed the economy, infra-structure, and housing in the Donbas; killed upward of 30,000 civilians and combatants; and created nearly 2 million IDPs and refugees. At the same time as record numbers of Ukrainians support NATO and EU membership, these two organizations have closed the door on further enlargement and for a country with some of its territory occupied by a foreign power.

During the nearly quarter century since Ukraine became an independent state, national integration progressed in the first decade, when national democrats and centrists were united, and declined during the second and third decades. Confrontation between Eastern and Western Ukraine dominated each election held from 2002 to 2012, especially in presidential elections, in which the second round was inevitably a contest between candidates from the two halves of Ukraine. The 2014 elections (similar to those held in December 1991) were an exception to this rule as a candidate won in the first round with support from throughout Ukraine (Kravchuk in 1991 and Poroshenko in 2014).

Whereas President Kuchma sought to build bridges between Eastern and Western Ukraine, national-identity policies pursued by Presidents Yushchenko and Yanukovych (coupled with antidemocratic policies against the opposition by the latter) deepened regional divisions and undermined national integration. Yushchenko focused excessively on memory politics which when dealing with the *holodomor* is not controversial but when dealing with Ukrainian nationalist groups is for Eastern Ukrainians; the latter focus also harmed relations with Poland. Yanukovych, in turn, went in the opposite direction and in line with Russian demands, Sovietized national identity and memory politics. Ukrainian nationalists were castigated using Soviet-style rhetoric, the *holodomor* was downplayed as one of many famines throughout the USSR brought about by collectivization, and the myth of the Great Patriotic War was reinstated with Soviet emblems. It is little wonder that Euromaidan protestors supported democratization, European integration, and national identity questions, and Ukrainian nationalists went to war with what they viewed as a Sovietophile regime.

Weak national integration harms the pursuit of declared objectives, be they political and economic reforms or European integration, and has the potential to lead to regional or ethnic conflict. Putin's aggression has through the greater integration of Russian speakers strengthened Ukrainian national integration between Eastern and Western Ukraine and helped to build a civic nation. The views of Eastern and Southern Ukrainians (outside the Donbas and Crimea) have become closer to those of Central Ukrainians. At the same time, the weakness of Ukrainian political parties has prevented the spread of their influence into the east and south where a political vacuum exists following the implosion of pro-Russian forces. Poroshenko's reliance on the discredited old guard to continue to run the east and south has not made the task of democratizing and Europeanizing the most Sovietized regions of Ukraine easier. The Euromaidan leaders and President Poroshenko also face the major task of building bridges to Russian-occupied Donbas.

The second critical challenge is facilitating the rule of law, which forms the basis of a democratic state and market economy, and fighting corruption. Lustration of Ukraine's judicial system began only after the Euromaidan. The bloated twenty-thousand-strong general prosecutor's office, the equivalent of the US attorney's office, should be disbanded and replaced as it cannot be reformed. The overwhelming majority of general prosecutors have been corrupted, including the first three appointed since the Euromaidan. The fourth, general prosecutor Yuriy Lutsenko, who was appointed in May 2016, had no legal training and was a Poroshenko loyalist. There has been progress with the establishment of new institutions—the National Anti-Corruption Bureau, e-declarations for state officials to declare their incomes and assets, and ProZorro to ensure transparency in competition for government contracts. But, the absence of criminal convictions shows that Ukrainian elites continue to remain above the law; hence, there is a need for a specialized anti-corruption court. High levels of graft and lack of elite accountability discourage the payment of taxes (as in Italy and Greece), encourage employment in the massive shadow economy, and lead to low levels of popular trust in state institutions.

European reforms of the Interior Ministry and SBU, including vast reductions in their manpower levels, are essential to prevent future potential authoritarians from dismantling democracy, as took place during Yanukovych's presidency. As noted above, there has been progress in transforming the bloated Soviet-era *Militsiya* into a smaller, more professional European police force, and public trust in the National Guard and police force is growing.

The third challenge is managing expectations about integration into transatlantic and European structures. Ukraine missed its opportunity to receive a MAP in 2006, and since then the opportunities for entering NATO's antechamber that prepares countries for membership have become more difficult. Although the 2008 NATO summit stated that Ukraine and Georgia would one day become members, it did not offer MAPs or an accession date. With opposition to NATO membership at an all-time low and support for membership at an all-time high, Ukraine has for more to offer to NATO than Montenegro or Macedonia, which were invited to join NATO despite their regional diversities.

Ukraine's only short-term option is therefore to pursue the same policy of NATO "enlargement-lite" as it has been forced to pursue in the case of the EU. That involves undertaking as much cooperation with NATO as possible, especially drawing on NATO expertise to modernize Ukraine's combined half million military and security forces.

The EU never offered Ukraine a membership path and, with the EU in crisis, enlargement is opposed by a large number of influential member states. With an association agreement, DCFTA, and visa-free regime, Ukraine has therefore been offered the most it can receive in the short term from the EU. Difficult and unpopular reforms demanded by the EU's "enlargement-lite" will over time have important and positive ramifications on Ukrainian society.

Successful policies toward these three critical challenges are more likely following the Euromaidan than they were after the Orange Revolution because of the desire not to repeat its failures, the strength of civil society, as well as the backing of the West in general, and reforms undertaken within the confines of the EU association agreement. As was the case in Ireland in its desire to overcome centuries of British colonialism and Spain, Portugal, and Greece when they overthrew fascist dictatorships and military juntas, European integration represents the only manner in which Ukraine can overcome its deep-seated totalitarian and colonial legacies.

Study Questions

1. Why is national integration important for the success of reforms and European integration in Ukraine and more broadly in other countries with regional diversity?
2. Compare the Orange Revolution and Euromaidan. What factors made the Euromaidan Revolution more violent, and will its aftermath produce more reforms and reduce corruption?
3. What in the Soviet experience makes Ukrainian political parties continue to be weak, as are parties throughout Central and Eastern Europe and in Eurasia?

4. Why have deep levels of corruption persisted in Ukraine, and how does this impact the rule of law, political system, and economy? What examples exist of successful policies implemented by similarly corrupt states to reduce corruption?
5. What were Putin's objectives in Ukraine, and did he achieve any of them when he annexed Crimea and unleashed military aggression against Ukraine?
6. How will Putin's aggression against Ukraine affect Ukrainian-Russian relations?
7. Why has the EU's response to Putin's actions in Ukraine been divided?

Suggested Readings

Alexeyeva, Lyudmilla. "Ukrainian National Movement," In *Soviet Dissent: Contemporary Movements for National, Religious, and Human Rights*. Middletown, CT: Wesleyan University Press, 1985.

Aslund, Anders. *Ukraine: What Went Wrong and How to Fix It*. Washington, DC: Peterson Institute of International Relations, 2015.

Bukkvoll, Tor. "Why Putin Went to War: Ideology, Interests and Decision-Making in the Russian Use of Force in Crimea and Donbas." *Contemporary Politics* 22, no. 3 (2016): 267–82.

Dragneva, Rilka, and Kataryna Wolczuk. *Ukraine between the EU and Russia. The Integration Challenge*. London: Palgrave Macmillan, 2015.

Fournier, Anna. "Mapping Identities: Russian Resistance to Linguistic Ukrainianisation in Central and Eastern Ukraine." *Europe-Asia Studies* 54, no. 3 (2002): 415–33.

Kudelia, Serhiy, and Taras Kuzio. "Nothing Personal: Explaining the Rise and Decline of Political Machines in Ukraine." *Post-Soviet Affairs* 30, no. 6 (December 2014): 1–29.

Kulyk, Volodymyr. "National Identity in Ukraine: Impact of Euromaidan and the War." *Europe-Asia Studies* 68, no. 4 (June 2016): 588–608.

Kuzio, T. "Impediments to the Emergence of Political Parties in Ukraine." *Politics* 34, no. 3 (2014): 1–15.

———. *Putin's War against Ukraine. Revolution, Nationalism, and Crime*. Toronto: Chair of Ukrainian Studies, 2017.

———. "Ukraine 'Experts' in the West and Putin's Military Aggression: A New Academic 'Orientalism'?" *Cicero Foundation Great Debate Paper*, no. 17/06 (September 2017). http://www.cicerofoundation.org/lectures/Kuzio_Western_Experts_on_Russian_Aggression_Ukraine.pdf.

Kuzio, T., and Paul D'Anieri. *The Sources of Russia's Great Power Politics: Ukraine and the Challenge to the European Order*. Bristol: E-International Relations, 2018.

Mitrokhin, Nikolay. "Infiltration, Instruction, Invasion: Russia's War in the Donbass." *Journal of Soviet and Post-Soviet Politics and Society* 1, no. 1 (2015): 219–49.

Wilson, Andrew. *Ukraine's Orange Revolution*. New Haven, CT: Yale University Press, 2005.

———. "The Donbas in 2014: Explaining Civil Conflict Perhaps, but Not Civil War." *Europe-Asia Studies* 68, no. 4 (2016): 631–52.

Websites

Chesno (Honesty): http://www.chesno.org (Ukrainian NGO that monitors members of parliament)

Kyiv Post: http://www.kyivpost.com (Ukraine's only English-language newspaper)

OpenDemocracy, "Ukraine": http://www.opendemocracy.net/countries/ukraine (analysis of democracy questions in the world)

Opora: http://oporaua.org/en (Ukrainian civil network that specializes in election monitoring)

Radio Free Europe/Radio Liberty, "Latest Ukraine News": http://www.rferl.org/section/ukraine/164.html

Transitions Online, "Ukraine": http://www.tol.org/client/search-by-country/26-ukraine.html

Vox Ukraine: https://voxukraine.org/en/

Notes

1. Timothy Snyder, "The Soviet Famines," chap. 1 in *Bloodlands: Europe between Hitler and Stalin.* (New York: Basic Books, 2010), 21–58.

2. Tadeusz A. Olszanski, *Ukraine: Ambitious De-Communization Laws and One Year of Ukraine's De-Communisation. A Change in the Historical Narrative* (Warsaw: Center for Eastern Studies, April 15, 2015, and May 18, 2016), https://www.osw.waw.pl/en/publikacje/analyses/2015-04-15/ukraine-ambitious-de-communisation-laws and https://www.osw.waw.pl/en/publikacje/osw-commentary/2016-05-18/one-year-ukraines-de-communisation-a-change-historical.

3. A full report on the implementation of the decommunization laws over the two years since their adoption was produced by the Agency for Legislative Initiatives NGO, http://parlament.org.ua/2017/11/01/reforma-u-sferi-polityky-pam-yati-promizhni-pidsumky-vykonannya-dekomunizatsijnyh-zakoniv-shadow-report/.

4. "Ukraine: Mounting Evidence of Abduction and Torture," Amnesty International, July 10, 2014, http://www.amnesty.ca/news/news-releases/ukraine-mounting-evidence-of-abduction-and-torture; "Ukraine: Rebel Forces Detain, Torture Civilians," Human Rights Watch, August 28, 2014, http://www.hrw.org/news/2014/08/28/ukraine-rebel-forces-detain-torture-civilians; and "New Evidence of Summary Killings of Ukrainian Soldiers Must Spark Urgent Investigations," Amnesty International, April 9, 2015, https://www.amnesty.org/en/latest/news/2015/04/ukraine-new-evidence-of-summary-killings-of-captured-soldiers-must-spark-urgent-investigations/.

5. See Lucan Way, "The Real Causes of the Color Revolutions," *Journal of Democracy* 19, no. 3 (2008): 55–69, and responses by Sharon Wolchik and Valeriy Bunce, Mark R. Beissinger, Martin K. Dimitrov, Charles H. Fairbanks, Vitalii Silitski, and L. Way, *Journal of Democracy* 20, no. 1 (2009): 69–97.

6 Nadia Diuk, "The Triumph of Civil Society" and Olena Prytula, "The Ukrainian Media Rebellion" in A. Aslund and Michael McFaul, *Revolution in Orange. The Origins of Ukraine's Democratic Breakthrough* (Washington DC: Carnegie Endowment for International Peace, 2006), 69–84, 103–24.

7. http://blogs.pravda.com.ua/authors/nayem/529a675c6dc20/.

8. Rosaria Puglisi, "Heroes or Villains? Volunteer Battalions in Post-Maidan Ukraine" (IAI working paper, no. 15, Instituto Affari Internazionali, Rome, March 8, 2015), http://www.iai.it/sites/default/files/iaiwp1508.pdf.

9. A. Aslund, *How Ukraine Became a Market Economy and Democracy* (Washington, DC: Peterson Institute of International Relations, 2009).

10. J.S. Hellman, "Winners Take All: The Politics of Partial Reform in Postcommunist Transitions," *World Politics* 50, no. 2 (1998): 203–34.

11. J.S. Hellman, "Winners Take All.'

12. http://www.heritage.org/index/.

13. R. Puglisi, "The Rise of the Ukrainian Oligarchs," *Democratization* 10, no. 3 (2003): 99–123.

14. Keith Darden, "The Integrity of Corrupt States: Graft as an Informal State Institution," *Politics and Society* 36, no. 1 (2008): 35–59.

15. Office of Public Affairs, "Six Defendants Indicted in Alleged Conspiracy to Bribe Government Officials in India to Mine Titanium Minerals," Department of Justice, April 2, 2014, http://www.justice.gov/opa/pr/2014/April/14-crm-333.html.

16. "Putin's Allies Channeled Billions to Ukraine Oligarch," *Reuters*, November 26, 2014, http://uk.reuters.com/article/russia-capitalism-gas-special-report-pix-idUKL3N0TF4QD20141126; and US Embassy Kyiv, "Ukraine: Firtash Makes His Case to the USG,"' *WikiLeaks*, December 10, 2008, https://wikileaks.org/plusd/cables/08KYIV2414_a.html.

17. "До 2050 року українців залишиться 36 мільйонів," *Pravda*, July 10, 2013, http://www.pravda.com.ua/news/2013/07/10/6993962.

18. "Ukraine," World Bank, http://www.worldbank.org/en/country/ukraine; and United Nations Development Program in Ukraine at http://www.ua.undp.org/ukraine/en/home.html.

19. http://web.worldbank.org/WBSITE/EXTERNAL/TOPICS/EXTPOVERTY/EXTPA/0,,contentMDK:20205446~menuPK:435735~pagePK:148956~piPK:216618~theSitePK:430367,00.html.

20. https://www.opendemocracy.net/5050/francesca-ebel/has-ukraines-revolution-of-dignity-left-women-behind.

21. https://www.theguardian.com/world/2010/mar/24/ukraine-mykola-azarov-women.

22. The argument was first developed by Paul R. Magocsi in his "The Ukrainian National Revival: A New Analytical Framework," *Canadian Review of Studies in Nationalism* 16, no. 102 (1989): 45–62.

23. T. Kuzio, *Russian–Ukrainian Relations: From Friendship of Peoples to War. Russian Analytical Digest no. 203* (Zurich: Centre for Security Studies, May 2017), http://www.css.ethz.ch/content/specialinterest/gess/cis/center-for-securities-studies/en/publications/rad/details.html?id=/n/o/2/0/no_203_russia_and_the_ukraine.

24. T. Kuzio, "Ukraine: Coming to Terms with the Soviet Legacy," *Journal of Communist Studies and Transition Politics* 14, no. 4 (1998): 1–27.

25. US Embassy Kyiv, "Ukraine: Crimea Update—Less Tense Than in 2006: Interethnic, Russia, Land Factors Remain Central," *WikiLeaks*, June 8, 2007, http://wikileaks.org/cable/2007/06/07KYIV1418.html.

26. T. Kuzio, "Crime, Politics and Business in 1990s Ukraine," *Communist and Post-Communist Politics* 47, no. 2 (2014): 195–210.

27. The open letter is available in Russian at "Послание Президенту Украины Виктору Ющенко," August 11, 2009, http://www.kremlin.ru/news/5158.

28. See polls by the Razumkov Center in *National Security and Defense*, nos. 8–9, 2015. http://old.razumkov.org.ua/eng/files/category_journal/UA_Rosiya_8_9-2015-ENG.compressed.pdf.

29. A. Aslund, *How Ukraine Became a Market Economy and Democracy*, 89.

30. http://uacrisis.org/58251-69-ukrayintsiv-pidtrymuyut-vstup-nato.

31. http://old.razumkov.org.ua/eng/poll.php?poll_id=1030.

32. http://old.razumkov.org.ua/eng/poll.php?poll_id=1030.

33. Slawomir Matuszak and Arkadiusz Sarna, *From Stabilisation to Stagnation: Viktor Yanukovych's Reforms*, Point of View 32 (Warsaw: Centre for Eastern Studies, March 2013). http://www.osw.waw.pl/en/publikacje/policy-briefs/2013-03-12/stabilisation-to-stagnation-viktor-yanukovychs-reforms.

34. Nicu Popescu and Andrew Wilson, *The Limits of Enlargement-Lite: European and Russian Power in the Troubled Neighbourhood* (London: European Council on Foreign Relations, June 2009), http://ecfr.eu/page/-/ECFR14_The_Limits_of_Enlargement-Lite._European_and_Russian_Power_in_the_Troubled_Neighbourhood.pdf.

Part IV

CONCLUSION

CHAPTER 18

Thirty Years after 1989

A BALANCE SHEET

Sharon L. Wolchik and Jane Leftwich Curry

Nearly thirty years after the fall of communism, as this volume was being completed, the miracle of the peaceful transformations of these states from communism to democracy and from in the Soviet bloc to, for most, in the North Atlantic Treaty Organization (NATO) and the European Union (EU) as members, remains. However, the rise of populist parties and their success in taking control in Poland and Hungary, which were among the first states to democratize, has demonstrated the fragility of democracy in these (and, potentially, other) Central and East European states. At the same time, while it is clear that most of these states, with the notable exceptions of Ukraine, firmly "returned to Europe," it is also clear that the legacies of their histories, particularly under communism, and their transitions keep them from being "just like Western Europe," even though they all sport sparkling malls, high rises, and all the accoutrements of democracy and capitalism—competitive elections, stock markets, critical media, and goods from Western Europe.

All of these initial changes seemed impossible dreams until 1989 when the collapse of communism and the disintegration of the Soviet bloc surprised almost everyone: the communist leaders and the oppositions of Central and Eastern Europe, Western and Soviet politicians, and observers and scholars of the area. The daily headlines of the *New York Times* heralded the changes as "the Year of Freedom." US and West European foreign policy initially turned from fighting communism to helping these new democracies develop their institutions through "democracy promotion" activities as well as move from command to market economies. Almost all of them, except the states of former Yugoslavia that fought with each other, seemed to have succeeded by the end of their first decade. The successful cases helped incipient democracies in the region make their transitions and established a model for Western assistance to states elsewhere in the world that wanted to democratize.

The end of communism throughout this region was followed by efforts to create or re-create democracy, establish market economies, and earn recognition once again as part of Europe. All these Central and East European states had bumps in the road to consolidating their democracies, but, until now, few have gone off the road. In part, these bumps reflected the legacies of their early histories and the communist period, whether they had "communism lite," as in Yugoslavia and, for significant periods, in Hungary and Poland, or the more draconian communism that Albania, Bulgaria, Czechoslovakia, East Germany, Romania, Ukraine, and the Baltic states experienced until after Mikhail Gorbachev came to power. They also reflected the complicated nature of the tasks leaders faced in simultaneously transforming their countries' politics, economies, social welfare systems, and foreign policies. In addition, ethnic divisions, papered over under communist rule, came to the fore with the transitions: Czechoslovakia split in a peaceful "Velvet Divorce," and Yugoslavia, following a series of wars and NATO intervention, broke up into seven separate states. Now, in the twenty-first century, the politics in a number of these states is increasingly bitterly split by the cultural and economic differences between those who gained from the economic transition and becoming part of the West and those who feel they lost because that transition undercut the social supports they depended on and undercut their positions in these societies. Many of them are now the base for populist parties that are challenging the democratic rules of their states.

The international environment changed dramatically as well. Within two years of the collapse of communism in Central and Eastern Europe, the Soviet Union no longer existed. The foreign policies of these new states turned to the West. But the shifts of power in Europe that began in 1989 in most of Central and Eastern Europe and continued in 1991 with the collapse of the Soviet Union were not set in stone. In the aftermath of the 2013–2014 Euromaidan demonstrations in Kyiv, the fragility of at least some parts of the new Europe was made more than clear. Vladimir Putin's illegal annexation of Crimea, following what was, at best, a sham referendum held after Russians fomented separatist actions, challenged the turn from the East to the West. After this annexation, the first forcible change of European borders since World War II, Russian separatists, armed and trained by Russia and, in late August 2014, joined by Russian troops, fought in eastern and southern Ukraine as additional Russian troops massed on the border. Putin's warning that he would, if necessary, intervene to protect Russians in other states put the Baltic states, particularly Latvia and Estonia which have significant Russian populations, on notice. NATO, the EU, and the United States responded with a series of sanctions and warnings to Russia that have had little impact on Putin's actions in Ukraine. It has thus become clear that Russia is now a player not just in the politics of Ukraine but in the security concerns of all of Central and Eastern Europe, as well as NATO, Western Europe, and the United States, as Putin's actions have challenged the post–World War II international order. As a result of Russian aggression in Ukraine, since 2017, NATO troops have been stationed on the Russian border in Poland, the Baltic states, Romania, and Bulgaria.

The return of Russia as a significant player in this area happened only recently. In 1989, the Soviet Union was too weak to hold back change in Central and Eastern Europe. Instead, with the implicit Soviet blessing of Gorbachev's Sinatra Doctrine, its former satellites simply ended communist rule and withdrew from the Warsaw Pact military alliance and the Comecon economic union, and the Baltic states began to reject Soviet control visibly. In the past quarter century, Russia regained its economic footing due, in large part, to the increased price of energy through the mid-2000s. Russia's ruler, Vladimir Putin, has used this new wealth and control of the oil and natural gas supplies to many of the countries in Central and Eastern Europe as well as several farther west to strengthen his base in Russia, expand his control to weaker post-Soviet states, and increase Russia's presence in international bodies. He also sought to definitively put down mass mobilization and protest in Russia. Although he clearly has not been able to turn back the clock in the states that have become part of NATO and the EU, Russia has been more and more bellicose. And, in recent years, Russia has begun to play a more direct role in other countries' domestic politics with "fake news" presented through apparently independent internet and standard media sources it controls and increased contacts with politicians in Central and East European states, including Hungary. Their intent has been clearly to destabilize these states' democracies.

Initial Gains and Later Setbacks

The euphoria of the men and women on the streets from Berlin to Bucharest and in the rest of the world was palpable in 1989 and 1991. Most thought creating or re-creating democracy would be a matter of shifting to life without the shackles and hardships of communism and would guarantee them prosperity and the "good life." In actuality, the change was not as easy as many expected. Prosperity did not necessarily follow for most in these populations and democracy proved hard to make work. The resulting disappointments and memories of the communist past have continued to impact politics in the area for the last three decades since communism collapsed. As the chapters in this book illustrate, the improvisations and reversals that marked the democratization process have, in many cases, been surprising, even agonizing, and continue even now, almost thirty years later.

The governing political institutions of the countries included in this volume are, on the whole, now similar to those of more established European democracies. The rule of law and guarantees of civil and political liberties and human rights have been formally instituted. Popular support for democracy as a general concept, if not for current political leaders or even institutions, is high, and there is little desire to turn back to communism, although some look back nostalgically to the "good old days" of communist cradle-to-grave social support.

It is also clear that these institutions and values are less stable than they are in most other European democracies. In the 2010 parliamentary election in Hungary, the radical right-wing party, FiDeSz (once a liberal youth movement that helped bring down communism), was voted into power. With a large majority of seats in the parliament, its leader, Viktor Orbán, as prime minister, pushed through limits on the courts, freedom of the media and of expression, as well as economic reforms that cut down on outside investment. Orbán's government encouraged attacks on minority groups such as Jews and Roma. Continued public support for these challenges to democratic structures was undeniable in 2014 when FiDeSz won the election, although it lost its supermajority, and an even more radical right-wing party, Jobbik, became a significant player in parliament. Poland, since the Law and Justice (PiS) victory in both the 2015 parliamentary and presidential elections, has followed the same path of de-democratization as Hungary but at a faster pace. Even the Czech Republic, the postcommunist country that had the most successful experience with democracy before World War II and one of the smoothest economic transitions after the end of communism in 1989, has had periods of division that left it with months of failed attempts to form governments, mired in a corruption scandal that has decreased the credibility of the government, and saw democratic candidates challenged by populists as well as the growth of anti-Islam and anti-refugee groups and activities. This has also happened in Romania, Bulgaria, and Albania.

The shift to a market economy has been completed in almost all of these states. Private enterprises account for the largest share of gross national product, and previously neglected sectors of the economy, such as the service sector, continue to grow, as have most of these economies as a whole. The worldwide economic crisis of 2008–2009 did reverberate throughout this area. As chapter 3 illustrates, the impact of this crisis and the severity of the resulting economic disruption varied within the region. It was most severe in Latvia, Hungary, and Ukraine, where gross domestic product plummeted, international investment and credit dried up, and people found themselves owing more than what their property was worth. By the time of this writing in 2017, most of the economies in the region—with the dramatic exception of Ukraine, which found itself deeply in debt and with empty state coffers already in 2013 and is held back by the loss of its industrial and mining area in the east as well as by the ongoing war in that region—have largely recovered, although unemployment remains high, especially among young people. Even prior to the global crisis, however, economic reform and progress had real costs: unemployment and rising inequality have caused hardships for the less well-positioned groups in these societies and led to political backlash in some countries.

Most of the countries examined in this volume—with the notable exception of Ukraine and a number of the states formed after the dissolution of Yugoslavia and Albania in the case of the EU—have also succeeded in joining Euro-Atlantic institutions, most importantly NATO and the EU. As members of these institutions, they achieved their original goal of returning to Europe. They have asserted their independence in the international realm and moved from being recipients of European aid to become players with their own agendas in the EU and, in some cases early on, providers of democracy assistance and other aid to countries to their east. Most recently, Poland and Hungary have been sharply criticized, formally and informally, by these European institutions for their moves away from democratic norms and institutions. Together with the Czech Republic, these states have also been subject to infringement procedures by the EU because of their failure to abide by quotas for accepting refugees determined by the majority of EU members.

The successes and failures of these states in achieving the major points in their political agendas following the end of communism raise new questions. Two of the most important of these concern how we should view these polities now. What role has the communist experience played? And what are the reasons for the pattern of two steps forward, one step back that seems to have emerged even in states that, in the first decade and a half, had been the most successful? These questions have been reflected in the scholarly debates over what frameworks are most useful in guiding the study of and research into politics in these countries now.

Postcommunist or "Normal" European Countries?

In the early years after the end of communism, as detailed in the introduction, the theoretical approaches that most frequently informed our study of these countries were based on the transitions from authoritarian rule in southern Europe and Latin America. These were used despite the many ways in which their earlier systems and these transitions differed from those in the postcommunist world.[1]

As the transitions continued and democratic institutions and processes were established, some scholars of politics in this region came to rely on concepts drawn from studies of politics in more established democracies. These included studies of political values and attitudes, legislatures and their processes, the roles of presidents and other political actors, and electoral behavior. Other scholars used approaches developed in the rest of Europe and the United States to study the development of political parties. Studies of the intersection of politics and the economy, in turn, employed concepts and approaches used by students of political economy in other regions of the world. Increasingly, we became aware of the need to include international actors, such as international and regional organizations and transnational actors and networks, in our analyses of political change in the postcommunist world. To do this, scholars have drawn on the literature on norms in international politics and the role of international organizations, as well as on the democracy-promotion literature.

Many of the studies based on these frameworks, including those by contributors to this volume, have yielded valuable insights into the political process in these countries. At the same time, it soon became clear that use of these approaches based on transitions from authoritarianism and political systems in Western Europe and the United States was not always fruitful. These postcommunist societies had their own problems, and although Central and East European countries had much in common with their Western neighbors and countries that underwent democratization elsewhere, there were and are important differences to consider.

Simply put, these new systems remain products of their special histories. Communist rule was different from the authoritarianism in southern Europe and Latin America. The political systems in place in the postcommunist European states today also differ in certain ways from those of their more established European neighbors. Although there are many similarities in the institutions of both sets of countries, and although the leaders of Central and East European countries face many of the same problems evident elsewhere, it would still be a mistake to lump these systems together with the more established democracies in what we used to call "Western" Europe. Due in part to their particular histories and in part to the demands and opportunities created by the transition, institutions that look similar in the two parts of Europe sometimes operate quite differently if one looks more closely. And, however far they have transitioned from communism, that history and the battles with neighboring states they had even before they were communist remain complicated and, sometimes, debilitating problems.

As the chapters in this book illustrate, the transition from communism seemed to be smoothest in Poland, Hungary, the Czech Republic, Slovenia, and the Baltic states for much of the first decade and a half. But these countries, like others in the region, continue to have weak political parties, fluid party systems, leaders who more often use their office to enrich or gain power for themselves than to serve the public good, and political cultures on the part of elites and citizens with elements at odds with democracy. They also suffer, as do most other countries in the region, from corruption in both the economic and political realms.

In all of these countries, to a greater or lesser extent, politics also has been affected by the economic disaffection of the population. That dissatisfaction has been mirrored by the demise of the political power of the old opposition; by a shift, particularly evident in Poland and Hungary but also in other countries, among many politicians and voters to radical, populist politics; and by the politics of accusations that others were agents or beneficiaries of the communist system. It is ironic that this shift occurred after these countries joined the EU and at a time when their economies were growing faster than most in Europe, until the global economic crisis hit. Poland was the only country in the EU with a gross domestic product that grew during this time period. In the process, its voters initially turned away from radical parties to a party that emphasized rational debate and efficient policy making and, then, in 2015, turned to what appeared to be a right-of-center party focused on ending corruption and ties to the old communist period, Law and Justice, only to have it, once its candidates won the presidency and, effectively, a majority in parliament, pass laws that ended the separation of powers and stripped freedoms away from the media and any who might oppose them. In both cases, international bodies such as the EU have condemned these steps away from democracy although they have not, to date, been able to impose effective sanctions on these backsliders. In the Polish case, there have been mass demonstrations against government moves to delegalize abortion and increased attempts to put the court system under the control of the ruling party. In both cases, at least initially, the national protests ended with some government concessions but did not lead to the formation of a cohesive and strong opposition movement.

In the other countries we have considered in this volume (Slovakia, Romania, Bulgaria, Albania, Ukraine, the Baltic states, and the successors to former Yugoslavia), the shift of power in the late 1980s and early 1990s was not so clear. In many, communist leaders maintained power while claiming to be democrats or nationalists for at least the first set of elections. In others, the initial victory of the opposition was quickly followed by the election of "old forces," or a period of de-democratization. Ostensibly democratic political institutions in these states often did not function democratically, and, as would happen elsewhere in the region later, democratically elected governments sometimes took actions that were decidedly not the norm in more established democracies. Efforts to account for this fact led scholars to describe many of these polities as "illiberal" or "hybrid" democracies.[2] Others termed these systems "semi-authoritarian" or "competitive-authoritarian" systems.[3] Whatever term was used, the basic elements were the same: governments, some of whose leaders were elected in relatively free and fair elections, that acted to restrict the freedom of action of their opponents, attempted to control the media and deny the opposition access, enacted legislation that disadvantaged minorities, worked to discourage the development of civil society, and reinforced values at variance with those supportive of democracy, such as compromise and tolerance.

Some of these states went through democratizing elections. Often termed "electoral" or "color revolutions" due to the tendency of their supporters and leaders to use certain colors as symbols, such as orange in the case of Ukraine, these events involved the mass mobilization of citizens by more unified oppositions in cooperation with nongovernmental organizations and campaigns to encourage citizens to participate in elections and, if necessary, protest in the streets if incumbents tried to steal the elections or failed to yield their offices if defeated. These events, which took place in Slovakia in 1998, Serbia and Croatia in 2000, and Ukraine in 2004, as well as in two countries not covered in this volume (Georgia in 2003 and Kyrgyzstan in 2005), have had different outcomes. With the exception of the latter two cases, the ouster of semi-authoritarian leaders was followed by initial movement, though not always linear or long-term, in a less corrupt and more democratic direction.[4] In Ukraine, these gains were reversed under Viktor Yanukovych, who was fairly elected president in 2010 and turned the country into an even more kleptocratic state than before the Orange Revolution. His turn to Russia precipitated the events that resulted in the Euromaidan protests in 2013 and 2014 and, with the help of Russia, led to the Russian annexation of Crimea after what was, at best, a sham referendum and to a violent conflict in the east and south of the country that is still going on.

Understanding "Democracy" in Central and Eastern Europe

If we adopt a minimal definition of democracy,[5] which requires free and fair elections and the alternation in power of different political groups, then all of the states considered in this volume, with the exception of those parts of former Yugoslavia still under international rule, are democracies. If we adopt a definition of democracy that requires not only democratic political institutions and the rule of law, but also a well-articulated, dense civil society, a well-developed political society that includes political parties and movements that structure political choice for citizens by articulating different policy perspectives and link citizens to the political process, and a functioning market economy to provide resources for individuals and groups independent of the state and to keep the government in check,[6] most of the states under consideration in this volume still have a way to go.

The question that remains is how we can best understand politics in the region now, particularly in those countries that have become part of the EU and NATO. Is it still useful, for example, to see these states as postcommunist? Or, as some have suggested and others fear, have they become "normal, boring European countries?" Václav Havel, for example, once noted that we no longer talk about the United States as a postcolonial country. Why then, he asked, should we continue to talk about the countries of Central and Eastern Europe as postcommunist? We have argued and continue to argue that the term still makes sense, at least in some areas. It is clear that the countries we have focused on in this book share certain characteristics and problems with the more established democracies of "Western" Europe. These similarities can, in fact, be expected to increase as these countries become more integrated into the EU and as generations of young people who have not had any experience with communism come of age politically. To date, though, these young people are focused not on politics but on getting jobs in their own countries or in Western Europe and are split between those who have gotten education and have hope for a prosperous future and those who are "stuck" at the bottom of the economic and social ladder.

At least until that generation comes to power, however, it appears the communist legacy will remain a strong force in politics. The countries analyzed in this book also face additional issues arising from their communist pasts and from the fact that they are newly established or reestablished democracies. Communism was a form of authoritarianism in which the state not only controlled politics but also the economy; communist leaders were not content merely to hold the reins of power but also wanted to transform their citizens into "new socialist men (and women)," at least initially. Mobilizing citizens was important in these systems in which leaders used propaganda, mass political demonstrations, and police control to ensure that there were no public questions or alternatives to the march they claimed to be making to "socialism."

The experience of democratization and the transformation of the economy were often not what people had either hoped for or expected. The lessons they learned under communism and during the period immediately after its collapse have stayed with them. Citizens learned, for example, that the system did not work as it said it did, that they needed to be part of informal groups that helped each other get the goods and services they needed but could not get on the market, and that they could have little voice in politics. In their lives, much happened behind the veil of the secret police and their informers or in a bureaucratic morass about which people had little information. Indeed, people often read the media not for what was said but for what was not. They assumed that democracy and prosperity would be instantly linked; they expected the remaking of the political system and the restructuring of the economy to bring about almost instant gains in their living standards. This improvement did not happen immediately or, for some groups of the population, at all. As a result, democratic institutions and traditions had to be built when people were disillusioned about what they were getting from their new governments. Political leaders also had to deal with citizens who had learned that politics was about appearing to support the top leadership's policies and not expressing their opinions or acting in groups to articulate interests or put pressure on political leaders to take action. Although many, if not most, citizens had seen through the claims of communism, they had also come, in some cases unconsciously, to expect the state to provide a wide array of services, however basic.

These legacies remain in the often high levels of popular alienation and anger at systems that did not meet their expectations, higher levels of corruption rooted in the lessons of surviving by "living outside the law," and high levels of distrust in politicians and democratic institutions. Some of their leaders, most clearly the new right-wing populist leaders in Hungary and Poland, have also fallen back on the old ways of government control of the courts and media, limits on free expression and association, and the use of police and other threats to control or attack the opposition which they see, as did the communist rulers, as a danger to their power rather than the norm in a democratic state. Although alienation and a loss of faith in politicians and political institutions as well as rulers' moves for control have appeared in other democratic systems, their roots are different and they have been less acute. These differences still make it difficult to simply use concepts and approaches borrowed from studies of political phenomena in more established democracies in some areas. And when these are used, differences often appear.

As the chapters in this volume indicate, even in states that were early democratizers, such as the Baltic states, Slovenia, Hungary, Poland, and the Czech Republic, the future is not entirely clear. To a greater or lesser degree, a gulf remains between the rulers and the ruled. Parties and party systems are still fluid in most states, and citizens have low levels of party identification and loyalty. They also tend to have lower levels of political efficacy than their counterparts in more established democracies.

Even prior to the recent economic crisis, when many of these economies had high growth rates, levels of economic performance and the functioning of social welfare systems did not please many citizens. This dissatisfaction has only increased as economic growth stopped or plummeted and governments struggled to stay afloat. Disenchantment with the "lived" democracy and capitalism that developed out of the transitions has led to a search, in most of these countries, for someone or something to blame. Ethnic conflicts are often more dramatic not only because they were allowed to fester by being papered over in the communist period but also because people search for the reason their systems are not doing what they hoped. Many citizens also question how best to deal with the past and puzzle about what to do about increasing inequality. The conflation of these two issues, egged on by the rhetoric of the right, has increased the sense among many that the systems are unfair and that punishing and lustrating former communists has not been done thoroughly enough. Other European governments also face a number of these questions, but they are particularly acute in the postcommunist region.

Membership in European and Euro-Atlantic institutions strengthened, at least initially, movement in a more democratic direction in many of these areas. Generational change may also accelerate this process, particularly as those young people who have made good use of ample opportunities to travel and study or work abroad come into positions of political responsibility. There is no guarantee of this, however, given the high unemployment levels of youth in many countries and the decrease in the number of young people both because of out-migration and the drop in the birthrate at the end of communism and during the first years of the transition. Further complicating all of this is the pressure by the EU on these countries to take in Syrian and other refugees since 2015. Most of their governments have been unwilling to do this given both the level of unemployment in their own countries and long-established biases against refugees from the Middle East and Africa.

EU membership itself also poses new issues and demands for leaders and citizens in these countries. As part of the broader community, political leaders in the postcommunist EU member states obviously will also face many of the same challenges as their counterparts in other advanced industrial societies. As the section to follow discusses more fully, the postcommunist states in particular also face challenges in the international realm.

Central and Eastern Europe in the World: New Roles and Concerns

Central and East European countries have, since 1989, shifted their sights and ties west and away from Russia. Even before communism collapsed in each of these states, European and American aid and trade with the states of the former Soviet bloc had increased substantially. In 1990, those in the Warsaw Pact military alliance and Comecon broke with what was then the Soviet Union. The goal of the new leaders was to go further and "return to Europe" by joining both NATO and the EU. Achieving this goal required significant changes in everything from their military equipment and training to their laws regarding civil rights to their economies. To accomplish all this, the states seeking membership received significant aid from the EU and NATO states. In the end, this created the incentives and resources for Central and East European states, as they entered, to meet West European standards and become full players in the politics of Europe and NATO. Yugoslavia, although it had, under Tito, the closest ties with the West, was not part of this process as it was mired in the wars of succession that ultimately, in the cases of Bosnia and Kosovo, resulted in a representative of the international community holding supreme power in Bosnia and NATO actions against the Serbs. These new states—with the exception of Slovenia, which joined the EU in 2004, and Croatia and Montenegro, which joined in 2013—are still in the process of preparing for EU membership. Slovenia, Croatia, and Montenegro are also the only states of former Yugoslavia that are members of NATO. Of the states covered in this volume, only Ukraine remains outside membership talks with the EU and NATO. Membership in the EU, much less NATO, was not seriously contemplated for Ukraine because of its long border with Russia. But the EU did provide aid and training to Ukraine and, after the Euromaidan protests, signed an agreement with Ukraine.

The states that have succeeded in joining Euro-Atlantic institutions, most importantly the EU and NATO, have achieved their original goal of returning to the European stage. Those that surrendered part of their sovereignty to an outside power, this time voluntarily, by joining the EU and NATO were, by the turn of the century, beginning to play significant roles in both organizations to the point that Donald Tusk of Poland became the President of the European Council. But the increasing strength of the Russian economy and Putin's control has begun to challenge a "new world order" in which the world is not divided between superpowers. The events in Ukraine and Russia's threat that it will protect Russians wherever they are have made clear that Russia can pose a real challenge to Europe and particularly to states like Ukraine and the Baltics, where there are significant Russian-speaking populations. The crisis in Ukraine has also pointed out the lack of viable responses to Russian power beyond sanctions—given the West's reluctance to engage directly in response to Russia's annexation of Crimea, fomenting of separatist unrest in eastern Ukraine, and invasion of Ukraine in 2014—due to the dependence of much of Europe, west and east, on Russian oil and natural gas, Europe's strong trade ties with Russia, and fear of the unpredictability of Russia's leaders, given Russia's status as a nuclear power.

Despite these challenges, membership in the EU has been a significant change in international relations for both those that have joined and others that have yet to accede or that are unlikely to become members in the near future. With membership, postcommunist European states, like earlier members, have voluntarily taken on obligations that impose certain limitations on their freedom of action.

Although the states of Central and Eastern Europe that have joined the EU hold fewer European Parliament seats than the older members, they have played a larger role in the politics of the EU than their numbers would suggest. A number of states like Poland have elected a significant proportion of Euroskeptic deputies who shifted the balance of power to the right. However, the EU remained committed to admitting more of the states covered in this volume, however costly this has been. Since the timetable for entrance had been set, Romania and Bulgaria were allowed to join in 2007, even though there were huge gaps between the formal standards for EU accession and actual practice in areas such as transparency, control of corruption, and judicial reform. These countries were accepted but remain subject to continued monitoring in these realms. In Bulgaria, in fact, failure to address the corruption that pervades economic and political life led to the temporary suspension of EU funds in 2008. Not only have representatives been active in pushing their agendas, but Poland, particularly, took on the role of serving as the "bridge to the east," advocating for more support for former Soviet states like Ukraine. In addition, by now, eight Central and East European states have held the presidency of the EU. In spite of their positions, though, the Central and East European states, along with Austria, have started the Three Seas Initiative to form a block of states between the Baltic, Adriatic, and Black Seas that will work to strengthen north–south links in the energy and transportation sectors as well as advocating for these smaller states in the EU.

Within the EU, some of the poorer states were concerned about the cost of preparing these former communist states for entrance. In addition, there was initially a fear among many of the original members that the local labor markets of the original states would be flooded with workers from the new member states, where unemployment is far higher and wages are far lower. In France, in fact, this fear of "Polish plumbers" was one reason for the defeat of the EU constitutional referendum in May 2005. A number of states were allowed to delay permanent work permits for those coming from Poland and elsewhere in Central and Eastern Europe for up to seven years. In the states that did not put restrictions on foreign workers—Ireland, England, and the Scandinavian countries—this influx occurred. Some stayed after the European recession took hold in 2008, but many others returned to their home countries with newfound skills. Then, workers who had taken jobs in England and stayed were part of the irritant that triggered the vote for Brexit in 2016.

Countries that border post-Soviet states other than the Baltics have created a porous border through which many desperate workers come from Ukraine and beyond. Although the EU funded one of the most secure border fences in the world between Poland and Ukraine, Poland has maintained a "good neighbor policy" with Ukraine and others. So Ukrainians and Belarusians can get visas to work in Poland for three months at a time at virtually no cost. Once in Poland, since the Schengen Treaty allows for the free flow of peoples within the EU, those who do not find jobs in Poland or who want to go further west travel freely on to Germany and elsewhere in Europe as their passports are not checked at borders. In addition, the border trade in cheap goods between Poland and Ukraine and Belarus has continued to help the poor, less industrialized regions of Poland survive. This is also the case, to a lesser degree, in Romania.

Even as they have succeeded in "returning to Europe," Central and East European states have been a key element of US foreign policy as well. Their transformation itself was a major issue in US foreign policy and also served as a platform and model for US aid to be used in democracy promotion. In the years immediately after 1989, non- and quasi-governmental organizations in the United States and Western Europe joined the US and European governments in providing funds and expertise related to many aspects of the transition. Activists from many of these countries, including, but not limited to, those that experienced early democratizing elections such as Slovakia and Serbia, have subsequently played important roles in supporting democratization in other semi-authoritarian countries by sharing their experiences, strategies, and techniques, in many cases with US funding. A number of countries in the region have committed their own resources to these efforts by targeting all or part of the development funds EU members are required to set aside for these efforts.

EU members, as well as those countries that still aspire to join that organization, also face the sometimes difficult task of reconciling their desire for, as many put it, "more Europe and more United States," or good relations both with other members of the EU and with the United States. A number of countries in the region sent troops or peacekeepers to Afghanistan; the governments of some also bucked both domestic public opinion and the attitudes of several other EU members, most notably France and Germany, by sending troops or otherwise supporting the US war in Iraq. Romania and Poland housed secret prisons where high-level terrorism subjects were tortured in the early years of the war on terrorism, and they were willing to house installations of the antimissile shield proposed by the George W. Bush administration in the United States, despite strong domestic as well as Russian opposition, until the plans were cancelled by the Barack Obama administration. Donald Trump's visit to Poland was seen, in 2017, as a demonstration of his commitment to strengthening US ties with some governments, like Poland's, that had been criticized for their retreat from democracy by Obama and a move to strengthen economic ties with this area. The leaders of several postcommunist members of the EU have expressed a desire for strong transatlantic relations, but this task can be expected to remain a difficult one when EU and US perspectives and objectives clash.

Although there is no way the clock will turn back for the states that are part of NATO and the EU, Russia's increased involvement poses new dilemmas for member countries. It is clear that Russia is now a player in the politics not just of Ukraine but in the security concerns and domestic politics of much, if not all, of Central and Eastern Europe, as well as NATO and the EU.

What Next?

As illustrated by this brief overview of some of this volume's main conclusions and of the utility of various theoretical frameworks for the study of the region's politics, including the very designation "postcommunist," leaders and citizens of the formerly communist countries in Central and Eastern Europe have achieved both more and less than might have been expected in 1989 or 1991; however, not all of their achievements have been permanent. The postcommunist European countries we have considered in this book face problems that are peculiar to postcommunist states and also ones that are common to other European or, more broadly, democratic governments. Their success in achieving the main goals outlined at the beginning of the transition period testifies to the ingenuity, sacrifice, and vision of both leaders and citizens. But while the gains made since 1989 are impressive in many ways, these countries still differ in important ways from their European counterparts that did not have a communist past.

In 2010, we concluded that despite these differences, these countries had become or were on their way to becoming "normal" European countries. In 2014 and to an even greater degree as we close this volume in 2017, this answer seems too optimistic, and their futures appear less clear. Although we would still argue that most of the countries in the region are on a trajectory to becoming "normal" European countries, the setbacks that have occurred in the recent past in some and the ongoing challenges all face suggest that their politics will be far from boring and that they will deserve our continued attention for some time to come.

Notes

1. For arguments that advocate this approach, see Philippe C. Schmitter with Terry Lynn Karl, "The Conceptual Travels of Transitologists and Consolidologists: How Far to the East Should They Attempt to Go?" *Slavic Review* 53, no. 1 (Spring 1994): 173–85. For arguments against this approach, see Valerie J. Bunce, "Should Transitologists Be Grounded?" *Slavic Review* 54, no. 1 (Spring 1995): 111–27. See also Juan J. Linz and Alfred Stepan, *Problems of Democratic Transition and Consolidation: Southern Europe, South America, and Post-Communist Europe* (Baltimore, MD: Johns Hopkins University Press, 1996); and Adam Przeworski, *Democracy and the Market* (New York: Cambridge University Press, 1991).

2. See Fareed Zakaria, *The Future of Freedom: Illiberal Democracy at Home and Abroad* (New York: W. W. Norton, 2004); Thomas Carothers, "The End of the Transition Paradigm," *Journal of Democracy* 13 (January 2002): 5–21; Larry Diamond, "Thinking about Hybrid Regimes," *Journal of Democracy* 13 (January 2002): 21–35; Andreas Schedler, "The Menu of Manipulation," *Journal of Democracy* 13 (January 2002): 36–50; and Steven Levitsky and Lucan A. Way, "The Rise of Competitive Authoritarianism," *Journal of Democracy* 13 (April 2002): 51–65.

3. See Levitsky and Way, "Rise of Competitive Authoritarianism."

4. For examples of the growing literature on these elections, see Valerie J. Bunce and Sharon L. Wolchik, "Favorable Conditions and Electoral Revolutions," *Journal of Democracy* 17, no. 4 (October 2006): 5–18; Taras Kuzio, "Kuchma to Yushchenko: Ukraine's 2004 Elections and the Orange Revolution," *Problems of Post-Communism* 52, no. 2 (April 2005): 117–30; and Sharon Fisher, *Political Change in Post-Communist Slovakia and Croatia: From Nationalist to Europeanist* (New York: Palgrave Macmillan, 2006).

5. See Adam Przeworski et al., *Democracy and Development: Political Institutions and Well-Being in the World, 1950–1990* (Cambridge: Cambridge University Press, 2000).

6. See Linz and Stepan, *Problems of Democratic Transition and Consolidation.*

Index

About the Contributors

Federigo Argentieri received a degree in political science from the University of Rome and a PhD in history from Eötvös Loránd University in Budapest. He also attended the Harvard Ukrainian Summer Institute and has been a member of the Association for Slavic, East European, and Eurasian Studies since 1989. He teaches political science and serves as director of the Guarini Institute for Public Affairs at John Cabot University, Rome, Italy. Scholarship and research interests are mostly focused on Central and Eastern Europe and international communism after Stalin, transatlantic relations, postcommunist Hungary and Ukraine, and Western views of Eastern Europe. A regular commentator for *Corriere della Sera* and other media on the region's current political events, he is an adviser to the Hungarian Europe Society and a member of the editorial board of *Limes*, a monthly Italian journal of geopolitics. Recent publications include chapters in the books *Il patto Ribbentrop-Molotov, l'Italia e l'Europa* (2013) and *1989: Il crollo del muro di Berlino e la nascita della nuova Europa* (2014), as well as two articles on the roots of Russian-inspired prejudice against Ukraine in Italian culture, politics, and diplomacy over a period of ninety years (2015 and 2016). He is currently working on a book about Palmiro Togliatti and international communism from 1949 to 1964.

Mark Baskin is director of the Peace and Conflict Studies Program at RIT-Kosovo in Prishtina, Kosovo. He was formerly research professor at the University at Albany's Department of Political Science and a senior fellow at the Center for International Development at the State University of New York. He has been a public policy scholar at the Woodrow Wilson International Center for Scholars in Washington, DC, and served as director of research at the Pearson Peacekeeping Centre in Canada from 2001 to 2002. From 1993 to 2000, he worked as a civil affairs and political officer for the United Nations Peace Operations in Croatia, Bosnia-Herzegovina, and Kosovo. He held Fulbright and IREX fellowships in Yugoslavia and Bulgaria in the 1970s and 1980s. His research has focused on ethnicity and nationalism in socialist Yugoslavia, the economic and political transitions in the Balkans, and institution building in conflict zones and developing countries. He recently coedited *Almost Pork: Distributive Politics in Developing Countries* (2014). He received his PhD in political science from the University of Michigan.

Elez Biberaj is director of Voice of America's (VOA) Eurasia Division. He is responsible for VOA's radio, television, and internet programming targeting Russia, Ukraine, Armenia, Georgia, and the Balkans. From 1986 to 2004, he served as chief of VOA's Albanian Service. He has authored three books on Albanian affairs, including *Albania in Transition: The Rocky Road to Democracy* (1998), and contributed chapters to several others. He has also published articles in the *World Today, Encyclopedia Britannica, Conflict Studies, Problems of Communism, Survey,* and *East European Quarterly.* Biberaj holds a PhD in political science from Columbia University. The views expressed herein are the author's and do not represent the views of Voice of America.

Janusz Bugajski is a senior fellow at the Center for European Policy Analysis (CEPA) in Washington, DC, and host of the television show *New Bugajski Hour* in Prishtina, Kosova. His previous shows in the region include *Bugajski Hour,* on Albanian Screen, in Tirana, Albania, and *Bugajski Time,* on Atlas TV, Podgorica, Montenegro. He is the author of twenty books on Europe, Russia, and transatlantic relations; contributor to various US and European newspapers and journals; and columnist for media outlets in Albania, Bosnia-Herzegovina, Bulgaria, Croatia, Georgia, Kosova, and Ukraine. His newest book is titled *Eurasian Disunion: Russia's Vulnerable Flanks* (2016). Other recent books include *Conflict Zones: North Caucasus and Western Balkans Compared* (2014), *Return of the Balkans: Challenges to European Integration and U.S. Disengagement* (2013), *Georgian Lessons: Conflicting Russian and Western Interests in the Wider Europe* (2010), *Dismantling the West: Russia's Atlantic Agenda* (2009), and *America's New European Allies* (2009).

Valerie Bunce is the Aaron Binenkorb Chair of International Studies and professor of government at Cornell University. Her research has addressed five issues, all involving comparisons among the postcommunist states: patterns of regime change, the relationship between democratization and economic reform, the impact of US democracy promotion, the role of nationalism in democratic politics and the dissolution of states, and the international diffusion of democracy and dictatorship. She is the author of over seventy articles and two single-authored books, most recently, *Subversive Institutions: The Design and the Destruction of Socialism and the State* (1999). She is also coeditor, with Kathryn Stoner-Weiss and Michael McFaul, of *Democracy and Authoritarianism in the Postcommunist World* (2009). Finally, she is coauthor with Sharon Wolchik of *Defeating Authoritarian Leaders in Postcommunist Countries* (2011). She received her PhD in political science from the University of Michigan.

Monica Ciobanu is a professor of criminal justice at the State University of New York at Plattsburgh. Dr. Ciobanu's current research is focused on issues of democratization, memory, truth, and justice in postcommunism and especially in Romania. Her work appeared in *Europe-Asia Studies, Comparative Sociology, International Journal of Politics, Culture and Society, Nationalities Papers,* and *Problems of Post-Communism.* She has also contributed to several edited volumes, including *Justice, Memory and Redress in Romania: New Insights* (edited by Lavinia Stan and Lucian Turcescu, 2017), *Post-Communist Transitional Justice: Lessons from 25 Years of Experience* (edited by Lavinia Stan and Nadya Nedelsky, 2015), the *Encyclopedia of Transitional Justice* (3 vols., edited by Lavinia Stan and Nadya

Nedelsky, 2013), and *International Crime and Justice* (edited by Mangai Natarajan, 2011). Currently, she is working on a manuscript on the memorialization of Stalinist repression in Romania. In fall 2017, she was a fellow in residency at Imre Kertesz Kolleg Institute in Jena, Germany, and in 2014–2015, she was the recipient of the Chancellor's Award for Excellence in Scholarship and Creative Activities granted by the State University of New York. Dr. Ciobanu received her PhD in sociology at the Graduate Faculty of Political and Social Science of the New School for Social Research in New York in 2005. She is currently serving on the board of the *Society for Romanian Studies*.

Zsuzsa Csergő is associate professor of political studies and graduate chair at Queen's University in Kingston, Canada. She is also president of the Association for the Study of Nationalities. She specializes in the study of nationalism in contemporary European politics, with particular focus on postcommunist Central and Eastern Europe. Csergő obtained her undergraduate education at the Babeş-Bolyai University in Cluj, Romania, and her graduate education at the George Washington University in Washington, DC (MA in Russian and East European studies, PhD in political science). Before joining the Queen's faculty, she was assistant professor of political science and coordinator of the Women's Leadership Program in US and International Politics at the George Washington University. She was also a regular lecturer at the US Foreign Service Institute. Csergő is currently working on a comparative book about minority inclusion in the enlarged European Union. She is author of *Talk of the Nation* (2007) and articles in *Perspectives on Politics, Foreign Policy, Nations and Nationalism, Europe-Asia Studies,* and *East European Politics and Societies*. She has received the Fernand Braudel Senior Fellowship from the European University Institute in Florence, Italy (fall 2006); the 2005 Sherman Emerging Scholar Award from the University of North Carolina, Wilmington; and research grants from the Woodrow Wilson International Center for Scholars, the Institute for the Study of World Politics, the American Council of Learned Societies, the Social Science Research Council, the George Hoffman Foundation, and the Social Sciences and Humanities Research Council of Canada.

Jane Leftwich Curry is professor of political science at Santa Clara University and at the Centre of East European Studies at University of Warsaw. She is the author of several books on Polish and Central and East European politics, including *Poland's Permanent Revolution* (1995), *Polish Journalists: Professionalism and Politics* (2011), *The Black Book of Polish Censorship* (1983), *The Left Transformed* (2004), and *Dissent in Eastern Europe* (1983). She has also written extensively on issues of civil society and pluralism in transitions, as well as transitional justice. In 2003 and 2004, she held the Fulbright–University of Warsaw Distinguished Chair in East European Politics. In 2006, she received a United States Institute of Peace grant to examine the dynamics of the colored revolutions in Serbia, Ukraine, and Georgia. Currently, she is also research director for the Cold War Communications Project. She holds a PhD in political science from Columbia University.

Kevin Deegan-Krause is an associate professor of political science at Wayne State University in Detroit, Michigan. He received a BA in economics from Georgetown University in 1990 and a PhD in government and international studies from the University of Notre Dame in 2000. He is the author of *Elected Affinities: Democracy and Party Competition in Slovakia and the Czech Republic* (2006) and from 2011 until 2017 served as coeditor of the *European Journal of Political Research Political Data Yearbook*. His research in comparative politics focuses on political parties and democracy, with emphasis on Europe's newer democracies and its newer parties.

Daina S. Eglitis is associate professor of sociology and international affairs at the George Washington University. Her research focuses on the social, economic, and cultural dimensions of postcommunist transformation in Central and Eastern Europe. Her articles have appeared in *Acta Sociologica, Cultural Sociology, East European Politics and Societies, Slavic Review, Nationalities Papers*, and the *Journal of Baltic Studies*, among others. She is the author of *Imagining the Nation: History, Modernity, and Revolution in Latvia* (2002) and coauthor of the introductory text *Discover Sociology* (2017). From 2007 to 2008, she was a Fulbright scholar in residence at the Latvian Academy of Culture in Riga, Latvia, and in the spring of 2015, she was a visiting fellow at the US Holocaust Memorial Museum's Mandel Center for Advanced Holocaust Studies. Her current work examines the history and memory of the Holocaust in the Baltic Countries. She received her PhD in sociology from the University of Michigan (1998).

Sharon Fisher is associate director with IHS Markit's economics and country risk group in Washington, DC. In that role, she oversees a team of economists focused on Central and Eastern Europe, providing economic and political analysis, risk assessment, and forecasting. During the mid-1990s, she spent four years as an analyst at the RFE/RL Research Institute in Munich and the Open Media Research Institute in Prague. She has also worked at the Institute for Public Affairs (IVO) in Bratislava and the Center for Economic Research and Graduate Education-Economics Institute (CERGE-EI) in Prague. Fisher has presented her work at numerous conferences and seminars in Europe and the United States, and her extensive list of publications includes *Political Change in Post-communist Slovakia and Croatia: From Nationalist to Europeanist* (2006). She holds a PhD from the School of Slavonic and East European Studies at University College London.

Taras Kuzio is a nonresident fellow at the Center for Transatlantic Relations, School of Advanced International Studies, Johns Hopkins University. His latest book is *Commissars into Oligarchs: A Contemporary History of Ukraine* (2014). He is the author and editor of seventeen books, including (with Paul D'Anieri) *The Sources of Russia's Great Power Politics: Ukraine and the Challenge to the European Order* (2018), *Putin's War against Ukraine. Revolution, Nationalism, and Crime* (2017), *Ukraine: Democratization, Corruption and the New Russian Imperialism* (2015), and *The Crimea: Europe's Next Flashpoint?* (2010), five think-tank monographs, thirty-eight book chapters, and one hundred scholarly articles on postcommunist and Ukrainian politics and European studies. He received a BA in economics from the University of Sussex, an MA in Soviet and East European studies from the University of London, and a PhD in political science from the University of Birmingham, England. He was a postdoctoral fellow at Yale University.

Ronald H. Linden is professor of political science at the University of Pittsburgh. From 2011 through 2016, he was director of the European Studies Center at Pitt, a National Resource Center, and Jean Monnet European Union Centre of Excellence. A Princeton PhD (1976), he was director of the Center for Russian and East European Studies at Pitt from 1984 to 1989 and from 1991 to 1998. From 1989 to 1991, Dr. Linden served as director of research for Radio Free Europe in Munich, Germany, with responsibility for observing and analyzing the extraordinary changes in Eastern Europe. Dr. Linden's research has focused on Central and Southeastern Europe including Turkey. His publications include *Turkey and Its Neighbors: Foreign Relations in Transition* (2012) and, with Yasemin Irepoğlu, "Turkey and the Balkans: New Forms of Political Community?" in *Turkish Studies* (2013). His publications on Eastern Europe include editing two special issues of *Problems of Post-Communism*, titled "The Meaning of 1989 and After" (2009) and "The New Populism in Central and Southeast Europe" (2008), and "The Burden of Belonging: Romanian and Bulgarian Foreign Policy in the New Era," *Journal of Balkan and Near Eastern Studies* (2009). Dr. Linden is a contributing author to *The Berlin Wall: 20 Years Later* (2009), published by the US Department of State. He has held fellowships and research grants from the German Marshall Fund, the United States Institute of Peace, the National Council for Eurasian and East European Research, the American Institute of Contemporary German Studies, and the Woodrow Wilson International Center for Scholars. During 2018, Dr. Linden will be a Fulbright-Schuman Scholar in Rome, Italy and Bruges, Belgium doing research on the impact on US–European relations of growing Chinese trade and investment in Europe.

Eva-Clarita Pettai is research associate at the Imre Kertész Kolleg, Friedrich-Schiller-University in Jena, Germany. She received her PhD in political science from the Free University of Berlin, and worked as a senior researcher for more than ten years at the University of Tartu, Estonia. She has published widely on the politics of memory, democratization, and transitional justice in postcommunist Central and Eastern Europe and, in particular, the Baltic states. Her most recent works have explored the relationship between postcommunist criminal trials and memory as well as the work of historical commissions as mediators in contemporary memory conflicts. Pettai is coauthor of *Transitional and Retrospective Justice in the Baltic States* (2015) as well as of *Demokratisierung der Geschichte in Lettland* (2003). She is also editor of the *Cultures of History Forum* (www.cultures-of-history.uni-jena.de), an online journal with a focus on how the societies in Central and Eastern Europe negotiate the history and memory of the twentieth century in museums, public debates, and state policies.

Vello Pettai is professor of comparative politics at the University of Tartu. Originally from the United States, he holds a PhD in political science from Columbia University. He has written widely on postcommunist political development in the Baltic states, including political parties, elections, ethnic politics, and transitional justice. He has published in the *Journal of Democracy*, *Nations and Nationalism*, *World Politics*, and elsewhere. He is the author of *Elections in Estonia, 1990–1992: Transitional and Founding* (2012) and coauthor of *Transitional and Retrospective Justice in the Baltic States* (2015). Since 2015, he is director of the V-Dem Regional Center for Eastern Europe and

Russia, conducting research on political change in the region using the Varieties of Democracy database.

Paula Pickering is associate professor of government at the College of William and Mary. Her research focuses on peace building, aid for good governance at the local level, ethnic politics in southeastern Europe, and the relationship between information and accountability. She is the author of *Peacebuilding in the Balkans: The View from the Ground Floor* (2007). Recent articles have been published in *Governance, East European Politics, Suedosteuropa, Problems of Post-communism, Democratization, Europe-Asia Studies, Communist and Post-communist Studies*, and *Ethnic and Racial Studies*. Between 1990 and 1994, she worked as the politico-military analyst for Eastern Europe at the US Department of State. She also worked as a human rights officer for the Organization for Security and Co-operation in Europe's Mission in Bosnia-Herzegovina (1996). She received her PhD in political science from the University of Michigan.

Joshua Spero is professor of international politics at Fitchburg State University, where he has taught since 2003, served as the director of the university's Regional Economic Development Institute, and also coordinates the International Studies Minor Program, the political science, and the Washington Center Internship Programs. He focuses on international security, international relations, government decision-making, and simulation crisis-management decision-making. Before transitioning to academia, he served as senior civilian strategic planner for the Joint Chiefs of Staff's J-5 Strategic Plans and Policy Directorate in the Europe-NATO Division (1994–2000), national security analyst at the Institute for National Strategic Studies (1990–1994), and deputy assistant for Europe and the USSR at the Office of the Secretary of Defense (1988–1990). From 1988 to 1994, he also served as the US Army's Ft. Leavenworth, Kansas–based Soviet Army/Foreign Military Studies Office liaison officer in Washington, DC. He received his PhD from the Johns Hopkins University's School for Advanced International Studies and has authored, among numerous publications, *Bridging the European Divide: Middle Power Politics and Regional Security Dilemmas* (Rowman and Littlefield, 2004).

Sharon L. Wolchik is professor of political science and international affairs at the George Washington University. She has also served as adjunct chair (contractor) of the Advanced Area Studies Seminar on East-Central Europe at the US Department of State's Foreign Service Institute. She has conducted research on the role of women in the transition to postcommunism in Central and Eastern Europe and the role of women leaders, as well as on ethnic issues and other aspects of politics. She is the author of *Czechoslovakia in Transition: Politics, Economics, and Society* (1991) and coeditor of *Women in Power in Postcommunist Parliaments*, with Marilyn Rueschemeyer (2009); *Women and Democracy: Latin America and Central and Eastern Europe*, with Jane S. Jaquette (1998); *Domestic and Foreign Policy in Eastern Europe in the 1980s*, with Michael Sodaro (1983); *Ukraine: In Search of a National Identity*, with Volodymyr Zviglyanich (2000); *The Social Legacy of Communism*, with James R. Millar (1994); and *Women, State and Party in Eastern Europe*, with Alfred G. Meyer (1985). She is a coauthor with Valerie Bunce of *Defeating Authoritarian Leaders in Postcommunist Countries* (2011). She received her PhD in political science from the University of Michigan.